A Kodansha Comics Trade Pap
Star-Crossed!! 4 copyright ©
English translation copyright © 2022 Junko

Published in the United States by Kodansha Comics, an imprint of
Kodansha USA Publishing, LLC, New York.

Publication rights for this English edition arranged through
Kodansha Ltd., Tokyo.

First published in Japan in 2020 by Kodansha Ltd., Tokyo
as *Wota Doru, Oshiga watashide watashiga oshide*, volume 4.

ISBN 978-1-64651-247-8

Original cover design by HASEPRO

Printed in the United States of America.

www.kodansha.us

1st Printing
Translation: Jessica Latherow / amimaru
Lettering: Mohit Dhiman / amimaru
Production assistants: Jessica Latherow, Monika Hegedusova, Adam Jankowski / amimaru
Additional lettering and layout: Scott O. Brown
Editing: Vanessa Tenazas
Kodansha Comics edition cover design by Phil Balsman

Publisher: Kiichiro Sugawara

Director of publishing services: Ben Applegate
Associate director of publishing operations: Stephen Pakula
Publishing services managing editors: Alanna Ruse, Madison Salters
Production managers: Emi Lotto, Angela Zurlo
Logo and character art ©Kodansha USA Publishing, LLC

THE SWEET SCENT OF LOVE IS IN THE AIR! FOR FANS OF OFFBEAT ROMANCES LIKE *WOTAKOI*

Sweat and Soap © Kintetsu Yamada / Kodansha Ltd.

In an office romance, there's a fine line between sexy and awkward... and that line is where Asako — a woman who sweats copiously — meets Koutarou — a perfume developer who can't get enough of Asako's, er, scent. Don't miss a romcom manga like no other!

A SMART, NEW ROMANTIC COMEDY FOR FANS OF *SHORTCAKE CAKE* AND *TERRACE HOUSE*!

LIVING ROOM

MATSUNAGA-SAN

Keiko Iwashita

KC KODANSHA COMICS

A romance manga starring high school girl Meeko, who learns to live on her own in a boarding house whose living room is home to the odd (but handsome) Matsunaga-san. She begins to adjust to her new life away from her parents, but Meeko soon learns that no matter how far away from home she is, she's still a young girl at heart — especially when she finds herself falling for Matsunaga-san.

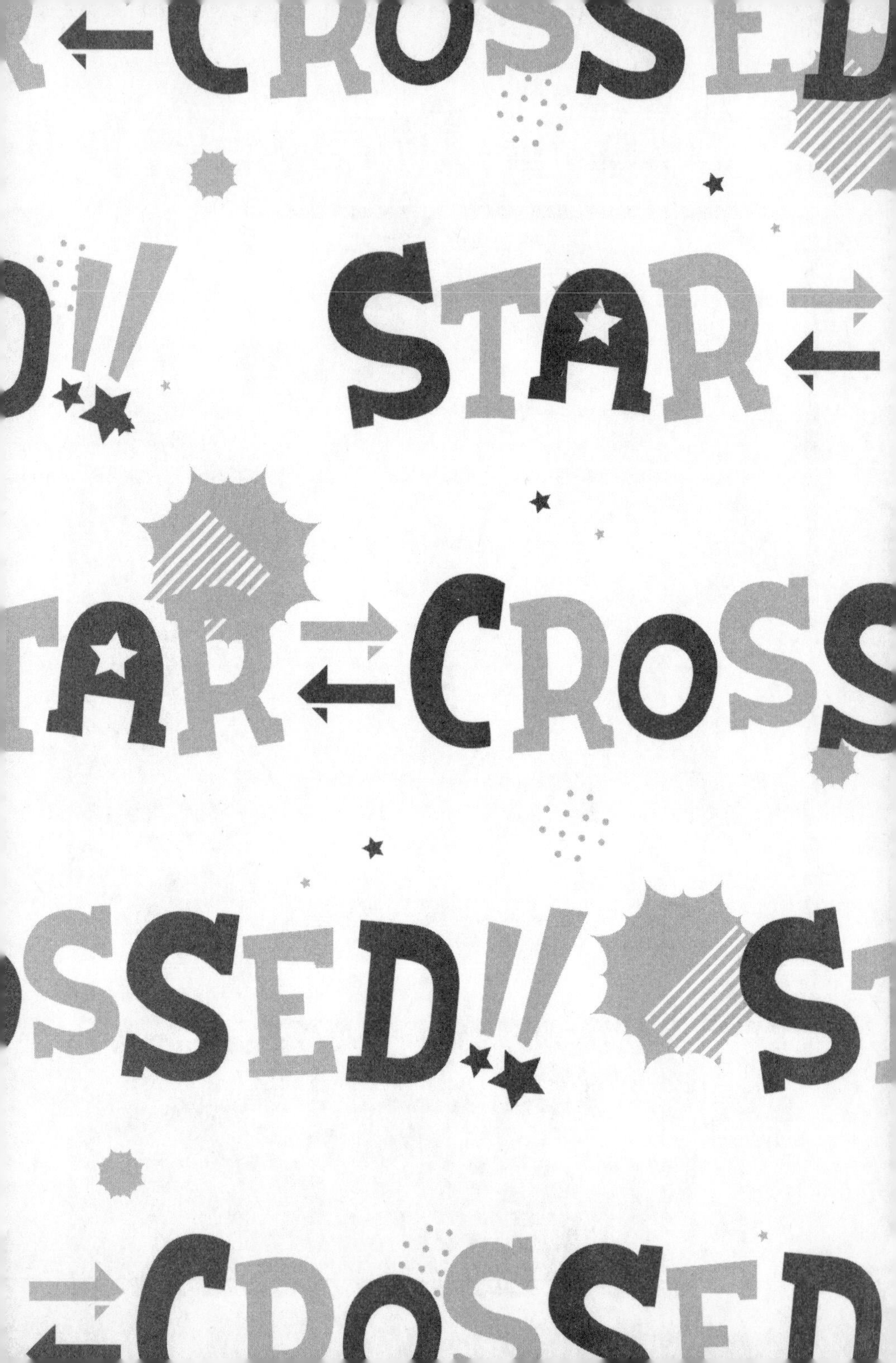
STAR-CROSSED!!

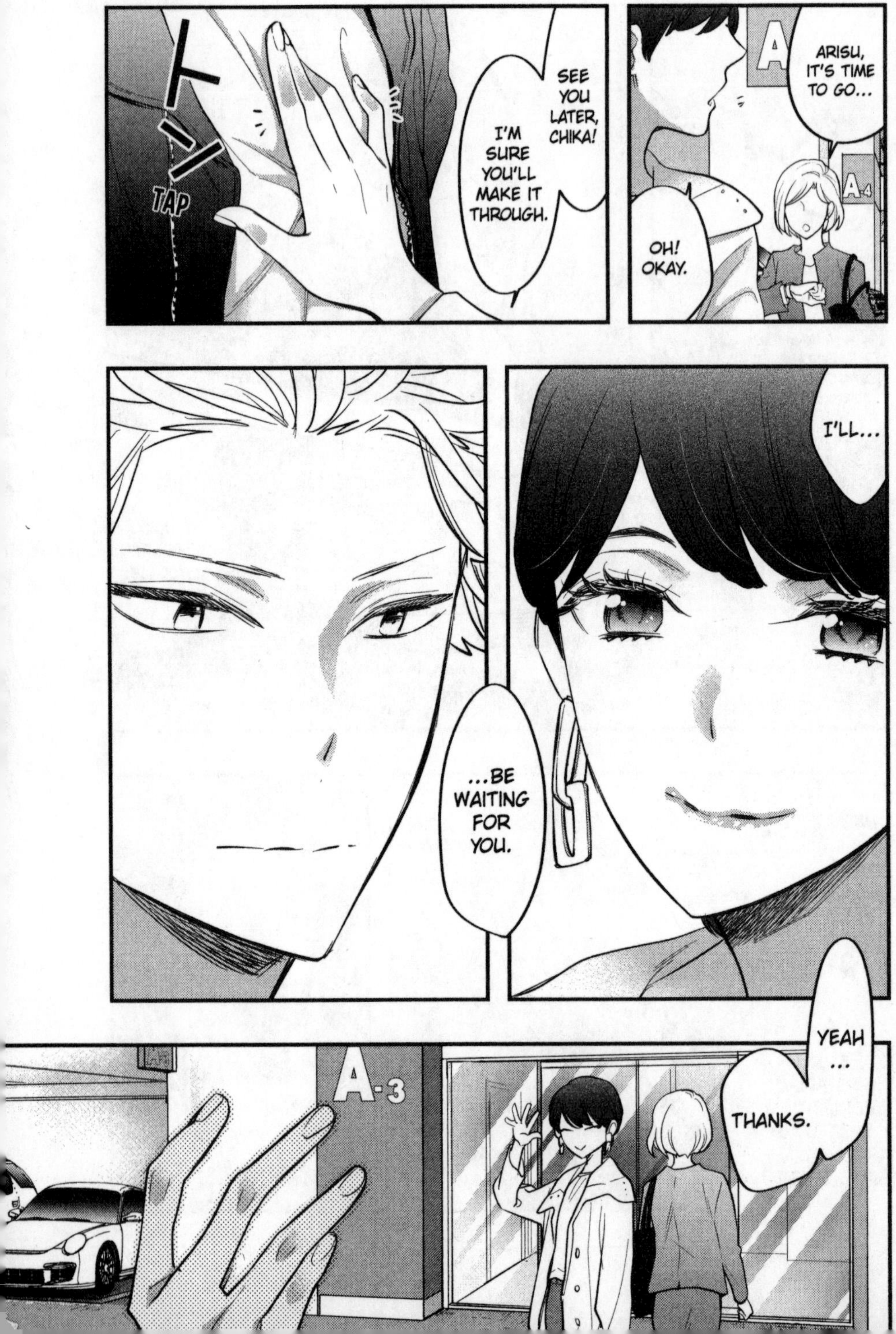
ARISU, IT'S TIME TO GO...
OH! OKAY.
SEE YOU LATER, CHIKA!
I'M SURE YOU'LL MAKE IT THROUGH.
TAP
I'LL...
...BE WAITING FOR YOU.
YEAH ... THANKS.

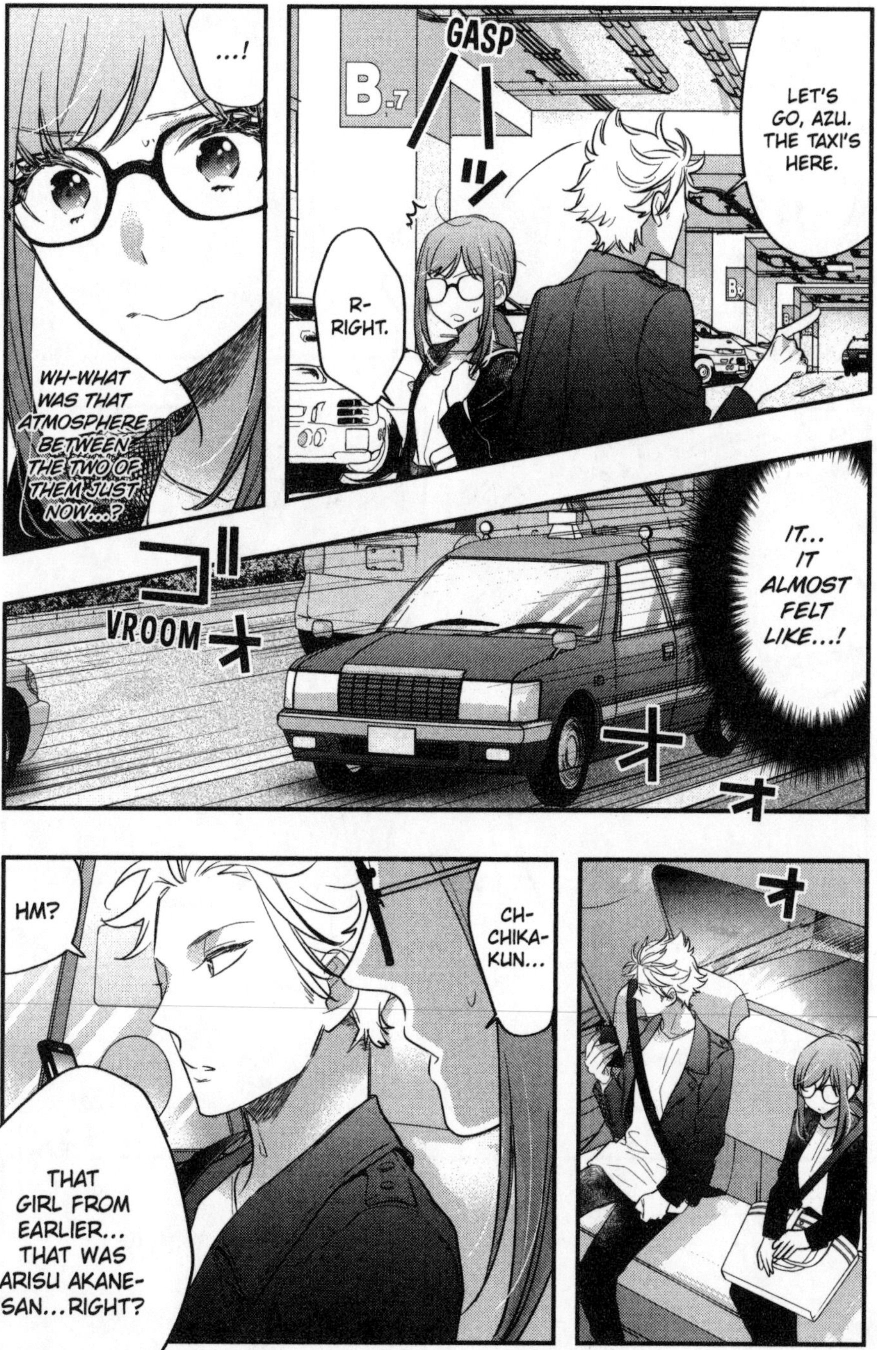
GASP
LET'S GO, AZU. THE TAXI'S HERE.
R-RIGHT.
...!
WH-WHAT WAS THAT ATMOSPHERE BETWEEN THE TWO OF THEM JUST NOW...?
IT... IT ALMOST FELT LIKE...!
VROOM
CH-CHIKA-KUN...
HM?
THAT GIRL FROM EARLIER... THAT WAS ARISU AKANE-SAN...RIGHT?

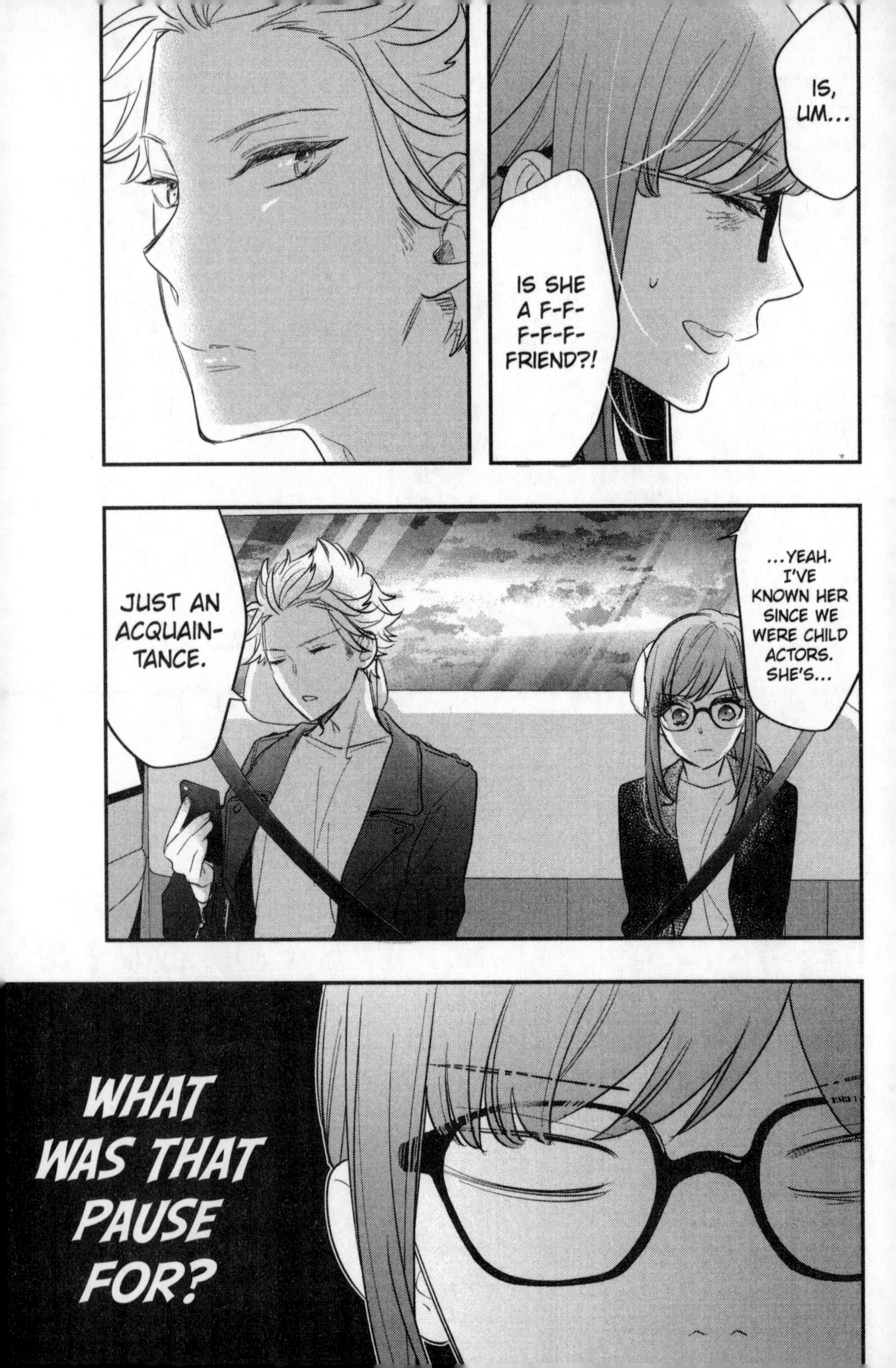
IS, UM...
IS SHE A F-F-F-F-F-FRIEND?!
...YEAH. I'VE KNOWN HER SINCE WE WERE CHILD ACTORS. SHE'S...
JUST AN ACQUAIN-TANCE.
WHAT WAS THAT PAUSE FOR?

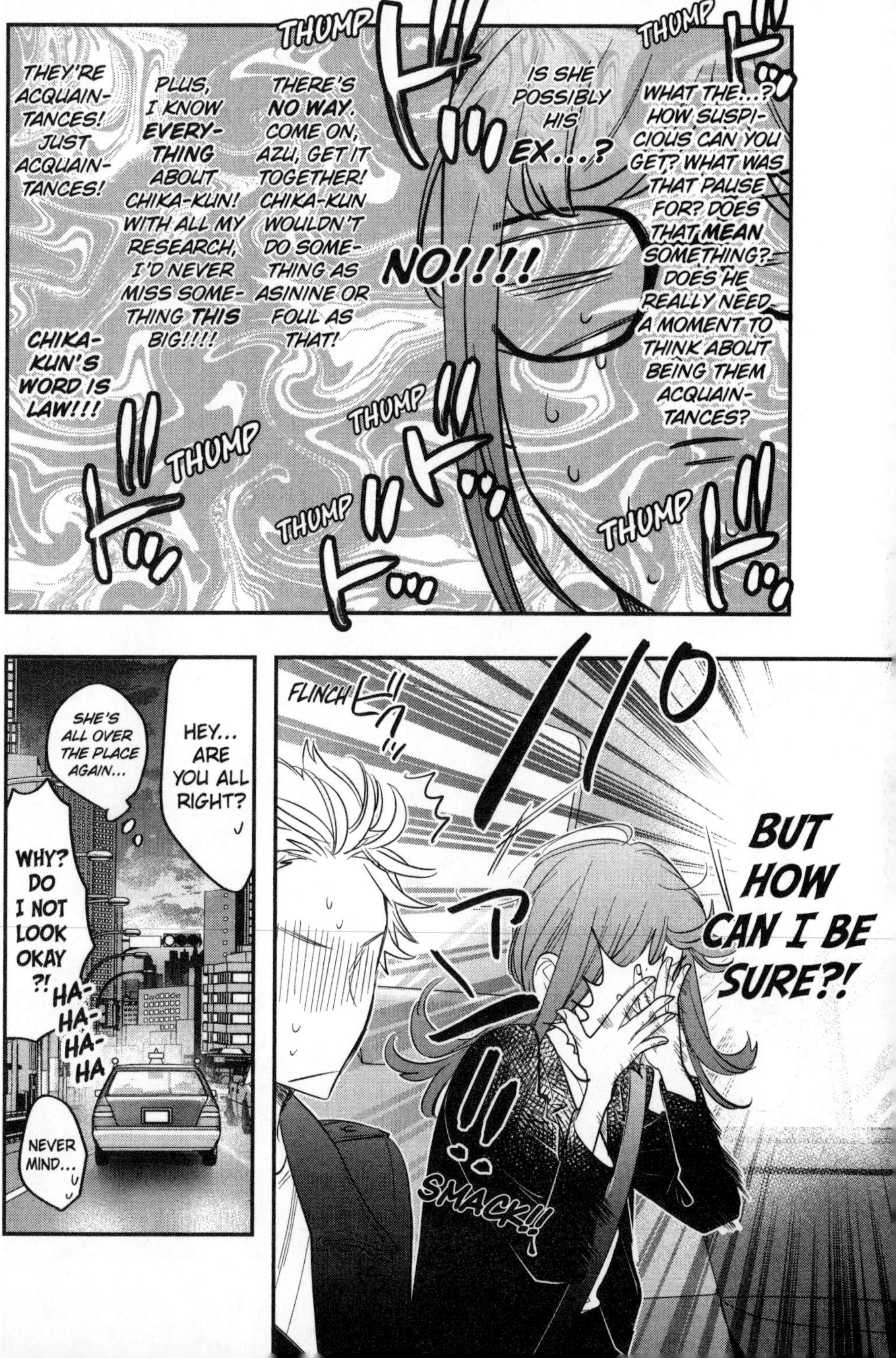
THUMP
THUMP
WHAT THE...? HOW SUSPICIOUS CAN YOU GET? WHAT WAS THAT PAUSE FOR? DOES THAT MEAN SOMETHING? DOES HE REALLY NEED A MOMENT TO THINK ABOUT BEING THEM ACQUAINTANCES?
IS SHE POSSIBLY HIS EX...?
NO!!!!
THERE'S NO WAY. COME ON, AZU, GET IT TOGETHER! CHIKA-KUN WOULDN'T DO SOMETHING AS ASININE OR FOUL AS THAT!
PLUS, I KNOW EVERYTHING ABOUT CHIKA-KUN! WITH ALL MY RESEARCH, I'D NEVER MISS SOMETHING THIS BIG!!!!
THEY'RE ACQUAINTANCES! JUST ACQUAINTANCES!
CHIKA-KUN'S WORD IS LAW!!!
THUMP
THUMP
THUMP
THUMP
FLINCH
BUT HOW CAN I BE SURE?!
SMACK!!
HEY... ARE YOU ALL RIGHT?
SHE'S ALL OVER THE PLACE AGAIN...
WHY? DO I NOT LOOK OKAY?!
HA-HA-HA-HA
NEVER MIND...

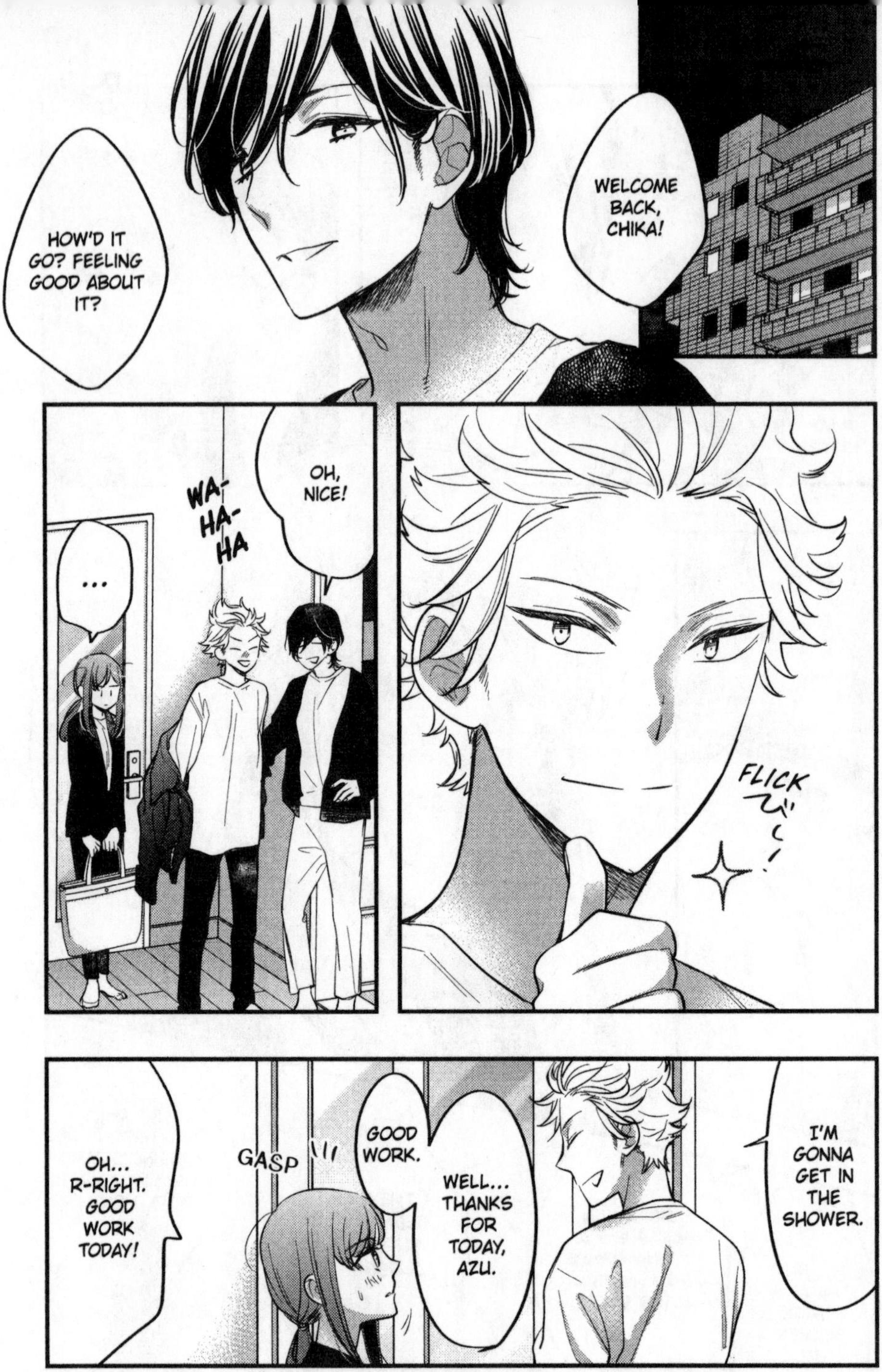
WELCOME BACK, CHIKA!
HOW'D IT GO? FEELING GOOD ABOUT IT?
FLICK
OH, NICE!
WA-HA-HA
...
I'M GONNA GET IN THE SHOWER.
WELL... THANKS FOR TODAY, AZU.
GOOD WORK.
GASP
OH... R-RIGHT. GOOD WORK TODAY!

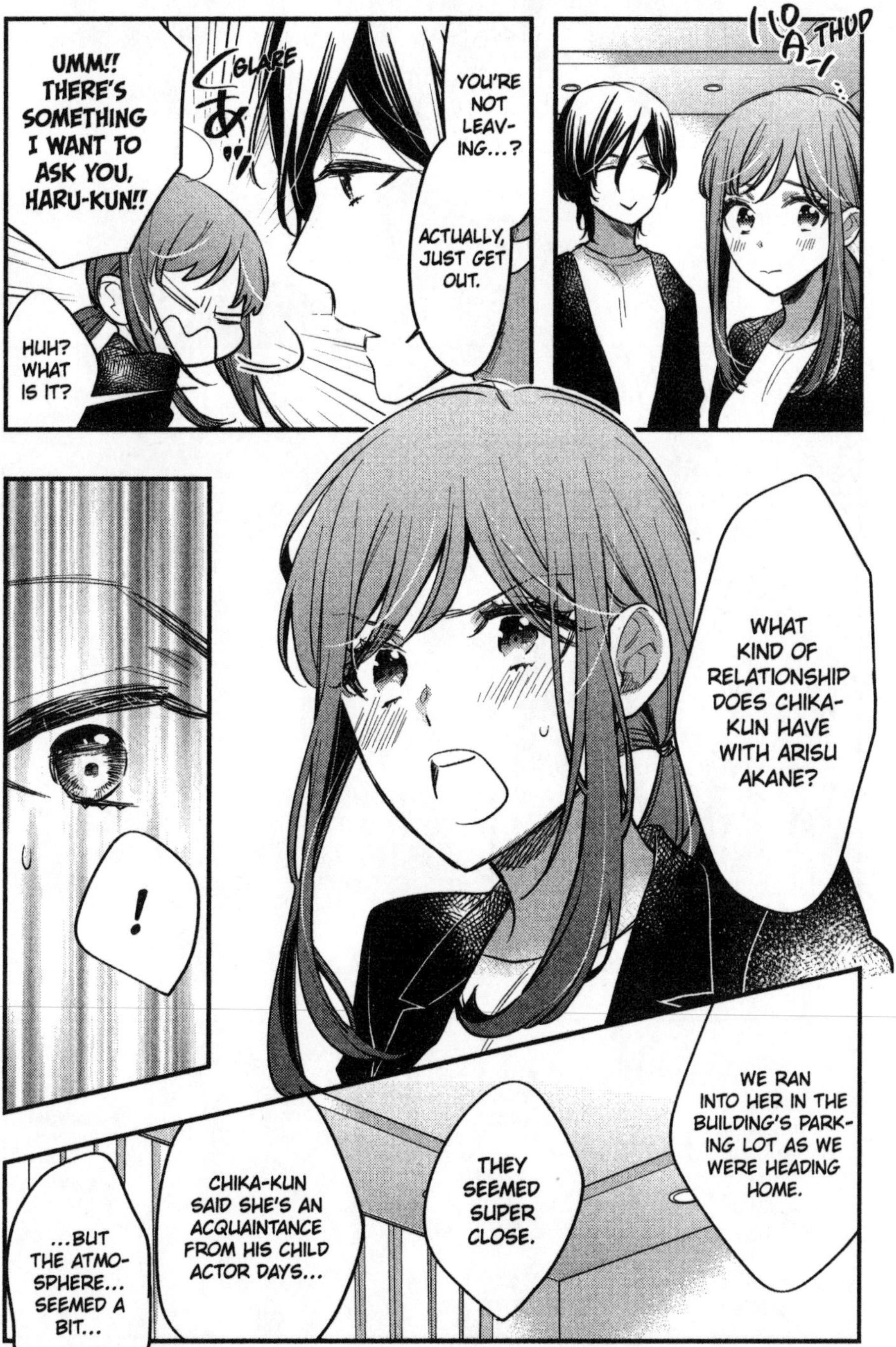
THUD
YOU'RE NOT LEAVING...?
ACTUALLY, JUST GET OUT.
GLARE
UMM!! THERE'S SOMETHING I WANT TO ASK YOU, HARU-KUN!!
HUH? WHAT IS IT?
WHAT KIND OF RELATIONSHIP DOES CHIKA-KUN HAVE WITH ARISU AKANE?
!
WE RAN INTO HER IN THE BUILDING'S PARKING LOT AS WE WERE HEADING HOME.
THEY SEEMED SUPER CLOSE.
CHIKA-KUN SAID SHE'S AN ACQUAINTANCE FROM HIS CHILD ACTOR DAYS...
...BUT THE ATMOSPHERE... SEEMED A BIT...

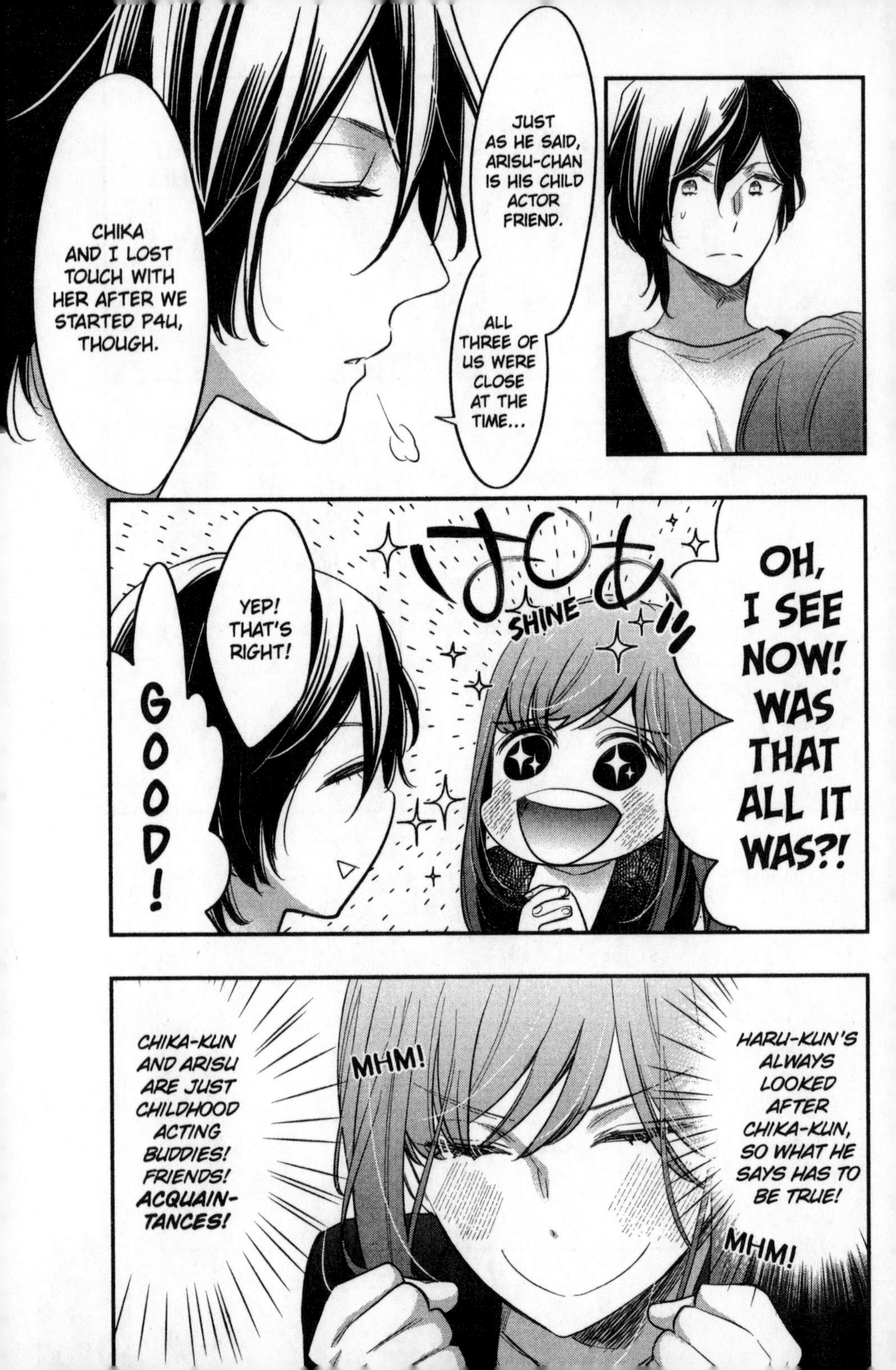
JUST AS HE SAID, ARISU-CHAN IS HIS CHILD ACTOR FRIEND.
ALL THREE OF US WERE CLOSE AT THE TIME...
CHIKA AND I LOST TOUCH WITH HER AFTER WE STARTED P4U, THOUGH.
OH, I SEE NOW! WAS THAT ALL IT WAS?!
SHINE
YEP! THAT'S RIGHT!
GOOD!
HARU-KUN'S ALWAYS LOOKED AFTER CHIKA-KUN, SO WHAT HE SAYS HAS TO BE TRUE!
MHM!
CHIKA-KUN AND ARISU ARE JUST CHILDHOOD ACTING BUDDIES! FRIENDS! ACQUAIN-TANCES!
MHM!

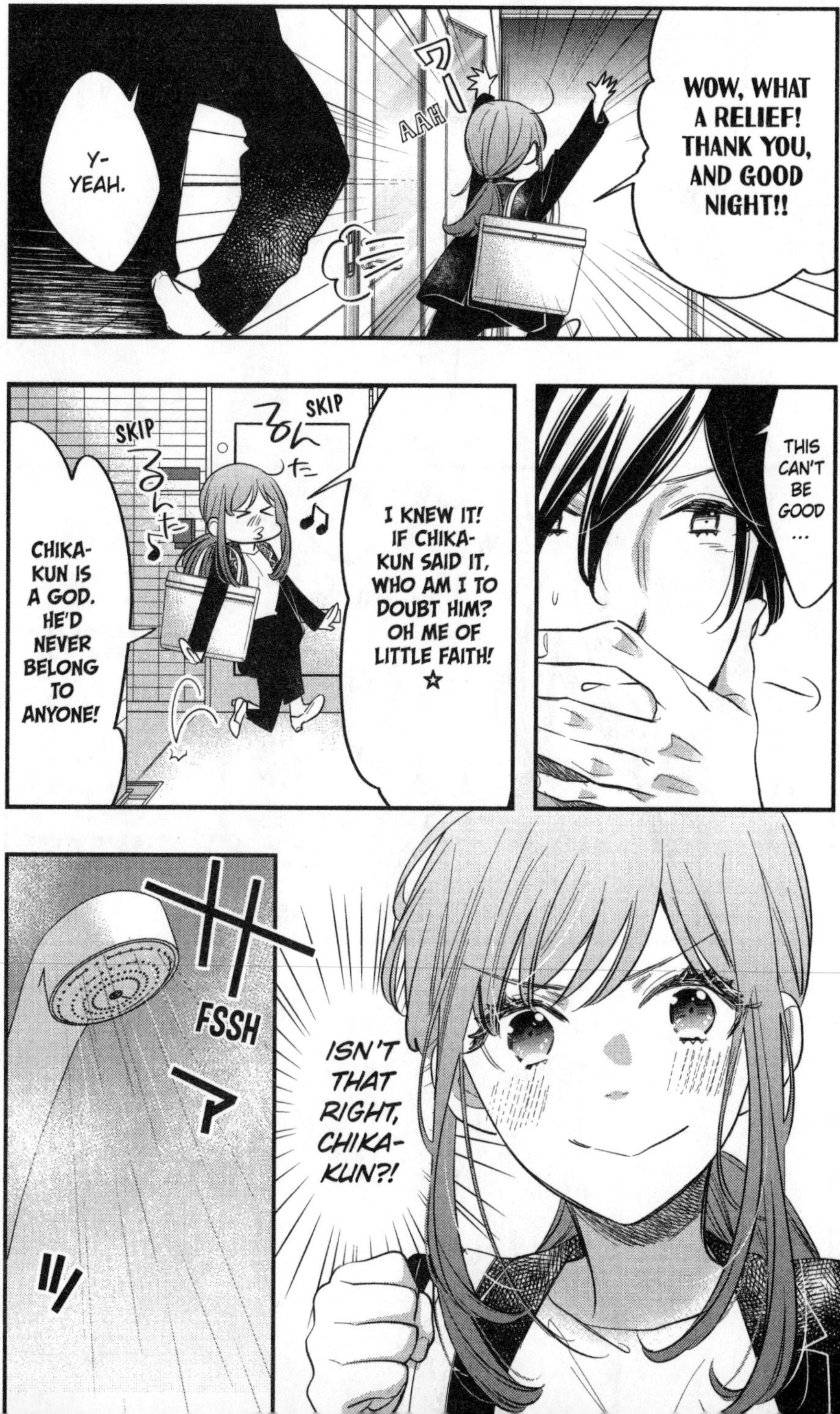
WOW, WHAT A RELIEF! THANK YOU, AND GOOD NIGHT!!
AAH
Y- YEAH.
THIS CAN'T BE GOOD...
SKIP
I KNEW IT! IF CHIKA-KUN SAID IT, WHO AM I TO DOUBT HIM? OH ME OF LITTLE FAITH! ☆
SKIP
CHIKA-KUN IS A GOD. HE'D NEVER BELONG TO ANYONE!
FSSH
ISN'T THAT RIGHT, CHIKA-KUN?!

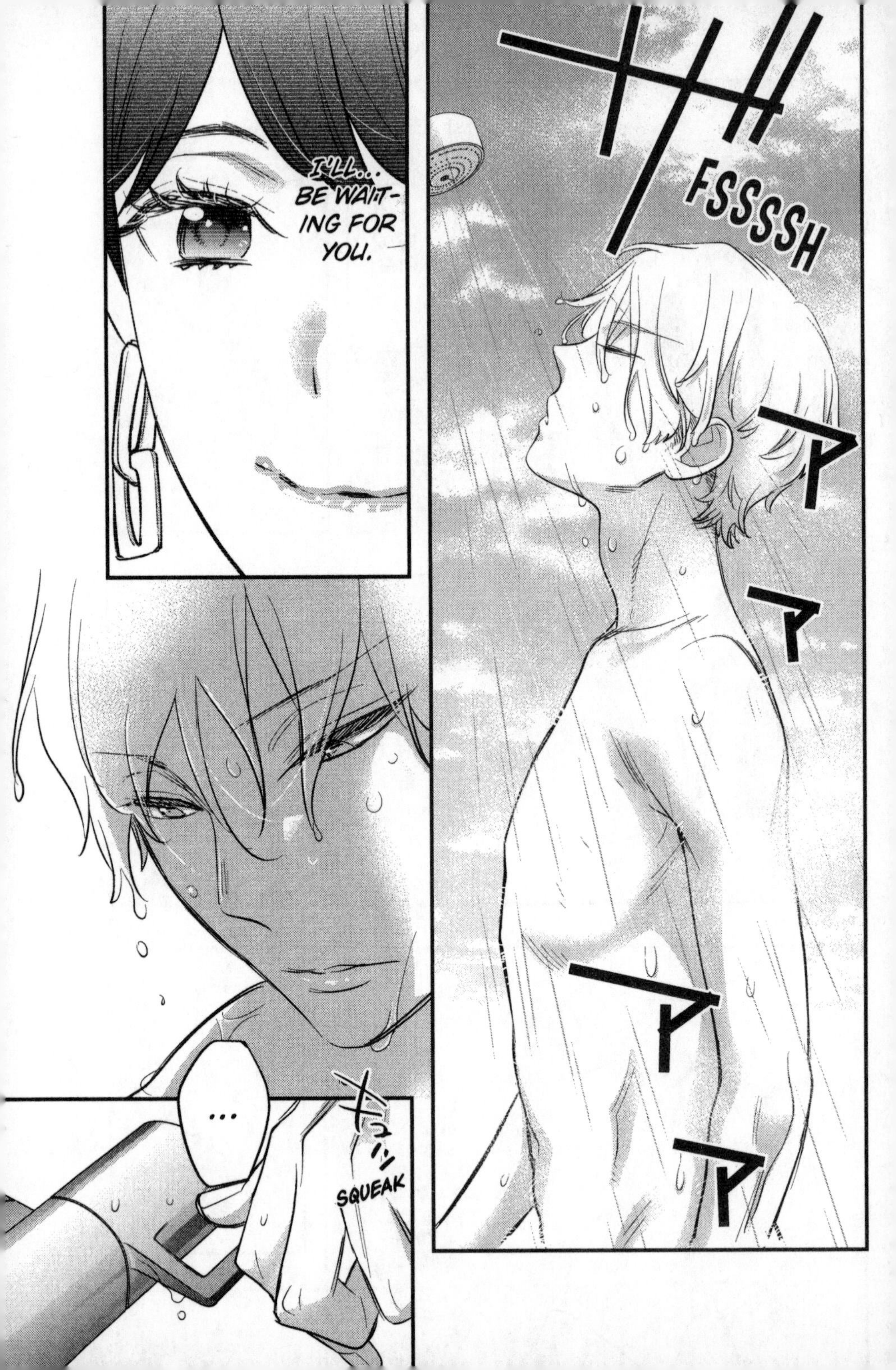
FSSSSH
I'LL... BE WAIT-ING FOR YOU.
...
SQUEAK

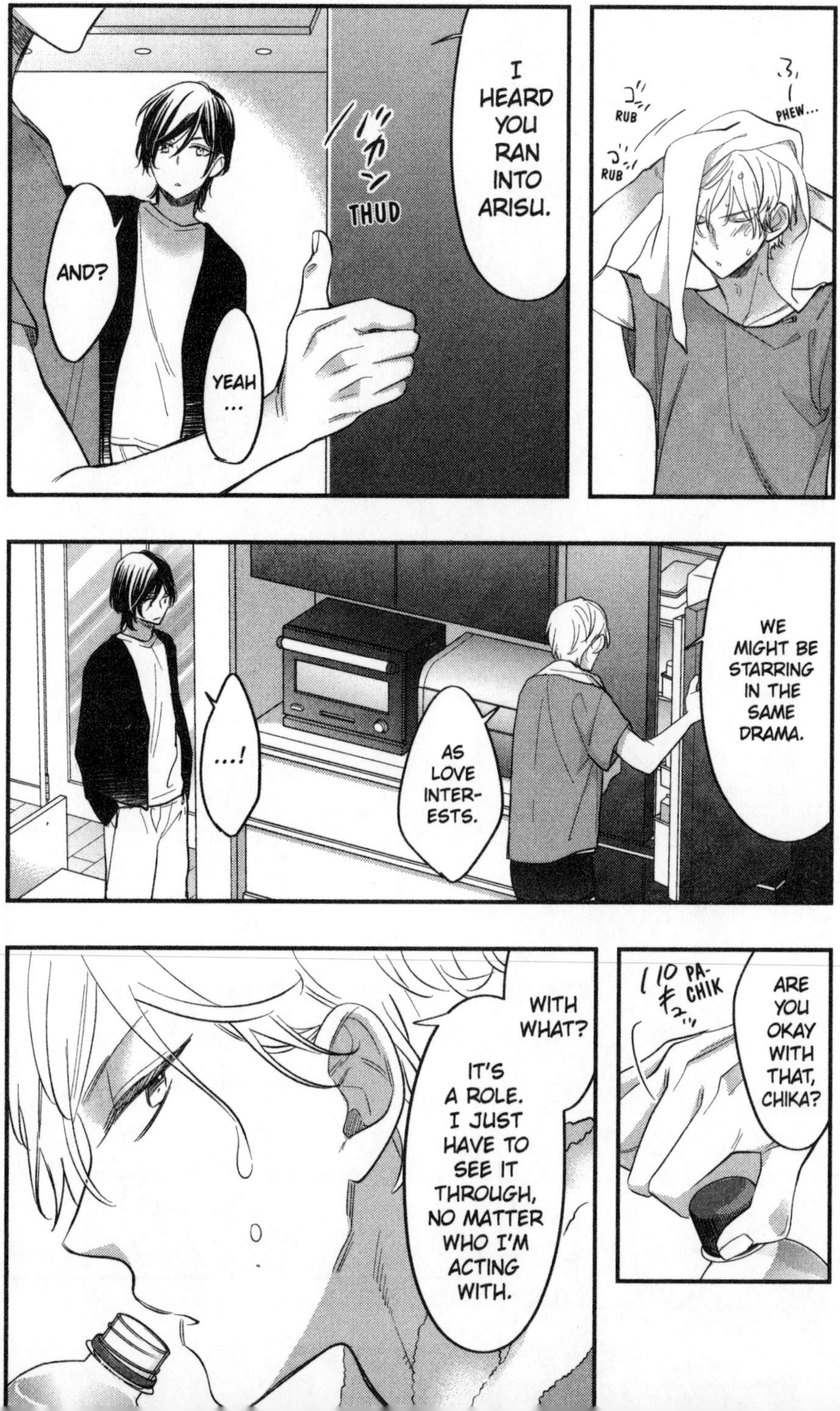
RUB
RUB
PHEW...
I HEARD YOU RAN INTO ARISU.
THUD
AND?
YEAH ...
WE MIGHT BE STARRING IN THE SAME DRAMA.
AS LOVE INTER-ESTS.
...!
PA-CHIK
ARE YOU OKAY WITH THAT, CHIKA?
WITH WHAT?
IT'S A ROLE. I JUST HAVE TO SEE IT THROUGH, NO MATTER WHO I'M ACTING WITH.

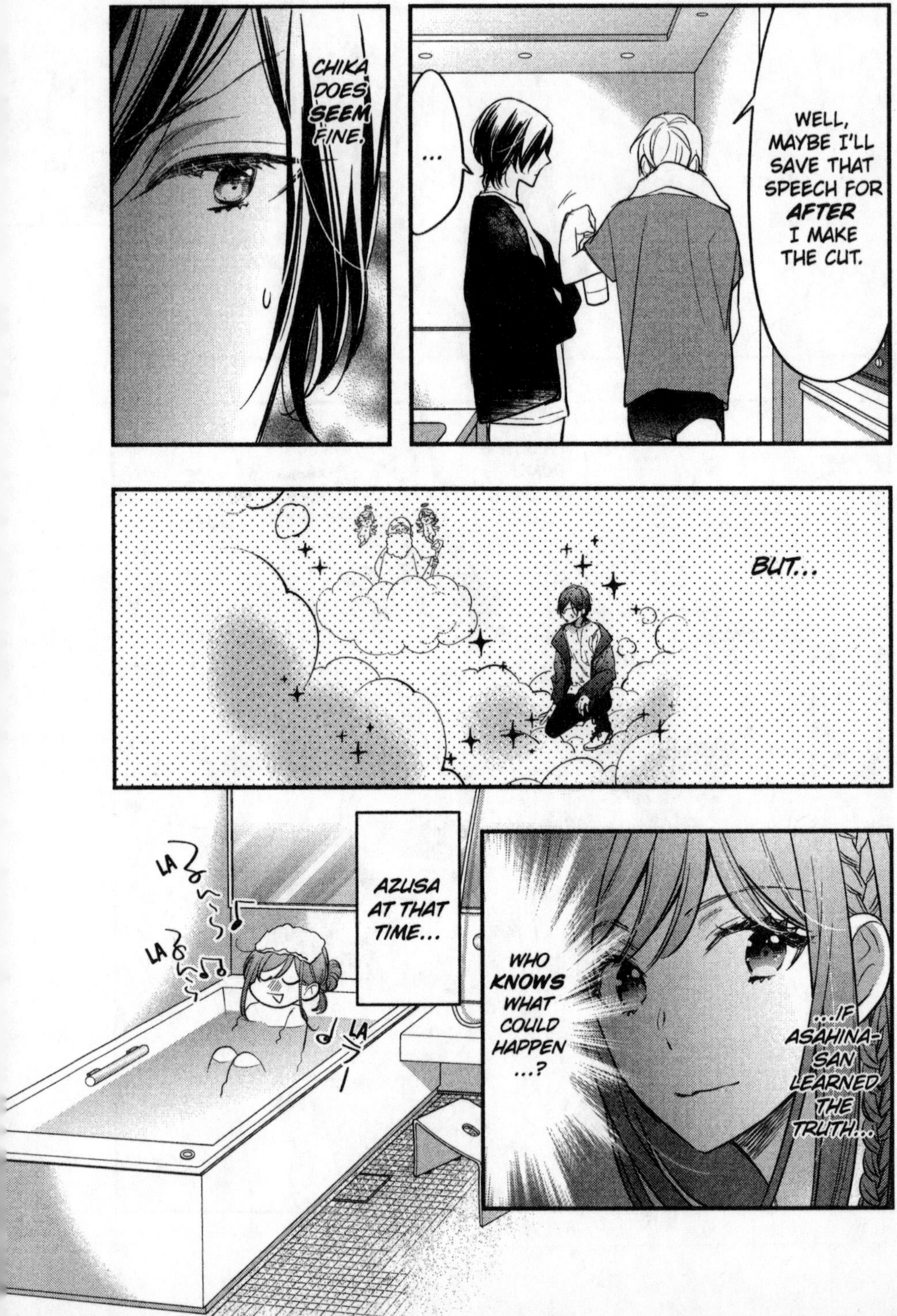

WELL, MAYBE I'LL SAVE THAT SPEECH FOR AFTER I MAKE THE CUT.
...
CHIKA DOES SEEM FINE.
BUT...
...IF ASAHINA-SAN LEARNED THE TRUTH...
WHO KNOWS WHAT COULD HAPPEN ...?
AZUSA AT THAT TIME...
LA
LA
LA

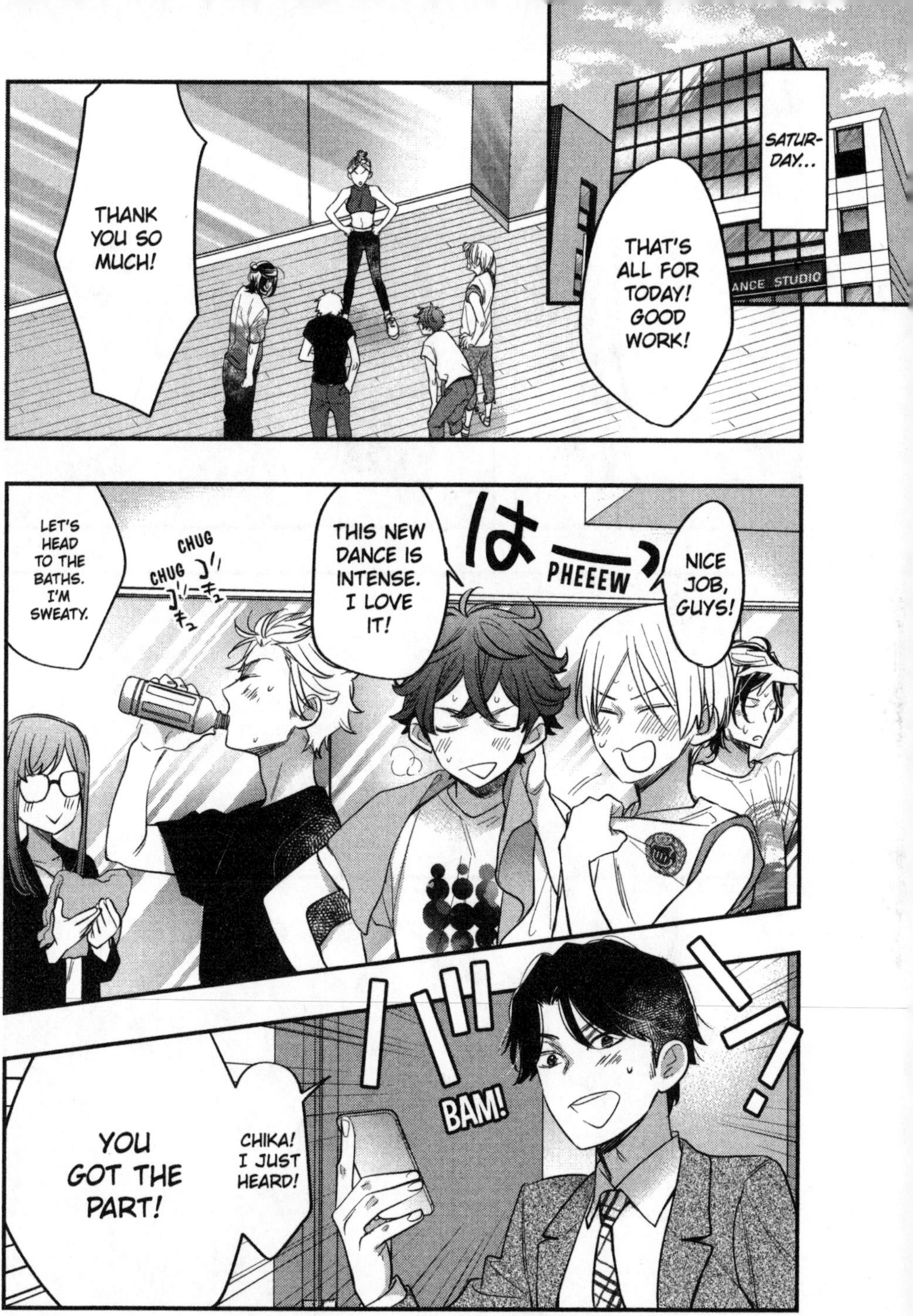
SATUR-DAY...
ANCE STUDIO
THAT'S ALL FOR TODAY! GOOD WORK!
THANK YOU SO MUCH!
NICE JOB, GUYS!
はーっ
PHEEEW
THIS NEW DANCE IS INTENSE. I LOVE IT!
CHUG CHUG
ゴキュ ゴキュ
LET'S HEAD TO THE BATHS. I'M SWEATY.
BAM!
CHIKA! I JUST HEARD!
YOU GOT THE PART!

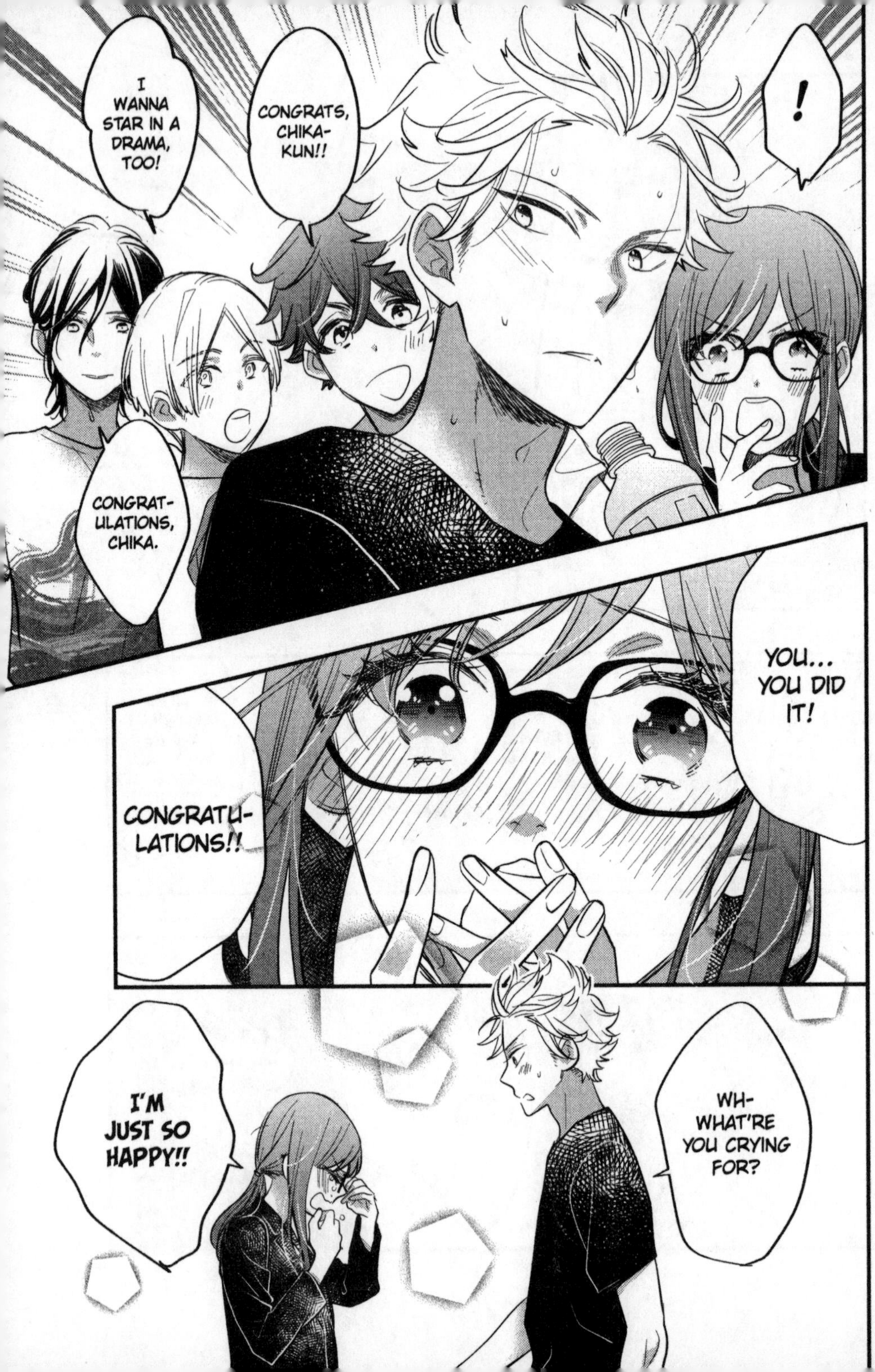
!
CONGRATS, CHIKA-KUN!!
I WANNA STAR IN A DRAMA, TOO!
CONGRATULATIONS, CHIKA.
YOU... YOU DID IT!
CONGRATULATIONS!!
WH-WHAT'RE YOU CRYING FOR?
I'M JUST SO HAPPY!!

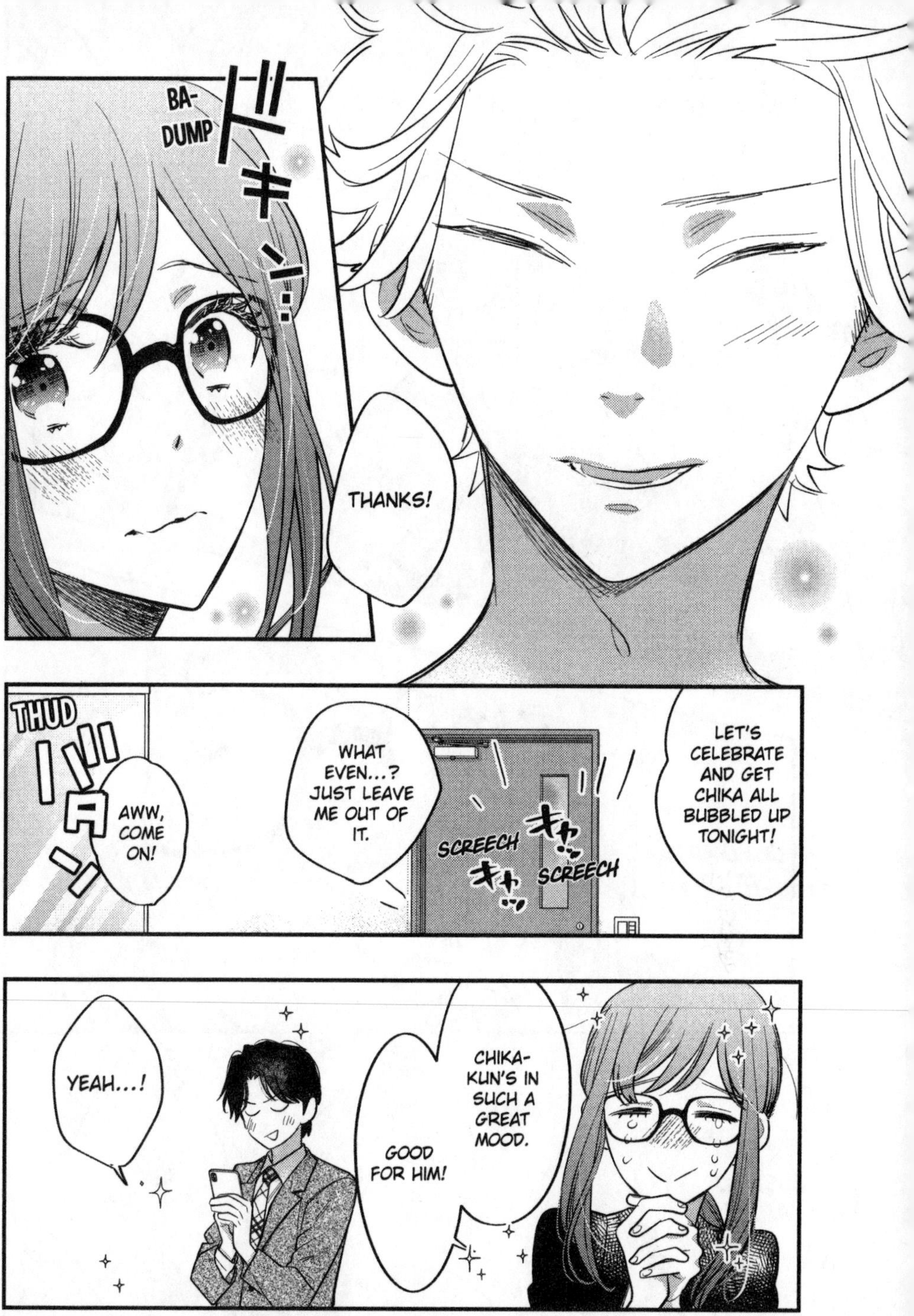
THANKS!
BA-DUMP
LET'S CELEBRATE AND GET CHIKA ALL BUBBLED UP TONIGHT!
SCREECH
SCREECH
WHAT EVEN...? JUST LEAVE ME OUT OF IT.
AWW, COME ON!
THUD
CHIKA-KUN'S IN SUCH A GREAT MOOD.
GOOD FOR HIM!
YEAH...!

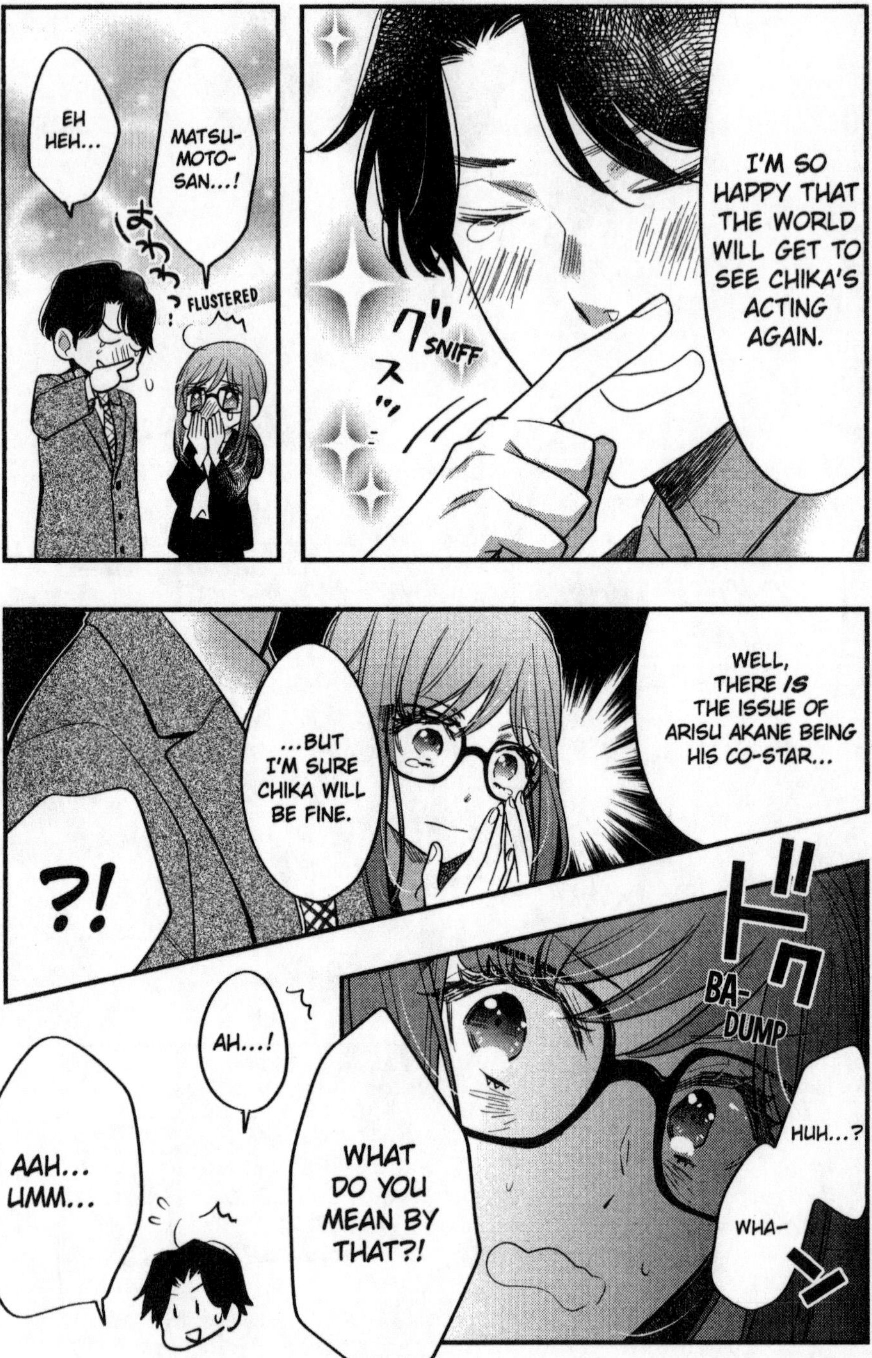
I'M SO HAPPY THAT THE WORLD WILL GET TO SEE CHIKA'S ACTING AGAIN.
グスッ
SNIFF
MATSU-MOTO-SAN...!
EH HEH...
はわわ
FLUSTERED
WELL, THERE *IS* THE ISSUE OF ARISU AKANE BEING HIS CO-STAR...
...BUT I'M SURE CHIKA WILL BE FINE.
?!
ドク
BA-DUMP
HUH...?
WHA-
WHAT DO YOU MEAN BY THAT?!
AH...!
AAH... UMM...

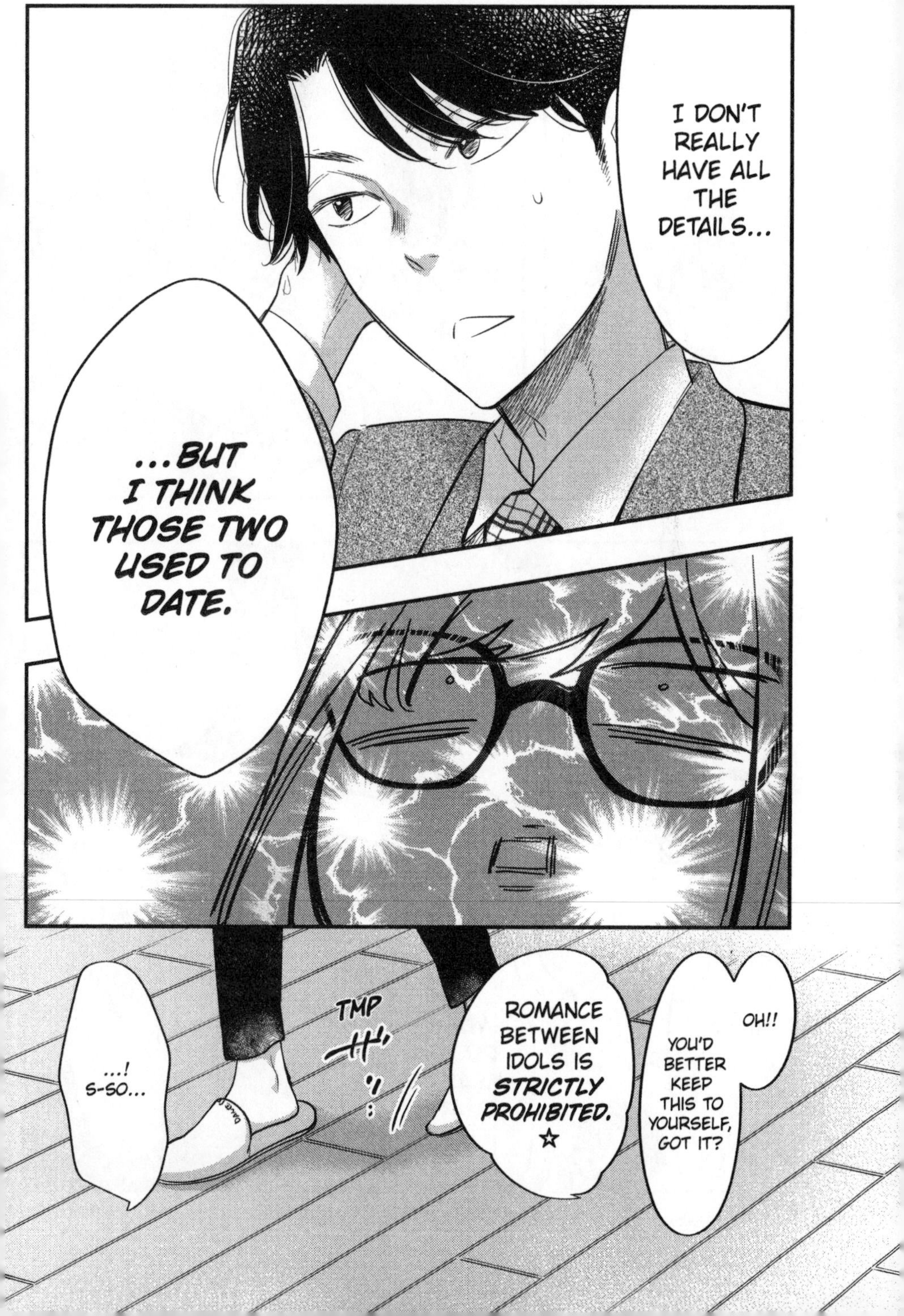
I DON'T REALLY HAVE ALL THE DETAILS...
...BUT I THINK THOSE TWO USED TO DATE.
OH!!
YOU'D BETTER KEEP THIS TO YOURSELF, GOT IT?
ROMANCE BETWEEN IDOLS IS STRICTLY PROHIBITED. ☆
TMP
...! S-SO...

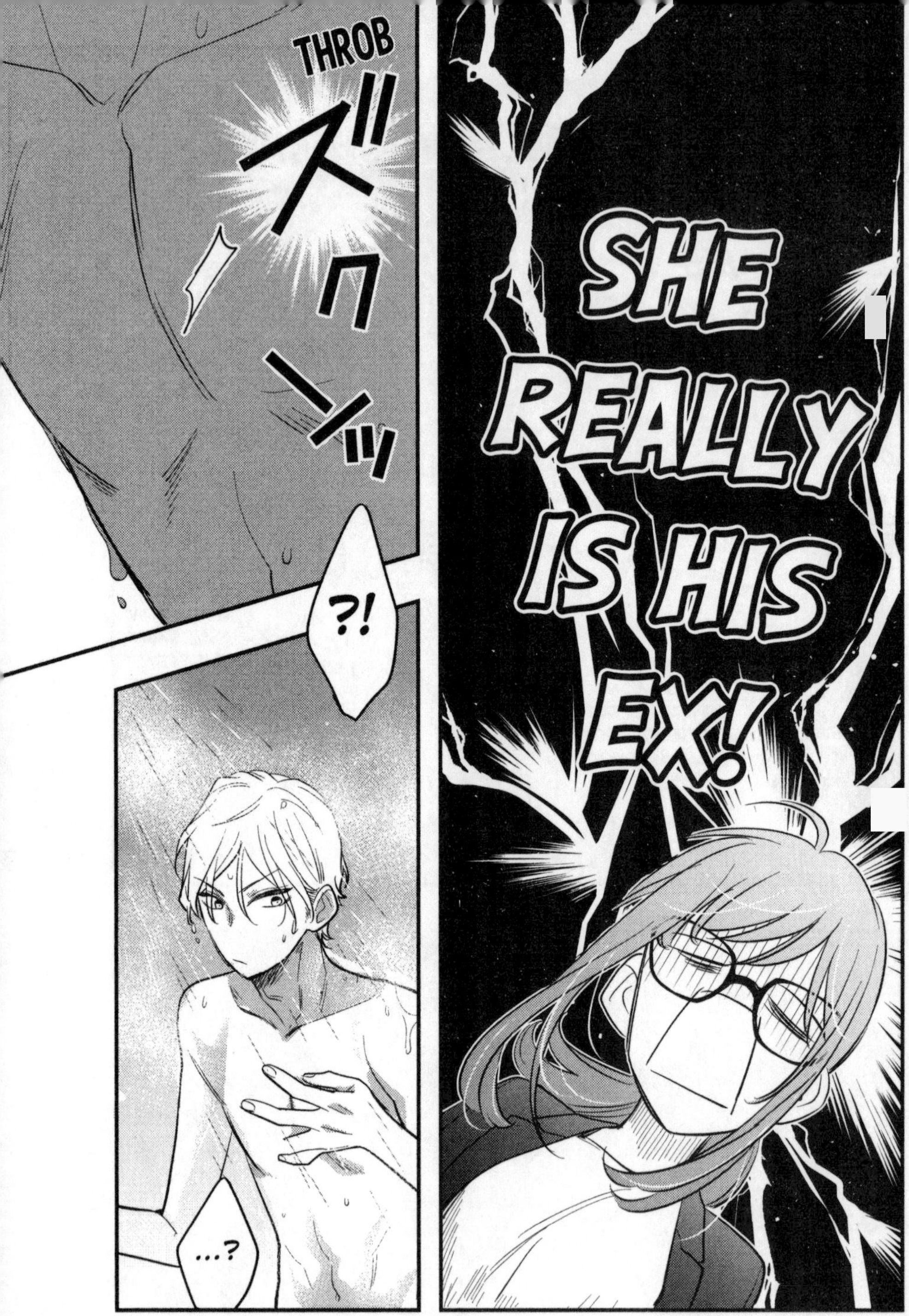
SHE REALLY IS HIS EX!
THROB
?!
...?

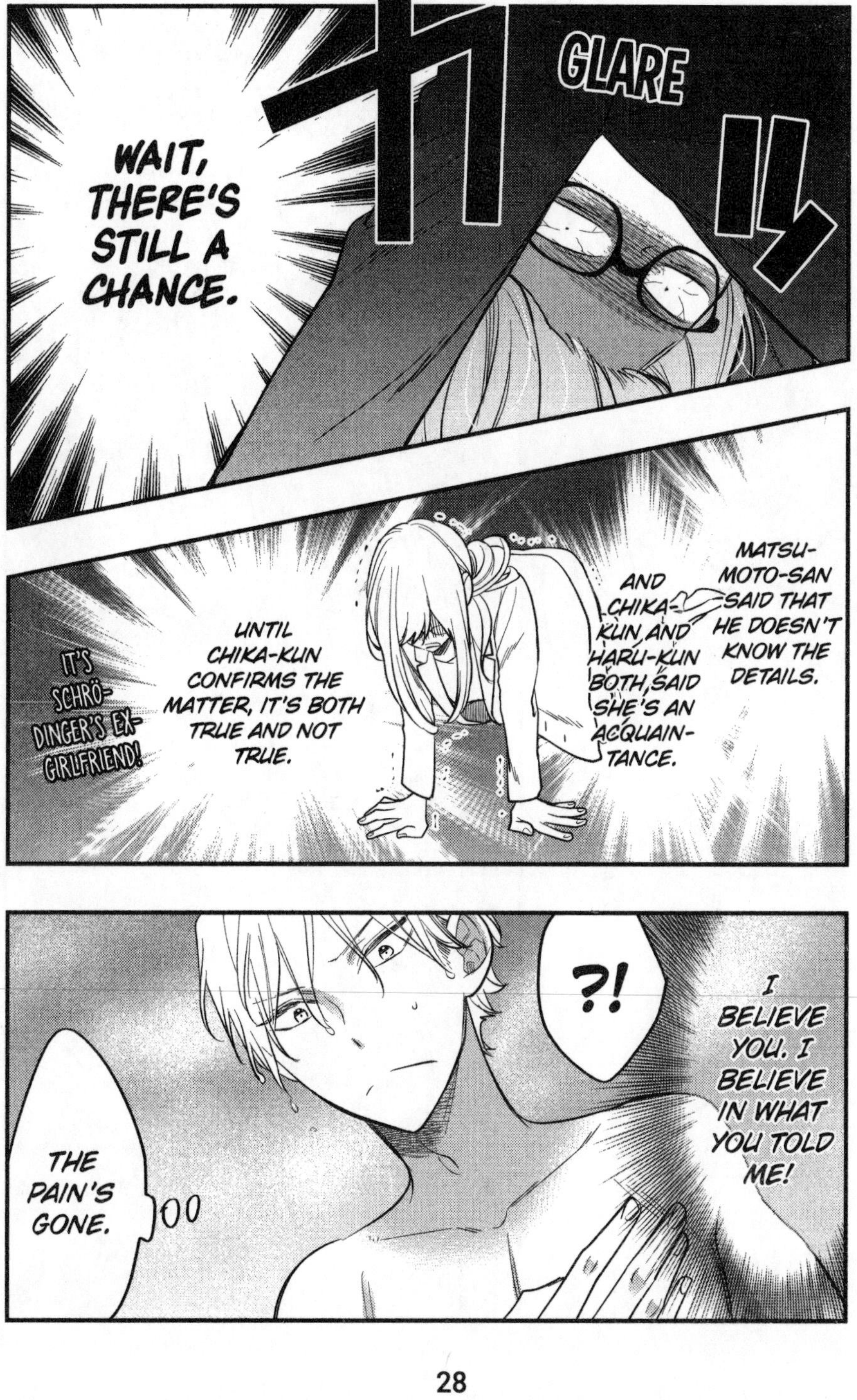
GLARE
WAIT, THERE'S STILL A CHANCE.
MATSU-MOTO-SAN SAID THAT HE DOESN'T KNOW THE DETAILS.
AND CHIKA-KUN AND HARU-KUN BOTH SAID SHE'S AN ACQUAIN-TANCE.
UNTIL CHIKA-KUN CONFIRMS THE MATTER, IT'S BOTH TRUE AND NOT TRUE.
IT'S SCHRÖ-DINGER'S EX-GIRLFRIEND!
?!
I BELIEVE YOU. I BELIEVE IN WHAT YOU TOLD ME!
THE PAIN'S GONE.

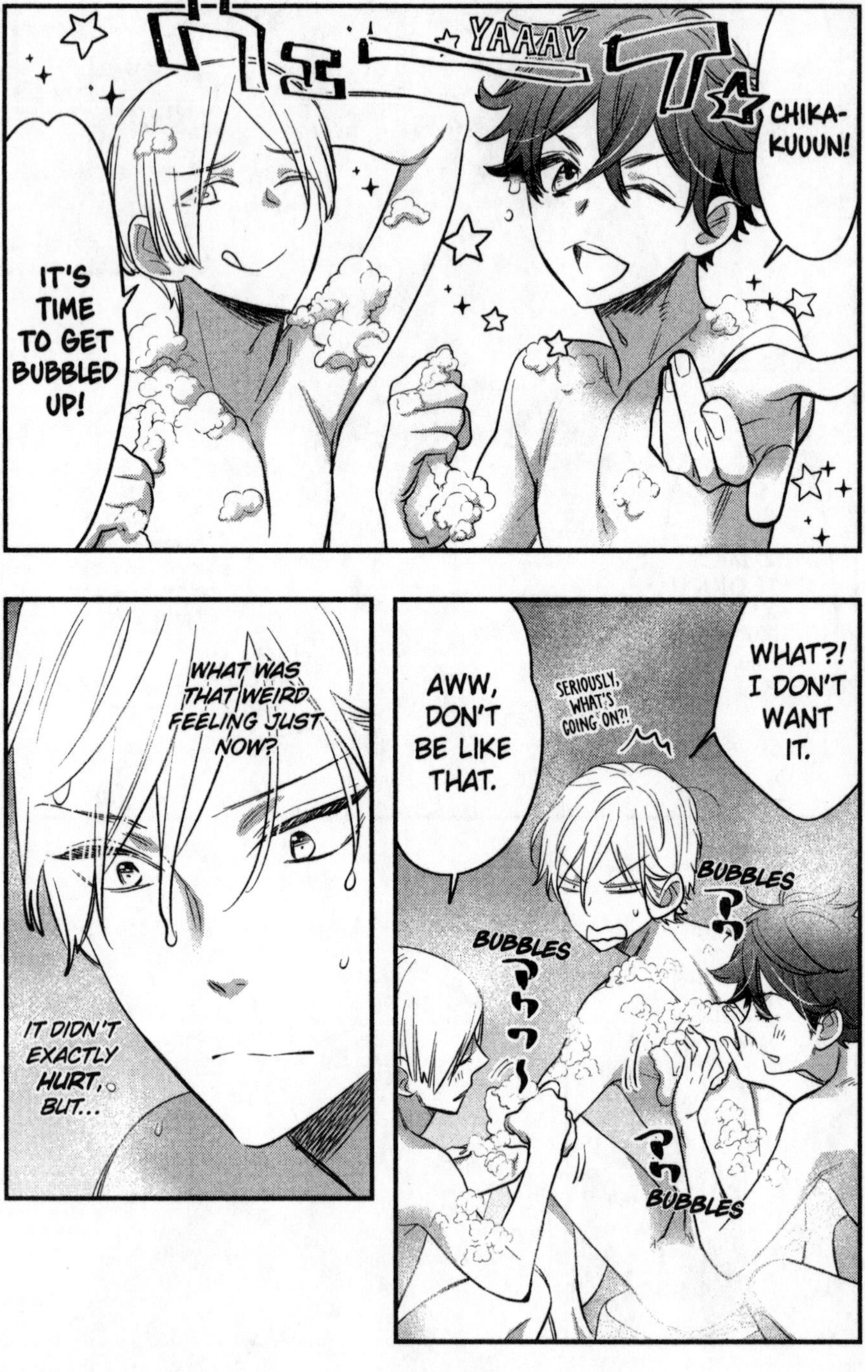
YAAAY
CHIKA-KUUUN!
IT'S TIME TO GET BUBBLED UP!
WHAT?! I DON'T WANT IT.
SERIOUSLY, WHAT'S GOING ON?!
AWW, DON'T BE LIKE THAT.
BUBBLES
BUBBLES
BUBBLES
WHAT WAS THAT WEIRD FEELING JUST NOW?
IT DIDN'T EXACTLY HURT, BUT...

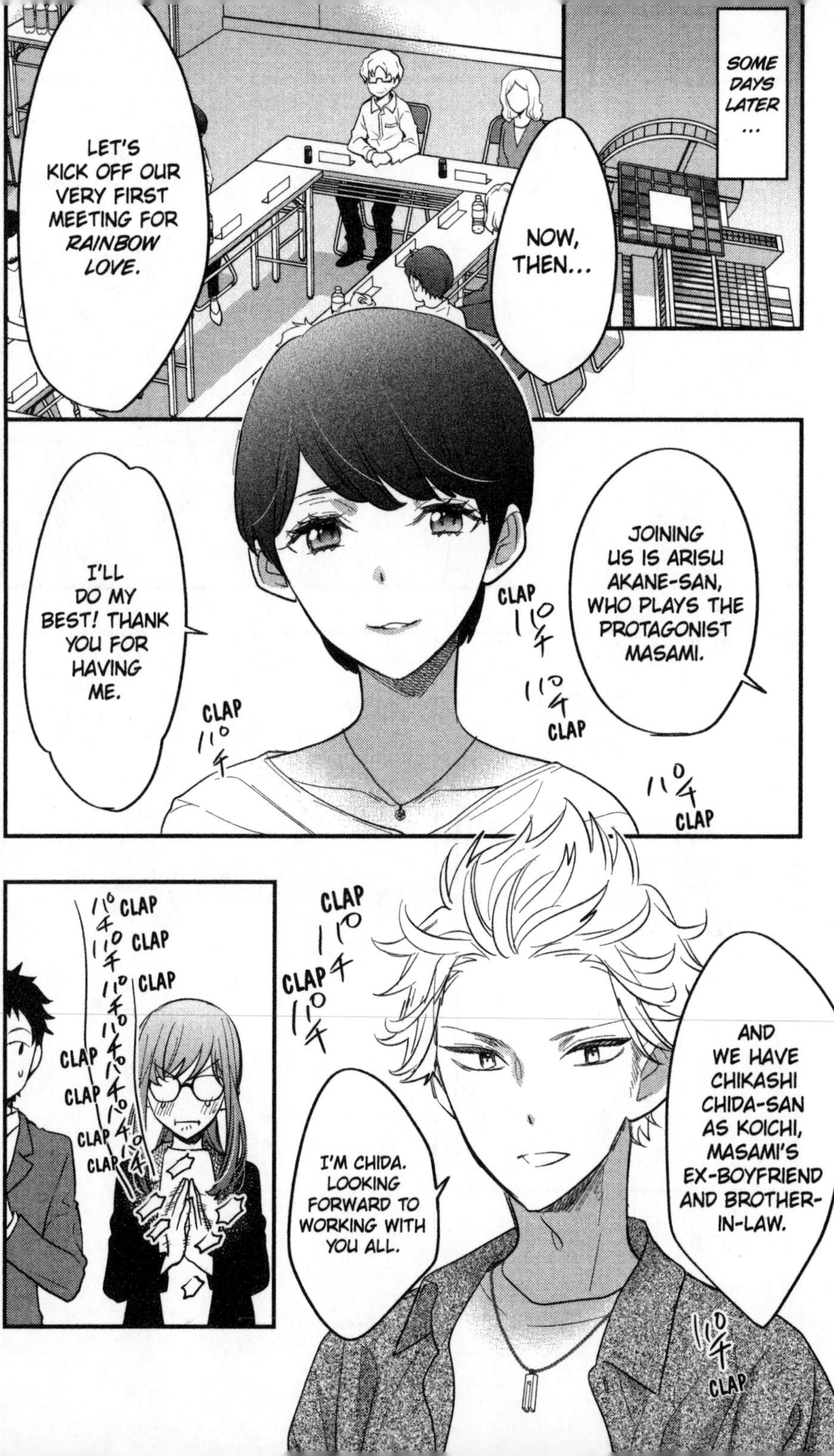
SOME DAYS LATER...
NOW, THEN...
LET'S KICK OFF OUR VERY FIRST MEETING FOR *RAINBOW LOVE.*
JOINING US IS ARISU AKANE-SAN, WHO PLAYS THE PROTAGONIST MASAMI.
パチ CLAP
パチ CLAP
パチ CLAP
パチ CLAP
I'LL DO MY BEST! THANK YOU FOR HAVING ME.
AND WE HAVE CHIKASHI CHIDA-SAN AS KOICHI, MASAMI'S EX-BOYFRIEND AND BROTHER-IN-LAW.
パチ CLAP
I'M CHIDA. LOOKING FORWARD TO WORKING WITH YOU ALL.
パチ CLAP
パチ CLAP
パチ CLAP
パチ CLAP
パチ CLAP
パチ CLAP
パチ CLAP
パチ CLAP
パチ CLAP

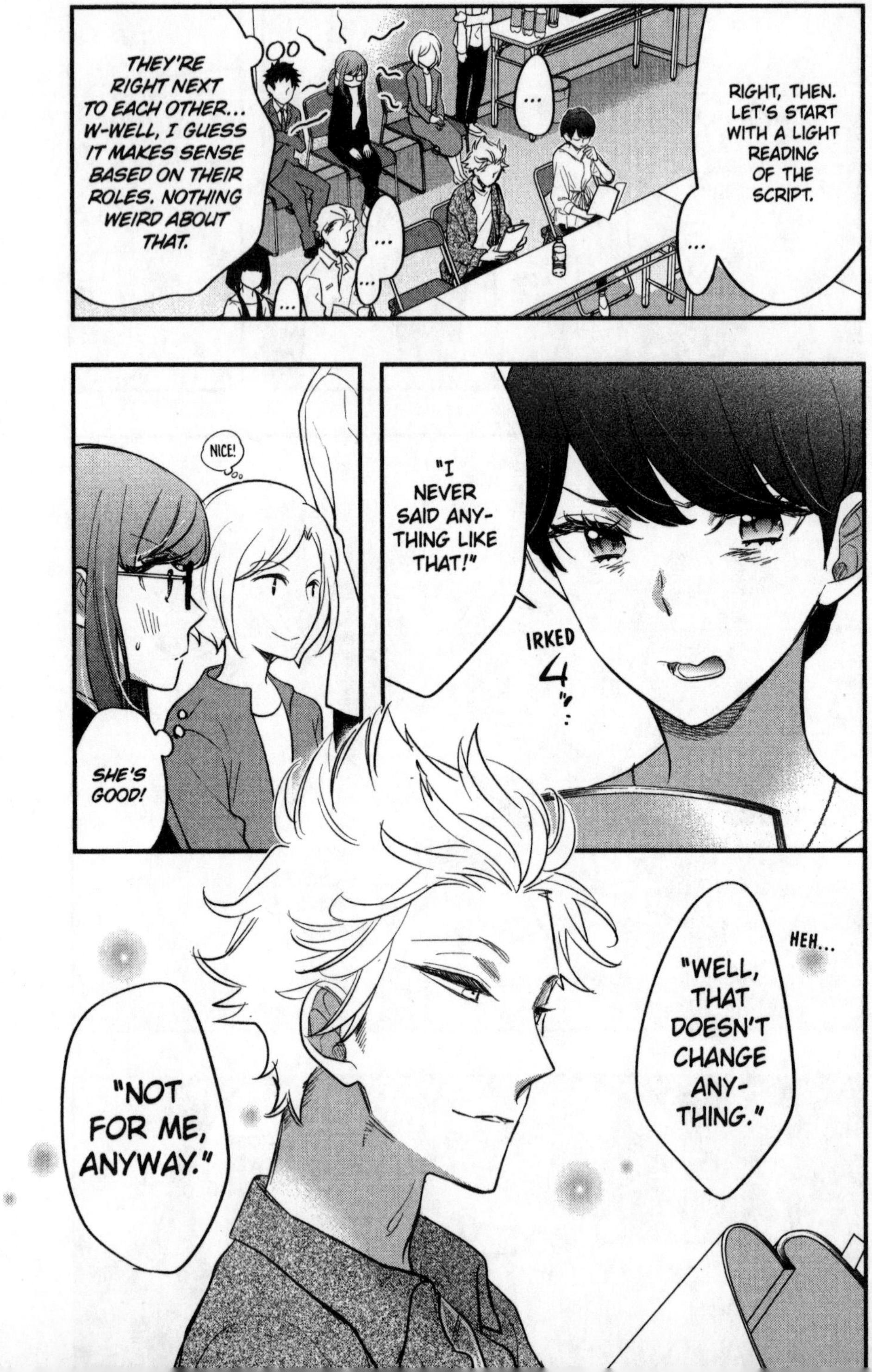
RIGHT, THEN. LET'S START WITH A LIGHT READING OF THE SCRIPT.
...
...
THEY'RE RIGHT NEXT TO EACH OTHER... W-WELL, I GUESS IT MAKES SENSE BASED ON THEIR ROLES. NOTHING WEIRD ABOUT THAT.
...
...
...
"I NEVER SAID ANYTHING LIKE THAT!"
IRKED
NICE!
SHE'S GOOD!
HEH...
"WELL, THAT DOESN'T CHANGE ANYTHING."
"NOT FOR ME, ANYWAY."

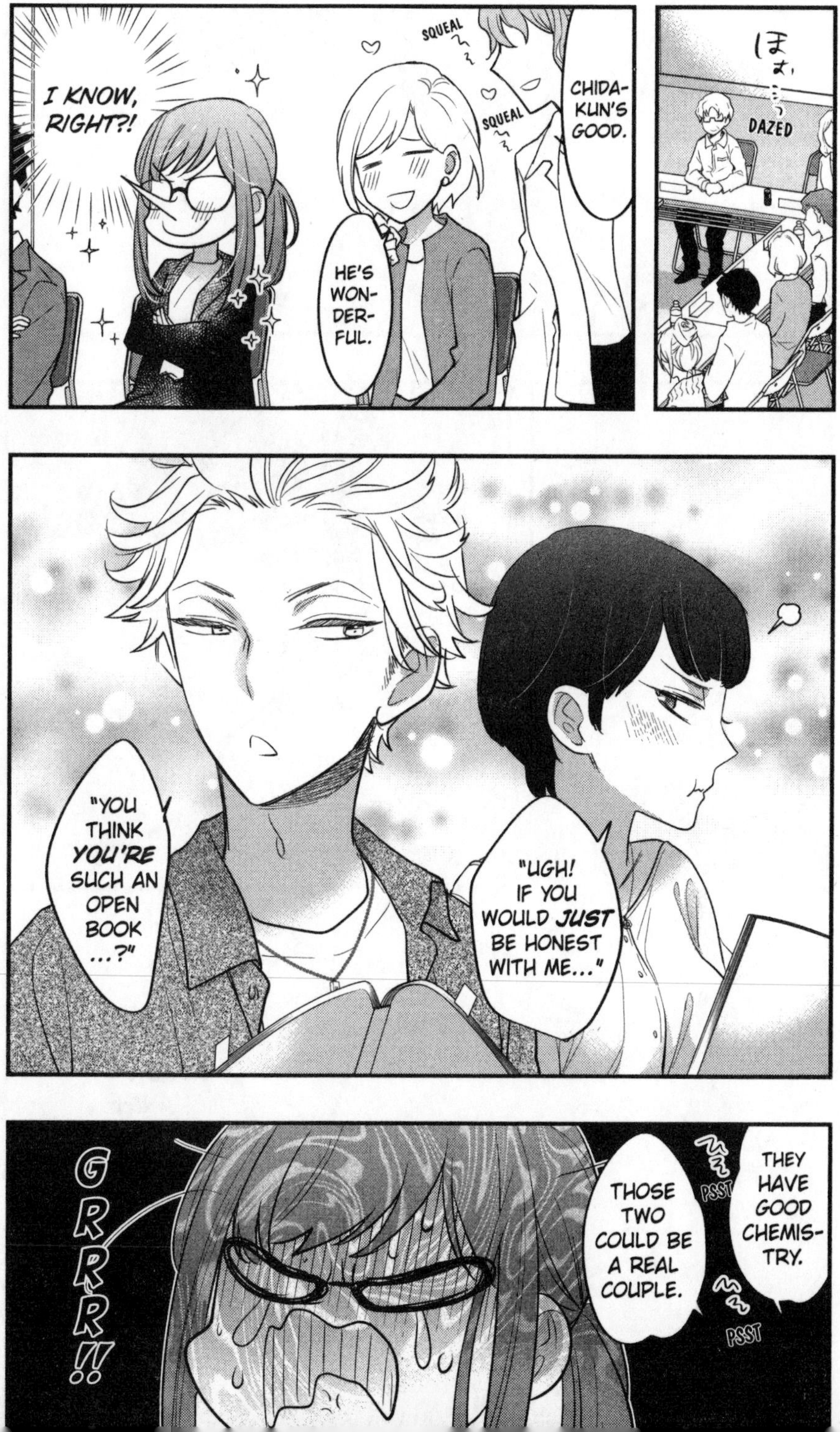
DAZED
CHIDA-KUN'S GOOD.
SQUEAL
SQUEAL
HE'S WONDER-FUL.
I KNOW, RIGHT?!
"UGH! IF YOU WOULD JUST BE HONEST WITH ME..."
"YOU THINK YOU'RE SUCH AN OPEN BOOK ...?"
THEY HAVE GOOD CHEMIS-TRY.
PSST
THOSE TWO COULD BE A REAL COUPLE.
PSST
GRRRR!!

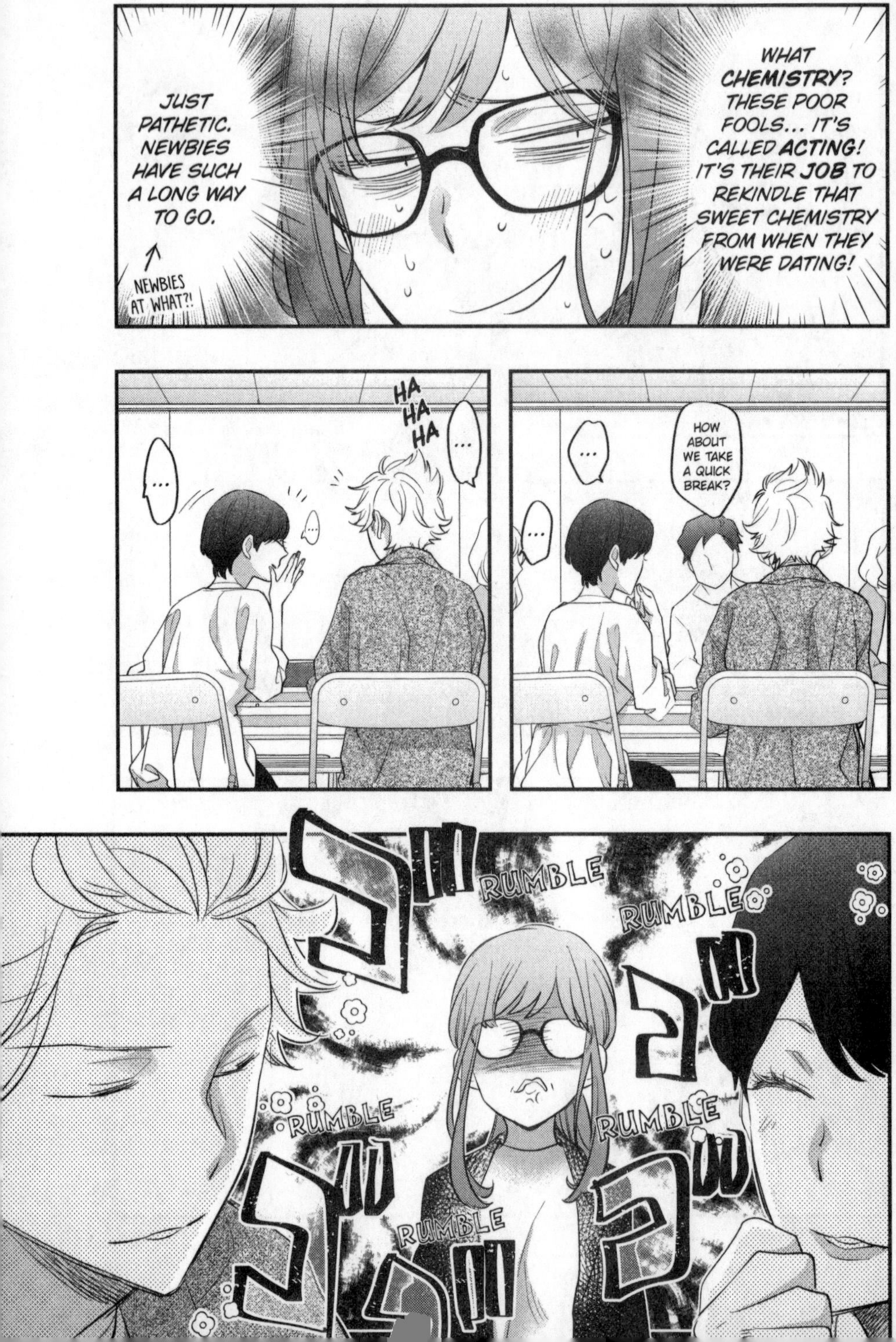
WHAT CHEMISTRY? THESE POOR FOOLS... IT'S CALLED ACTING! IT'S THEIR JOB TO REKINDLE THAT SWEET CHEMISTRY FROM WHEN THEY WERE DATING!
JUST PATHETIC. NEWBIES HAVE SUCH A LONG WAY TO GO.
NEWBIES AT WHAT?!
HOW ABOUT WE TAKE A QUICK BREAK?
...
...
HA HA HA
...
...
...
RUMBLE
RUMBLE
RUMBLE
RUMBLE
RUMBLE

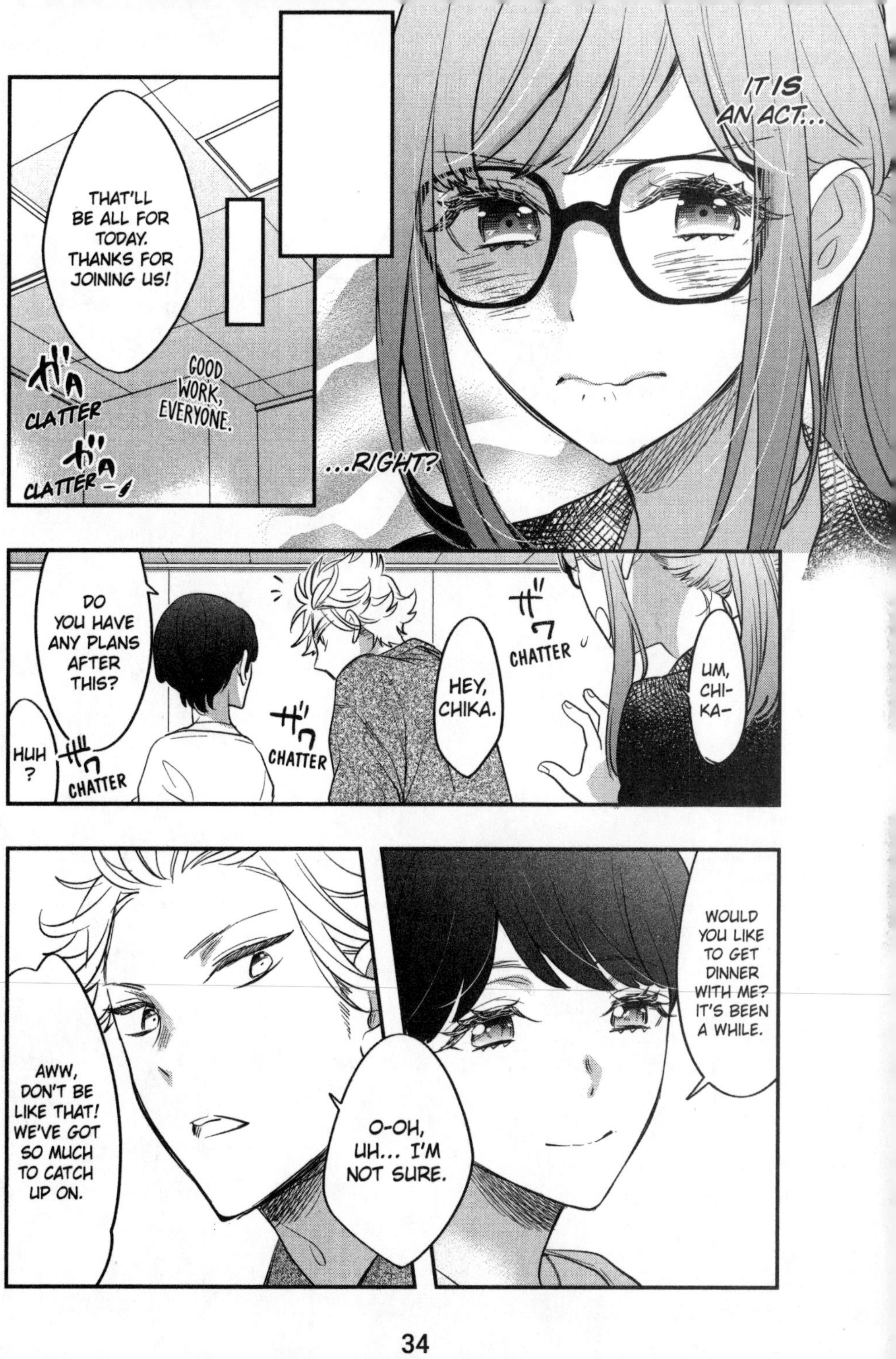
IT IS AN ACT...
...RIGHT?
THAT'LL BE ALL FOR TODAY. THANKS FOR JOINING US!
GOOD WORK, EVERYONE.
ガタ CLATTER
ガタ CLATTER
UM, CHI-KA-
ザワ CHATTER
HEY, CHIKA.
ザワ CHATTER
DO YOU HAVE ANY PLANS AFTER THIS?
HUH?
ザワ CHATTER
WOULD YOU LIKE TO GET DINNER WITH ME? IT'S BEEN A WHILE.
O-OH, UH... I'M NOT SURE.
AWW, DON'T BE LIKE THAT! WE'VE GOT SO MUCH TO CATCH UP ON.

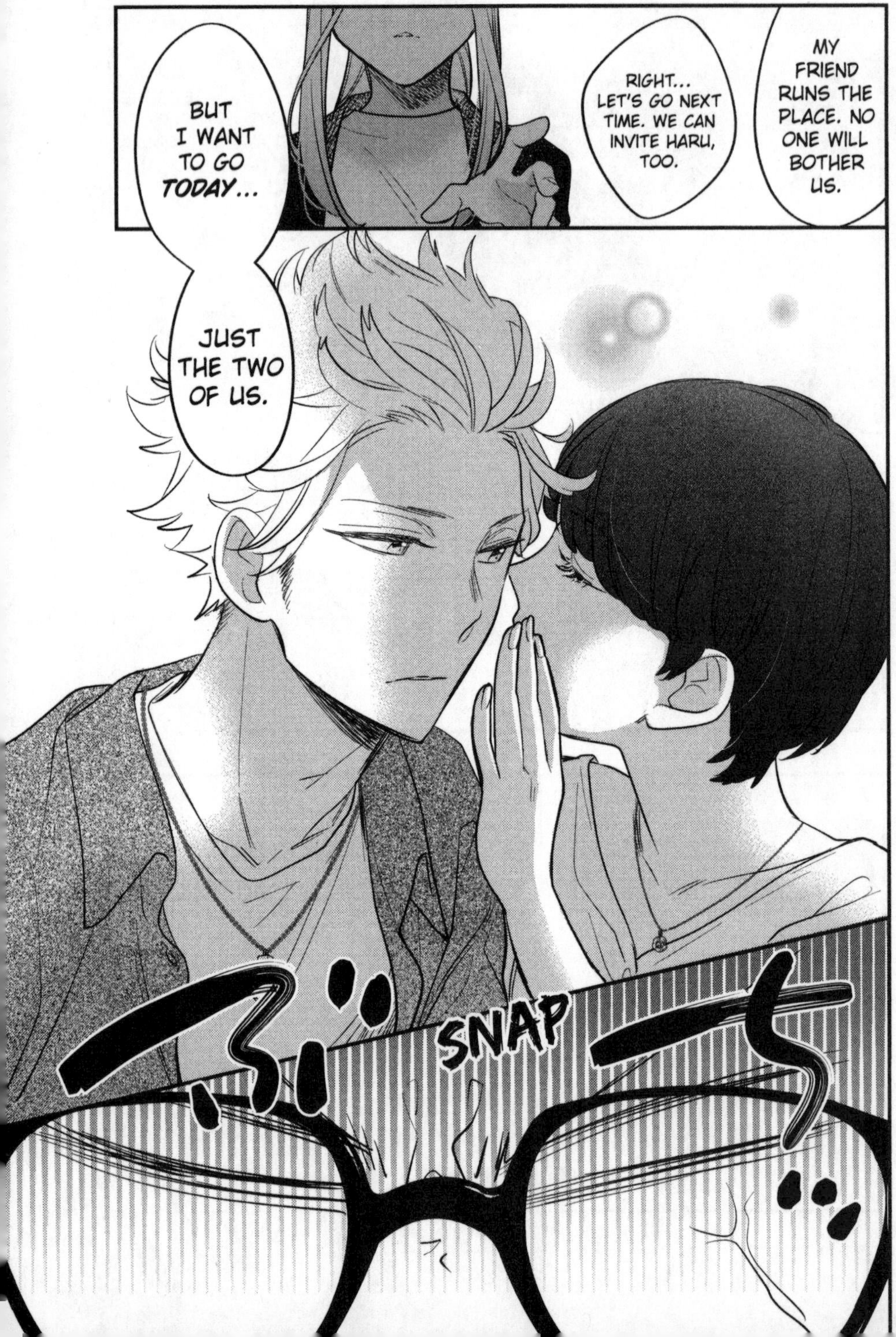
MY FRIEND RUNS THE PLACE. NO ONE WILL BOTHER US.
RIGHT... LET'S GO NEXT TIME. WE CAN INVITE HARU, TOO.
BUT I WANT TO GO *TODAY*...
JUST THE TWO OF US.
SNAP

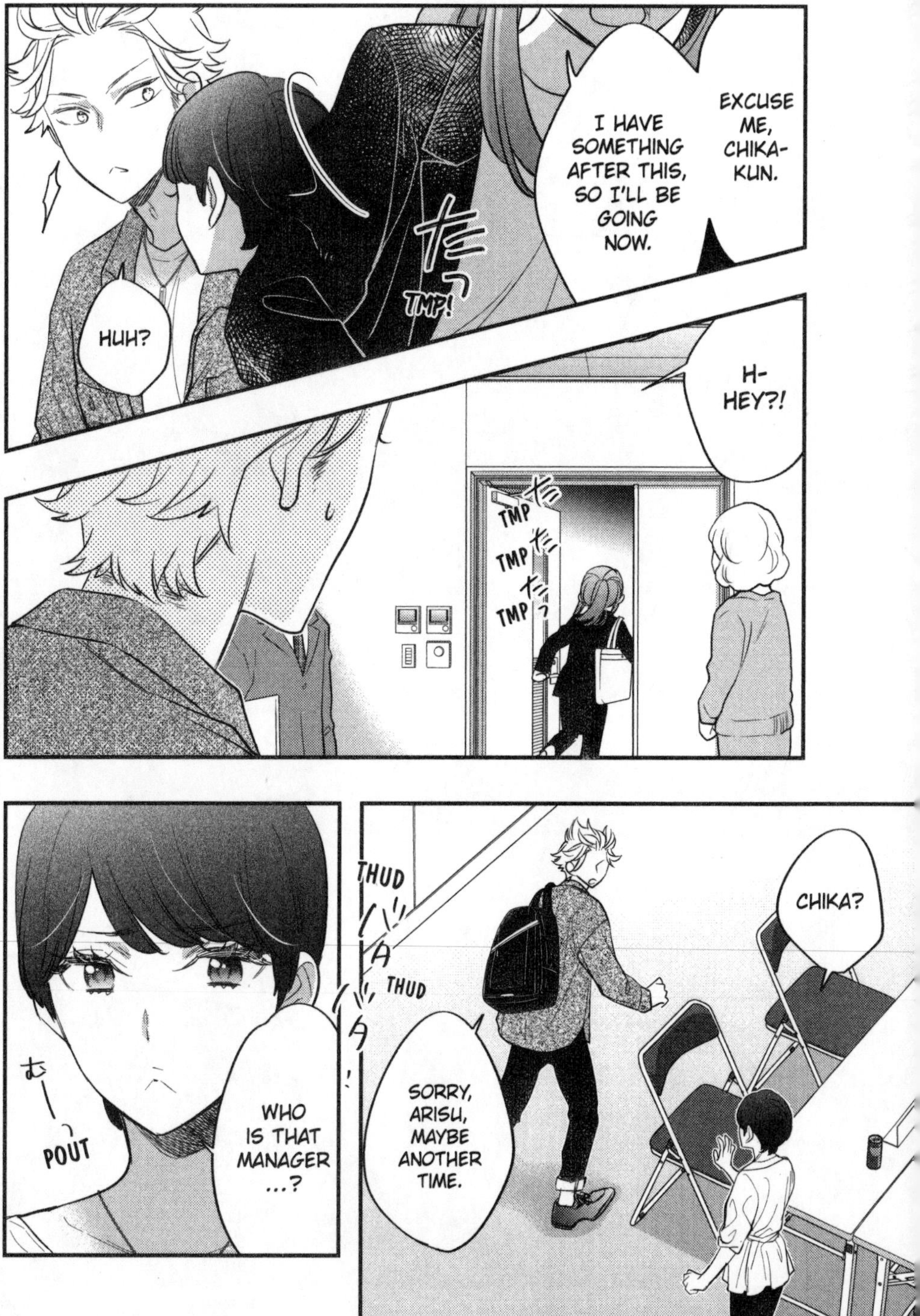
EXCUSE ME, CHIKA-KUN.
I HAVE SOMETHING AFTER THIS, SO I'LL BE GOING NOW.
TMP!
HUH?
H- HEY?!
TMP
TMP
TMP
CHIKA?
SORRY, ARISU, MAYBE ANOTHER TIME.
THUD
THUD
WHO IS THAT MANAGER ...?
POUT

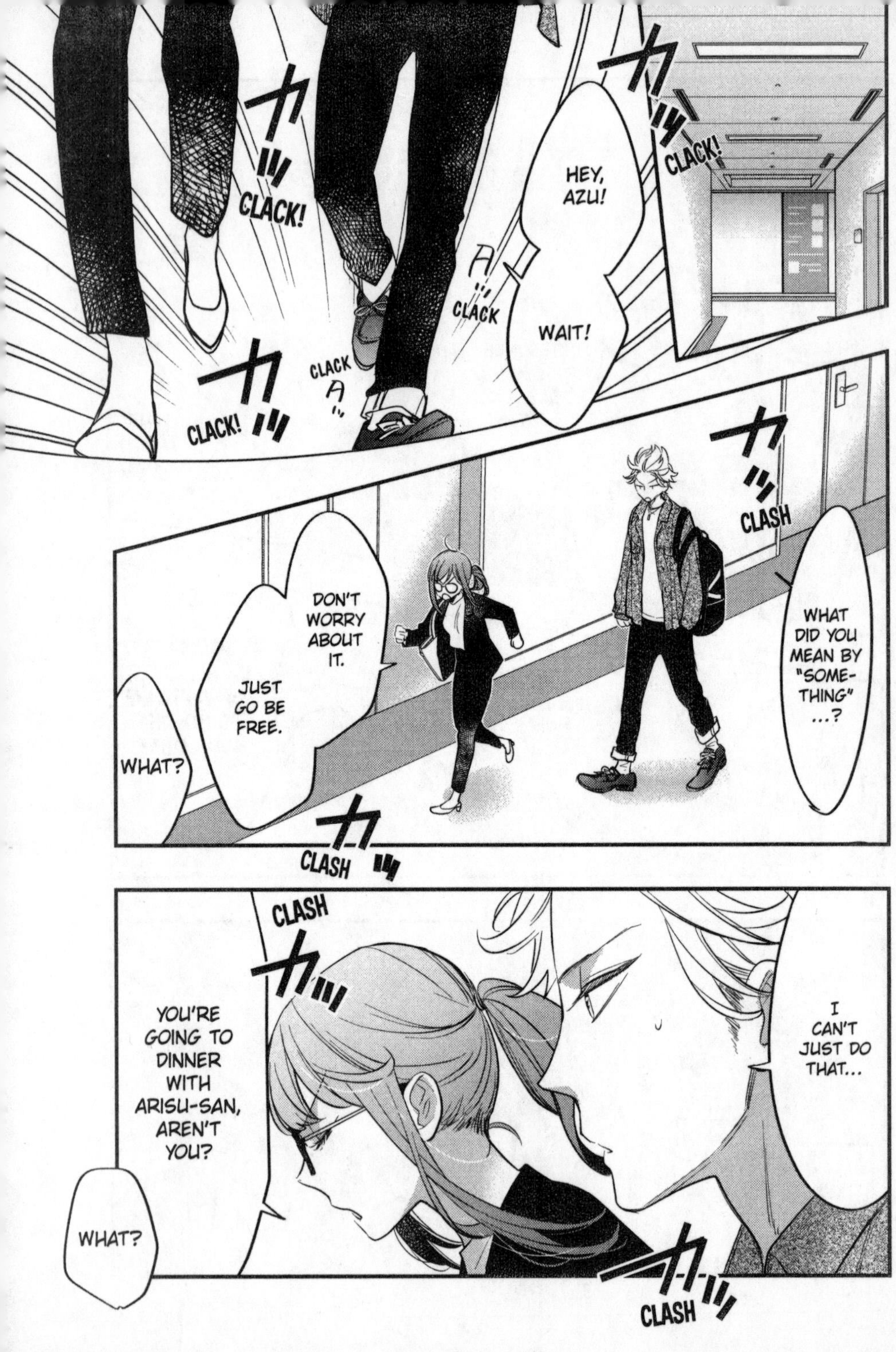
CLACK!
HEY, AZU!
WAIT!
CLACK
CLACK!
CLACK
CLACK!
CLASH
WHAT DID YOU MEAN BY "SOME-THING"...?
DON'T WORRY ABOUT IT.
JUST GO BE FREE.
WHAT?
CLASH
I CAN'T JUST DO THAT...
CLASH
YOU'RE GOING TO DINNER WITH ARISU-SAN, AREN'T YOU?
WHAT?
CLASH

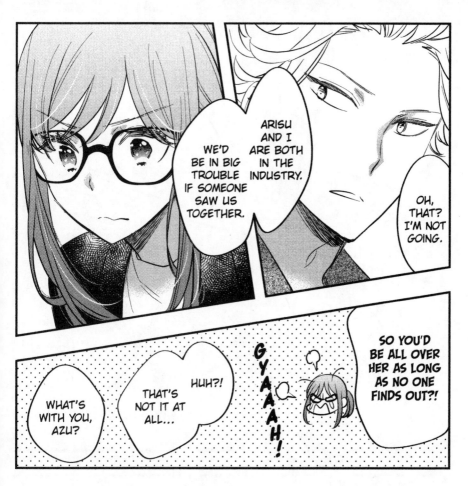

OH, THAT? I'M NOT GOING.
ARISU AND I ARE BOTH IN THE INDUSTRY.
WE'D BE IN BIG TROUBLE IF SOMEONE SAW US TOGETHER.
SO YOU'D BE ALL OVER HER AS LONG AS NO ONE FINDS OUT?!
GYAAAH!
HUH?!
THAT'S NOT IT AT ALL...
WHAT'S WITH YOU, AZU?
...!
WELL ...
OH–

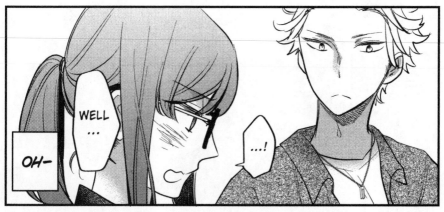

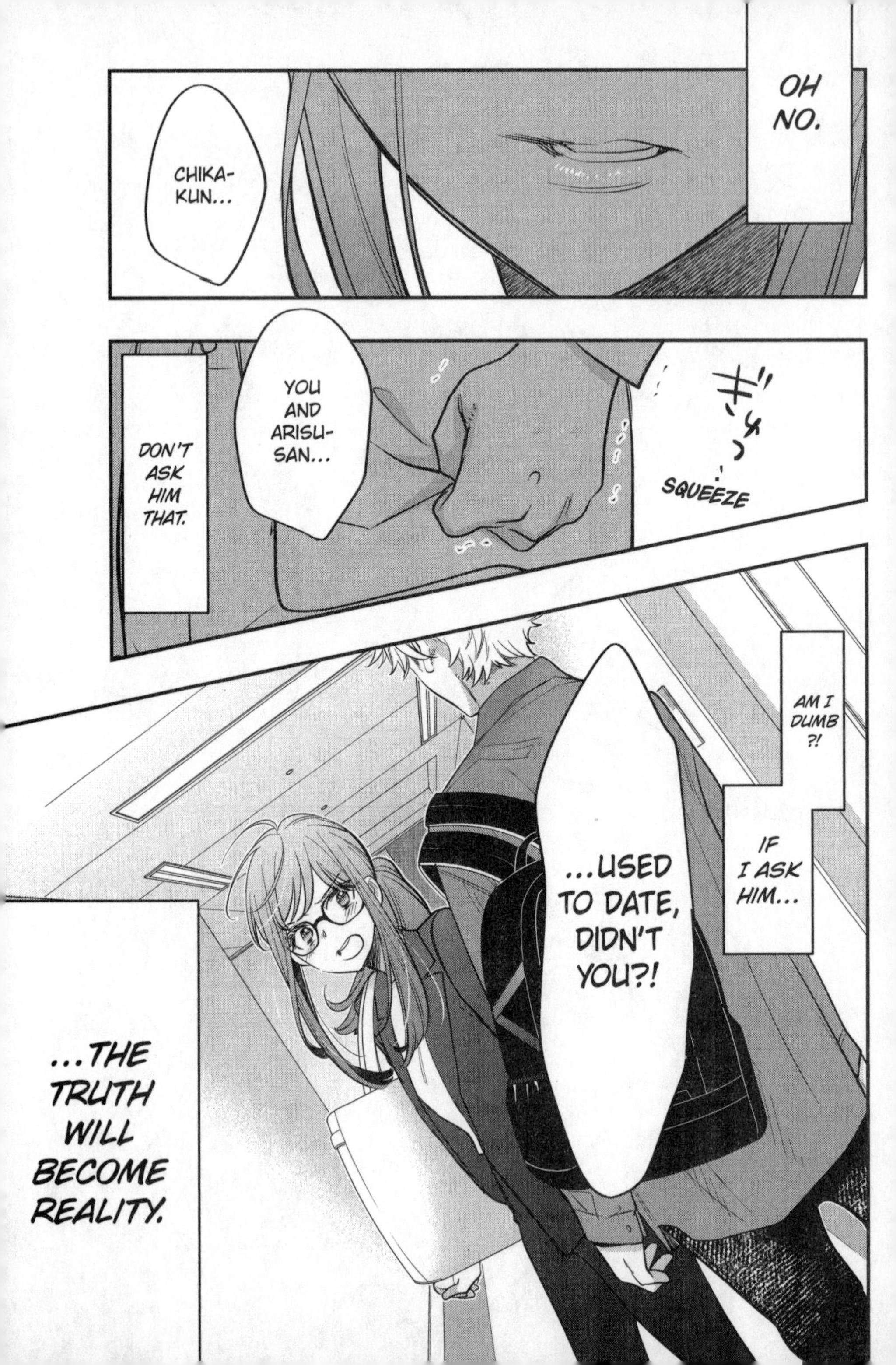
OH NO.
CHIKA-KUN...
ぎゅっ
SQUEEZE
YOU AND ARISU-SAN...
DON'T ASK HIM THAT.
AM I DUMB?!
IF I ASK HIM...
...USED TO DATE, DIDN'T YOU?!
...THE TRUTH WILL BECOME REALITY.

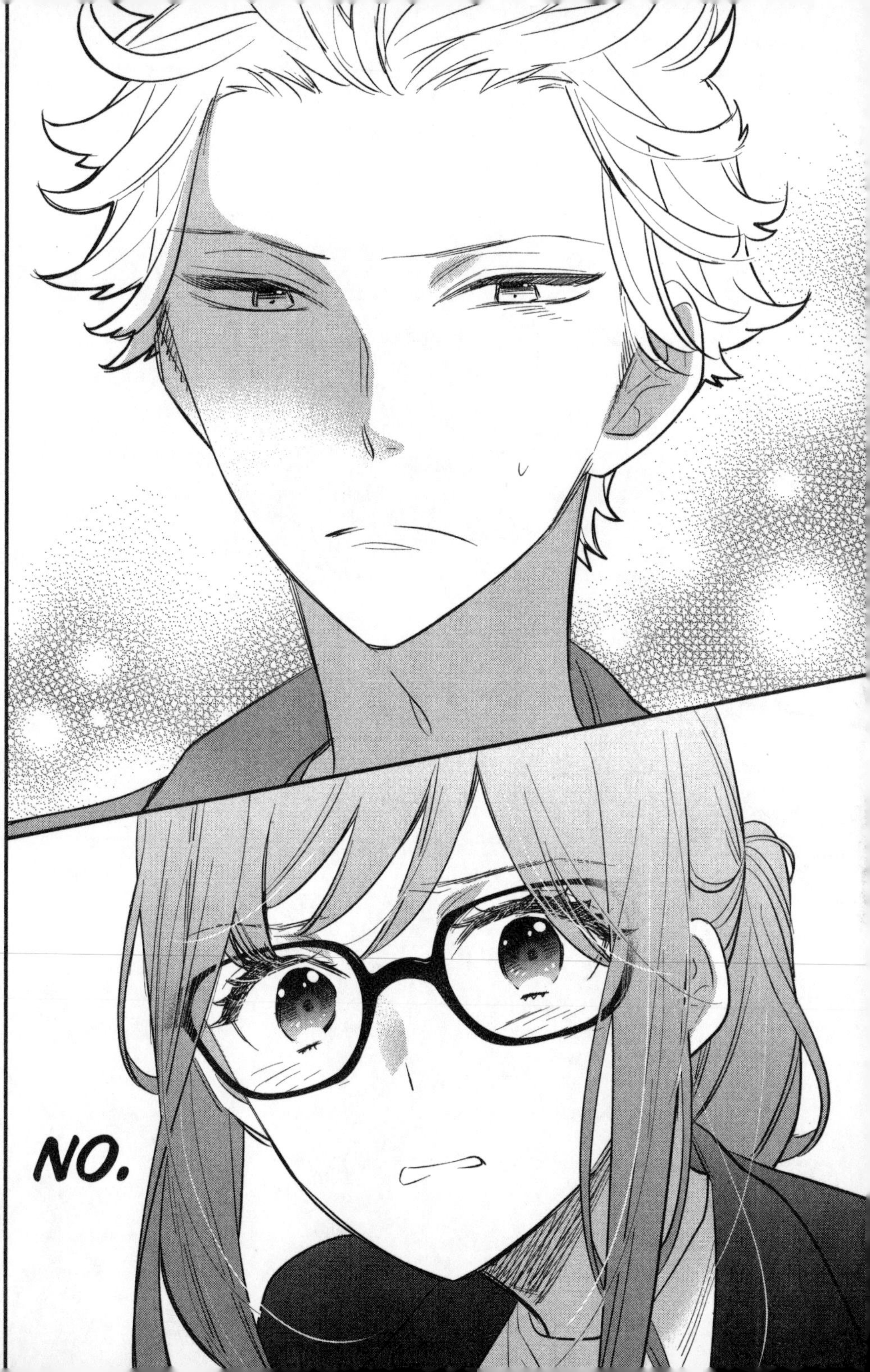
NO.

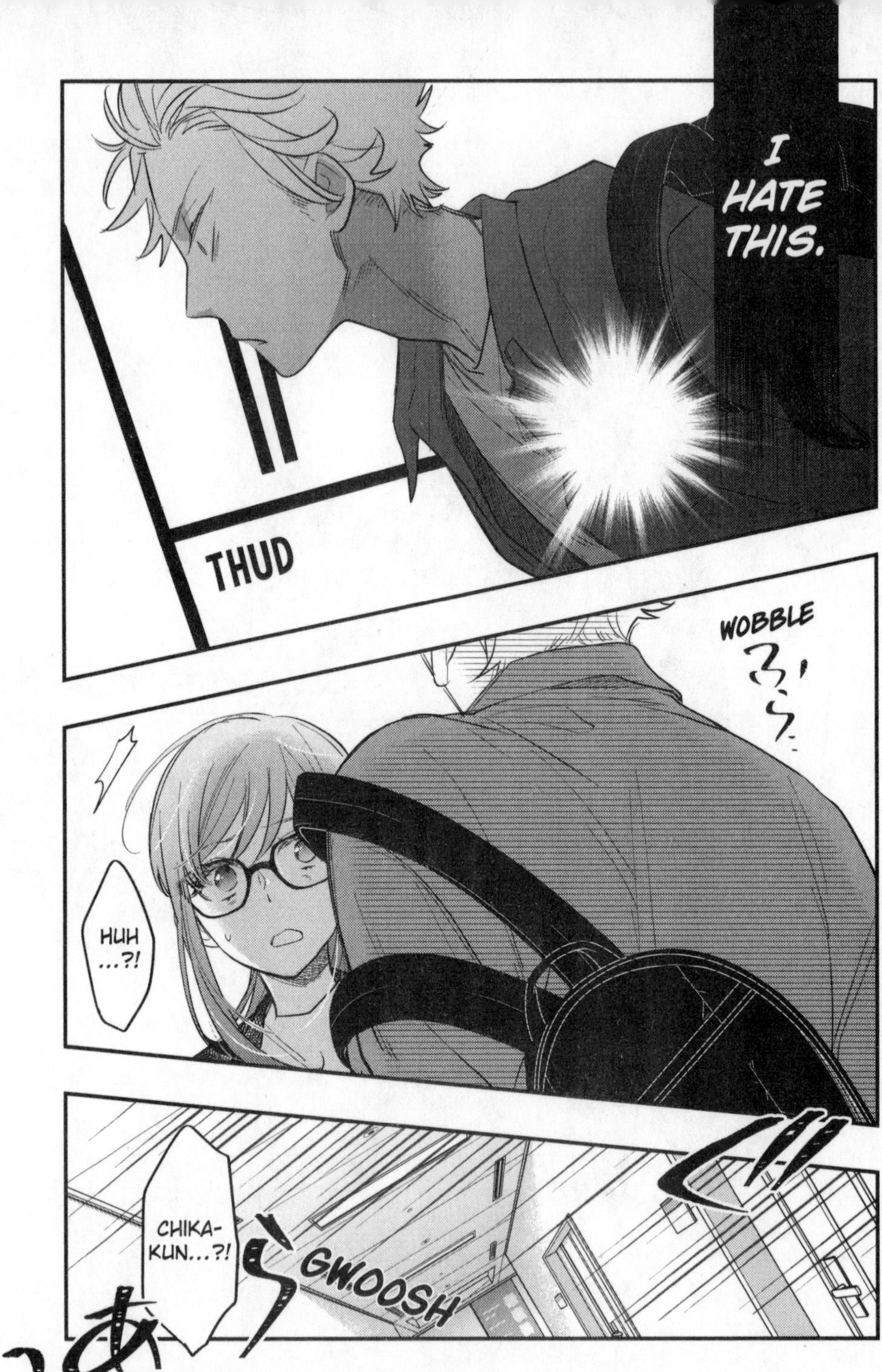
I HATE THIS.
THUD
WOBBLE
HUH ...?!
GWOOSH
CHIKA-KUN...?!

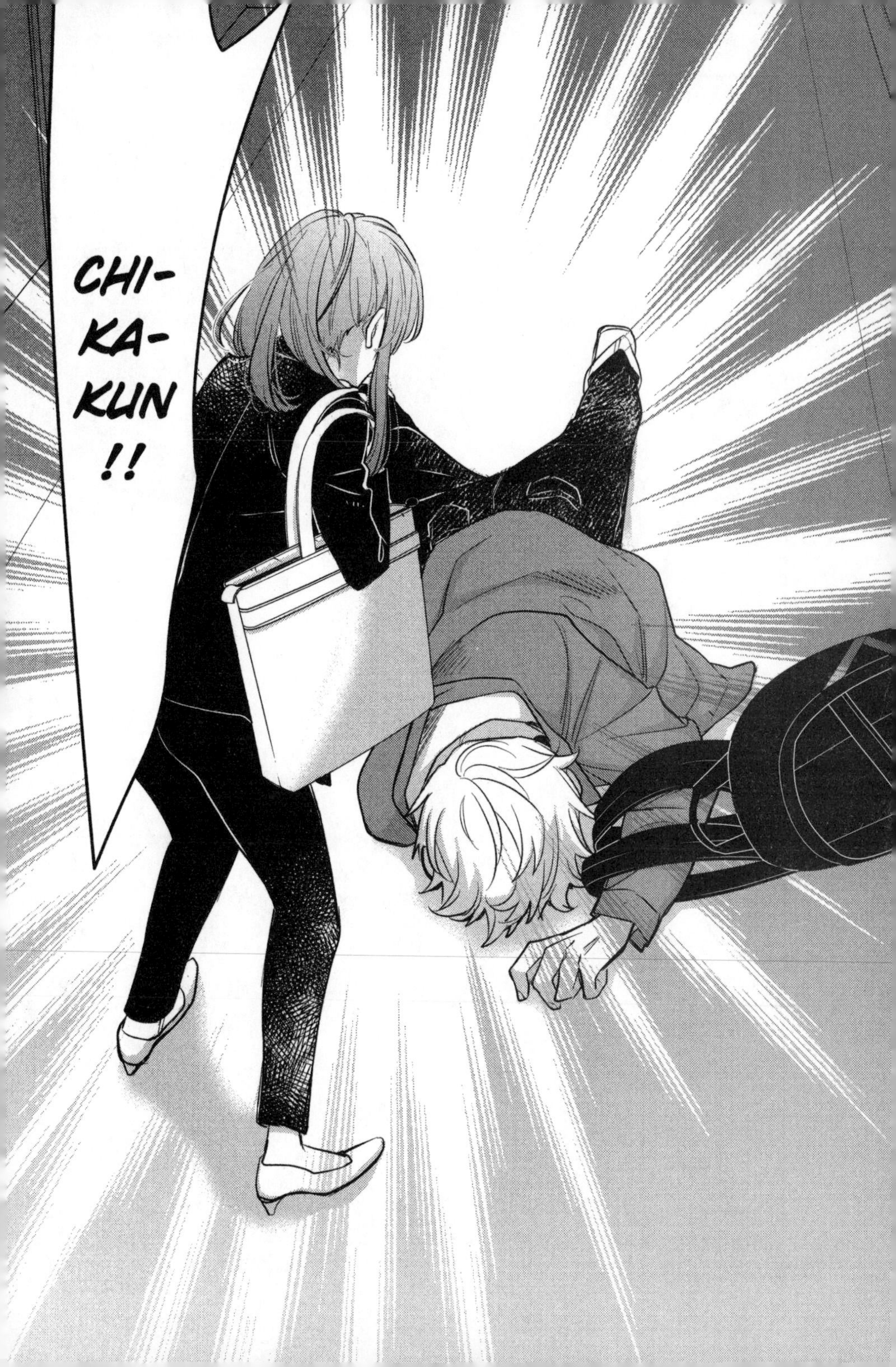
CHI-
KA-
KUN
!!

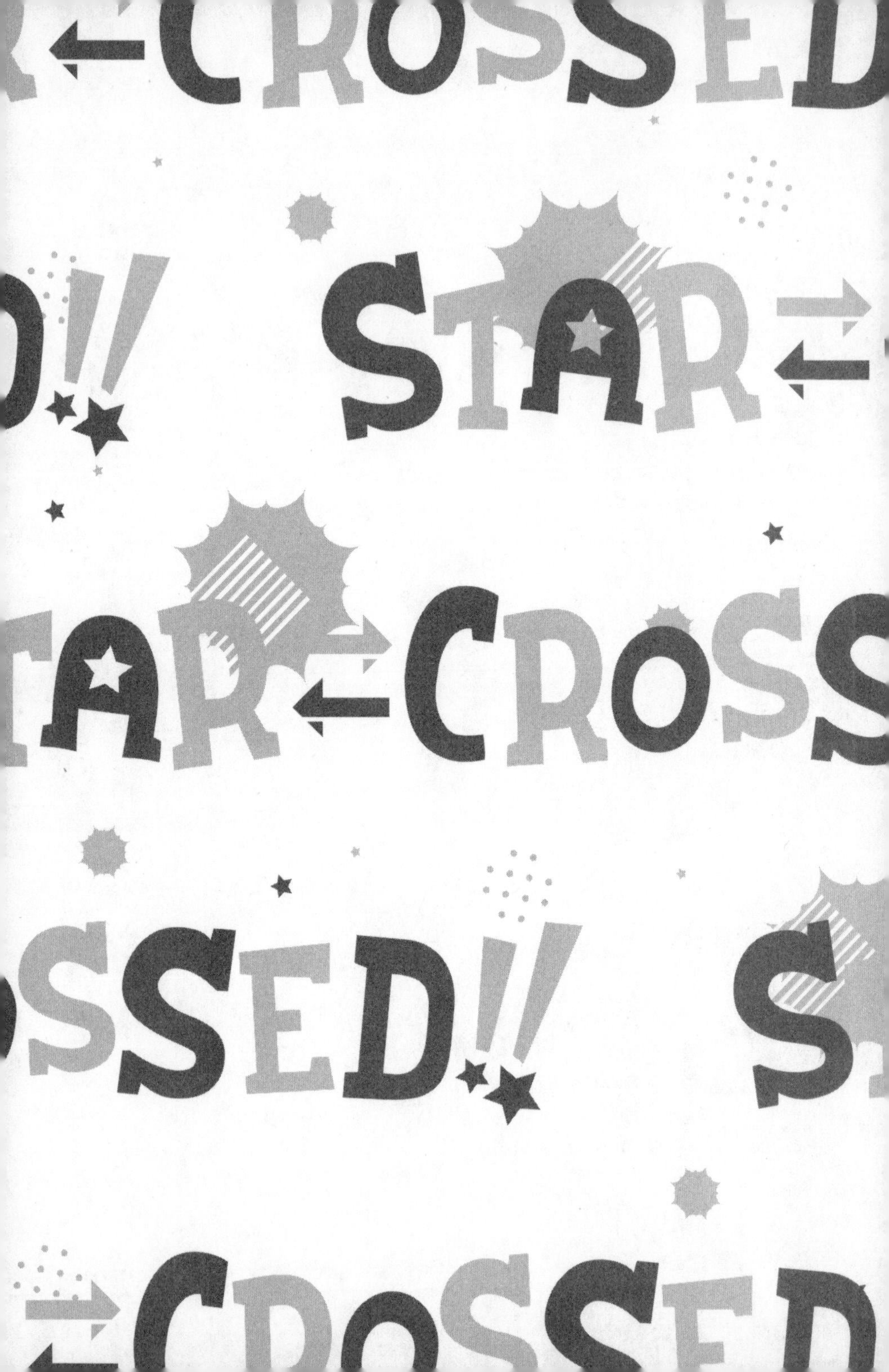
STAR-CROSSED!!

STAR⇄CROSSED!!

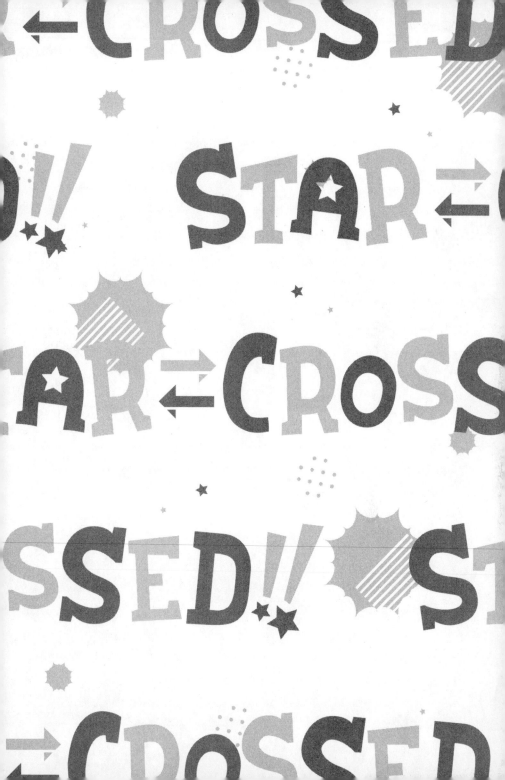

STAGE. 12 | SOMEONE SPECIAL

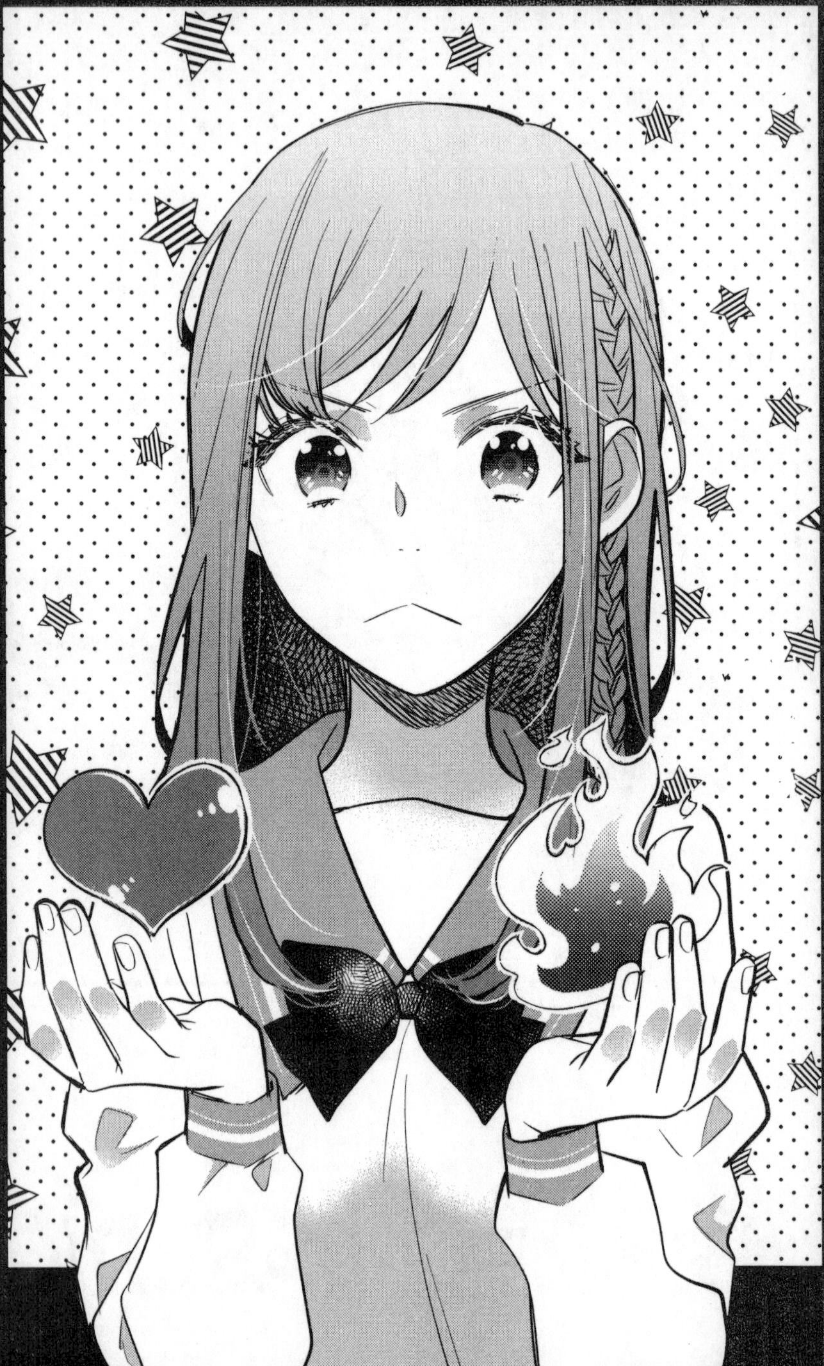

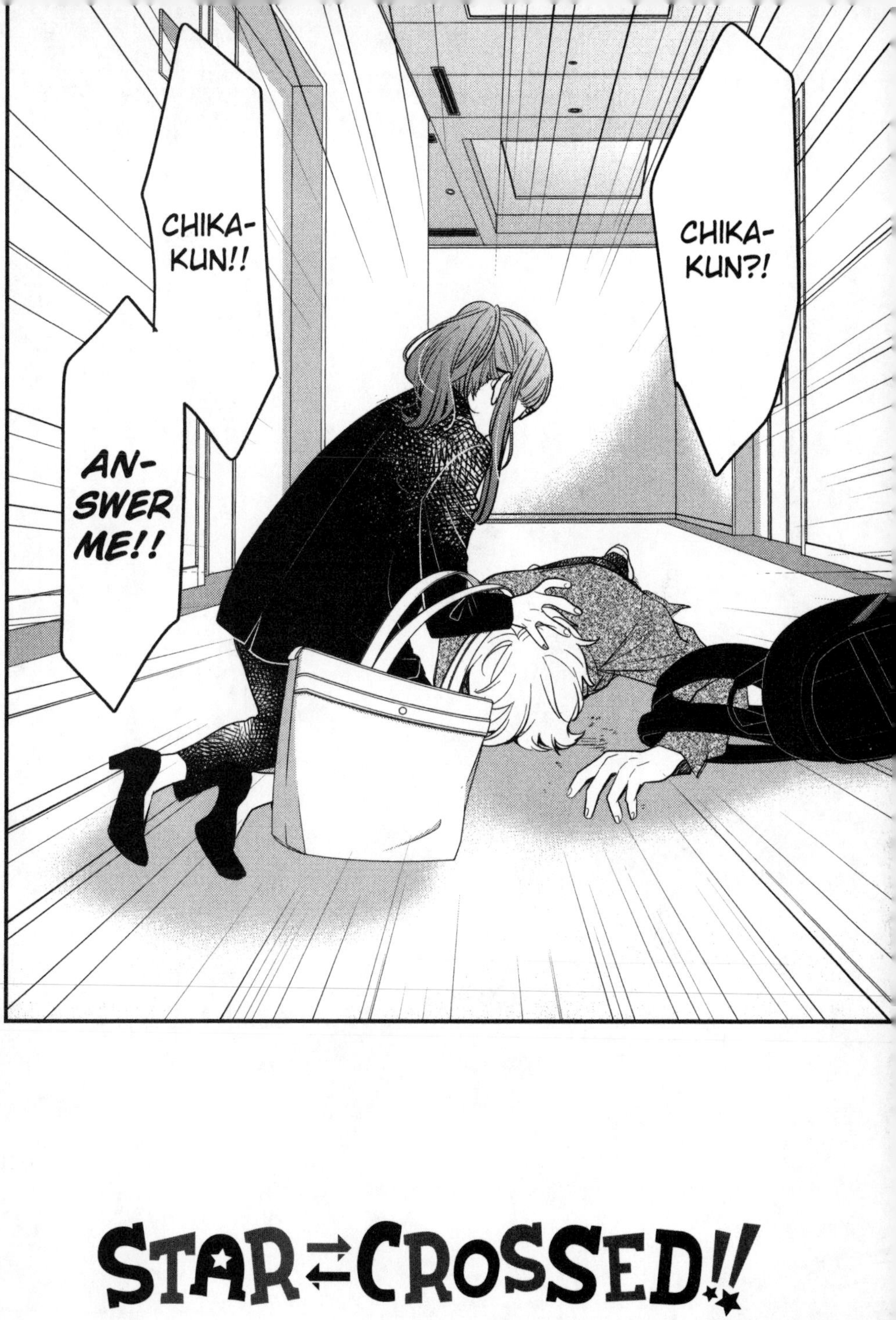
CHIKA-KUN?!
CHIKA-KUN!!
AN-SWER ME!!

STAR⇄CROSSED!!

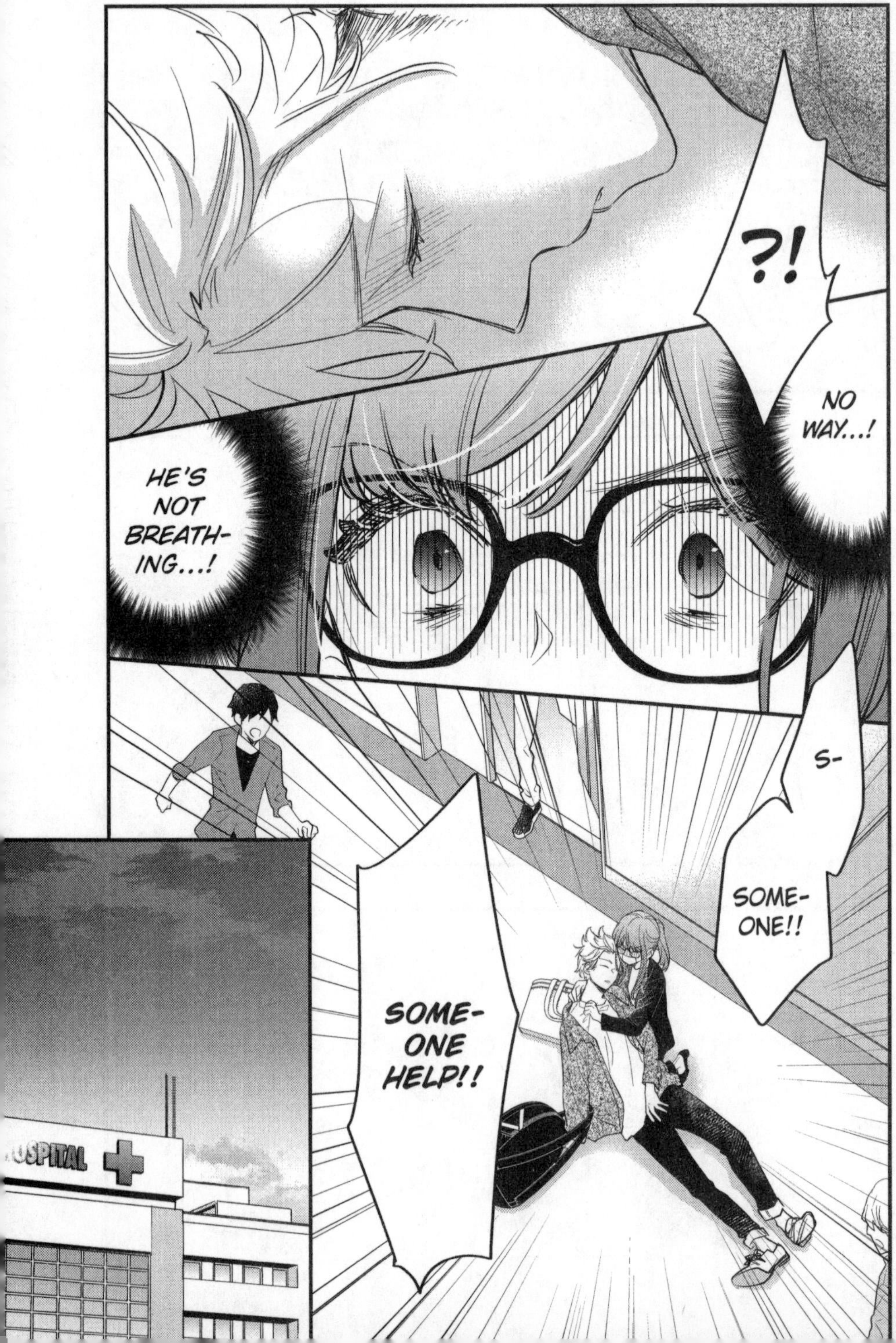
?!
NO WAY...!
HE'S NOT BREATHING...!
S-
SOME-ONE!!
SOME-ONE HELP!!
OSPITAL

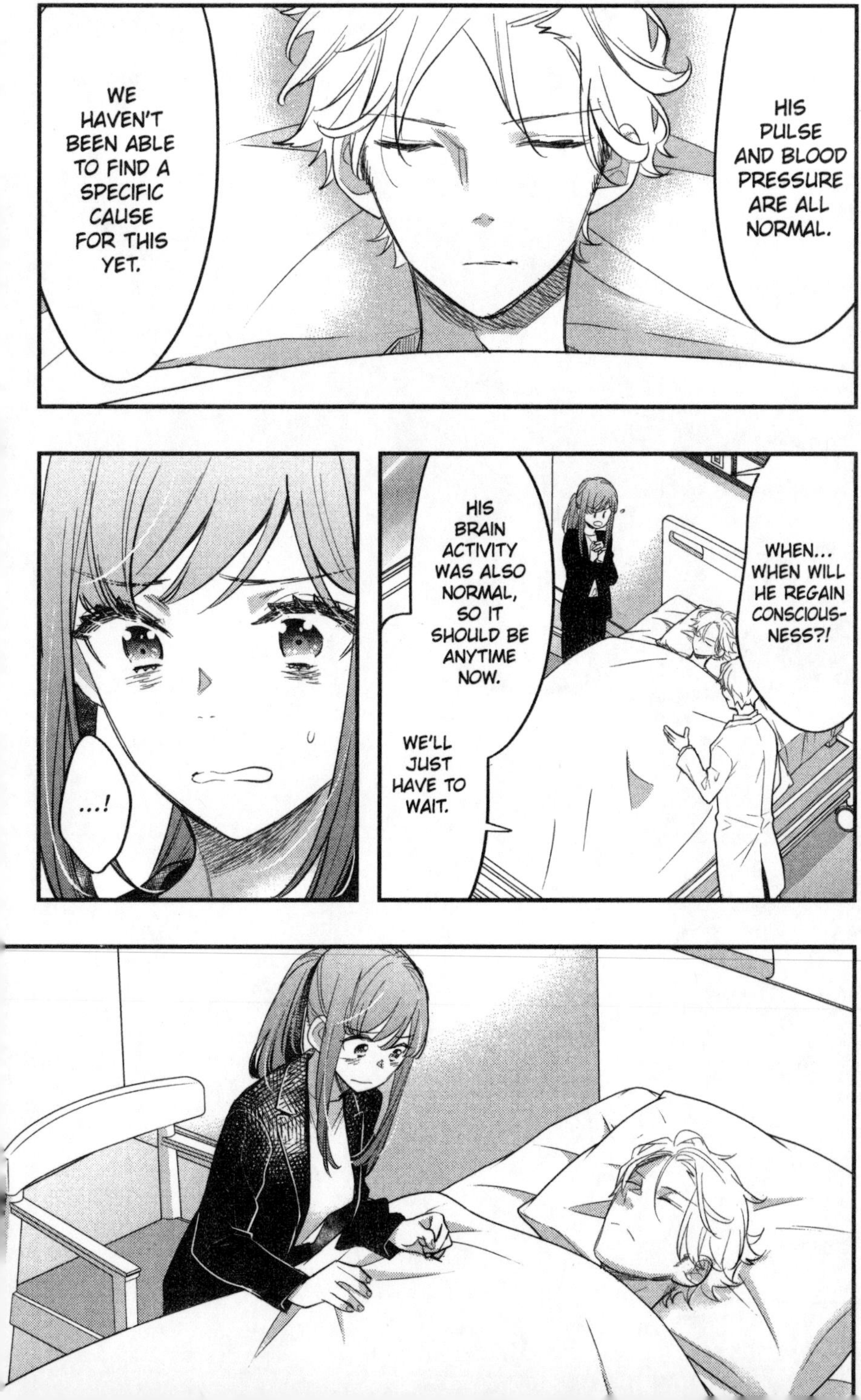
HIS PULSE AND BLOOD PRESSURE ARE ALL NORMAL.
WE HAVEN'T BEEN ABLE TO FIND A SPECIFIC CAUSE FOR THIS YET.
WHEN... WHEN WILL HE REGAIN CONSCIOUS-NESS?!
HIS BRAIN ACTIVITY WAS ALSO NORMAL, SO IT SHOULD BE ANYTIME NOW.
WE'LL JUST HAVE TO WAIT.
...!

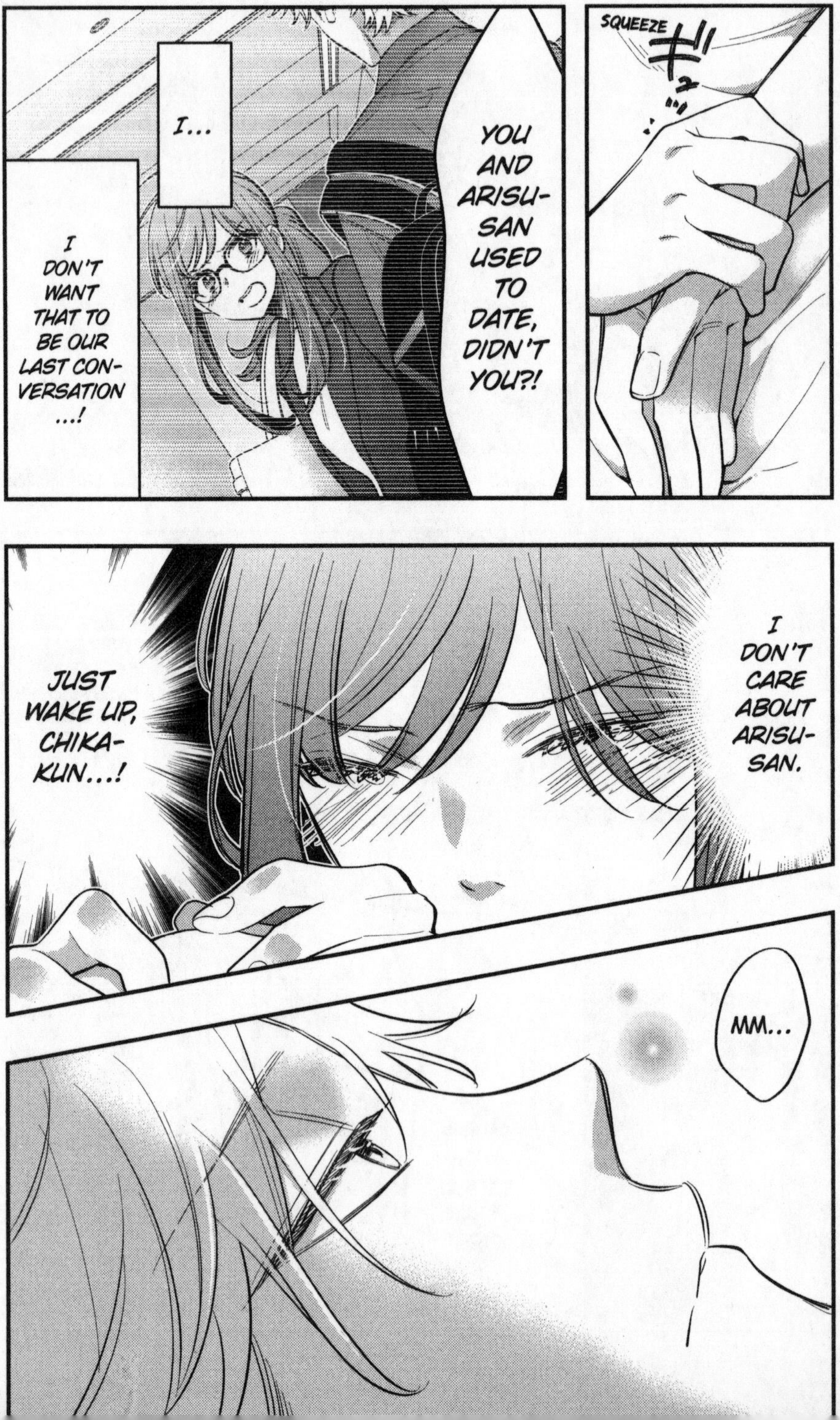
SQUEEZE
YOU AND ARISU-SAN USED TO DATE, DIDN'T YOU?!
I...
I DON'T WANT THAT TO BE OUR LAST CONVERSATION ...!
I DON'T CARE ABOUT ARISU-SAN.
JUST WAKE UP, CHIKA-KUN...!
MM...

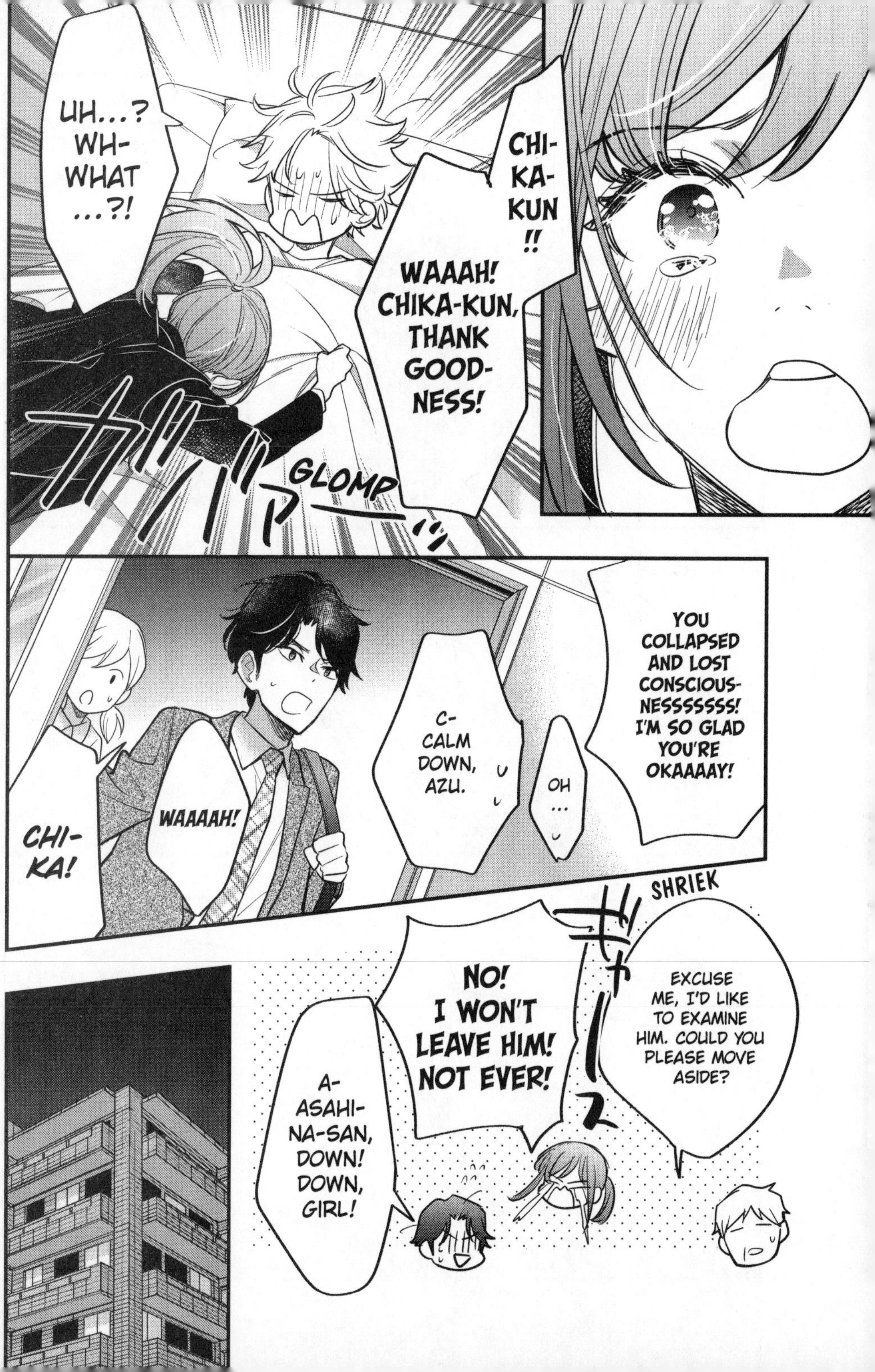
CHI-KA-KUN!!
WAAAH! CHIKA-KUN, THANK GOODNESS!
UH...? WH-WHAT...?!
GLOMP
YOU COLLAPSED AND LOST CONSCIOUS-NESSSSSSS! I'M SO GLAD YOU'RE OKAAAAY!
OH...
C-CALM DOWN, AZU.
WAAAAH!
CHI-KA!
SHRIEK
EXCUSE ME, I'D LIKE TO EXAMINE HIM. COULD YOU PLEASE MOVE ASIDE?
NO! I WON'T LEAVE HIM! NOT EVER!
A-ASAHI-NA-SAN, DOWN! DOWN, GIRL!

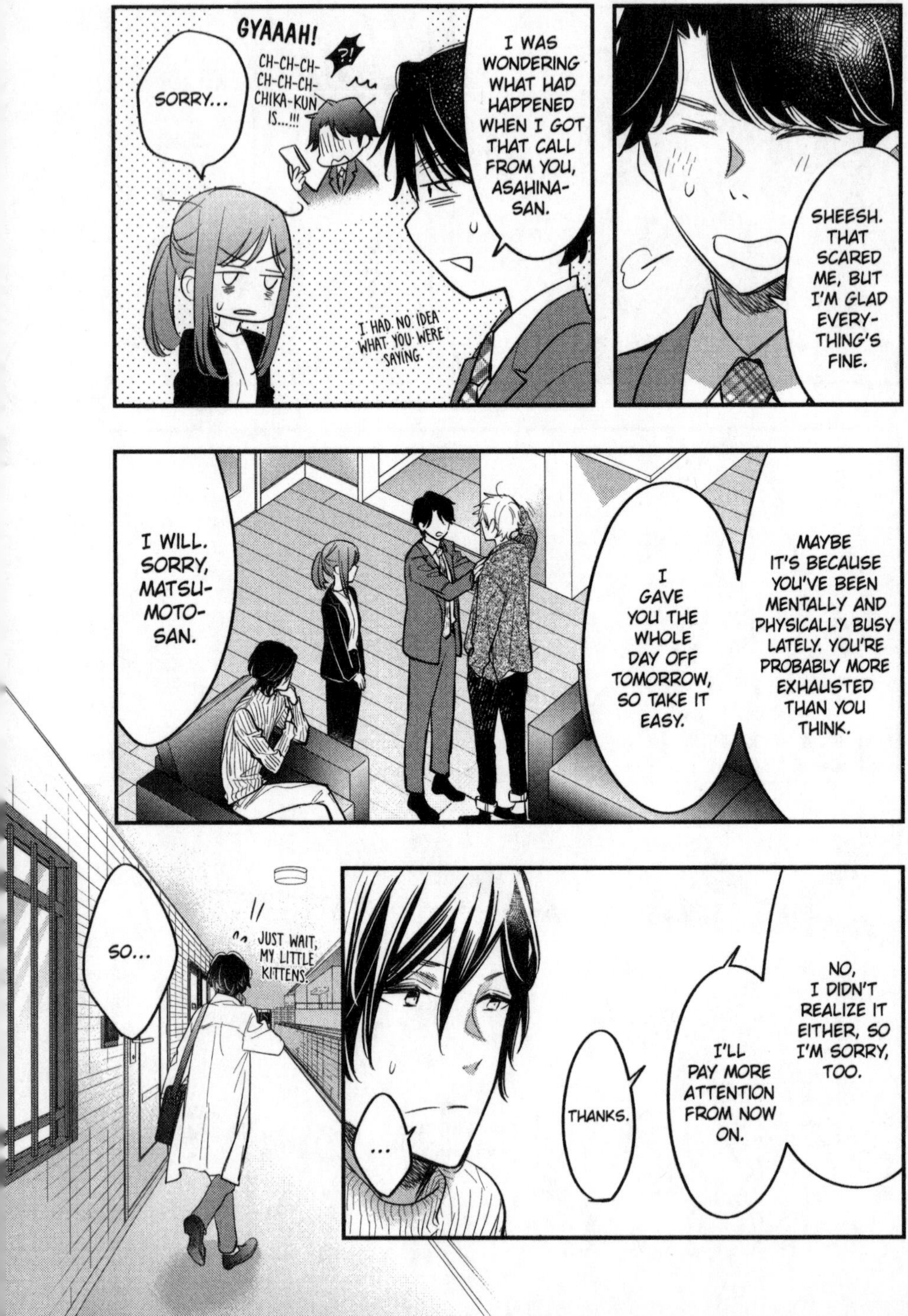
SHEESH. THAT SCARED ME, BUT I'M GLAD EVERY-THING'S FINE.
I WAS WONDERING WHAT HAD HAPPENED WHEN I GOT THAT CALL FROM YOU, ASAHINA-SAN.
GYAAAH!
CH-CH-CH-CH-CH-CH-CHIKA-KUN IS...!!!
?!
SORRY...
I HAD NO IDEA WHAT YOU WERE SAYING.
MAYBE IT'S BECAUSE YOU'VE BEEN MENTALLY AND PHYSICALLY BUSY LATELY. YOU'RE PROBABLY MORE EXHAUSTED THAN YOU THINK.
I GAVE YOU THE WHOLE DAY OFF TOMORROW, SO TAKE IT EASY.
I WILL. SORRY, MATSU-MOTO-SAN.
NO, I DIDN'T REALIZE IT EITHER, SO I'M SORRY, TOO.
I'LL PAY MORE ATTENTION FROM NOW ON.
THANKS.
...
JUST WAIT, MY LITTLE KITTENS.
SO...

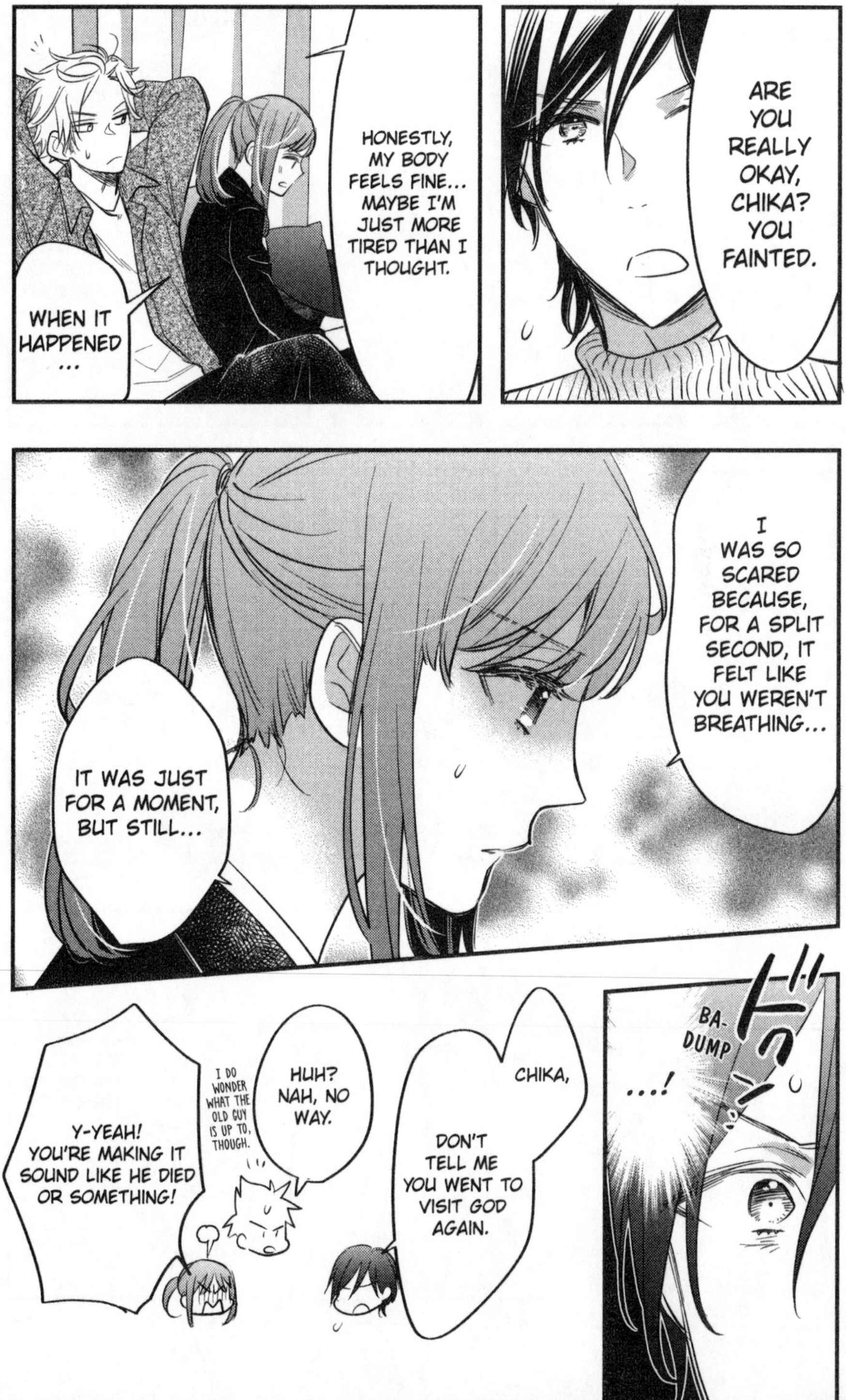
ARE YOU REALLY OKAY, CHIKA? YOU FAINTED.
HONESTLY, MY BODY FEELS FINE... MAYBE I'M JUST MORE TIRED THAN I THOUGHT.
WHEN IT HAPPENED ...
I WAS SO SCARED BECAUSE, FOR A SPLIT SECOND, IT FELT LIKE YOU WEREN'T BREATHING...
IT WAS JUST FOR A MOMENT, BUT STILL...
BA-DUMP
...!
CHIKA,
DON'T TELL ME YOU WENT TO VISIT GOD AGAIN.
HUH? NAH, NO WAY.
I DO WONDER WHAT THE OLD GUY IS UP TO, THOUGH.
Y-YEAH! YOU'RE MAKING IT SOUND LIKE HE DIED OR SOMETHING!

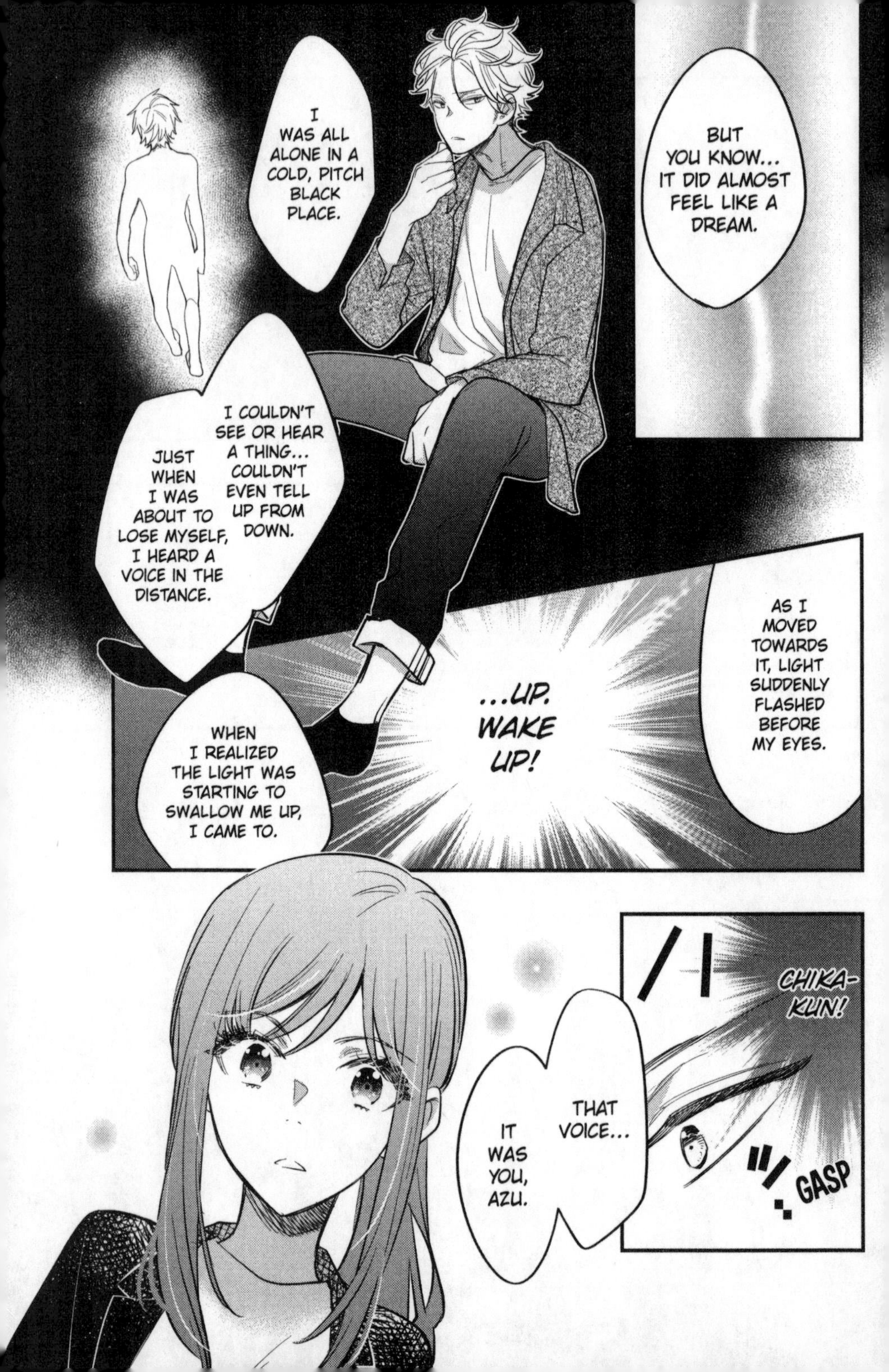
BUT YOU KNOW... IT DID ALMOST FEEL LIKE A DREAM.
I WAS ALL ALONE IN A COLD, PITCH BLACK PLACE.
I COULDN'T SEE OR HEAR A THING... COULDN'T EVEN TELL UP FROM DOWN.
JUST WHEN I WAS ABOUT TO LOSE MYSELF, I HEARD A VOICE IN THE DISTANCE.
AS I MOVED TOWARDS IT, LIGHT SUDDENLY FLASHED BEFORE MY EYES.
...UP. WAKE UP!
WHEN I REALIZED THE LIGHT WAS STARTING TO SWALLOW ME UP, I CAME TO.
CHIKA-KUN!
GASP
THAT VOICE...
IT WAS YOU, AZU.

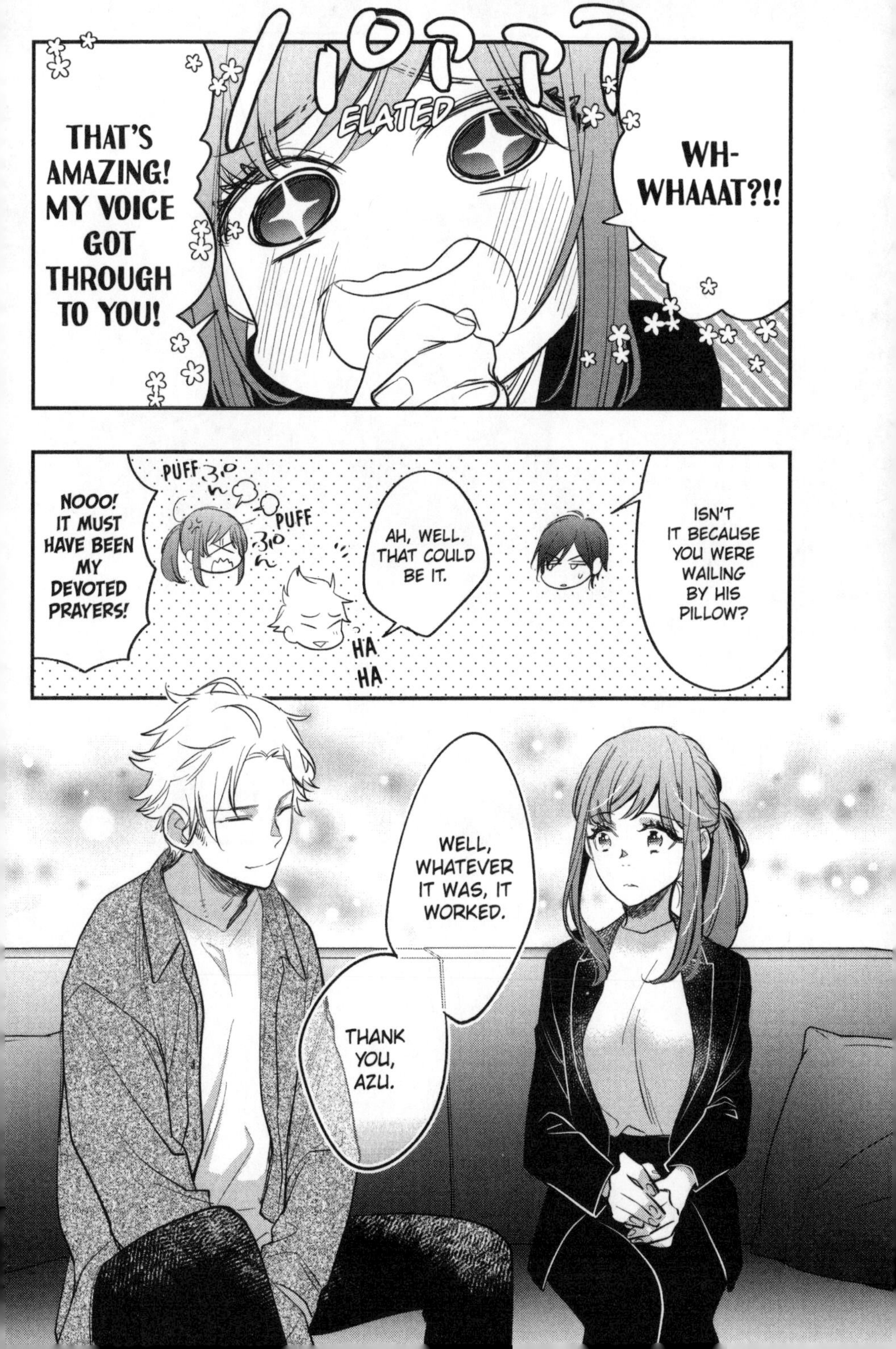
WH-WHAAAT?!!
ELATED
THAT'S AMAZING! MY VOICE GOT THROUGH TO YOU!
ISN'T IT BECAUSE YOU WERE WAILING BY HIS PILLOW?
AH, WELL. THAT COULD BE IT.
HA HA
NOOO! IT MUST HAVE BEEN MY DEVOTED PRAYERS!
PUFF
PUFF
WELL, WHATEVER IT WAS, IT WORKED.
THANK YOU, AZU.

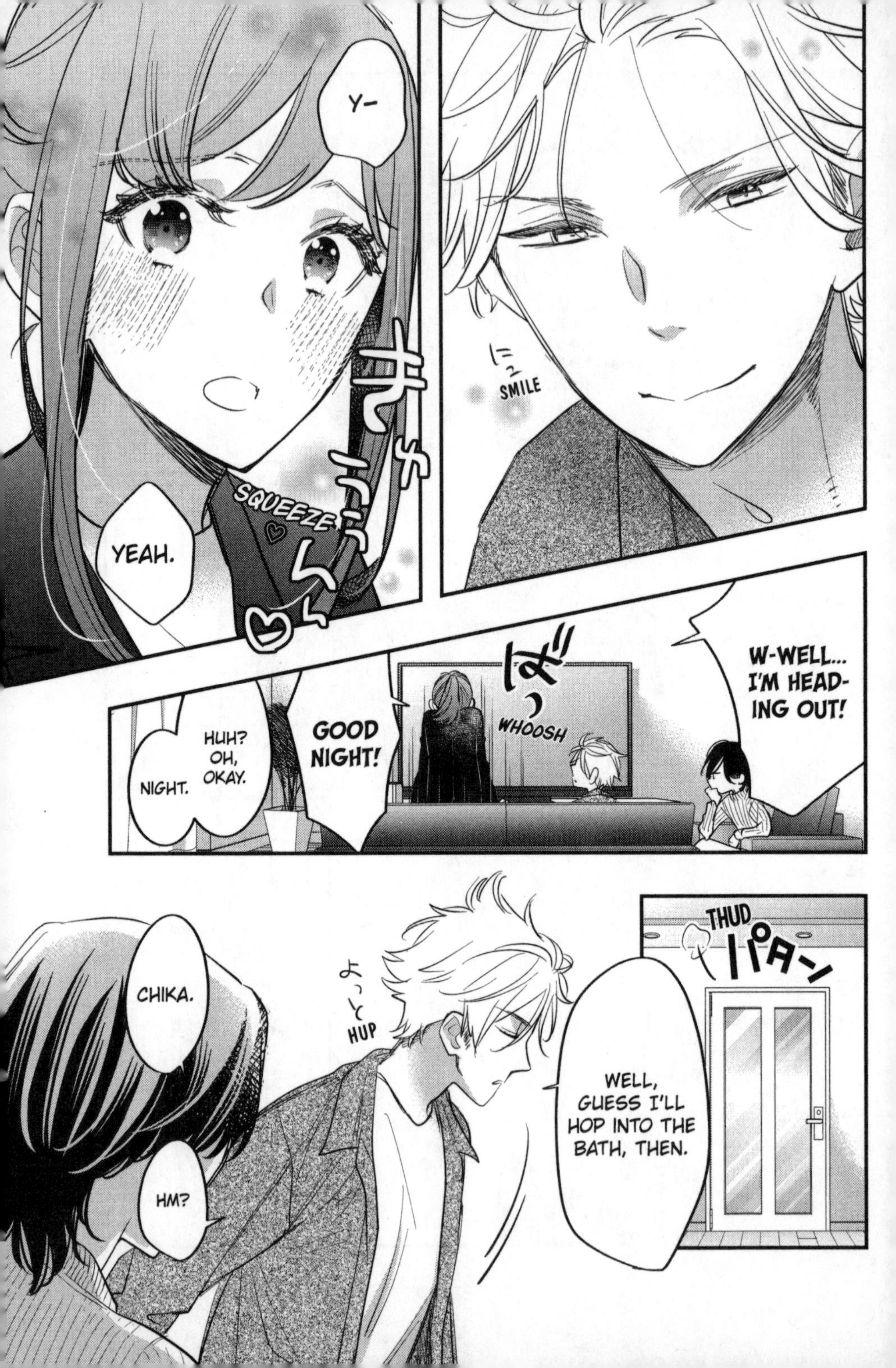
にっ
SMILE
Y-
きゅううん
SQUEEZE
YEAH.
W-WELL... I'M HEADING OUT!
ばっ
WHOOSH
GOOD NIGHT!
HUH? OH, OKAY.
NIGHT.
THUD
パタン
WELL, GUESS I'LL HOP INTO THE BATH, THEN.
よっと
HUP
CHIKA.
HM?

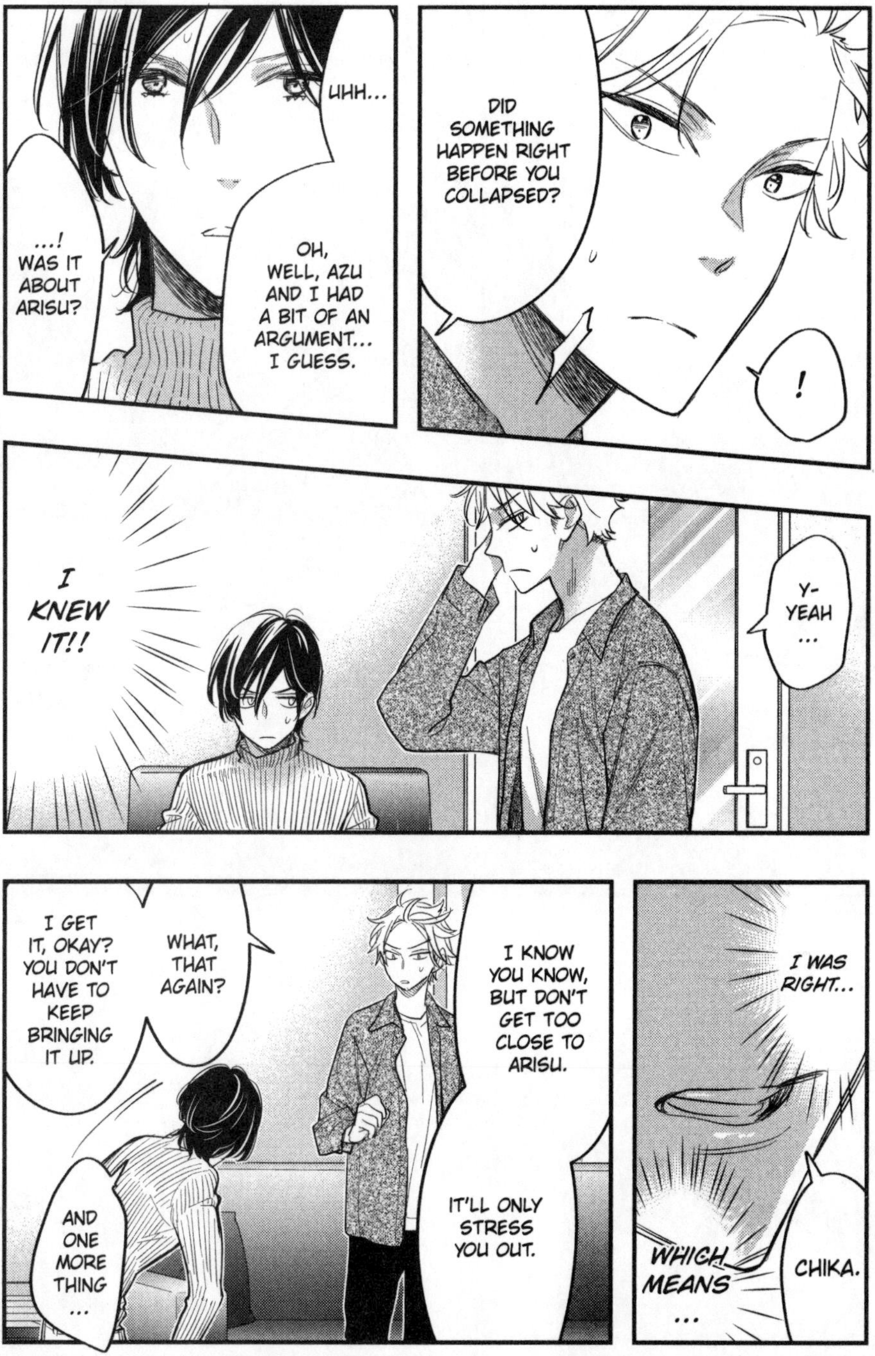
DID SOMETHING HAPPEN RIGHT BEFORE YOU COLLAPSED?
!
UHH...
OH, WELL, AZU AND I HAD A BIT OF AN ARGUMENT... I GUESS.
...! WAS IT ABOUT ARISU?
Y-YEAH...
I KNEW IT!!
I WAS RIGHT...
WHICH MEANS...
CHIKA.
I KNOW YOU KNOW, BUT DON'T GET TOO CLOSE TO ARISU.
IT'LL ONLY STRESS YOU OUT.
WHAT, THAT AGAIN?
I GET IT, OKAY? YOU DON'T HAVE TO KEEP BRINGING IT UP.
AND ONE MORE THING...

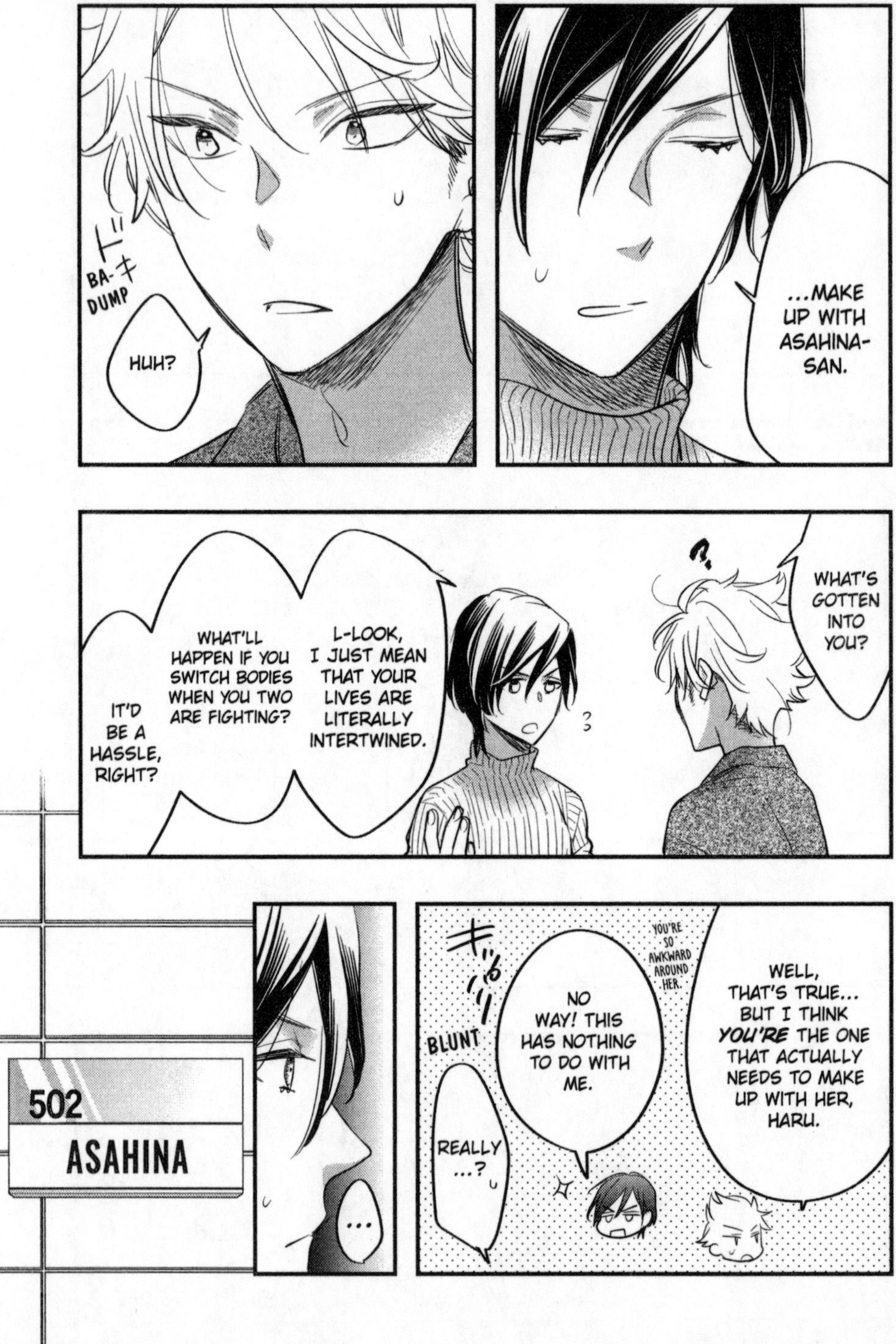
...MAKE UP WITH ASAHINA-SAN.
BA-DUMP
HUH?
WHAT'S GOTTEN INTO YOU?
L-LOOK, I JUST MEAN THAT YOUR LIVES ARE LITERALLY INTERTWINED.
WHAT'LL HAPPEN IF YOU SWITCH BODIES WHEN YOU TWO ARE FIGHTING?
IT'D BE A HASSLE, RIGHT?
WELL, THAT'S TRUE... BUT I THINK *YOU'RE* THE ONE THAT ACTUALLY NEEDS TO MAKE UP WITH HER, HARU.
YOU'RE SO AWKWARD AROUND HER.
NO WAY! THIS HAS NOTHING TO DO WITH ME.
BLUNT
REALLY...?
...
502
ASAHINA

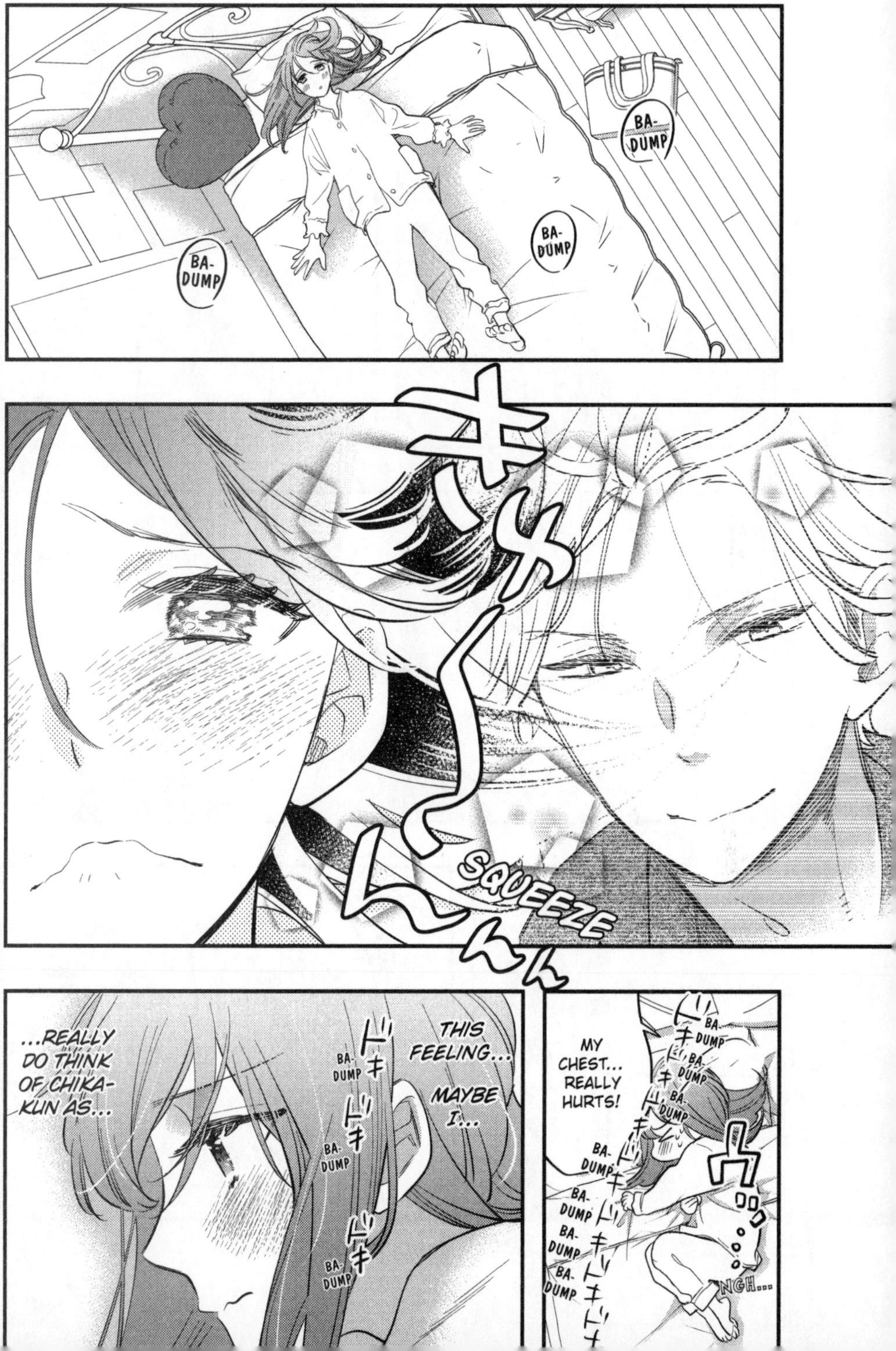

BA-DUMP
BA-DUMP
BA-DUMP
SQUEEZE
MY CHEST... REALLY HURTS!
BA-DUMP
BA-DUMP
BA-DUMP
BA-DUMP
BA-DUMP
BA-DUMP
BA-DUMP
NGH...
THIS FEELING...
MAYBE I...
...REALLY DO THINK OF CHIKA-KUN AS...
BA-DUMP
BA-DUMP
BA-DUMP

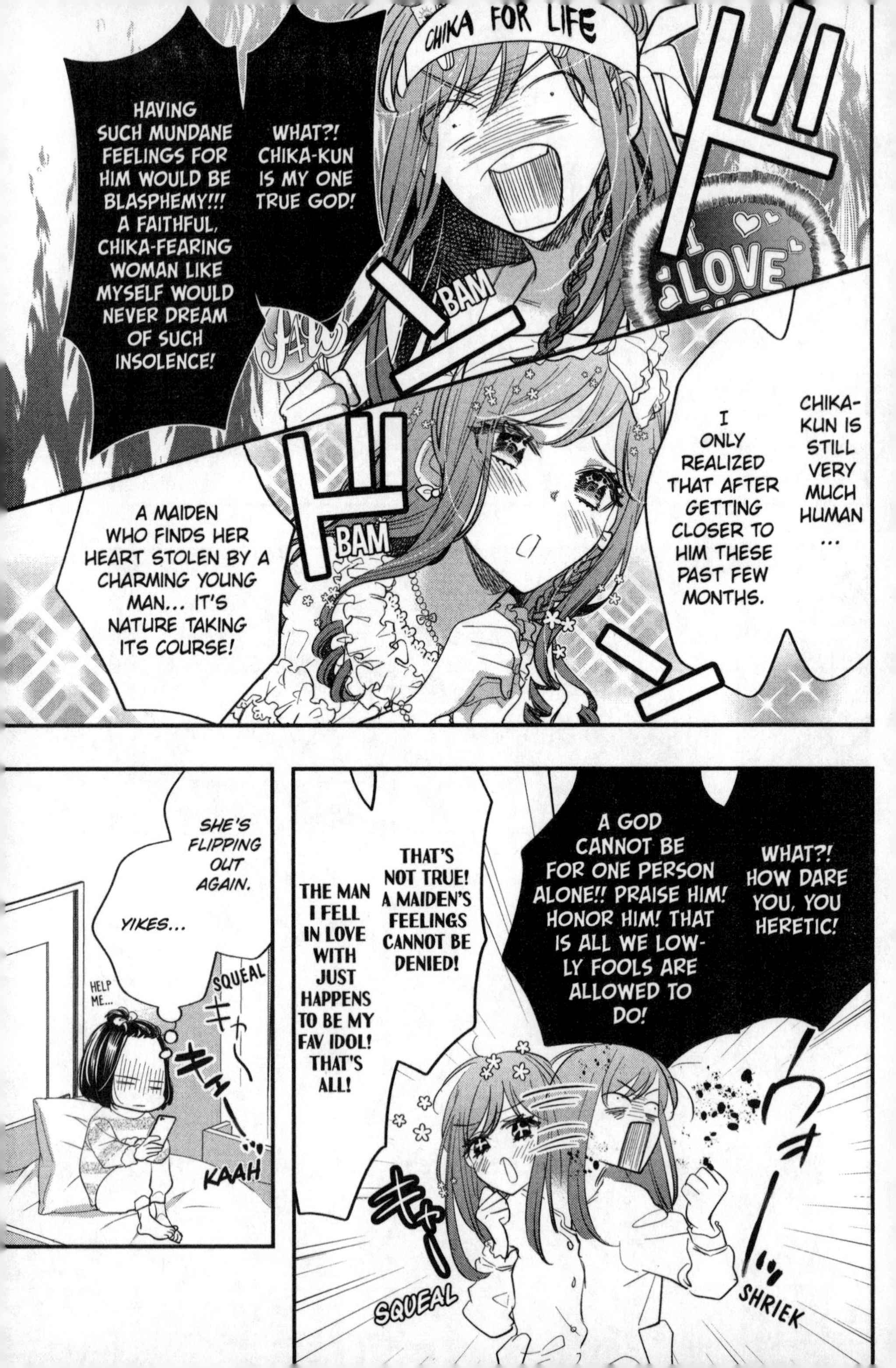
CHIKA FOR LIFE
WHAT?! CHIKA-KUN IS MY ONE TRUE GOD!
HAVING SUCH MUNDANE FEELINGS FOR HIM WOULD BE BLASPHEMY!!! A FAITHFUL, CHIKA-FEARING WOMAN LIKE MYSELF WOULD NEVER DREAM OF SUCH INSOLENCE!
I LOVE
BAM
CHIKA-KUN IS STILL VERY MUCH HUMAN...
I ONLY REALIZED THAT AFTER GETTING CLOSER TO HIM THESE PAST FEW MONTHS.
BAM
A MAIDEN WHO FINDS HER HEART STOLEN BY A CHARMING YOUNG MAN... IT'S NATURE TAKING ITS COURSE!
WHAT?! HOW DARE YOU, YOU HERETIC!
A GOD CANNOT BE FOR ONE PERSON ALONE!! PRAISE HIM! HONOR HIM! THAT IS ALL WE LOWLY FOOLS ARE ALLOWED TO DO!
THAT'S NOT TRUE! A MAIDEN'S FEELINGS CANNOT BE DENIED!
THE MAN I FELL IN LOVE WITH JUST HAPPENS TO BE MY FAV IDOL! THAT'S ALL!
SHRIEK
SQUEAL
SHE'S FLIPPING OUT AGAIN.
YIKES...
HELP ME...
SQUEAL
KAAH

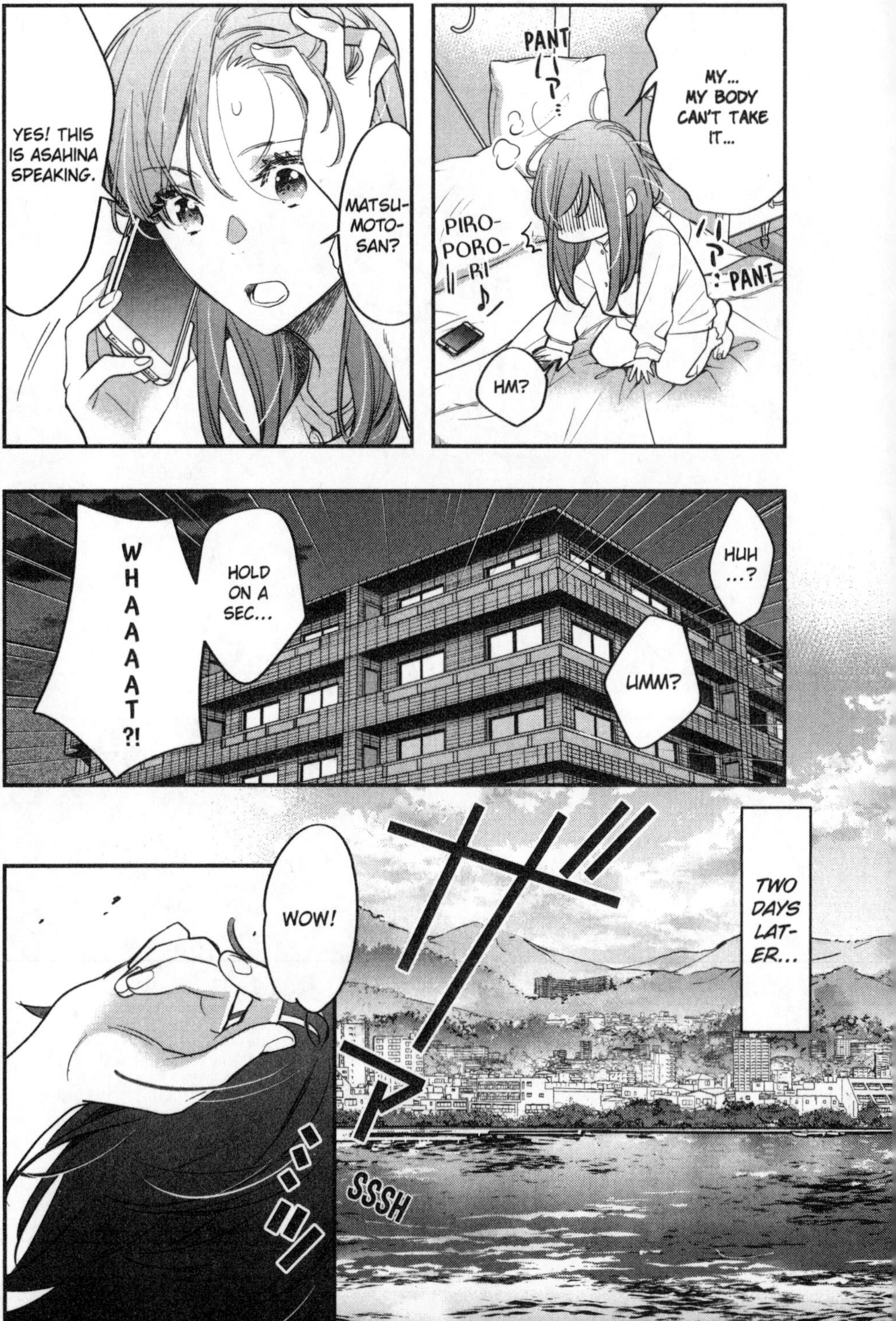

PANT
MY... MY BODY CAN'T TAKE IT...
PIRO-PORO-RI ♪
PANT
HM?
YES! THIS IS ASAHINA SPEAKING.
MATSU-MOTO-SAN?
HUH ...?
UMM?
HOLD ON A SEC...
WHAAAAAT?!
TWO DAYS LATER...
WOW!
SSSH

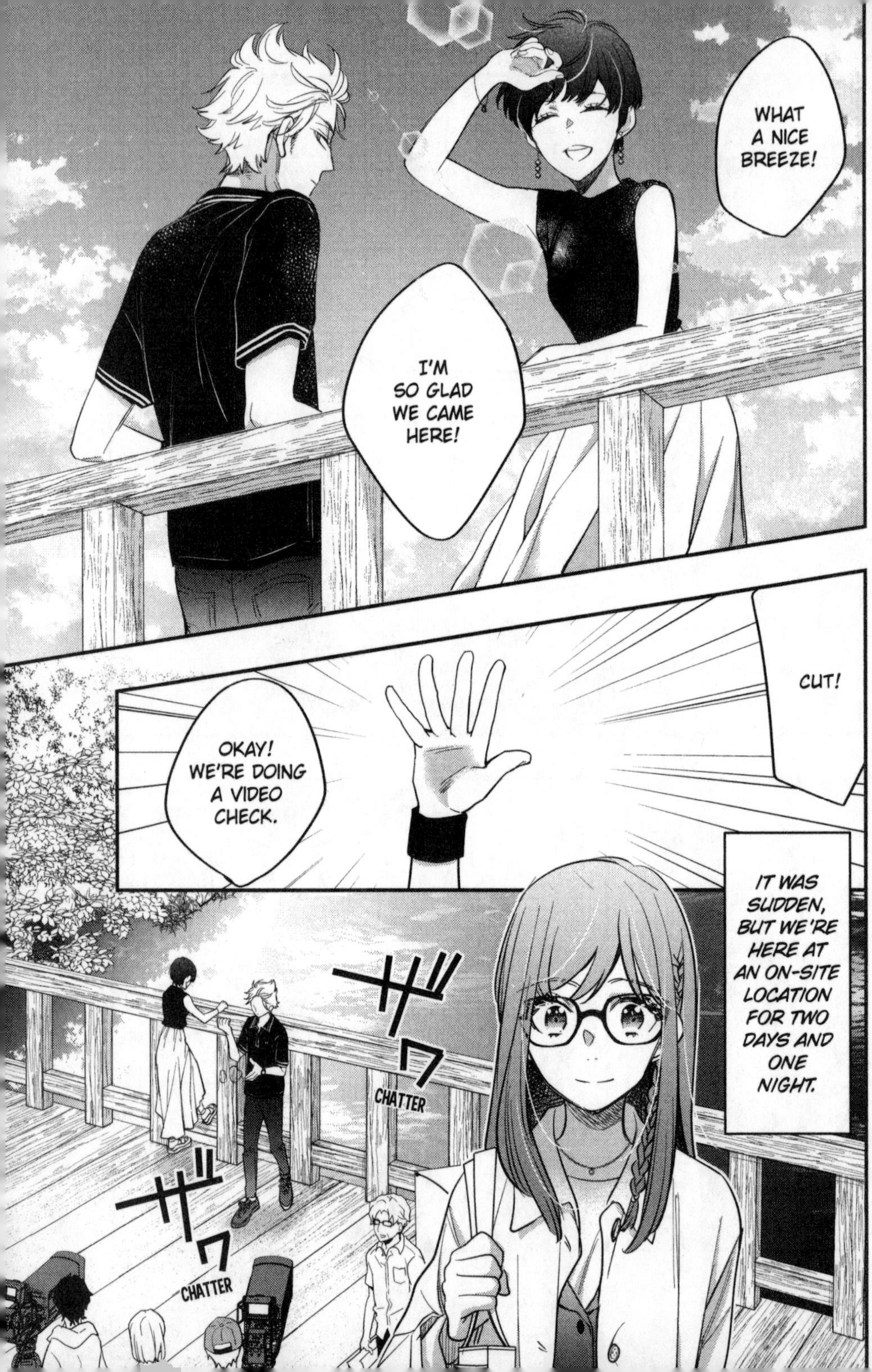
WHAT A NICE BREEZE!
I'M SO GLAD WE CAME HERE!
CUT!
OKAY! WE'RE DOING A VIDEO CHECK.
IT WAS SUDDEN, BUT WE'RE HERE AT AN ON-SITE LOCATION FOR TWO DAYS AND ONE NIGHT.
CHATTER
CHATTER

"I FORGOT TO TELL YOU, BUT CHIKA'S GOING TO BE ON LOCATION FOR A SCENE IN A COUPLE OF DAYS."

"I'D GO WITH HIM, BUT I'M STILL BALANCING THE OTHER THREE MEMBERS' SCHEDULES... SO MAYBE YOU CAN GO INSTEAD?!"

WHAT A MESS, MATSUMOTO!

THIS IS WAY TOO SUDDEN! I'M A STU-DENT, YOU KNOW?!

BUT...

HEY, CHIKA. DO YOU HA-

HMPH ...!

STARE

OH, THANKS.

WHOOSH

GOOD WORK, CHIKA-KUN! THERE'S A SEAT AND DRINK OVER THERE FOR YOU. THIS WAY!

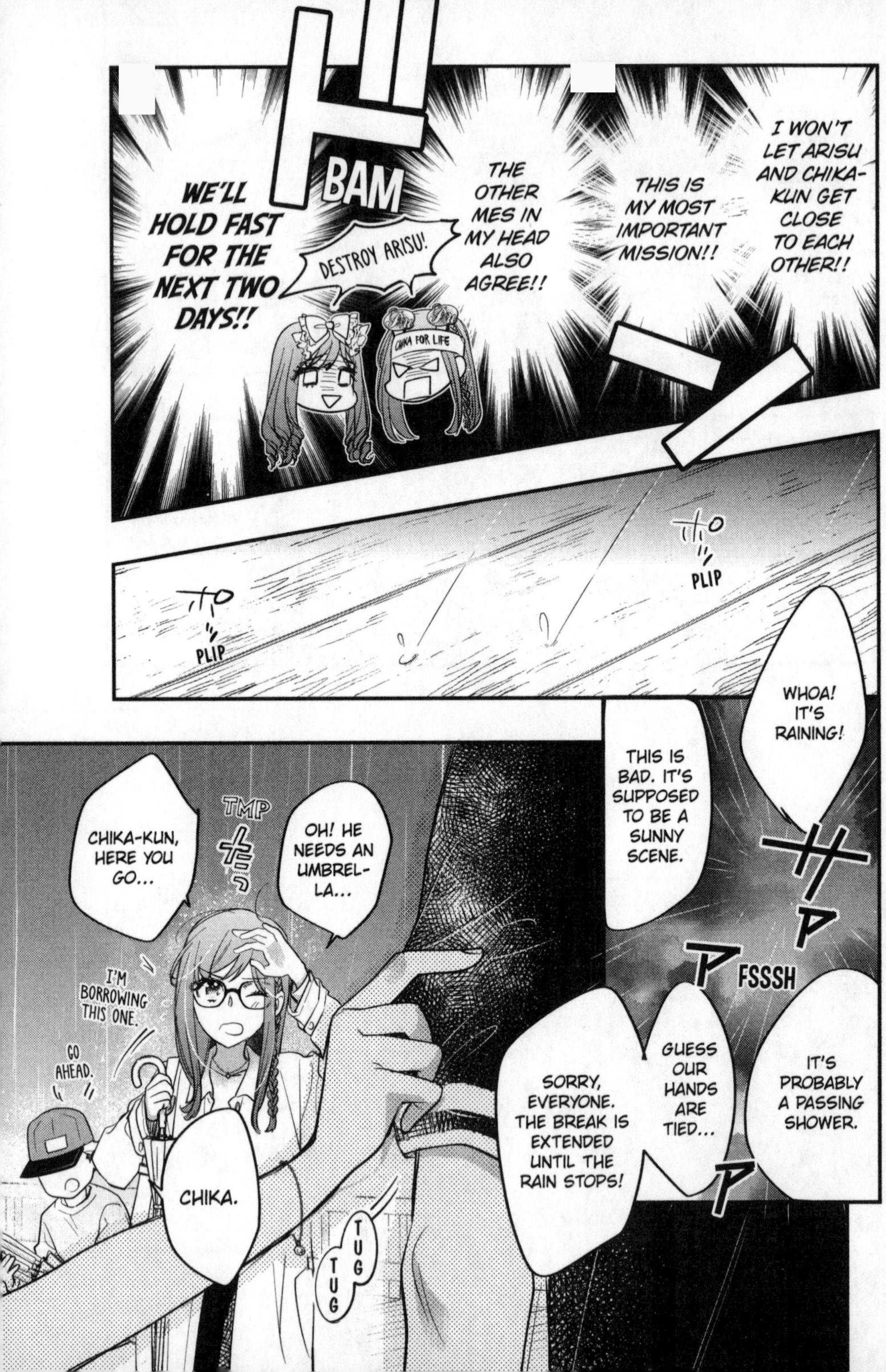

I WON'T LET ARISU AND CHIKA-KUN GET CLOSE TO EACH OTHER!!
THIS IS MY MOST IMPORTANT MISSION!!
THE OTHER MES IN MY HEAD ALSO AGREE!!
BAM
DESTROY ARISU!
WE'LL HOLD FAST FOR THE NEXT TWO DAYS!!
CHIKA FOR LIFE
PLIP
PLIP
WHOA! IT'S RAINING!
THIS IS BAD. IT'S SUPPOSED TO BE A SUNNY SCENE.
FSSSH
IT'S PROBABLY A PASSING SHOWER.
GUESS OUR HANDS ARE TIED...
SORRY, EVERYONE. THE BREAK IS EXTENDED UNTIL THE RAIN STOPS!
OH! HE NEEDS AN UMBREL-LA...
TMP
CHIKA-KUN, HERE YOU GO...
I'M BORROWING THIS ONE.
GO AHEAD.
TUG TUG
CHIKA.

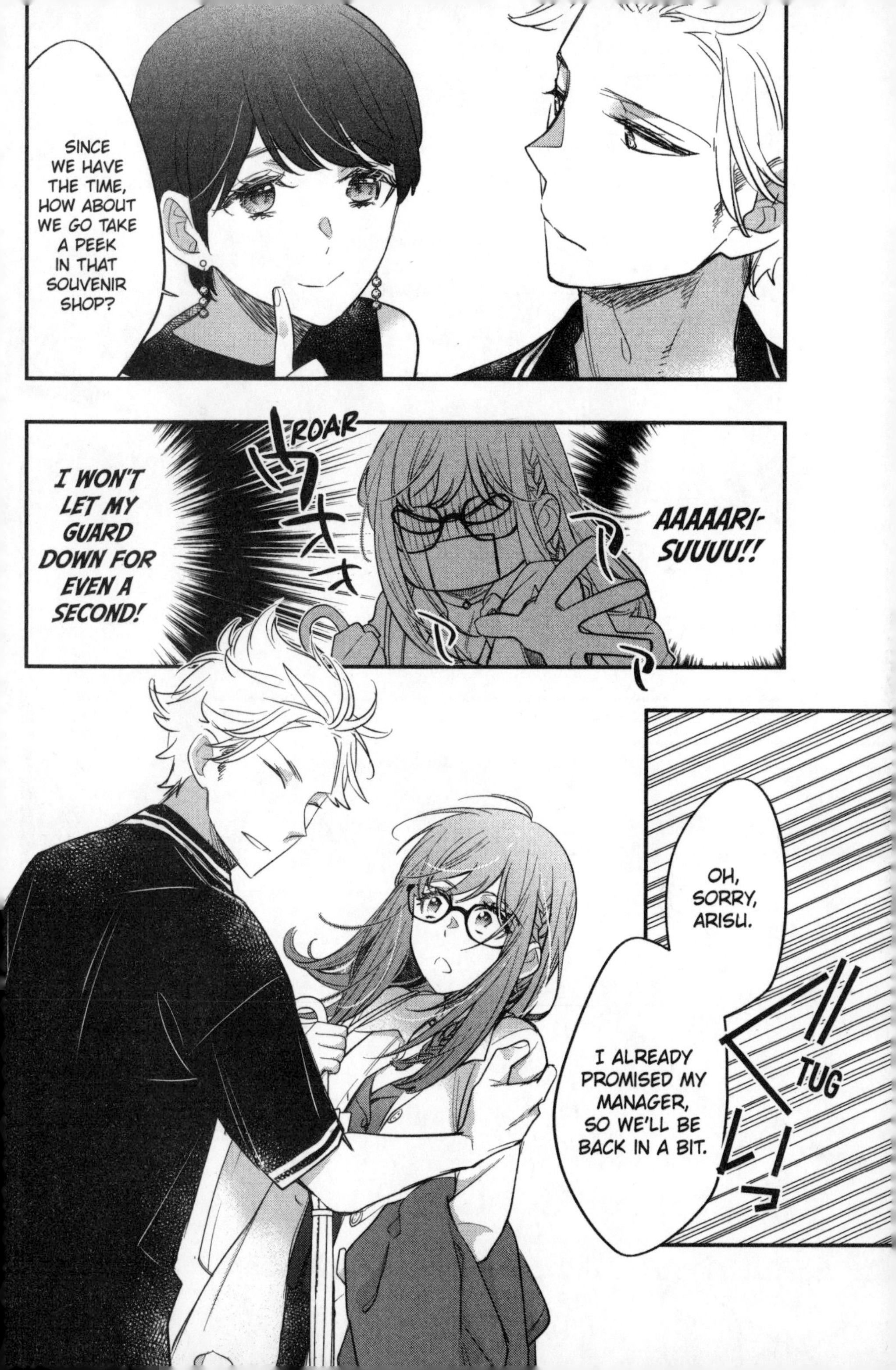
SINCE WE HAVE THE TIME, HOW ABOUT WE GO TAKE A PEEK IN THAT SOUVENIR SHOP?
AAAAARI-SUUUU!!
ROAR
I WON'T LET MY GUARD DOWN FOR EVEN A SECOND!
TUG
OH, SORRY, ARISU.
I ALREADY PROMISED MY MANAGER, SO WE'LL BE BACK IN A BIT.

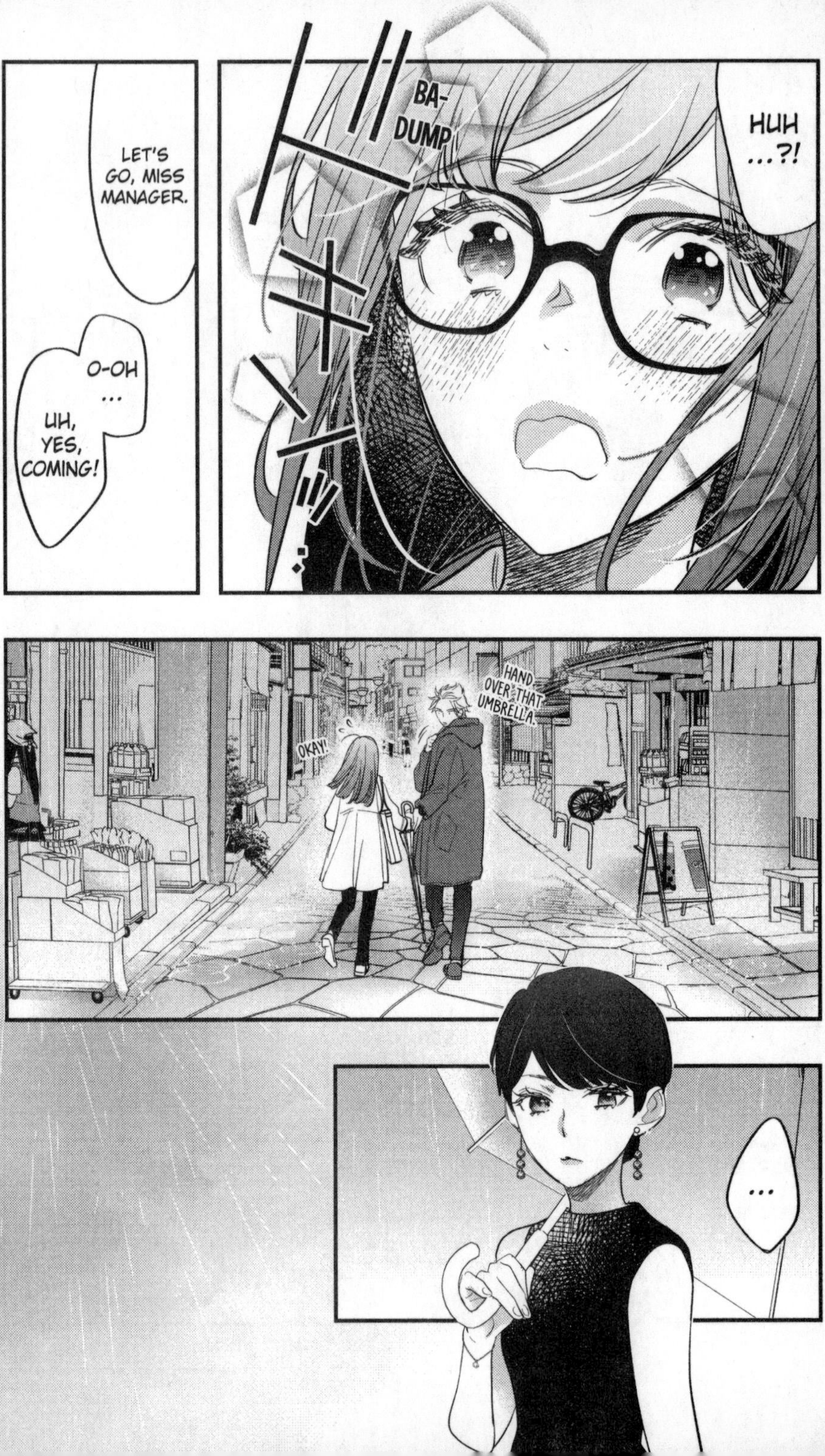
HUH ...?!
BA-DUMP
LET'S GO, MISS MANAGER.
O-OH ... UH, YES, COMING!
HAND OVER THAT UMBRELLA.
OKAY!
...

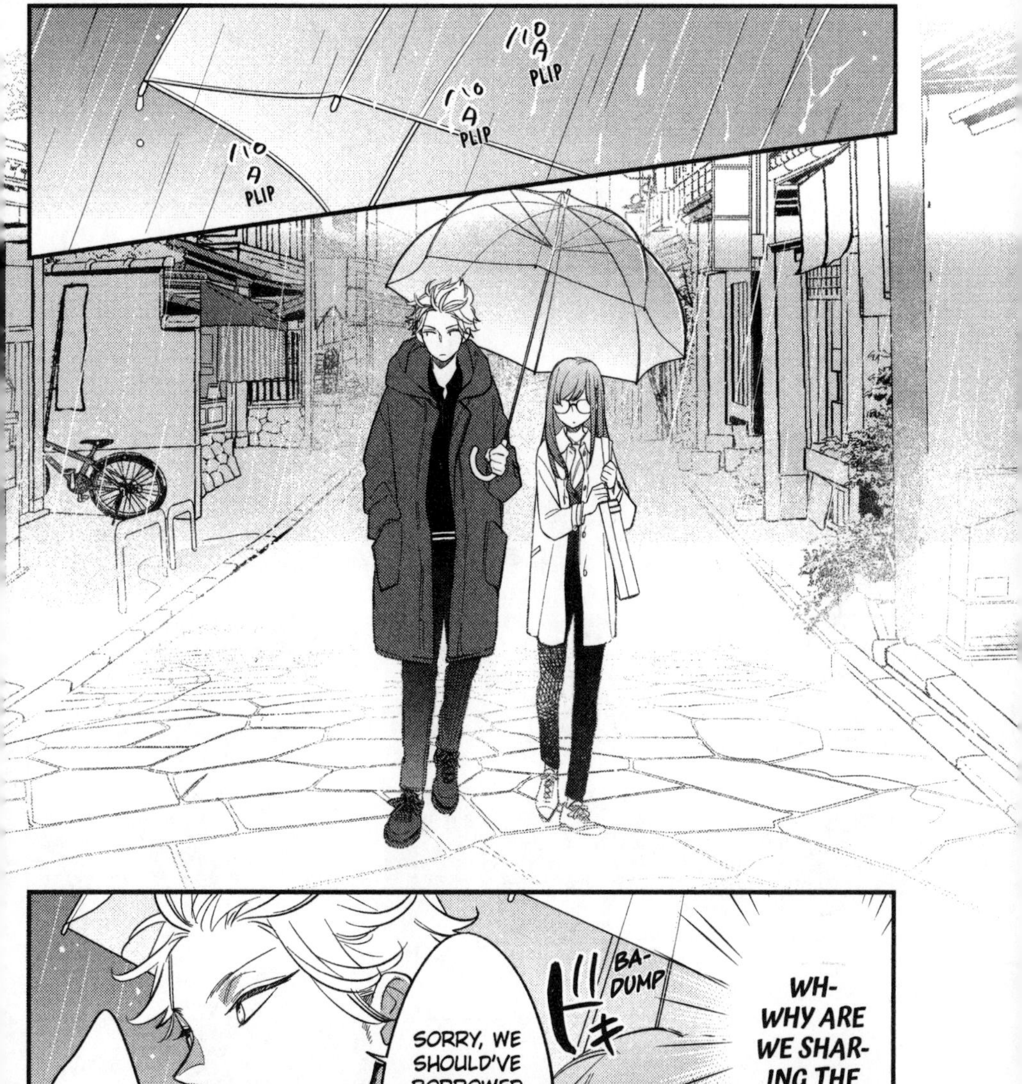
PLIP
PLIP
PLIP

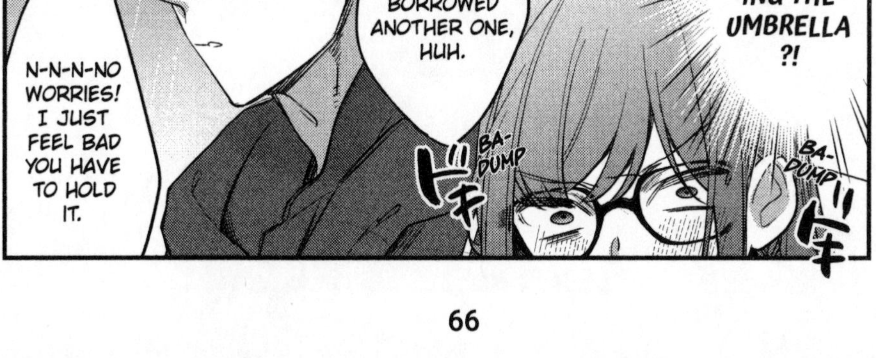
BA-DUMP
WH- WHY ARE WE SHARING THE UMBRELLA ?!
BA-DUMP
SORRY, WE SHOULD'VE BORROWED ANOTHER ONE, HUH.
BA-DUMP
N-N-N-NO WORRIES! I JUST FEEL BAD YOU HAVE TO HOLD IT.

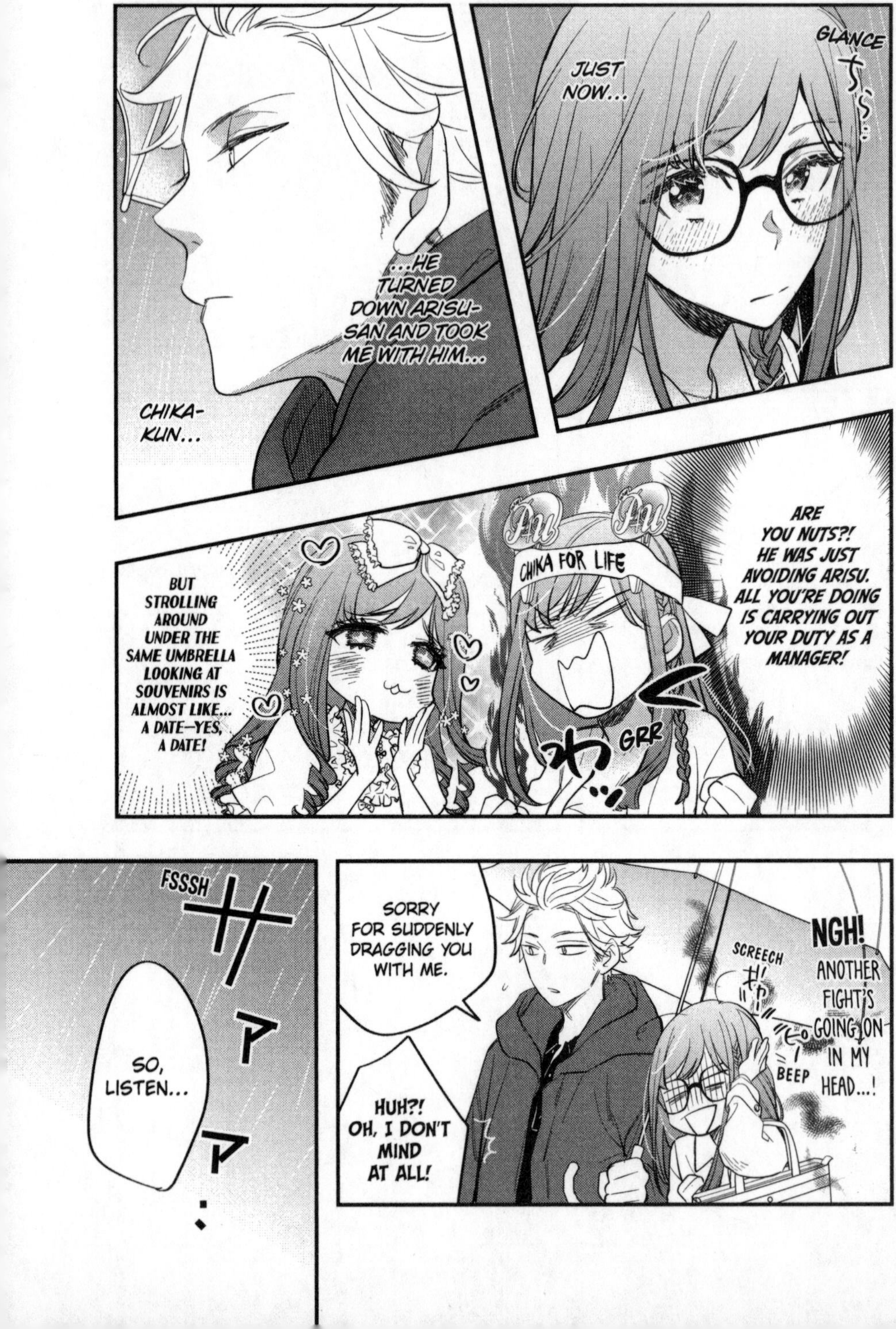
GLANCE
JUST NOW...
...HE TURNED DOWN ARISU-SAN AND TOOK ME WITH HIM...
CHIKA-KUN...
CHIKA FOR LIFE
ARE YOU NUTS?! HE WAS JUST AVOIDING ARISU. ALL YOU'RE DOING IS CARRYING OUT YOUR DUTY AS A MANAGER!
GRR
BUT STROLLING AROUND UNDER THE SAME UMBRELLA LOOKING AT SOUVENIRS IS ALMOST LIKE... A DATE—YES, A DATE!
SORRY FOR SUDDENLY DRAGGING YOU WITH ME.
NGH! ANOTHER FIGHT'S GOING ON IN MY HEAD...!
SCREECH
BEEP
HUH?! OH, I DON'T MIND AT ALL!
FSSSH
SO, LISTEN...

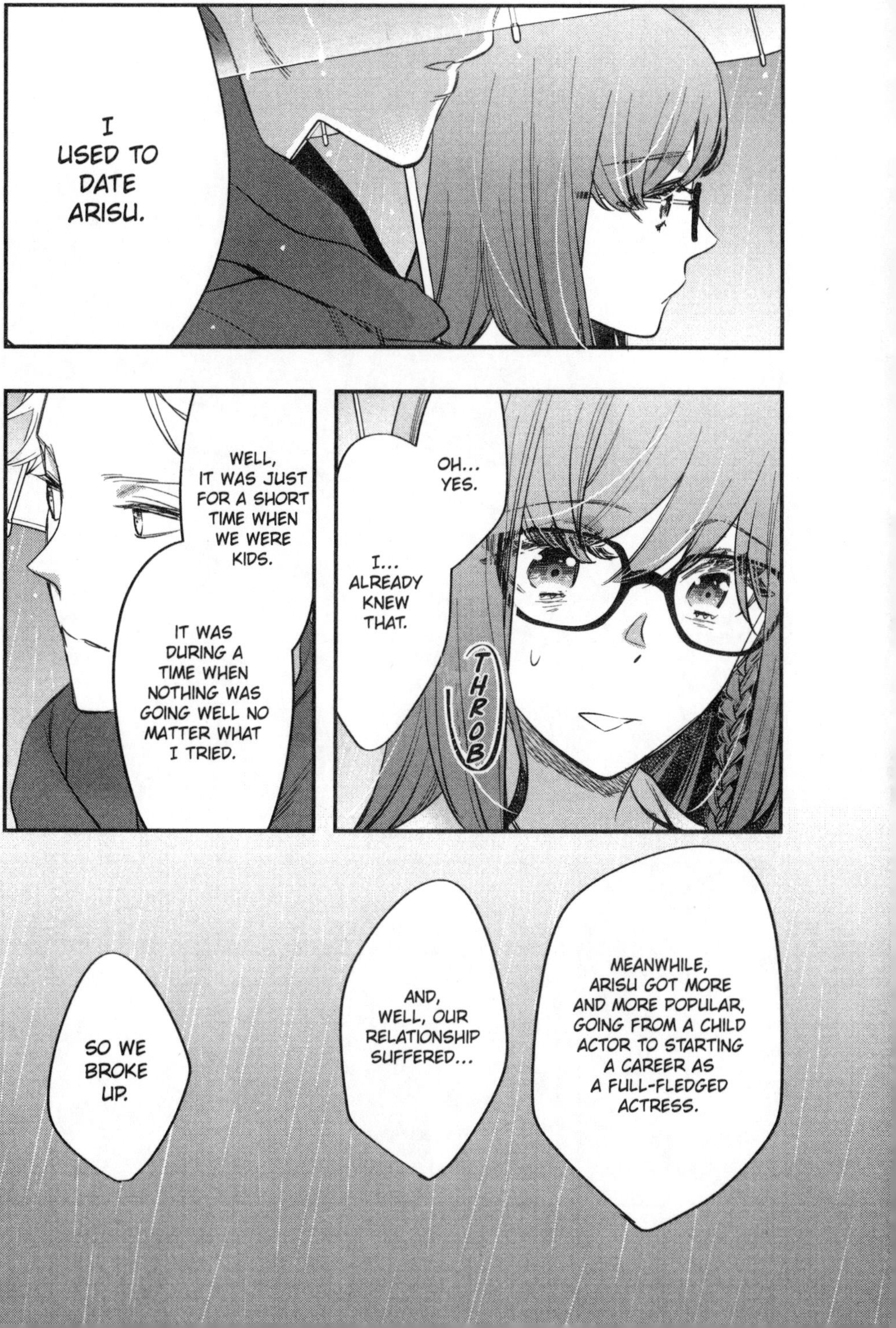
I USED TO DATE ARISU.
OH... YES.
I... ALREADY KNEW THAT.
THROB
WELL, IT WAS JUST FOR A SHORT TIME WHEN WE WERE KIDS.
IT WAS DURING A TIME WHEN NOTHING WAS GOING WELL NO MATTER WHAT I TRIED.
MEANWHILE, ARISU GOT MORE AND MORE POPULAR, GOING FROM A CHILD ACTOR TO STARTING A CAREER AS A FULL-FLEDGED ACTRESS.
AND, WELL, OUR RELATIONSHIP SUFFERED...
SO WE BROKE UP.

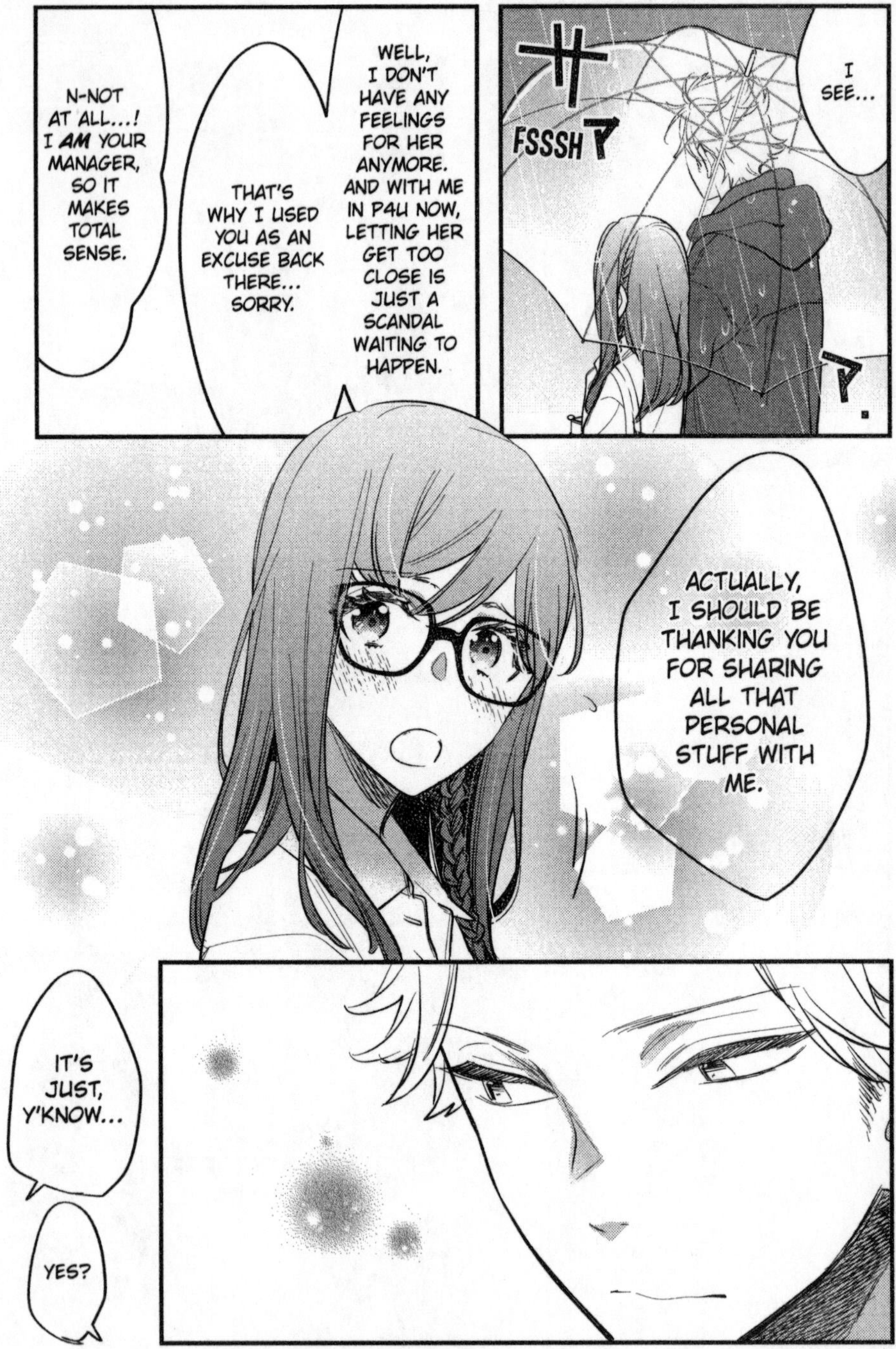

I SEE...
FSSSH
WELL, I DON'T HAVE ANY FEELINGS FOR HER ANYMORE. AND WITH ME IN P4U NOW, LETTING HER GET TOO CLOSE IS JUST A SCANDAL WAITING TO HAPPEN.
THAT'S WHY I USED YOU AS AN EXCUSE BACK THERE... SORRY.
N-NOT AT ALL...! I *AM* YOUR MANAGER, SO IT MAKES TOTAL SENSE.
ACTUALLY, I SHOULD BE THANKING YOU FOR SHARING ALL THAT PERSONAL STUFF WITH ME.
IT'S JUST, Y'KNOW...
YES?

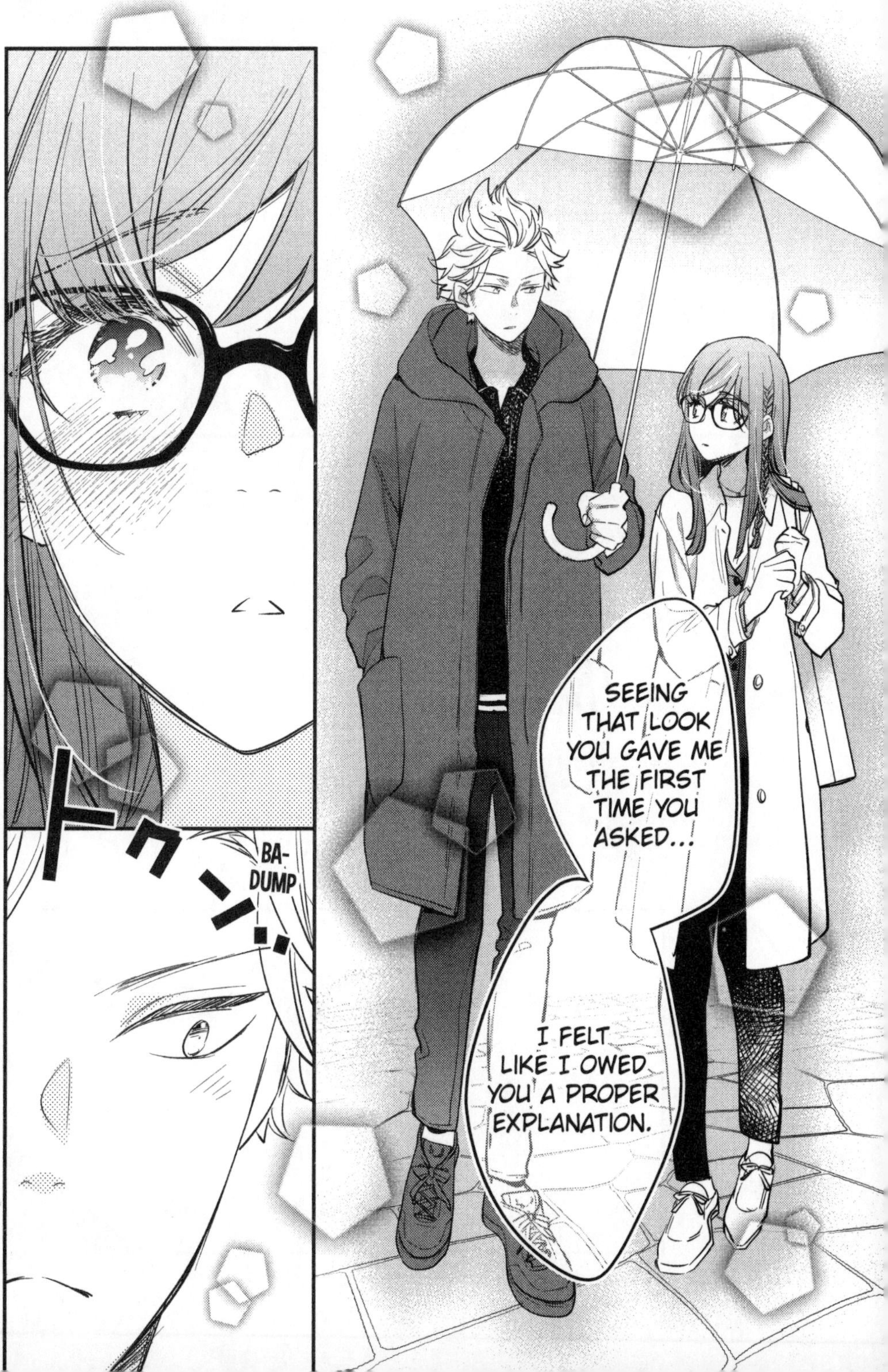
SEEING THAT LOOK YOU GAVE ME THE FIRST TIME YOU ASKED...
I FELT LIKE I OWED YOU A PROPER EXPLANATION.
BA-DUMP

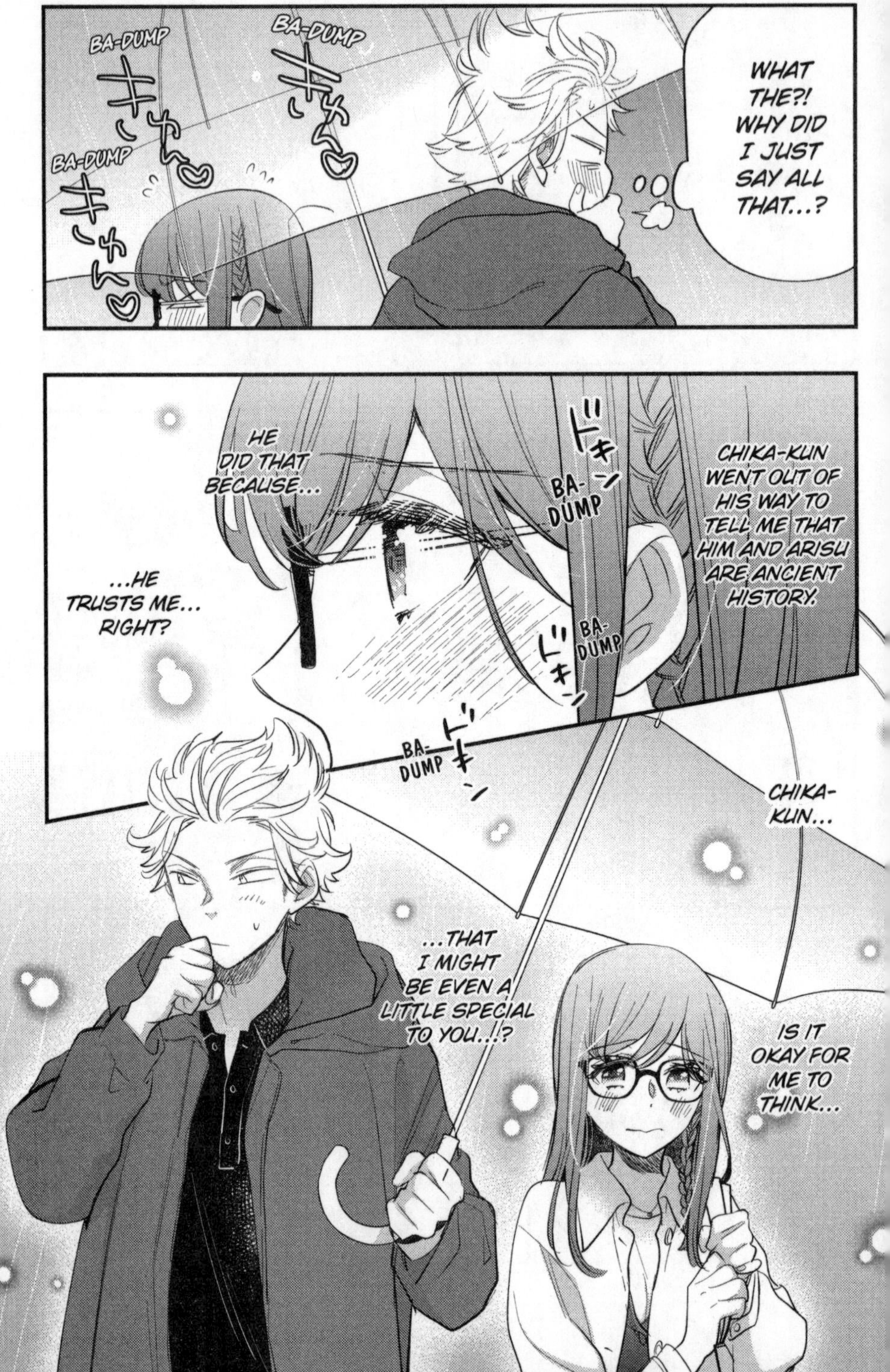
WHAT THE?! WHY DID I JUST SAY ALL THAT...?
BA-DUMP
BA-DUMP
BA-DUMP
CHIKA-KUN WENT OUT OF HIS WAY TO TELL ME THAT HIM AND ARISU ARE ANCIENT HISTORY.
BA-DUMP
BA-DUMP
HE DID THAT BECAUSE...
...HE TRUSTS ME... RIGHT?
BA-DUMP
CHIKA-KUN...
IS IT OKAY FOR ME TO THINK...
...THAT I MIGHT BE EVEN A LITTLE SPECIAL TO YOU...!?

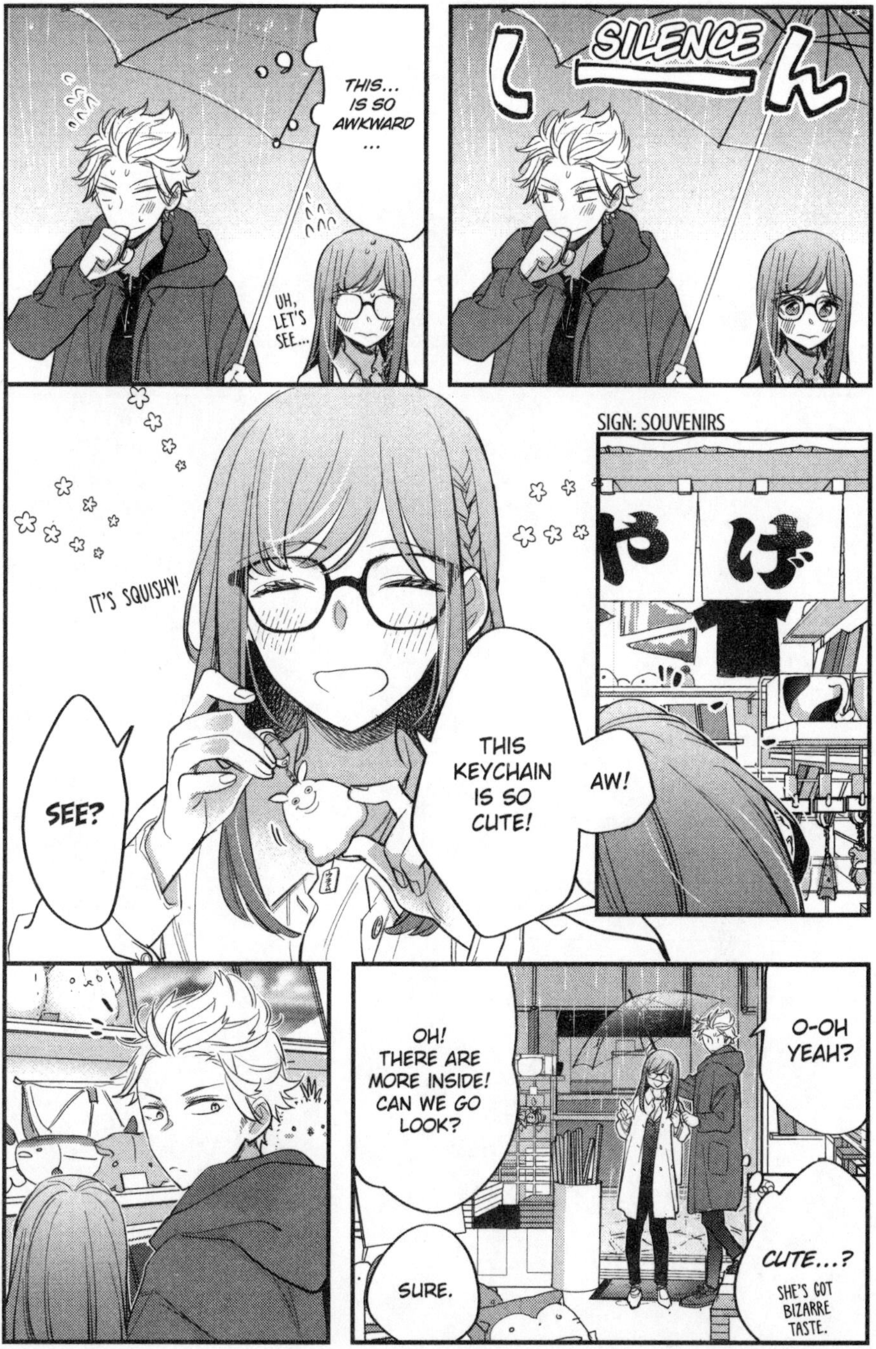
SILENCE
THIS... IS SO AWKWARD ...
UH, LET'S SEE...
SIGN: SOUVENIRS
AW!
THIS KEYCHAIN IS SO CUTE!
IT'S SQUISHY!
SEE?
O-OH YEAH?
OH! THERE ARE MORE INSIDE! CAN WE GO LOOK?
CUTE...?
SHE'S GOT BIZARRE TASTE.
SURE.

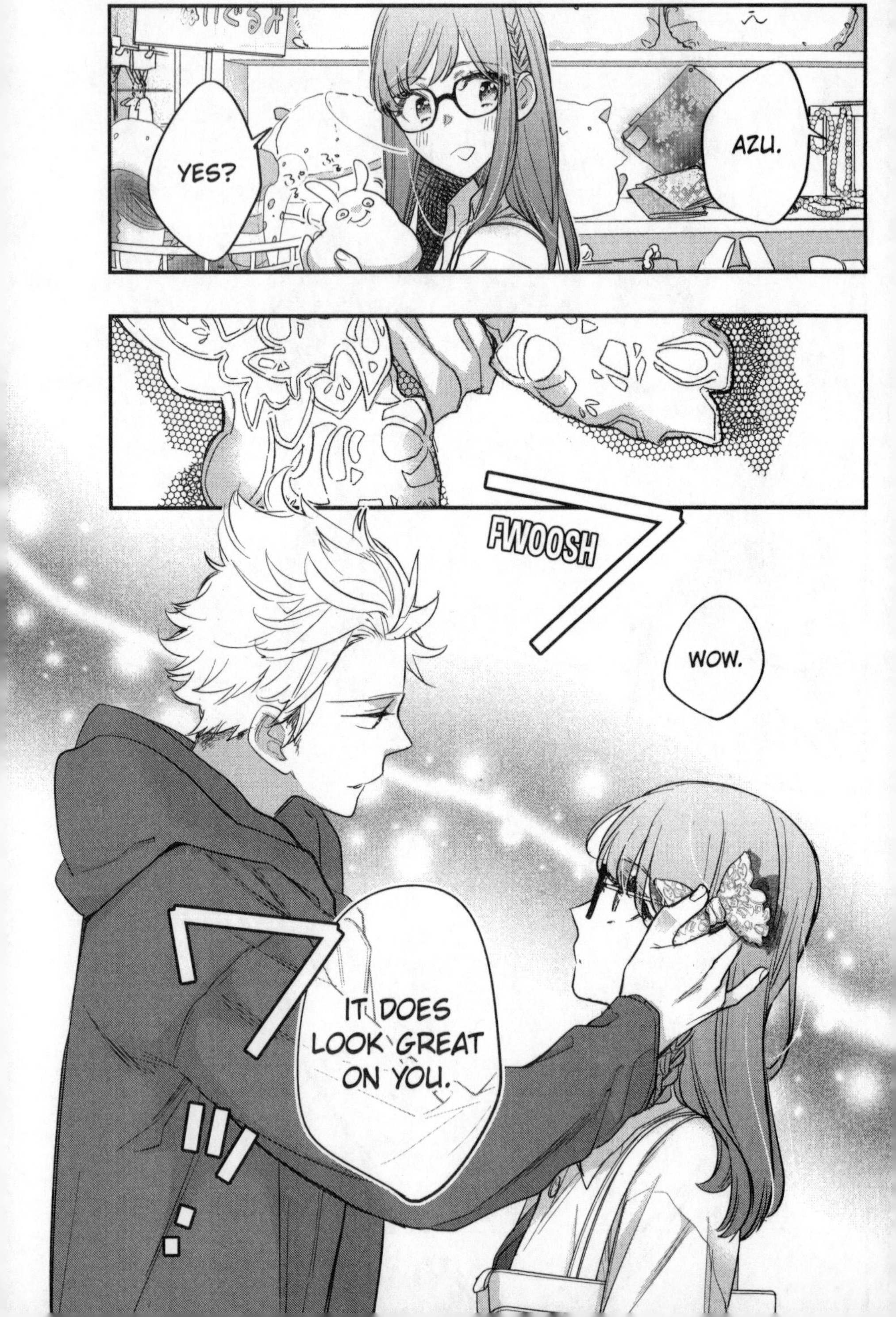
AZU.
YES?
FWOOSH
WOW.
IT DOES LOOK GREAT ON YOU.

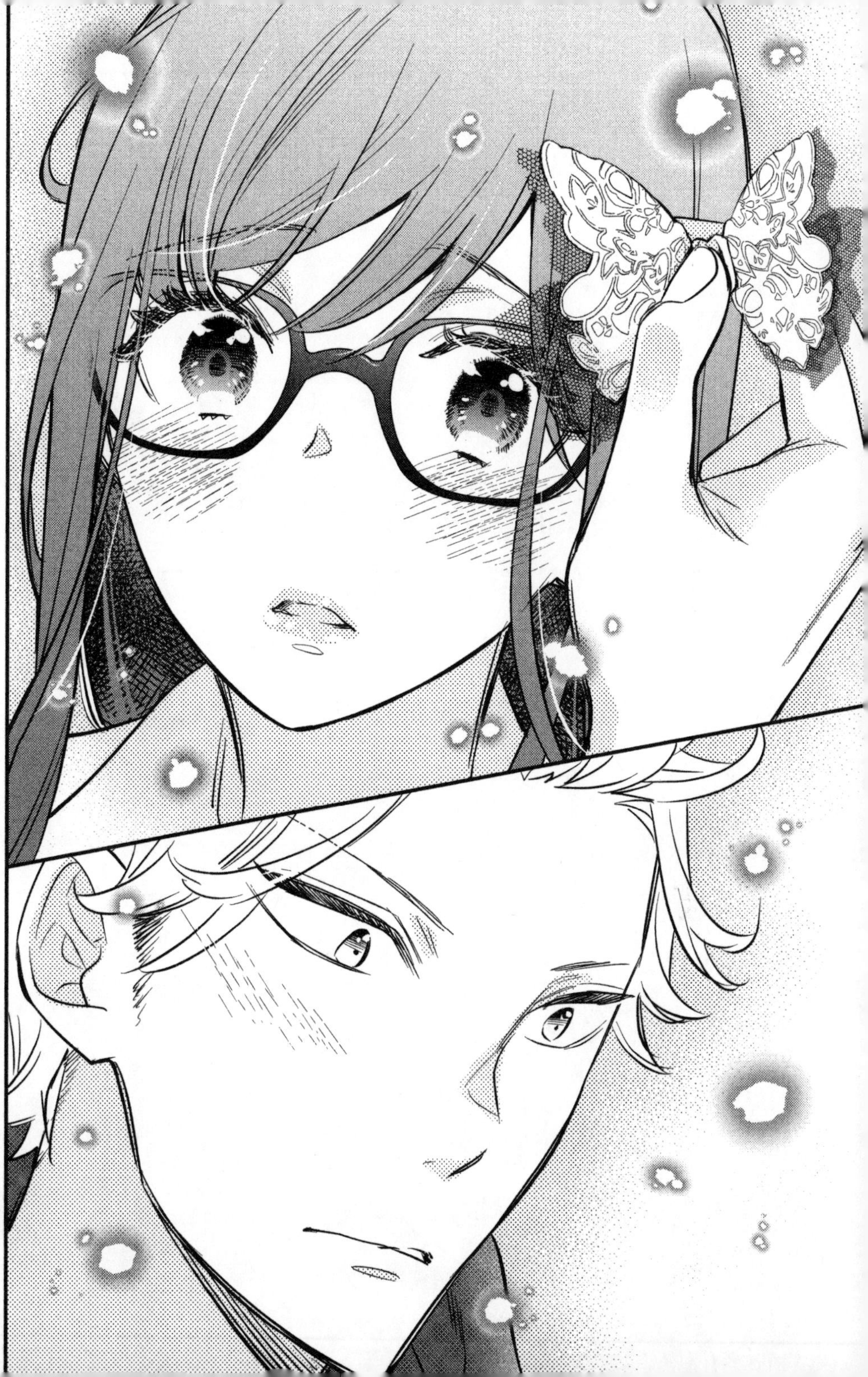

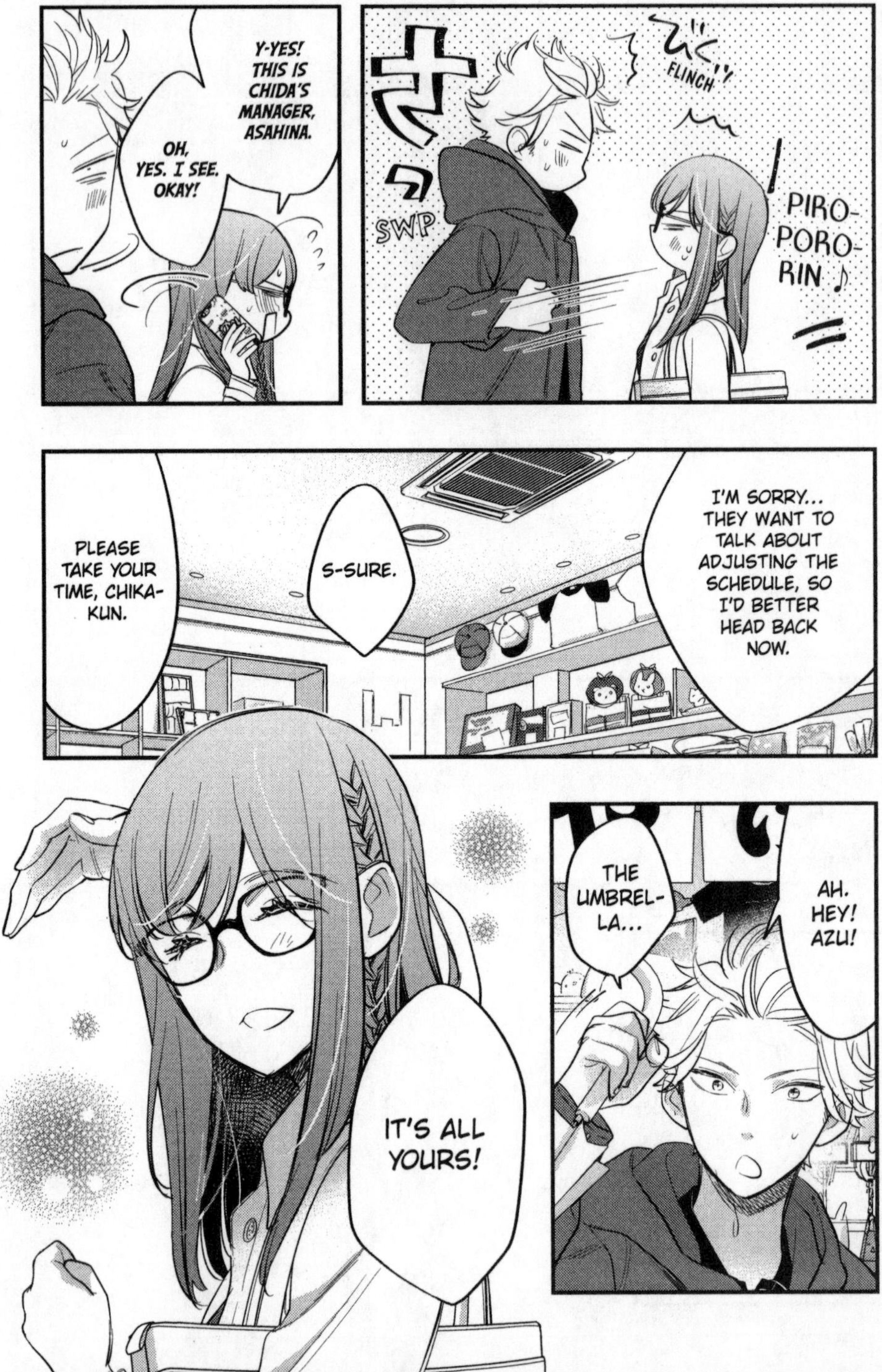
FLINCH
PIRO-PORO-RIN ♪
SWP
Y-YES! THIS IS CHIDA'S MANAGER, ASAHINA.
OH, YES. I SEE. OKAY!
I'M SORRY... THEY WANT TO TALK ABOUT ADJUSTING THE SCHEDULE, SO I'D BETTER HEAD BACK NOW.
S-SURE.
PLEASE TAKE YOUR TIME, CHIKA-KUN.
AH. HEY! AZU!
THE UMBREL-LA...
IT'S ALL YOURS!

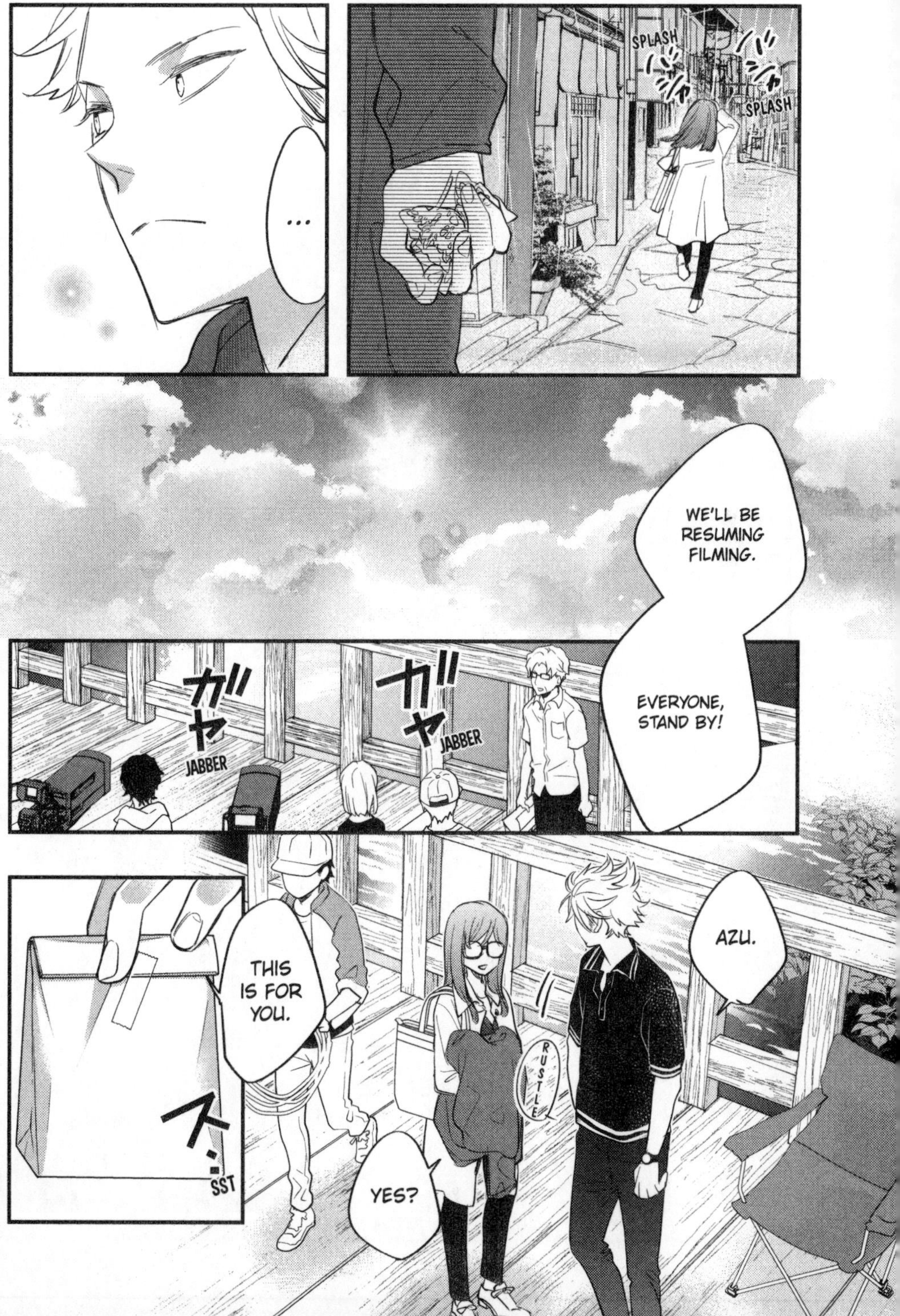

SPLASH
SPLASH
...
WE'LL BE RESUMING FILMING.
EVERYONE, STAND BY!
JABBER
JABBER
AZU.
RUSTLE
YES?
THIS IS FOR YOU.
SST

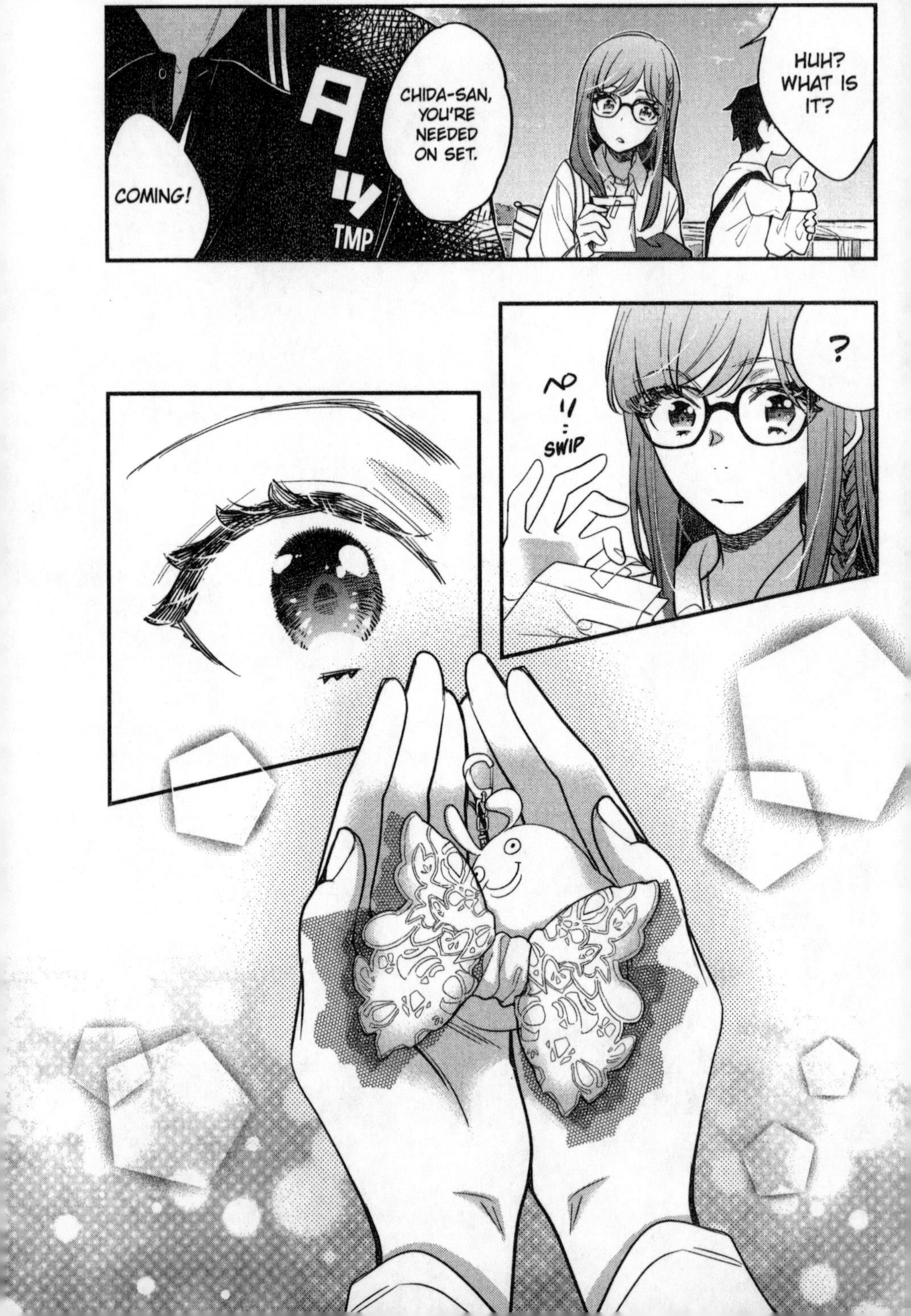
HUH? WHAT IS IT?
CHIDA-SAN, YOU'RE NEEDED ON SET.
TMP
COMING!
?
SWIP

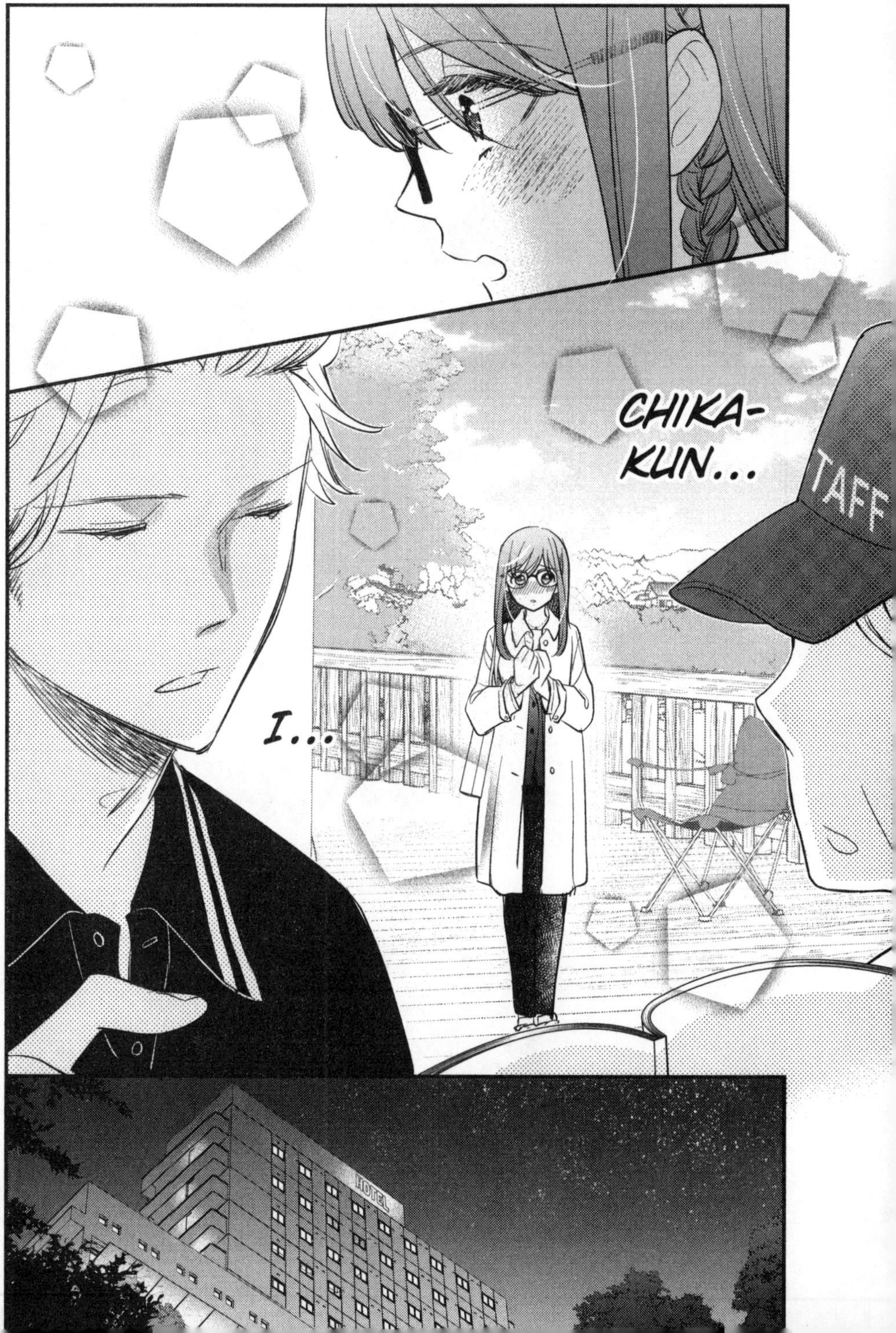
CHIKA-KUN...
TAFF
I...
HOTEL

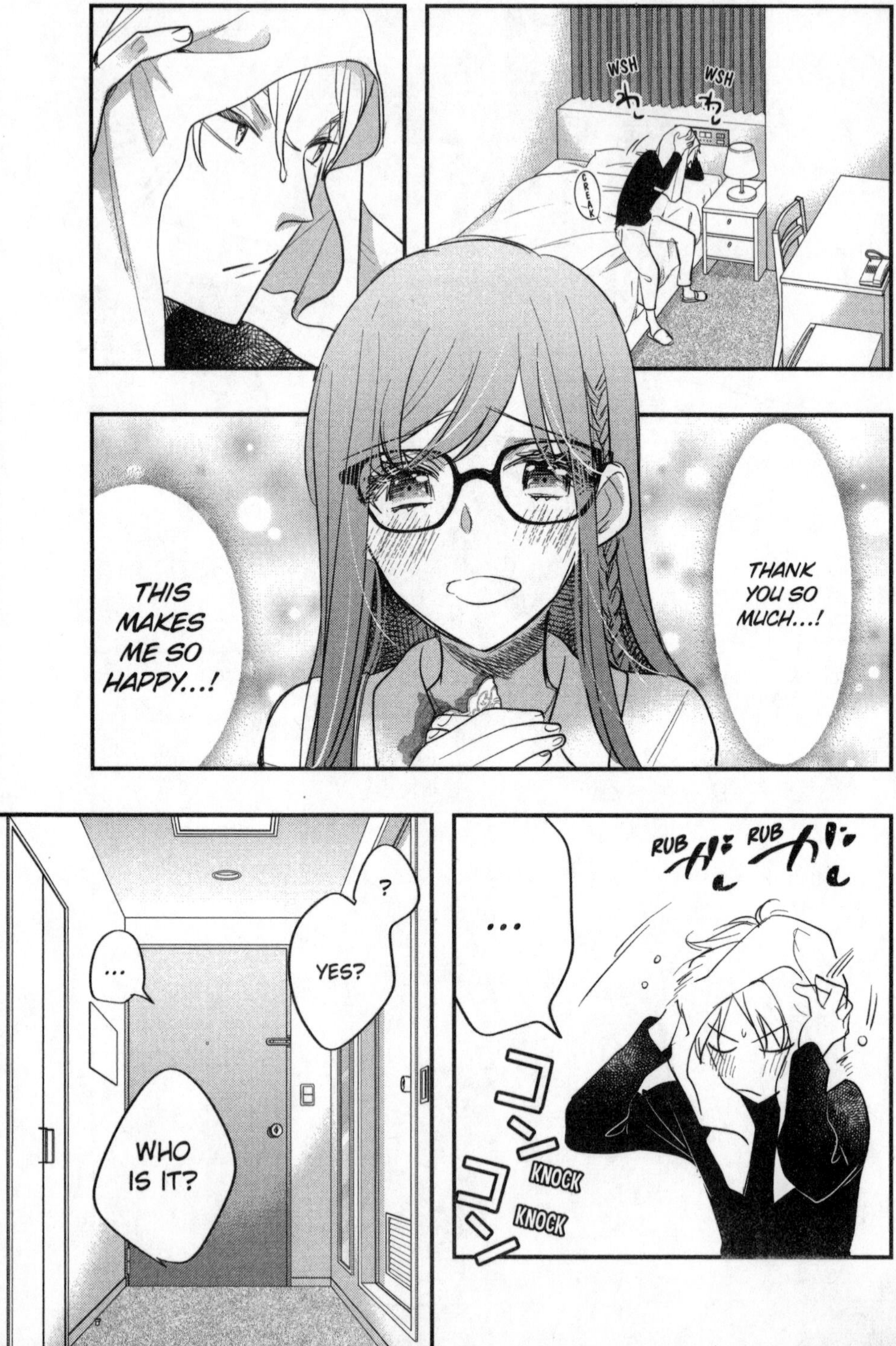
WSH
WSH
CREAK
THIS MAKES ME SO HAPPY...!
THANK YOU SO MUCH...!
RUB RUB
...
KNOCK
KNOCK
?
YES?
...
WHO IS IT?

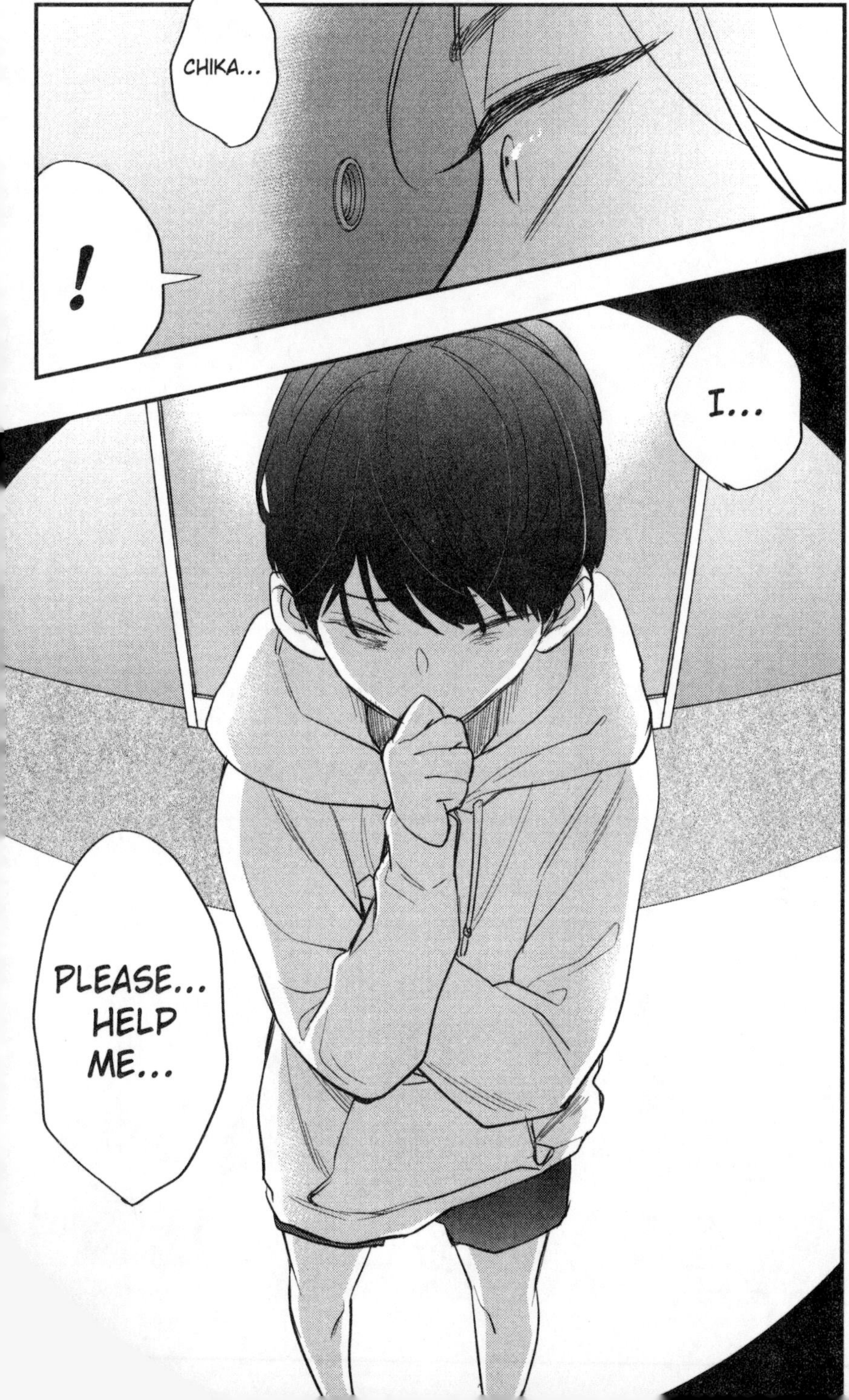
CHIKA...
!
I...
PLEASE... HELP ME...

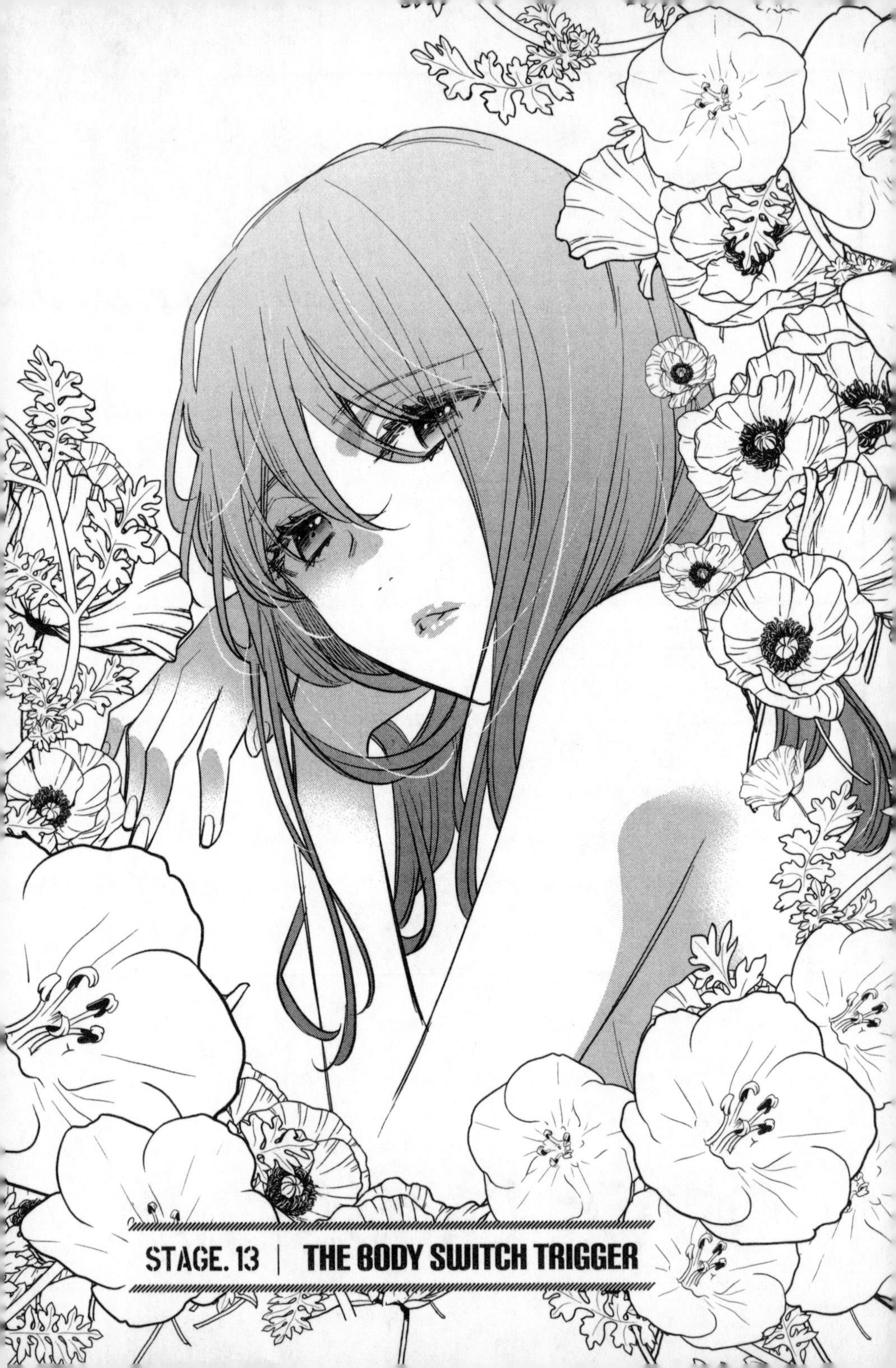
STAGE. 13 | THE BODY SWITCH TRIGGER

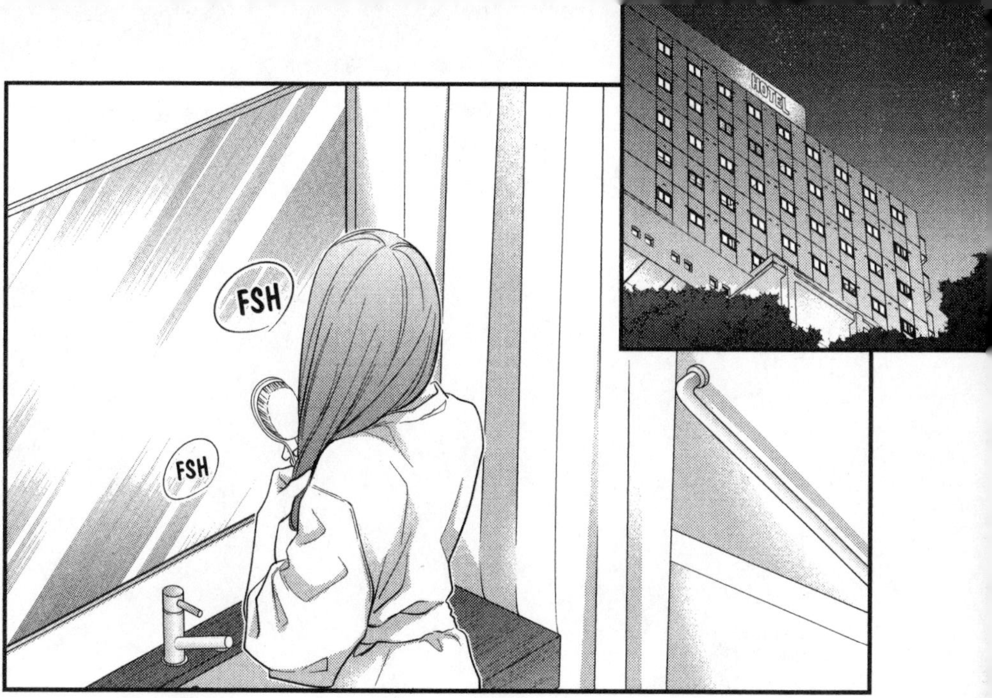
HOTEL
FSH
FSH

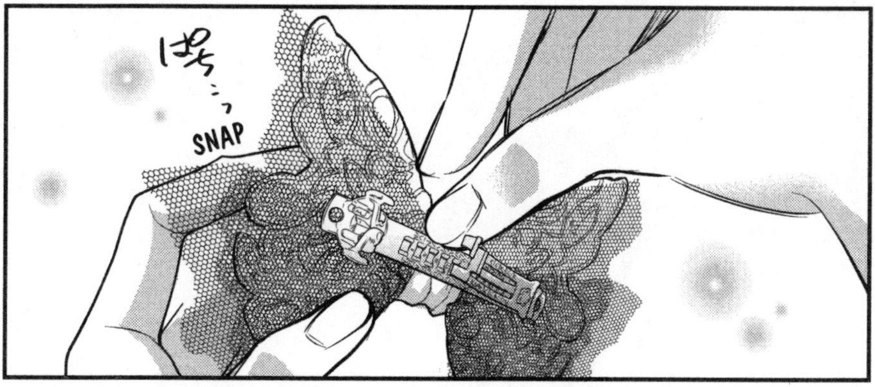
ぱちっ
SNAP

STAR⇄CROSSED!!

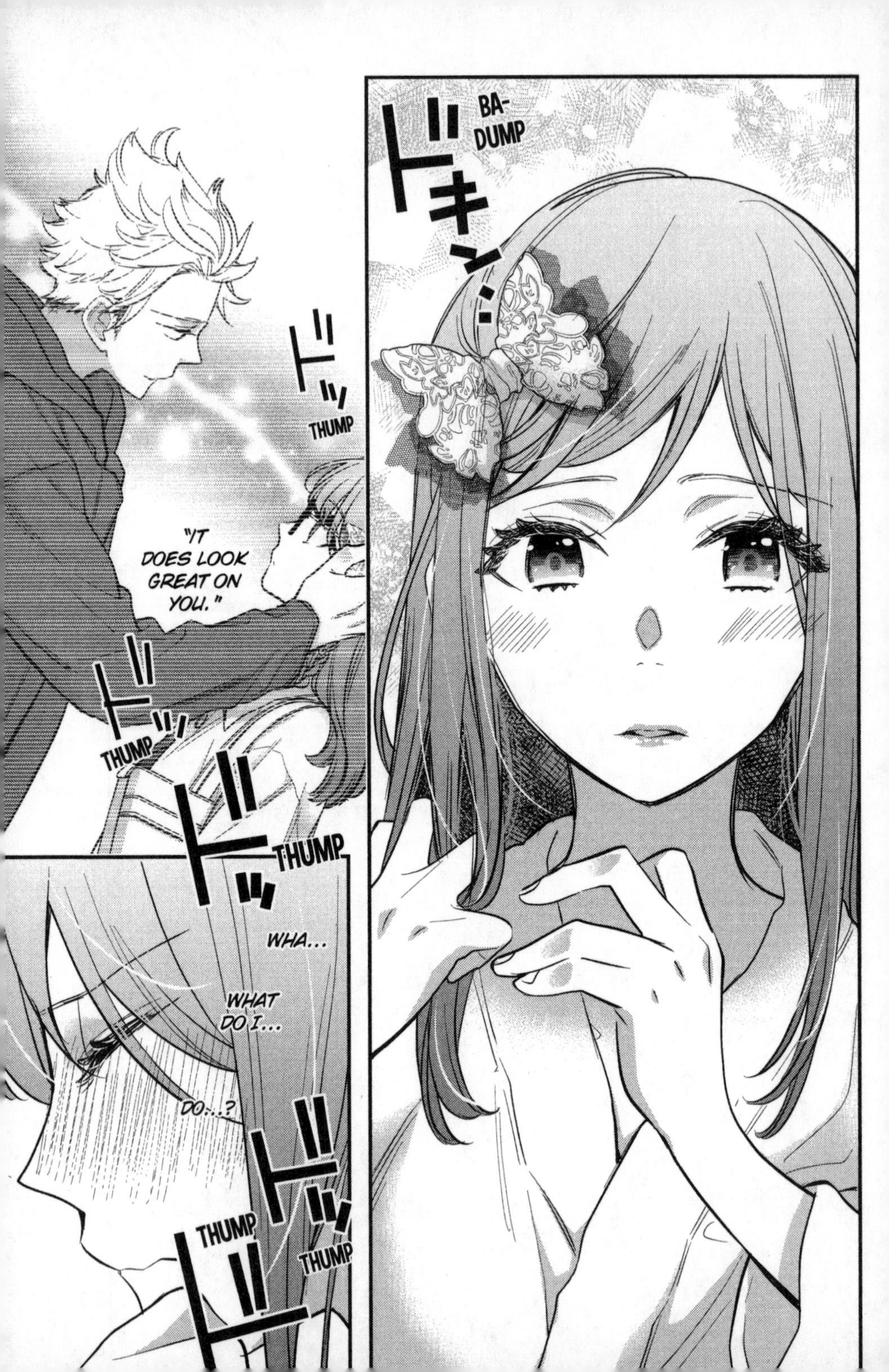
ドキン
BA-DUMP
ドッ
THUMP
"IT DOES LOOK GREAT ON YOU."
ドッ
THUMP
ドッ
THUMP
WHA...
WHAT DO I...
DO...?
ドッ
THUMP
ドッ
THUMP

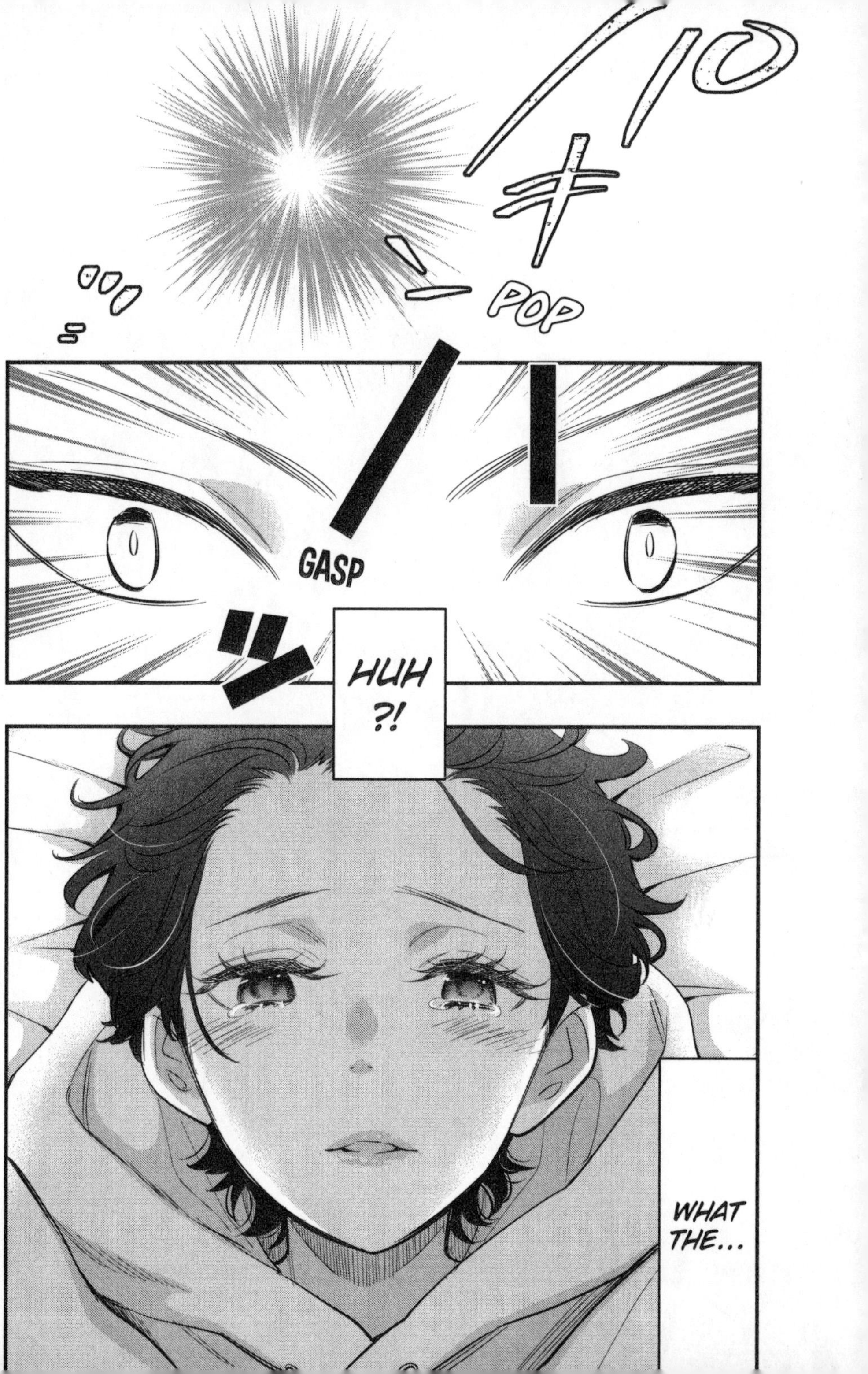
POP
GASP
HUH ?!
WHAT THE...

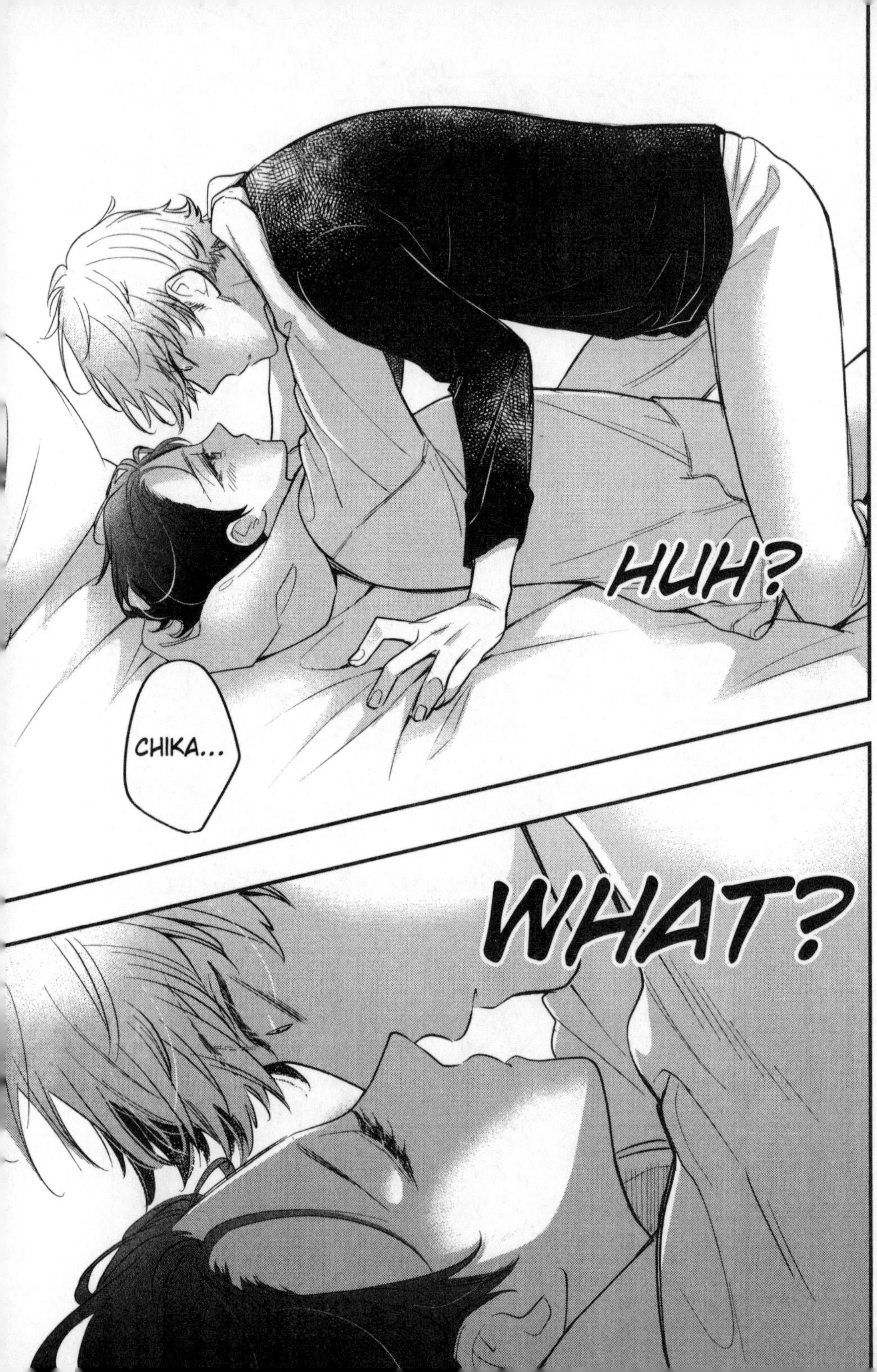
HUH?
CHIKA...
WHAT?

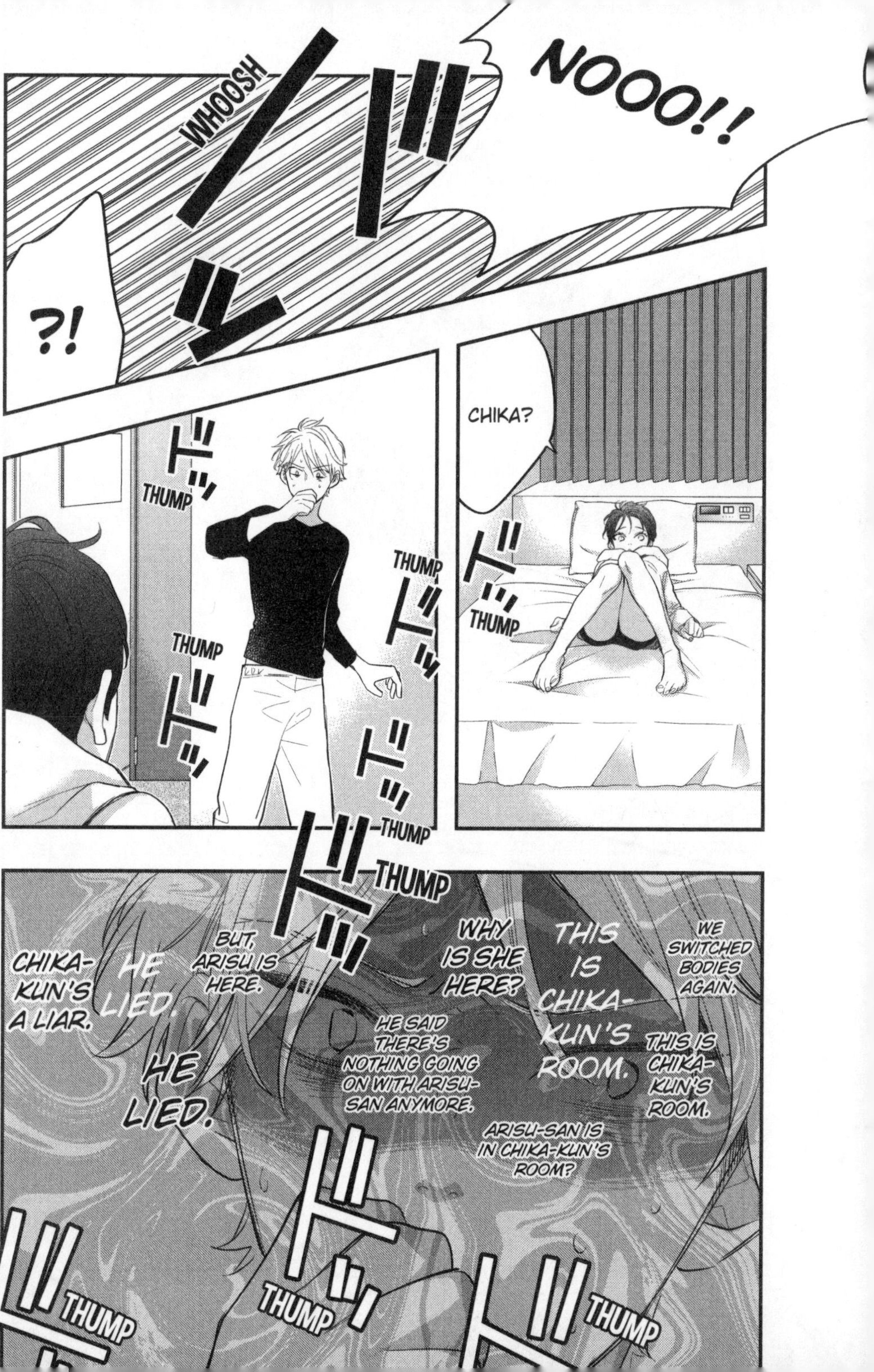
NOOO!!
WHOOSH
?!
CHIKA?
THUMP
THUMP
THUMP
THUMP
THUMP
THUMP
WE SWITCHED BODIES AGAIN.
THIS IS CHIKA-KUN'S ROOM.
THIS IS CHIKA-KUN'S ROOM.
WHY IS SHE HERE?
HE SAID THERE'S NOTHING GOING ON WITH ARISU-SAN ANYMORE.
ARISU-SAN IS IN CHIKA-KUN'S ROOM?
BUT, ARISU IS HERE.
HE LIED.
HE LIED.
CHIKA-KUN'S A LIAR.
THUMP
THUMP
THUMP

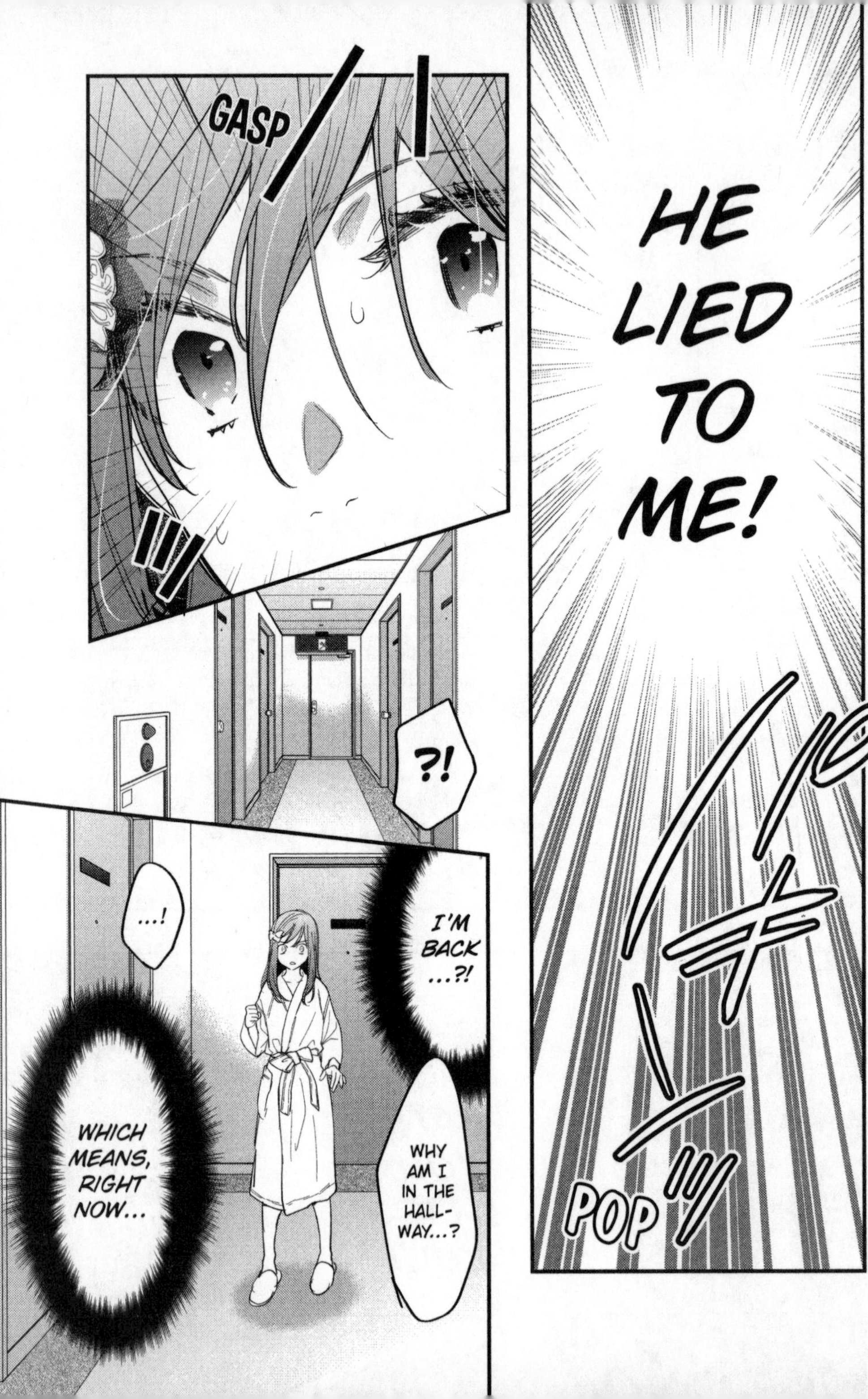
GASP
?!
I'M BACK ...?!
...!
WHY AM I IN THE HALL-WAY...?
WHICH MEANS, RIGHT NOW...
HE LIED TO ME!
POP

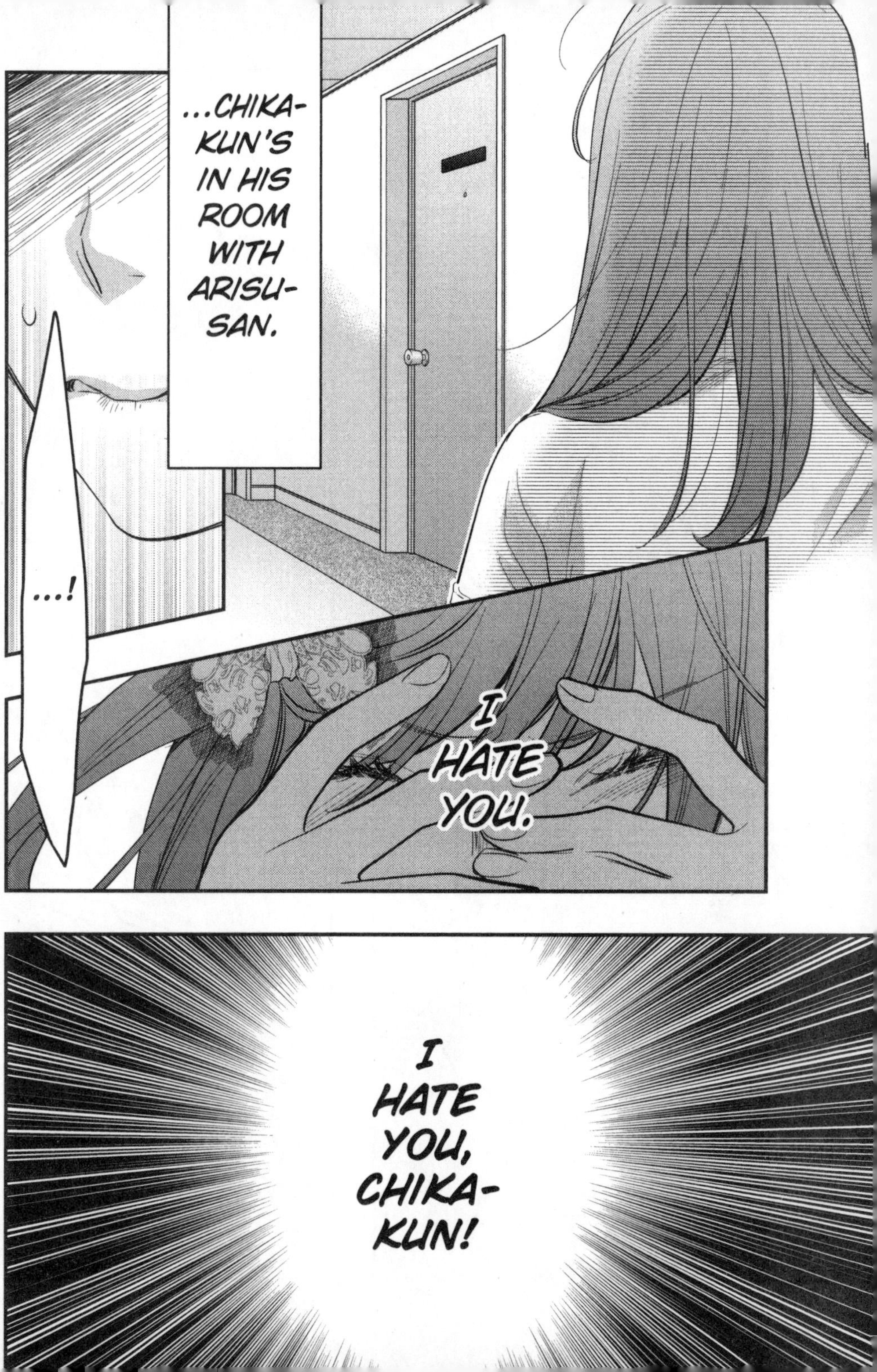
...CHIKA-KUN'S IN HIS ROOM WITH ARISU-SAN.
I HATE YOU.
...!
I HATE YOU, CHIKA-KUN!

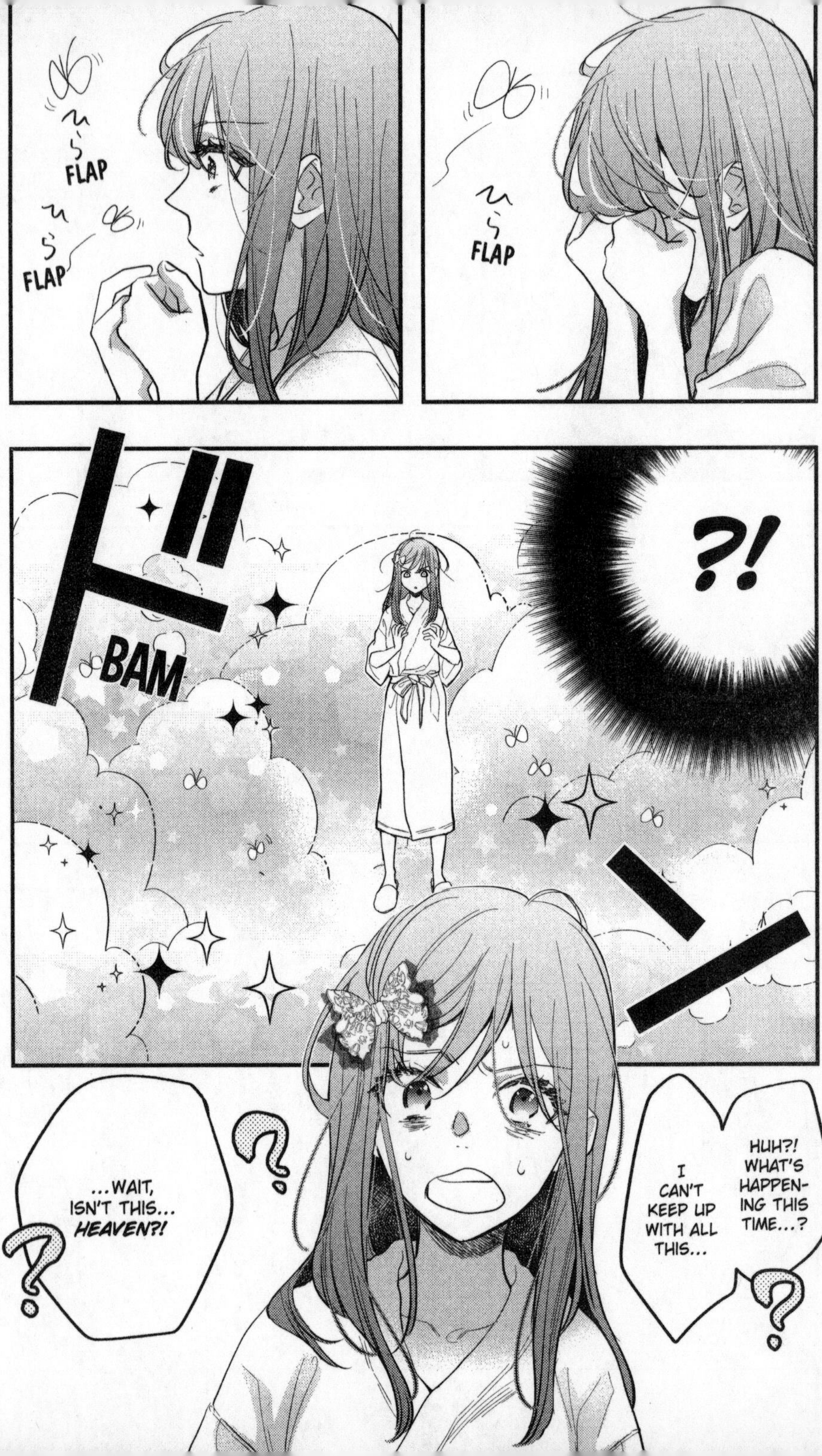
ひら
FLAP
ひら
FLAP
ひら
FLAP
?!
ド
BAM
HUH?! WHAT'S HAPPENING THIS TIME...?
I CAN'T KEEP UP WITH ALL THIS...
...WAIT, ISN'T THIS... *HEAVEN?!*

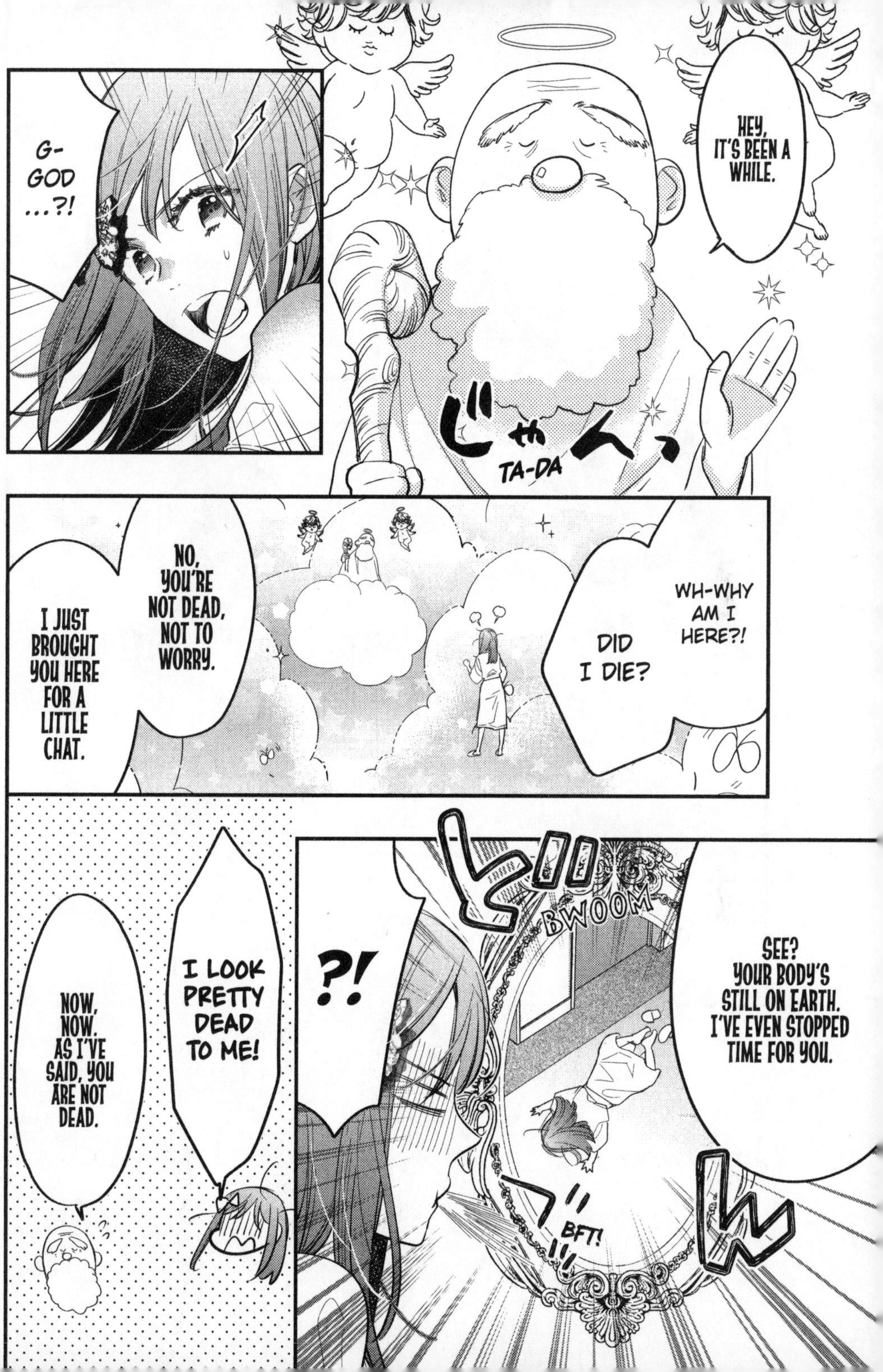
HEY, IT'S BEEN A WHILE.
TA-DA
G-GOD...?!
WH-WHY AM I HERE?!
DID I DIE?
NO, YOU'RE NOT DEAD, NOT TO WORRY.
I JUST BROUGHT YOU HERE FOR A LITTLE CHAT.
BWOOM
SEE? YOUR BODY'S STILL ON EARTH. I'VE EVEN STOPPED TIME FOR YOU.
?!
BFT!
I LOOK PRETTY DEAD TO ME!
NOW, NOW. AS I'VE SAID, YOU ARE NOT DEAD.

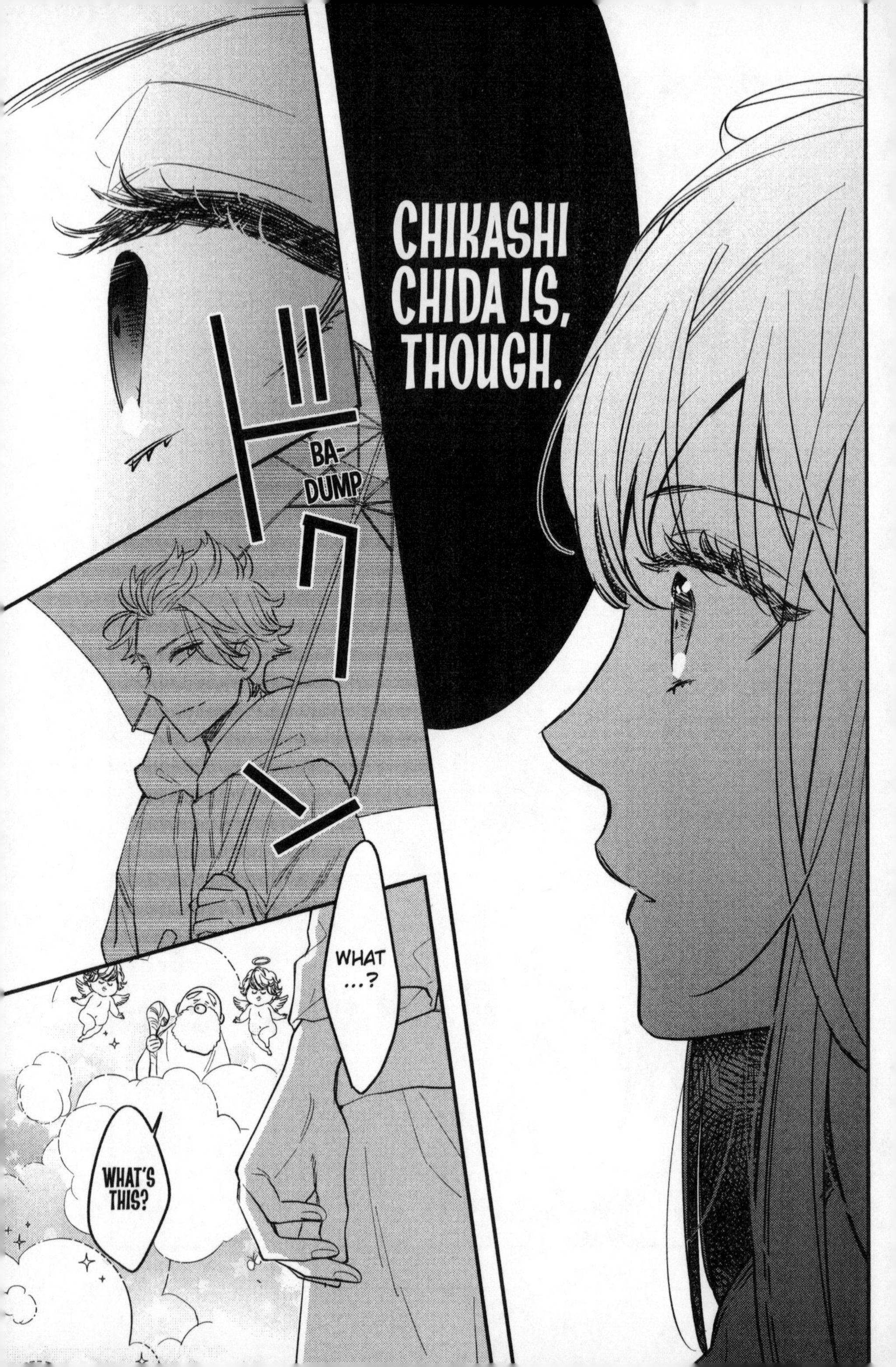
CHIKASHI CHIDA IS, THOUGH.
BA-DUMP
WHAT ...?
WHAT'S THIS?

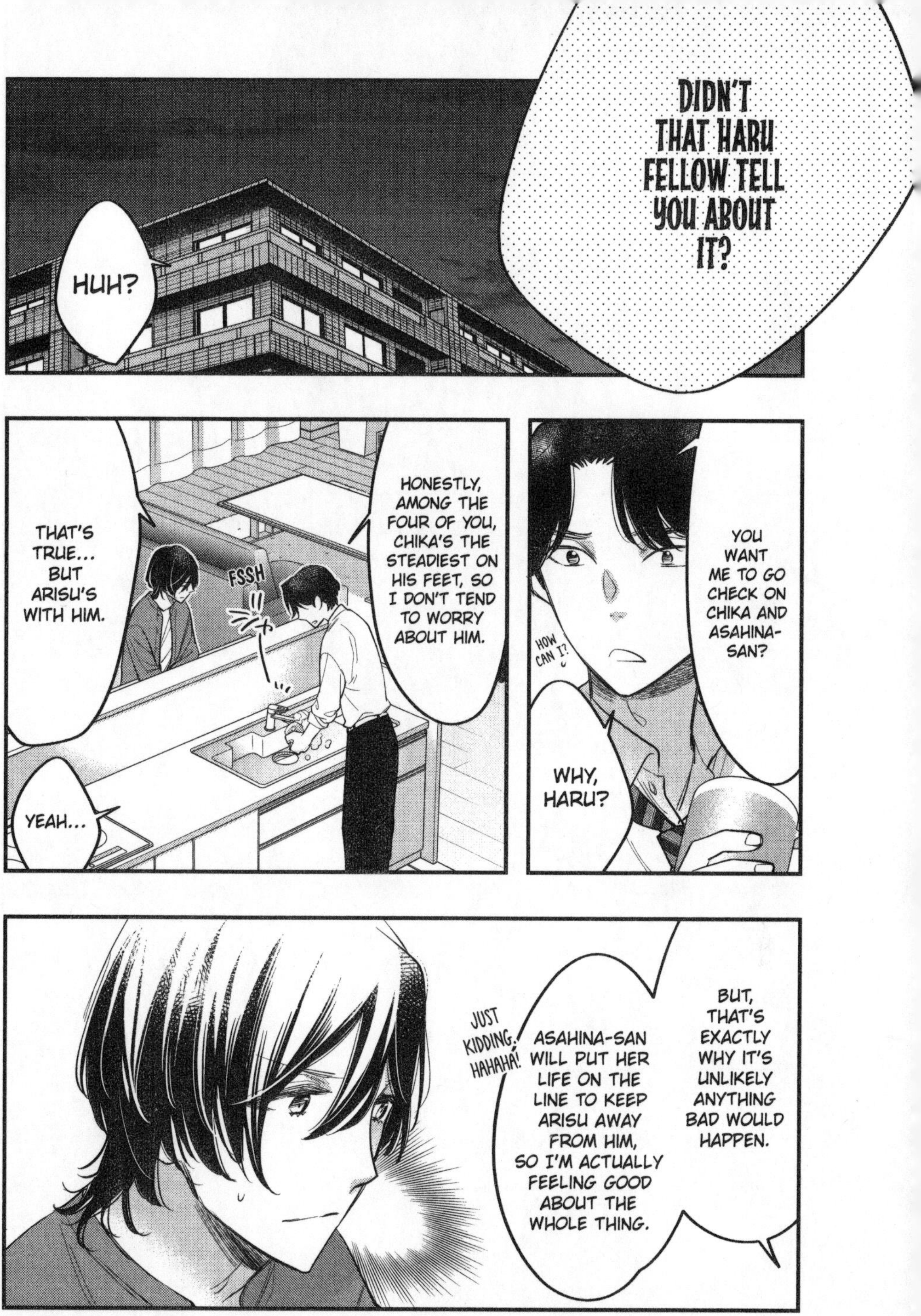
DIDN'T THAT HARU FELLOW TELL YOU ABOUT IT?
HUH?
YOU WANT ME TO GO CHECK ON CHIKA AND ASAHINA-SAN?
HOW CAN I?
WHY, HARU?
HONESTLY, AMONG THE FOUR OF YOU, CHIKA'S THE STEADIEST ON HIS FEET, SO I DON'T TEND TO WORRY ABOUT HIM.
FSSH
THAT'S TRUE... BUT ARISU'S WITH HIM.
YEAH...
BUT, THAT'S EXACTLY WHY IT'S UNLIKELY ANYTHING BAD WOULD HAPPEN.
ASAHINA-SAN WILL PUT HER LIFE ON THE LINE TO KEEP ARISU AWAY FROM HIM, SO I'M ACTUALLY FEELING GOOD ABOUT THE WHOLE THING.
JUST KIDDING. HAHAHA!

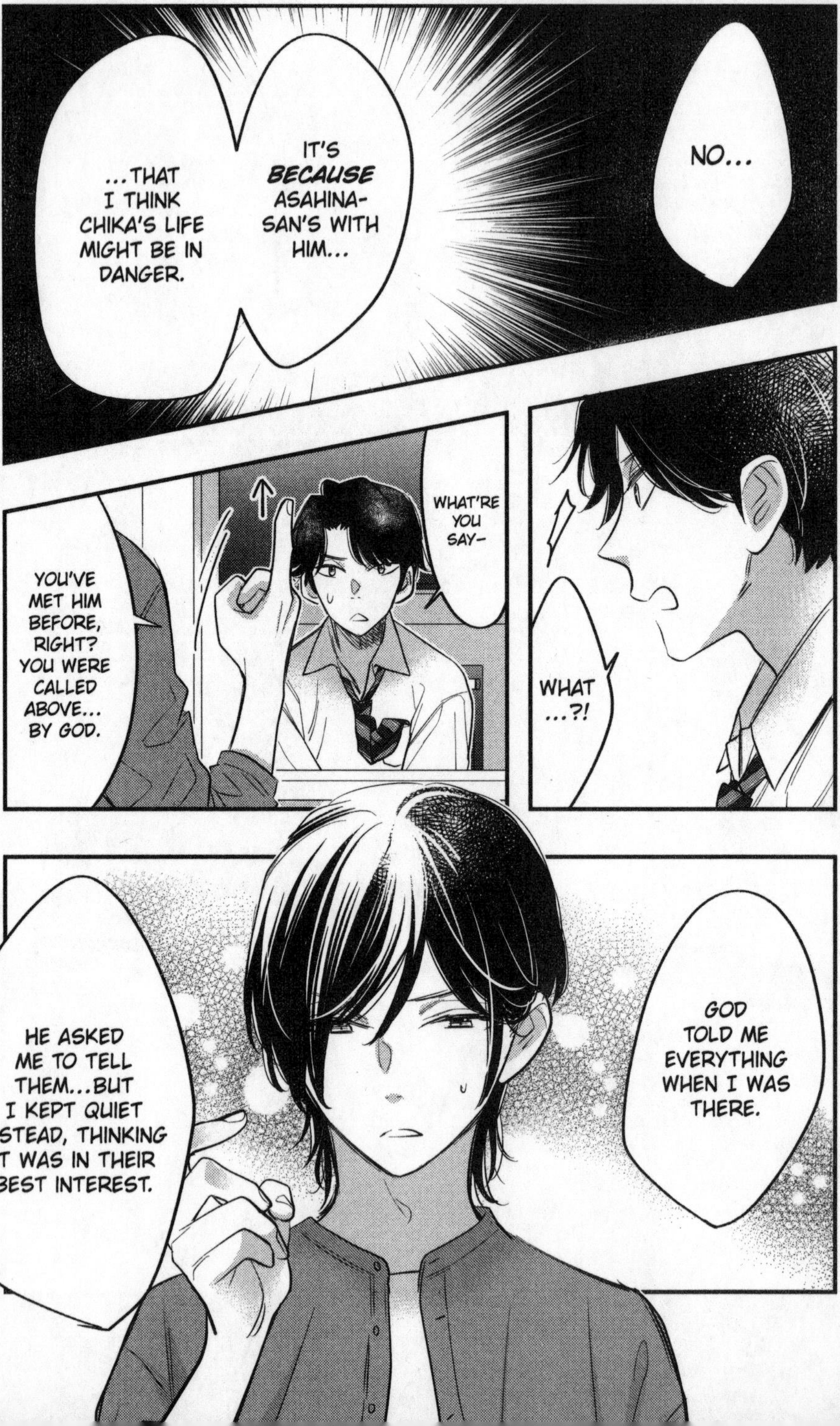
NO...
IT'S *BECAUSE* ASAHINA-SAN'S WITH HIM...
...THAT I THINK CHIKA'S LIFE MIGHT BE IN DANGER.
WHAT...?!
WHAT'RE YOU SAY-
YOU'VE MET HIM BEFORE, RIGHT? YOU WERE CALLED ABOVE... BY GOD.
GOD TOLD ME EVERYTHING WHEN I WAS THERE.
HE ASKED ME TO TELL THEM...BUT I KEPT QUIET INSTEAD, THINKING IT WAS IN THEIR BEST INTEREST.

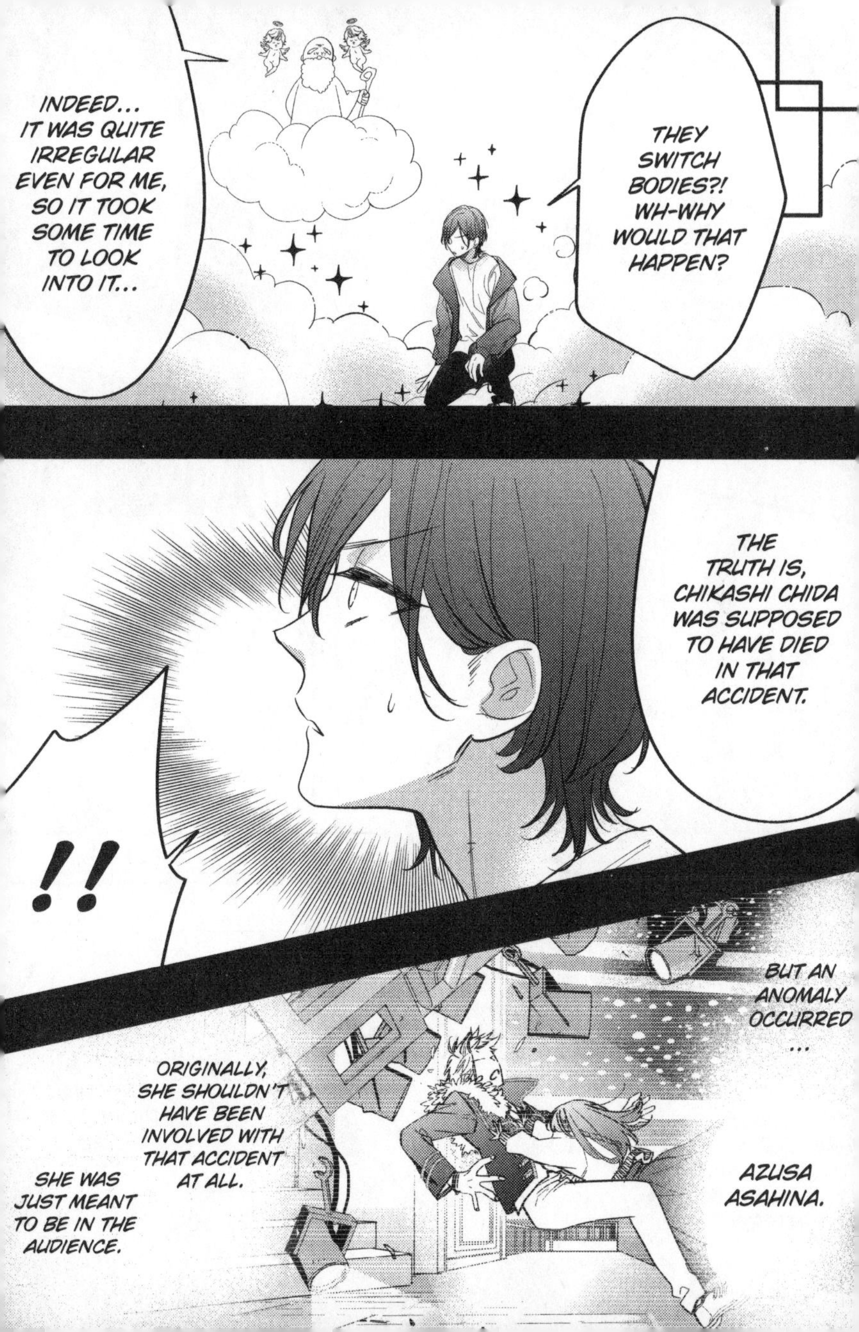
THEY SWITCH BODIES?! WH-WHY WOULD THAT HAPPEN?
INDEED... IT WAS QUITE IRREGULAR EVEN FOR ME, SO IT TOOK SOME TIME TO LOOK INTO IT...
THE TRUTH IS, CHIKASHI CHIDA WAS SUPPOSED TO HAVE DIED IN THAT ACCIDENT.
!!
BUT AN ANOMALY OCCURRED...
AZUSA ASAHINA.
ORIGINALLY, SHE SHOULDN'T HAVE BEEN INVOLVED WITH THAT ACCIDENT AT ALL.
SHE WAS JUST MEANT TO BE IN THE AUDIENCE.

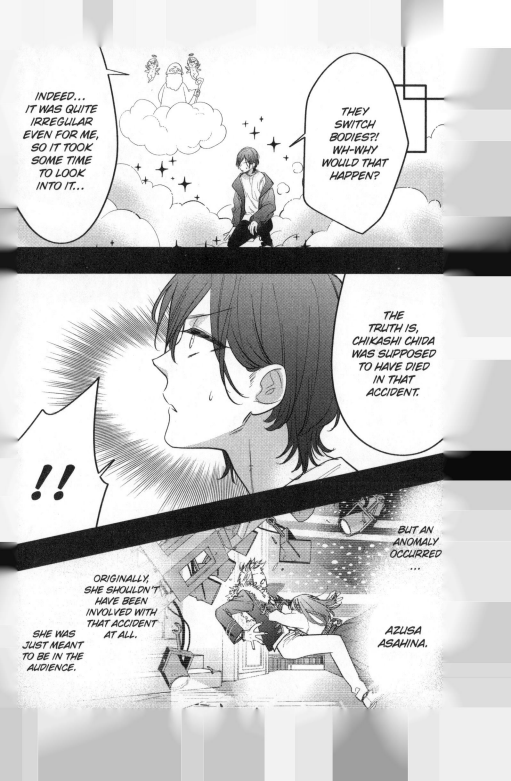

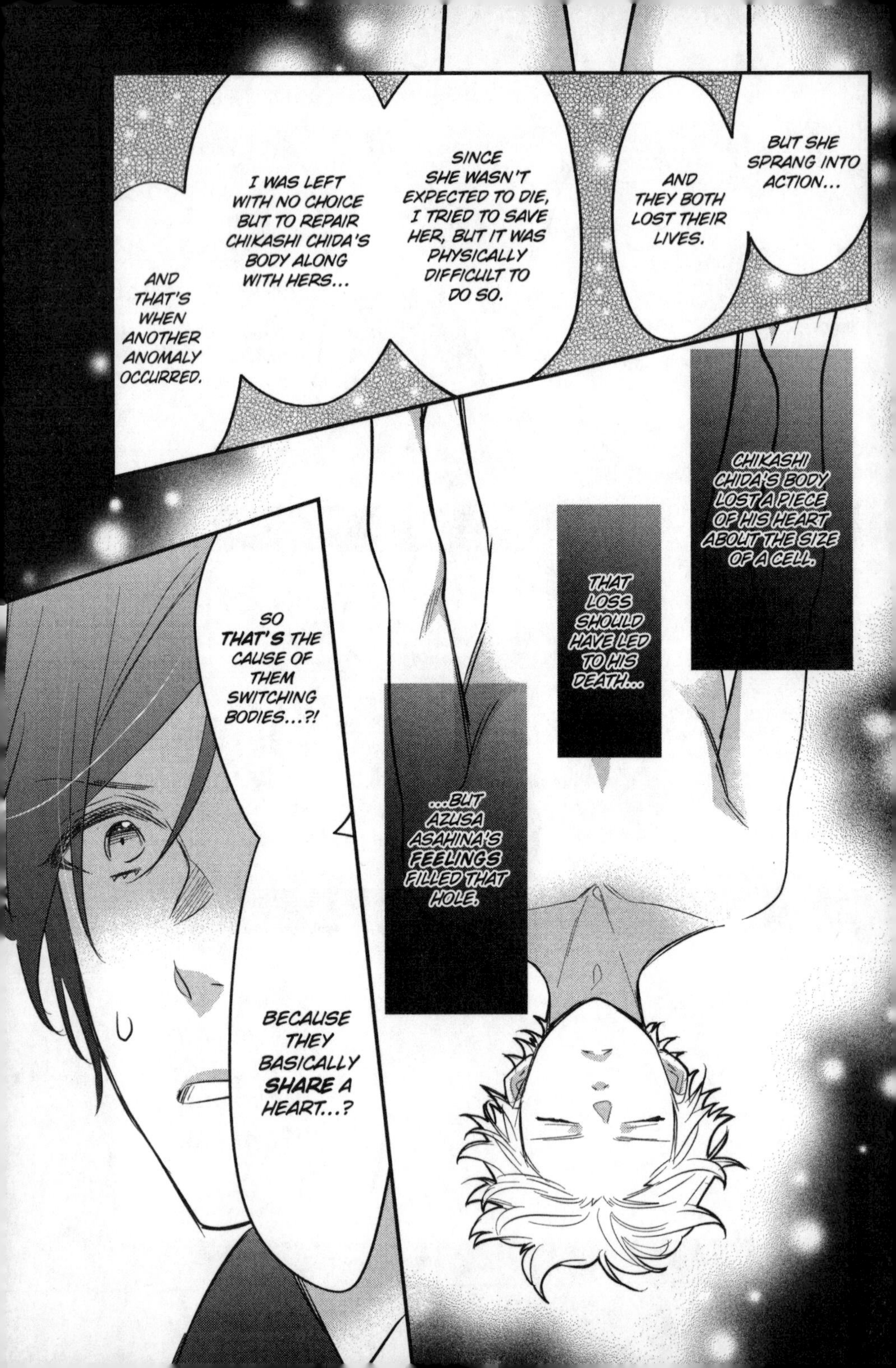
BUT SHE SPRANG INTO ACTION...
AND THEY BOTH LOST THEIR LIVES.
SINCE SHE WASN'T EXPECTED TO DIE, I TRIED TO SAVE HER, BUT IT WAS PHYSICALLY DIFFICULT TO DO SO.
I WAS LEFT WITH NO CHOICE BUT TO REPAIR CHIKASHI CHIDA'S BODY ALONG WITH HERS...
AND THAT'S WHEN ANOTHER ANOMALY OCCURRED.
CHIKASHI CHIDA'S BODY LOST A PIECE OF HIS HEART ABOUT THE SIZE OF A CELL.
THAT LOSS SHOULD HAVE LED TO HIS DEATH...
...BUT AZUSA ASAHINA'S FEELINGS FILLED THAT HOLE.
SO THAT'S THE CAUSE OF THEM SWITCHING BODIES...?!
BECAUSE THEY BASICALLY SHARE A HEART...?

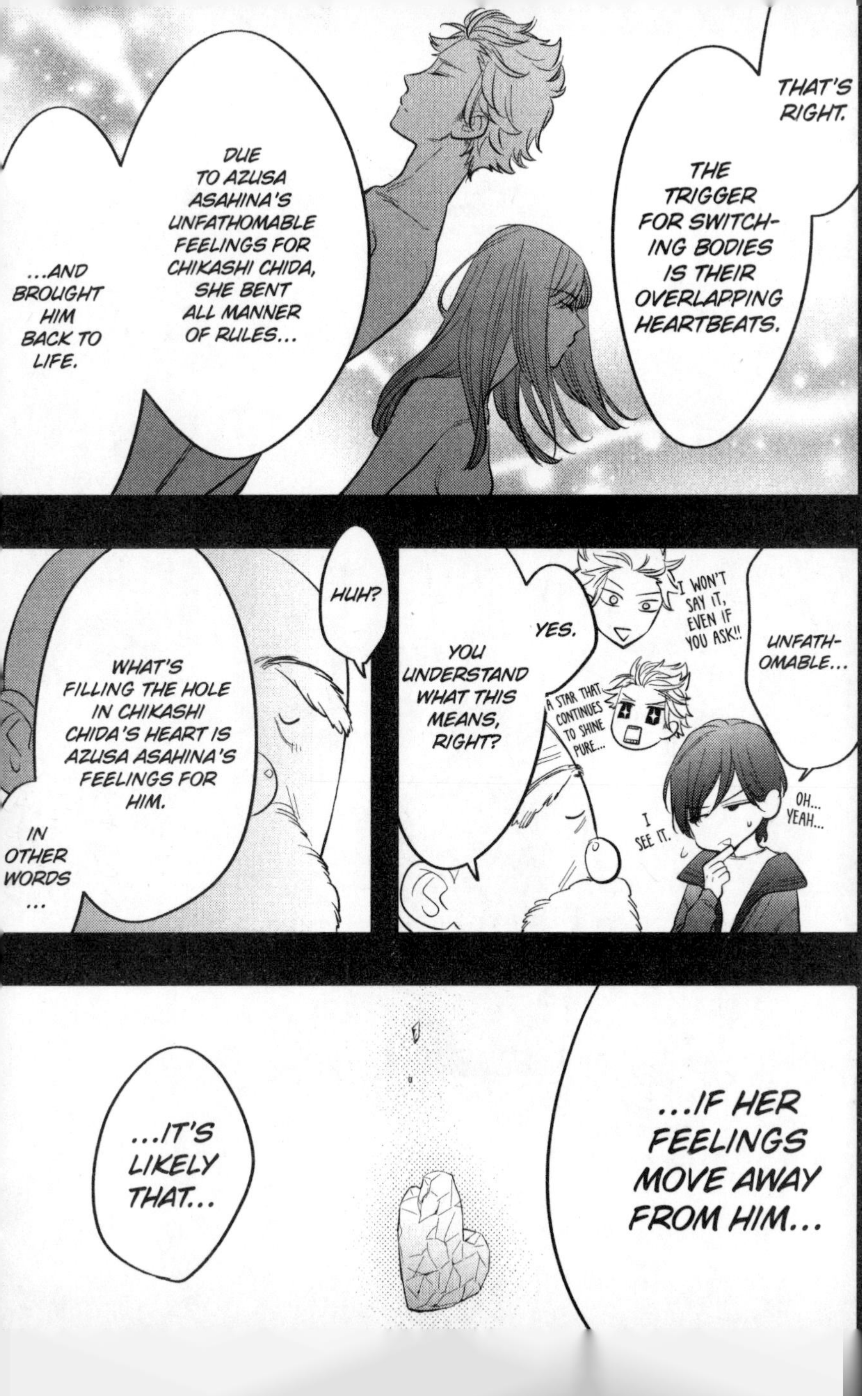
THAT'S RIGHT.
THE TRIGGER FOR SWITCHING BODIES IS THEIR OVERLAPPING HEARTBEATS.
DUE TO AZUSA ASAHINA'S UNFATHOMABLE FEELINGS FOR CHIKASHI CHIDA, SHE BENT ALL MANNER OF RULES...
...AND BROUGHT HIM BACK TO LIFE.
UNFATHOMABLE...
I WON'T SAY IT, EVEN IF YOU ASK!!
OH... YEAH...
I SEE IT.
A STAR THAT CONTINUES TO SHINE PURE...
YES.
YOU UNDERSTAND WHAT THIS MEANS, RIGHT?
HUH?
WHAT'S FILLING THE HOLE IN CHIKASHI CHIDA'S HEART IS AZUSA ASAHINA'S FEELINGS FOR HIM.
IN OTHER WORDS...
...IF HER FEELINGS MOVE AWAY FROM HIM...
...IT'S LIKELY THAT...

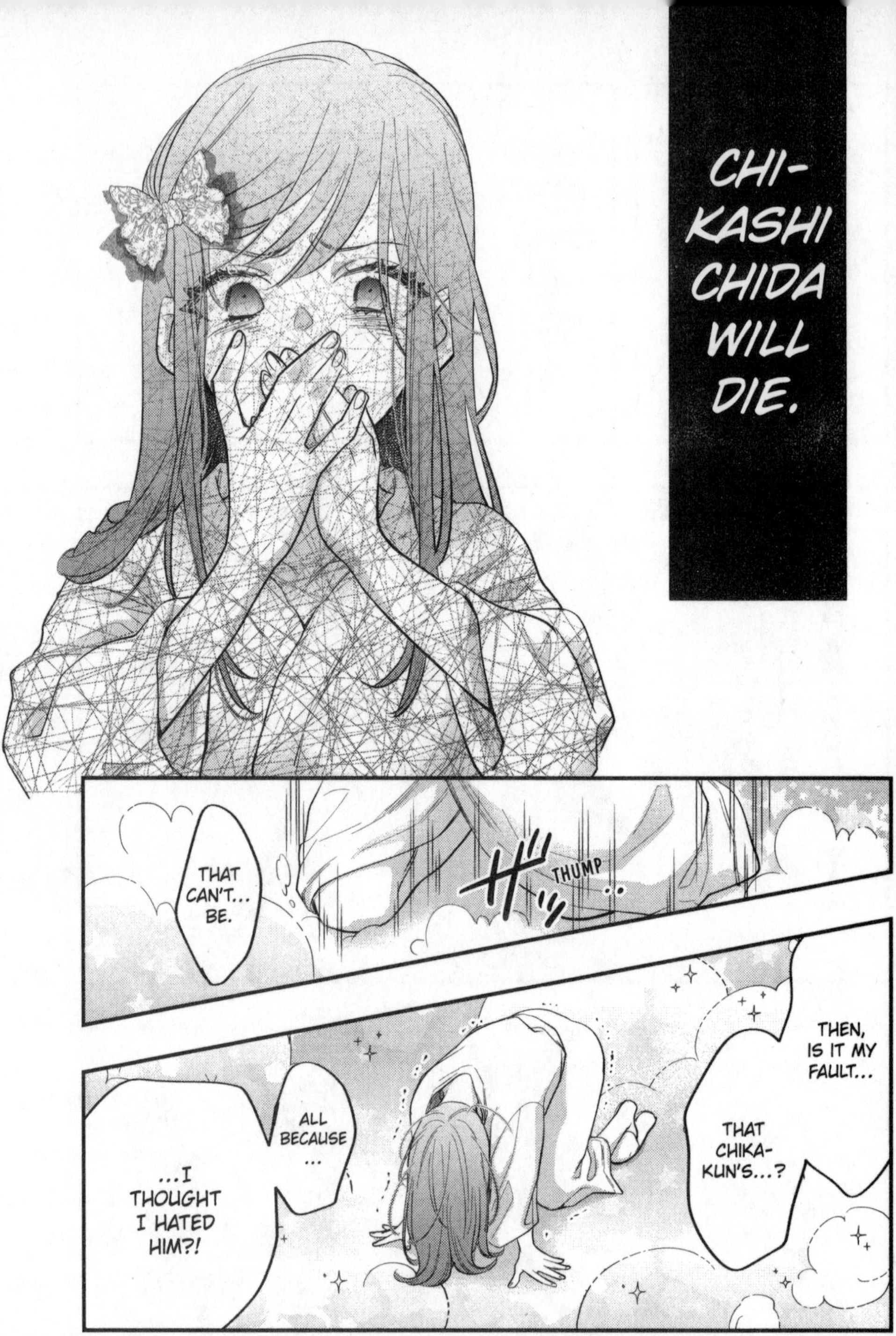
CHI-KASHI CHIDA WILL DIE.
THAT CAN'T... BE.
THUMP
THEN, IS IT MY FAULT...
THAT CHIKA-KUN'S...?
ALL BECAUSE ...
...I THOUGHT I HATED HIM?!

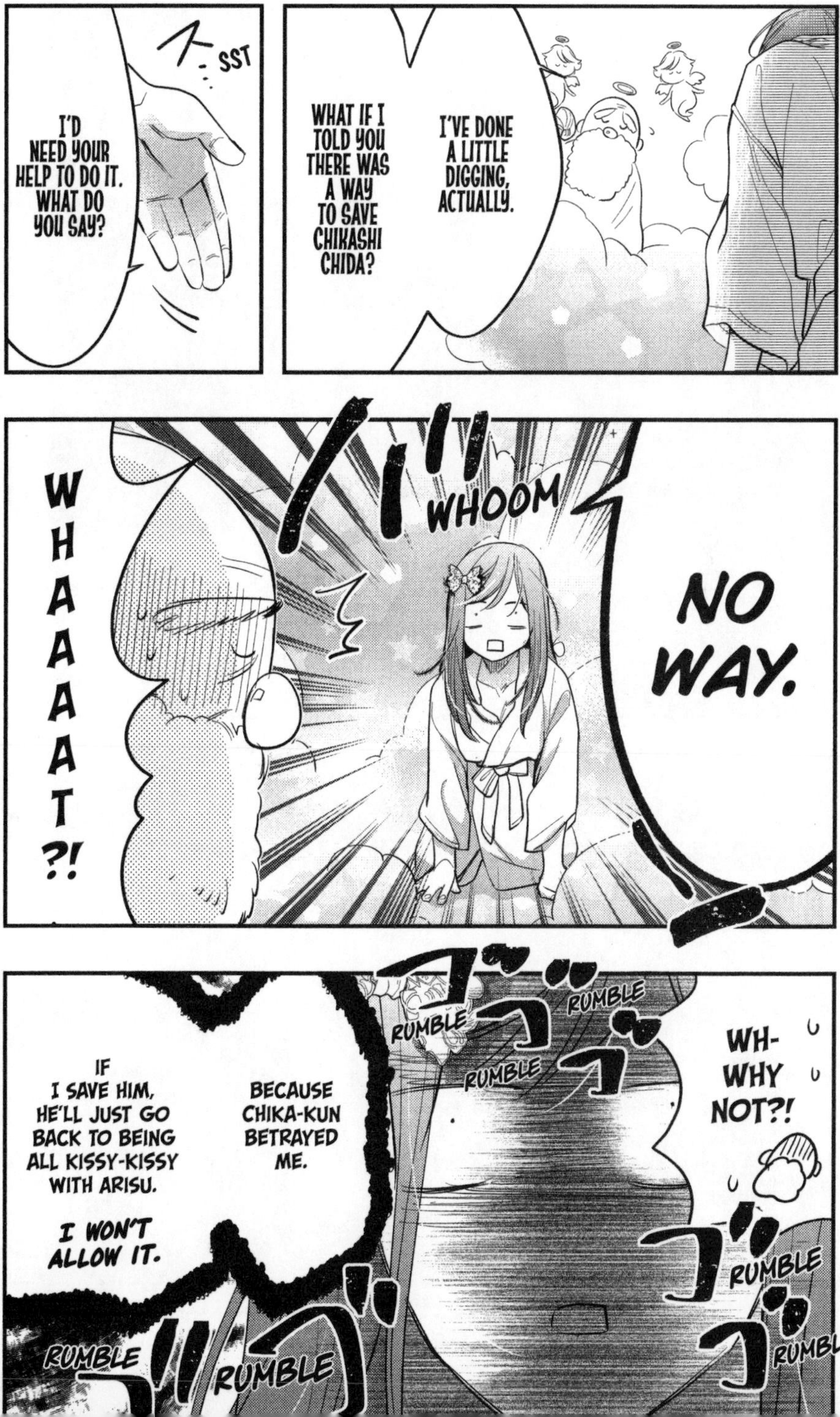
I'VE DONE A LITTLE DIGGING, ACTUALLY.
WHAT IF I TOLD YOU THERE WAS A WAY TO SAVE CHIKASHI CHIDA?
SST
I'D NEED YOUR HELP TO DO IT. WHAT DO YOU SAY?
NO WAY.
WHOOM
WHAAAAAT?!
WH- WHY NOT?!
RUMBLE
RUMBLE
RUMBLE
RUMBLE
RUMBLE
BECAUSE CHIKA-KUN BETRAYED ME.
IF I SAVE HIM, HE'LL JUST GO BACK TO BEING ALL KISSY-KISSY WITH ARISU.
I WON'T ALLOW IT.
RUMBLE
RUMBLE

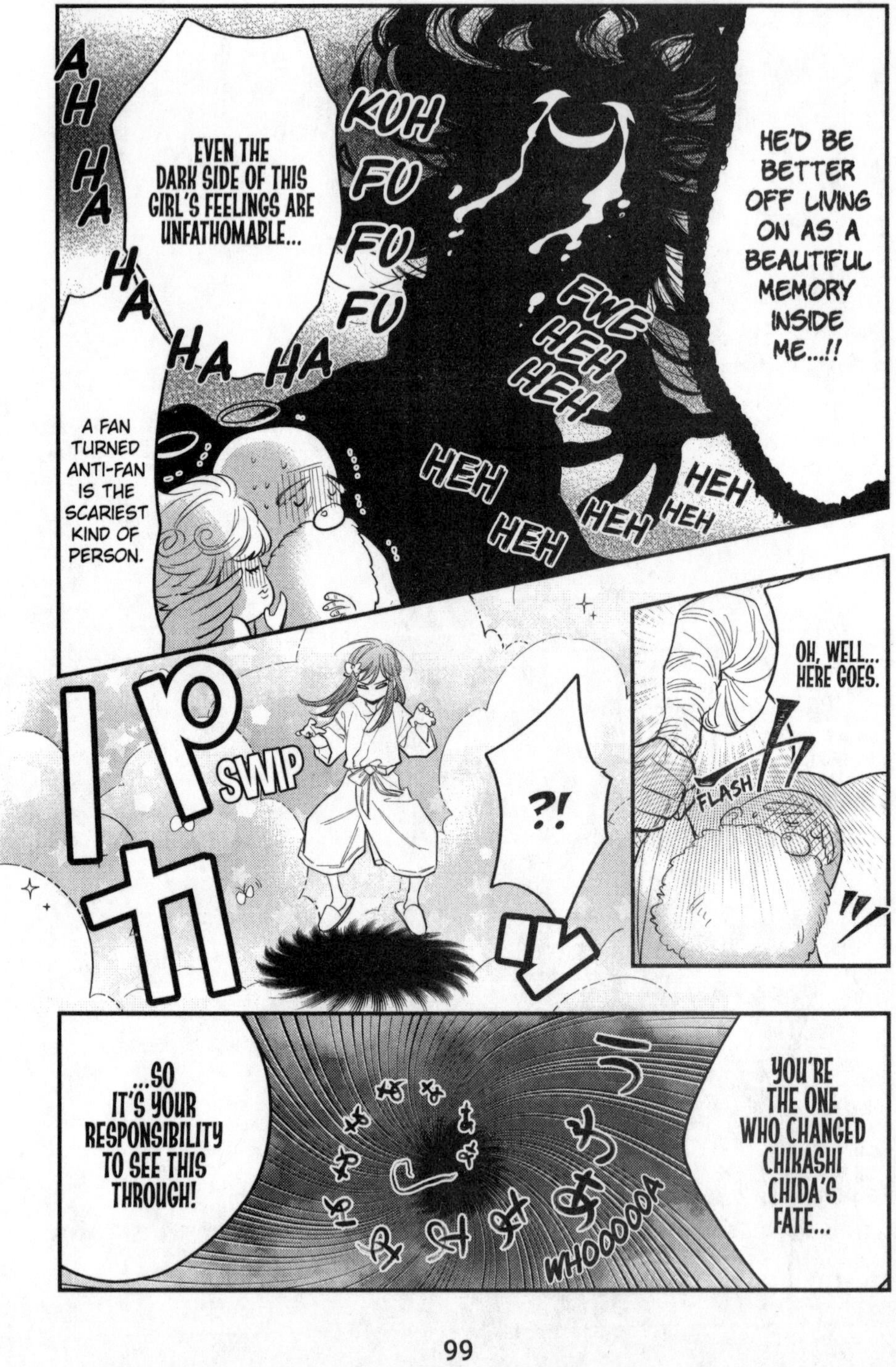
HE'D BE BETTER OFF LIVING ON AS A BEAUTIFUL MEMORY INSIDE ME...!!
FWE HEH HEH
HEH HEH HEH HEH HEH
KUH FU FU FU FU
EVEN THE DARK SIDE OF THIS GIRL'S FEELINGS ARE UNFATHOMABLE...
AH HA HA HA HA HA HA HA
A FAN TURNED ANTI-FAN IS THE SCARIEST KIND OF PERSON.
OH, WELL... HERE GOES.
FLASH
?!
SWIP
YOU'RE THE ONE WHO CHANGED CHIKASHI CHIDA'S FATE...
WHOOOOOA
...SO IT'S YOUR RESPONSIBILITY TO SEE THIS THROUGH!

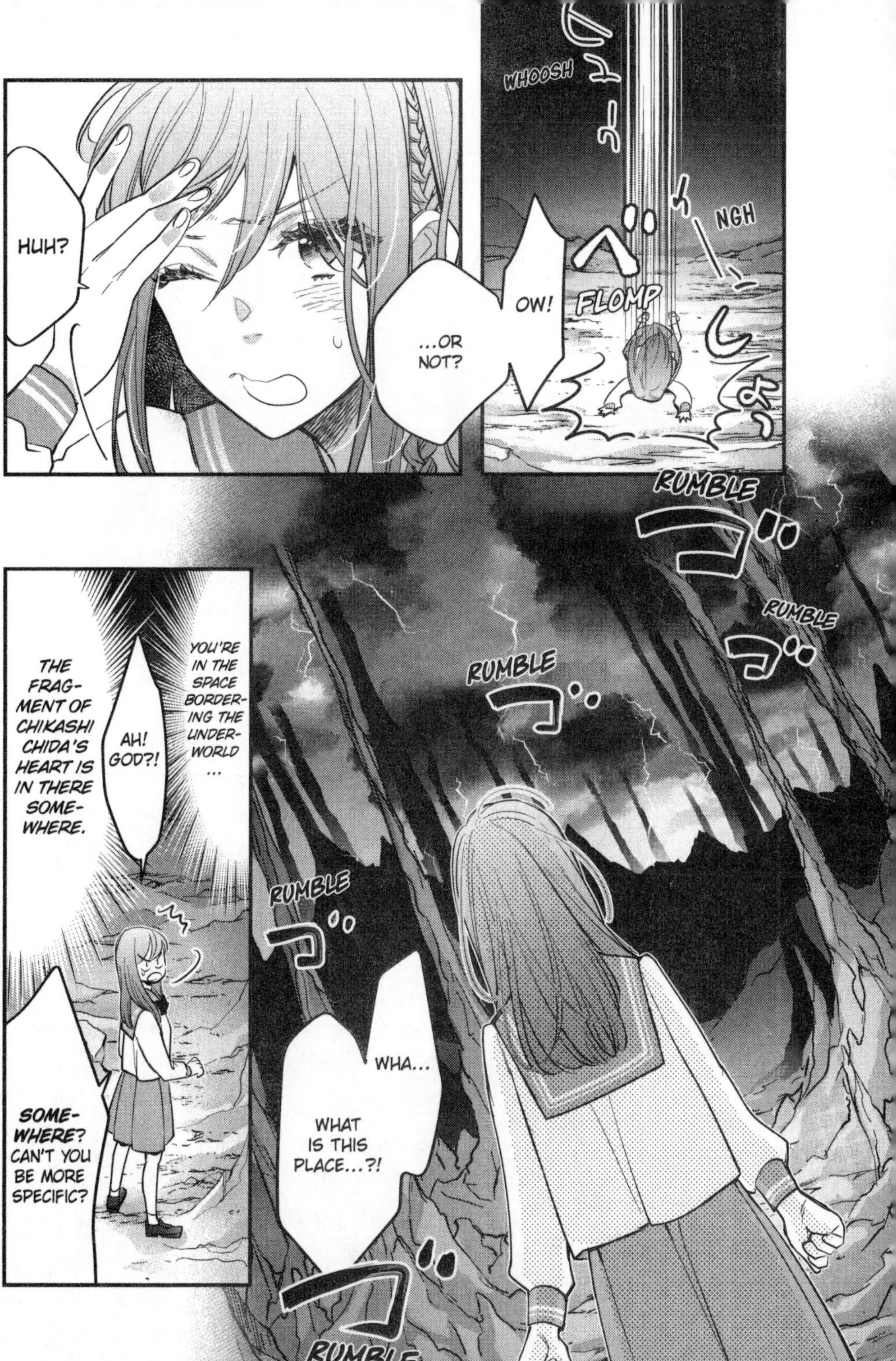
WHOOSH
NGH
FLOMP
OW!
...OR NOT?
HUH?
RUMBLE
RUMBLE
RUMBLE
RUMBLE
WHA...
WHAT IS THIS PLACE...?!
RUMBLE
YOU'RE IN THE SPACE BORDERING THE UNDERWORLD...
AH! GOD?!
THE FRAGMENT OF CHIKASHI CHIDA'S HEART IS IN THERE SOMEWHERE.
SOMEWHERE? CAN'T YOU BE MORE SPECIFIC?

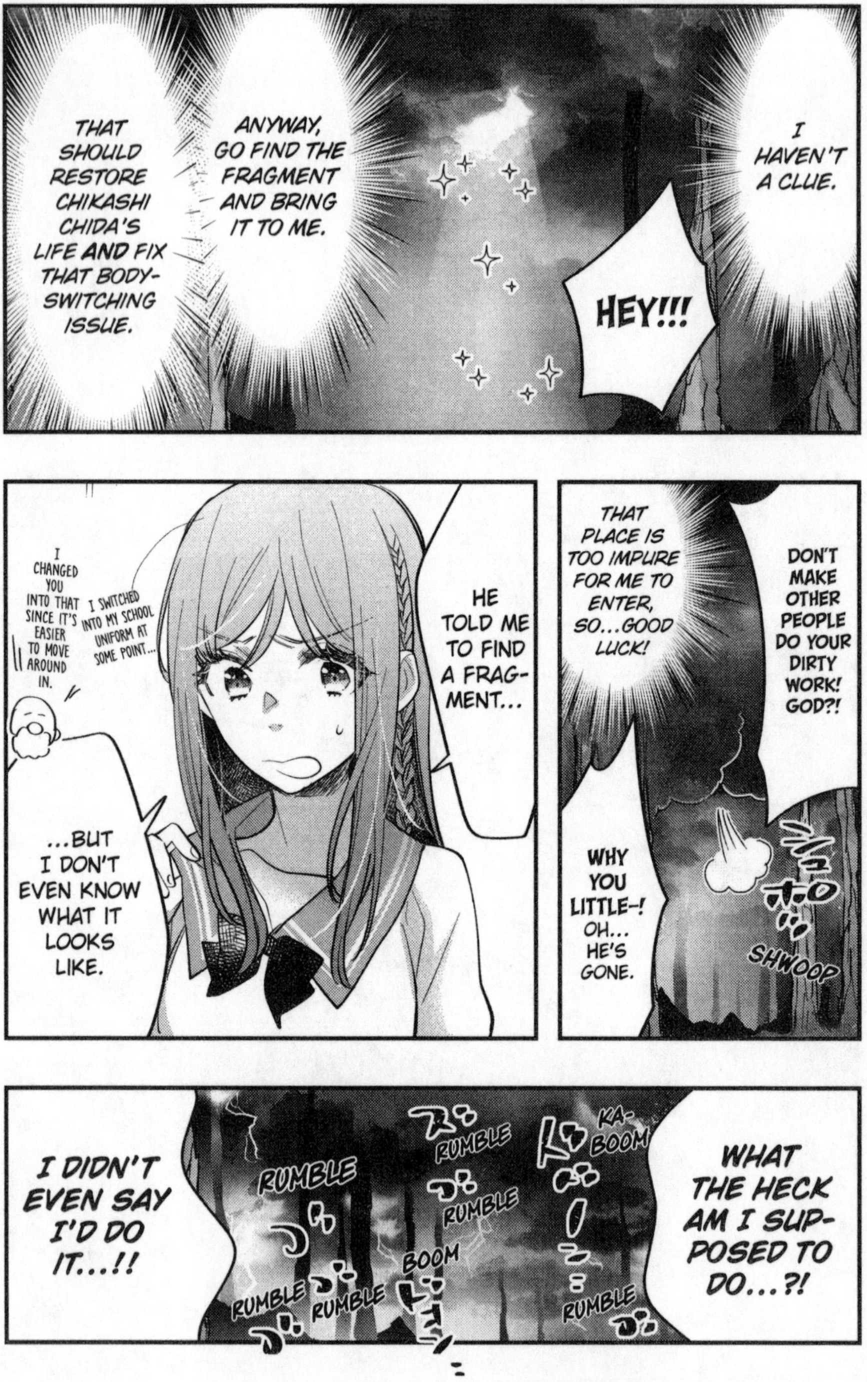
I HAVEN'T A CLUE.
HEY!!!
ANYWAY, GO FIND THE FRAGMENT AND BRING IT TO ME.
THAT SHOULD RESTORE CHIKASHI CHIDA'S LIFE AND FIX THAT BODY-SWITCHING ISSUE.
THAT PLACE IS TOO IMPURE FOR ME TO ENTER, SO...GOOD LUCK!
DON'T MAKE OTHER PEOPLE DO YOUR DIRTY WORK! GOD?!
SHWOOP
WHY YOU LITTLE-! OH... HE'S GONE.
HE TOLD ME TO FIND A FRAGMENT...
I SWITCHED INTO MY SCHOOL UNIFORM AT SOME POINT...
I CHANGED YOU INTO THAT SINCE IT'S EASIER TO MOVE AROUND IN.
...BUT I DON'T EVEN KNOW WHAT IT LOOKS LIKE.
WHAT THE HECK AM I SUPPOSED TO DO...?!
KA-BOOM
RUMBLE
RUMBLE
RUMBLE
RUMBLE
BOOM
RUMBLE
RUMBLE
RUMBLE
I DIDN'T EVEN SAY I'D DO IT...!!

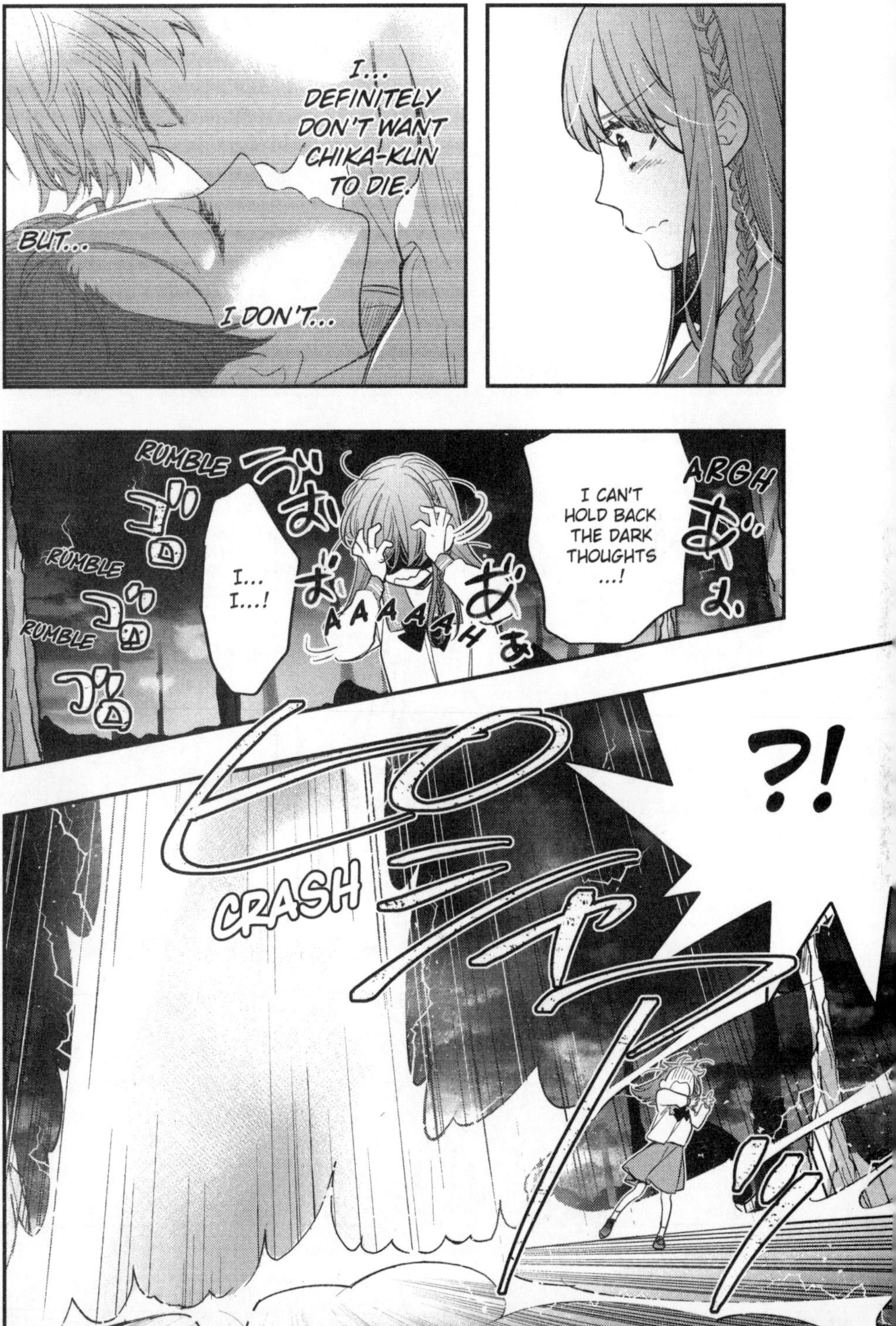
I... DEFINITELY DON'T WANT CHIKA-KUN TO DIE.
BUT...
I DON'T...
ARGH
I CAN'T HOLD BACK THE DARK THOUGHTS ...!
AAAAAAH
I... I...!
RUMBLE
RUMBLE
RUMBLE
?!
CRASH

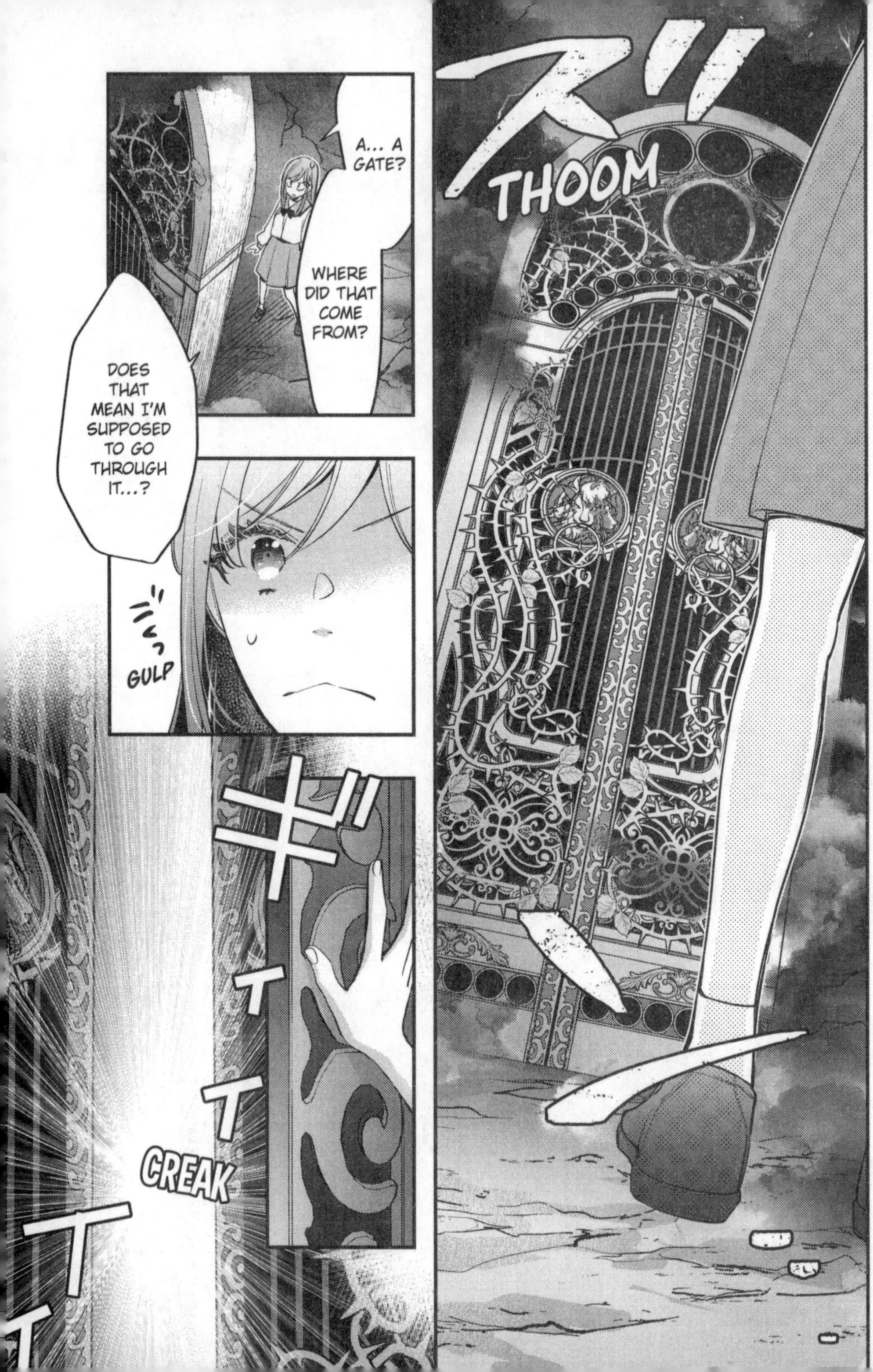
THOOM
A... A GATE?
WHERE DID THAT COME FROM?
DOES THAT MEAN I'M SUPPOSED TO GO THROUGH IT...?
GULP
CREAK

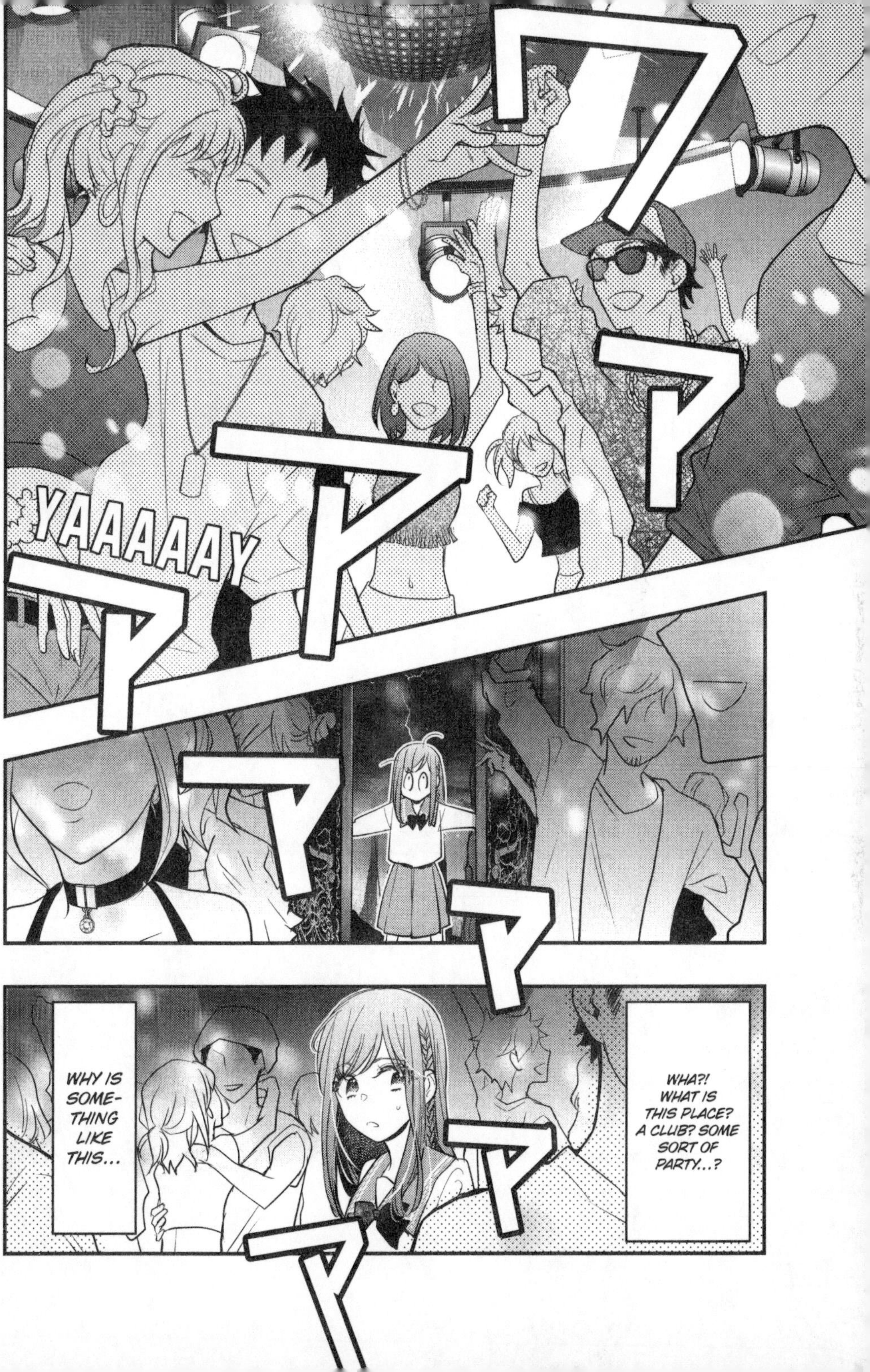
ワアアアアアアア
YAAAAAY
WHA?! WHAT IS THIS PLACE? A CLUB? SOME SORT OF PARTY...?
WHY IS SOME-THING LIKE THIS...

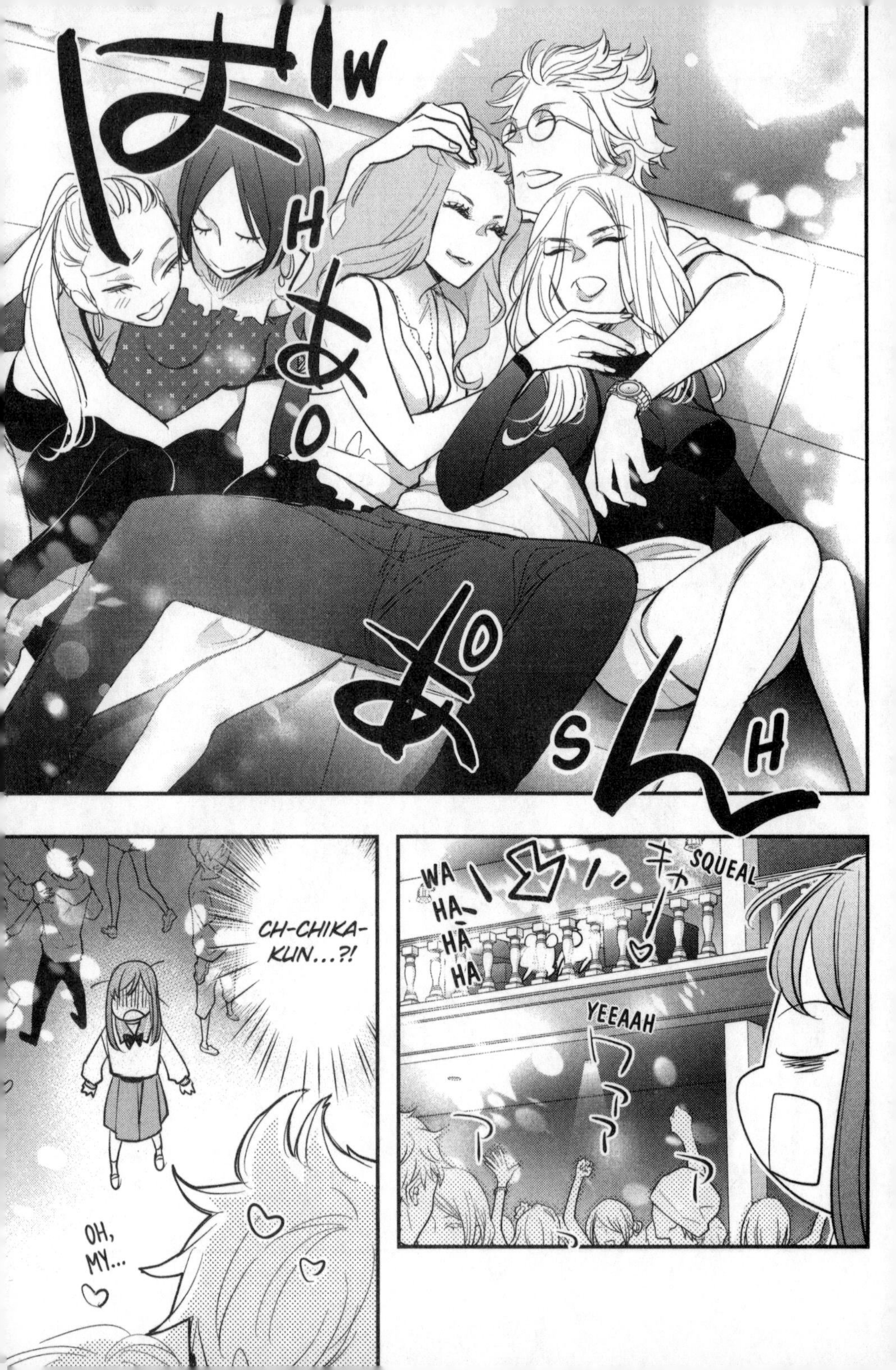
WHOOSH
WA HA HA HA
SQUEAL
YEEAAH
CH-CHIKA-KUN...?!
OH, MY...

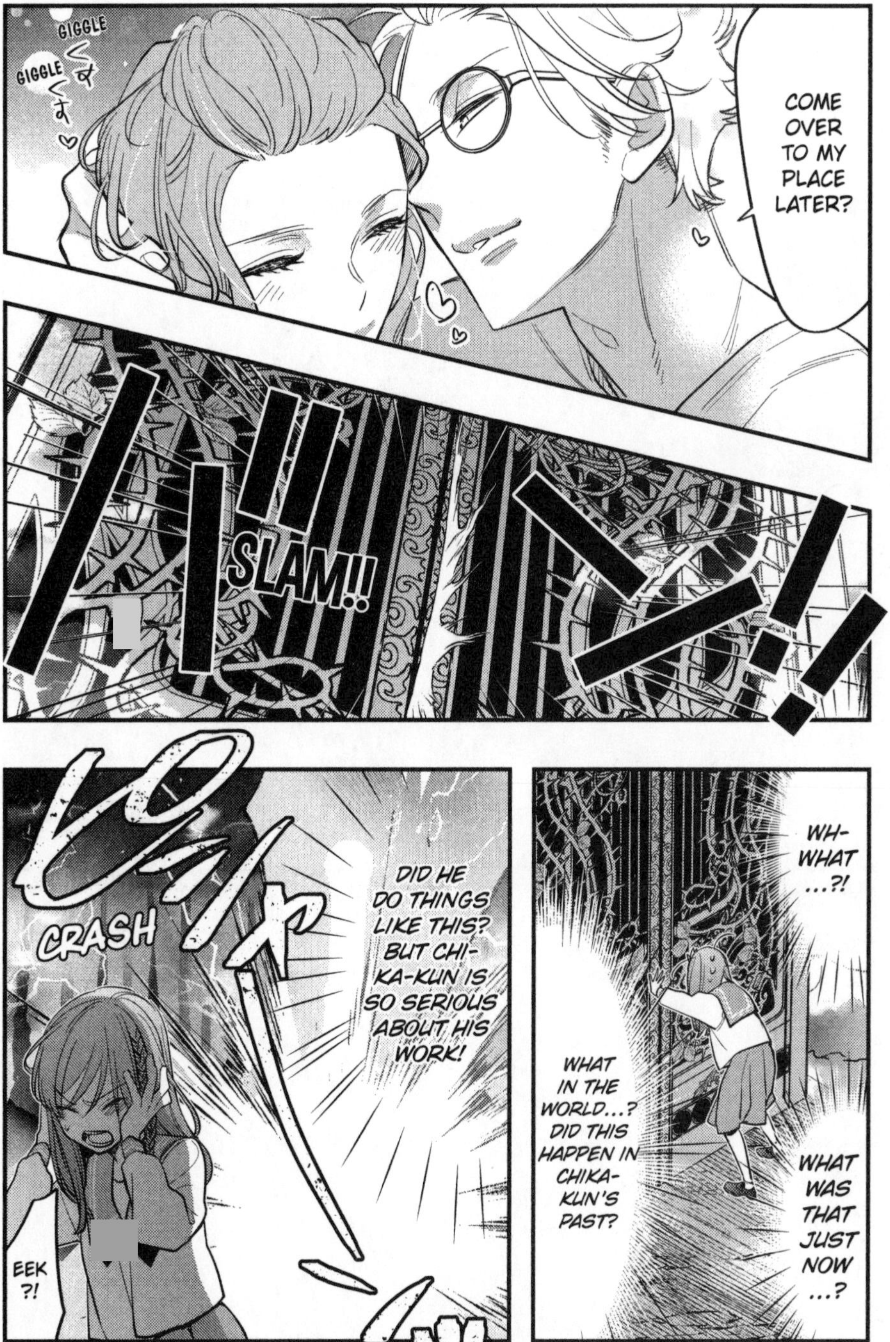

COME OVER TO MY PLACE LATER?
GIGGLE
GIGGLE
SLAM!!
WH- WHAT ...?!
WHAT WAS THAT JUST NOW ...?
WHAT IN THE WORLD...? DID THIS HAPPEN IN CHIKA-KUN'S PAST?
DID HE DO THINGS LIKE THIS? BUT CHI-KA-KUN IS SO SERIOUS ABOUT HIS WORK!
CRASH
EEK ?!

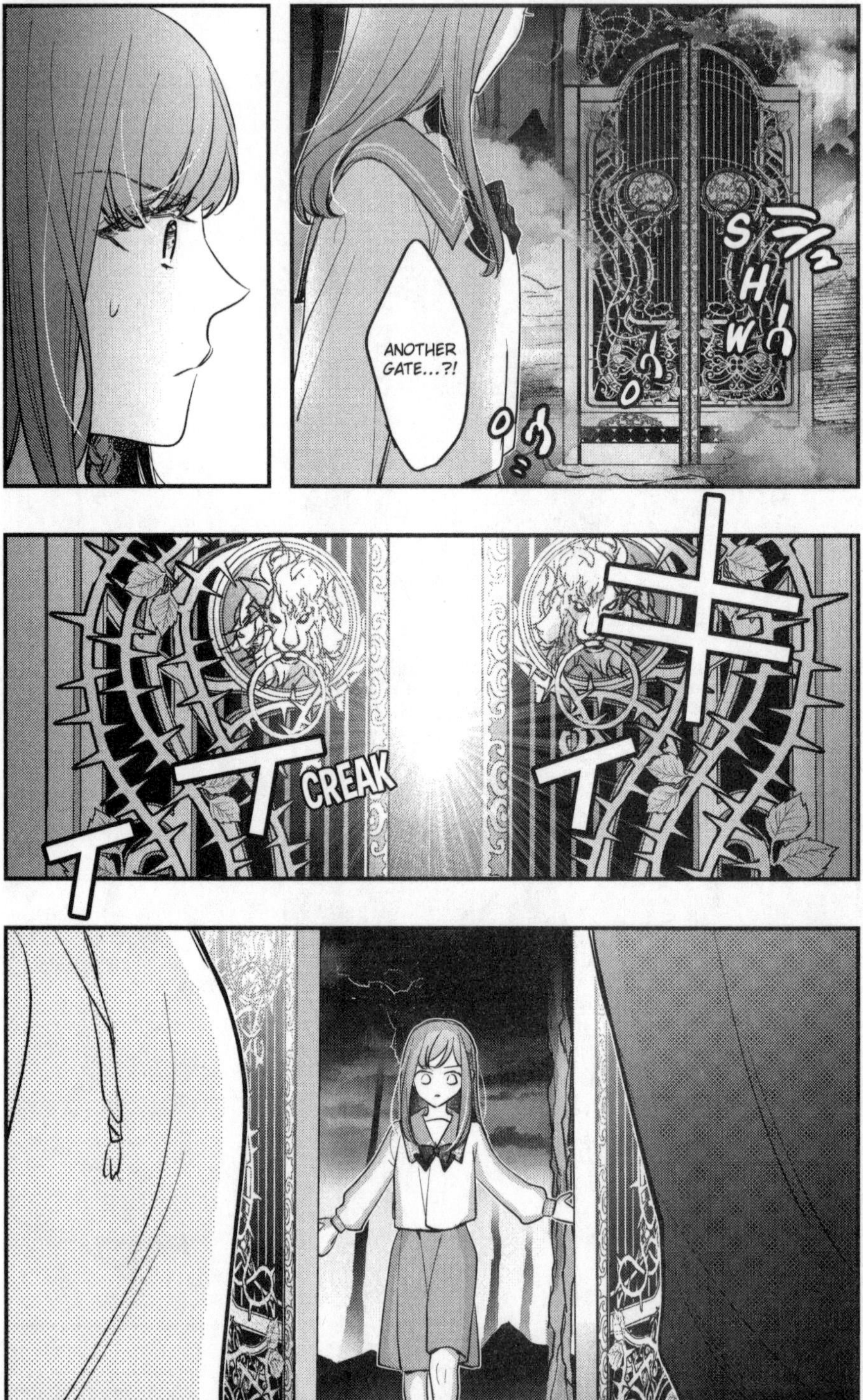
SHWOO
ANOTHER GATE...?!
CREAK

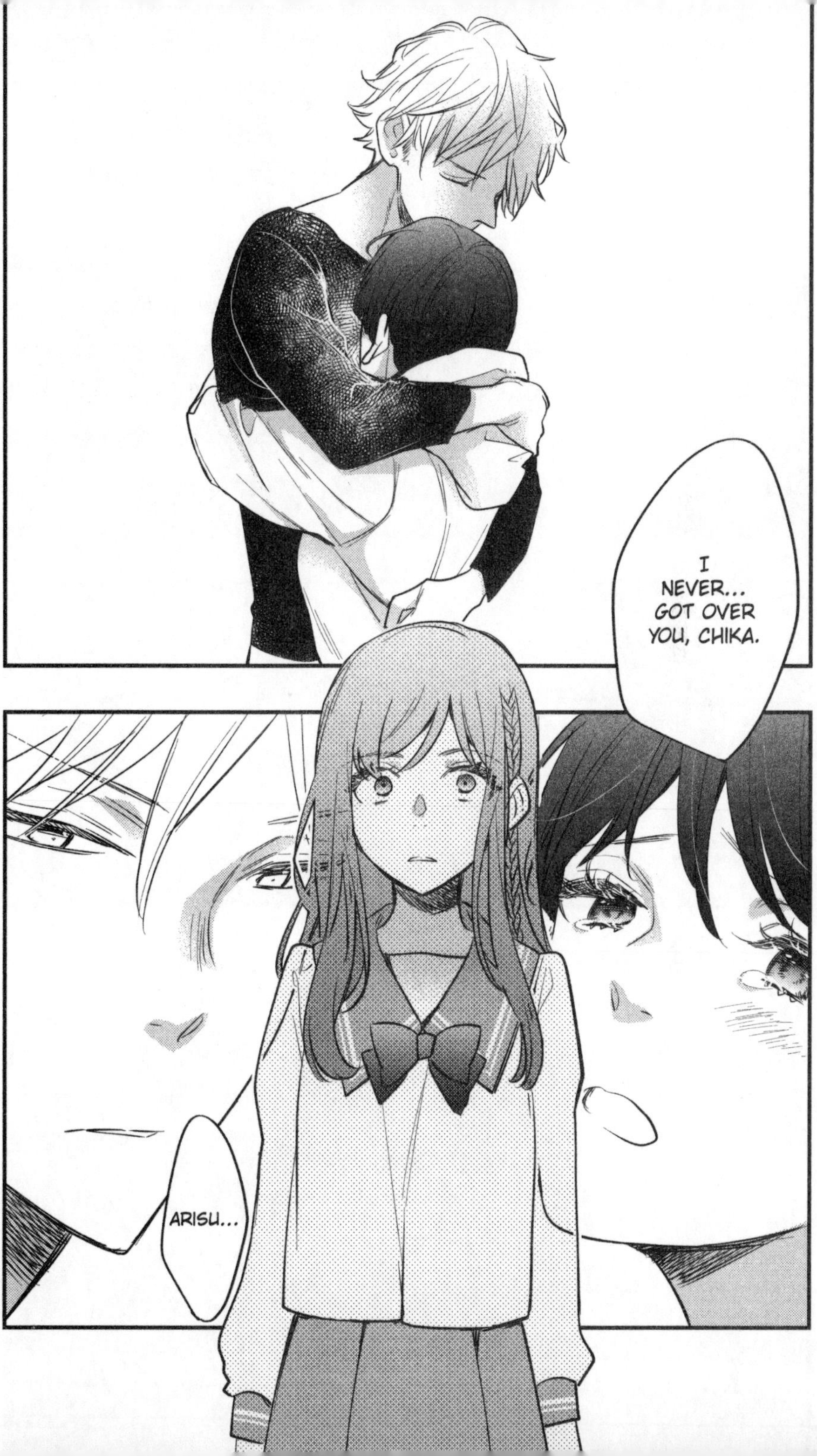
I NEVER... GOT OVER YOU, CHIKA.
ARISU...

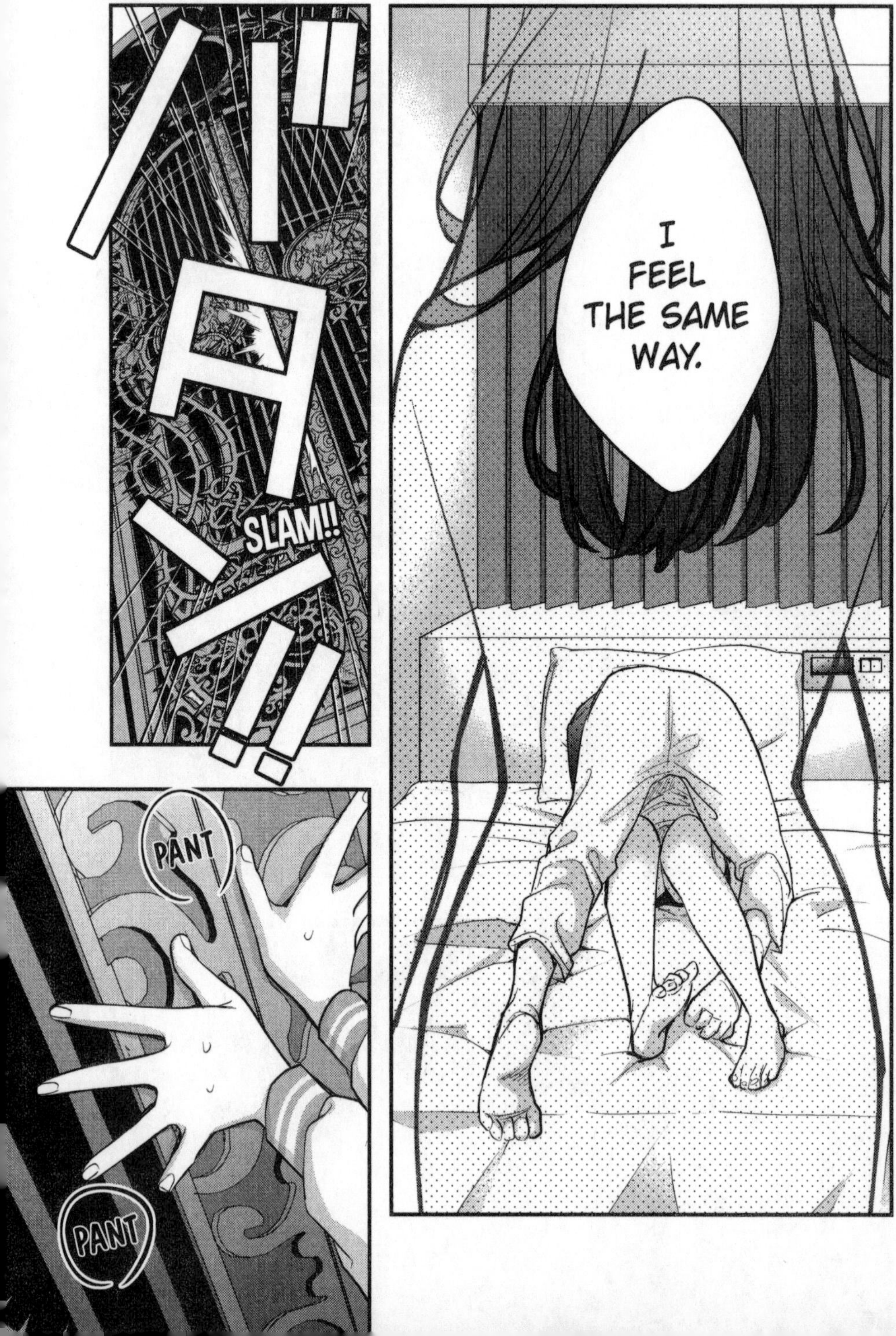
I FEEL THE SAME WAY.
SLAM!!
PANT
PANT

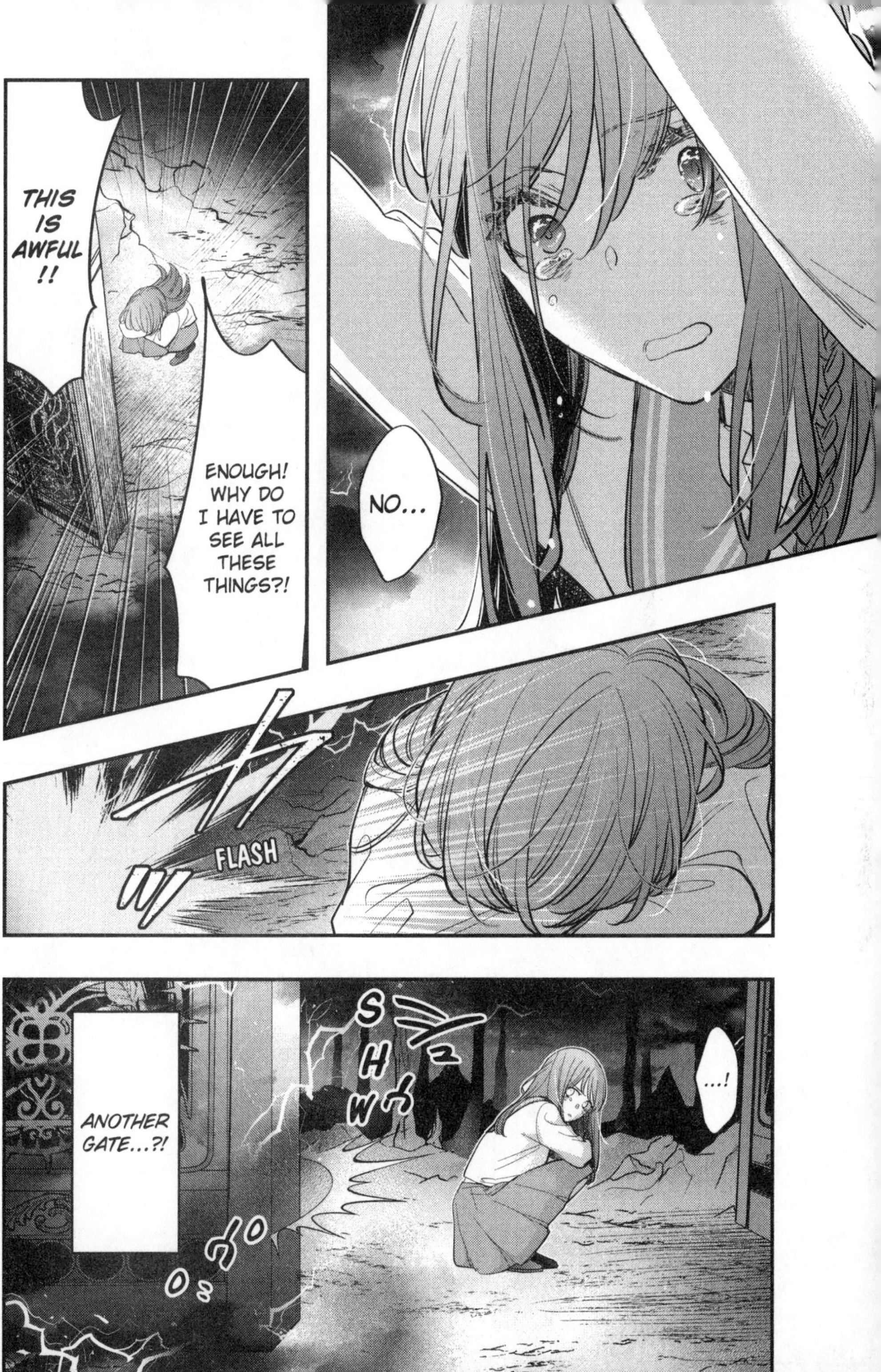
NO...
THIS IS AWFUL!!
ENOUGH! WHY DO I HAVE TO SEE ALL THESE THINGS?!
FLASH
...!
SHWW
ANOTHER GATE...?!

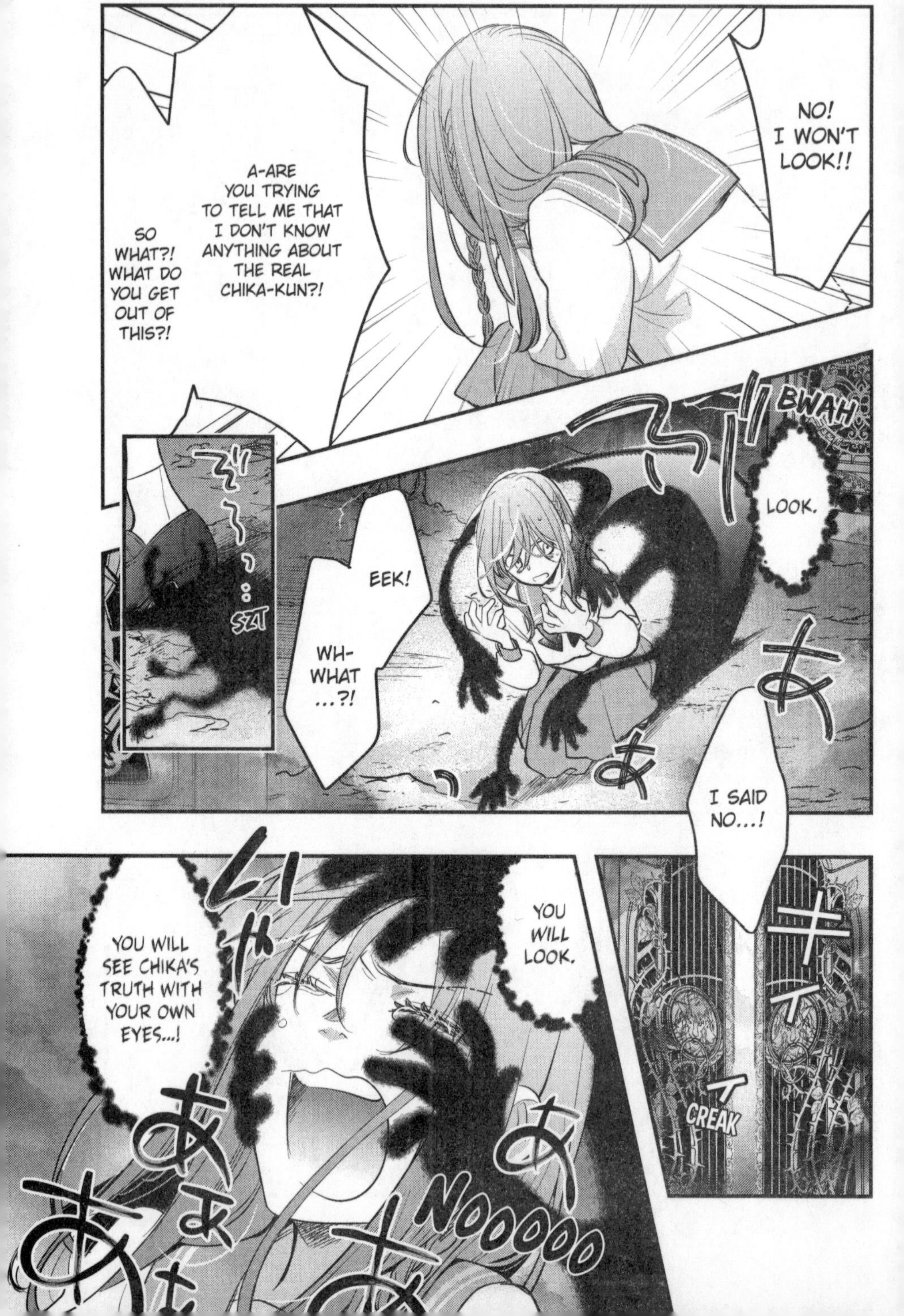
NO! I WON'T LOOK!!
A-ARE YOU TRYING TO TELL ME THAT I DON'T KNOW ANYTHING ABOUT THE REAL CHIKA-KUN?!
SO WHAT?! WHAT DO YOU GET OUT OF THIS?!
BWAH
LOOK.
EEK!
WH-WHAT...?!
SZT
I SAID NO...!
CREAK
YOU WILL LOOK.
YOU WILL SEE CHIKA'S TRUTH WITH YOUR OWN EYES...!
NOOOOO

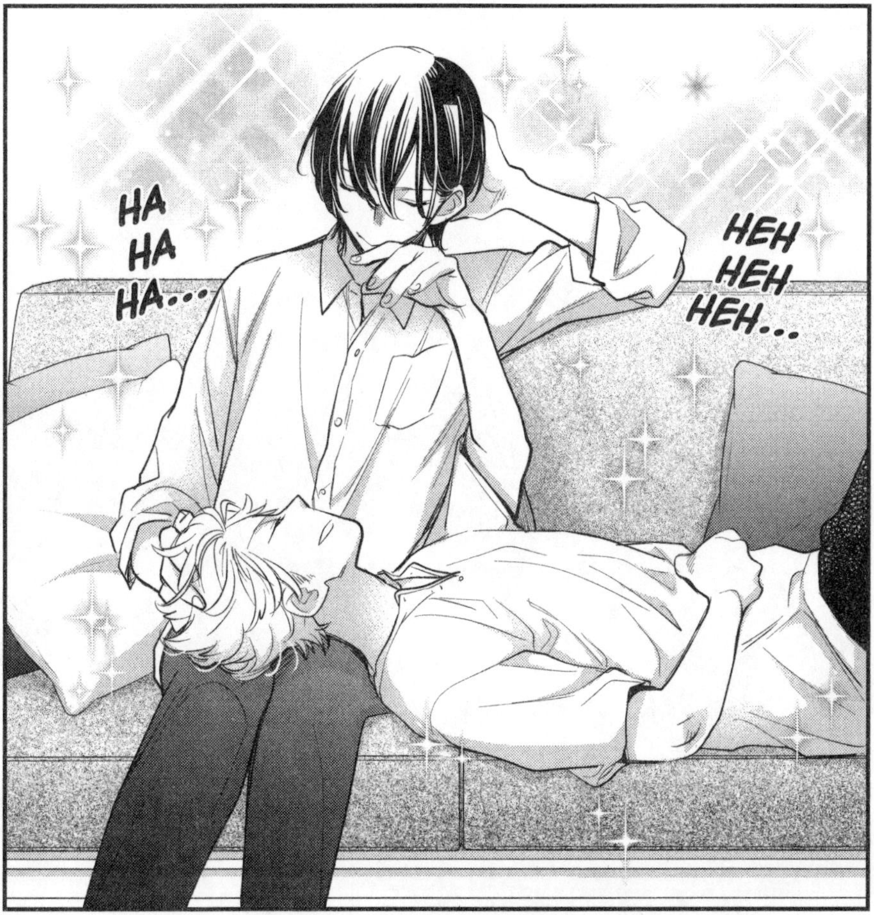
HEH HEH HEH...
HA HA HA...

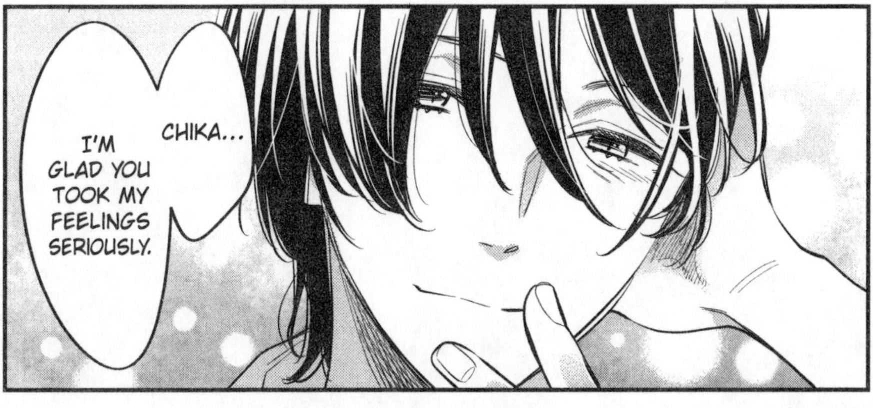
CHIKA... I'M GLAD YOU TOOK MY FEELINGS SERIOUSLY.

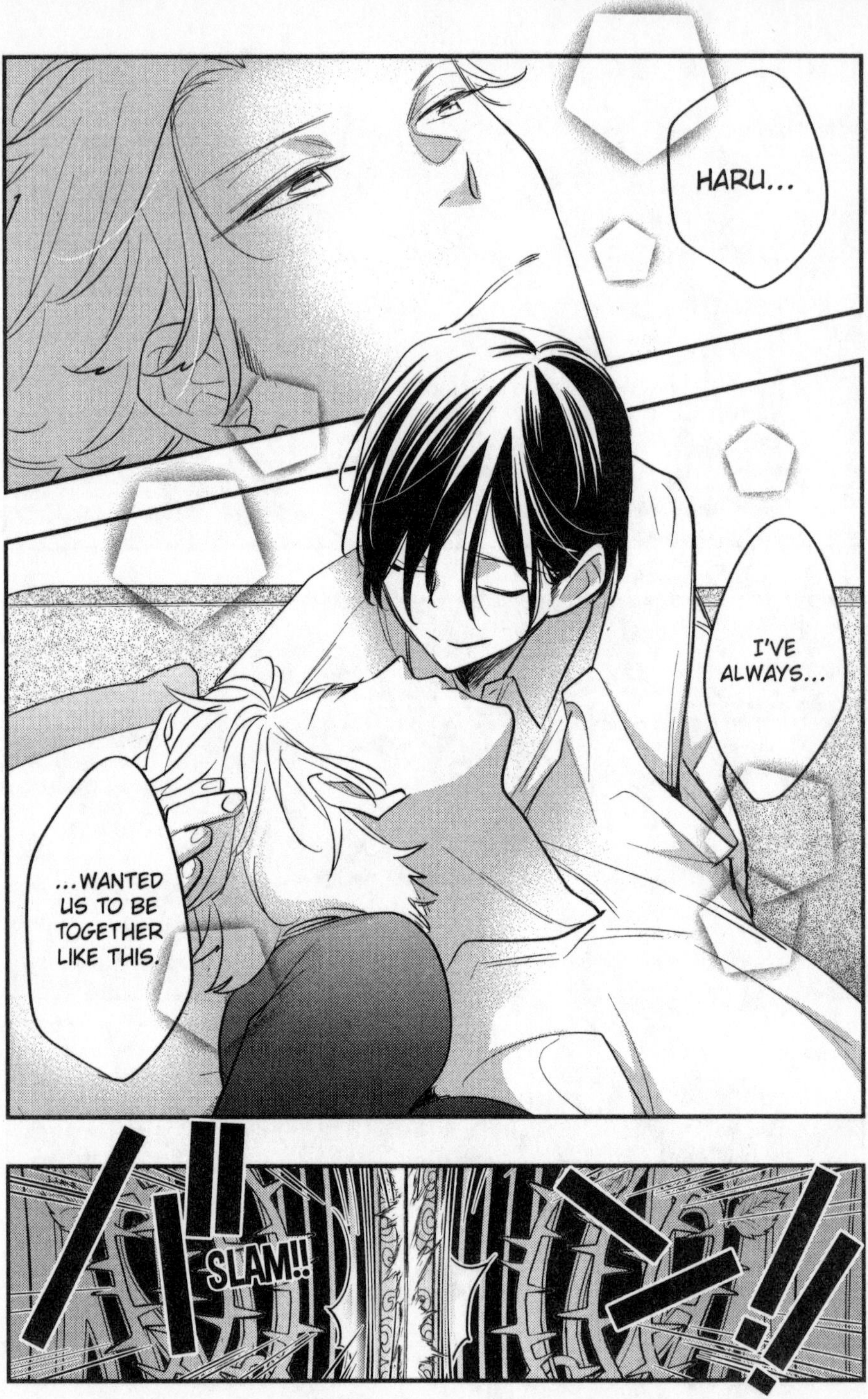
HARU...
I'VE ALWAYS...
...WANTED US TO BE TOGETHER LIKE THIS.
SLAM!!

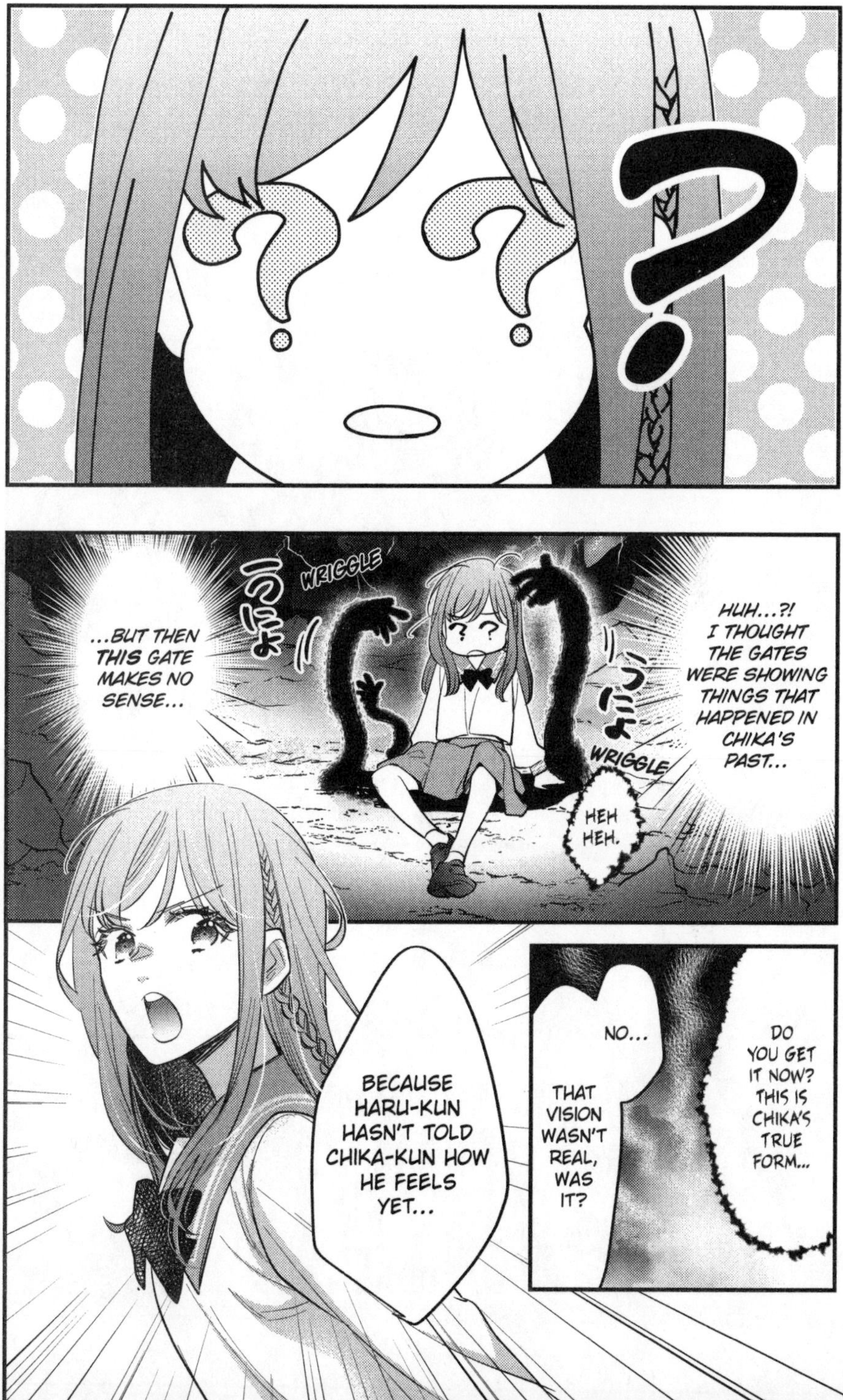
?
HUH...?! I THOUGHT THE GATES WERE SHOWING THINGS THAT HAPPENED IN CHIKA'S PAST...
うにょ
WRIGGLE
HEH HEH.
うにょ
WRIGGLE
...BUT THEN THIS GATE MAKES NO SENSE...
DO YOU GET IT NOW? THIS IS CHIKA'S TRUE FORM...
NO...
THAT VISION WASN'T REAL, WAS IT?
BECAUSE HARU-KUN HASN'T TOLD CHIKA-KUN HOW HE FEELS YET...

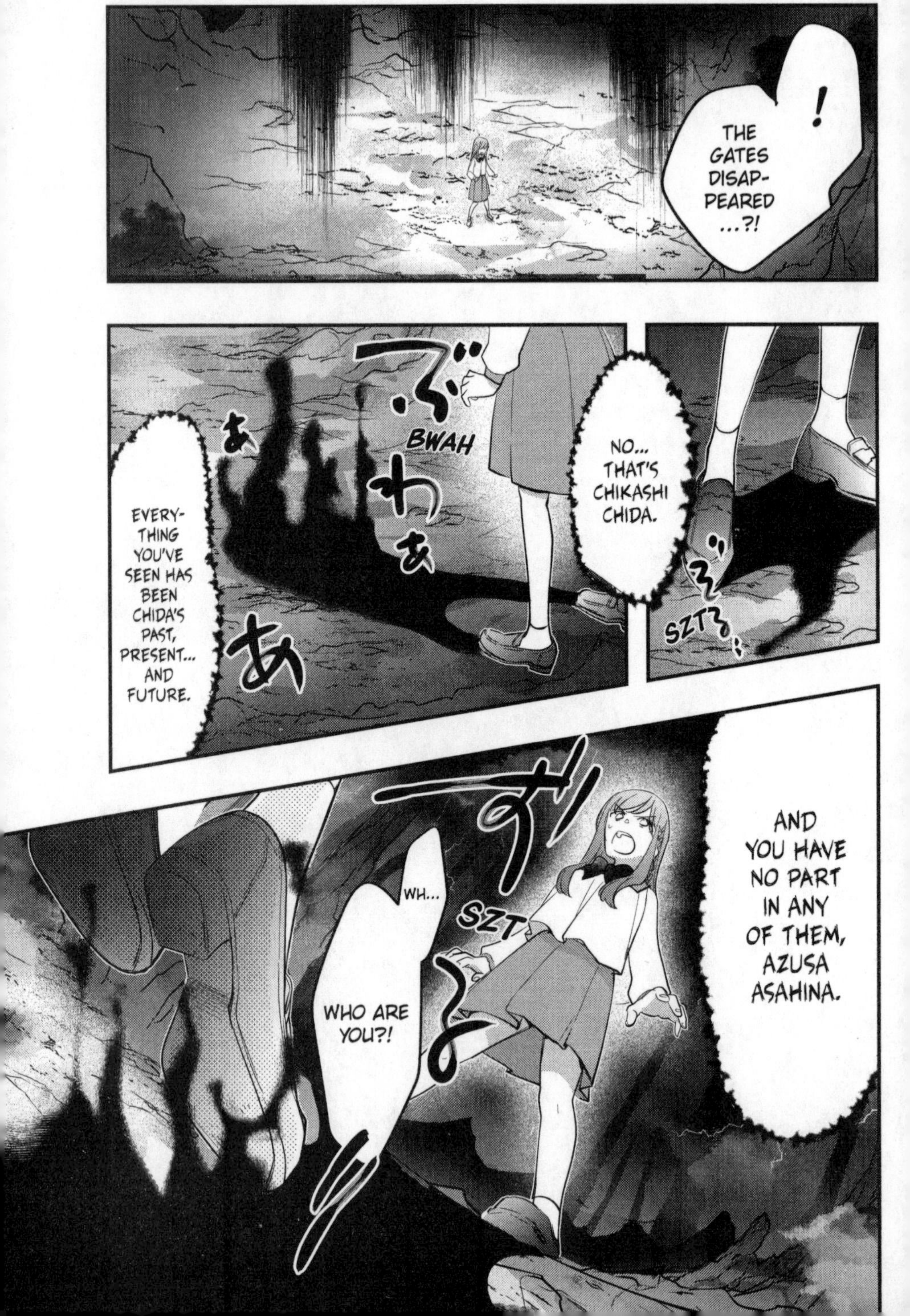
!
THE GATES DISAPPEARED...?!
SZT
NO... THAT'S CHIKASHI CHIDA.
BWAH
EVERYTHING YOU'VE SEEN HAS BEEN CHIDA'S PAST, PRESENT... AND FUTURE.
AND YOU HAVE NO PART IN ANY OF THEM, AZUSA ASAHINA.
WH...
SZT
WHO ARE YOU?!

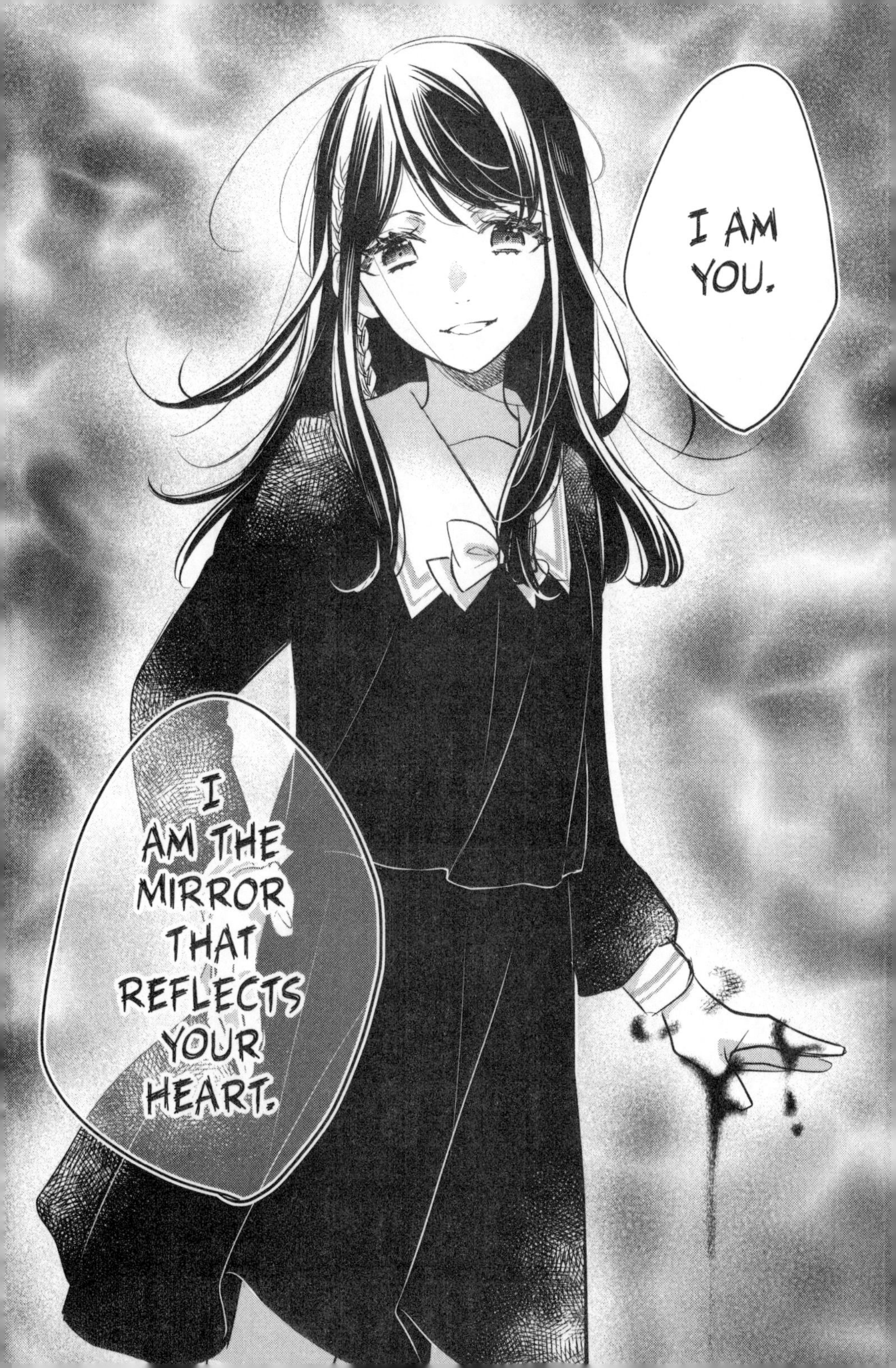
I AM YOU.
I AM THE MIRROR THAT REFLECTS YOUR HEART.

STAGE. 14 | STAR-CROSSED!!

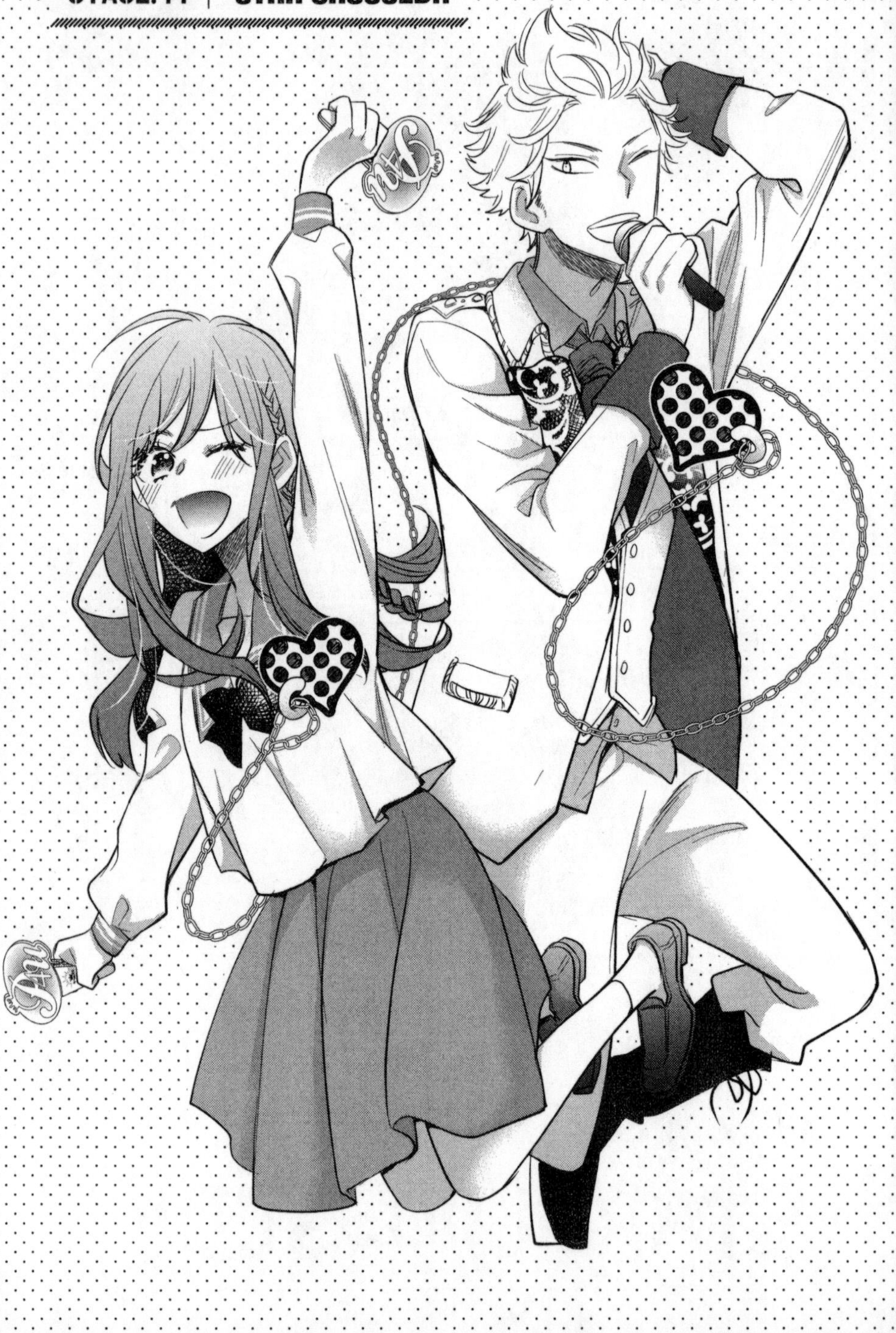

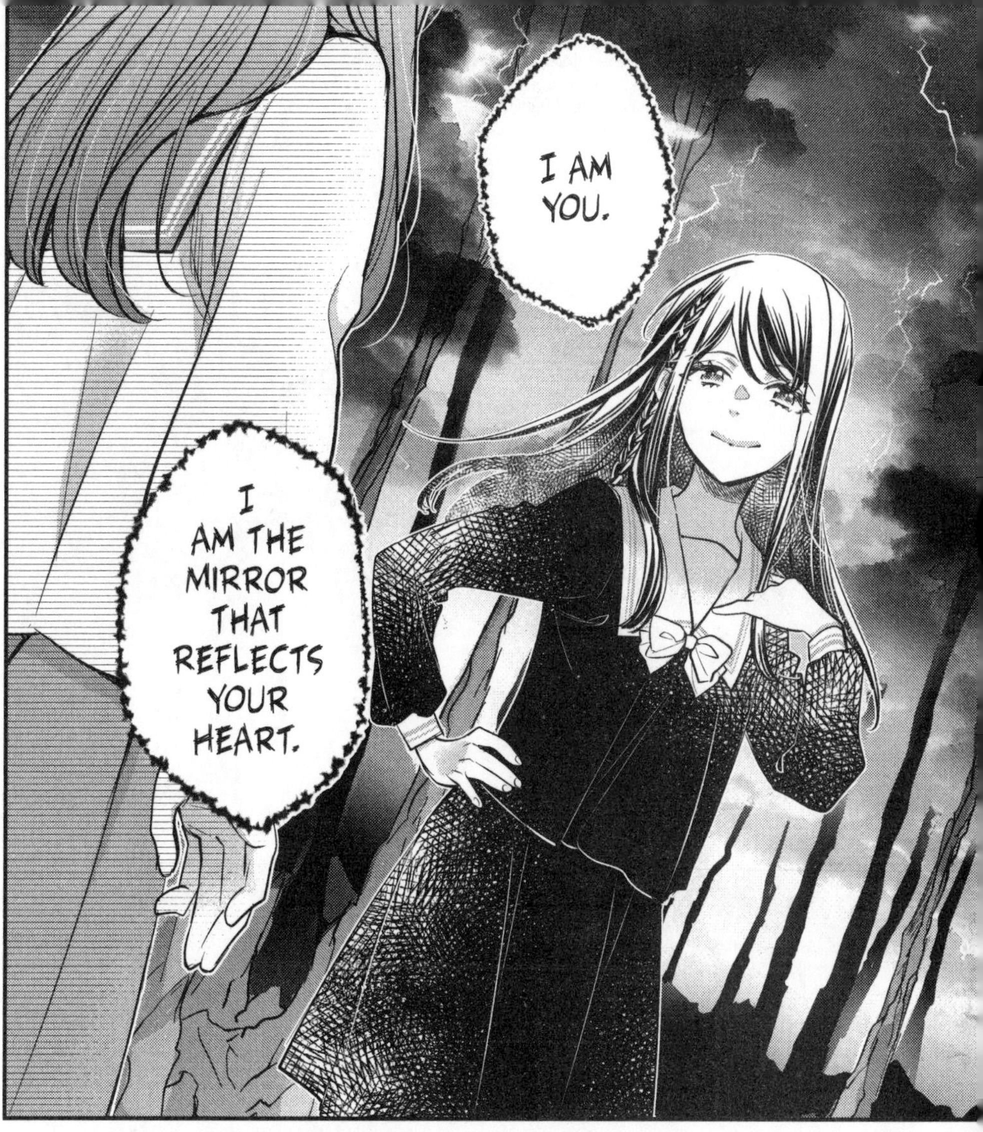
I AM YOU.
I AM THE MIRROR THAT REFLECTS YOUR HEART.

STAR⇄CROSSED!!

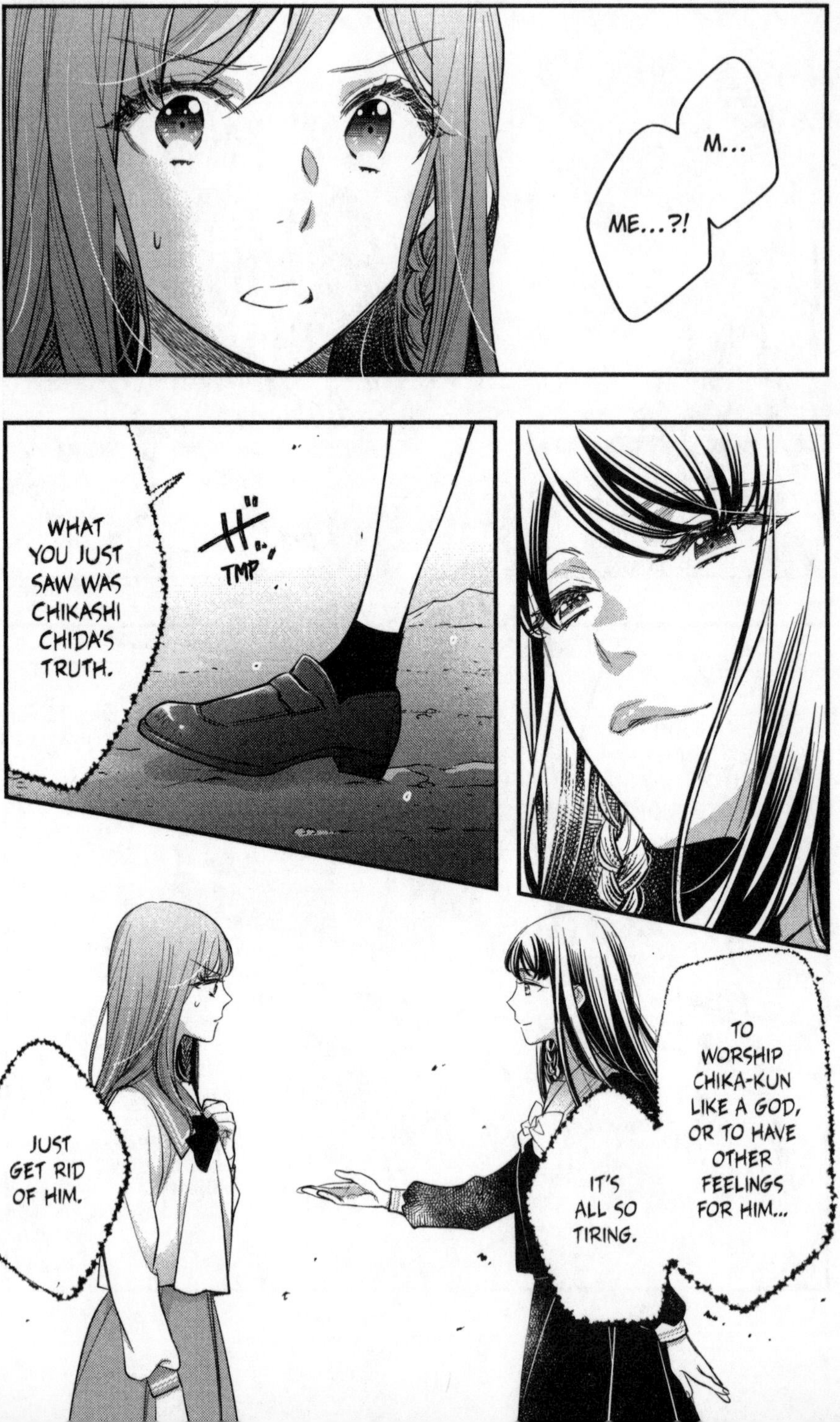
M... ME...?!
TMP
WHAT YOU JUST SAW WAS CHIKASHI CHIDA'S TRUTH.
TO WORSHIP CHIKA-KUN LIKE A GOD, OR TO HAVE OTHER FEELINGS FOR HIM...
IT'S ALL SO TIRING.
JUST GET RID OF HIM.

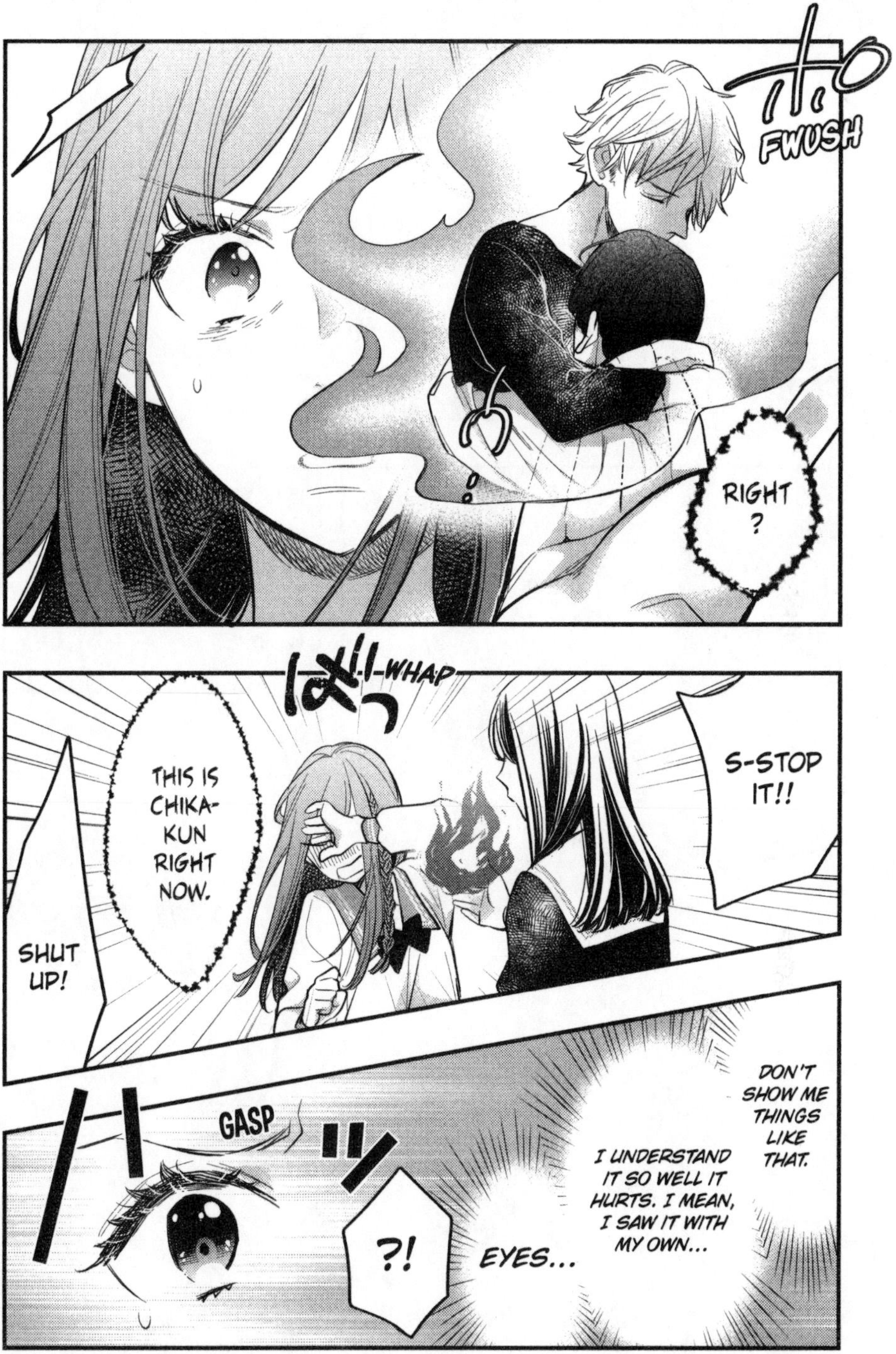
FWUSH
RIGHT ?
WHAP
S-STOP IT!!
THIS IS CHIKA-KUN RIGHT NOW.
SHUT UP!
DON'T SHOW ME THINGS LIKE THAT.
I UNDERSTAND IT SO WELL IT HURTS. I MEAN, I SAW IT WITH MY OWN...
EYES...
?!
GASP

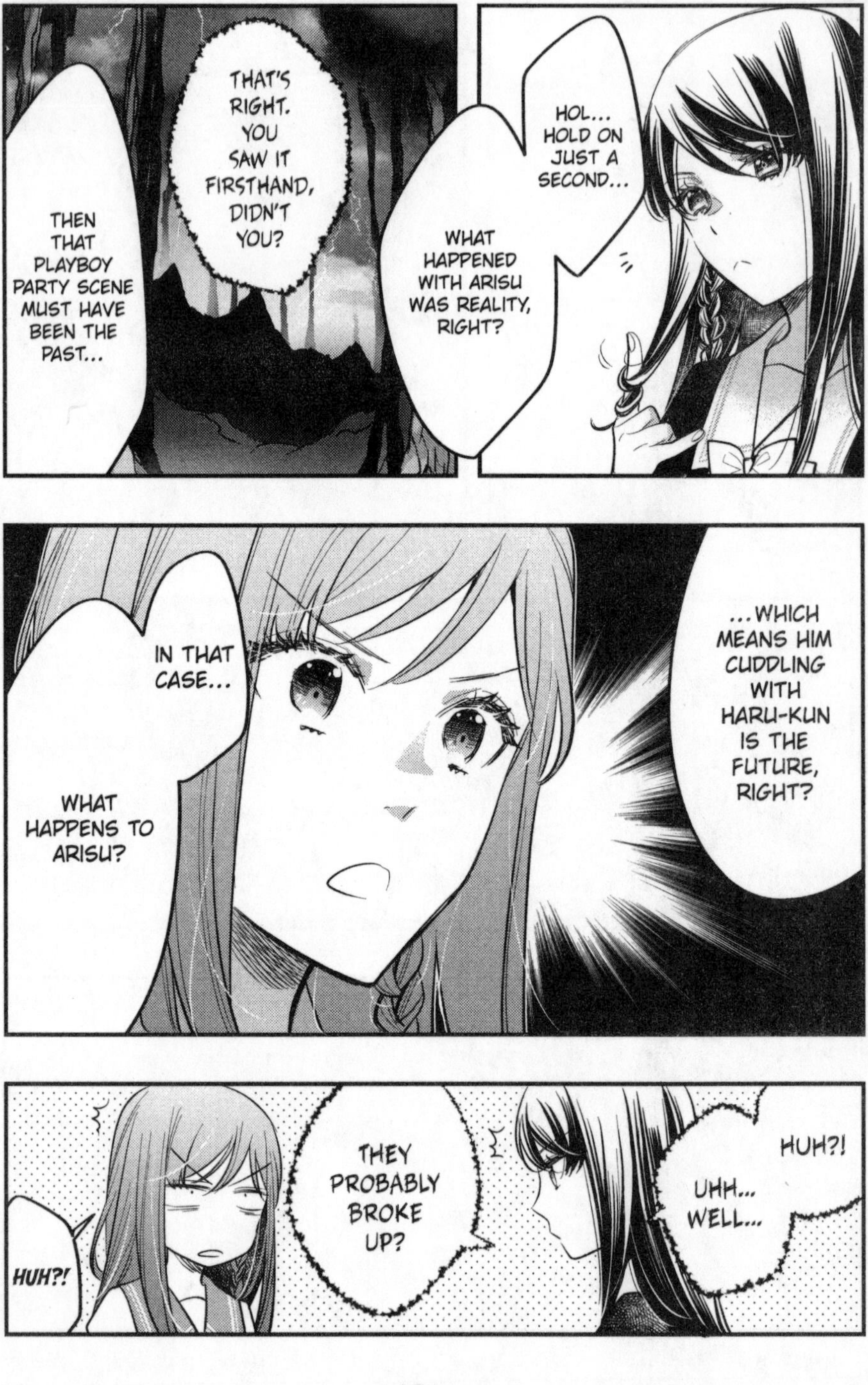
HOL... HOLD ON JUST A SECOND...
WHAT HAPPENED WITH ARISU WAS REALITY, RIGHT?
THAT'S RIGHT. YOU SAW IT FIRSTHAND, DIDN'T YOU?
THEN THAT PLAYBOY PARTY SCENE MUST HAVE BEEN THE PAST...
...WHICH MEANS HIM CUDDLING WITH HARU-KUN IS THE FUTURE, RIGHT?
IN THAT CASE...
WHAT HAPPENS TO ARISU?
HUH?!
UHH... WELL...
THEY PROBABLY BROKE UP?
HUH?!

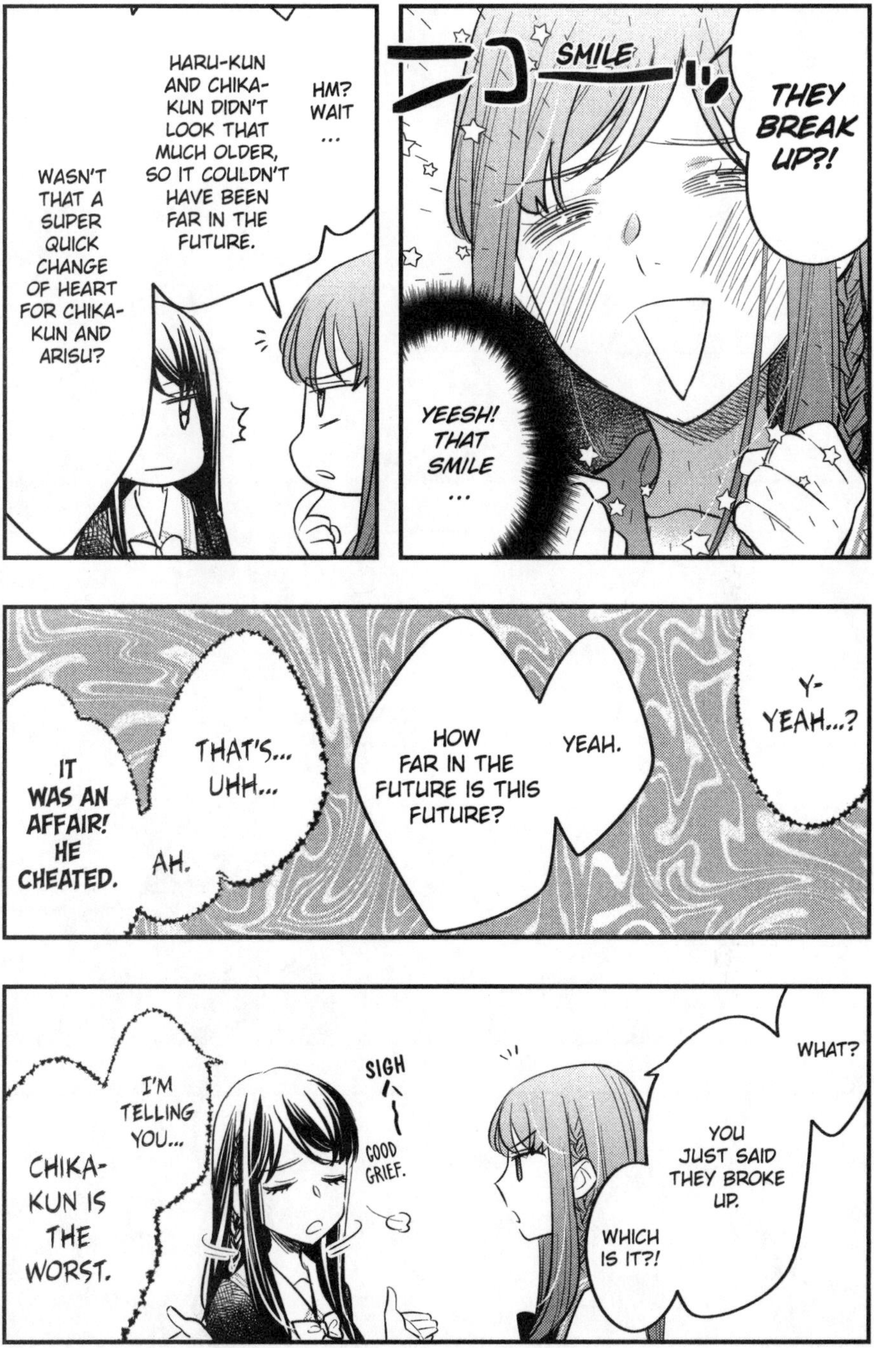
THEY BREAK UP?!
SMILE
YEESH! THAT SMILE...
HM? WAIT...
HARU-KUN AND CHIKA-KUN DIDN'T LOOK THAT MUCH OLDER, SO IT COULDN'T HAVE BEEN FAR IN THE FUTURE.
WASN'T THAT A SUPER QUICK CHANGE OF HEART FOR CHIKA-KUN AND ARISU?
Y-YEAH...?
YEAH.
HOW FAR IN THE FUTURE IS THIS FUTURE?
THAT'S... UHH...
AH.
IT WAS AN AFFAIR! HE CHEATED.
WHAT?
YOU JUST SAID THEY BROKE UP.
WHICH IS IT?!
SIGH
GOOD GRIEF.
I'M TELLING YOU...
CHIKA-KUN IS THE WORST.

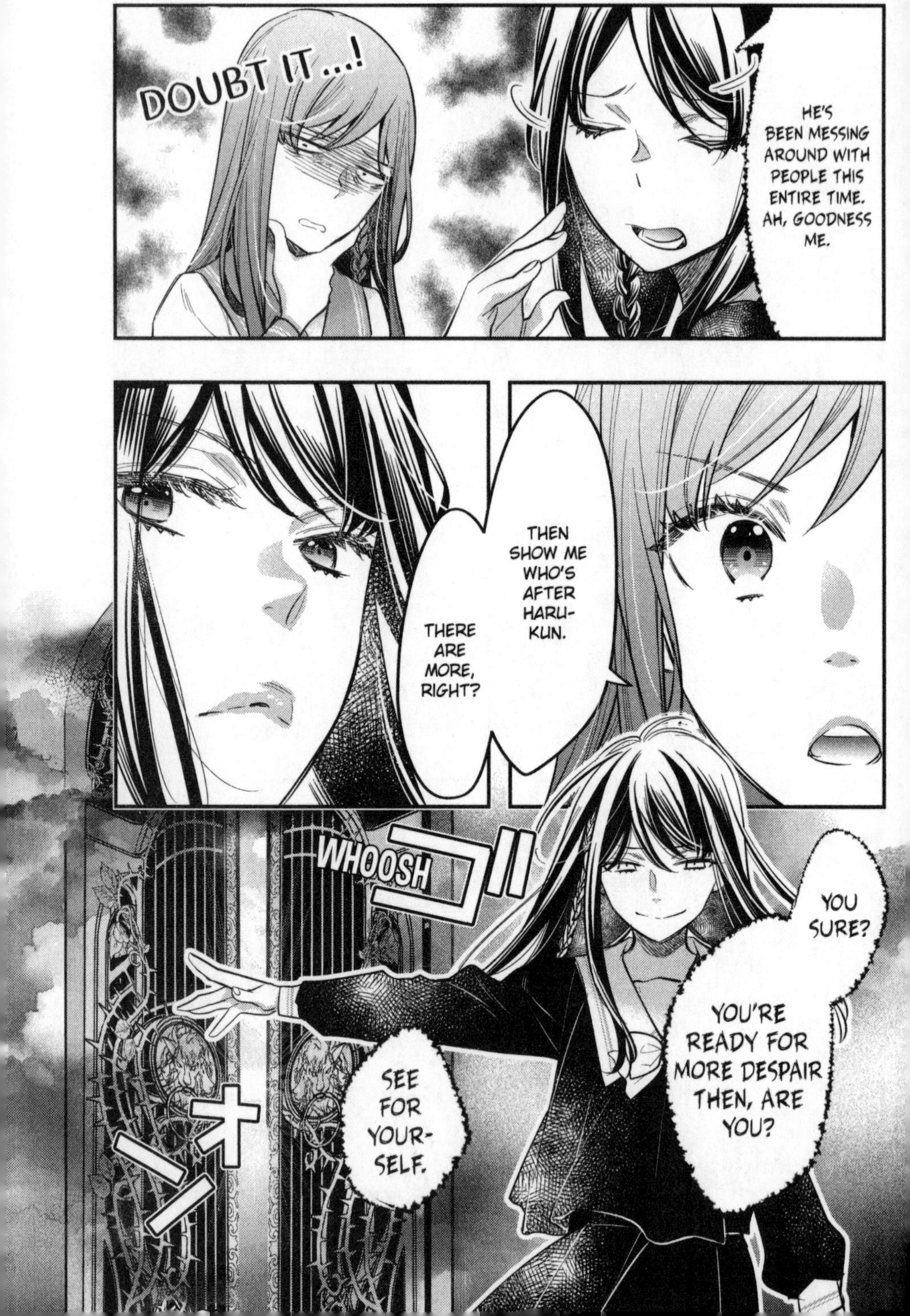
HE'S BEEN MESSING AROUND WITH PEOPLE THIS ENTIRE TIME. AH, GOODNESS ME.
DOUBT IT...!
THEN SHOW ME WHO'S AFTER HARU-KUN.
THERE ARE MORE, RIGHT?
YOU SURE?
YOU'RE READY FOR MORE DESPAIR THEN, ARE YOU?
WHOOSH
SEE FOR YOUR-SELF.

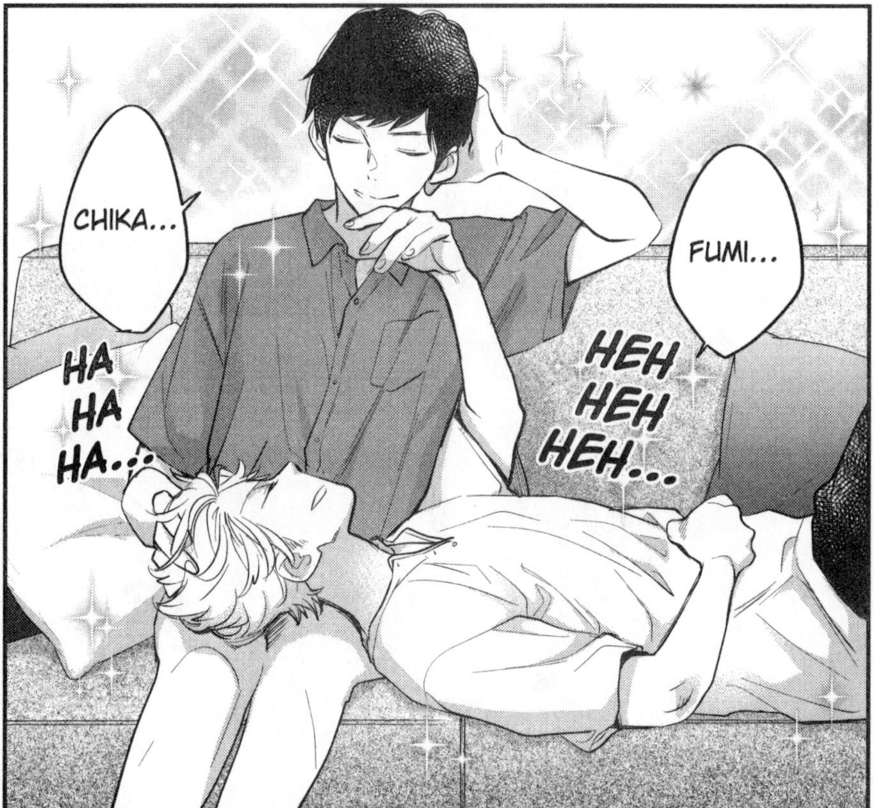
FUMI...
HEH HEH HEH...
CHIKA...
HA HA HA...!
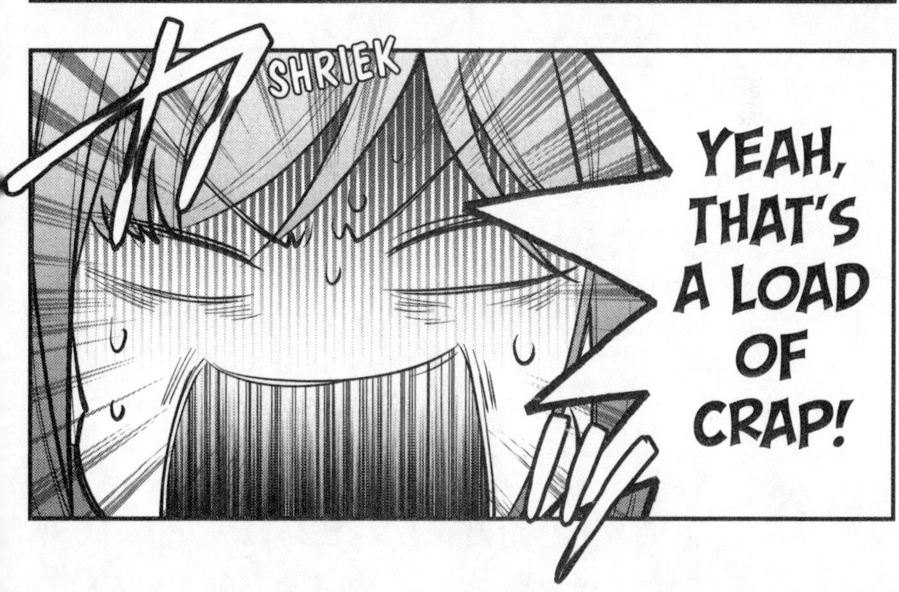
YEAH, THAT'S A LOAD OF CRAP!
SHRIEK

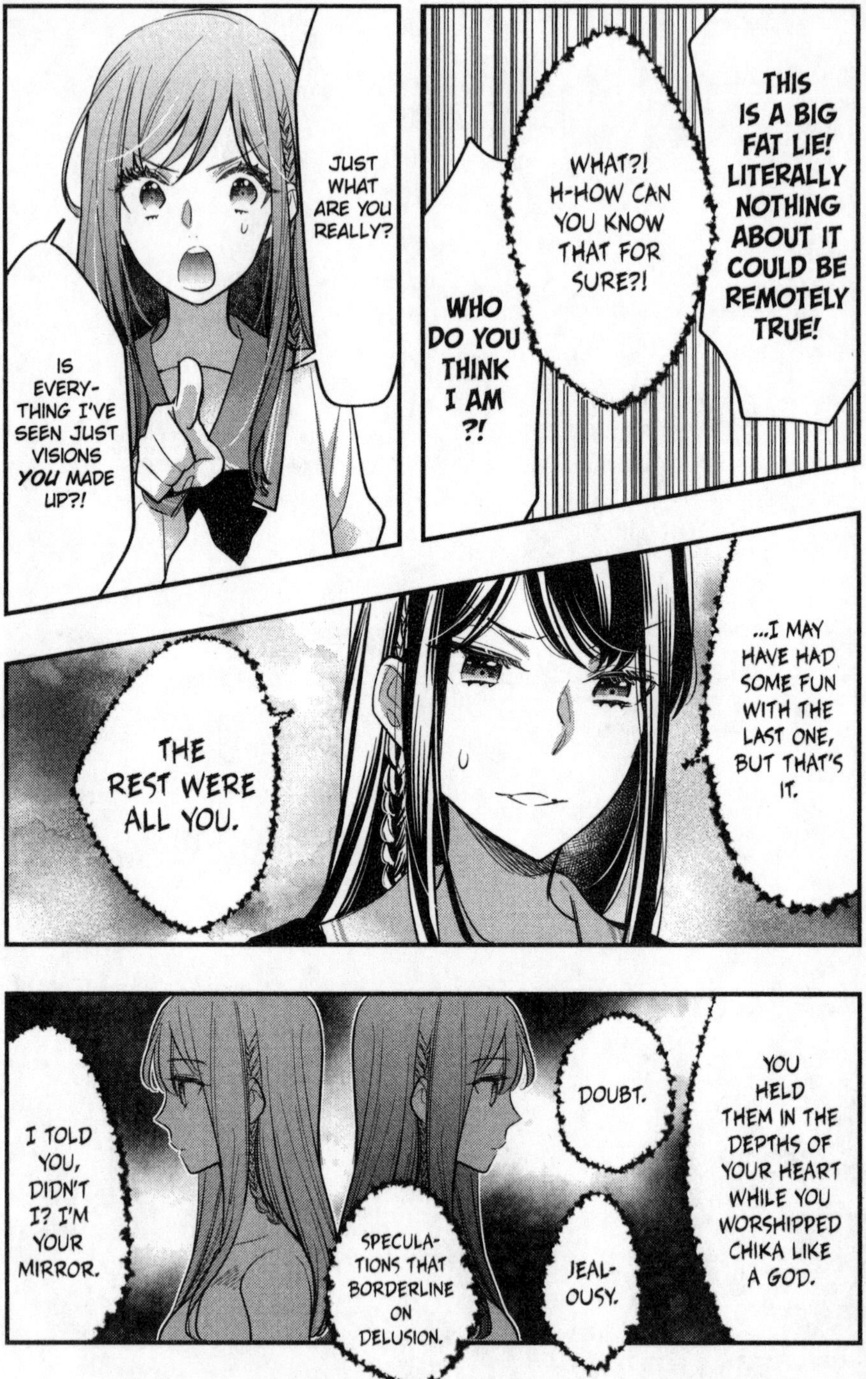
THIS IS A BIG FAT LIE! LITERALLY NOTHING ABOUT IT COULD BE REMOTELY TRUE!
WHAT?! H-HOW CAN YOU KNOW THAT FOR SURE?!
WHO DO YOU THINK I AM ?!
JUST WHAT ARE YOU REALLY?
IS EVERYTHING I'VE SEEN JUST VISIONS *YOU* MADE UP?!
...I MAY HAVE HAD SOME FUN WITH THE LAST ONE, BUT THAT'S IT.
THE REST WERE ALL YOU.
YOU HELD THEM IN THE DEPTHS OF YOUR HEART WHILE YOU WORSHIPPED CHIKA LIKE A GOD.
DOUBT.
JEALOUSY.
SPECULATIONS THAT BORDERLINE ON DELUSION.
I TOLD YOU, DIDN'T I? I'M YOUR MIRROR.

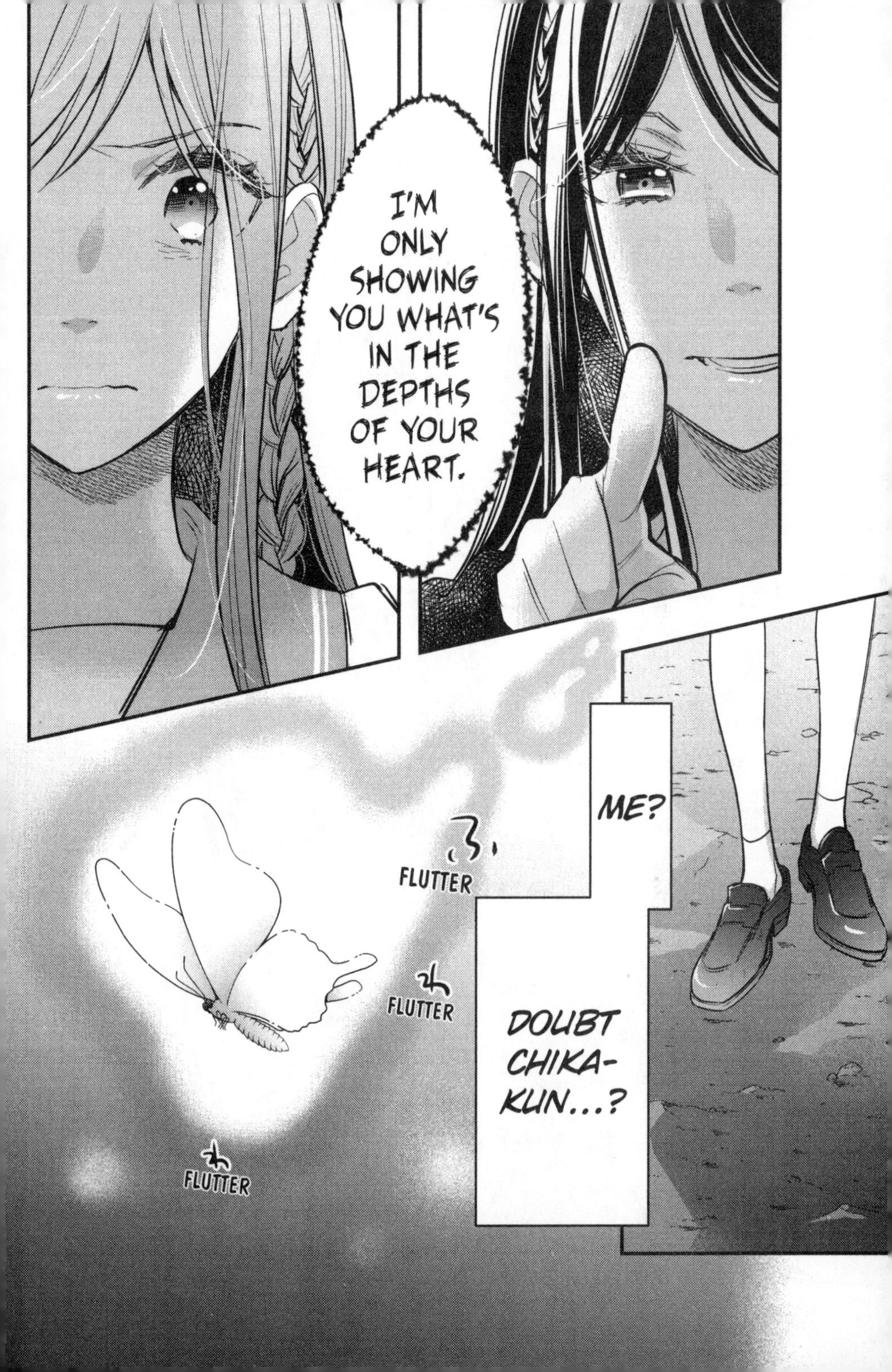
I'M ONLY SHOWING YOU WHAT'S IN THE DEPTHS OF YOUR HEART.
ME?
DOUBT CHIKA-KUN...?
ふ FLUTTER
ふわ FLUTTER
ふわ FLUTTER

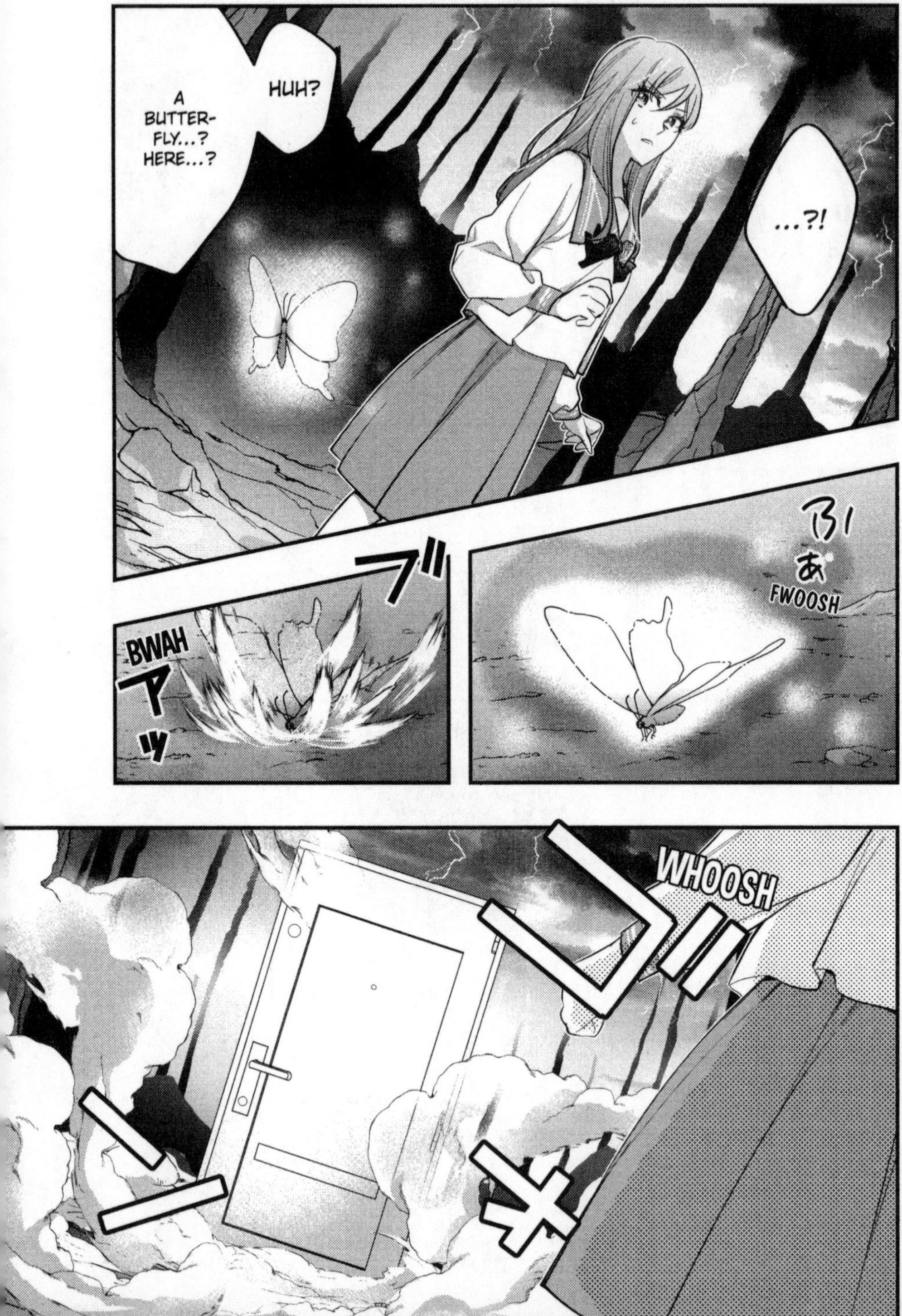
...?!
HUH?
A BUTTER-FLY...? HERE...?
FWOOSH
BWAH
WHOOSH

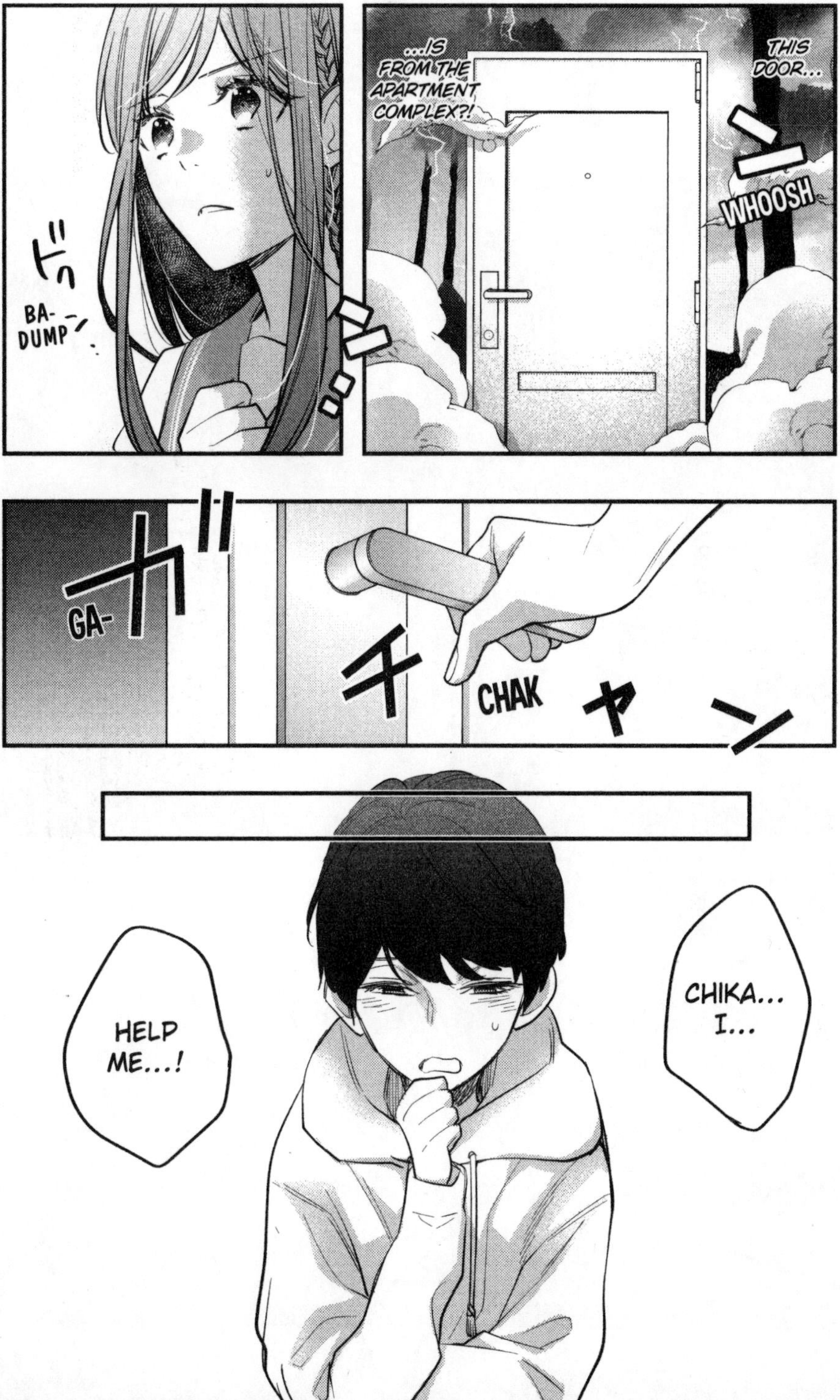
THIS DOOR...
...IS FROM THE APARTMENT COMPLEX?!
WHOOSH
BA-DUMP
GA-
CHAK
CHIKA... I...
HELP ME...!

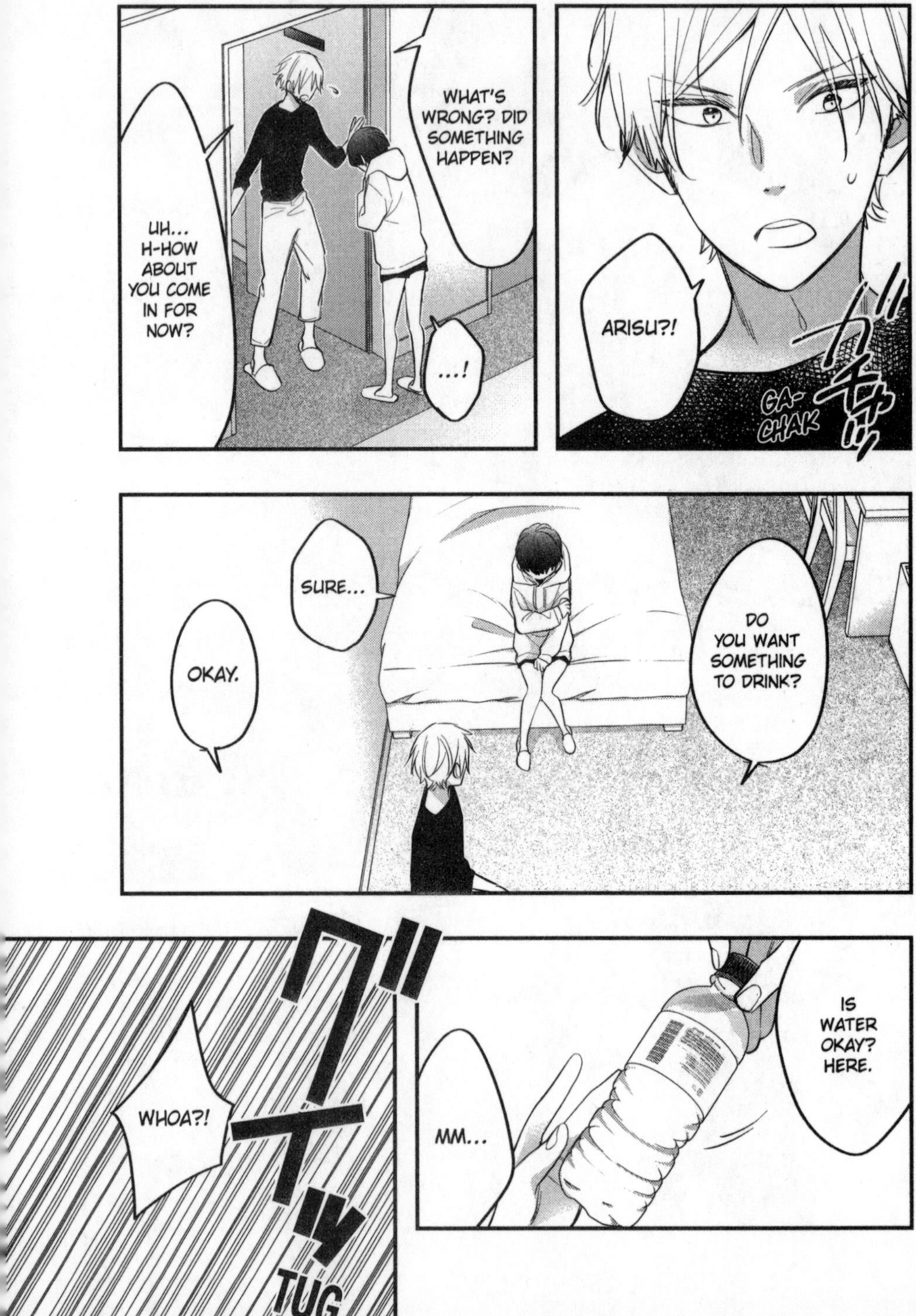
ARISU?!
GA-CHAK
WHAT'S WRONG? DID SOMETHING HAPPEN?
...!
UH... H-HOW ABOUT YOU COME IN FOR NOW?
DO YOU WANT SOMETHING TO DRINK?
SURE...
OKAY.
IS WATER OKAY? HERE.
MM...
WHOA?!
TUG

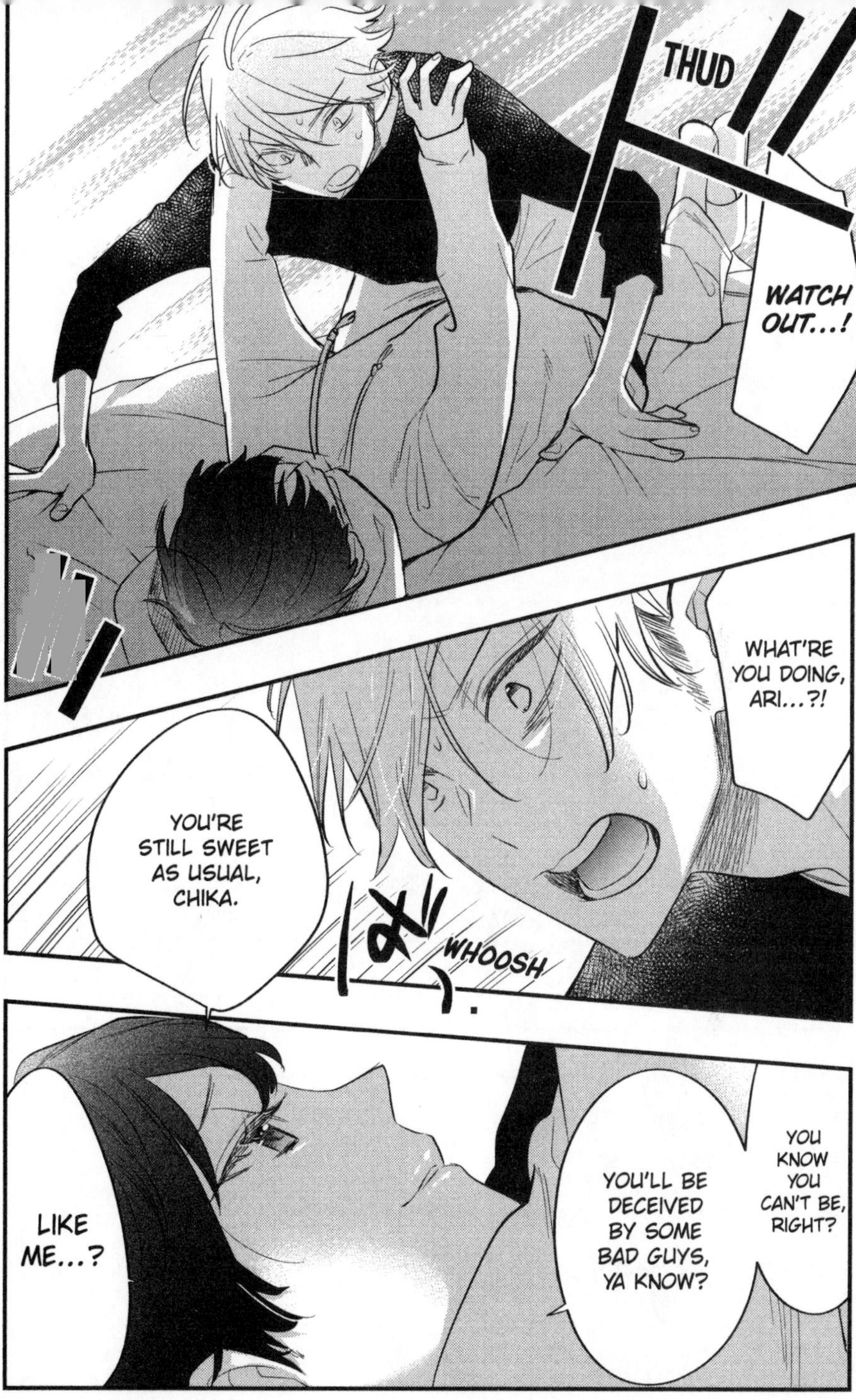
THUD
WATCH OUT...!
WHAT'RE YOU DOING, ARI...?!
WHOOSH
YOU'RE STILL SWEET AS USUAL, CHIKA.
YOU KNOW YOU CAN'T BE, RIGHT?
YOU'LL BE DECEIVED BY SOME BAD GUYS, YA KNOW?
LIKE ME...?

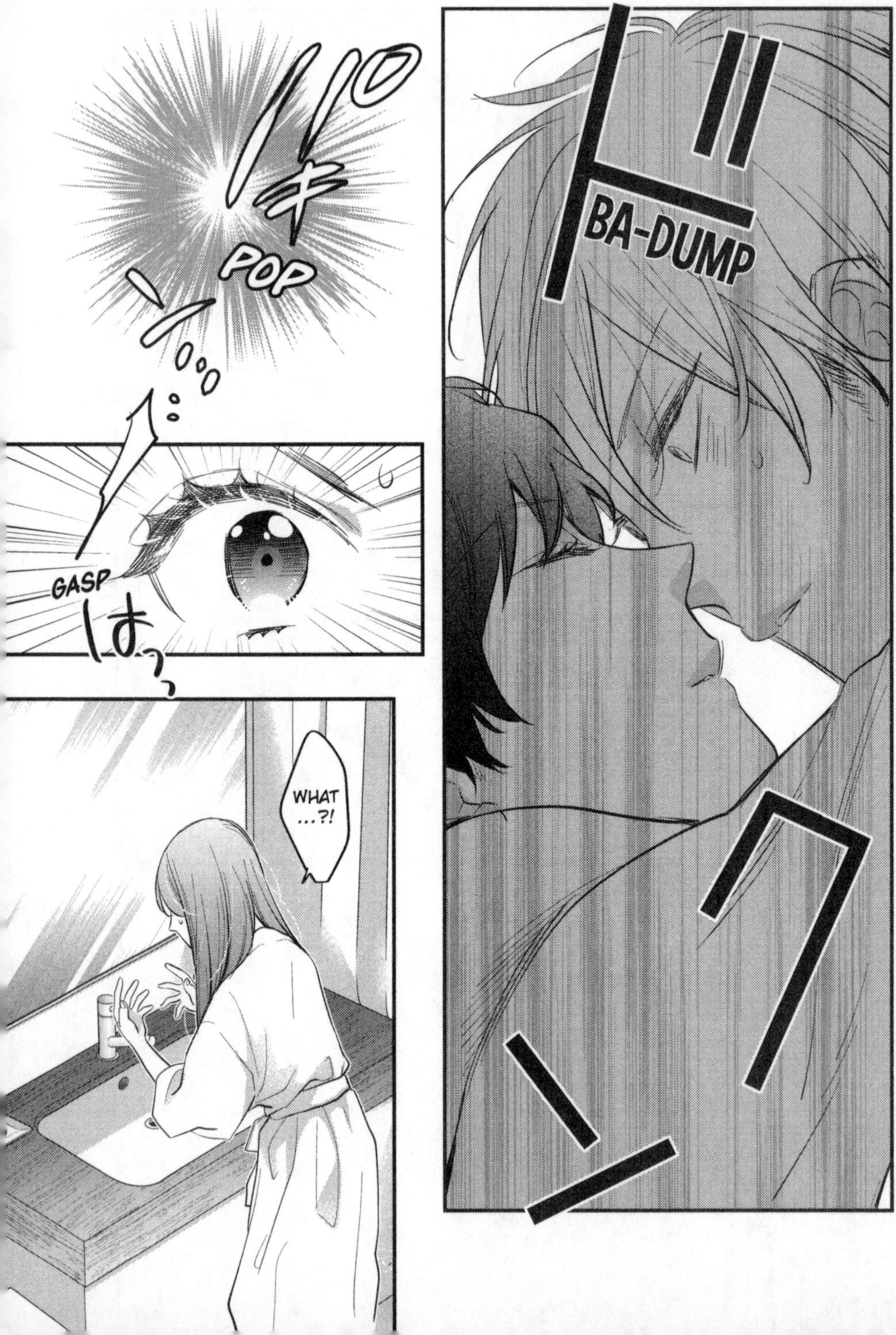
ドクン
BA-DUMP
パキーン
POP
はっ
GASP
WHAT ...?!

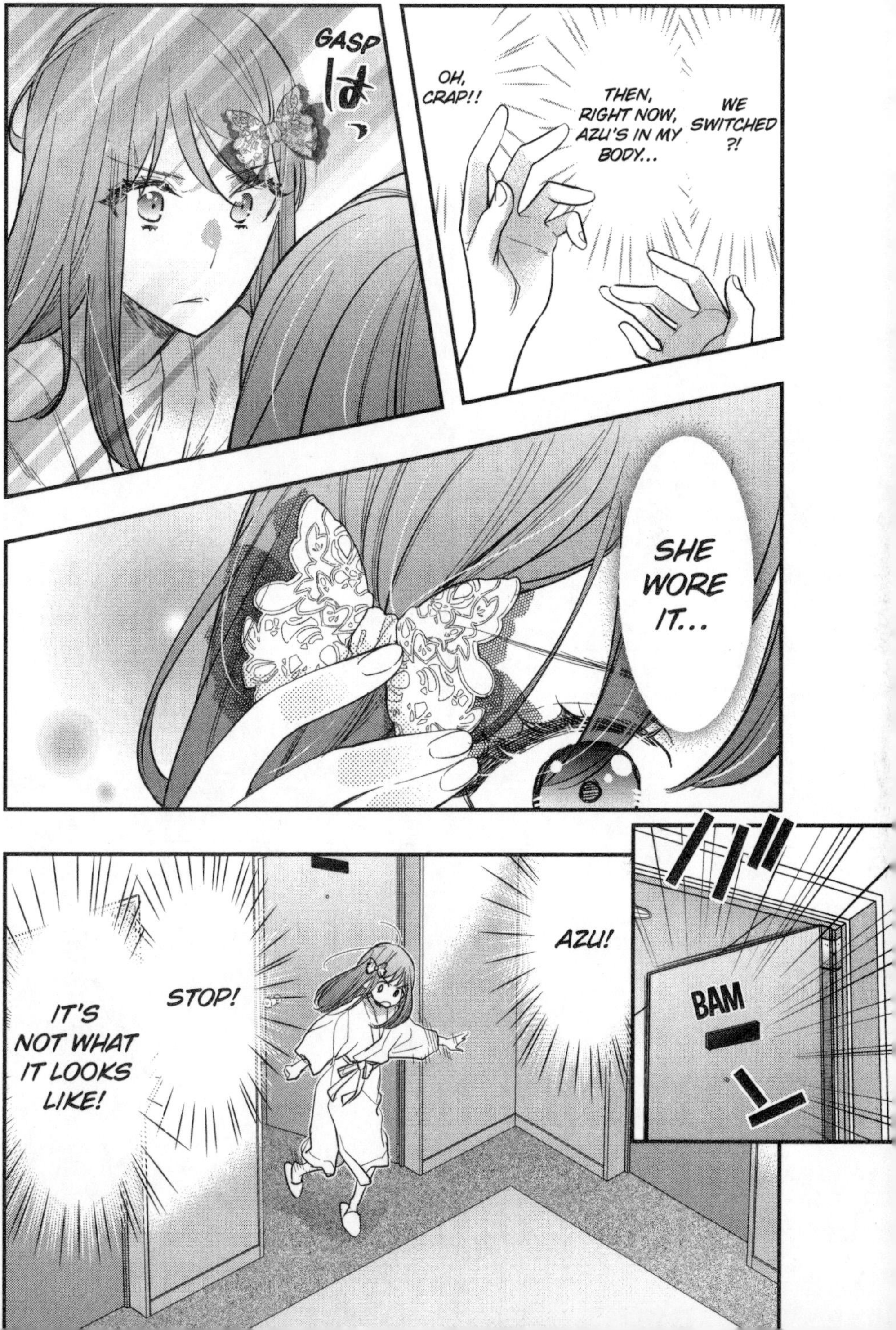
WE SWITCHED ?!
THEN, RIGHT NOW, AZU'S IN MY BODY...
OH, CRAP!!
GASP
はっ
SHE WORE IT...
BAM
AZU!
STOP!
IT'S NOT WHAT IT LOOKS LIKE!

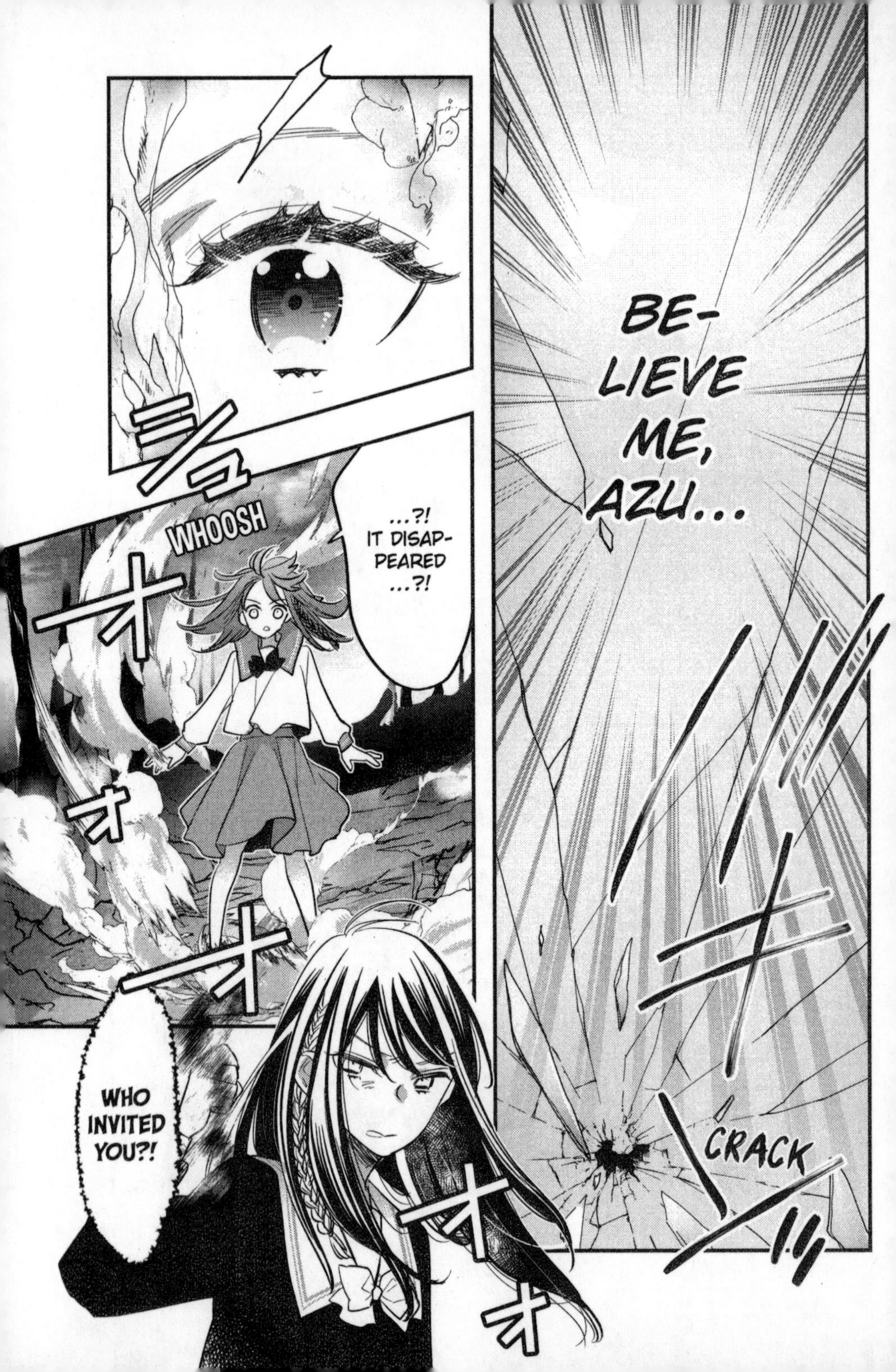
BE-
LIEVE
ME,
AZU...
CRACK
WHOOSH
...?! IT DISAP-PEARED ...?!
WHO INVITED YOU?!

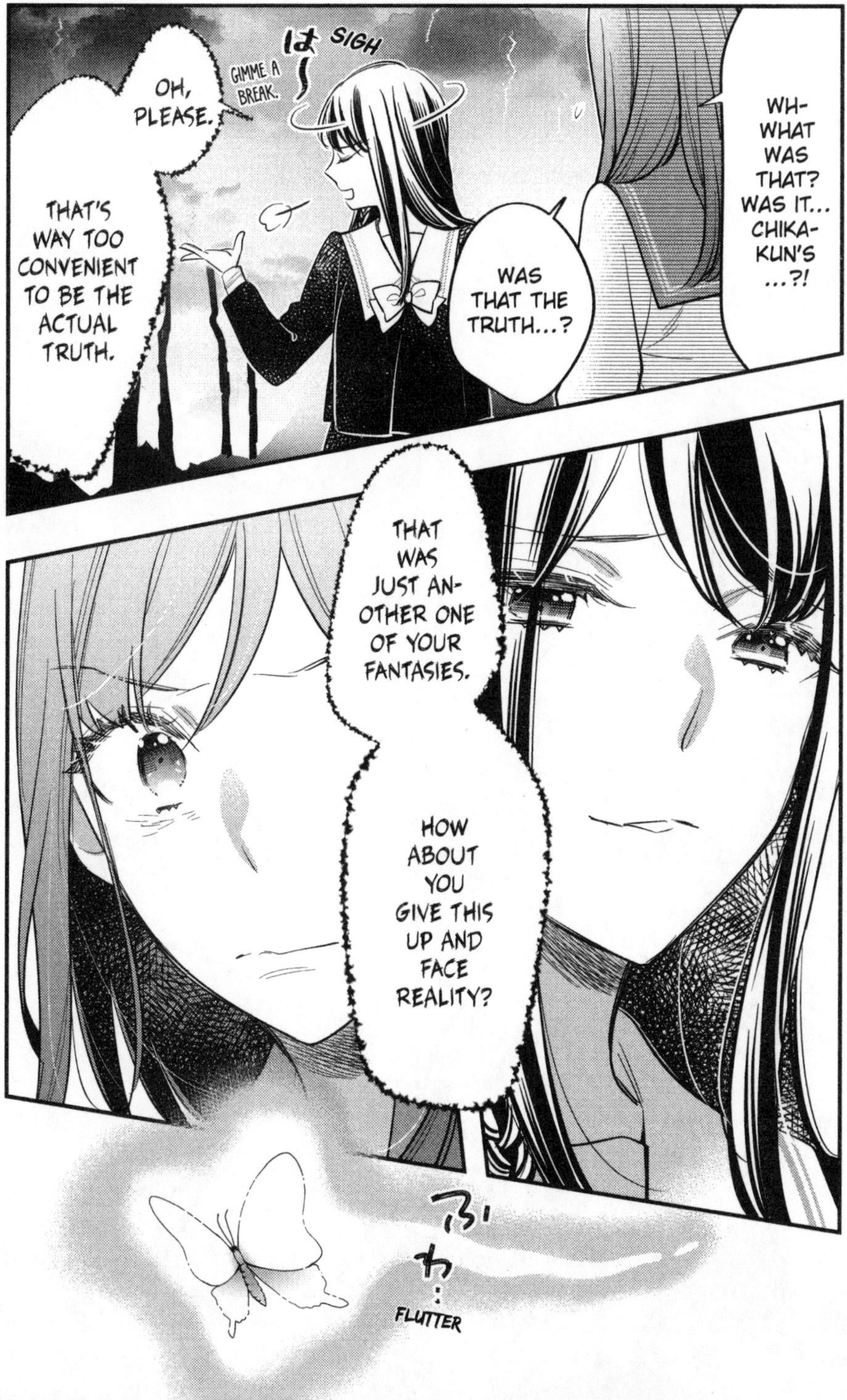
WH-WHAT WAS THAT? WAS IT... CHIKA-KUN'S ...?!
WAS THAT THE TRUTH...?
は～
SIGH
GIMME A BREAK.
OH, PLEASE.
THAT'S WAY TOO CONVENIENT TO BE THE ACTUAL TRUTH.
THAT WAS JUST AN-OTHER ONE OF YOUR FANTASIES.
HOW ABOUT YOU GIVE THIS UP AND FACE REALITY?
ふわ
FLUTTER

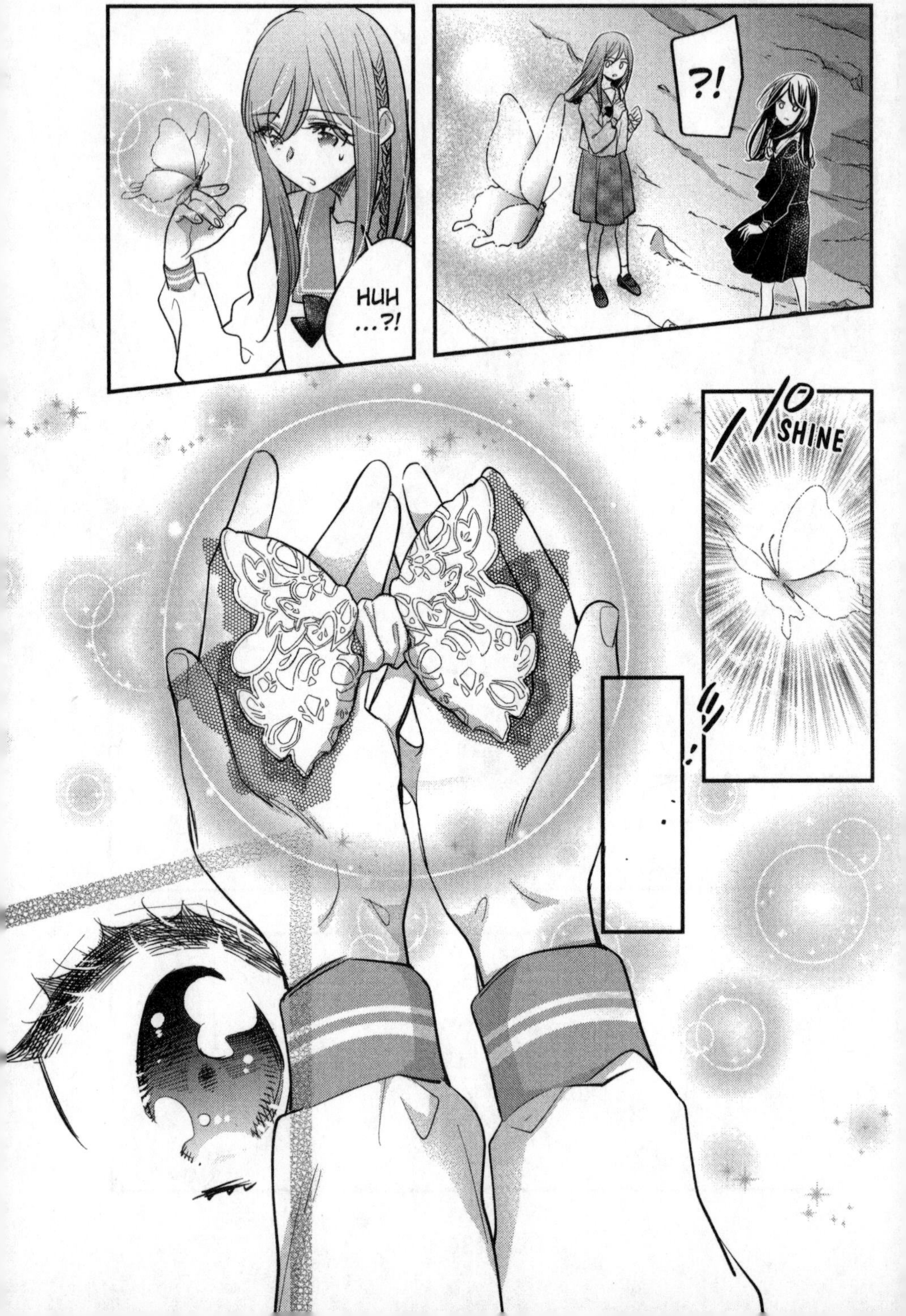
?!
HUH ...?!
SHINE
...

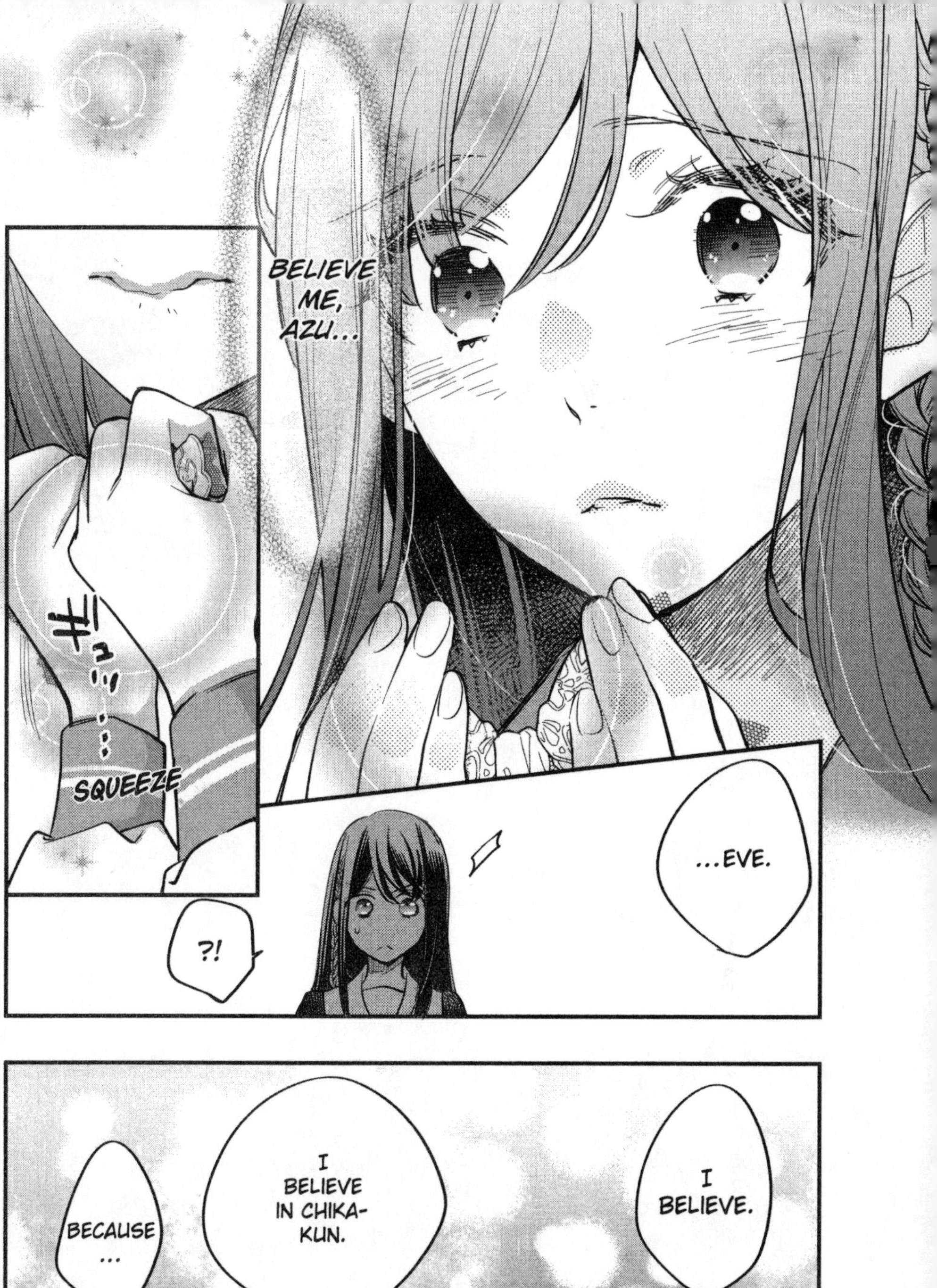
BELIEVE ME, AZU...
SQUEEZE
...EVE.
?!
I BELIEVE.
I BELIEVE IN CHIKA-KUN.
BECAUSE...

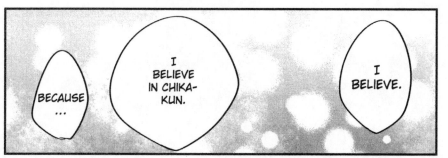

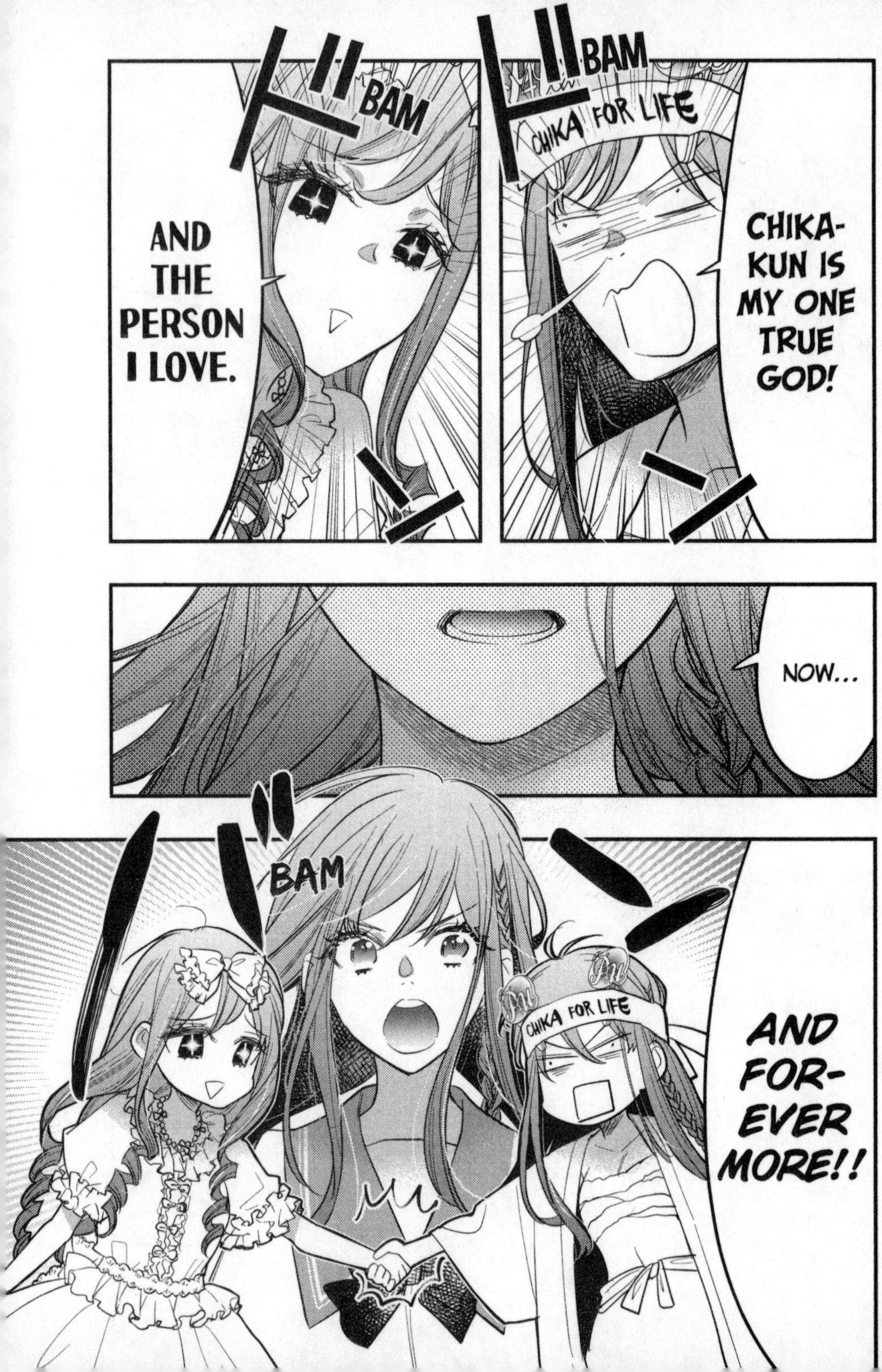
BAM
CHIKA FOR LIFE
CHIKA-KUN IS MY ONE TRUE GOD!
BAM
AND THE PERSON I LOVE.
NOW...
AND FOR-EVER MORE!!
CHIKA FOR LIFE
BAM

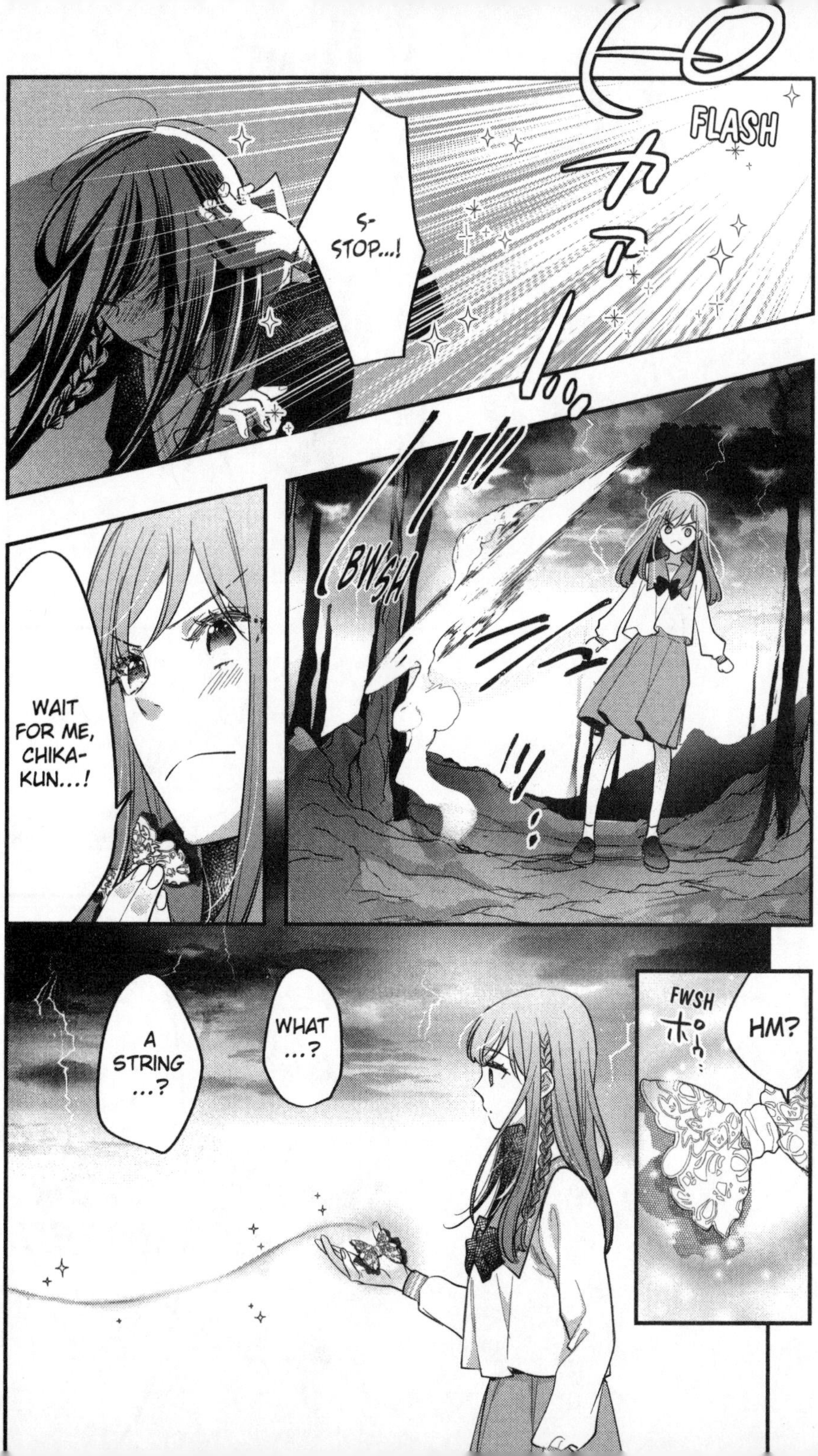

FLASH
S-STOP...!
BWSH
WAIT FOR ME, CHIKA-KUN...!
FWSH
HM?
WHAT...?
A STRING...?

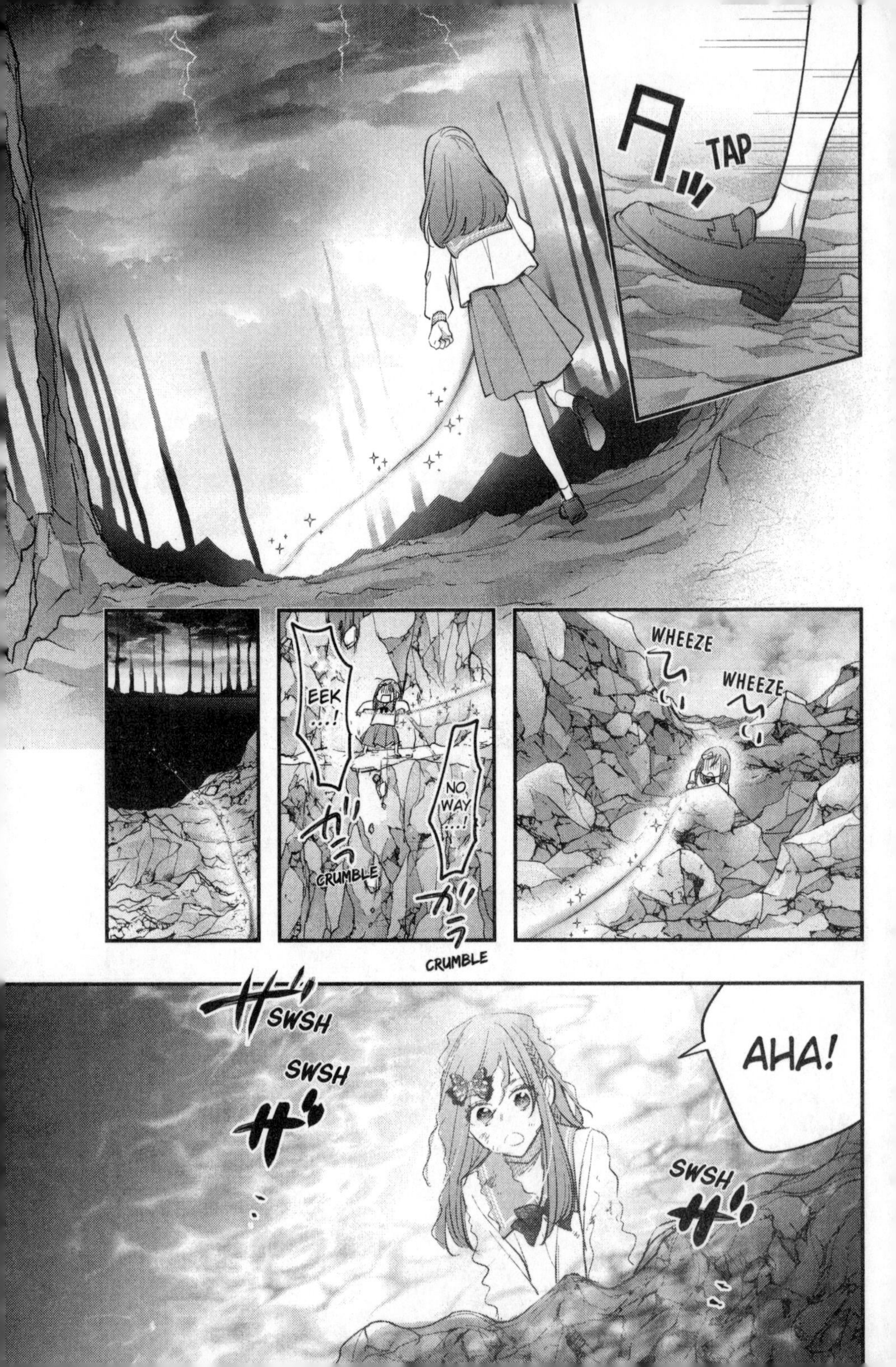
TAP
WHEEZE
WHEEZE
EEK...!
NO WAY...!
CRUMBLE
CRUMBLE
AHA!
SWSH
SWSH
SWSH

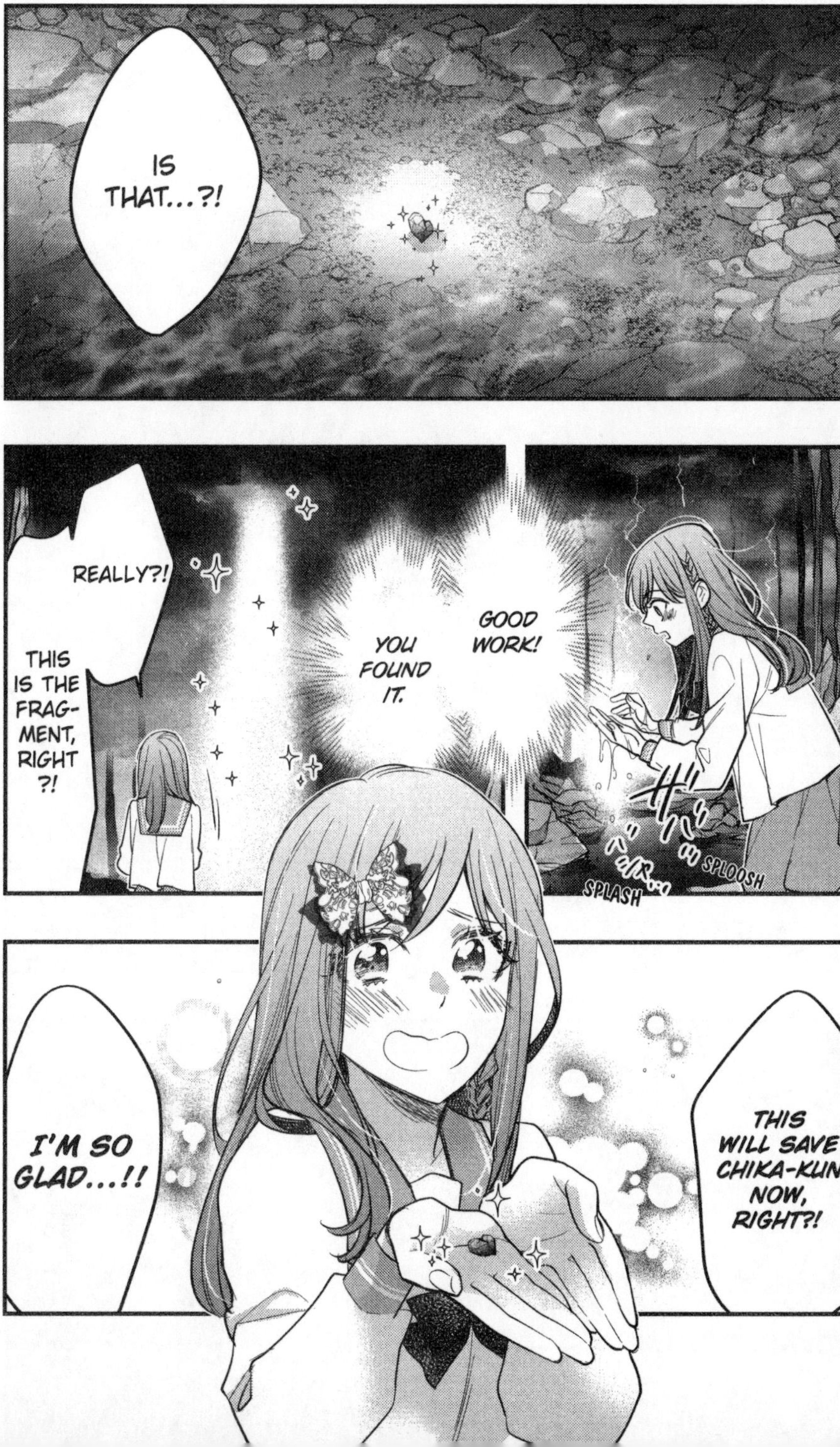
IS THAT...?!
SPLOOSH
SPLASH
GOOD WORK!
YOU FOUND IT.
REALLY?!
THIS IS THE FRAGMENT, RIGHT?!
THIS WILL SAVE CHIKA-KUN NOW, RIGHT?!
I'M SO GLAD...!!

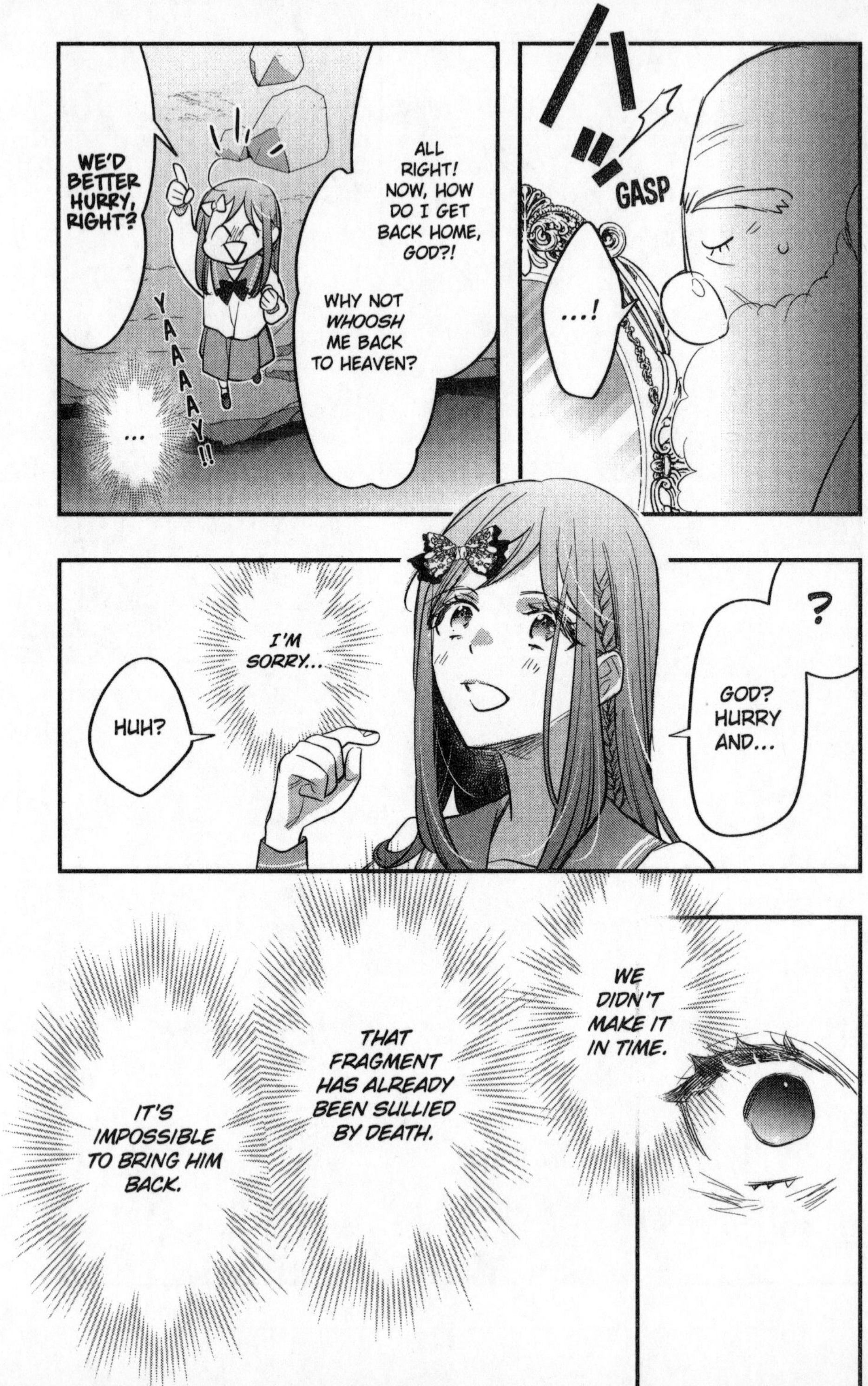
GASP
...!
ALL RIGHT! NOW, HOW DO I GET BACK HOME, GOD?!
WHY NOT *WHOOSH* ME BACK TO HEAVEN?
WE'D BETTER HURRY, RIGHT?
YAAAAAAY!!
...
?
GOD? HURRY AND...
I'M SORRY...
HUH?
WE DIDN'T MAKE IT IN TIME.
THAT FRAGMENT HAS ALREADY BEEN SULLIED BY DEATH.
IT'S IMPOSSIBLE TO BRING HIM BACK.

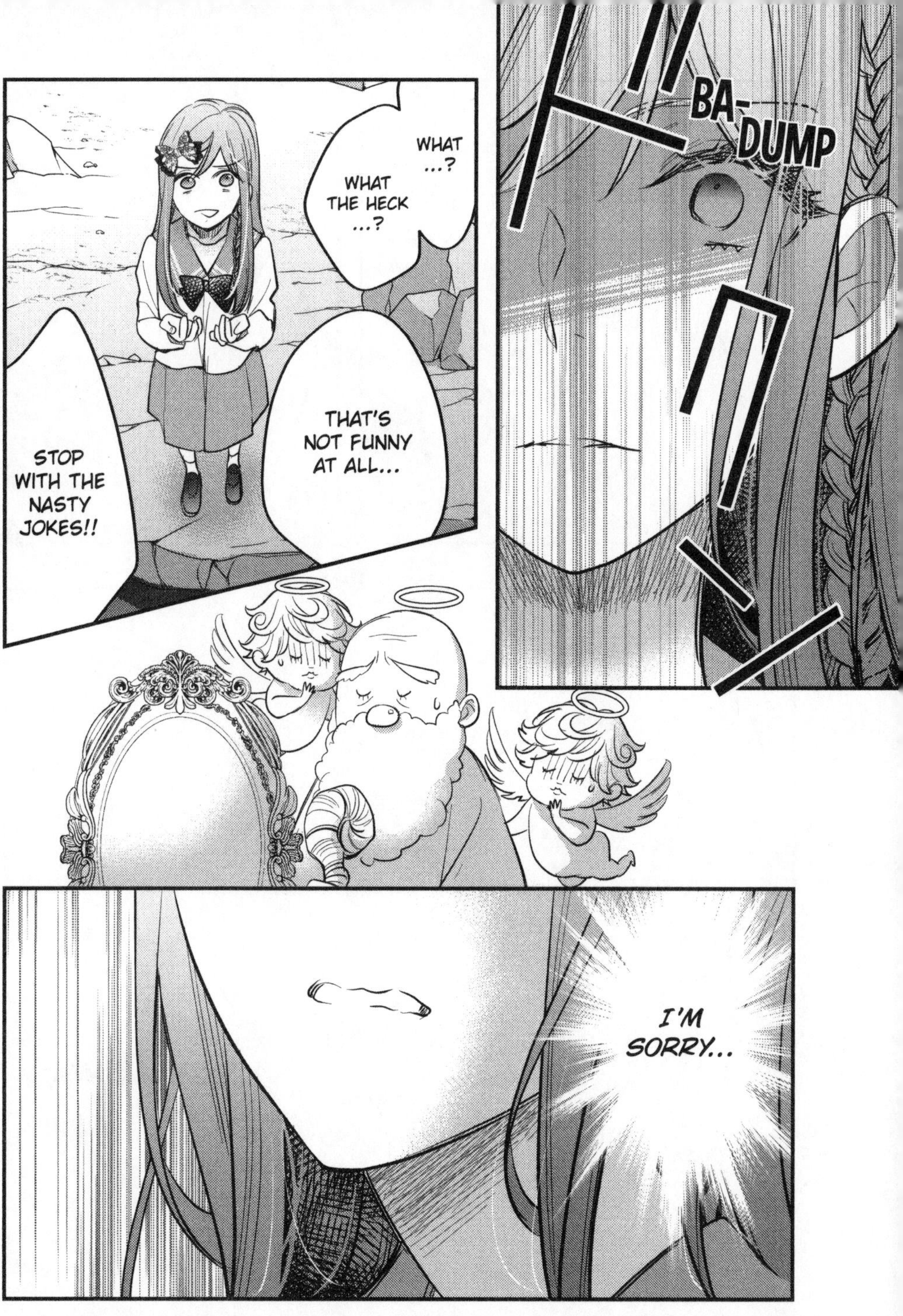
BA-DUMP
WHAT ...?
WHAT THE HECK ...?
THAT'S NOT FUNNY AT ALL...
STOP WITH THE NASTY JOKES!!
I'M SORRY...

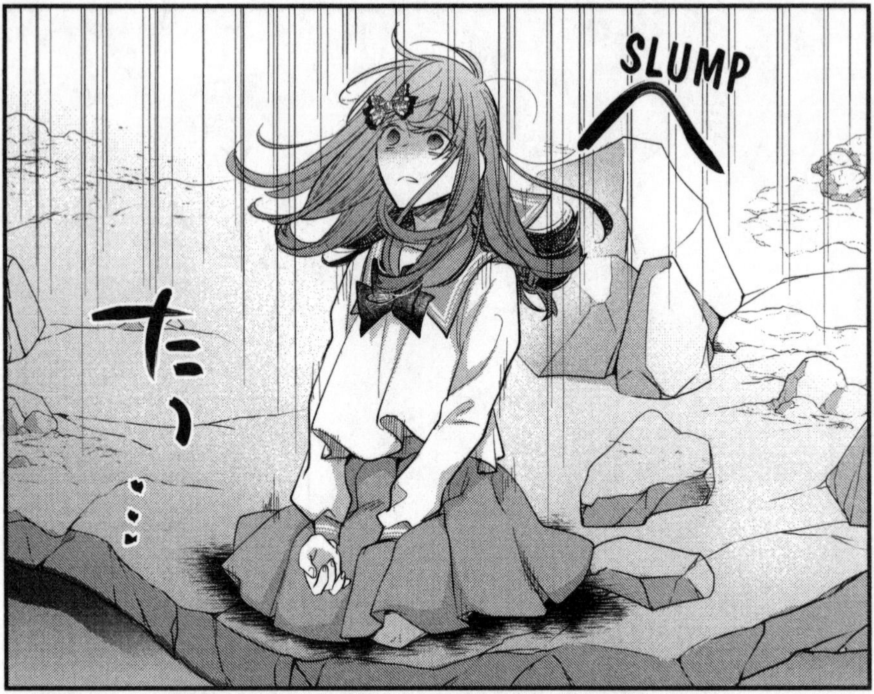
SLUMP

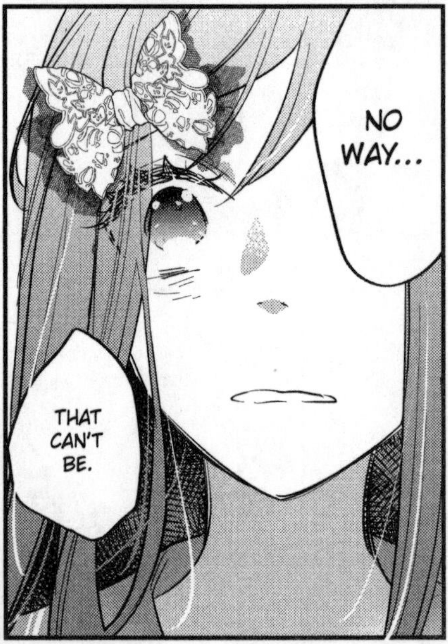
NO WAY...
THAT CAN'T BE.

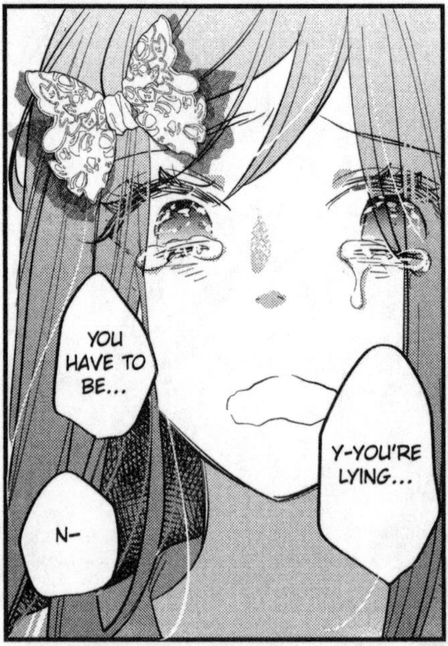
Y-YOU'RE LYING...
YOU HAVE TO BE...
N-

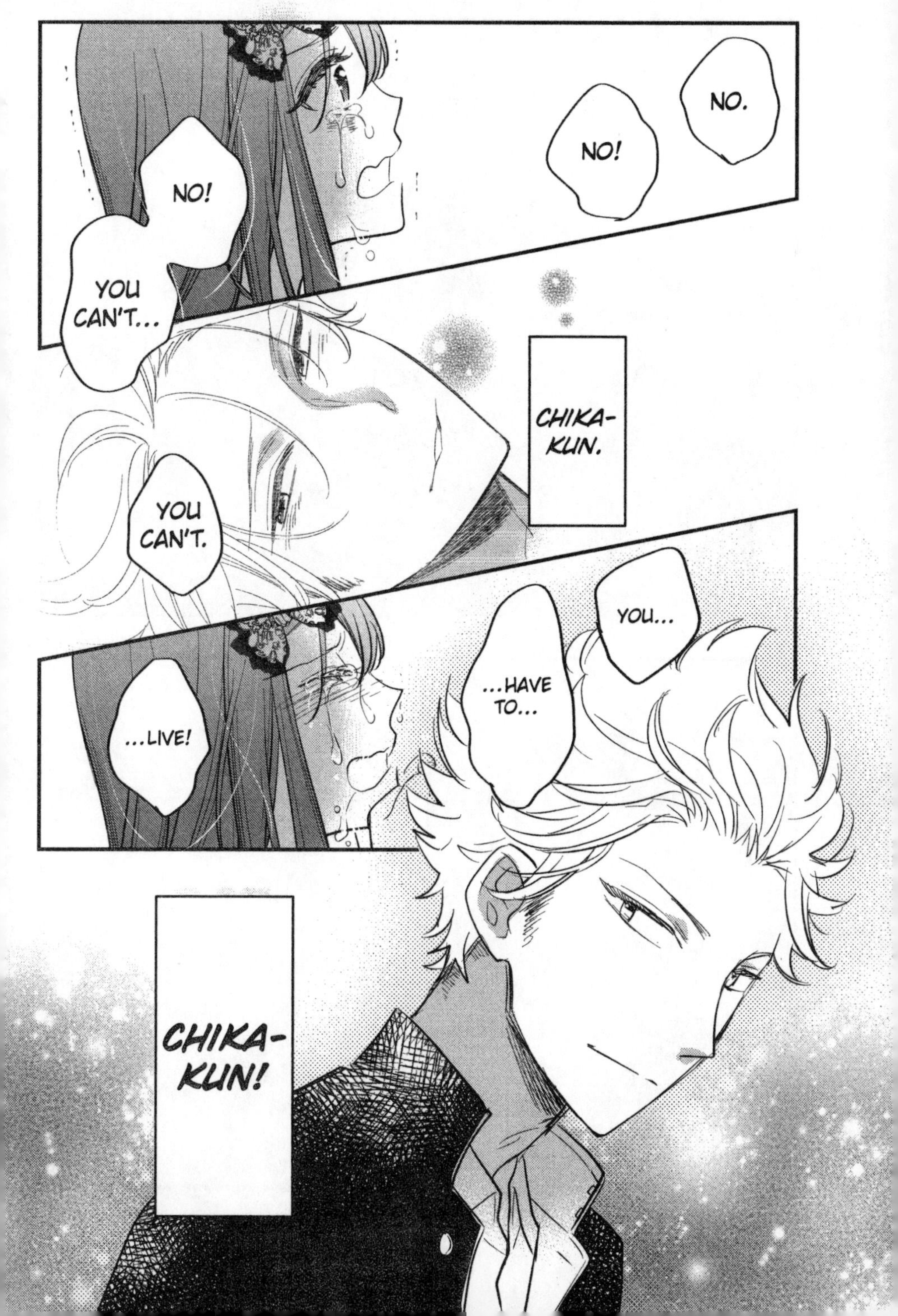
NO.
NO!
NO!
YOU CAN'T...
CHIKA-KUN.
YOU CAN'T.
YOU...
...HAVE TO...
...LIVE!
CHIKA-KUN!

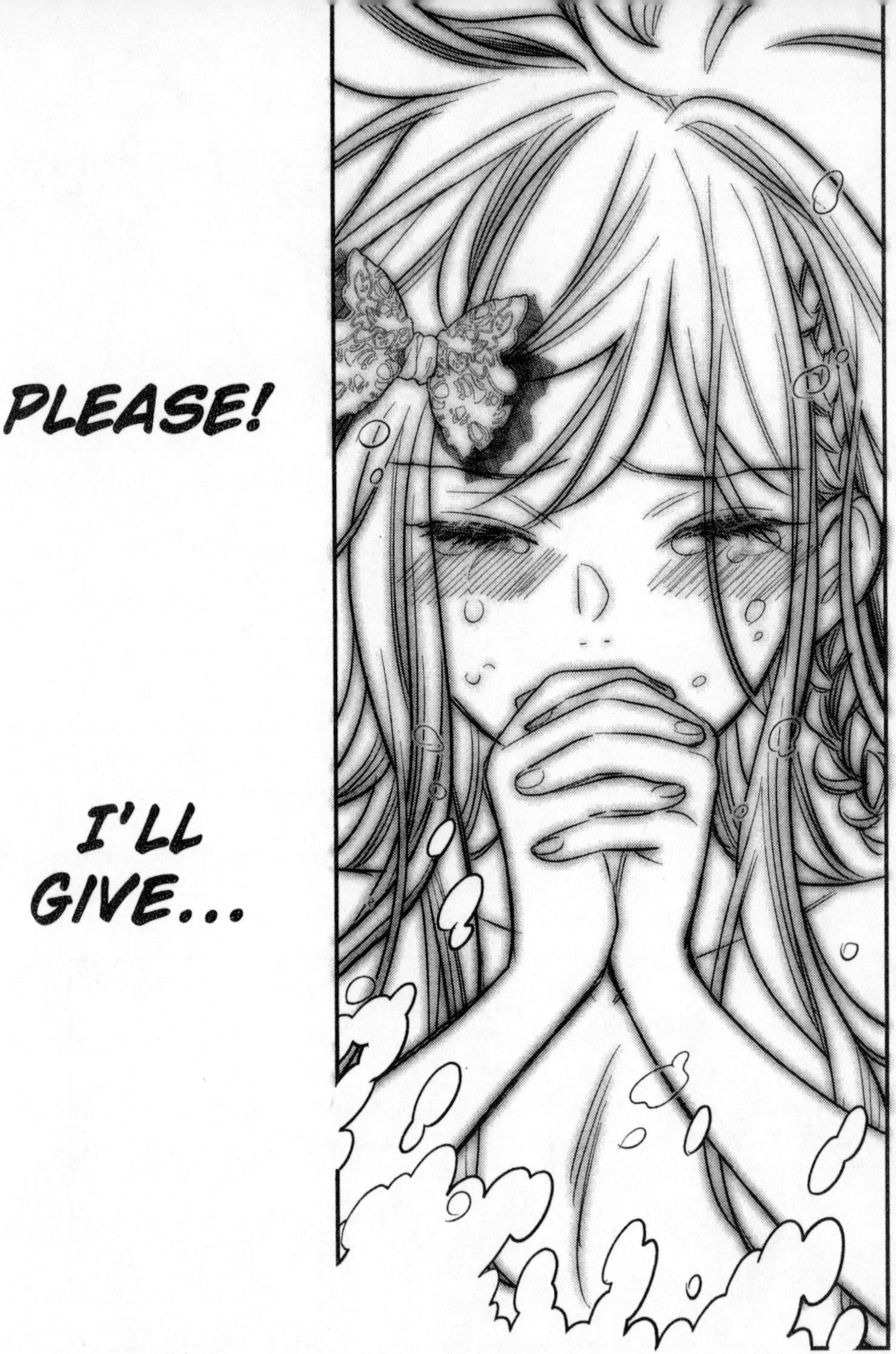
PLEASE!
I'LL GIVE...

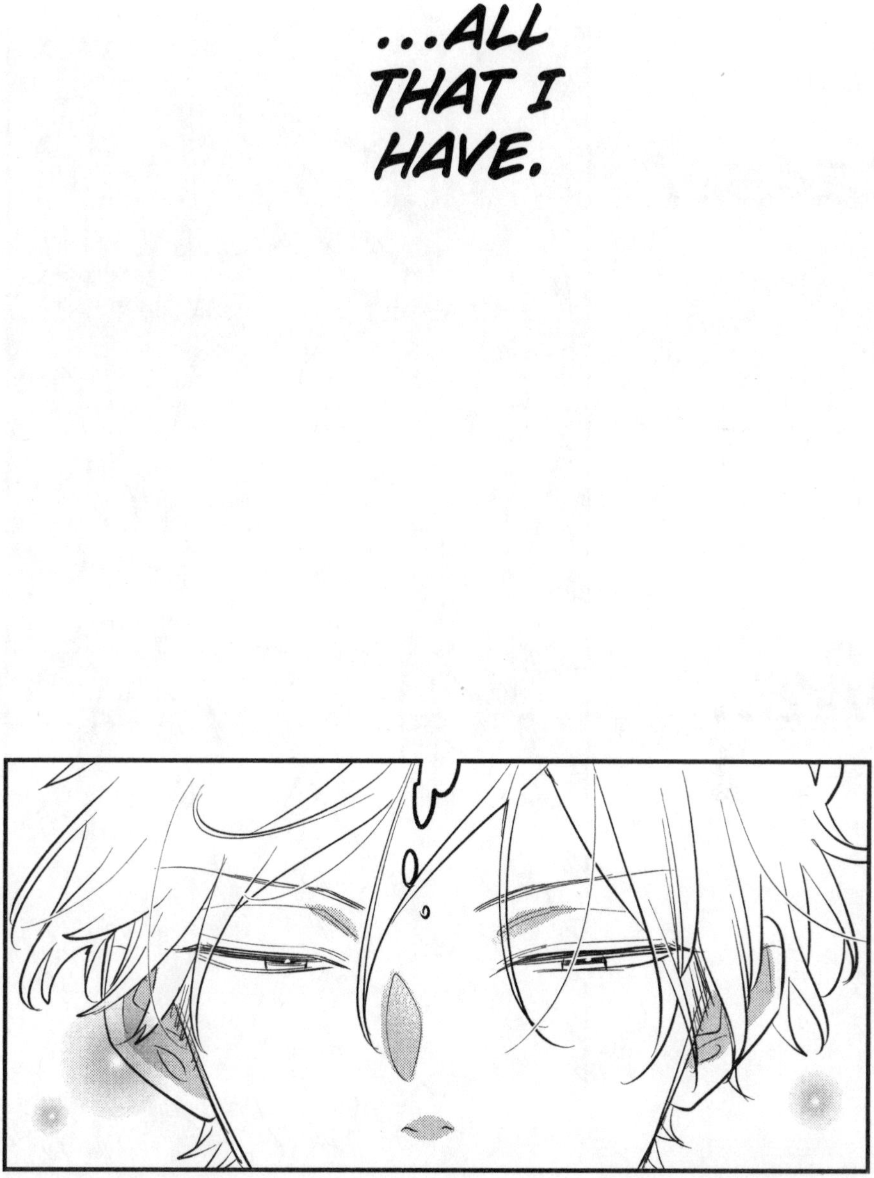
...ALL THAT I HAVE.

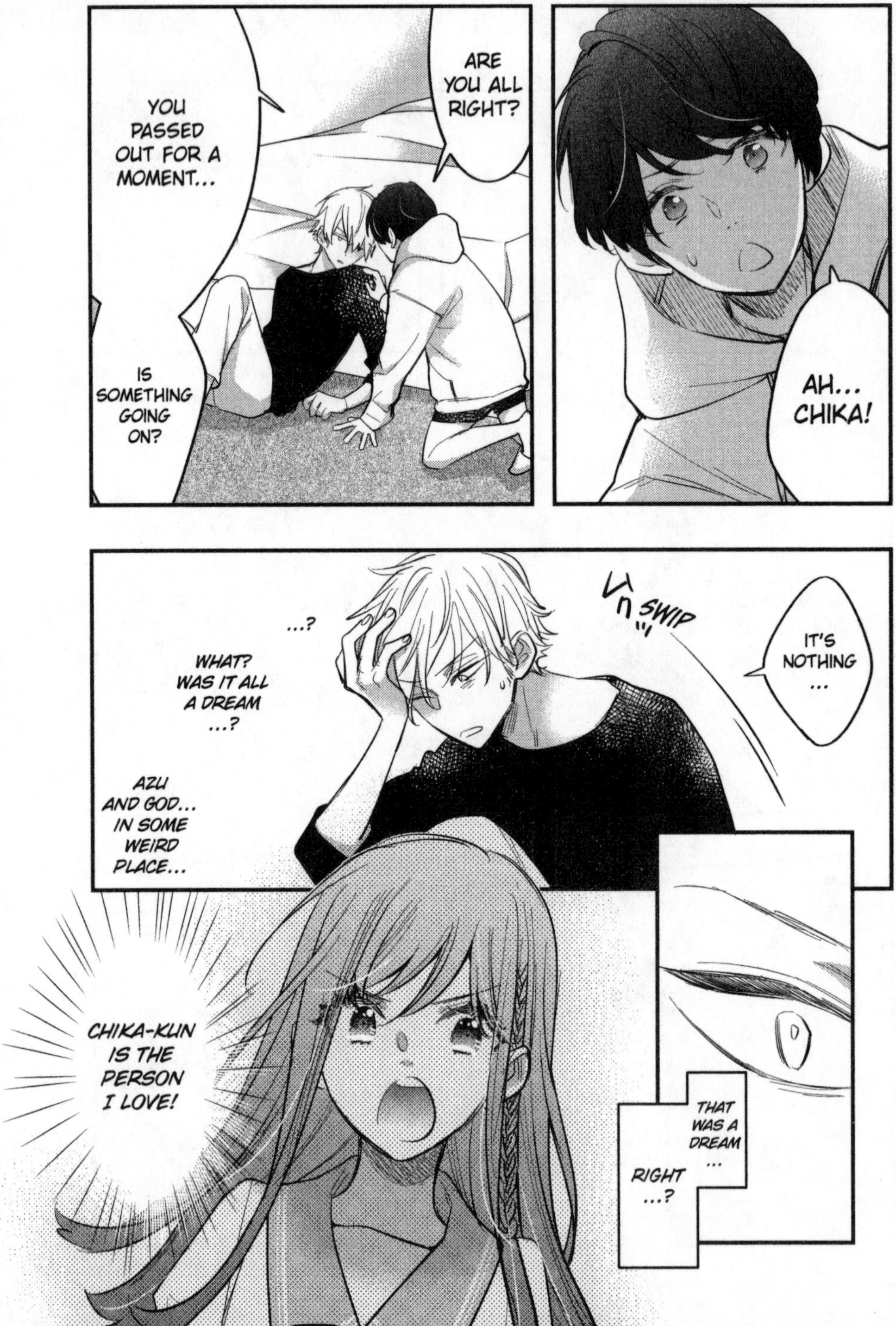
AH... CHIKA!
ARE YOU ALL RIGHT?
YOU PASSED OUT FOR A MOMENT...
IS SOMETHING GOING ON?
IT'S NOTHING...
SWIP
...?
WHAT? WAS IT ALL A DREAM...?
AZU AND GOD... IN SOME WEIRD PLACE...
THAT WAS A DREAM...
RIGHT...?
CHIKA-KUN IS THE PERSON I LOVE!

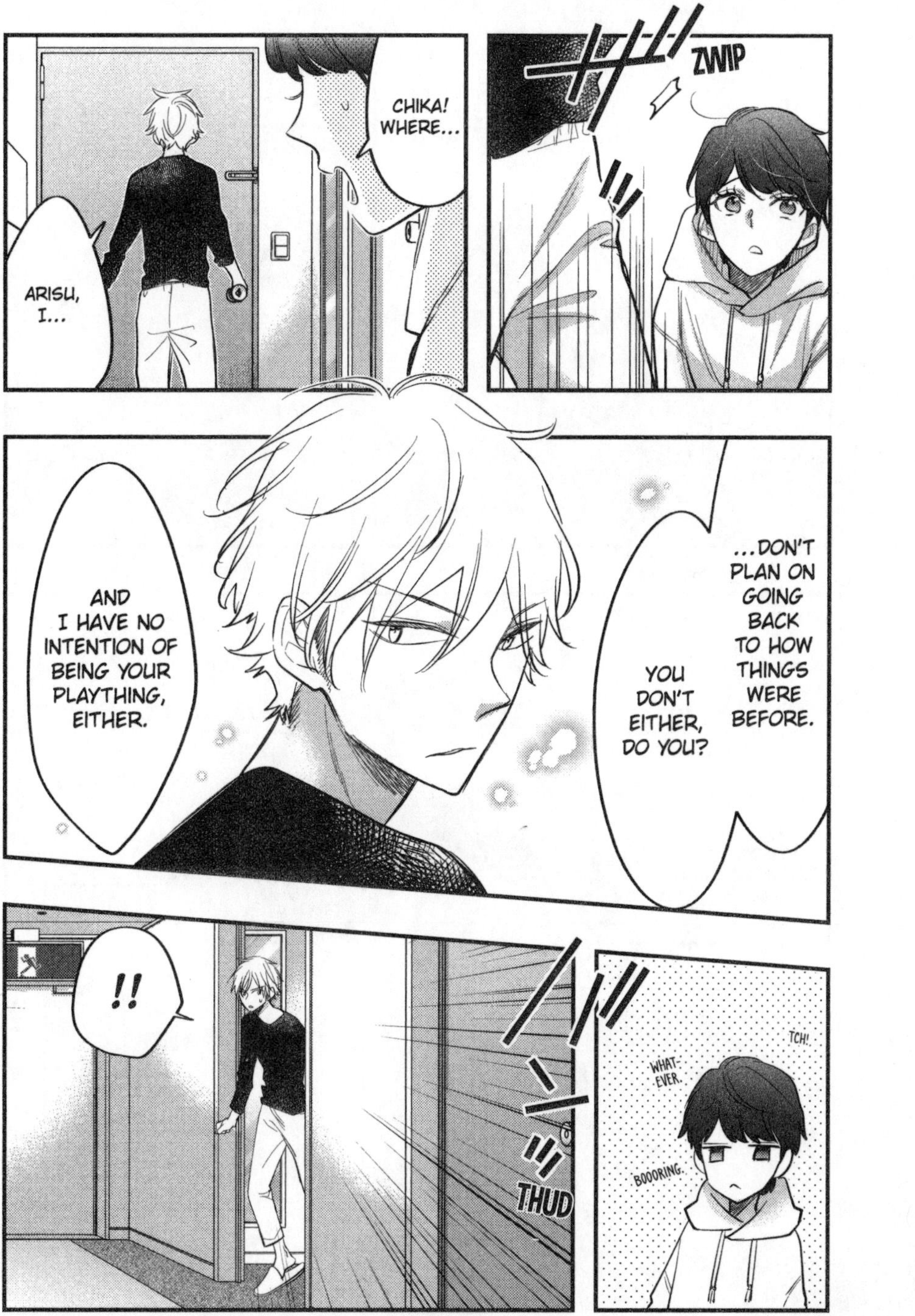
ZWIP
CHIKA! WHERE...
ARISU, I...
...DON'T PLAN ON GOING BACK TO HOW THINGS WERE BEFORE.
YOU DON'T EITHER, DO YOU?
AND I HAVE NO INTENTION OF BEING YOUR PLAYTHING, EITHER.
TCH!
WHAT-EVER.
BOOORING.
THUD
!!

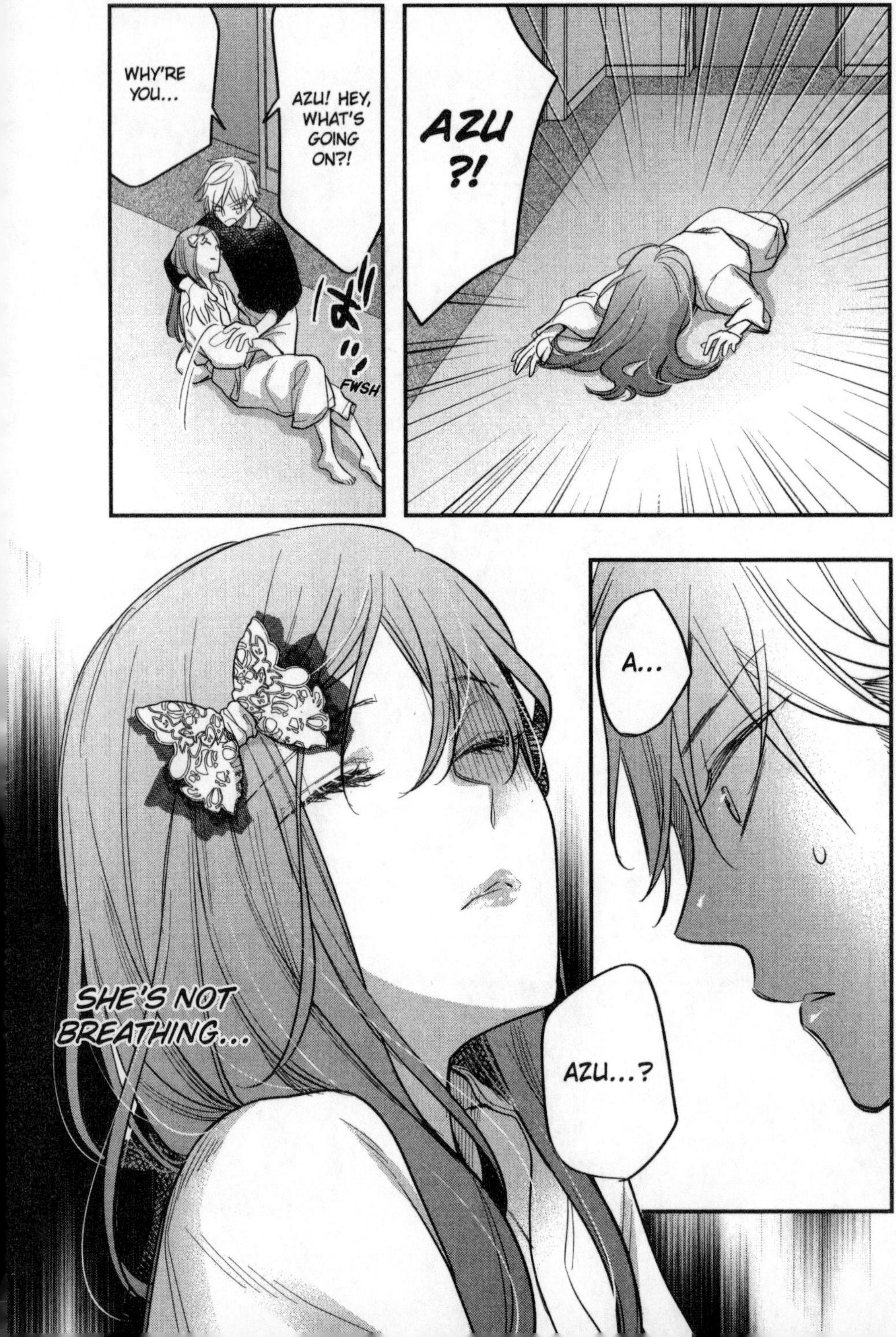
AZU ?!
AZU! HEY, WHAT'S GOING ON?!
WHY'RE YOU...
FWSH
A...
AZU...?
SHE'S NOT BREATHING...

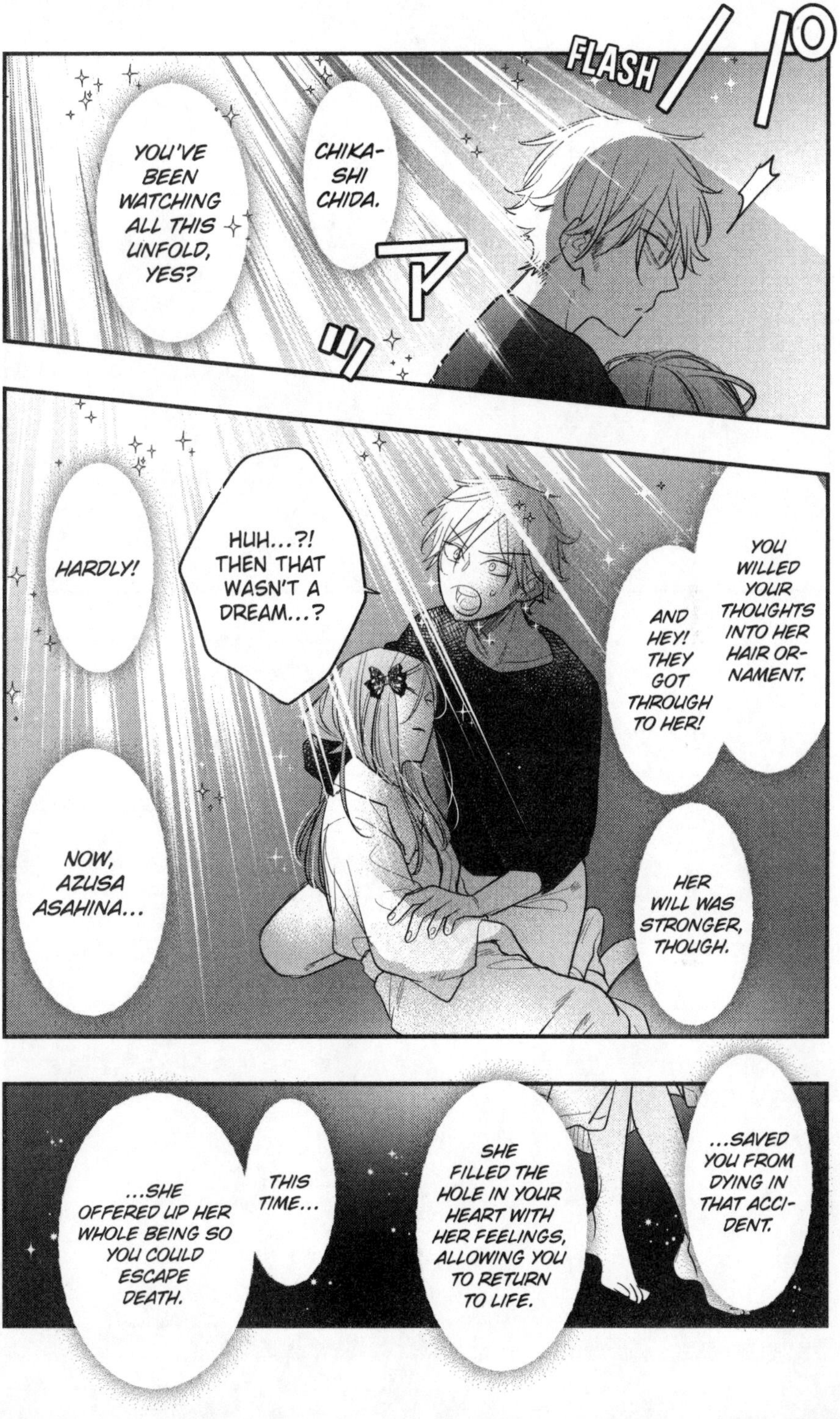
FLASH
CHIKA-SHI CHIDA.
YOU'VE BEEN WATCHING ALL THIS UNFOLD, YES?
YOU WILLED YOUR THOUGHTS INTO HER HAIR OR-NAMENT.
AND HEY! THEY GOT THROUGH TO HER!
HUH...?! THEN THAT WASN'T A DREAM...?
HARDLY!
HER WILL WAS STRONGER, THOUGH.
NOW, AZUSA ASAHINA...
...SAVED YOU FROM DYING IN THAT ACCI-DENT.
SHE FILLED THE HOLE IN YOUR HEART WITH HER FEELINGS, ALLOWING YOU TO RETURN TO LIFE.
THIS TIME...
...SHE OFFERED UP HER WHOLE BEING SO YOU COULD ESCAPE DEATH.

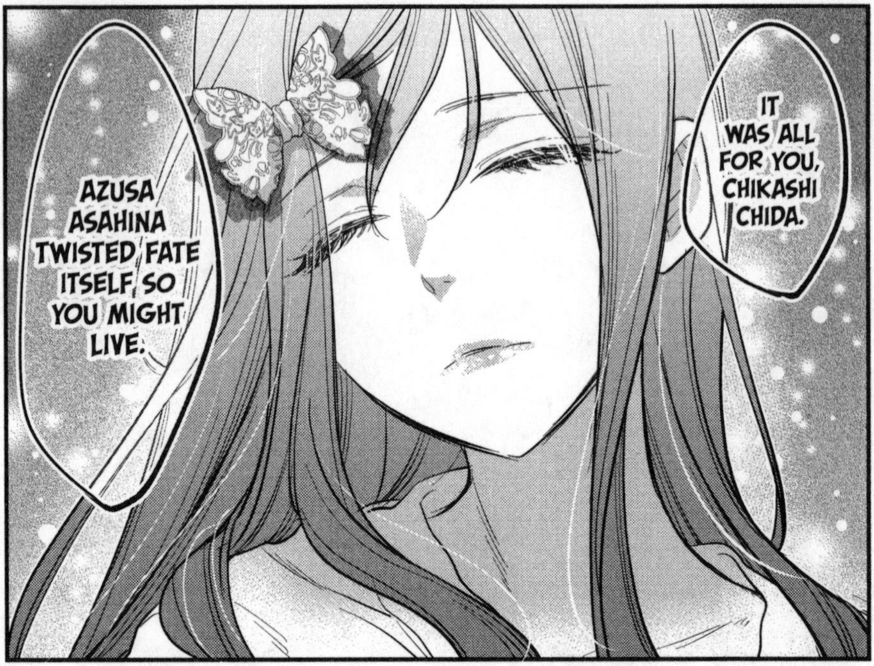
IT WAS ALL FOR YOU, CHIKASHI CHIDA.
AZUSA ASAHINA TWISTED FATE ITSELF SO YOU MIGHT LIVE.

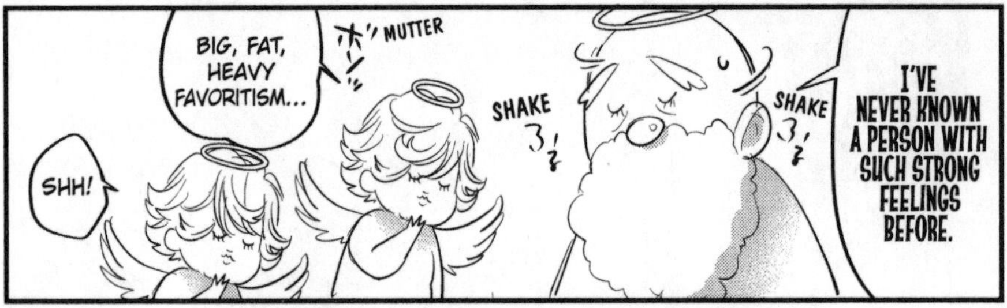
I'VE NEVER KNOWN A PERSON WITH SUCH STRONG FEELINGS BEFORE.
SHAKE
SHAKE
MUTTER
BIG, FAT, HEAVY FAVORITISM...
SHH!

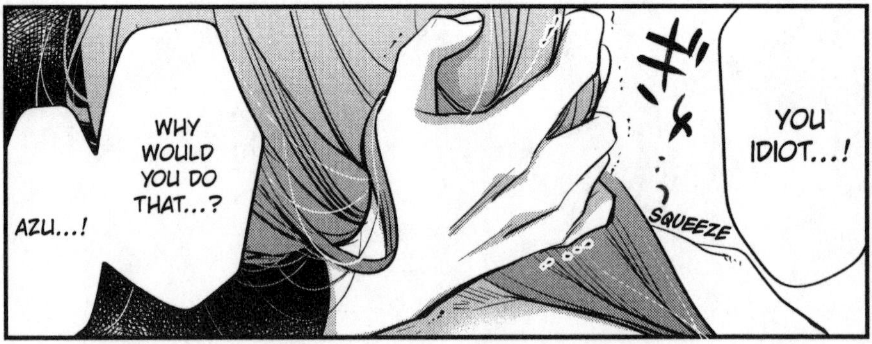
YOU IDIOT...!
SQUEEZE
WHY WOULD YOU DO THAT...?
AZU...!

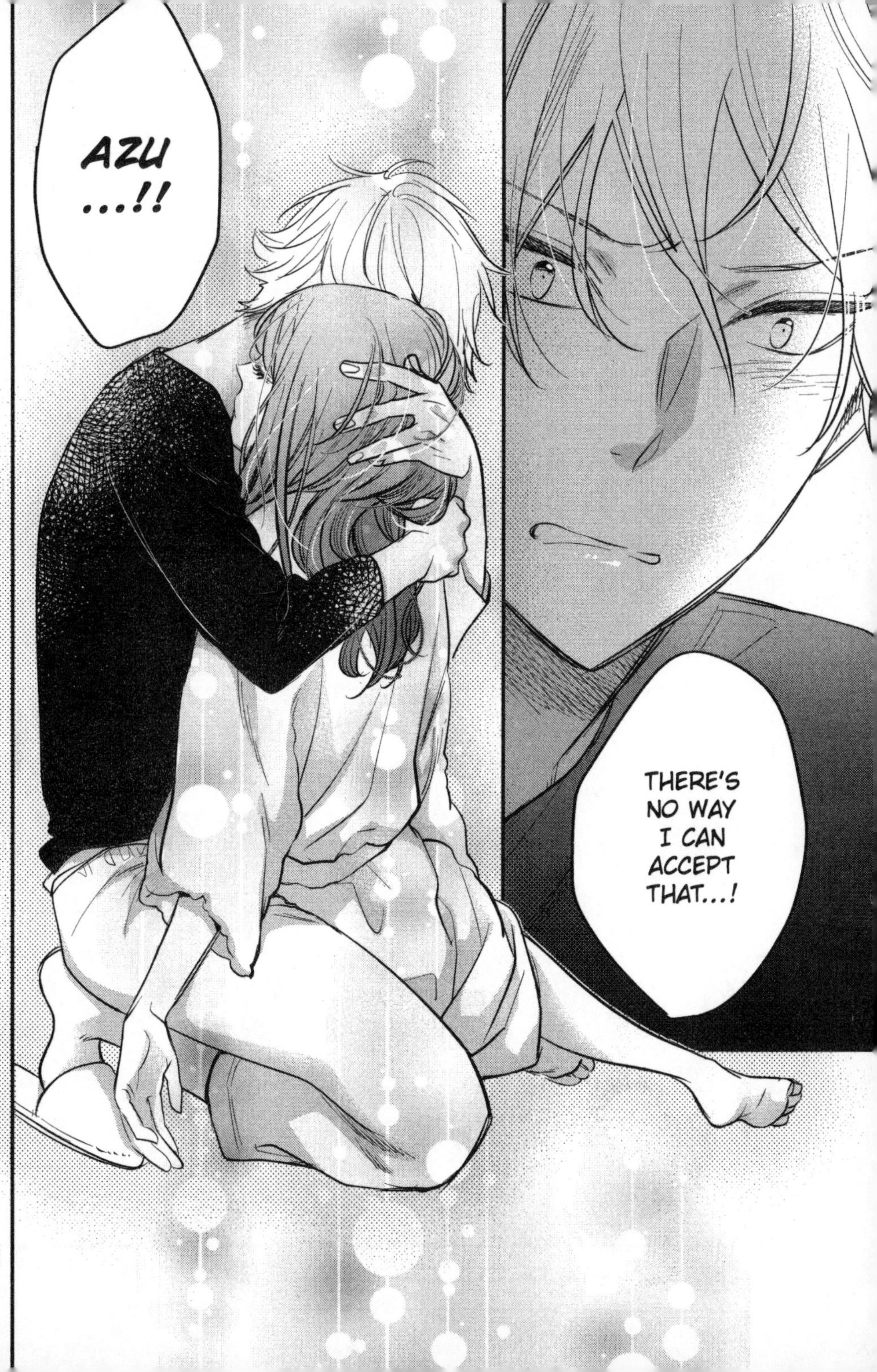
THERE'S NO WAY I CAN ACCEPT THAT...!
AZU ...!!

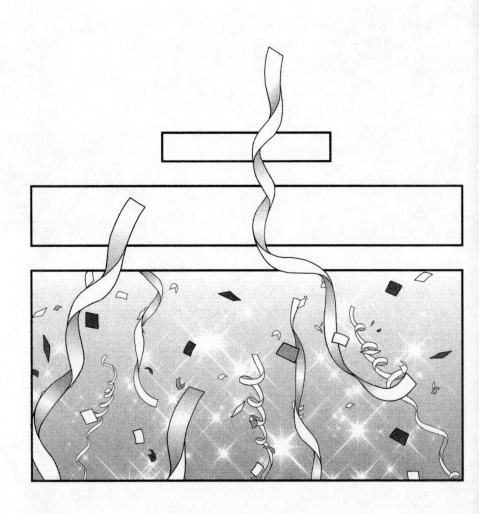

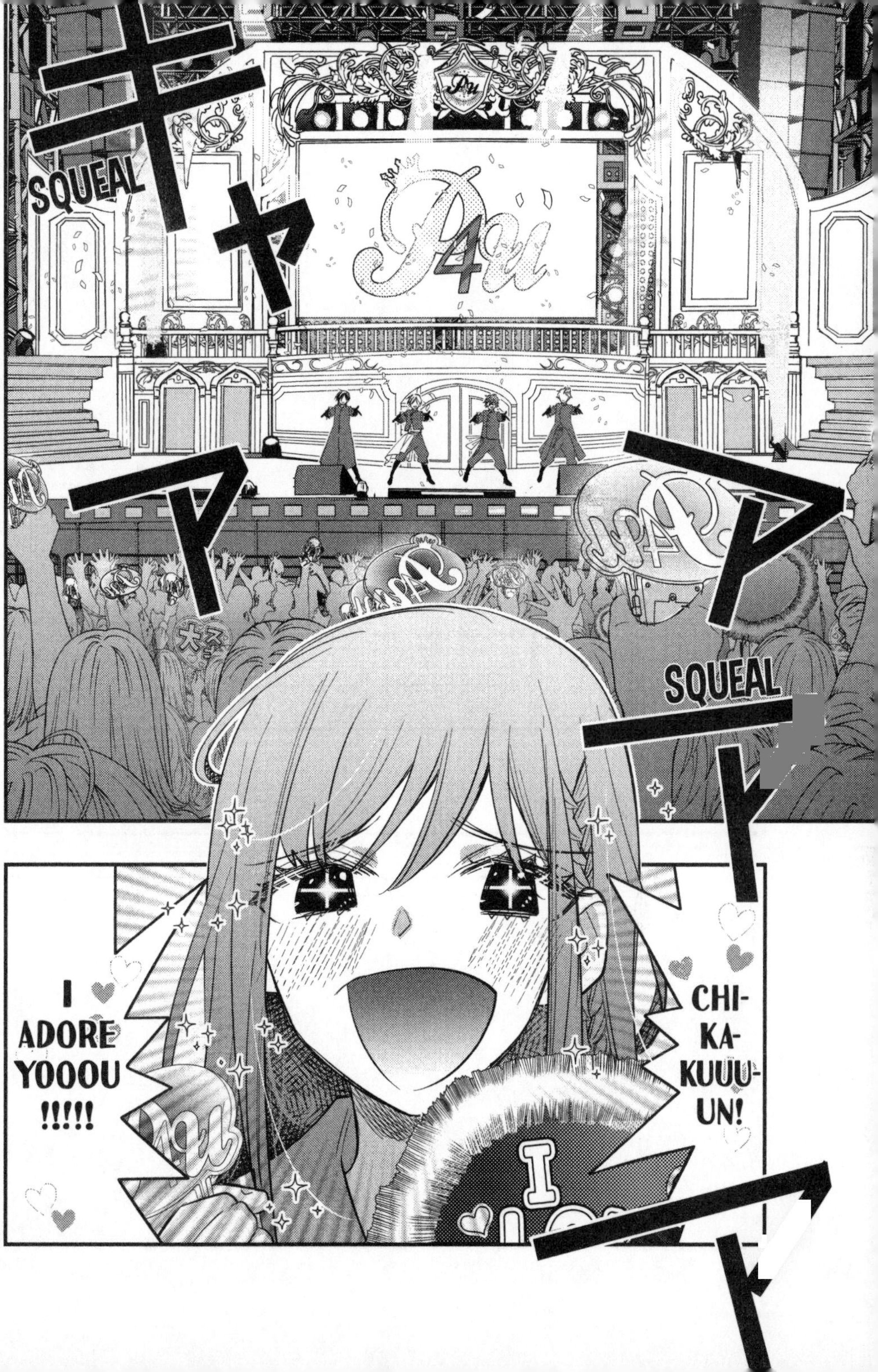

SQUEAL
SQUEAL
CHI-KA-KUUU-UN!
I ♥ ADORE YOOOU!!!!!

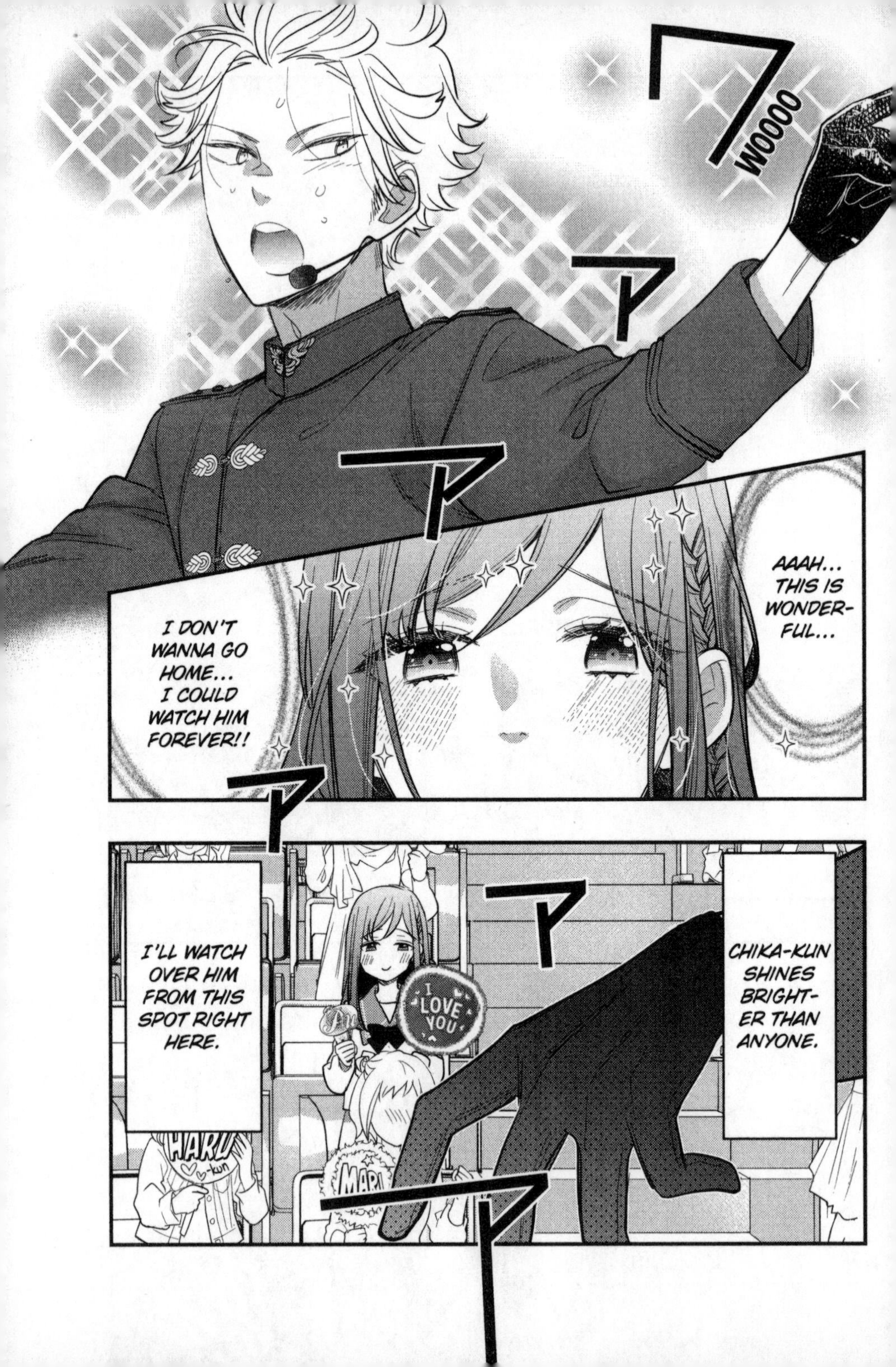
WOOOOW
AAAH... THIS IS WONDERFUL...
I DON'T WANNA GO HOME... I COULD WATCH HIM FOREVER!!
CHIKA-KUN SHINES BRIGHTER THAN ANYONE.
I LOVE YOU
I'LL WATCH OVER HIM FROM THIS SPOT RIGHT HERE.
HARU -kun

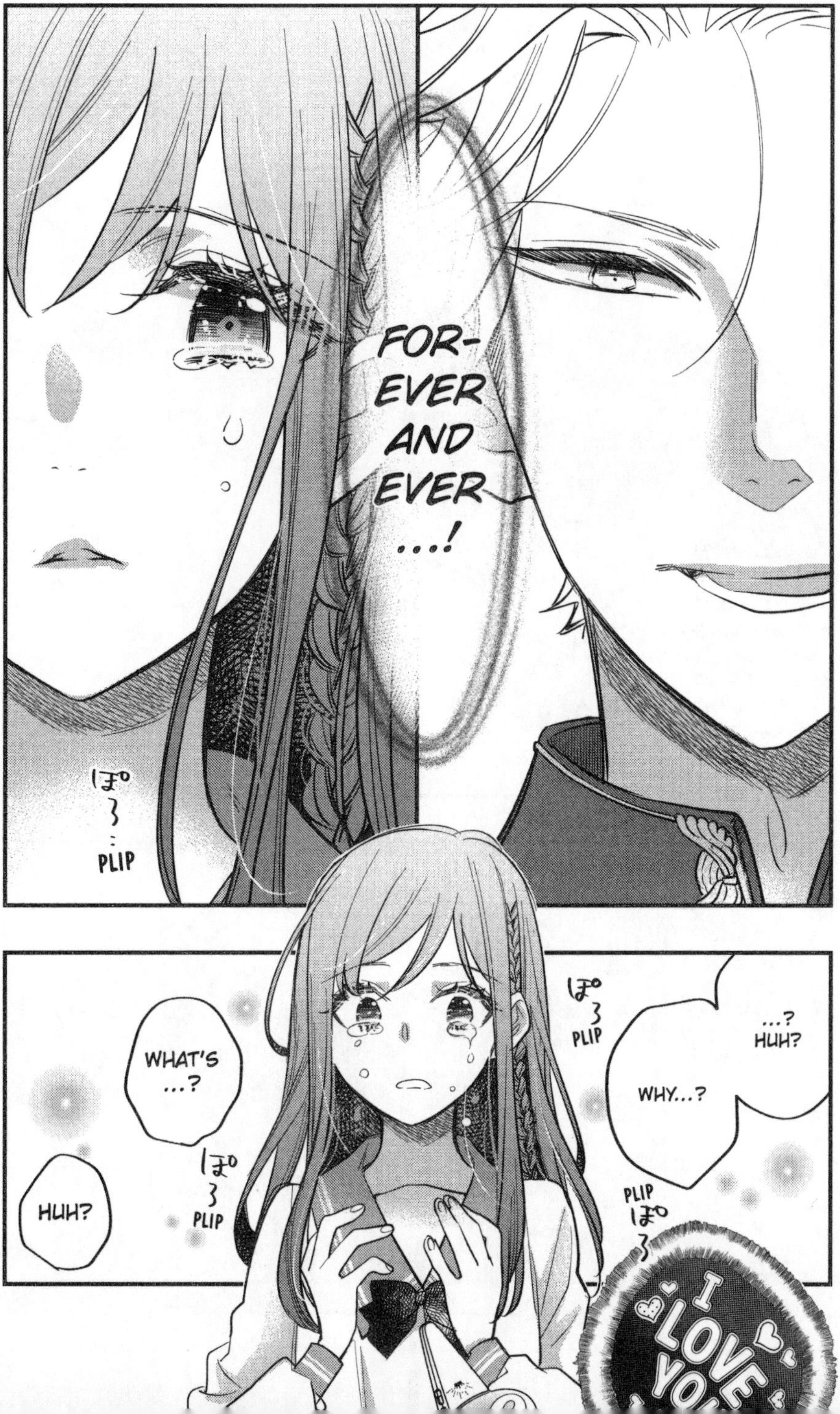
FOR-EVER AND EVER ...!
ぽろ PLIP
...? HUH?
WHY...?
ぽろ PLIP
PLIP ぽろ
WHAT'S ...?
ぽろ PLIP
HUH?

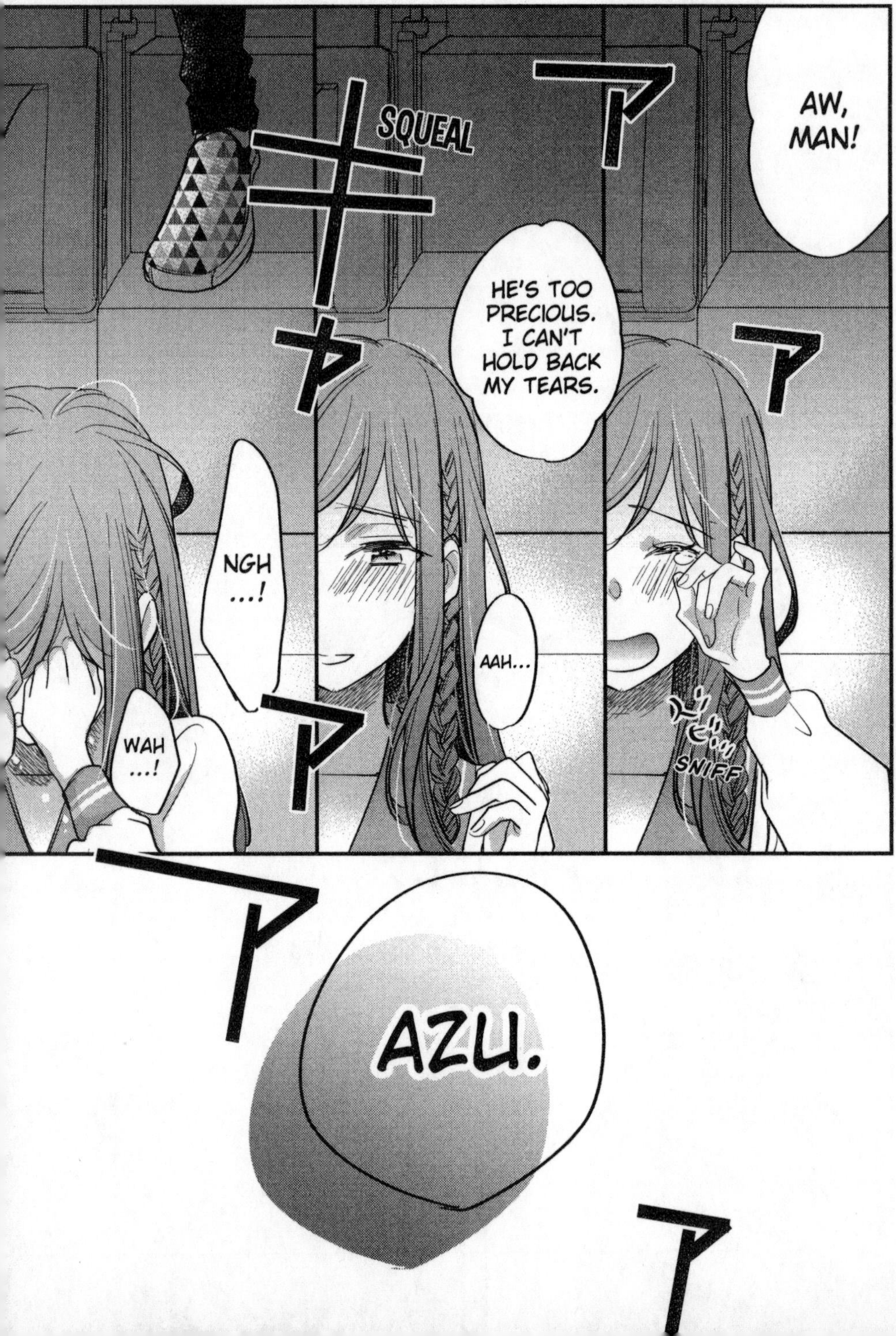
AW, MAN!
SQUEAL
HE'S TOO PRECIOUS. I CAN'T HOLD BACK MY TEARS.
SNIFF
AAH...
NGH ...!
WAH ...!
AZU.

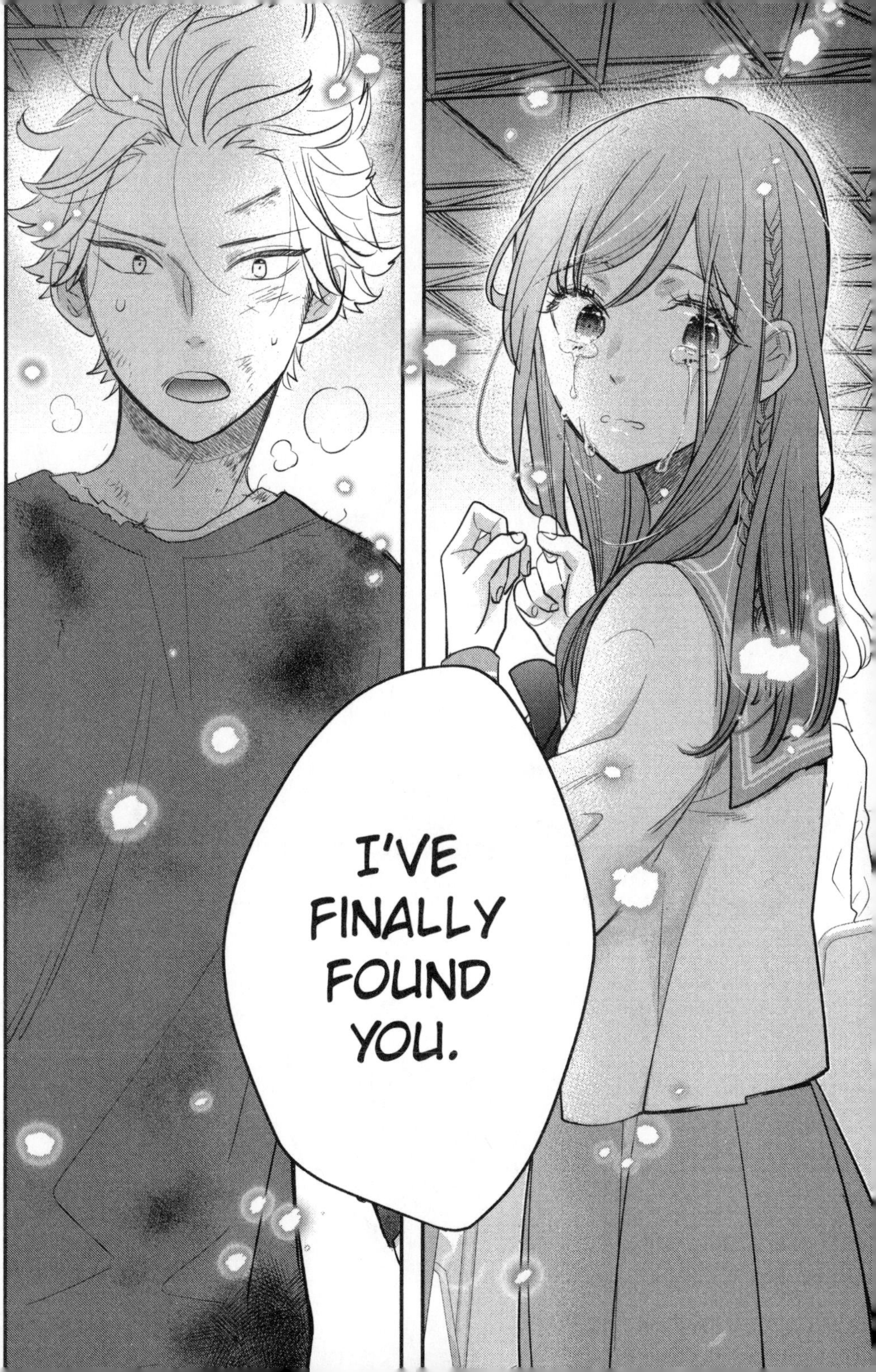
I'VE FINALLY FOUND YOU.

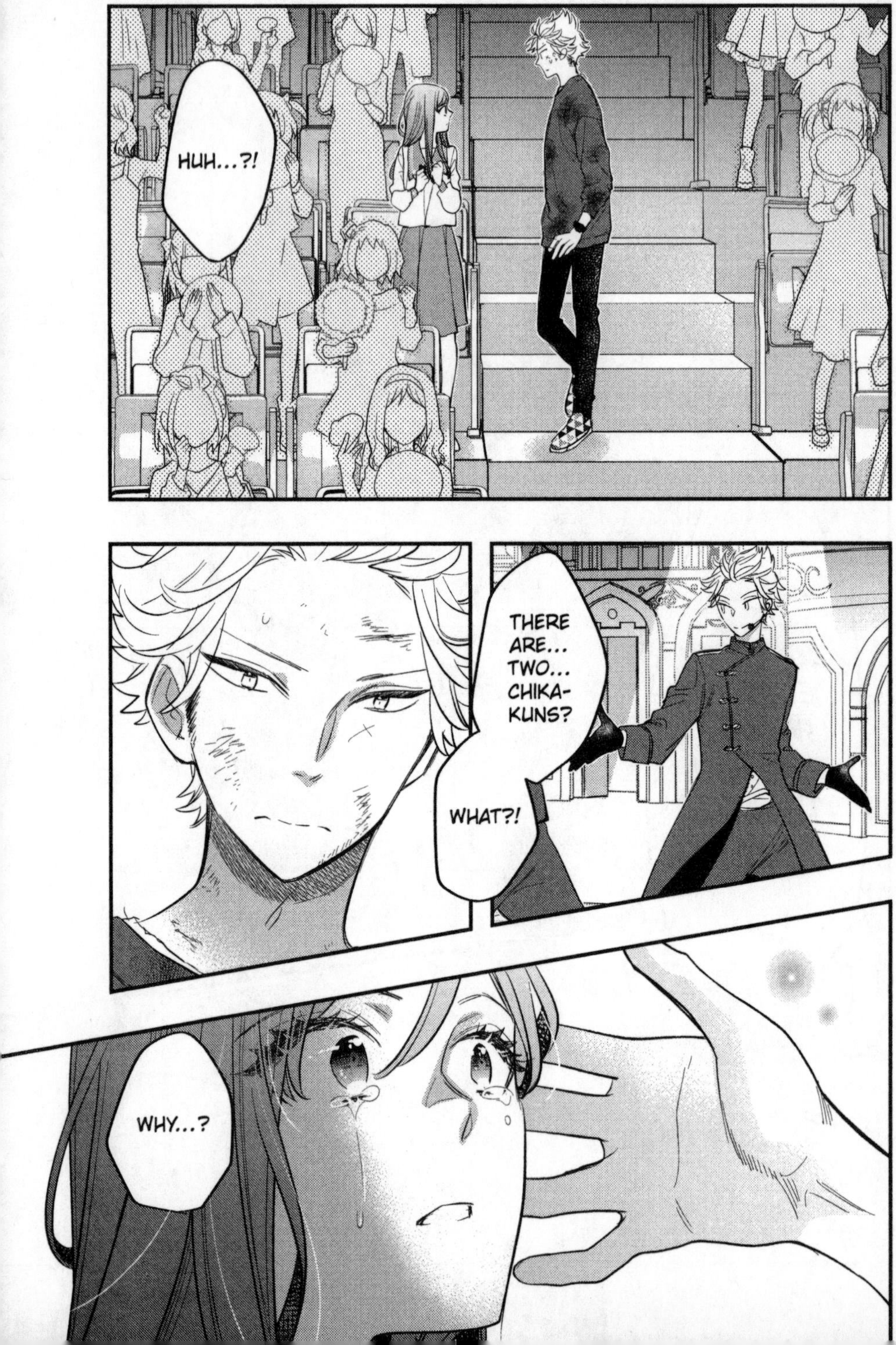
HUH...?!
THERE ARE... TWO... CHIKA-KUNS?
WHAT?!
WHY...?

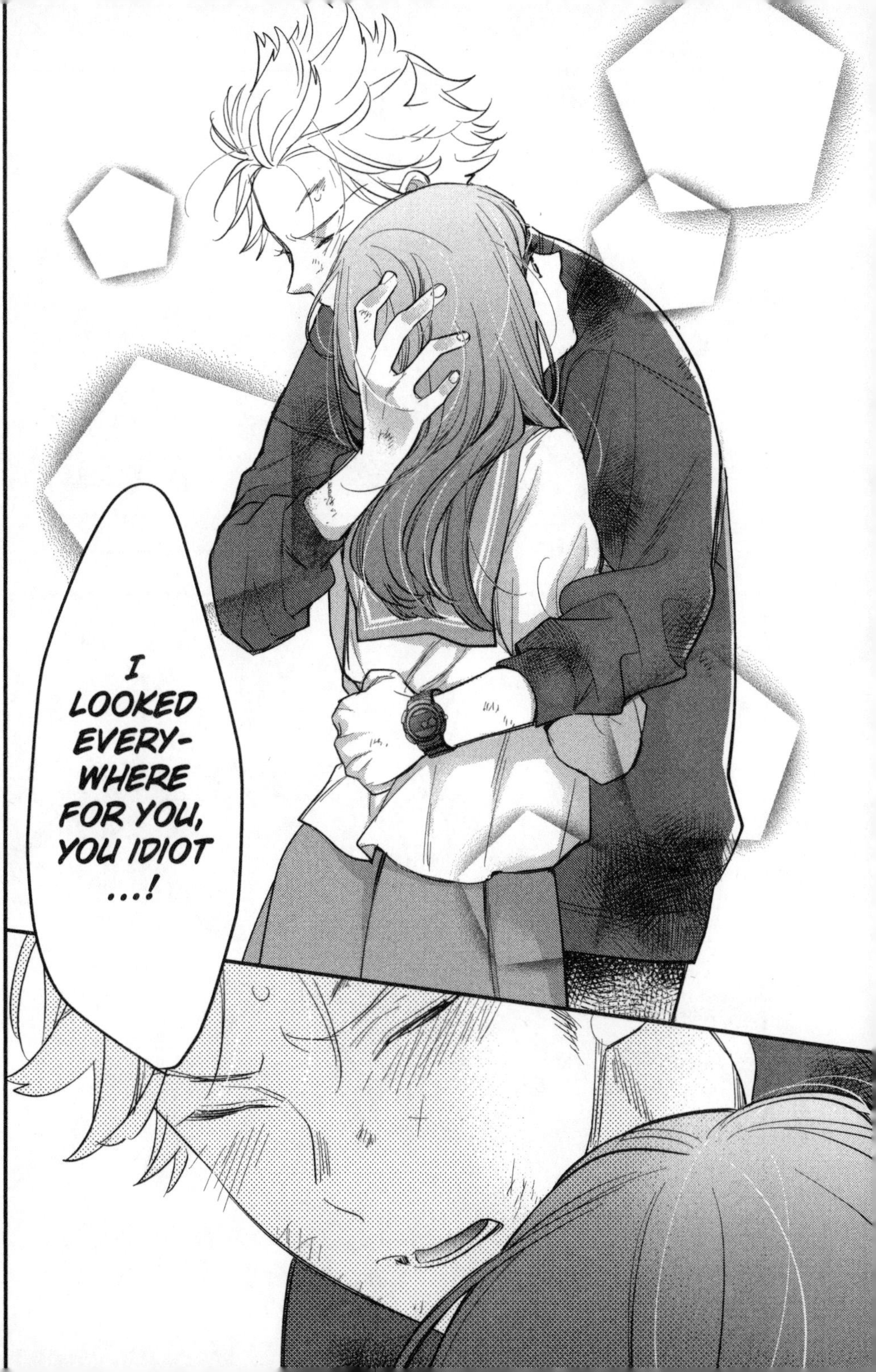
I LOOKED EVERY-WHERE FOR YOU, YOU IDIOT ...!

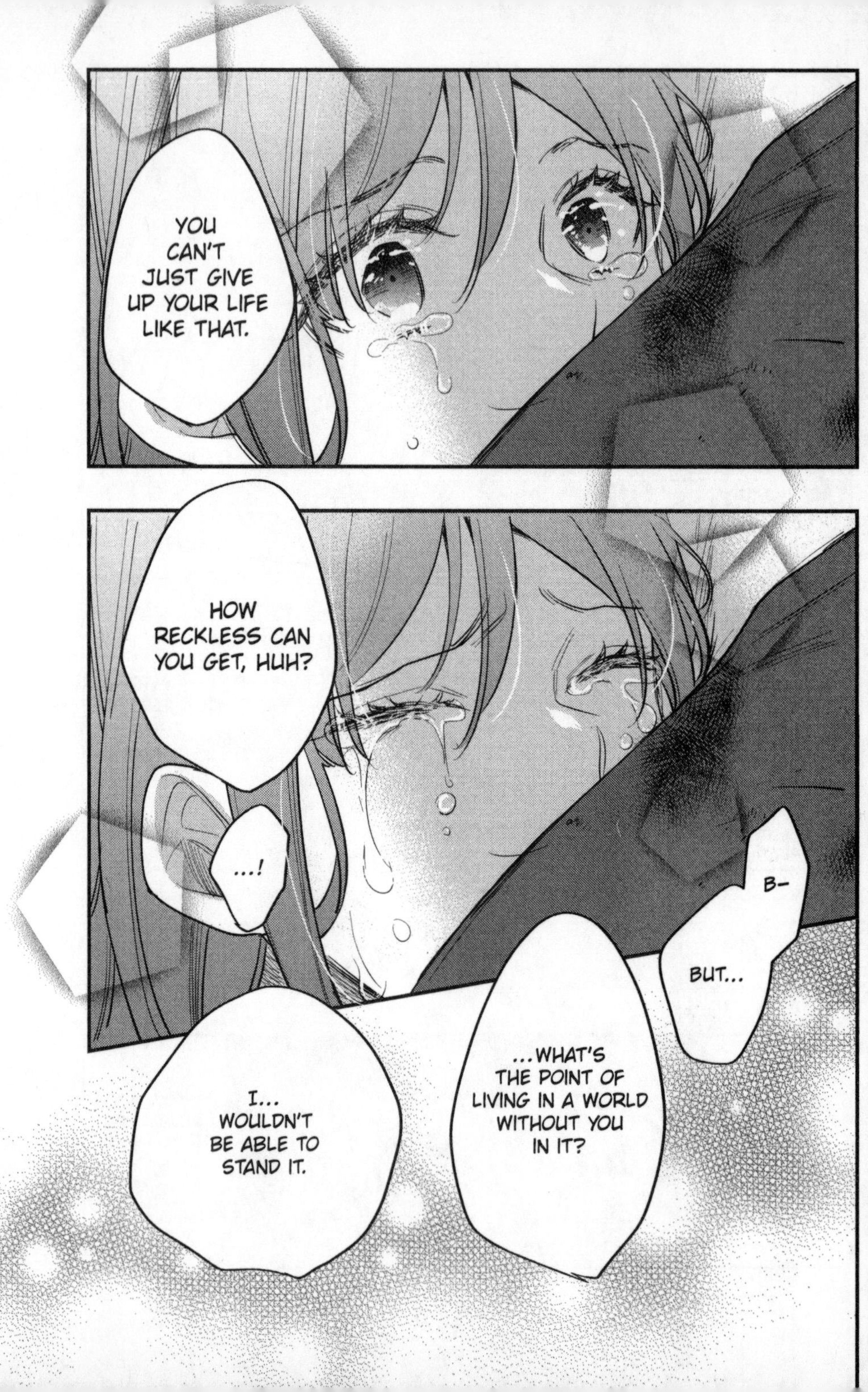
YOU CAN'T JUST GIVE UP YOUR LIFE LIKE THAT.
HOW RECKLESS CAN YOU GET, HUH?
...!
B—
BUT...
...WHAT'S THE POINT OF LIVING IN A WORLD WITHOUT YOU IN IT?
I... WOULDN'T BE ABLE TO STAND IT.

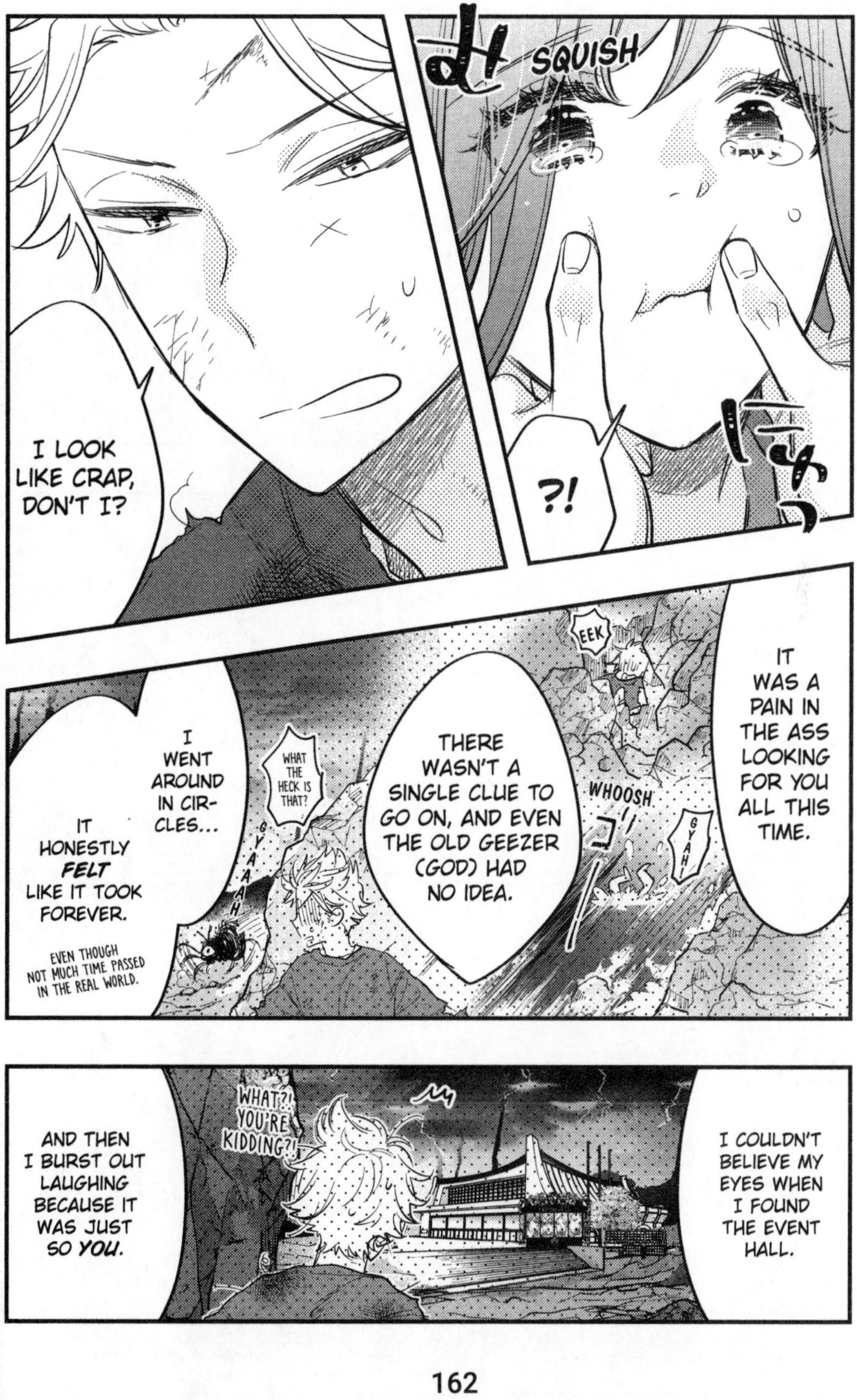
SQUISH
?!
I LOOK LIKE CRAP, DON'T I?
IT WAS A PAIN IN THE ASS LOOKING FOR YOU ALL THIS TIME.
EEK
GYAH!
WHOOSH
THERE WASN'T A SINGLE CLUE TO GO ON, AND EVEN THE OLD GEEZER (GOD) HAD NO IDEA.
WHAT THE HECK IS THAT?
GYAAAAH
I WENT AROUND IN CIR-CLES...
IT HONESTLY *FELT* LIKE IT TOOK FOREVER.
EVEN THOUGH NOT MUCH TIME PASSED IN THE REAL WORLD.
I COULDN'T BELIEVE MY EYES WHEN I FOUND THE EVENT HALL.
WHAT?! YOU'RE KIDDING?!
AND THEN I BURST OUT LAUGHING BECAUSE IT WAS JUST SO *YOU*.

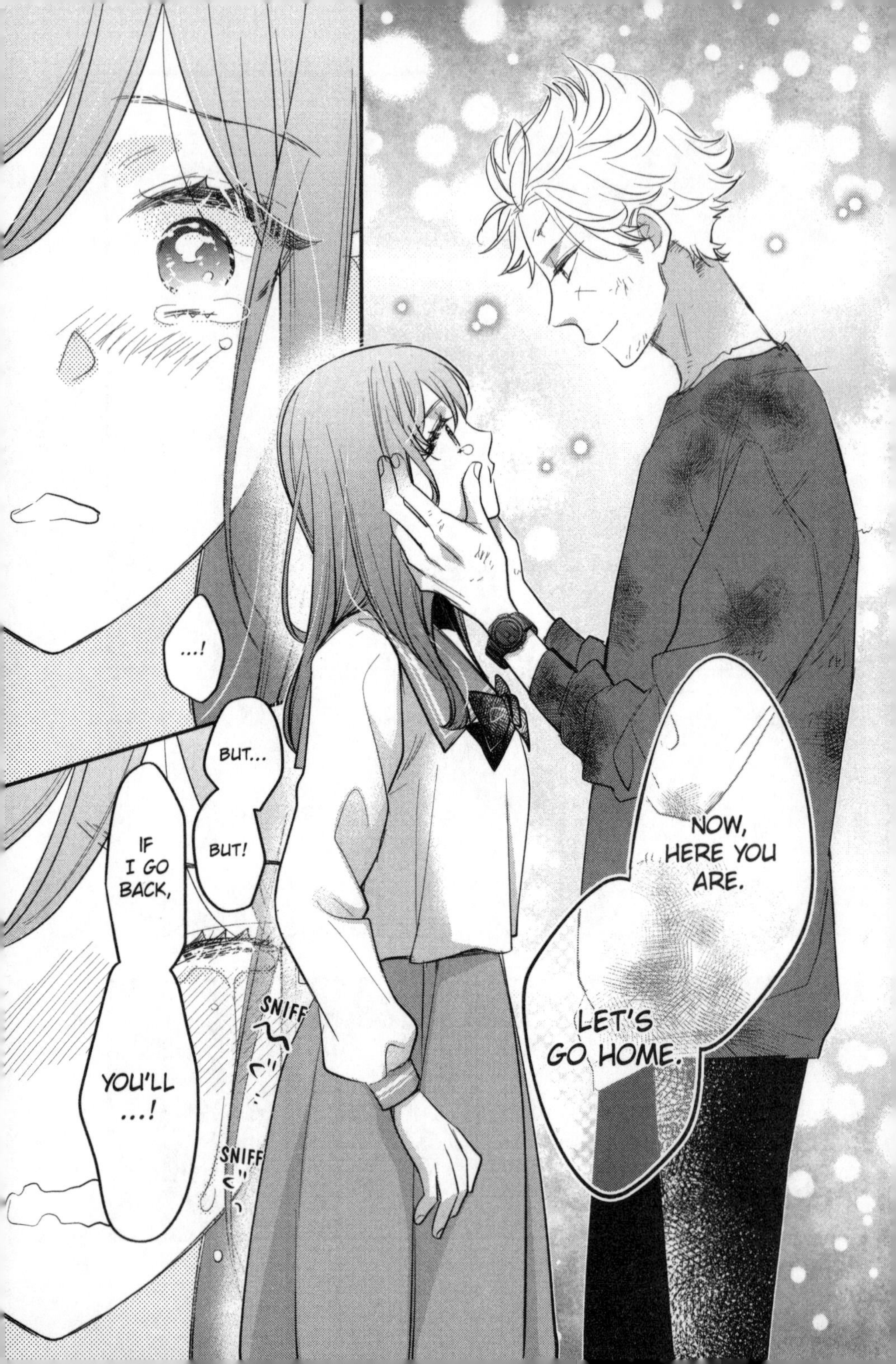
NOW, HERE YOU ARE.
LET'S GO HOME.
...!
BUT...
BUT!
IF I GO BACK,
YOU'LL ...!
SNIFF
SNIFF

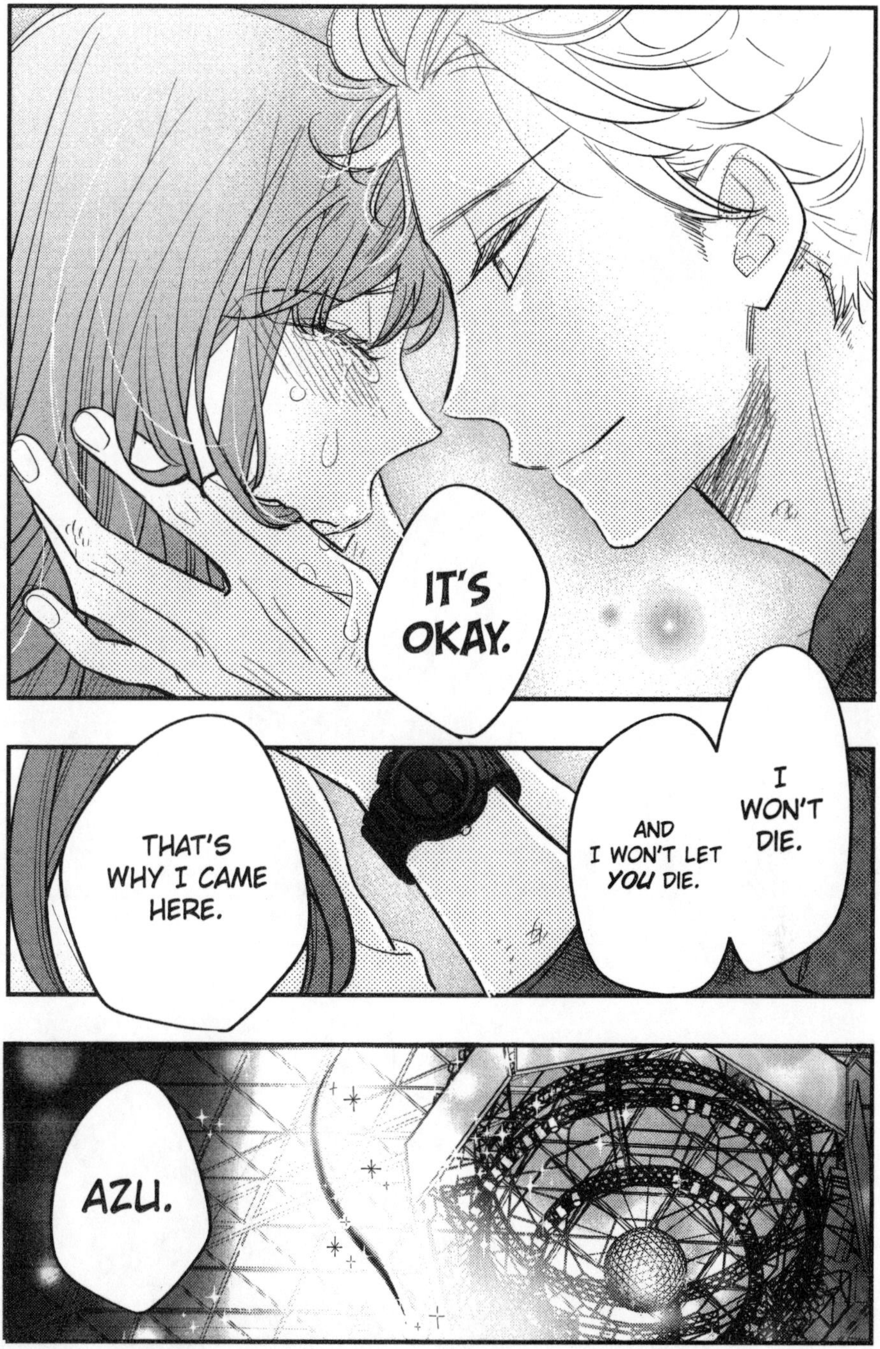
IT'S OKAY.
I WON'T DIE.
AND I WON'T LET YOU DIE.
THAT'S WHY I CAME HERE.
AZU.

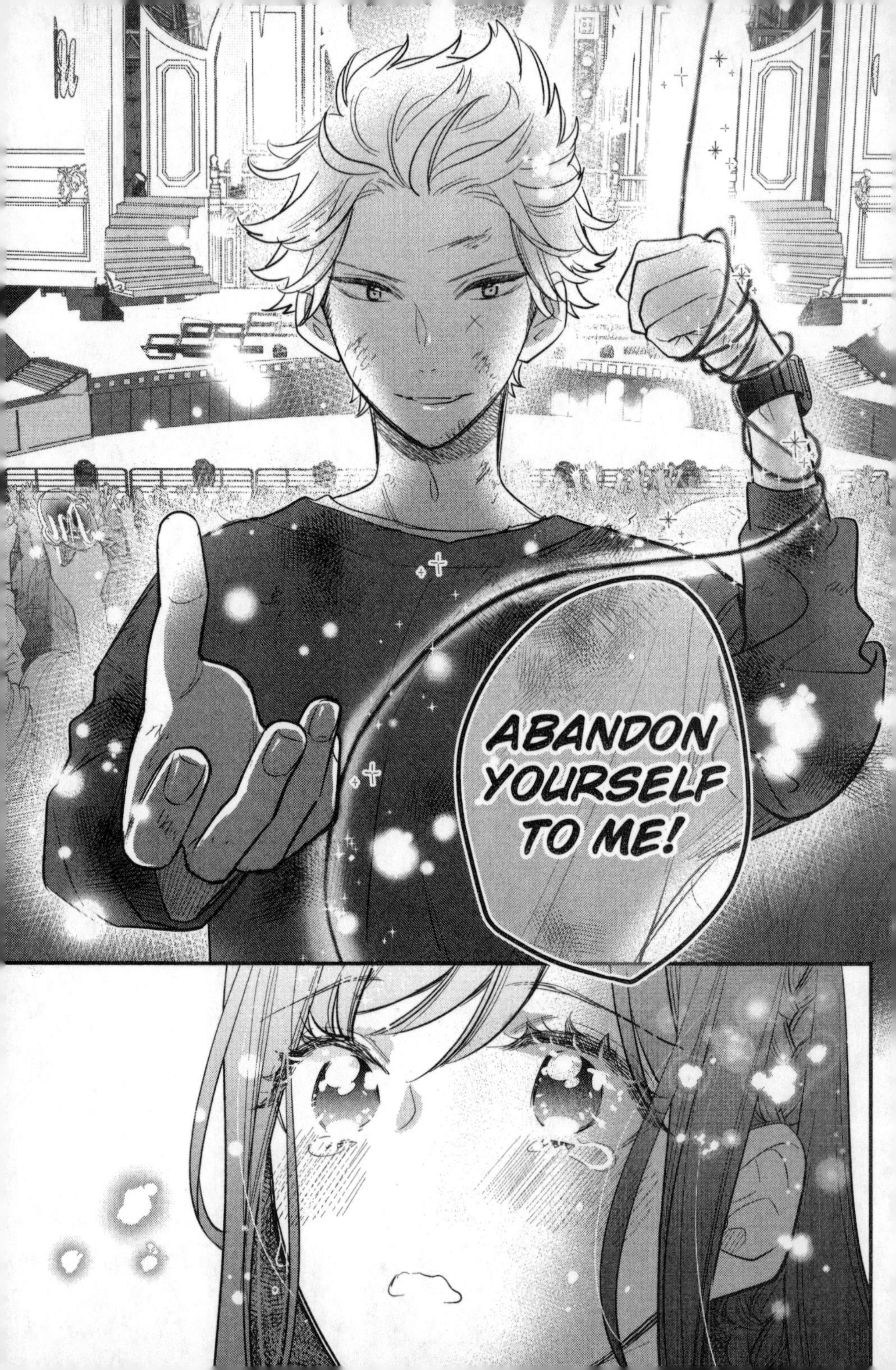
ABANDON YOURSELF TO ME!

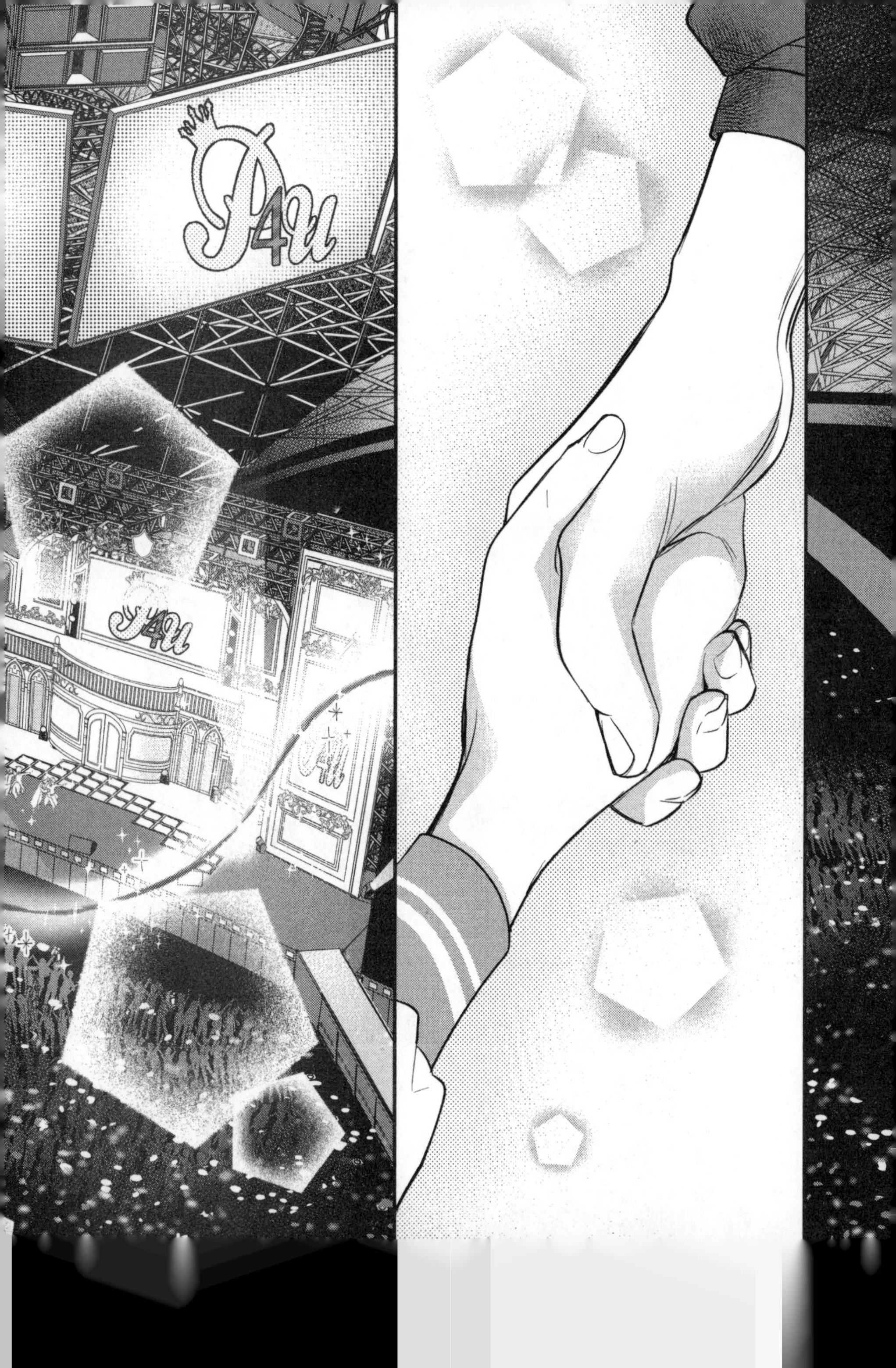
P4U

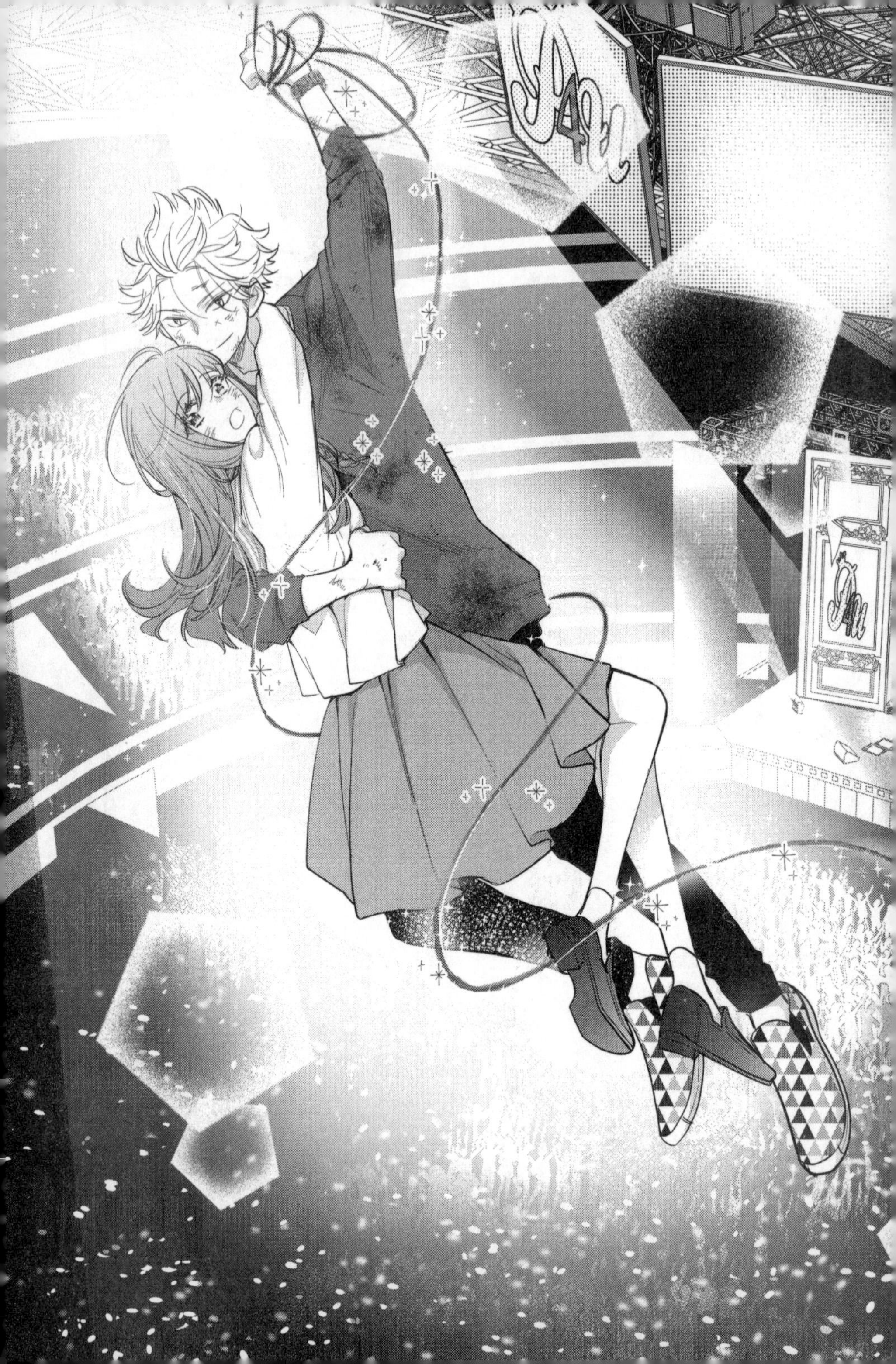

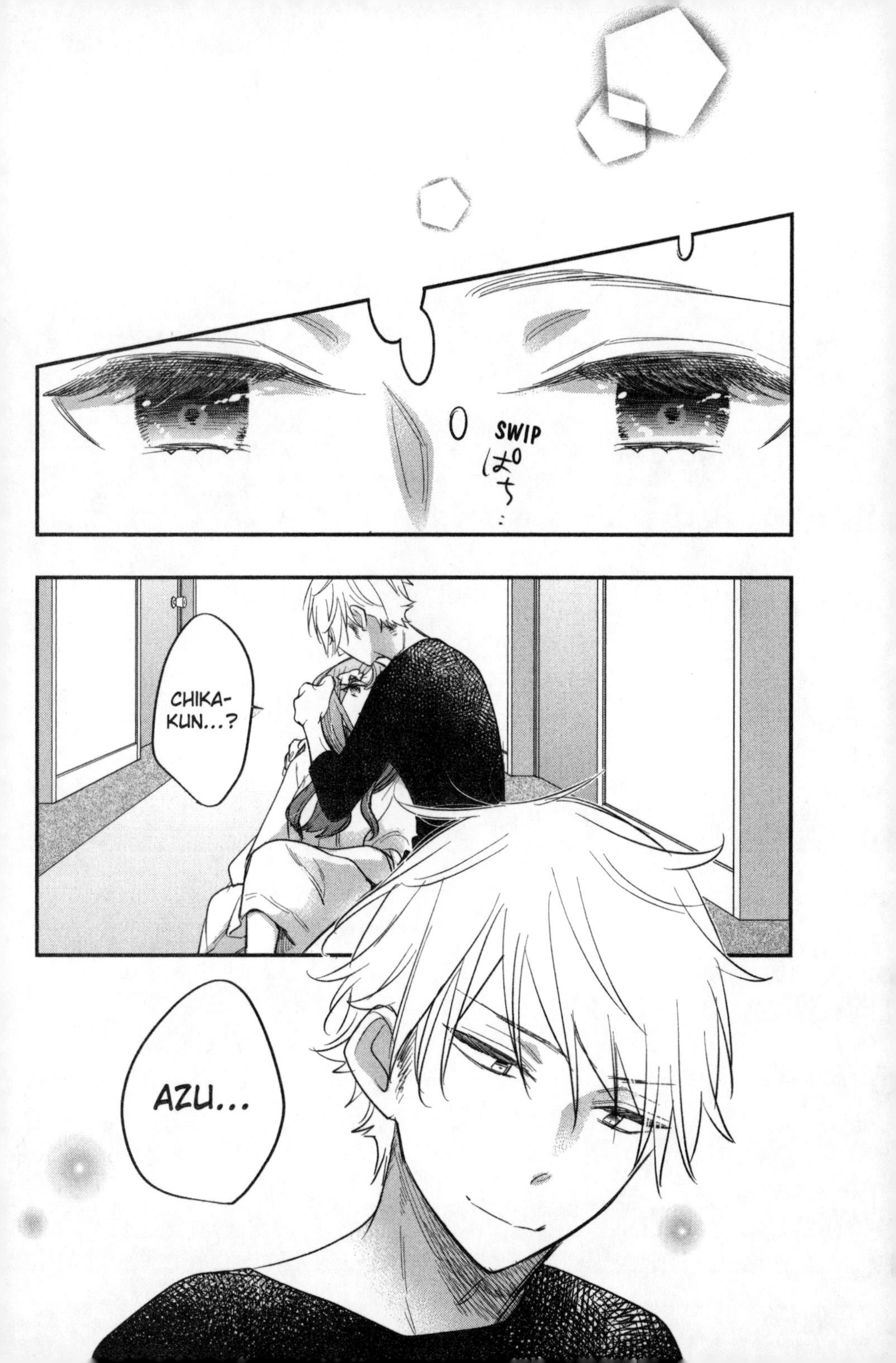
SWIP
ぱち…
CHIKA-KUN...?
AZU...

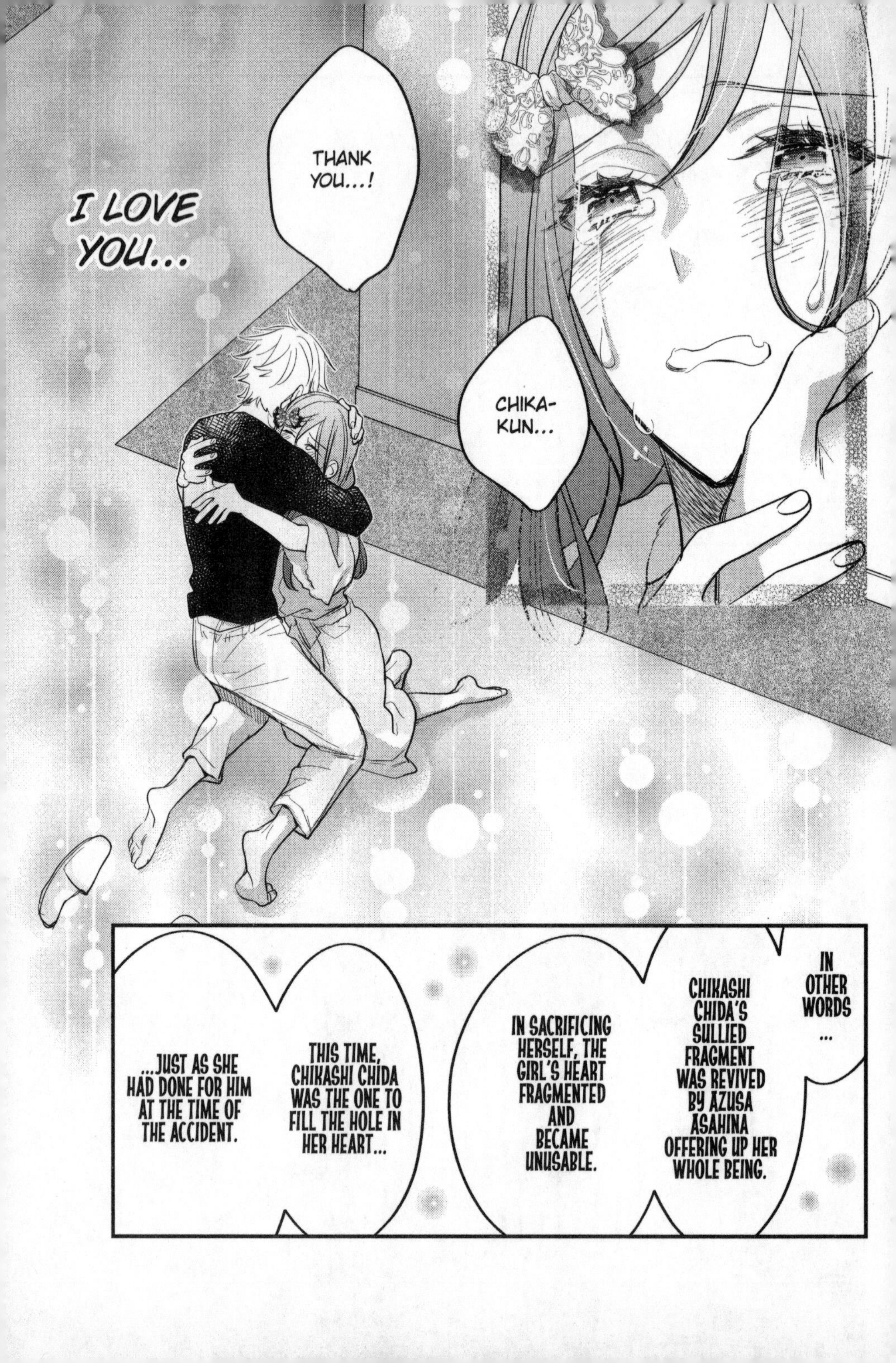

CHIKA-KUN...
THANK YOU...!
I LOVE YOU...
IN OTHER WORDS...
CHIKASHI CHIDA'S SULLIED FRAGMENT WAS REVIVED BY AZUSA ASAHINA OFFERING UP HER WHOLE BEING.
IN SACRIFICING HERSELF, THE GIRL'S HEART FRAGMENTED AND BECAME UNUSABLE.
THIS TIME, CHIKASHI CHIDA WAS THE ONE TO FILL THE HOLE IN HER HEART...
...JUST AS SHE HAD DONE FOR HIM AT THE TIME OF THE ACCIDENT.

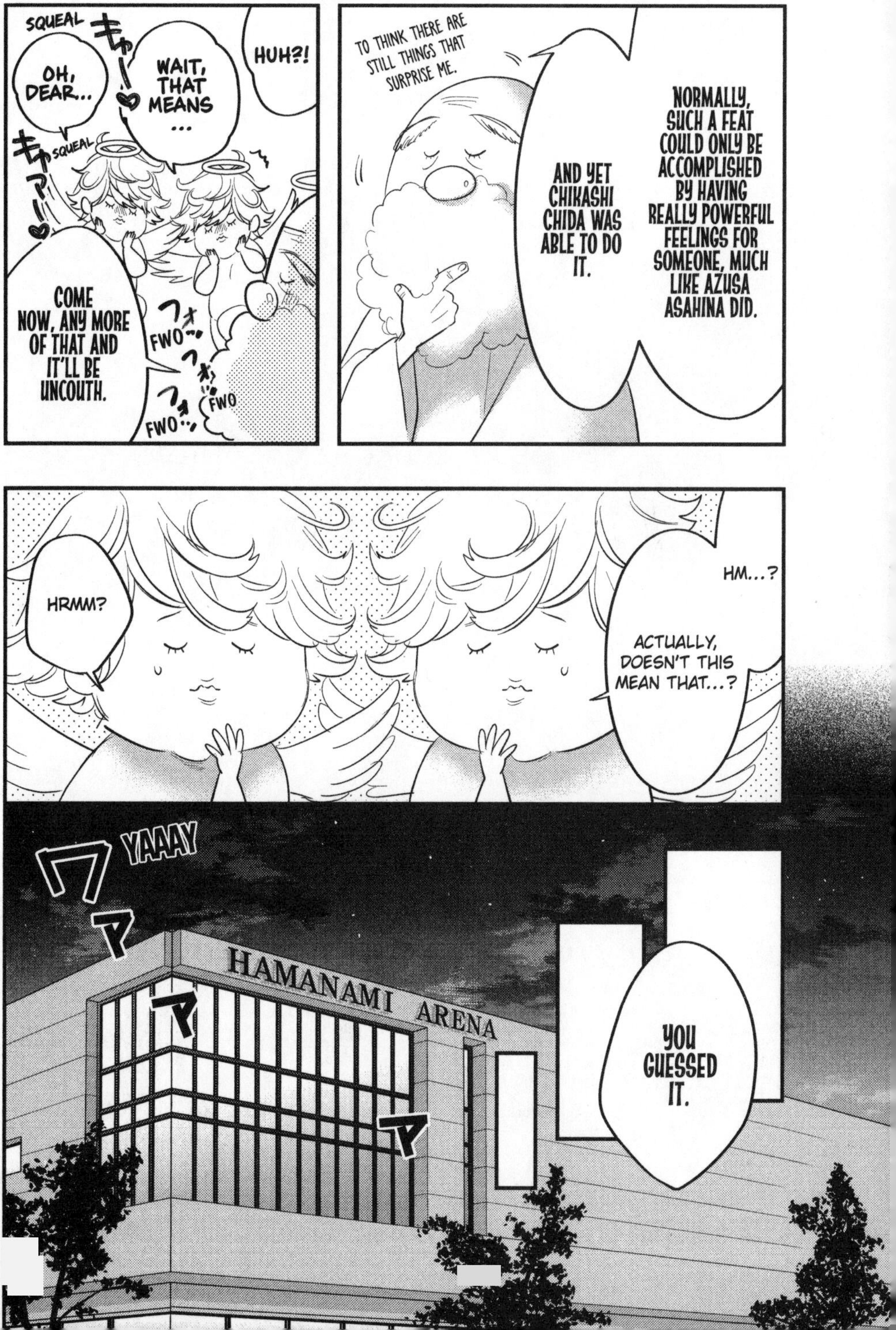
NORMALLY, SUCH A FEAT COULD ONLY BE ACCOMPLISHED BY HAVING REALLY POWERFUL FEELINGS FOR SOMEONE, MUCH LIKE AZUSA ASAHINA DID.
AND YET CHIKASHI CHIDA WAS ABLE TO DO IT.
TO THINK THERE ARE STILL THINGS THAT SURPRISE ME.
HUH?!
WAIT, THAT MEANS...
キャー♥
SQUEAL
OH, DEAR...
キャア!!♥
SQUEAL
COME NOW, ANY MORE OF THAT AND IT'LL BE UNCOUTH.
フォ FWO
フォ FWO
フォ FWO
HM...?
ACTUALLY, DOESN'T THIS MEAN THAT...?
HRMM?
YOU GUESSED IT.
HAMANAMI ARENA
ワアアア
YAAAY

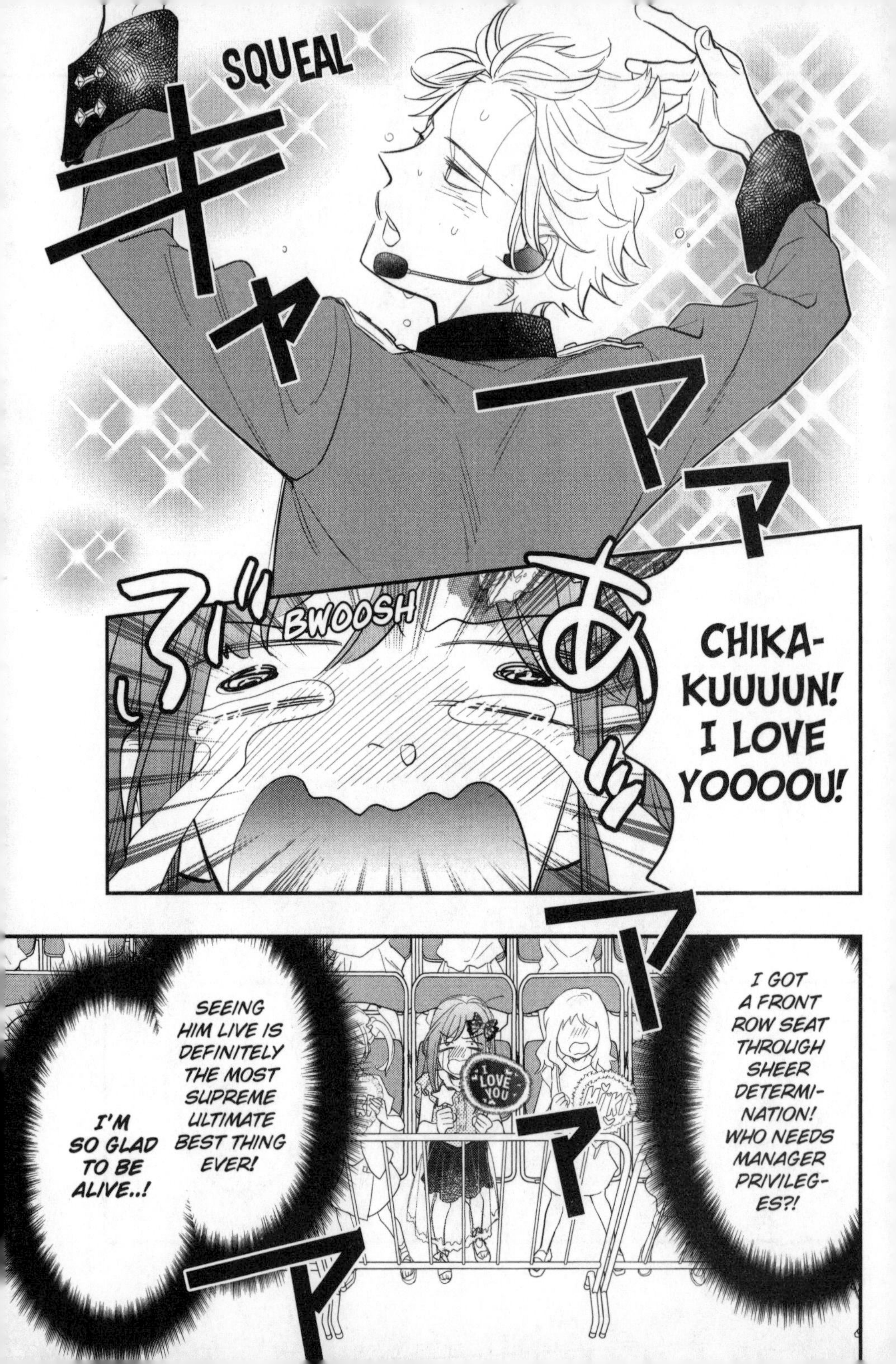
SQUEAL
BWOOSH
CHIKA-KUUUUN! I LOVE YOOOOU!
I GOT A FRONT ROW SEAT THROUGH SHEER DETERMI-NATION! WHO NEEDS MANAGER PRIVILEG-ES?!
SEEING HIM LIVE IS DEFINITELY THE MOST SUPREME ULTIMATE BEST THING EVER!
I'M SO GLAD TO BE ALIVE..!
I LOVE YOU
MIKI

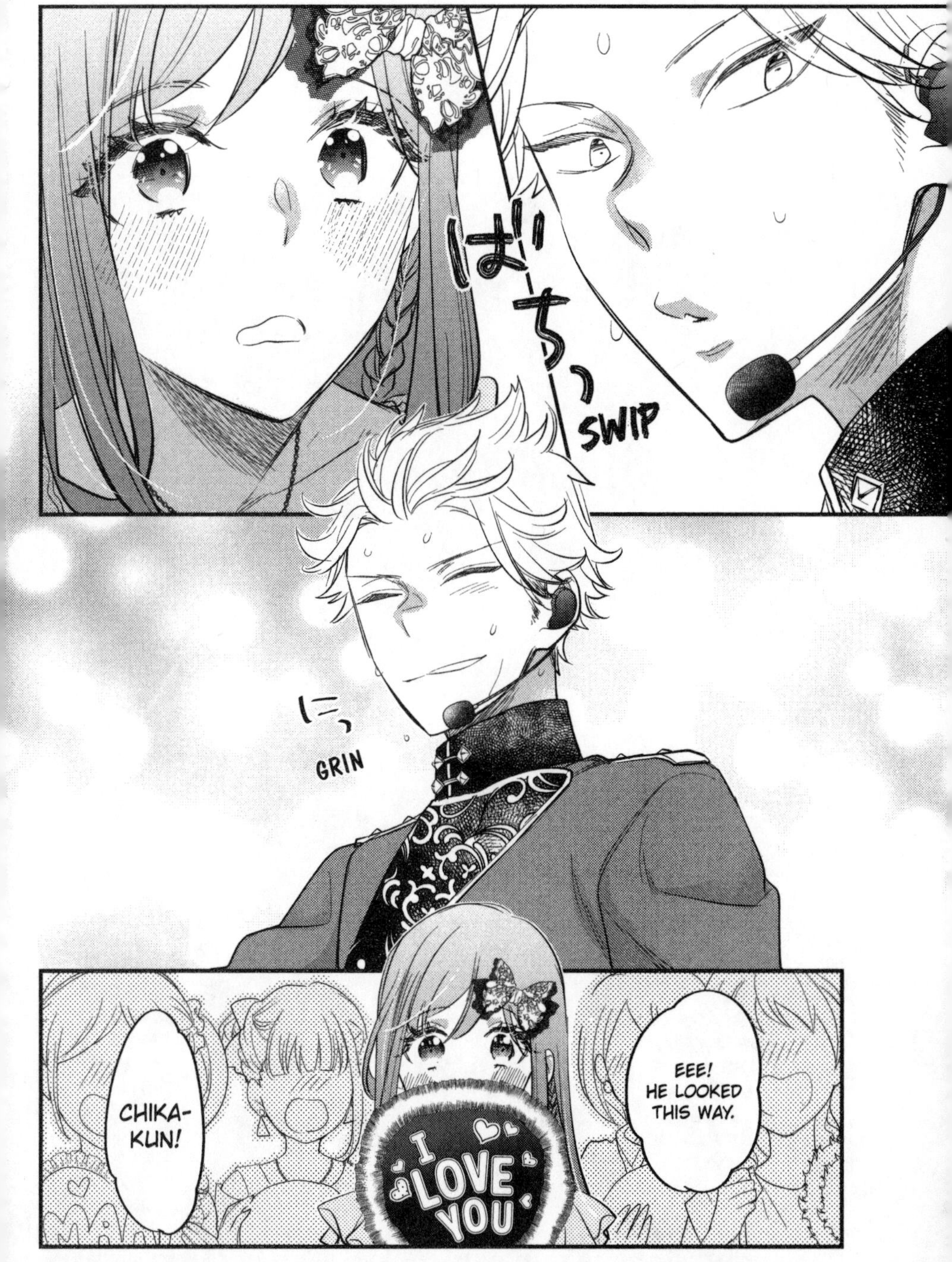
ぱちっ
SWIP
にっ
GRIN
EEE! HE LOOKED THIS WAY.
CHIKA-KUN!
I LOVE YOU

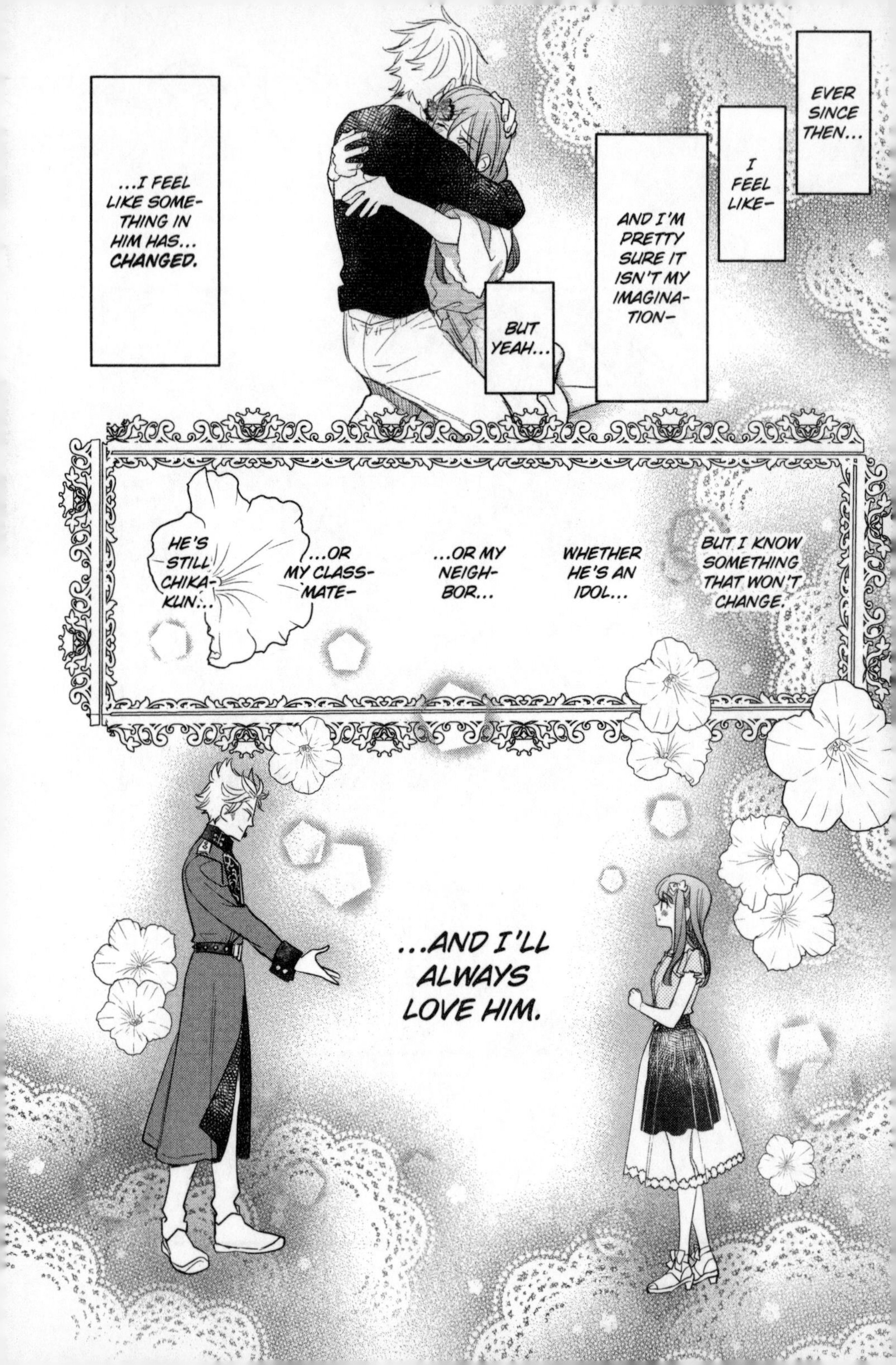
EVER SINCE THEN...
I FEEL LIKE-
AND I'M PRETTY SURE IT ISN'T MY IMAGINATION-
BUT YEAH...
...I FEEL LIKE SOMETHING IN HIM HAS... CHANGED.
BUT I KNOW SOMETHING THAT WON'T CHANGE.
WHETHER HE'S AN IDOL...
...OR MY NEIGHBOR...
...OR MY CLASSMATE-
HE'S STILL CHIKA-KUN...
...AND I'LL ALWAYS LOVE HIM.

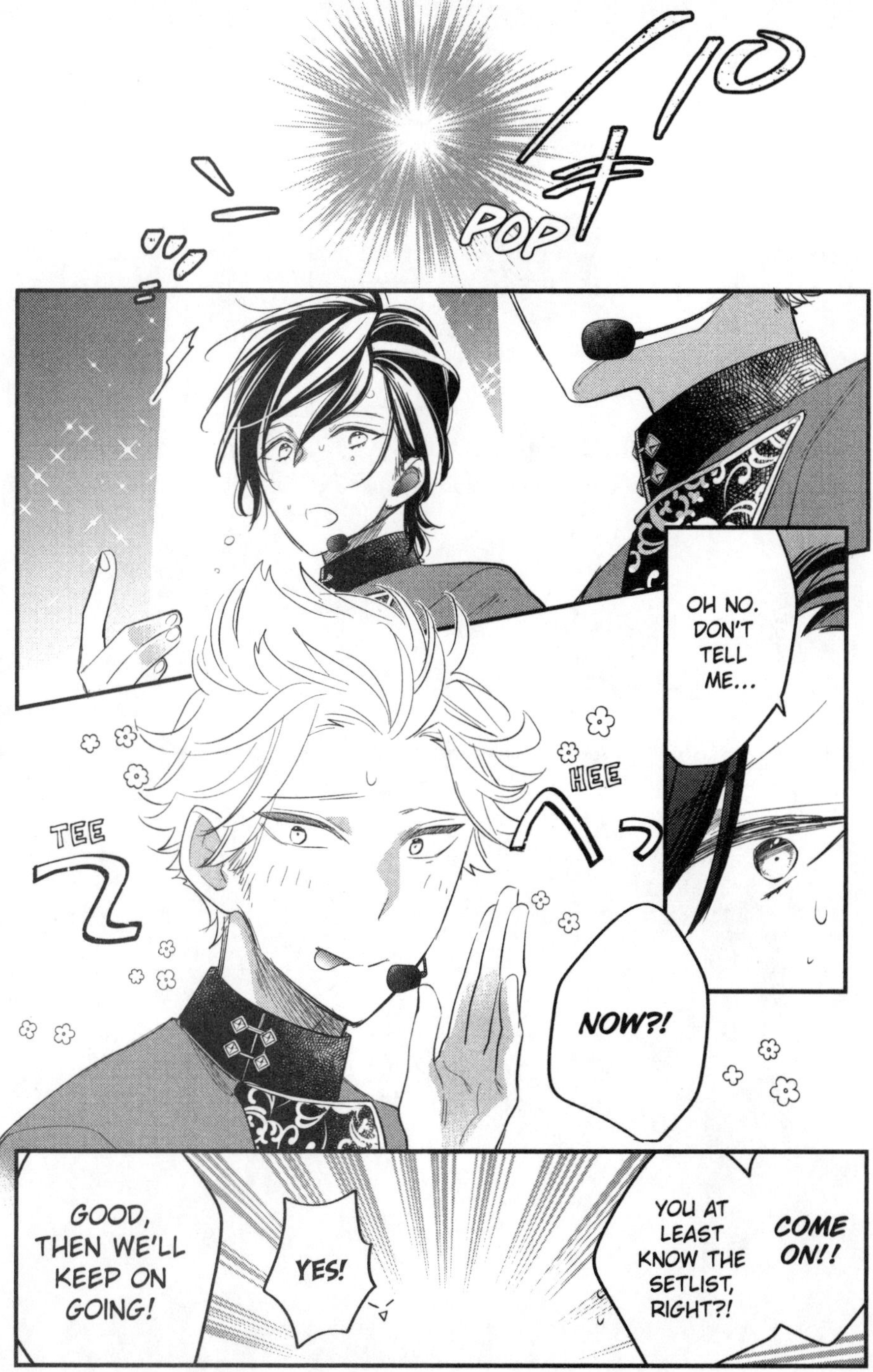
POP
OH NO. DON'T TELL ME...
HEE
TEE
NOW?!
COME ON!!
YOU AT LEAST KNOW THE SETLIST, RIGHT?!
YES!
GOOD, THEN WE'LL KEEP ON GOING!

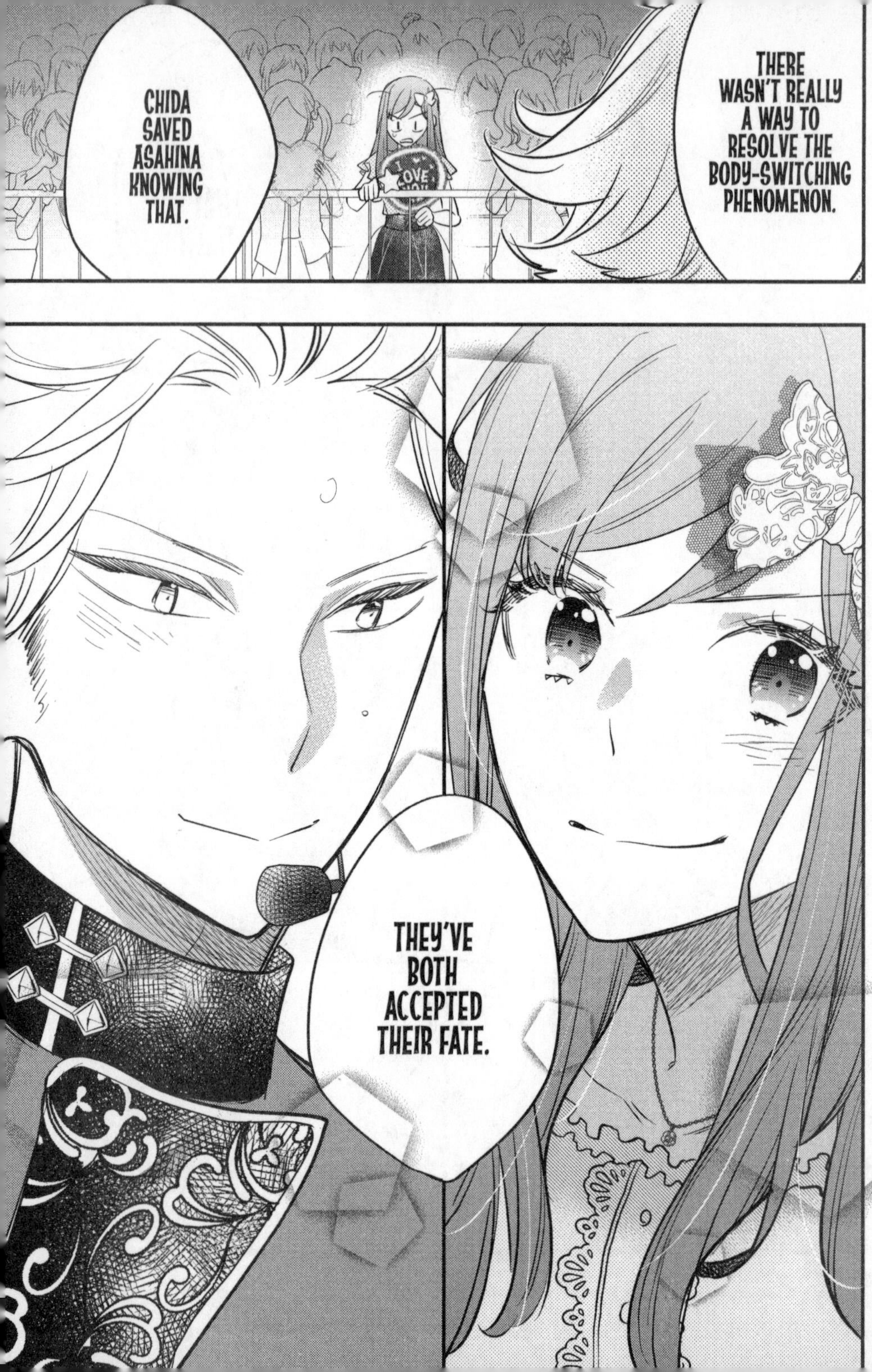
THERE WASN'T REALLY A WAY TO RESOLVE THE BODY-SWITCHING PHENOMENON.
CHIDA SAVED ASAHINA KNOWING THAT.
THEY'VE BOTH ACCEPTED THEIR FATE.

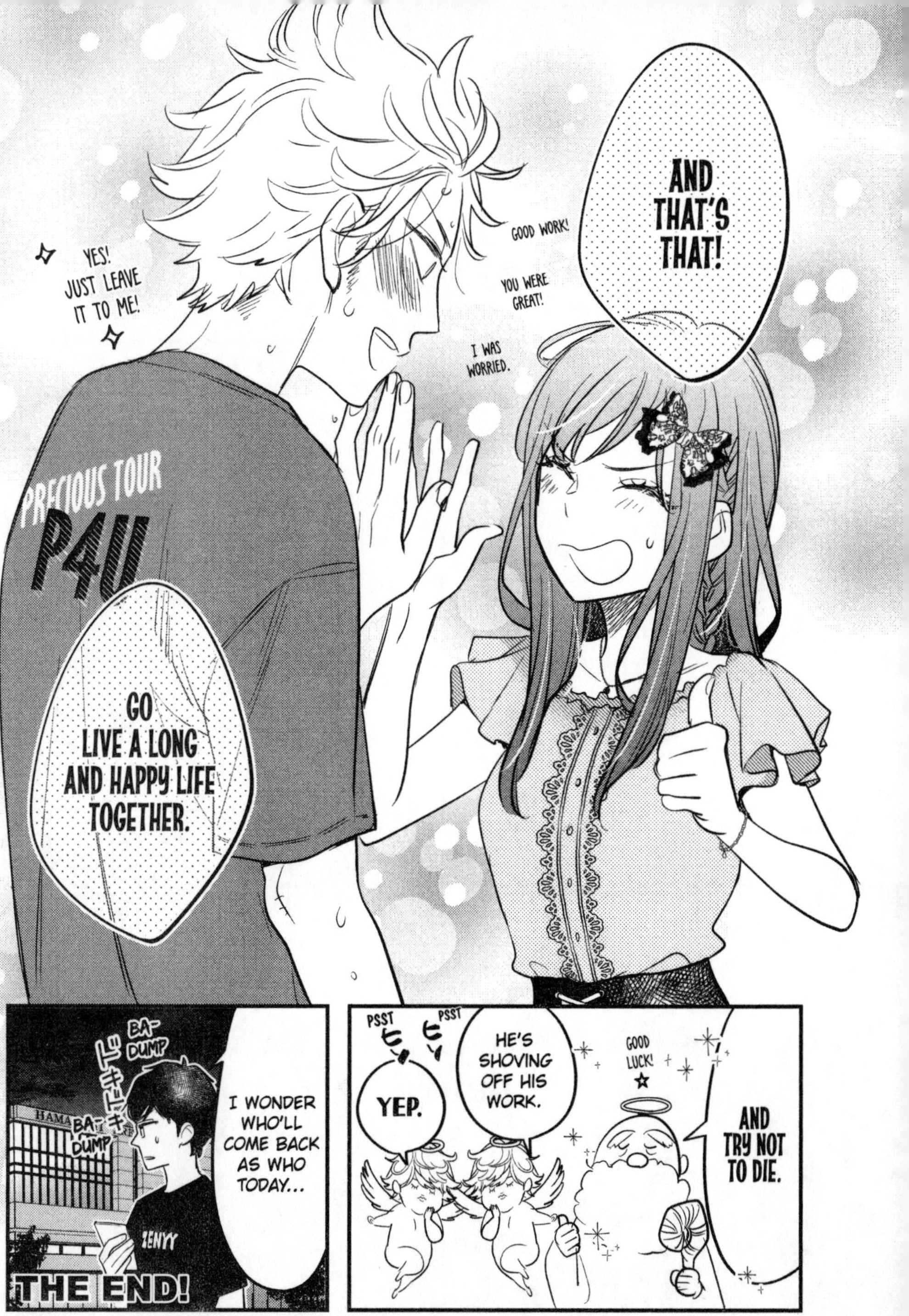
AND THAT'S THAT!
GOOD WORK!
YOU WERE GREAT!
I WAS WORRIED.
YES! JUST LEAVE IT TO ME!
PRECIOUS TOUR P4U
GO LIVE A LONG AND HAPPY LIFE TOGETHER.
AND TRY NOT TO DIE.
GOOD LUCK! ☆
HE'S SHOVING OFF HIS WORK.
PSST ヒソ PSST ヒソ
YEP.
I WONDER WHO'LL COME BACK AS WHO TODAY...
BA-DUMP ドキドキ BA-DUMP
ZENYY
THE END!

STAR⇄CROSSED!!

The End

CROSSED

D!! STAR

TAR CROSS

SSED!! ST

CROSSED

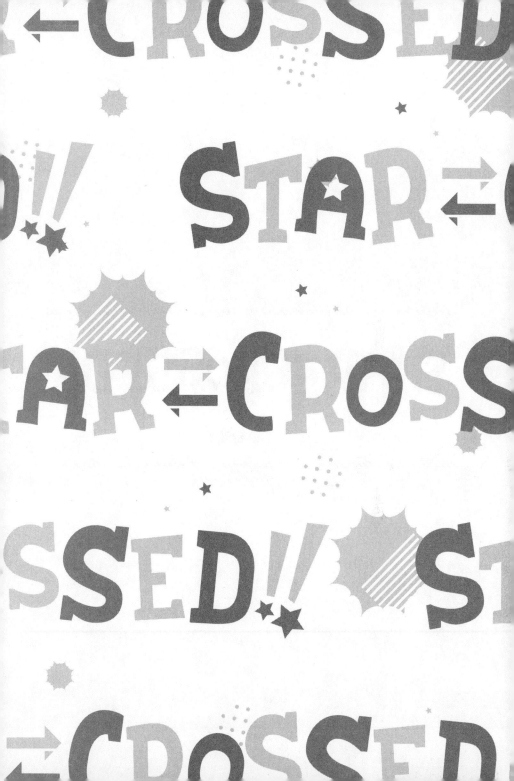

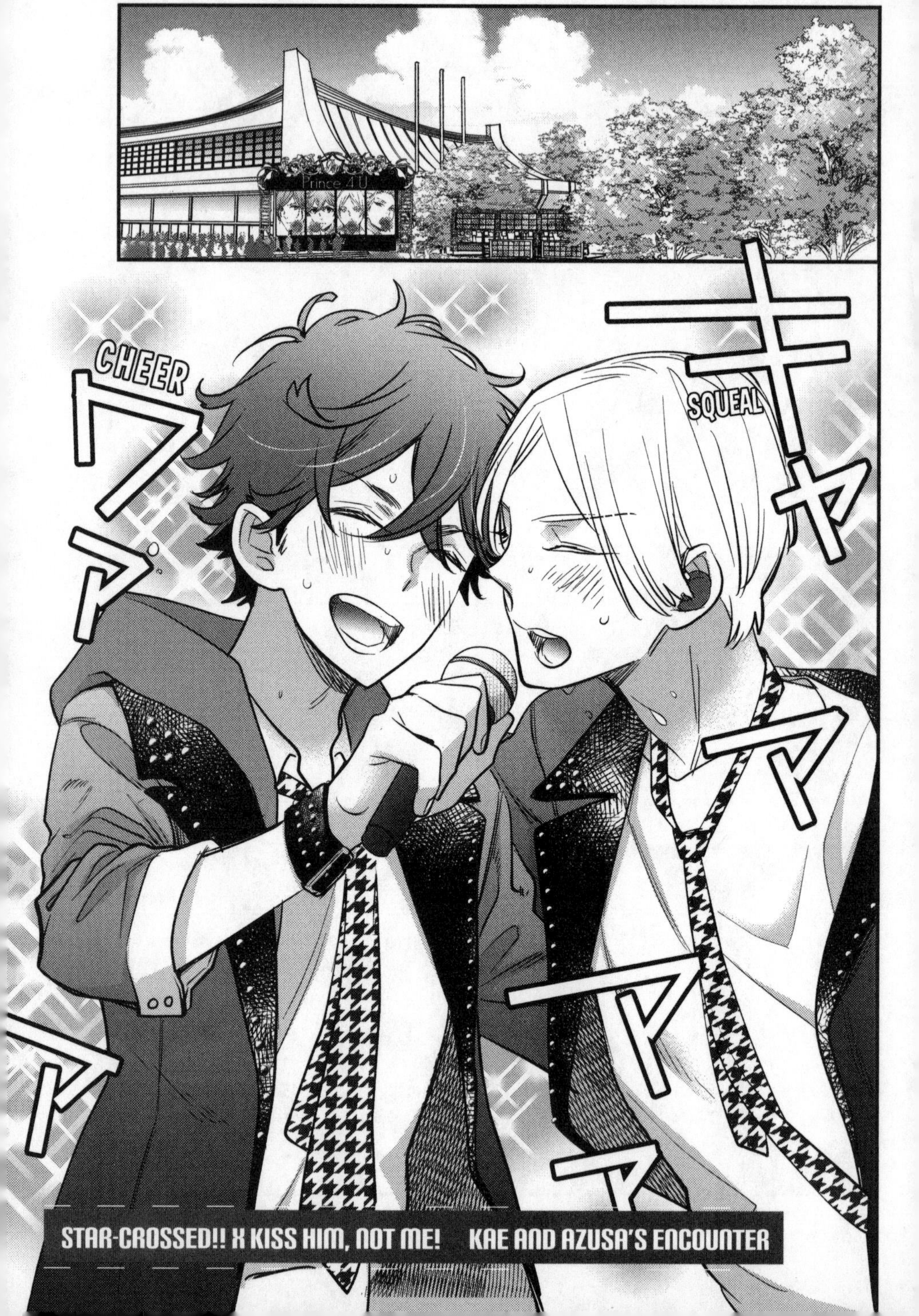
Prince 4 U
キャアアア
SQUEAL
ワアア
CHEER

STAR-CROSSED!! X KISS HIM, NOT ME! KAE AND AZUSA'S ENCOUNTER

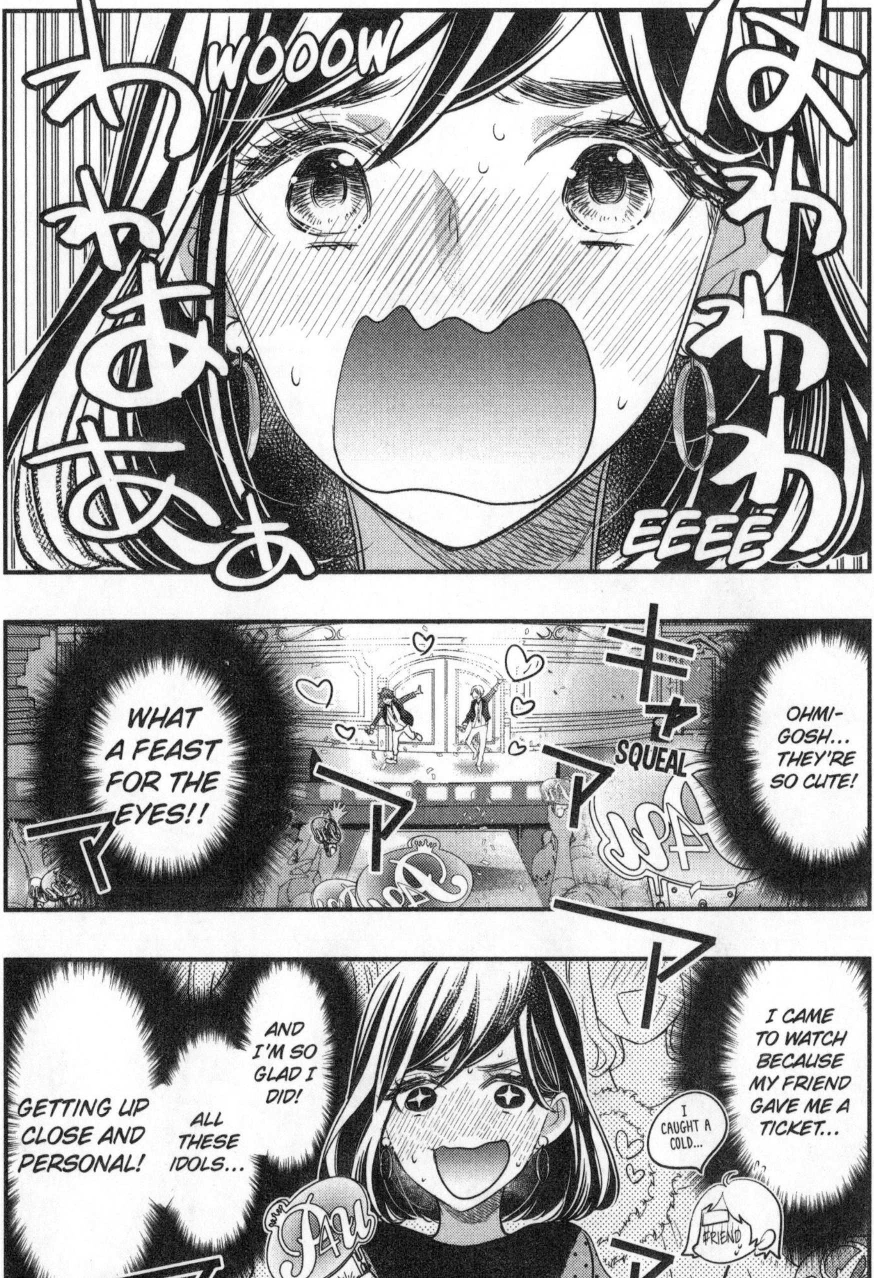
EEEEE
WOOOW
OHMI-GOSH... THEY'RE SO CUTE!
SQUEAL
WHAT A FEAST FOR THE EYES!!
I CAME TO WATCH BECAUSE MY FRIEND GAVE ME A TICKET...
I CAUGHT A COLD...
#FRIEND
AND I'M SO GLAD I DID!
ALL THESE IDOLS...
GETTING UP CLOSE AND PERSONAL!

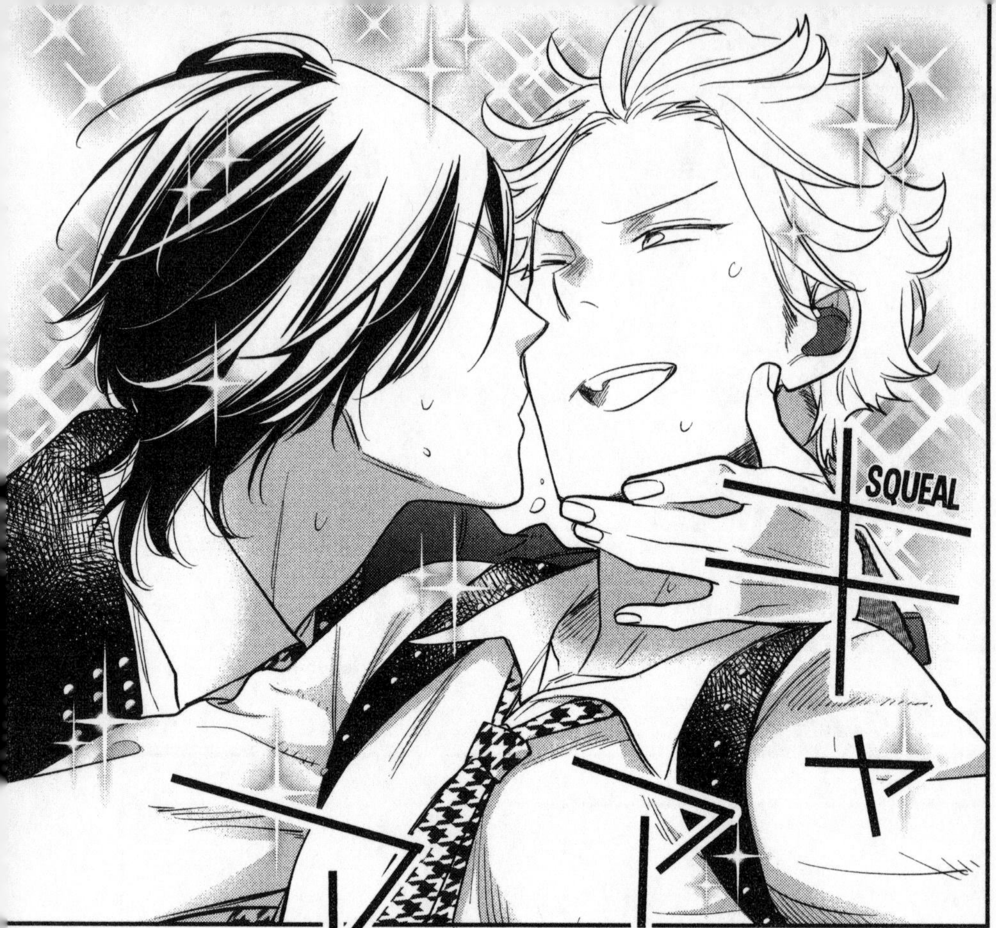
SQUEAL
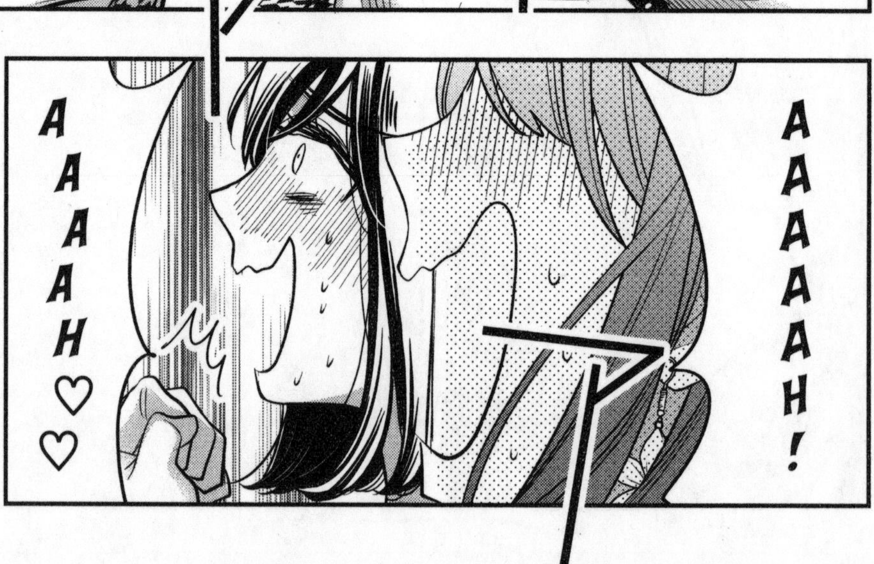
AAAAAAH!
AAAAH♡♡

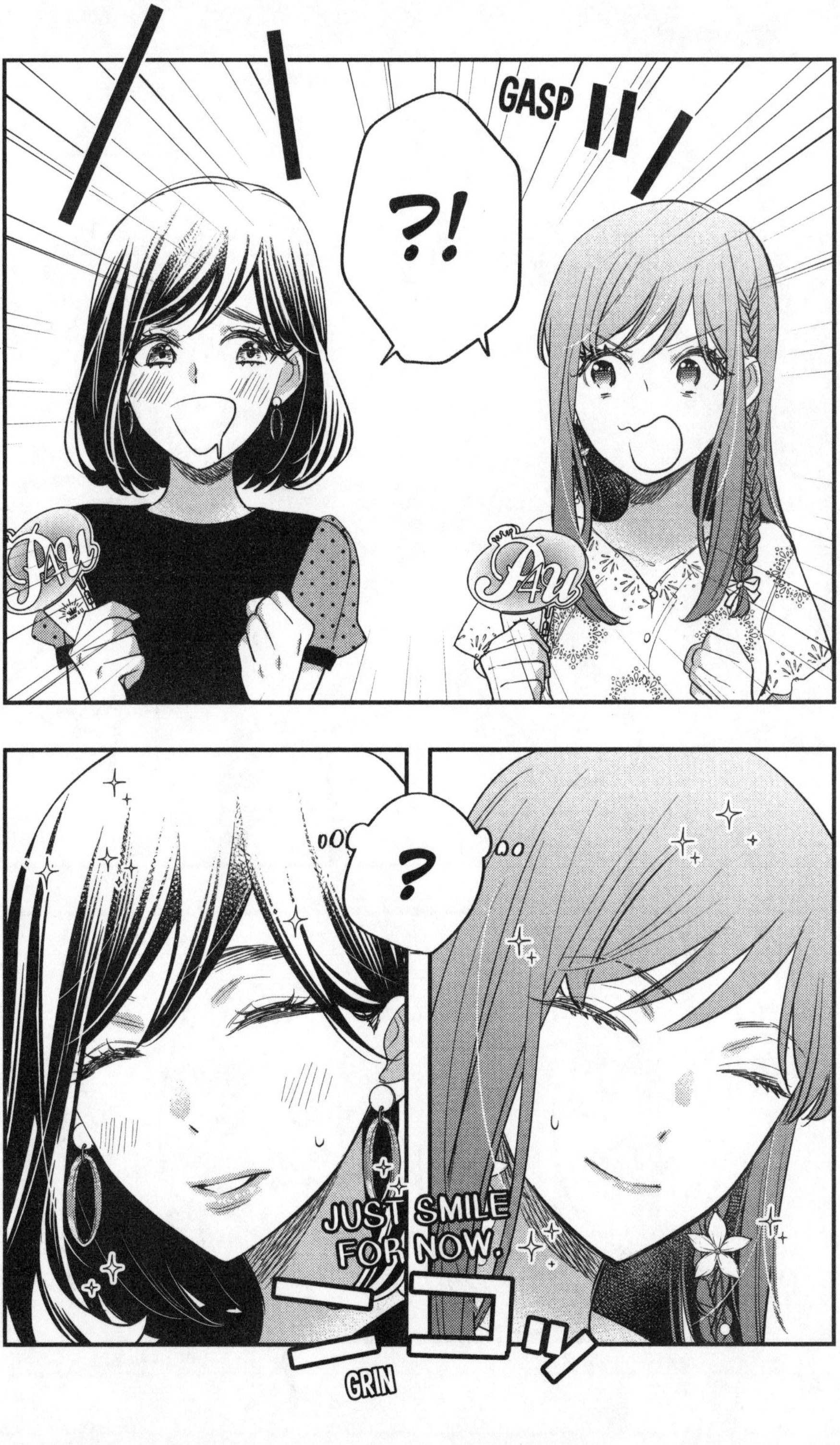
GASP
?!
?
JUST SMILE FOR NOW.
GRIN

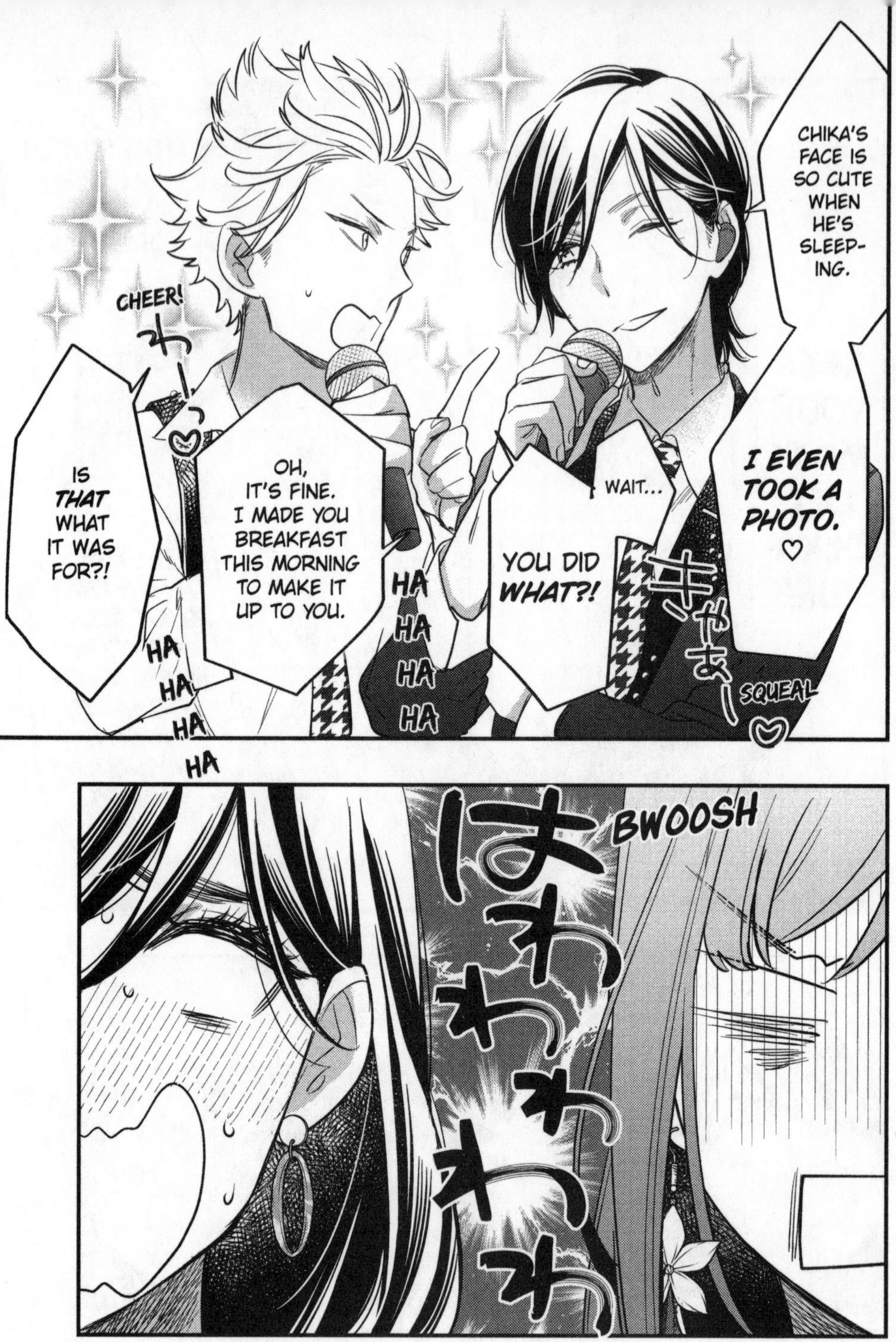
CHIKA'S FACE IS SO CUTE WHEN HE'S SLEEP- ING.
I EVEN TOOK A PHOTO. ♡
SQUEAL ♡
WAIT...
YOU DID WHAT?!
HA HA HA HA
OH, IT'S FINE. I MADE YOU BREAKFAST THIS MORNING TO MAKE IT UP TO YOU.
HA HA HA HA
IS THAT WHAT IT WAS FOR?!
CHEER! ♡
BWOOSH

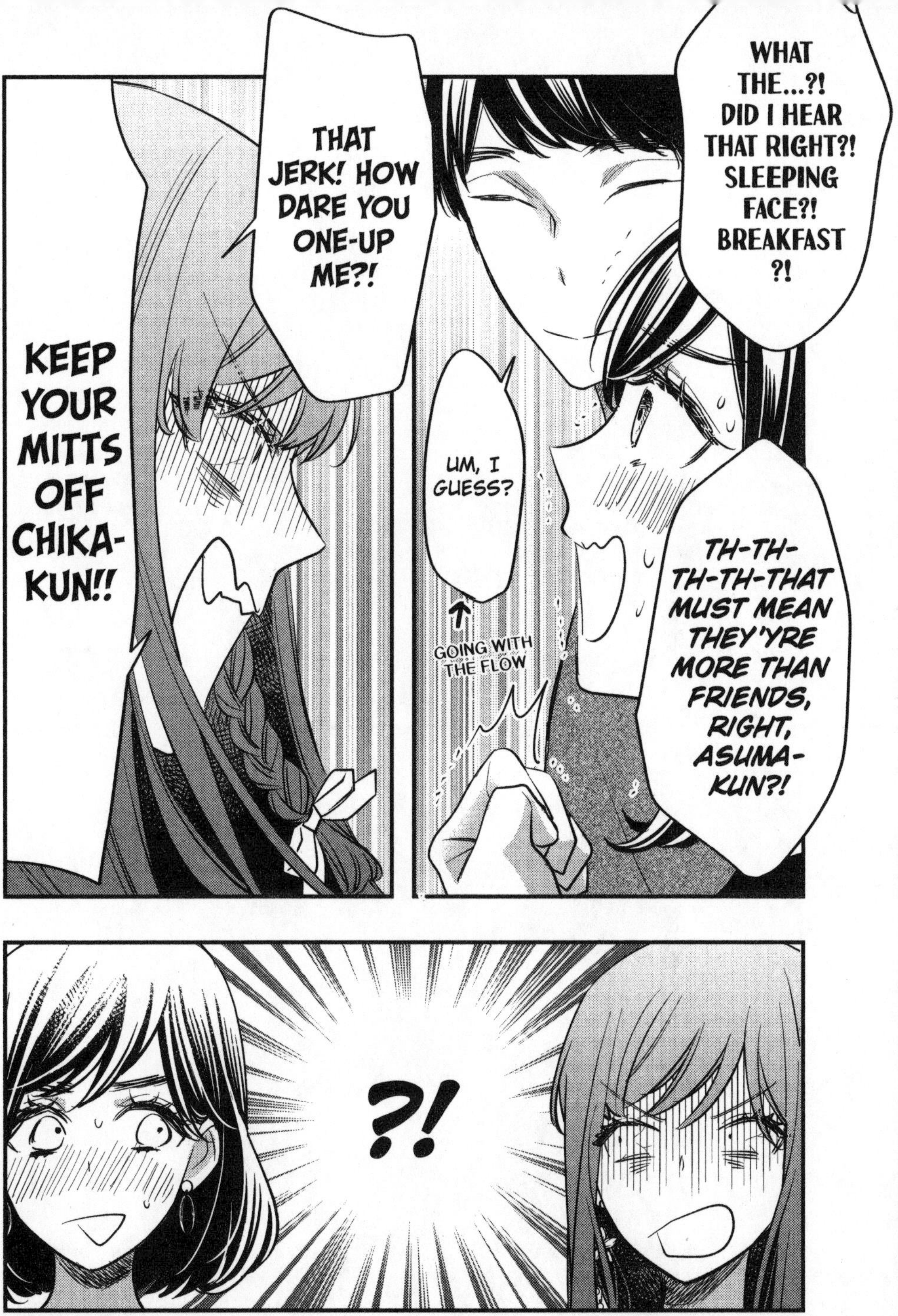
WHAT THE...?! DID I HEAR THAT RIGHT?! SLEEPING FACE?! BREAKFAST ?!
TH-TH-TH-TH-THAT MUST MEAN THEY'RE MORE THAN FRIENDS, RIGHT, ASUMA-KUN?!
UM, I GUESS?
GOING WITH THE FLOW
THAT JERK! HOW DARE YOU ONE-UP ME?!
KEEP YOUR MITTS OFF CHIKA-KUN!!
?!

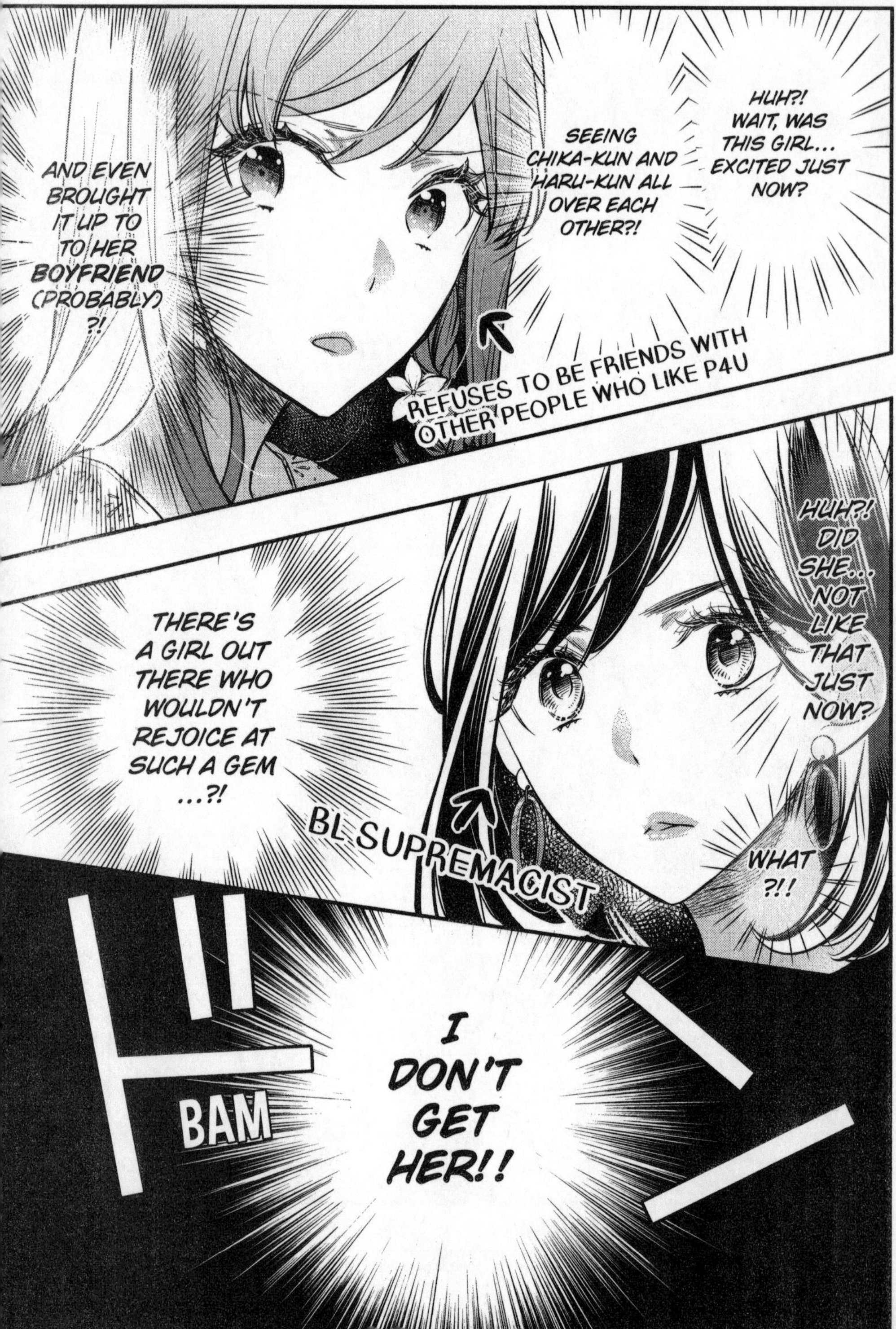
HUH?! WAIT, WAS THIS GIRL... EXCITED JUST NOW?
SEEING CHIKA-KUN AND HARU-KUN ALL OVER EACH OTHER?!
AND EVEN BROUGHT IT UP TO TO HER BOYFRIEND (PROBABLY) ?!
REFUSES TO BE FRIENDS WITH OTHER PEOPLE WHO LIKE P4U
HUH?! DID SHE... NOT LIKE THAT JUST NOW?
WHAT ?!!
THERE'S A GIRL OUT THERE WHO WOULDN'T REJOICE AT SUCH A GEM ...?!
BL SUPREMACIST
I DON'T GET HER!!
BAM

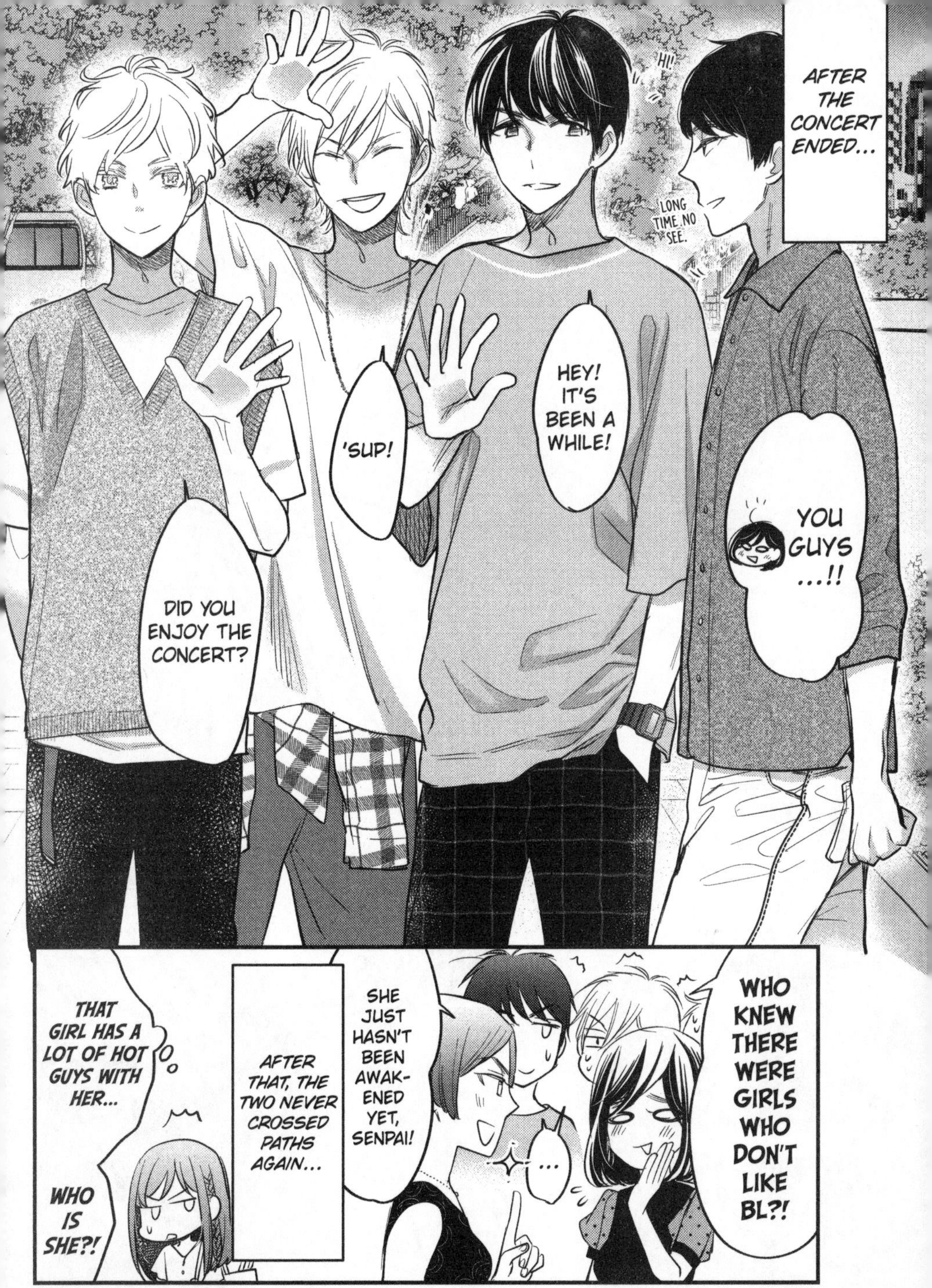
AFTER THE CONCERT ENDED...
LONG TIME, NO SEE.
HI!
YOU GUYS ...!!
HEY! IT'S BEEN A WHILE!
'SUP!
DID YOU ENJOY THE CONCERT?
WHO KNEW THERE WERE GIRLS WHO DON'T LIKE BL?!
...
SHE JUST HASN'T BEEN AWAK-ENED YET, SENPAI!
AFTER THAT, THE TWO NEVER CROSSED PATHS AGAIN...
THAT GIRL HAS A LOT OF HOT GUYS WITH HER...
WHO IS SHE?!

■ORIGINALLY PUBLISHED IN *BESSATSU FRIEND*, JULY 2020.

~END~

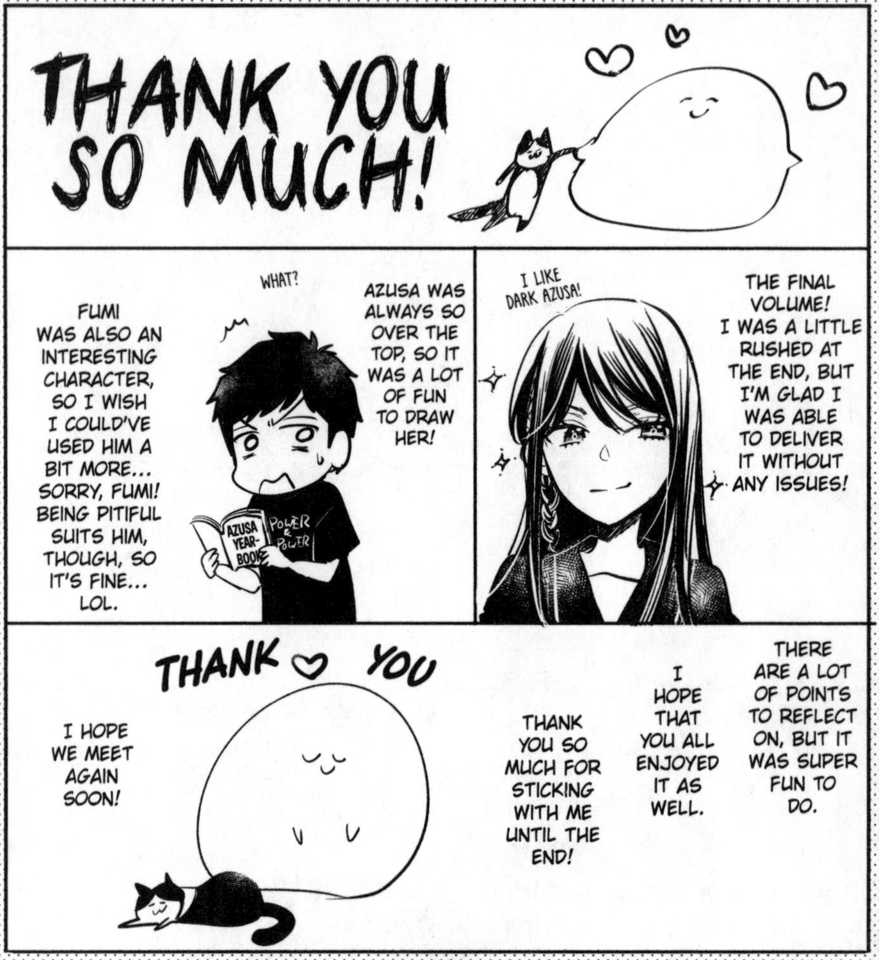
THANK YOU SO MUCH!
THE FINAL VOLUME! I WAS A LITTLE RUSHED AT THE END, BUT I'M GLAD I WAS ABLE TO DELIVER IT WITHOUT ANY ISSUES!
I LIKE DARK AZUSA!
AZUSA WAS ALWAYS SO OVER THE TOP, SO IT WAS A LOT OF FUN TO DRAW HER!
WHAT?
FUMI WAS ALSO AN INTERESTING CHARACTER, SO I WISH I COULD'VE USED HIM A BIT MORE... SORRY, FUMI! BEING PITIFUL SUITS HIM, THOUGH, SO IT'S FINE... LOL.
AZUSA YEAR-BOOK
POWER & POWER
THANK ♡ YOU
THERE ARE A LOT OF POINTS TO REFLECT ON, BUT IT WAS SUPER FUN TO DO.
I HOPE THAT YOU ALL ENJOYED IT AS WELL.
THANK YOU SO MUCH FOR STICKING WITH ME UNTIL THE END!
I HOPE WE MEET AGAIN SOON!

THANKS!

SPECIAL ADVISOR
EIKI EIKI-SENSEI

ASSIST
UZUKI-SAN, AKI-SAN, MIKAN-SAN, SHIROE-SAN

COVER DESIGNER
HASE PRO-SAMA

SUPERVISING EDITOR
SATO-SAN

EVERYONE ELSE WHO WAS INVOLVED, AND **YOU!**♡

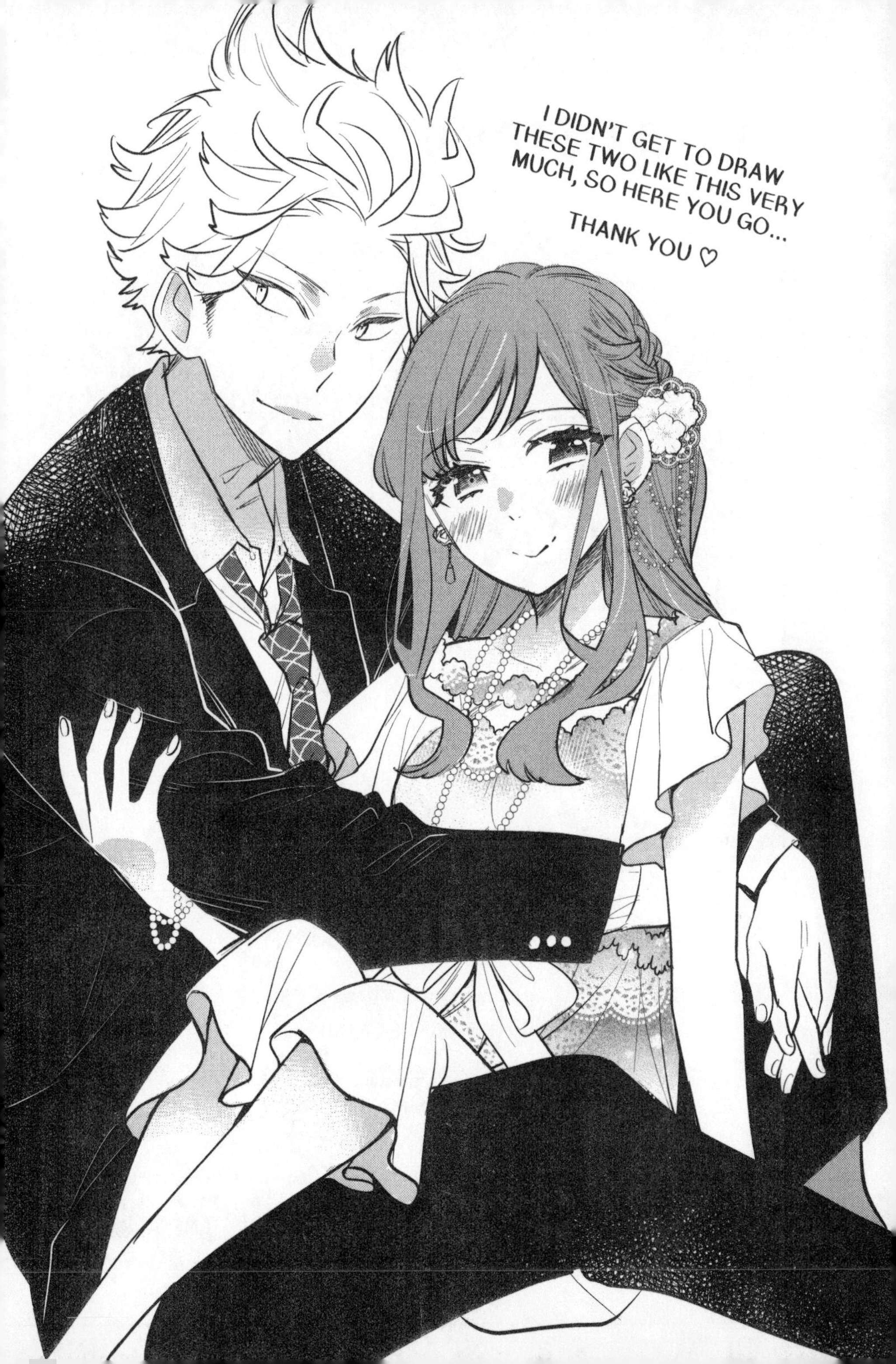
I DIDN'T GET TO DRAW THESE TWO LIKE THIS VERY MUCH, SO HERE YOU GO...
THANK YOU ♡

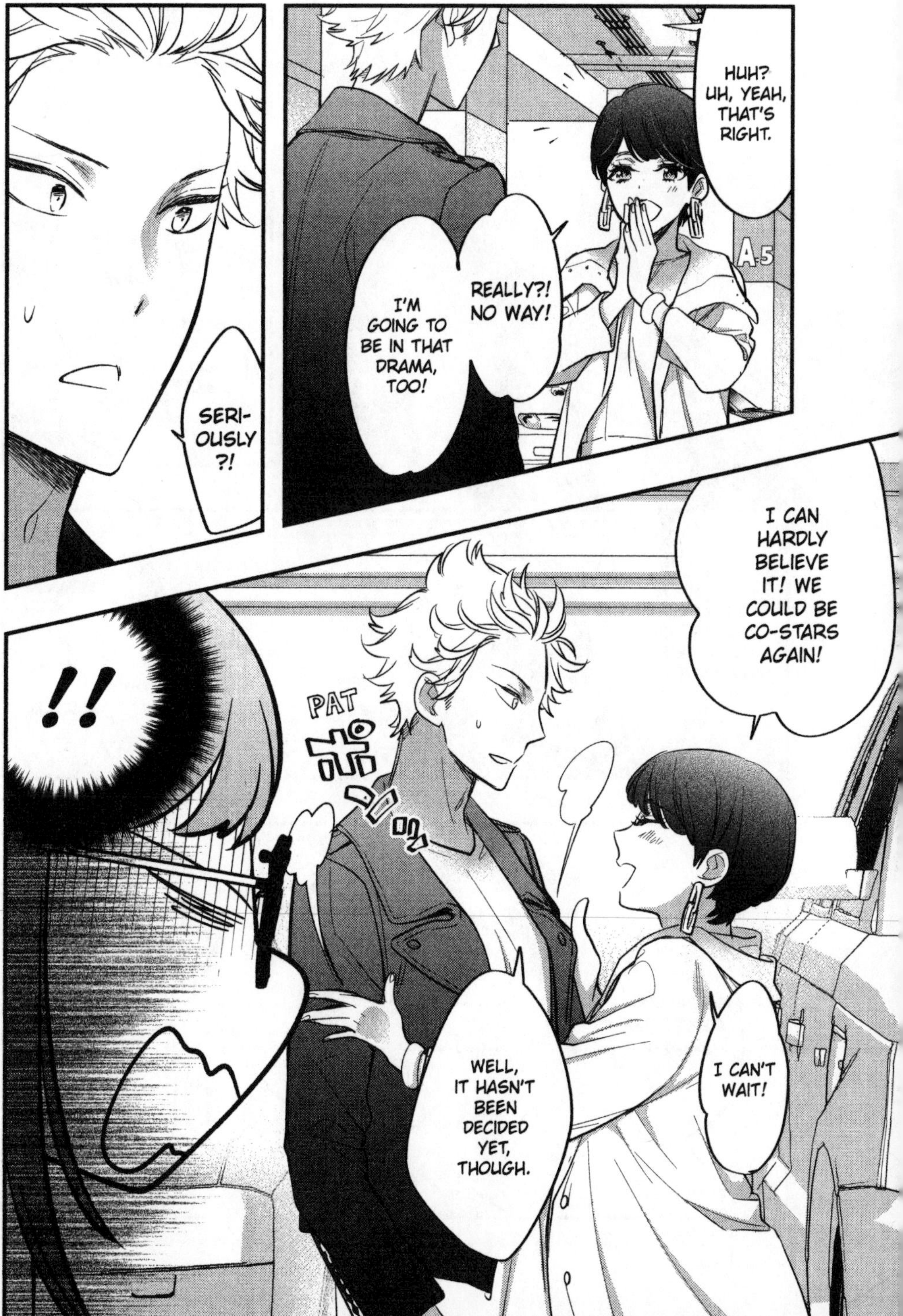
HUH? UH, YEAH, THAT'S RIGHT.
REALLY?! NO WAY!
I'M GOING TO BE IN THAT DRAMA, TOO!
SERI-OUSLY?!
I CAN HARDLY BELIEVE IT! WE COULD BE CO-STARS AGAIN!
PAT
!!
I CAN'T WAIT!
WELL, IT HASN'T BEEN DECIDED YET, THOUGH.

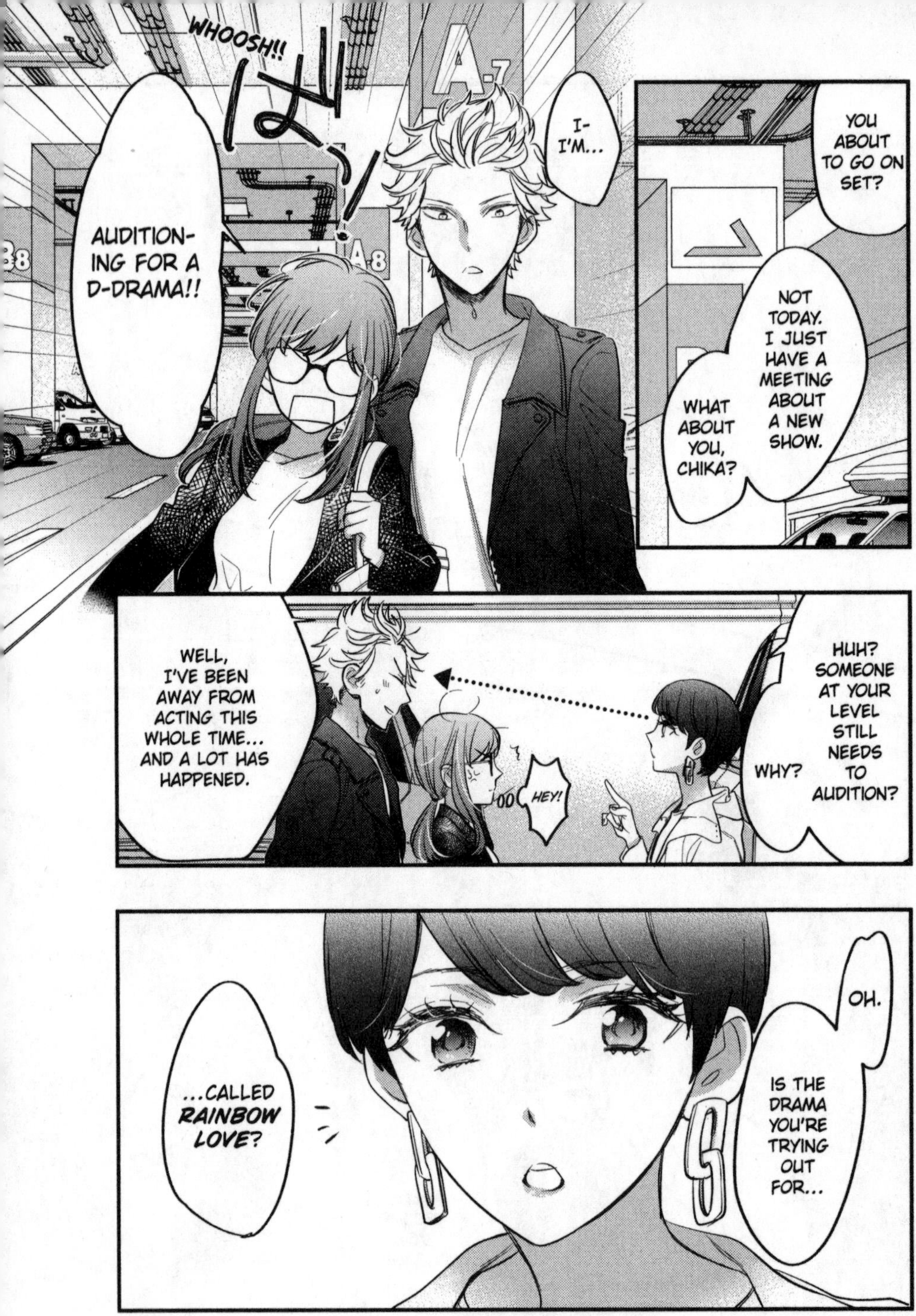
YOU ABOUT TO GO ON SET?
NOT TODAY. I JUST HAVE A MEETING ABOUT A NEW SHOW.
WHAT ABOUT YOU, CHIKA?
I- I'M...
WHOOSH!!
AUDITION-ING FOR A D-DRAMA!!
HUH? SOMEONE AT YOUR LEVEL STILL NEEDS TO AUDITION?
WHY?
HEY!
WELL, I'VE BEEN AWAY FROM ACTING THIS WHOLE TIME... AND A LOT HAS HAPPENED.
OH.
IS THE DRAMA YOU'RE TRYING OUT FOR...
...CALLED *RAINBOW LOVE*?

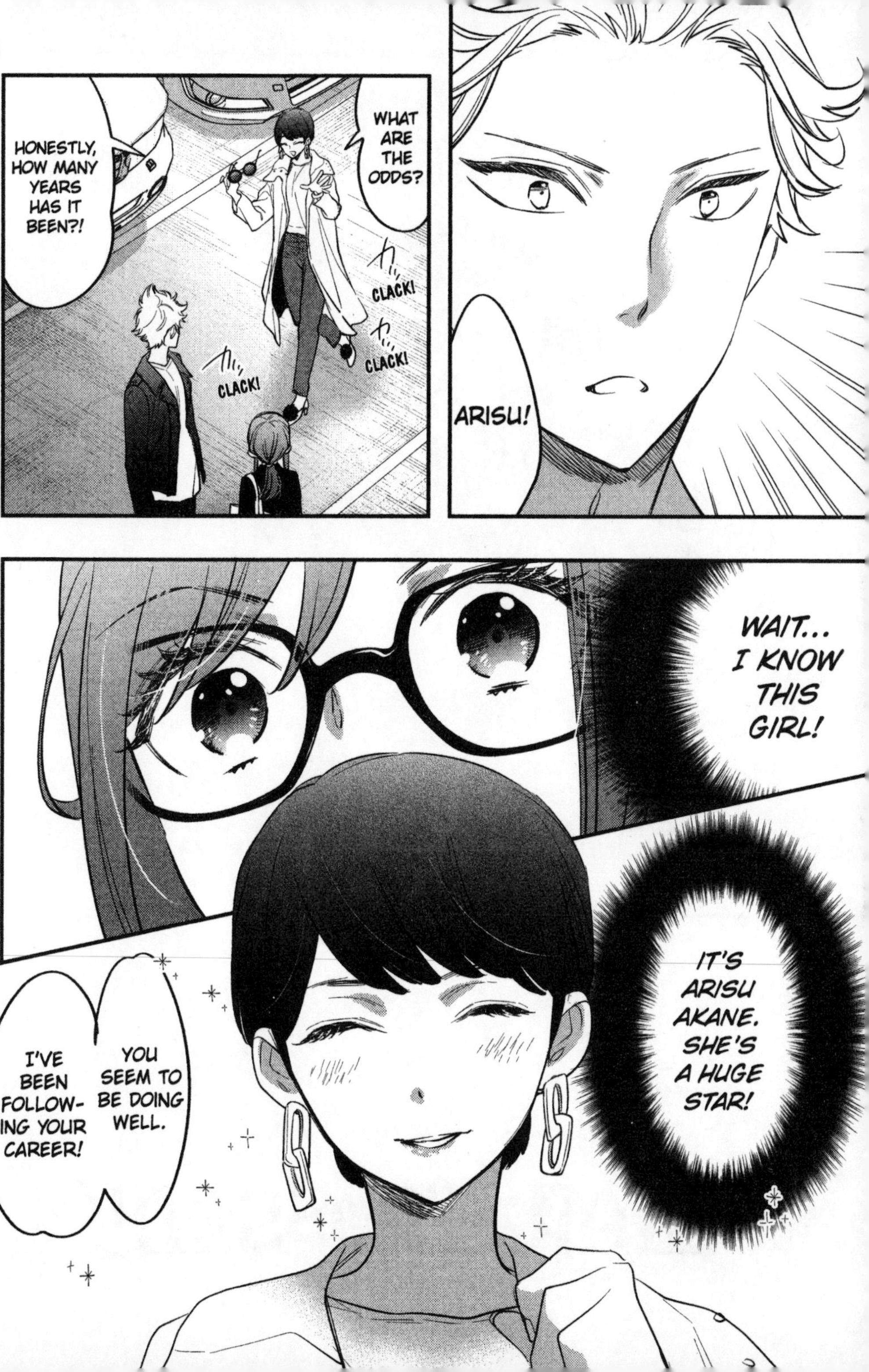
ARISU!
WHAT ARE THE ODDS?
HONESTLY, HOW MANY YEARS HAS IT BEEN?!
CLACK!
CLACK!
CLACK!
WAIT... I KNOW THIS GIRL!
IT'S ARISU AKANE. SHE'S A HUGE STAR!
YOU SEEM TO BE DOING WELL.
I'VE BEEN FOLLOW-ING YOUR CAREER!

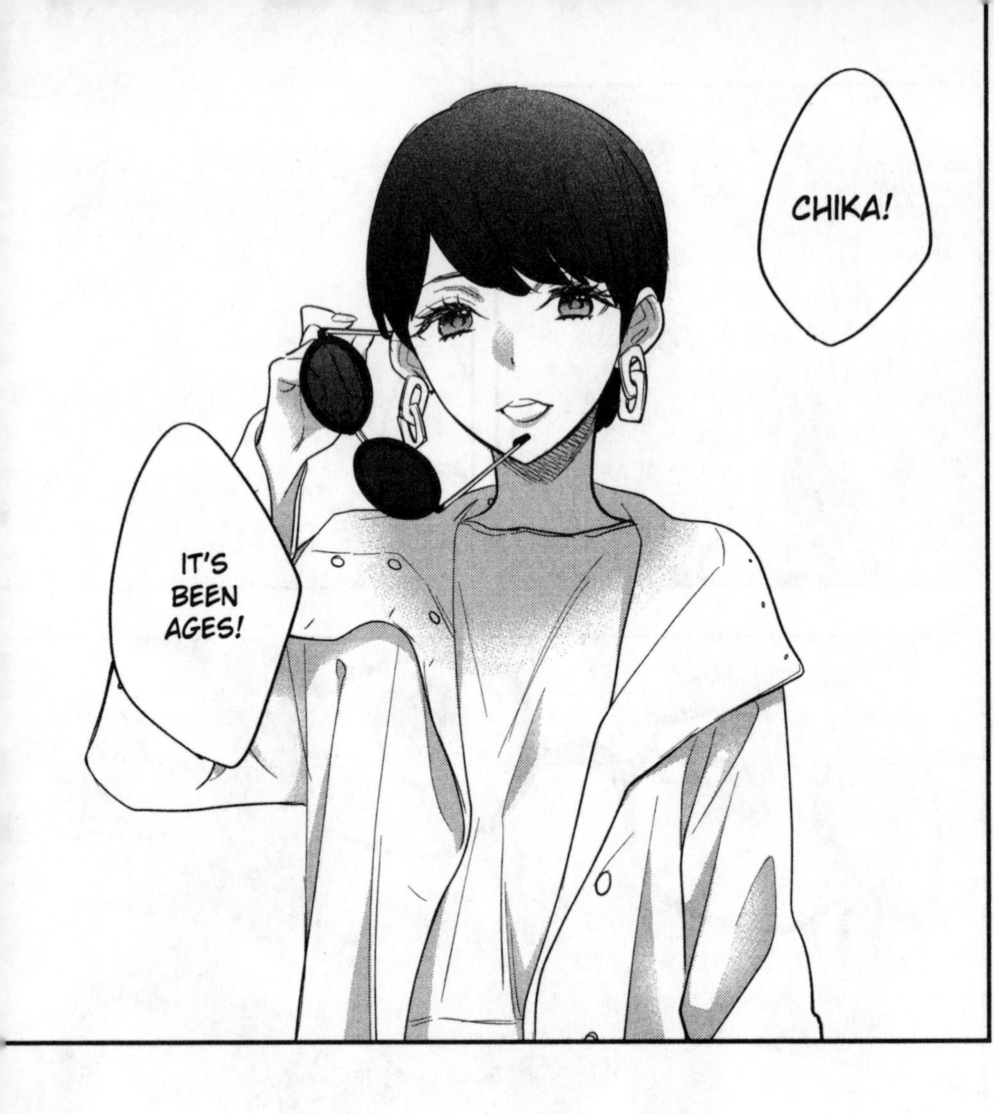
CHIKA!
IT'S BEEN AGES!

STAR⇄CROSSED!!

CROSSED

D!! STAR

TAR CROSS

OSSED!! ST

CROSSED

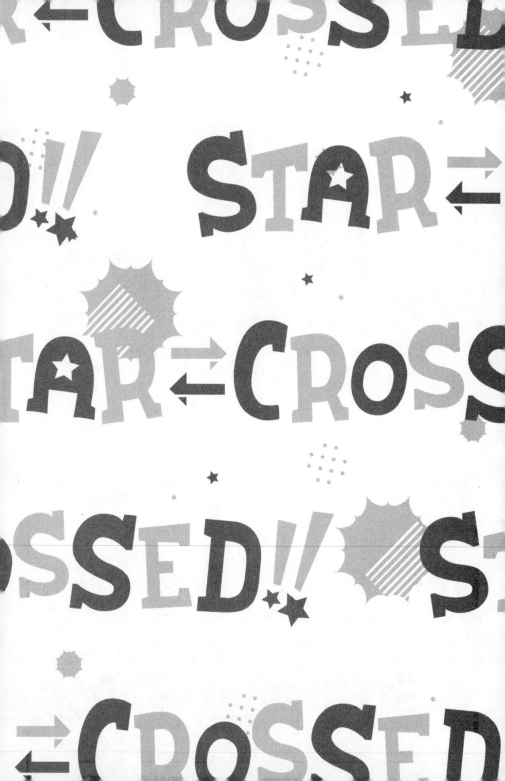

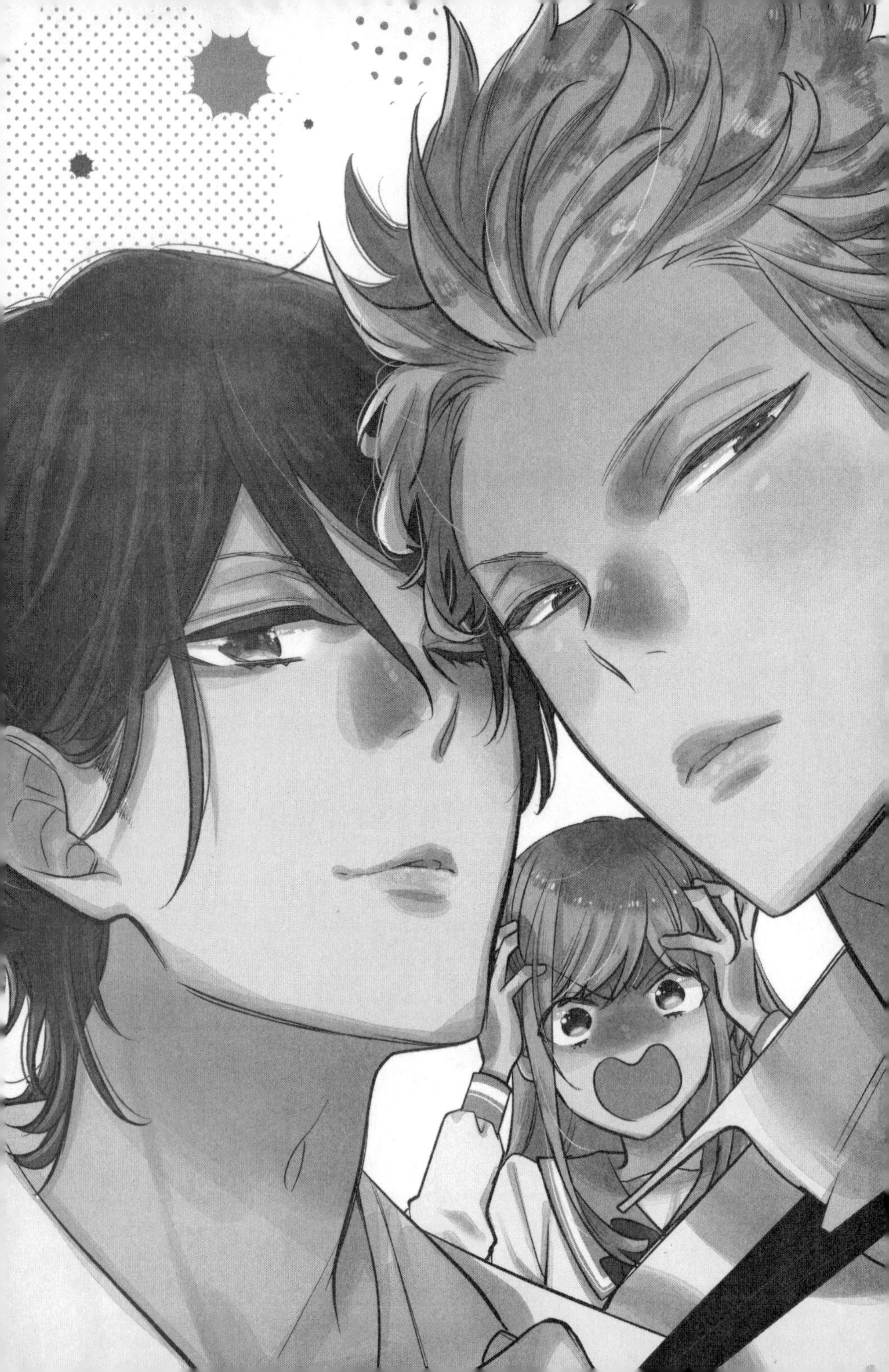

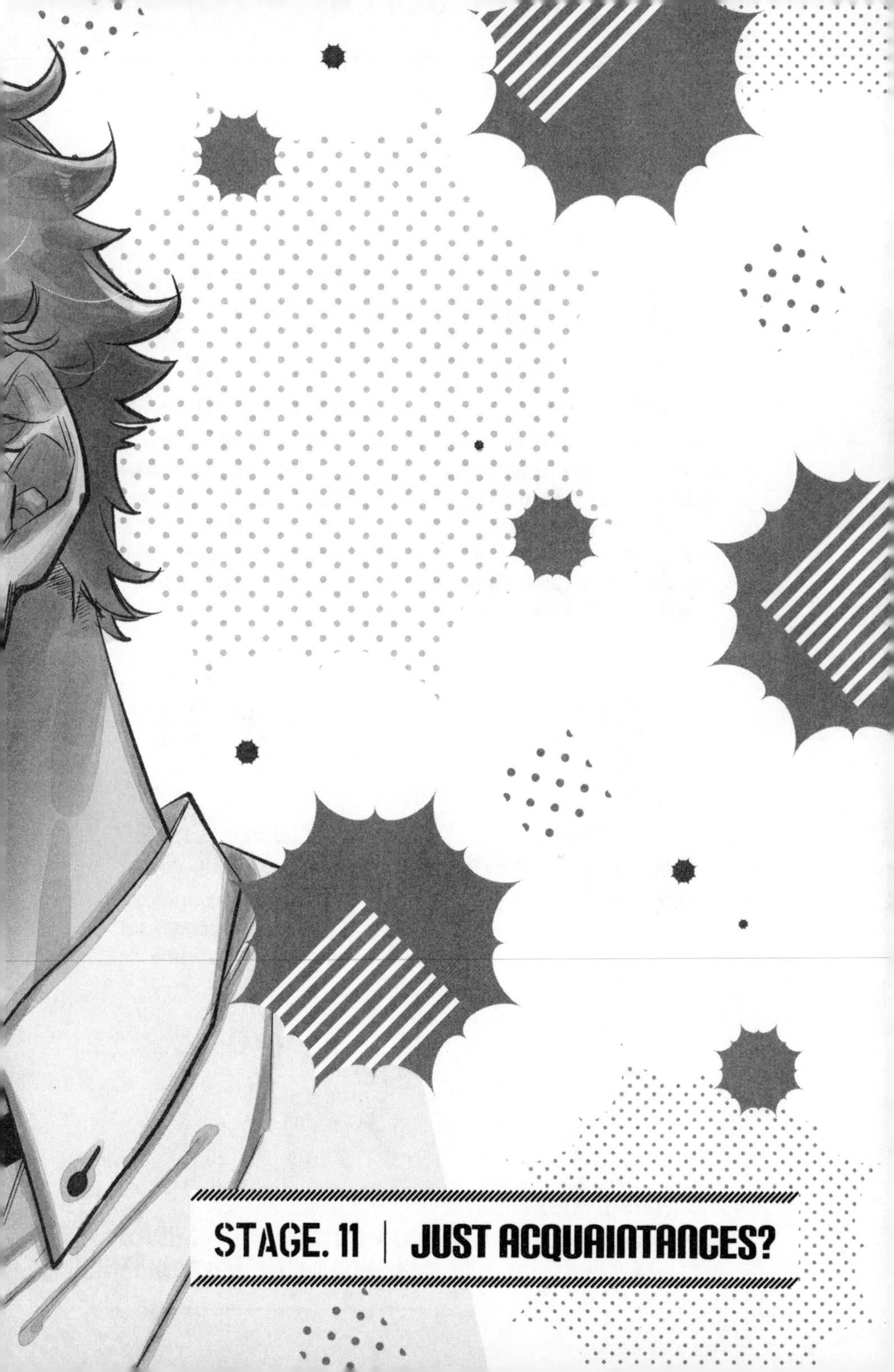

STAGE. 11 | JUST ACQUAINTANCES?

CHARACTER

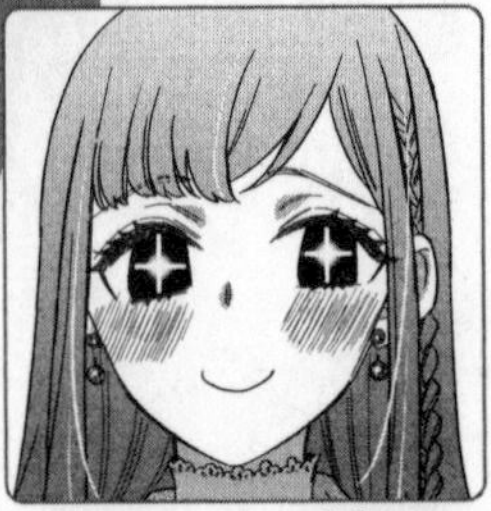

Azusa Asahina

A picture-perfect high school girl—with the looks, grades, and student council president title to match. In reality, she's a rabid fangirl who's crafted an elaborate image to be a worthy superfan of her favorite idol, Chikashi Chida.

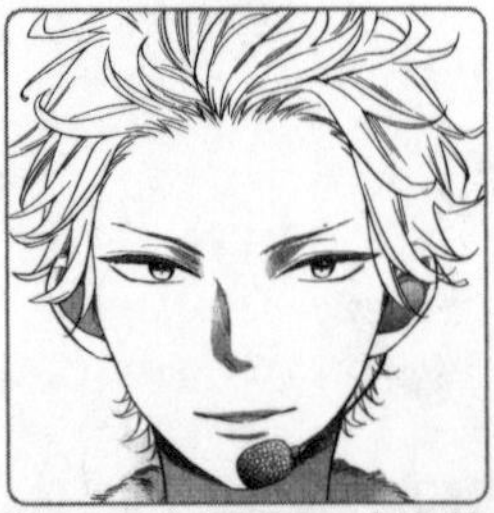

Chikashi Chida (Chika)

A member of the four-man idol group P4U, and Azusa's favorite. He died in an accident during a concert, but was restored to life by God. He's put off by Azusa's idol obsession.

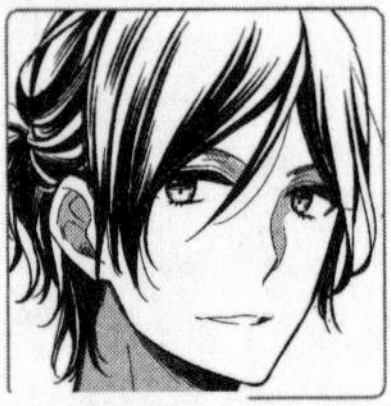

Haruki Haijima (Haru)

P4U's leader. He has feelings for Chikashi?!

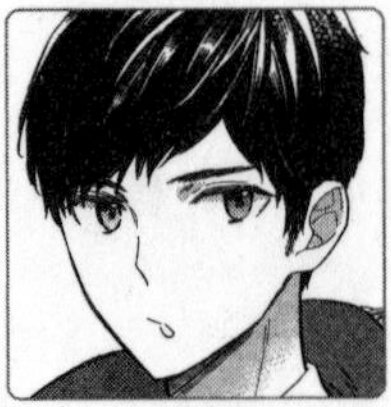

Fumi

Azusa's hapless childhood friend who is zealously and obnoxiously in love with her.

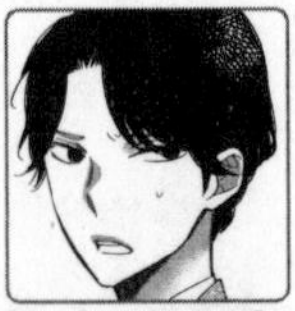

Matsumoto

P4U's manager. Loves cats.

P4U

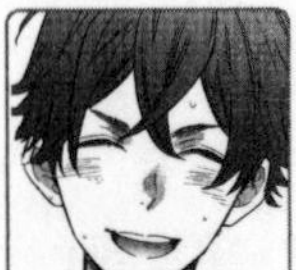

Mariya Manaka (Mari)

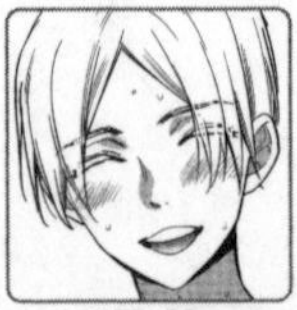

Mikito Miyama (Miki)

C O N T E N T S

S T O R Y

Azusa is a hardcore idol fangirl, but when she's caught in a freak
accident with her favorite idol, Chikashi, they end up swapping bodies!

When Azusa learns that Haru, the leader of P4U, is in love with
Chikashi, she tries to keep him at arm's length to protect Chikashi's
chastity, but Haru won't leave Chikashi's side at all!

As she's bickering with Haru, Azusa realizes that she's starting to
embrace her romantic feelings for Chikashi. Meanwhile, Chikashi
sets out to become an actor, a dream he had long given up on.

By combining forces with Azusa, Chikashi makes it through his first audition.
But, just as their bond deepens, a beautiful woman
from Chikashi's past appears...?!

STAR⇄CROSSED!!

04
JUNKO

CRAIG D. KAIN, PhD

POSITIVE

HIV Affirmative Counseling

AMERICAN
COUNSELING
ASSOCIATION

5999 Stevenson Avenue
Alexandria, VA 22304-3300

Positive: HIV Affirmative Counseling

10 9 8 7 6 5 4 3 2 1

American Counseling Association
5999 Stevenson Avenue
Alexandria, VA 22304

Acquisitions and Development Editor
Carolyn Baker

Managing Editor
Michael Comlish

Copyeditor
Lucy Blanton

Cover design by Brian Gallagher
Back cover photograph by Denver Stedman

Library of Congress Cataloging-in-Publication Data

Kain, Craig D.
    Positive: HIV affirmative counseling / Craig D. Kain.
      p.   cm.
    Includes bibliographical references and index.
    ISBN 1-55620-147-8
    1. AIDS (Disease)—Patients—Counseling of.   2. HIV-positive
persons—Counseling of.   I. Title.
RC607.A26K349   1995
362.1′969792—dc20

                                      95-20787
                                         CIP

FOR ROBERT,
MY
LOVE

ACKNOWLEDGMENTS

Gratitude is the memory of the heart.

—JEAN BAPTISTE MASSIEU

My heartfelt appreciation to the following people for their invaluable support and assistance: Peter Quinn, Sara Winter, Frances Sawaya, Ian Stulberg, Gloria Bleezarde, Jane Wagner, Carolyn Baker, Mary Ellen Ciptak, Tim Dunn, my colleagues at Antioch University Los Angeles, Marlon Guzman, my family, and Robert L. Smith.

Blest Are the Sorrowing:
They Shall Be Consoled

And what does it mean to mourn?
I asked the multitude.
And an old man stepped forward.

To mourn, he said, is to be given a second heart.
It is to care so deeply
that you show your ache in person.

To mourn is to be unashamed of tears.
It is to be healed
and broken
and built-up
all in the same moment.

Blessed are you if you can minister to others
with a heart that feels
with a heart that hurts
with a heart that loves
and blessed are you if you can minister to others
with a heart that serves
and a heart that sees need before it's spoken.

To mourn is to forget yourself for a moment and get lost
in someone else's pain
and then, to find yourself
in the very act of getting lost.

To mourn is to be an expert
in the miracle
of being careful with another's pain.

It is to be full of the willingness
of forever reaching out to
and picking up
and holding carefully
those who hurt.

To mourn is to sing with the dying
and to be healed
by the song
and the death.

—AUTHOR UNKNOWN.

TABLE OF CONTENTS

Positive: HIV Affirmative Counseling brings together an incredible amount of both experiential and scientific data and presents a revolutionary approach to counseling. That it accomplishes this in language accessible to therapists, medical practitioners, legislators, caregivers of all kinds, and people with HIV disease is of enormous benefit to all and is the next important step in a struggle that has claimed so many lives.

We live in what has been called the Information Age. Daily, it seems, there is another way to send information, punch a personal code to pay bills, order goods, or vote for our favorite song on the radio. Most major newspapers these days offer the reader an Internet address for each major article so additional analysis or background information can be tapped into from the comfort of one's own home. However, it also seems that along with this avalanche of data, we have a corresponding sense of there being no way to organize all that is knowable, no way to make sense of the flood of details available at our fingertips.

Additionally, how to discriminate between what is useful or important and what is simply available is a key issue for anyone attuned to contemporary life, whether that be in the electronic cultures we increasingly find ourselves navigating, in the books we read, or in the interactions we have with friends, family, and associates. The issue of the language in which information arrives and what meaning the language contains is crucial. Here, at the end of the 20th century, the dynamics of HIV disease and AIDS have created a contemporary Babel of languages almost unimaginably intricate and intense. The ramifi-

xii POSITIVE: HIV Affirmative Counseling

cations of this disease are discussed in terms of the medical, the psychological, the interpersonal, the cultural, the political, and on and on. Unfortunately, because of a complex constellation of demonizing factors regarding HIV/AIDS in Western culture, noise and negativity have reigned over various reasoned and reasonable approaches to the human devastation visited upon people who have contracted HIV disease.

Although I am not a therapist, my colleague and friend Dr. Craig Kain asked me to write a foreword to his book, *Positive: HIV Affirmative Counseling*, a work I feel falls into the category of the necessary and the visionary, different classifications to be sure, but because of the nature of the situation, intimately wedded.

Like many people, my understanding of HIV/AIDS is highly personal. My friends have died. My students have died. My fellow writers and artists have died. Others have continued to live, create, love, and triumph in the face of the unexpected—a physical condition that affects every human expectation we have about how our lives should logically progress.

Last night I did a poetry reading, and as usual, I stood around and chatted with my poet friends who were on the same bill. As I thought about this occasion in the light of Craig's book, I realized HIV/AIDS is always a part of my creative life and my personal life. At least two of the poets I read with yesterday are people beset with a condition that will eventually silence them.

As a poet, here's how I would refer to it in language—silence and creating in the face of silence—my experience being that many fellow writers and artists have had their creative lives truncated by AIDS-related illnesses. Many others have had their experiences denied or ignored. Many have not been able to speak for fear of retribution, betrayal, or shame.

But, as my friends last night show to all of us, they have also transformed their lives and the lives of others with the explainable and unexplainable knowledge they carry and communicate. My friends keep appearing at events like these, sometimes physically fragile, sometimes at a pretty good level of health, but always strong in their focus on their lives and their art.

Often I think of the poet John Keats and his early death. He was a young man caught in the grip of a deadly disease of his day, tuberculosis. He, too, faced a life cut short of its full potential, but something he said in one of his letters frequently enters my mind for its numerous points of application. Keats said poetry is a vale of soul making, and what I find remarkable about the book Craig has written is that it implicitly recognizes the crucible at the center of each person's life, client and counselor alike, in which a soul is being formed and forged. Covering the progression of steps from testing positive until life ceases, Craig's book recognizes and honors the amalgam of physical, emotional, and spiritual complexities present in a human life. The focus here is on the multifaceted process in the *making of a life*. This clearly is the central wisdom of *Positive: HIV Affirmative Counseling*.

No person creates a self without others. A human being is a series of participatory acts which our various cultures ritualize, honor, allow, or forbid. When a person faces illness, often there is an accompanying fear of loneliness and loss of connection. The fear of being alone, of not being able to communicate and connect is a great human fear.

For the person with HIV disease, as many writers and artists have so ably characterized, the specifics of life must be honored. The fact of being an individual must be held onto at all costs, because the cultural definitions of HIV disease seek to obliterate the individual with a strength and method as virulent as the virus itself.

Recently I heard a news report about the Names Quilt. The reporter was eager to list all the statistics about the size of the quilt and how it has grown too large to be exhibited all at once. I thought about the number of acres it would cover and thought, too, of the small farms and the city blocks where the people with HIV disease came from. I thought of how the media often changes neighbors into numbers. I thought of how, as Craig's book says, we need to change our minds and move on to the next step in dealing with the facts of HIV disease. People are going to be living with HIV disease and not simply dying from it; each of them deserves to be known and dealt with as a full human being, not just a statistic or a victim.

While reading *Positive: HIV Affirmative Counseling*, I noted the differentiation between healing and curing. Not only is this an important distinction for counselors and those living with HIV disease, it is important that those of us who have lost friends and family find ways to heal. It is important for our society to move toward a concept of healing which presupposes a new attitude toward what we mean by living. Many times in reading this book I was startled to realize how much of what we mean by a good life has been altered by this disease. The fact that HIV disease has cut a path across social classes, racial groups, age groups, ethnic communities, and people of different sexual orientations means that the question about what life really demands of us has reached to the very heart of humanity worldwide. There is no place the nature of existence is not being dealt with in a new light.

Likewise, as you will see in this book, the nature of hope and time and what it means to have a future are clearly addressed. I was particularly struck by this statement: "In Western culture, it is nearly impossible to live without plans." It is true that we are magnetized to the clock and calendar, sometimes with no clear sense of content. In the poem I wrote for a former student who had died of AIDS-related causes, I reflected on having lived, mindless of how long it had been since I had seen him before realizing he was gone. And then, for me, there was a change in that kind of mindlessness forever. Dealing with HIV disease, we become acquainted with an array of intimate information about our friends and family members—where they are and what medicines they are taking, their cell counts, their changing hopes and dreams.

This book is full of insights about basic changes in awareness we need to have. In reading through the chapters, I would find sentence after sentence opening out, unfolding more and more things to reflect upon. The marvel of Craig's work is that all this wisdom is delivered in such a straightforward and practical manner. And I found myself thinking, "of course this is how to deal with such impossibilities."

In all the time since we have known about HIV disease, there has been information at the street level which hasn't risen to the level of public discourse. What I admire most about this book is that an important set of issues which is usually ignored is presented in a direct and comprehensive way. For example, men and women do not have the same experiences with HIV disease. Their symptoms, treatment, and availability of medications differs. Young people aren't the same as middle-aged people in what they understand by "quality of life." African Americans may not have the same reactions to the stresses of disclosure of HIV status as Anglos or Chicanos/Chicanas.

Something so simple as making these distinctions clear, really clear, is brand new. And something so complicated as showing how to handle all the differences is another of the remarkable features of this book.

Besides presenting practical approaches in dealing with diverse populations, a basic and profound respect for differences is evident as the chapters unfold. For people who have not only had to suffer from HIV disease but from being made into something less than human for having contracted it, the clear-eyed affirmation of the special nature of each person's struggle is heartening. Usually I tend to seek attention to women's issues in what I read, and usually I come away dispirited and disappointed. Not so here. Both the text and the generous listing of resources pay heed to giving supportive assistance to counselor and client alike. As a teacher, I felt helped by the case studies. This is material I can use in my women's studies courses.

Sometimes it is hard to remember that even with all the information about HIV/AIDS, there can still be so much ignorance and bad will about it. Recently, there was another ugly reminder of downright stupidity at the highest levels of government when a group of gay activists meeting at the White House had their briefcases and bags searched by security staff wearing protective gloves. If it weren't such a tragic display of wrongheadedness and a venal lack of judgment, this kind of behavior would be laughable. Why not visit playgrounds wearing latex gloves? Children have HIV disease. Why not chaperone the prom in your tux and protective hand coverings? Kids at dances have HIV disease. Unfortunately, these kinds of battles over blatant stupidity still need to be fought.

Fortunately, Craig's book will arm many in this ongoing struggle, practitioners and clients alike, and heal many wounded spirits along the way. There is an answer and a blessing for everyone in these pages, and everyone is included here at last.

—Eloise Klein Healy
Los Angeles, California

Eloise Klein Healy is a poet, an educator, and a member of the Core Faculty at Antioch University in Los Angeles. She has taught at Immaculate Heart College, the California School of Professional Psychology, the Wright Institute, and in the Feminist Studio Workshop at the Women's Building in Los Angeles where she served on the board of directors.

Ms. Healy is the author of four books of poetry, the most recent being Artemis in Echo Park *(Firebrand Books). Her work is also available from New Alliance Records.*

INTRODUCTION

The Tenets of HIV Affirmative Counseling

Positive always meant something good when I was growing up. Now *the word seems almost synonymous with despair. Why not another* *word for being infected with HIV? Maybe* subjected, *you know, like* *being subjected to a bad perm.*

—MIKE DONNICI
(Hitchens, 1992, p. 148)

A new connotation for the word *positive* has entered into the popular lexicon: to live with HIV disease. Daily we hear rumors, reports, and stories that yet another person is positive, and immediately we assume we understand what that means. But do we? Do we really know what the experience of living with HIV disease is like?

Certainly, as Donnici suggested, part of what it means to be positive is to despair. Living with HIV disease often brings an end to old ways of thinking, old ways of acting, and old ways of living. Often hope is also lost. Ironically, at the same time, to be positive means to be hopeful. This paradox—to have hope destroyed while at the same time becoming increasingly reliant on it—defines the experience of being HIV positive more than anything. And it is this profound paradox that we, as counselors, must come to understand.

For many people, remaining hopeful after they test positive demands great strength. Society still stigmatizes people who live with HIV disease. Life adaptations caused by the progression of the disease often strain people's self-concepts. Relationships can become drastically altered. As these things happen, long-term psychological support becomes crucial. More and more frequently, people living with HIV disease and their loved ones call upon us, whether we call ourselves counselors, therapists or psychologists, social workers or nurses, professionals or paraprofessionals, to provide such support.

What it means to be positive in the 1990s differs from what it meant in the 1980s. To work effectively with HIV-positive clients, we must understand the differences. In the early days of the AIDS pandemic, our focus was primarily on helping our HIV-positive clients overcome the shock of testing positive and preparing them for their death. By the late 1980s, we had expanded our notion of what working with HIV-infected people involved. We broadened our practice to include the concerns of women with HIV disease. We began to attend to infected children. We became more sensitive to the special issues of substance abusers. Yet in the late 1980s our own narrow and disjointed therapeutic vision often prevented us from fully understanding what it really meant to be positive.

By the end of the 1980s, we continued, for the most part, to lack an integrated approach to counseling people living with HIV disease. Many of us treated our HIV-positive clients as though they were mirrors that had fallen to the ground and shattered into a thousand pieces. Rather than try to put the mirror together again, many of us looked at one piece here and another piece there. Often we counseled people living with HIV disease as if their illness separated them from their lives. For example, many of us assumed that talking with our clients about how they were handling their HIV status was sufficient; we overlooked inquiring about how living with HIV disease affected their sex life, their work, or their spiritual beliefs.

This book describes the experience of counseling people in the 1990s who are living with HIV disease. The major premise of the book is simple: to counsel HIV-positive clients we must come to understand their experience and must affirm it, as it is. We must not make their experience into what we want it to be, into what we think it should be, or into what we need it to be. Instead we must handle their experience of being positive with great respect and with great compassion.

This book pushes the art of counseling people living with HIV disease into the second half of the 1990s. It defines a new counseling approach—HIV affirmative counseling—that takes into consideration the medical advances of the last decade. Today, unlike 10 years ago, testing HIV positive no longer means the immediate end of a client's life. Our clients often live many productive years, and we are called upon to accompany them along the complex journey that comprises their life with HIV disease. Because the breadth and scope of our work has changed, so too must our approach. HIV affirmative counseling provides a new integrated basis for working with HIV-positive clients. The basic tenets of this approach, described in the following sections, are that HIV affirmative counseling is atheoretical; developmental; sensitive to issues of sexual and affectional orientation as well as of gender, culture, class, and age; and contextual. It takes a bifocal approach and is systemic, sex affirmative, relationship centered, validating, realistic, and tolerant of anxiety. HIV affirmative counseling also focuses on quality not quantity of life, and on healing, not the cure. It respects a client's choice to live or die, is spiritual, and is about being therapeutic, not acting therapeutic.

HIV Affirmative Counseling Is Atheoretical

Working effectively with our clients living with HIV disease and their loved ones does not depend upon our knowledge of a particular theoretical orientation. HIV affirmative counseling strategies draw from the basic need of people living with HIV disease to be understood. To understand what a person living with HIV feels and thinks, we must turn to many sources. At times our clients' emotional reactions reflect a reinjury of some early childhood experience. At other times, their outlook reflects an irrational thought pattern. HIV affirmative counseling strategies are most effective when we allow ourselves to break through any self-imposed theoretical restrictions we may hold and approach our clients' problems with an open mind and an open heart.

Sadly, today's graduate programs in counseling rarely cover working with people living with HIV disease. Few programs in counseling, psychology, social work, and other related disciplines require a course on HIV affirmative counseling as part of the curriculum. Although we may be highly prepared to counsel people with many different types of problems, this lack of additional education often leaves us unprepared to work with many of the issues with which people living with HIV disease struggle. In addition, many generations of us received our clinical training before the start of the AIDS crisis. Therefore, whether novice or experienced, we can benefit from incorporating the strategies of HIV affirmative counseling into our established theoretical orientation.

HIV Affirmative Counseling Is Developmental

HIV affirmative counseling strategies reflect the changes made in the medical treatment of HIV disease in the late 1980s and early 1990s. Greater advances in prophylactic treatment of HIV-related infections and more effective drugs for treating the infections that do arise have extended the life-span of those living with HIV disease. Doctors and researchers now consider HIV disease a continuum that begins with being infected, runs through people's first opportunistic infection, and ends with death. As many as 10 to 15 years may pass from the time people become infected with HIV until the time they first exhibit overt, physically disruptive symptoms of illness. Given the increased life expectancy of HIV-positive people, a new set of psychological issues have arisen. Like medical issues, these psychological issues can be placed on a developmental continuum.

Some issues weigh more heavily on our clients when they first decide to get tested. Understanding these issues in the context of this decision is important. The shock of receiving positive test results gives rise to a whole series of issues, including adjusting to being positive, telling others, and continuing relationships with partners. Clients often experience these issues as more pressing at the earlier stages of their illness than when they have grown more accustomed to living with HIV disease.

Although they can affect clients at any time, some issues generally cause more trouble for our clients when they are asymptomatic. These middle-stage issues include dating, sex and sexuality, planning for the future, preventative treatment decisions, strategies for living healthier, workplace issues, and spiritual issues. We can anticipate that the importance of these issues to our clients will wax and wane with time.

Some issues become pertinent to our clients only when they reach the advanced stages of their illness and receive an AIDS diagnosis. Issues of hospitalization and loss, severe neurological decline, and the inability to care for themselves overwhelm many newly diagnosed clients. We err when we think our clients must address all of the issues related to living with HIV in early counseling sessions. Issues like dying with dignity, hospice care, and letting go are best discussed when our clients are ready, not because we are ready.

Although some of the concerns addressed in one stage may spill over to another stage, and some concerns may bridge all stages, the appearance of a concern from a later stage early on in a client's life with HIV disease often serves as an indication of more complex, underlying issues. For instance, some clients who first test positive entertain thoughts of suicide; the thoughts, however, typically do not endure. If a client seems obsessed with suicide at this early stage, it may indicate a deeper psychological disturbance that needs our immediate attention. Similarly, the absence of timely discussion of an early stage issue (e.g., how to negotiate safer sex) may alert us to a client's difficulty in handling that particular issue.

The developmental approach of HIV affirmative counseling reflected in the structure of this book allows us to normalize our clients' feelings. Clients who first test positive have good reasons for feeling concerned about whom to inform that they are HIV positive. Clients who have begun to experience some physiological effects of HIV disease have good reasons for questioning whether to continue work or apply for disability. Clients who can no longer care for themselves have good reasons for beginning the letting-go process. Knowing that our clients' thoughts, feelings, and actions are developmentally appropriate can help us to validate their experiences.

HIV Affirmative Counseling Is Sensitive to Issues of Sexual and Affectional Orientation as Well as of Gender, Culture, Class, and Age

In the early days of the AIDS crisis, counselors, researchers, and even activists separated people into categories. We talked about "high-risk groups," which euphemistically referred to a person's sexual and affectional orientation or ethnicity. Today, we have come to recognize the shared experience of people living with HIV disease. At the same time we need to acknowledge the uniqueness of each of our clients.

In the past, counseling approaches for working with people living with HIV disease tended to focus more on group specifics than on universals. The book, *No Longer Immune: A Counselor's Guide to AIDS* (Kain, 1989) and others that followed its lead exemplified this approach with separate chapters on women with AIDS, adolescents with AIDS, and on culturally diverse people with AIDS. In contrast, this book and the counseling approach it presents reflect the significance of a client's identity as a whole person living with HIV disease. Wherever possible, it avoids artificial distinctions between men and women, homosexual and heterosexual, whites and people of color, young and old.

At the same time, it is inevitable that our clients' experiences with HIV reflect their sexual and affectional orientation, gender, ethnicity, or age. Tragically, today's society still fosters inequality between the genders. Women are paid less, have less privilege and less power. Similarly, gay men and lesbians face great hatred and violence in their day-to-day life. Members of ethnic communities contend with institutional and individual racism, marginalization, and oppression that persist and thrive across this country. Young people, too, must overcome ageist attitudes that restrict vital information because "they are too young to know" and prevent them from making intelligent choices. Tragically, being HIV positive often magnifies the incidence of prejudice. Whenever necessary, special sections in the chapters of this book illustrate these unique concerns.

If we do not feel comfortable working with people who identify with one of these groups, for example, gay men, it behooves us to avoid engaging them in HIV affirmative counseling (or any counseling, for that matter). Gender, age, ethnicity, social class, and sexual and affectional orientation are core elements of our clients' personality structures and therefore invariably involved in how they live with HIV disease. We cannot affirm their experience of living with HIV disease without affirming their experience of being gay, a woman, a poor person, an ethnic person, or a youth. Counseling should never be used as a vehicle for converting our clients, for getting our clients to act less gay, less ethnic, less (or even more) religious. Before beginning this work, we should examine our motives—our own sexual, cultural, and gender identity. It is crucial that we remain sensitive to all of our clients' hopes, dreams, and fears.

HIV Affirmative Counseling Is Contextual

HIV affirmative counseling exists in the context of social and political forces. Drawing from the tenets of feminist psychology, we cannot conduct HIV affirmative counseling without working to change the political and social system that oppresses people living with HIV disease. For example, we cannot work to instill hope for the future in a client without also working for the allocation of more funds for AIDS research. By virtue of our training, education, and experience, we can be powerful spokespeople in the fight against AIDS. We have an obligation to use the power associated with our position to fight for HIV-related services, HIV-related prevention programs, and HIV-related research on local, state, and national levels.

For most HIV-positive people, the political and social transformation needed to improve their lives comes too slowly. Validating the frustration and anger our clients feel when budgets get cut, agencies close, and programs end plays a big part in HIV affirmative counseling.

When people live with HIV disease, the personal becomes political and the political personal.

HIV Affirmative Counseling Takes a Bifocal Approach

Clients present some issues clearly related to their HIV status. Other issues result from non-HIV-related influences. HIV affirmative counseling recognizes the distinctions and responds accordingly.

As counselors, we must work as though we are wearing bifocals. Bifocals allow both long-range vision and close vision, although not at the same time. We need to differentiate between our clients' HIV-related dynamics and their characterological dynamics. The dangers inherent in dropping this bifocaled approach can be seen in the following example.

> A counselor in supervision was describing a client he saw for a few sessions. The client had tested positive 6 months earlier and came into counseling because he was having problems getting along with his friends. Whenever they went out, he drank and nobody wanted to be with him. The counselor was convinced that the client was pushing away his friends because of his unconscious abandonment issues and his ambivalence about his friends' ability to stay with him when he got sick. Not once did the counselor ask about the client's drinking or make any attempt to determine whether the client was a practicing alcoholic. When asked about this oversight, the counselor replied that he didn't think the client's drinking was as important as his HIV positivity.

We must remember that an alcoholic who tests HIV positive is still an alcoholic. We can only effectively work with the HIV-related issues after addressing the alcohol-related issues. We must remain alert for clients whose characterological issues must take precedence over HIV-related issues.

Good HIV affirmative counseling interventions take into account both clients' personal dynamics and their HIV-related dynamics. We must avoid assuming that every issue our HIV-positive clients want to discuss in sessions is about AIDS. Similarly, we must explore with clients issues that could be HIV related but which our clients avoid addressing in HIV-related terms. We want to take care to avoid either shortsightedness or farsightedness.

HIV Affirmative Counseling Is Systemic

HIV affirmative counseling strategies acknowledge the far-reaching effect of a client's HIV-positive status. The progression of a client's HIV disease impinges upon a client's spouse or partner, friends, and family and often necessitates their inclusion in counseling sessions. HIV affirmative counseling strategies recognize that people living with HIV often create their own families and do not necessarily rely on blood relatives for support.

A major task of HIV affirmative counseling is the assessment of our clients' support systems. This is addressed throughout this book, particularly in the chapters on continuing relationships with partners, on dementia, and on letting go. Whenever possible, we want to make sure that those who take on the role of caregiver receive adequate physical, emotional, psychological, and spiritual support. At times we need to provide additional sessions to clients and their partners, friends, and family or to provide referrals to other counselors or support groups.

Surviving the loss of a loved one to AIDS-related complications often prompts people to call upon counselors to help ease their pain. The unique dynamics of HIV disease can result in numerous complications to the bereavement process. The chapters in Part 4: Renewal address ways in which we can validate and support our grieving clients.

Friends, partners, and family members who have repeatedly lost those close to them may suffer from multiple loss syndrome. These people often need to engage in psychic numbing, and we must not see their lack of traditional bereavement reactions as pathological. At the same time, we must help them to create the opportunities necessary for processing their grief.

HIV Affirmative Counseling Is Sex Affirmative

HIV disease combines two things most people refuse to talk about: death and sex. Sadly, many of us (and our clients) mistakenly believe that with respect to HIV disease, sex and death are one and the same. We incorrectly think that once clients test HIV positive their sex life ends.

Sex can provide people with powerful ways of expressing themselves. The sexual act can offer the opportunity to connect with others in an extremely intimate way. Therefore, we must support our HIV-positive clients in continuing to pursue an active sex life. Certainly accommodations must be made to prevent the transmission of HIV, and we need to take a hard stance regarding the importance of safer sex practices.

As counselors, we need to explore our own resistances to talking openly about sex and sexual activities. Those of us who work with clients living with HIV disease must be able to speak directly and explicitly about everything from how to put on a condom before engaging in anal intercourse to how to use a dental dam when engaging in cunnilingis. We need to be equally comfortable listening to gay and nongay clients describe their sexual desires. We need to speak comfortably with our clients using their own words. Using clinical textbook language to describe important and pleasurable activities for our clients rarely coveys acceptance.

Many of us naturally assume that we are comfortable discussing sex. However, unless we have worked hard to break through cultural and familial taboos related to discussing sexuality openly, we may fall short of the degree of ease needed to support and encourage our HIV-positive clients. Our clients will pick up on the smallest sign of discomfort we may display and decide never to talk about sex again. Our clients are then left to struggle alone with their own feelings about being HIV positive and having sex; unfortunately many of their feelings may prohibit them from having a fulfilling sex life. We must constantly strive to ensure that this does not happen.

HIV Affirmative Counseling Is Relationship Centered

HIV affirmative counseling focuses on the relationship between the counselor and the client. Living with HIV disease often strips clients of their humanity. People, even those dearest to them, become afraid to touch them, to work with them, to get close to them. The counseling relationship can provide the antidote to the social, emotional, and spiritual isolation many people living with HIV disease experience.

HIV affirmative counseling strategies rely on the development of a supportive, validating relationship. To develop such a relationship we must "get wet" with our clients. We cannot remain emotionally distant; to do so recreates inside the consulting room the isolation of the outside world. We must drop any preconceived notions of how a client should respond to his or her illness (even the examples given in this book must be sacrificed for the real life experience of the client sitting across from the us). We must accompany our clients using what Spiegal (1993) referred to as *rafter's wisdom*:

This approach to coping with the tragedy of having a life-threatening illness may be likened to a lesson my wife and I learned on a rafting trip on the Salmon River in Idaho some years ago. . . . The exhilaration of negotiating our way around the rocks made us acutely interested in the skills of our guides in steering the rafts. They pointed out that the most common mistake novices make is to waste energy pulling against the current of the river. . . . The way a good guide steers is by moving the boat perpendicular to the flow of the stream. This means that you accept the direction, but the quality of your trip is influenced enormously by which portion of the onrushing flow you ride. . . . It struck me that there was a lesson in life in that river. Coping with cancer or another serious illness can benefit from this rafter's wisdom. The ultimate direction has been determined, and opposing it is exhausting and futile. However, the nature of the trip and how safe and pleasant it is can be enormously influenced by maneuvering within this fundamental direction. (pp. 7–8)

We must become good guides. We must be willing to ride the rapids of our HIV-positive clients' lives without complaining about the cold temperature of the water or the heat of the sun. We must remain present at our clients' side from the time they first set into the water until the time they are lifted out.

The importance of the counseling relationship demands that we avoid injuring clients in the same way as others in our clients' lives do. If clients feel rejected by others in their life, it behooves us to determine what we may have done to reject them. We must take care not to deny our clients' views of the counseling relationship. If clients perceive us as rejecting, then we must assume that the feeling is based in reality in some way. Here the distinction between effect and intent is often helpful. Although we may not have intentionally rejected our clients, our words or actions may have had this effect. We must affirm our clients' reality, own the effect of our actions, and address any ruptures in the therapeutic relationship that occurred. We must always keep in mind that the counseling relationship may be the only relationship that provides our clients with support, affirmation, and validation. Thus preserving the counseling relationship must be our primary goal.

HIV Affirmative Counseling Is Validating

Showing true validation for our clients is more difficult than most of us realize. To do so, we need to affirm their so-called positive thoughts and feelings and their negative thoughts and feelings. Both express clients' essence, and both need validation. Validating our clients' positive and negative sides becomes even more challenging when they are living with HIV disease.

On a deep level, most of us want our clients to feel better and to live happier, more productive lives. Most of us can readily validate our clients when they behave the way we want them to (e.g., when they act more assertive, less depressed, more active, less isolated). We can easily validate clients living with HIV disease when things are going well. We rejoice when they stop worrying about their CD_4 cells (a commonly used marker for HIV progression—a significant drop reflects the amount of damage to the immune system). We smile when they talk about feeling hopeful and optimistic. We feel happy when they let go of their anger. But this comprises only half the picture.

Typically, clients have numerous sources of validation that are conditional upon their acting positive. Their partners, families, and friends may all encourage them to remain optimistic. This constant reinforcement of the positive causes many clients to split off and repress what they consider to be their negative side. If we only act in the same way as others in the clients' life, clients may have no place to express and fully experience anger, fear, and despair.

HIV affirmative counseling recognizes that the validation of negative feelings can have a powerful effect on people's sense of self. For many clients, our office is the only place in which they can express their fear of dying, their anger at their partner, or their boredom over repeating uplifting sayings. However, our clients can only express the wide range of their feelings when we make it absolutely clear to them that we consider all of their feelings equally significant. We may find it difficult to sit with HIV-positive clients who feel hopeless and helpless without wanting to rescue them from their feelings, but we must do so. We cannot lose sight of the value people living with HIV disease find in having at least one place where they can receive affirmation and validation for the totality of who they are.

HIV Affirmative Counseling Is Realistic

As counselors, we must maintain realistic goals both for our clients and for ourselves. It is unrealistic to think that our clients will totally and drastically transform their lives because they test HIV positive, even though this has been known to happen. Most clients live with HIV disease the same way they lived before becoming infected. Counseling goals need to reflect the reality of clients' past histories and current life situations.

We must take care not to indulge in unrealistic fantasies that our work helps clients live longer. The life-span of clients living with HIV disease is so multidetermined that even the best HIV affirmative counseling may have little effect. However, it is realistic to think that HIV affirmative counseling improves the quality of our clients' lives.

In the counseling relationship it is important that one member remain grounded in reality at all times. If our clients become convinced that a cure for AIDS will made be available within the next year, we need to provide the reality check. Without discouraging our clients' feelings of hope, we must invite them to explore what may happen if a cure is not discovered. This is particularly important when our clients' unrealistic beliefs seduce them into acting in a potentially harmful way (e.g., going against their physician's orders). At the same time, when clients take a limited view of reality (e.g., an effective cure for AIDS will never be found so there is no reason to continue to fight), it is up to us to present an alternative version of reality (e.g., remembering that researchers conduct new studies every day). We must carefully present this alternative view in a way that avoids invalidating our clients' thoughts and feelings. At the same time, we must also avoid offering clients unrealistic reasons for optimism (e.g., people who are fighters like you don't get sick). We must strive to strike the balance between maintaining hope and accepting painful realities.

HIV Affirmative Counseling Is Tolerant of Anxiety

Living with HIV disease produces extreme anxiety. However, HIV-positive people are often told to stop being stressed. Our clients become trapped in a double bind; concern over the functioning of their immune system leads to stress, which they are told weakens their immune system. Ironically, this secondary stress, or stress about stress, often proves most harmful to clients.

HIV affirmative counseling strategies help clients learn to better tolerate anxiety. We need to help our clients understand that although they can eliminate some sources of anxiety, they cannot eliminate others. To do this, we need to provide our clients with an environment in which they can safely feel anxious.

Working effectively with clients living with HIV disease obligates us to explore our own tolerance for anxiety. If we are to be truly present with our clients, then we need to contain their anxiety. To do this, we must remain nonreactive. However, we can act as a container only to the degree that we can tolerate our own anxious feelings. The more anxiety-tolerant we become, the more we can work productively with our HIV-positive clients' anxiety.

HIV Affirmative Counseling Focuses on Quality Not Quantity of Life

HIV affirmative counseling strategies concentrate on helping to improve the quality of our clients' lives. We must remember that most clients do not need our help to find ways to extend their lives. Our clients' physicians or holistic practitioners make more than enough life-extending suggestions. Most clients' friends or support networks eagerly share the latest cure for AIDS. Other people, however, rarely provide a sounding board for the examination of ways to make life more enjoyable regardless of its length. Thus this task gets relegated to us.

Some people living with HIV disease may have never given much attention to issues of life quality prior to becoming infected. Developmentally, they may be unprepared for the psychological search that constitutes discovering what gives their life meaning. We can assist these clients with this process. Other clients may find their previously determined notions of a quality life drastically altered by their HIV status. We also can support these clients as they work to find new ways to fill their life with meaning.

HIV Affirmative Counseling Focuses on Healing Not Cure

Before we can focus on curing we must ask, "Of what do our clients need to be cured?" Certainly, we cannot cure clients of HIV disease. Nor will counseling cure clients of their fear, sadness, hopelessness, or helplessness. These are all natural reactions to living with a life-threatening illness. Therefore, HIV affirmative counseling does not seek to cure clients.

Instead, HIV affirmative counseling focuses on healing, on encouraging clients to grow whole. To become healed, our clients must integrate the part of themselves from which they have become separate—the part that they rejected. This may be their illness, their anger, their depression. It may be their hope, their joy, and their love. It may be their relationship with self or others. We must work to help our clients see value in all of their parts and in all of their experiences.

Often our clients (and we) confuse what it means to be healed with what it means to be cured. Clients sometimes believe that if they work hard to develop themselves, to enlighten themselves, they will become free from HIV disease. Intensive counseling and self-reflection may help free our clients from dis-ease (i.e., uneasiness with themselves), but counseling and self-reflection rarely free them from the physical attack of the HIV virus. We must help our clients (and ourselves) come to see healing, or wholeness, as a valid goal in and of itself, regardless of its effect on the physiological functioning of the immune system.

Another important aspect of healing is that it can occur even while our clients are in the process of dying, of letting go. HIV affirmative counseling recognizes the importance of preparing for death, of healing those things that may make death difficult. Whereas cures are of the flesh, healing is of the spirit. Even when our clients near death and the time for cures is over, time still remains for healing.

HIV Affirmative Counseling Respects a Client's Choice to Live or Die

If we plan to work with HIV-positive clients, we must learn to respect them when they choose to die with dignity. Although the ethical and legal implications of intentional suicide may temper the way we respond to their wishes to end their life, we should hold as a core belief our clients' right to determine their own lifecourse. To do so, we need to make every effort possible to understand how they arrive at the decision to stop living. We need to resist making value judgments about intentional suicide and concede that as much as we may empathize, we can never know what it is truly like to be in our clients' situation.

We must also respect clients who choose to live. This may seem like an easy task, but often it is not. The severe toll of HIV on our clients' body and mind may leave us (and their loved ones) wishing that death comes quickly and ends their suffering. We need to understand and help our clients understand their reasons for holding on. Paradoxically, when our clients acknowledge their reasons for holding on, they may be better able to let go.

HIV Affirmative Counseling Is Spiritual

Counseling people living with HIV disease is a spiritual endeavor. Questions about existence and the meaning of life are concerns of the soul. A client's life with HIV disease undoubtedly raises many spiritually oriented questions. Although some clients turn for guidance to clergy instead of, or in addition to, a counselor, many clients living with HIV disease feel estranged from organized sources of spiritual comfort. We may be a client's only source of spiritual guidance.

To create an atmosphere that encourages clients to aspire to goals spiritual in nature, we need clarity about our own religious and spiritual beliefs, or lack of beliefs. This is equally important for those of us who hold devout religious beliefs and those of us who have rejected all forms of religion or spirituality. Often these religious beliefs (or lack of beliefs) prevent us from understanding and attending to our clients' needs for spiritual sustenance. We need to be open to the deeply personal tones our clients' spirituality may take. If we are, we may be amazed by the myriad ways our clients' spirituality expresses itself.

HIV Affirmative Counseling Is About Being Therapeutic, Not Acting Therapeutic

It is not uncommon to worry about what we should do with our HIV-positive clients. The answer is *do* nothing. We should instead *be* with our clients.

In his book *Affirmation and Reality*, Ofman (1976) gave a concise description of the difference between being therapeutic and acting therapeutic:

> I believe that the model for the therapeutic enterprise is not the distant, hierarchical relationship that exists in most of orthodox psychotherapy, but rather in an intimately engaged encounter between the therapist and the person. . . . This kind of situation ought to be as natural, pedestrian, direct, and free from artifice as is possible in the paradox of a relationship lived within the constraints of a therapist's office. (p. 178)

Ofman elaborated upon the distinction between the therapeutic act and acting therapeutic by quoting a 1973 statement by Lomas that this way of counseling is

> an ordinary interpersonal activity and the special technical procedures to which psychotherapists resort are, at best, of secondary importance and, at worst, inhibiting factors. The belief that it is primarily a technique is, to a large extent, a defensive maneuver . . . designed to avoid the pain, risk, and uncertainty of emotional involvement. (p. 178)

HIV affirmative counseling strategies encourage a genuine encounter between human beings. Our clients typically feel assaulted by their humanness and by their illness, and they therefore try to deny their vulnerabilities and their human frailties. What clients need is another human to mirror the act of being human. Our clients need us—not for the brilliance of our interventions but for the humanness of our actions.

Conclusion

As counselors, we often wonder what we have to offer our clients. Usually we tie our worth as a counselor to our education, our training, and our experience. At no time are these sources of worth more challenged than when we are working with clients living with HIV disease.

By now it should be clear that we need not feel obligated to offer our clients living with HIV disease flashy techniques or interventions. The vast and ever-changing expanse of information about the physiological and psychological aspects of HIV disease virtually ensures that this is impossible. Instead, we can offer our clients ourselves. Simply put, HIV affirmative counseling is about providing our clients an experience of respect and validation for their lives with HIV.

This book offers a way of approaching the course of our clients' HIV disease and working with the issues that arise along the way. As is always the case, there are many ways to get from start to finish. Each of our clients' journeys is distinctive. Therefore, HIV affirmative counseling is always a unique endeavor, and we should always stay open to its newness.

The need for additional, qualified HIV affirmative counselors increases each day. Tragically, because people continue to become infected with HIV, counselors will continue to be needed in the future. Tragically, because some of us have been working with HIV-positive clients for well over a decade, we are burning out. The final chapter of this book addresses the issues of counselor grief and burnout. It looks at the many things we (and others who provide emotional support to people living with HIV disease) must do for ourselves in order to ensure that we sustain our ability to care for those who need us.

And what does it mean to mourn?
I asked the multitude.
And an old man stepped forward.

In spite of the mourning we ourselves do, we should take great care so as not to forget that HIV affirmative counseling can be an extremely rewarding enterprise. If we are open, we can learn much about life from our clients, many of whom become wise beyond their years. Our HIV-positive clients touch us, enliven us, and inspire us.

To mourn is to be an expert
in the miracle
of being careful with another's pain.

It is to be full of the willingness
of forever reaching out to
and picking up
and holding carefully
those who hurt.

To mourn is to sing with the dying
and to be healed
by the song
and the death.

When we practice HIV affirmative counseling we are given a second heart. We learn to be careful with another's pain. We learn to reach out. We learn to pick up and to hold carefully those who hurt. We sing with the dying and are healed by the song. When this happens, HIV affirmative counseling is positive—in the best sense of the word—both for our clients and for us.

PART ONE

BEGINNINGS

CHAPTER 1

Deciding to Get Tested

It all starts with the test.

Few decisions are more intimidating than deciding to get tested for HIV. Deciding to get tested often brings people into counseling. Some clients begin seeing us because they have already decided to get tested. Other clients work with us for a long time in an attempt to reach a decision. Still other clients make appointments to see us because merely anticipating getting tested makes them severely anxious. The many aspects of the decision to get tested—the call for the appointment, the drive to the test site, clinic, or doctor's office, and the drawing of blood—all mark a turning point in clients' lives.

Counseling can help clients address the various aspects of their decision to get tested. Clients who are unfamiliar with where to get tested may need our help to find a test site that is appropriate to their needs. Clients who are waiting for their results may need our help to ease their anxiety. Clients who anticipate the outcome of their tests may need our help to stay grounded until they receive the actual results.

Pretest Decisions

In the early 1980s, many health educators advised against getting tested. They correctly feared the possible (at that time, perhaps even probable) harm that awaited people if others found out their HIV-positive status. In addition, many people questioned the security and privacy of test results. Many counselors who then believed that positive test results almost certainly produced negative psychological reactions urged their clients to "live as though they were negative but

3

act as though they were positive." In that way, many counselors in the 1980s advocated safer sexual practices but not testing.

A shift in thinking occurred in the 1990s. This is most visible in advertising campaigns geared at gay men: "HIV . . . Afraid of knowing? If you have ever thought about being tested for HIV, it is time to do it now" (HIV. . ., 1993). This change in approach reflects advances in the early treatment of HIV infection. The rationale of the 1980s—not getting tested because there was nothing people could do if they tested positive—is outdated. It has been replaced by a spectrum of early interventions including but not limited to the use of nucleoside analogues. These antiviral drugs inhibit the replication of the HIV virus. Examples are ZDV (zidovudine—also known as AZT), ddC, ddI (didanosine), and stavidue (d4T). Drugs with high anti-HIV activity are also prescribed. Examples include alpha interferon, foscarnet, and ribavirin.

Today many physicians think that early intervention may be crucial to the successful long-term treatment of HIV infection (Marks & Goldblum, 1989). Still, some clients reject the use of prophylactic drugs based on their toxicity and therefore do not see early drug intervention as a benefit to early testing. However, recent theories about treatment suggest that the negative side effects of any particular drug may be alleviated by alternating several drugs or by using them in tandem (Baker, 1994). Thus, clients' concern over the side effects of medications may also be their way of expressing their fear of testing. When this occurs, directly addressing the intensity of clients' feelings regarding testing is often a good counseling strategy.

Once our clients have decided to get tested, they must choose a test site. This choice alone raises many questions: Should the test be taken at an alternative testing site? Is a trusted doctor's office more appropriate? What if a health clinic is the only setting available for testing? Each of these settings has benefits and costs that must be acknowledged. Although an alternative testing site at a gay and lesbian center may provide a comfortable environment for our gay and lesbian clients, it may not feel right to heterosexual clients. A doctor's office may provide privacy but is likely to be more expensive than a clinic; in order to protect their anonymity, clients getting tested at many doctors' offices have to avoid using their insurance carrier and pay for the test themselves. Many people in this country without insurance get tested at a county health clinic where care is free. There they often are subject to long waits, impersonal attention, and rude treatment that results from an overwhelmed system inadequate to handle the amount of work demanded of it.

Clients must also decide whether they want anonymous or confidential test results. Many of our clients may not even be aware of the difference between getting results that will not be shared with anyone but will be recorded under their name (confidential) and results that cannot be traced back to them (anonymous). As counselors, we may find ourselves in the position of educating our clients about their options. Most alternative test sites provide anonymous results relying on a random set of digits to code a client's identity. In a private medical setting, doctors commonly provide confidential results. In this setting, clients who want anonymous results may have to ask that they be given a pseudonym for use with the test and may have to pay cash to avoid creating any written record. Charting the clients' results under their own name but in a separate set of private records may provide some measure of confidentiality, but this method is not foolproof. Cases exist where this second set of records has inadvertently been released to others, such as an insurance company. Clients should learn to ask how their results will be handled and not just assume that their privacy will be maintained.

At alternative testing sites, pre- and posttest counseling is almost always required. The extent of this counseling varies from state to state and from site to site. It can take the form of sitting with someone who is trained to answer questions or of simply viewing a videotape. Although this counseling may be well intentioned, it does not always help relieve clients of their anxiety; indeed it may actually increase anxiety. Briefing our clients about what to expect from the pre- and posttest counseling sessions is often helpful and may minimize the possibility that work done in treatment will be undermined.

The Wait

Some clients may find that getting tested brings about some immediate relief. At the very least, a decision was made. However, the wait between the time blood is drawn and the time results are given is almost always psychologically uncomfortable. In the documentary *Common Threads: Stories From the Quilt* (Epstein & Friedman, 1989), Sara Lewinstein, describes this limbo period: "There's something to that wait that can really drive you crazy. I mean, it makes you crazy if you weren't already." Although the time varies between test and results (from as little as 24 hours to several weeks), enough time always exists for clients to worry. Issues that heretofore were unapproachable during counseling may come to the forefront. This is often an opportune time for us to explore (or reexplore) with clients the meanings they attribute to positive results.

Anticipating Results

At this stage, clients often view positive results as a death sentence. It is critical that we hear out and affirm our clients' fears even if they are not realistic. Our clients need the space to explore their worst fears in order to prepare emotionally for their results.

Anticipating positive results stirs up numerous emotions in most clients, but some may experience strong feelings about the possibility of negative results. When clients have lost a large number of friends and lovers to AIDS, anticipating not being infected may evoke both relief and intense survivor's guilt (Marks, 1994c). These clients may question how they escaped becoming infected. They may wonder why they should look forward to living, having lost their loved ones and closest friends.

When we counsel gay male clients who believe they will test negative, we need to be sensitive to another important phenomenon first recognized in the early 1990s. Some gay male clients may feel disappointed when anticipating or when informed that they are not HIV positive. Though the gay community has done much to provide a supportive environment for people living with HIV, many gay men who are HIV negative feel isolated, without support, and without a place to belong. One harmful consequence of these feelings is the increasing trend among HIV-negative men to return to unsafe sexual practices so as to join the supported ranks of the infected (Dilley & Moon, 1994).

We can do much to prevent this relapse behavior by working with our gay male clients before they even receive their results. If we sense that clients will feel disappointed if they receive negative results, we should address it directly. Many times these men do not feel entitled to speak about feeling left out and unsupported. They often compare themselves to friends who are HIV positive and say, "What do I have to complain about?" We should affirm these clients' experience of displacement and find ways for them to receive support if, in fact, they do test negative. In some cities, groups have formed for gay men who are HIV negative and who find it difficult to consistently practice safer sex. We can make our clients aware of these groups before they get their results and before they act unsafely.

This discussion of testing has assumed that the decision to take the test was made freely. Such is not always the case. Although illegal in many states, some insurance companies require an HIV-antibody test when issuing new policies. They employ a third-party company to administer the HIV-antibody test thus overcoming legal restrictions. Clients in this situation not only may face the same issues as those just described but may also confront feelings of anger about having no choice in the matter. The waiting period and the feelings associated with anticipating results may be exaggerated, given that most people screened for an insurance policy do not get the results of their test directly; they are simply told whether or not they are insurable. In these situations anonymity is not provided, and new concerns about never being able to gain health coverage may arise. Finally, clients may have to confront issues of how to explain a denied policy to prospective employers, families, and friends.

As overwhelming as these issues may feel to our clients (and to us), there are additional issues surrounding getting tested if our client is a woman, poor, or a youth.

Women's Issues

Whereas men, particularly gay men, are frequently urged to get tested, many women face the strange situation of getting talked out of testing. Women clients may have to demand their right to be tested. Often there is a failure on the part of physicians to acknowledge women's risk for HIV infection and to recommend that they get tested. At times women clients may confide their fear of having AIDS to us but not to their medical doctors. We should take their concerns seriously and should encourage them to get tested if they so desire.

When women have had negative experiences with medical clinics and doctors, the creation of a solid client-counselor relationship is not easy. Many times we are viewed as members of the health care establishment regardless of our gender. Clients have to come to trust that we will not treat them in the same disrespectful ways they already may have experienced. This trust building can only occur slowly over time.

The process of deciding to get tested may also differ for women and men. Because society still holds tight to a sexual double standard, labeling those women who are unmarried and sexually active as promiscuous, strong feelings may arise around getting tested. If women were infected via sexual contact prior to their current relationship, they may feel guilty and assume blame for something that involved a previous partner. They may avoid getting tested if their current partner has not been informed about their past activities. When counseling these clients, we need to be especially careful not to inadvertently reinforce any "my fault" feelings they may have. Even what may seem to us to be an innocuous question (e.g., "How did you get infected?") may be hurtful.

When women do not have a regular health care provider, or prefer not to use their regular health care provider for testing, other alternative sites are needed. Just as gay men may feel more comfortable getting tested at a clinic that provides services for gay men, women may find themselves more at ease being tested at a women's clinic if such a site is available and provides testing. Thus it is important that we become knowledgeable about various places close to us that offer HIV-antibody testing especially for women.

Some women clients who may be at high-risk for HIV disease may be reluctant to allow the testing of their biological children for fear of self-incrimination. If a woman's young children test positive, there is a good chance that she is also infected. Thus, in addition to the overwhelming fears these women may have for their children, they also harbor fears for themselves. The multiple consequences of allowing or not allowing their children to be tested may be heartbreaking to women in this situation. We should not underestimate the anguish accompanying any decision they make under these circumstances. Neither choice—allowing or prohibiting the children's test—is without pain. It is the pain, not the choice, that we should validate.

Women who have sex with women also face unique issues with regards to being tested for HIV infection. From the beginning of the AIDS crisis, lesbians have considered themselves immune (Braine, 1994; Vasquez, C., 1994). Recently, an increasing number of cases of HIV-infected women who have sex with women have been recognized (Vasquez, C., 1994). Lesbian AIDS projects have been created in many metropolitan cities. Perhaps the biggest issue facing lesbians is denial of the necessity for testing. Thus we should not avoid raising the issue of HIV testing with lesbian clients who engage in high-risk activities. When lesbian clients do decide to get tested, we should ensure that the site they go to is sensitive to their health issues.

Class, Cultural, and Language Considerations

Access to health care is a prominent problem for clients who are poor, unemployed, or marginalized by racism within society. In the United

States, the burden of the lack of an organized health-care system rests on poor people, including members of many ethnic communities. With regard to testing for HIV infection, poor clients may have no choice but to utilize public health facilities. The current rationale for getting tested rests on the need for early intervention. However, much of this treatment, particularly the more experimental protocols, is expensive and may not be offered through public health clinics. In particular, poor clients may justifiably question whether it is worth getting tested if no prophylactic treatment is available. We may need to work with our clients to find ways to gain access to early intervention. We may also need to inform impoverished clients of nonmedical interventions that could be implemented if they were to know they were HIV positive. For example, cigarette smoking has been linked to decreased life-span in individuals infected with HIV (Siano, 1993). If clients knew they were positive, they might want to work toward giving up smoking.

Special care may be needed to ensure that clients whose first language is not English are tested at a setting that is culturally sensitive. Many questions arise: Does the test site have bilingual staff? Are directions for getting tested, including information on keeping results anonymous, given in the client's own language if it is not English? Will the person drawing the client's blood be able to speak to the client in her or his own language? Is pretest and posttest counseling done solely in English or are other languages provided? If a video is shown, is it understandable to clients for whom English is not their first language? Are risk-reduction materials available in languages other than English? If our clients cannot read, is there someone competent enough to help them understand written material? A good strategy is to investigate personally a site before referring any client with special needs such as these.

Another barrier to seeking testing for clients from some ethnic communities is that they may fail to perceive themselves at risk. Since the onset of the AIDS epidemic, homophobia has prevented many people in ethnic groups from seeing AIDS as potentially affecting them (Dalton, 1991; Dowd, S., 1994; Parés-Avila & Montano-López, 1994). For example, in many Latino communities, it is not uncommon for men who have sex with men, and who are therefore at higher risk for HIV infection, to view themselves as immune if they are married or otherwise not gay-identified. We have to work with these clients both to explore cultural stereotypes of homosexuality and to educate them about the transmission of HIV. We need to inform clients that

HIV does not discriminate; transmission is a function of behavior, not belief.

Youth Issues

As teenage sexual behavior becomes more widely acknowledged, so too does the need for HIV testing for youth. Today's youth grow up in a society that besieges them with contradictions: they are asked to act like young adults yet are provided with few of the powers and privileges that accompany adult status. Adult society restricts information given to teens and then punishes them for making the wrong choices.

> The forces that control information, from education in the schools to public service messages on TV or on buses and subways, are unwilling to start from the premise that teenagers desire sex, teenagers have sex, and teenagers, like the rest of us, are at risk for HIV. (Lurie, 1992, p. 135)

In most cases, youth do not have independent access to health care. The question of HIV testing becomes increasingly complex when a youth wishes to be tested with complete anonymity. Issues of confidentiality are a concern to many adolescent clients, particularly in light of the realistic fears concerning parental access to records (Slater, 1989).

Legislation regarding disclosure of HIV-antibody test results varies from state to state. In states with legislation about medical record confidentiality, disclosure of HIV-antibody test results may be prohibited. This protection is generally extended to youth older than the age of consent (Wood, Marks, & Dilley, 1992a). Of course, young clients may not be aware of the confidential nature of their test results and may still fear that results will be disclosed to parents and others. In addition, if an inappropriate disclosure is made, they may not have the power to pursue the legal channels necessary for compensation. Even if they do take legal action, it may be too late to mitigate harm and stigmatization. When working with young clients, we need to listen carefully for any concerns they may have about confidentiality. Keeping current with legislation governing our particular states helps us accurately explain to clients their rights. State counseling and psychological associations are often valuable resources in assisting us to stay current.

Not perceiving oneself at risk also prevents many youth from being tested. Although developmentally appropriate, the typical adolescent perspective of invulnerability allows teenagers to engage in high-risk activities without considering the consequences. Alex Champion, a gay teen, described this dynamic vividly:

> I'm HIV positive and I'm 16 years old. I thought that I could never get it because I was too cute. I broke up with the guy who gave it to me. He didn't even tell me that he had it. (Hitchens, 1992, p. 241)

In working with youth, we should focus on overcoming the obstacle of invulnerability. To do this, young clients' fantasies of omnipotence should first be explored. The importance of these fantasies to young clients must be acknowledged. It is crucial that this exploration be a dialog, not a lecture. In that way we separate ourselves from others in their lives who may be trying to force them to get tested. By siding with young clients, and at the same time offering them a more mature approach to reasoning, we stand a better chance of allowing them to come to their own conclusion that testing is needed.

Conclusion

Many issues arise when clients contemplate being tested for HIV. Regardless of the intricacies of the clients' situation—whether they are male or female, rich or poor, European-American or African-American, young or old—we have three main counseling tasks. First, we must help clients overcome any ambivalence they may have about taking the test. The best way for us to help is to not discount the ambivalence but rather to acknowledge how difficult it is to decide to get tested. Second, we need to support clients while they wait for results. Their fears need to be valued and discussed, not discounted. Third, we should prepare clients for the results of the test. Even clients who predict they are not infected need guidance. Regardless of how well they prepare, clients still often need help coming to terms with the feelings that arise when they receive their results. The need for help is often greater when the results are positive.

CHAPTER 2

Receiving Positive Results

*Receiving positive results is both
the end and the beginning of a client's life.*

Reactions to testing HIV positive vary. Some clients view their results as a confirmation of what they intuitively knew. Other clients take their results as a complete surprise. How clients respond to positive results is a function of many components: their personality structure, their way of dealing with illness, and their work in counseling.

The days and weeks of adjustment following positive results may seem like just a short step on the journey of living with HIV disease. Clients often prefer to rush past their immediate reactions. At times we may collude with them, pushing them toward accepting their positive status without fully exploring the wide range of emotional responses embedded in the adjustment process. However, this stage is crucial and can provide a wealth of material for counseling sessions.

Clients' responses to testing positive can be characterized by two divergent positions. One group of clients considers their positive results a death sentence. Another group of clients engages in denial and acts as though the results change nothing (Lynch & Palacios-Jimenez, 1993). Although these are extreme responses, understanding them allows us to better support clients whose responses are more moderate.

Positive Results as a Death Sentence

Clients who consider their positive results a death sentence often engage in "never thinking." They begin to recite, either to themselves or in session, a litany of things they believe will never happen now that they are positive: "I will never have a relationship; I will never finish school; I will never go to Europe; I will never see my daughter married; I will never live to be 40; I will never find anyone who wants to have sex with me again." We may be tempted to counter these thoughts quickly by labeling them irrational, but a better strategy is to affirm them. Frequently our clients need to experience these thoughts. Once experienced, the thoughts become less troubling and less all consuming. Rian Neves, a gay filmmaker in his mid-30s, captured this phenomenon in his description of first receiving positive results:

> Needless to say, that night was crazy. . . . I had that feeling in my stomach, like the world was going to end. It didn't go away for weeks and weeks. Going through it, you wonder if it will ever go away, but it does. You get used to the idea of it, and in time, you begin to think of other things again. (Hitchens, 1992, p. 218)

Because most clients who engage in never thinking are not at that point capable of considering things rationally, an effective counseling strategy is to focus on the feelings that fuel the thoughts. Helping clients withstand the onslaught of thoughts and feelings that follow testing positive helps them develop an inner strength that will serve them well as their HIV disease progresses.

Just as clients get overwhelmed when they hear their results, we also may become emotional when clients we care for tell us they are HIV positive. When this happens it is critical that we contain our own anxiety, sadness, and despair. Otherwise, we risk trying to cheer up clients as a way of dealing with our own feelings.

In response to their positive results, clients may also begin taking inventory to determine what they did to deserve AIDS (Lynch & Palacios-Jimenez, 1993). Guilt and remorse for past behaviors may be overwhelming. We must be careful not to talk clients out of these feelings. A more beneficial strategy is to begin by encouraging clients to explore their feelings of self-blame. Then we can help clients draw the distinction between blame and responsibility.

For clients infected via sexual contact, moving away from a position of self-blame may result in intense feelings of anger at the person they hold responsible for infecting them. Counseling should provide a place for our clients to express the depth of their rage appropriately. Although it is often important to help clients determine the source of infection, we must gauge when their constant dwelling on the source prevents them from discussing deeper fears and concerns.

When clients first receive positive results, we must attend to any signs of suicidal ideation. Suicidal thoughts are not uncommon for people living with HIV disease. The sentiments expressed by Don Hagan, an HIV-positive doctor, are common to people who have tested positive:

> I'm very realistic about this disease, and I don't have a problem with dying, but I really wonder about my future. I wonder if I will live in horrible pain, and if so, should I endure the pain? (Hitchens 1992, p. 113)

When clients express feelings like this, we must remember that thinking about taking one's life is different from acting. A few cases in which people have actually succeeded in killing themselves upon receiving positive test results have been well publicized, causing undue alarm. Suicidal thoughts should always be taken seriously; the severity of the threat should always be assessed. However, clients should not be made to feel wrong for having such thoughts. Exploration of the intent behind suicide often provides us and our clients with valuable insights that are otherwise inaccessible.

Denial of Positive Results

In contrast to our clients who view their positive results as a death sentence, other clients may respond to their results little or not at all. It is not uncommon for these clients to numb themselves to their feelings. We may experience our clients' test results with more feeling than they do. Thus these clients are usually more difficult for us to work with.

Often clients who deny their results attempt to justify why the results are incorrect. Some clients may blame the lab, convinced that a mix-up of tested blood occurred. Others may simply reject the results outright. Before dying in 1992, Sonia Singleton, an African-American woman, recounted how she was informed of testing positive. Her statement provides an example of the process of denial and justification:

> I was also numb. When you're given information that powerful, I think one goes into shock. And then, of course, there's denial. That couldn't be *me*. That's the first thing I thought, because I can remember in the early 1980s, in the community from which I came, the only people who were supposed to have this infection

were gay white men. I certainly wasn't gay. And I certainly wasn't white. And I certainly wasn't a man! (Hitchens, 1992, p. 244)

In traditional counseling denial is often considered a defense mechanism that needs to be directly confronted, but in HIV affirmative counseling a different strategy is employed: our clients' denial is viewed as protective, shielding them from feelings too overwhelming for them to comprehend. Our task is to explore our clients' good reasons for needing to deny their results. In reality, our HIV-positive clients' denial is rarely complete. On some level clients do know the significance and the validity of their results; otherwise there would be no reason to be strongly protected. The challenge for us is to be able to trust that in time our clients will be able to explore their feelings.

Some clients may not deny their results but may avoid acknowledging that the results affect them. These clients treat their results with the same attention they treat having a flat tire. They may not even inform us of their results until weeks after receiving them. When we ask about the delay, they may respond that the results weren't important and that nothing has changed.

Clients are both correct and mistaken when they say that nothing has changed as a result of their results. They are correct in that many aspects of life continue much as they always have. They are mistaken in that many things do change. Bill Hanson, a 47-year-old man living with HIV, recalled:

What I didn't expect was the subtle change in the way I now perceive and prioritize *everything* and *everyone*. So much just doesn't matter anymore. So much else is equally and simply priceless, such as friends (sick or well) and my own health. (Hitchens, 1992, p. 17)

Helping clients come to acknowledge fully how things have and have not changed can take some time. Unless the consequences of denying testing positive is harmful to clients, there is no reason for us to rush the process.

In its most extreme form, denial can interfere with our clients' ability to process and organize information. Lynch and Palacios-Jimenez (1993) called this *pervasive denial*. When clients engage in pervasive denial, they create a false reality that contains a good deal of their anxiety and fear but leaves high-risk activities unaffected (Lynch & Palacios-Jimenez, 1993). How we respond to clients who engage in pervasive denial often reflects our concerns about our legal duty to warn HIV-positive clients' partners.

Much of the anxiety aroused for us by clients in pervasive denial stems from the case of *Tarasoff v. Regents of the University of California* (1976), which established a counselor's duty to warn or protect an endangered third party. We may find it reassuring to know that although recent trends regarding negligent exposure have become more litigious, counselors have been spared. *Judicious Practice: An Update to AIDS Law for Mental Health Professionals* (Wood, Marks, & Dilley, 1992b) stated

> There have been no reported cases in which a mental health professional has been held liable under a *Tarasoff* or duty-to-warn analysis for failing to inform a third party that his or her client is HIV infected and might expose the third party to the virus. Indeed, . . . cases . . . indicate a reluctance by courts to require a health care provider to violate the confidentiality of a patient or client even when there is a possibility of HIV exposure. Underlying this reluctance is the assessment that health care providers cannot reasonably predict incidents in which HIV might be transmitted or people who might be exposed. (p. 9)

Feeling anxious while working with clients who engage in pervasive denial signals us to examine our own feelings further. This is particularly true when we find ourselves directing clients to break through their denial. Sometimes, in spite of court rulings to the contrary, we feel we may be sued if we allow this type of denial to continue. When our feelings interfere with our ability to affirm our clients' reality, we should seek out consultation.

How Results Are Presented

The manner in which clients receive notification of being HIV positive strongly influences how they respond. When Sonia Singleton received her results, she was hospitalized on a chemical dependency unit:

> The way I was told was very nonchalant. The doctor who gave me my posttest results acted like it didn't really matter that I was HIV positive. He acted like I should decide whether or not I wanted to continue with the rehabilitation program because I was going to die in a year anyway. I felt betrayed. I felt like this man was willfully telling me, You might as well *not* use the tools

we've given you, and go out and kill yourself, drink yourself to death, drug yourself to death, because it's not going to matter anyway. (Hitchens, 1992, p. 244)

Like Sonia Singleton, many people receive positive test results as an unrequested byproduct of some other activity. When this occurs, clients often feel angry about the test results, the fact that they were tested, and how they were informed.

Some people are naturally drawn to clinics or services that provide quick test results, usually within 24 hours with results relayed over the telephone. The great disadvantage to these operations is that, because results are not given in person, people are left to absorb the impact of the results alone. Even at clinics that include more extensive posttest counseling as part of the routine procedure of receiving re-sults, treatment may feel impersonal; clients may experience them-selves as simply one more person who tested positive.

Many times posttest counseling merely informs people of the im-portance of engaging in protected safer sexual activities. This warning may be clinical in tone and may not include any mention of how to eroticize safer sexual behavior. Instead of being helpful, such posttest counseling may act to reinforce HIV-positive people's feelings of being sexually undesirable or untouchable.

When we counsel clients who recently tested positive, we will do well to ask them what they were told at the time they were given their results. We may have to work hard to counter the explicit and implicit messages clients received along with their results. We also need to consider how fears, anxieties, and unconscious projections influence the ways in which clients hear and make sense of what they were told in posttest counseling.

Accepting Positive Results

Although it is not a perspective most clients arrive at readily, receiving positive test results eventually comes to be accepted as a milestone. This acceptance can be seen in Rian Neves' description of what it felt like to find out he was HIV positive:

A couple of weeks ago, my mother asked me, "How do you feel?" And I said, "Well, Mom, the only way I can describe it to you is like this: You know the feeling you get when you've gotten off the bus and you realize that you've left your wallet on the seat, and the bus is taking off? You realize that it's *that* close to you, but the bus is taking off and you'll never see it again. That's how I feel being HIV positive. My life is never, ever going to be the same again. The bus has taken off. (Hitchens, 1992, p. 217)

In the process of accepting that they are HIV positive, clients often lose hope. Because it is important that someone in the therapeutic relationship maintain the element of hope (Fortunato, 1993), we have to. We may not talk about it at this point, but we need to believe that though HIV disease will present our clients with many challenges, it also will provide them with many opportunities for growth. Not all clients are willing or able to persevere through the challenges and reap their rewards, but we must think that our clients can and will.

Women's Concerns

The issues described in preceding sections may be exacerbated for women. Sometimes people who provide test results to women possess little understanding of a woman's concerns and display little sensitivity to her needs. Sharon Lund, a 42-year-old spokesperson for women with HIV disease, described the general lack of sensitivity women face:

When I was diagnosed, the counselor who gave me the news looked at me with tears in his eyes. He said, "I don't know what to tell you. I've never experienced having to tell a woman she's infected." He then proceeded to hand me a handful of pamphlets on AIDS. They were all directed to men. (Hitchens, 1992, p. 29)

Women must frequently contend with biased attitudes. For example, often women are portrayed as vectors for the transmission of HIV to their children and male sexual partners. The bias inherent in this portrait becomes clear when it is acknowledged that these women "are themselves frequently victims of transmission from the men in their lives" (Anastos & Marte, 1991, p. 195). Another image depicts pregnant women with HIV disease as "incubators of sick babies who are destined to become a burden to society" (Anastos & Marte, 1991, p. 195). This biased view overlooks the struggle and pain these women experience. It fails to acknowledge that not all babies born to HIV-positive mothers will themselves be HIV positive.

In our work with HIV-positive women, we should remain sensitive to the fact that their choices regarding pregnancy are often made in the context of cultural attitudes that view childbearing as the most valuable contribution they can make to their family or community.

Having a baby may provide them with their primary means of attaining a sense of identity and status (Anastas & Marte, 1991).

When we counsel HIV-positive women, one of our tasks is to explore how exposure to society's negative messages affects their self-esteem. It is important for us to know how much our clients have accepted and incorporated common distortions. We must help our clients develop their own opinions about the many issues facing them as HIV positive (e.g., whether it is acceptable for a pregnant HIV-positive woman to carry her baby to term).

To work effectively with HIV-positive women, we should be honest about the opinions we hold; we too may have been bombarded with messages that HIV-positive women are bad. Thus we may need to reexamine and challenge our own beliefs. If in our work a values conflict arises that prevents us from understanding and empathizing with our clients, we should make an appropriate referral.

Youth Considerations

In his article, "Counseling for HIV-Infected Adolescents," Elliot (1993) provided a framework for understanding the experience of adolescents with HIV disease. Elliot pointed out that unlike adults, teenagers may find it difficult to understand and believe they are HIV infected in the absence of overt signs of infection. Because the ability to think in abstract terms occurs slowly during adolescence, teens do not yet possess a developmentally matured cognitive capacity capable of fully accepting or understanding the implications of their infected status (Elliot, 1993). It is important that we readily provide teens with a more mature perspective when they are unable to provide it for themselves.

Children and adolescents may also differ from adults in the amount of knowledge they have about HIV disease. What may be basic knowledge to adults may be new information to youth who have just tested positive. We need to find age-appropriate ways to convey information about HIV disease and to dispel fears. The following example illustrates the way one mother, Shevawn Avila, explained to her 8-year-old son Troy his positive test results:

> I waited a little longer until I brought it up again. Finally, I took Troy into the bathroom, and we were sitting there talking when I said, "Troy, remember when we talked about AIDS? What would you do if you knew somebody who had it?" And he said,

"Well I don't know. I don't know if I'd play with them any-more." Then we talked about how you can get it, and I said, "Well, there's somebody we know who has it." He said, "Who?" And I said, "You."

I told him how he had gotten it, and he wanted to know who knew about it. Then he said, "Well, I don't want to tell my friends. I don't want them to know. Because if they know they'll tease me and say things like, 'Troy has AIDS.' And I don't want them to do that."

And then I told him, "I love you very much, and any time you need to talk about it, we can talk about it." Later on he came to me and said, "Do I *really* have it?" And I said, "Yeah." Then he asked me, "Am I going to die?" And I said, "Well, some people live a long time with it. And some people die." I just left it like that. (Hitchens, 1992, p. 57)

Shevawn Avila's explanation possesses many important qualities: di-rectness, simplicity, and an openness to talking further. These qualities should also be present in our work with our younger clients.

If HIV-positive youth are disenfranchised from the mainstream cul-ture due to homelessness, ethnicity, or sexual and affectional orien-tation, the lack of information regarding HIV disease is magnified (Elliot, 1993). Traditional outreach efforts may overlook these youth. Parents may be unavailable, unwilling, or unable to explain positive test results. In these cases, we are often left to fill the role of supportive educator as well as the role of supportive parent.

Conclusion

Receiving and accepting positive results marks the first hurdle in clients' lives with HIV disease. Responses to receiving positive results can range from intense fatalism to protective denial. Our work with clients should help them bridge these two extremes. It should include exploring how much clients know about HIV disease. It should also explore the personal meaning clients attach to their positive results.

One of the primary goals of HIV affirmative counseling is the cre-ation of supportive and validating relationships with our clients. To do this we need to set aside any notions we may have for how clients should react to testing positive. Though it may be a struggle, clients must find their own means to accepting their results.

CHAPTER 3

Adjusting to Being Positive

*Adjusting to being HIV positive
is a lifelong process.*

L iving with HIV disease is best approached as a developmental process (Gutierrez & Perlstein, 1992). As time passes, the major issues HIV-positive people face change, taking on new and different meanings. This chapter looks at six major psychological issues in light of how they first manifest at the time of testing positive. Although these issues are examined many times throughout this book, how clients first work through these issues is integral to how they adjust to being HIV positive.

In his book, *AIDS-Related Psychotherapy*, Winiarski (1991) questioned whether goals and themes of HIV-related psychotherapy differ from those in other psychotherapies. Although many of the themes appear similar, the sense of imminence and sharp urgency that HIV illness imposes makes the issues qualitatively different. When counseling clients who are trying to adjust to being HIV positive, we can expect to feel this urgency. This may be particularly salient in sessions that focus on blame, abandonment, and death. Urgency is often also present when clients explore how to cope with uncertainty, live fully, and make connections.

Overcoming Blame

Our work with newly diagnosed clients often revolves around overcoming feelings of guilt and shame. "Why me?" is a frequently asked question at this stage that clouds our clients' deeper questions: "How could I have done this?" and "What bad thing did I do to deserve this?" Because having AIDS is still very highly stigmatized, we have to help clients realize the many harmful beliefs they may have internalized.

Often it can be quite emotionally difficult for clients to recognize and overcome internalized blame. Roxy Ventola, an HIV-positive AIDS educator who lost her husband and baby to AIDS complications spoke to the importance of working to overcome negative introjects:

> I would also say to get rid of the blame. That's going to be your biggest struggle. Don't blame yourself, don't blame others, don't blame the world. Get rid of the phase of anger that you are going to be [going] through, because you're just poisoning your own quality of life with it. Use those feelings constructively. Know that you've done nothing wrong. We don't even execute serial killers in this country. Don't buy into anybody else's trip. Let your life prove their attitudes to be a lie. Let your life be so wonderful, so full of love and joy and happiness and good feelings that the light is going to blind those in the dark. (Hitchens, 1992, p. 266)

As difficult as this process is in general, if clients are members of oppressed groups the difficulty sometimes becomes compounded. Gay and lesbian clients are often subject to homophobic attacks that may increase their feelings of self-blame. Similarly, society's negative view of drug users often exacerbates feelings of guilt in clients who were infected through injecting drug use (Gretzel & Mahony, 1993). With these clients it becomes even more important that feelings of guilt and shame are explored.

Our clients' acceptance of being positive is a movement away from questioning why they were infected and toward dealing with and finding meaning in the realities of life with HIV disease. Schwartzberg (1992) noted that the trauma of becoming positive affects clients at a fundamental psychological level by shattering basic, underlying assumptions they held about themselves and the world prior to testing. Once clients move past self-blame, their primary challenge becomes how to "reascribe meaning to life and their place in the world" (p. 483).

Fear of Abandonment

When clients first test positive, the fear that they will never be able to love or be loved again can be overwhelming. Clients often become anxious in anticipation of rejection from friends, family, and loved

ones. Our clients' fears of abandonment need to be acknowledged—
even when we believe they will not be abandoned. In supposedly
tolerant communities, people living with HIV disease still face rejection. Christopher Esposito, a gay man in his 30s, described his experiences in the gay popular city of West Hollywood, California:

> Now I know what it's like to be in a prison camp. It's not the
> disease; it's the way people have responded to it. I feel ostracized.
> . . . I wanted to be popular, and I was. After I found out I had
> AIDS, I was rejected by the gay community in West Hollywood.
> Suddenly they had no time for me, these people whom I thought
> were my friends. One day this guy came up to me at the gym
> and said, "You know Chris, you'd better not spread this dis-
> ease"—as if I needed to be told that! That really hurt me. The
> attitude is, I don't have it yet, so I'm going to stay away from
> you. I thought that I would've been welcomed with open arms.
> Since that day I have not gone back to the gym. (Hitchens, 1992,
> p. 49)

For many clients, the loss of others is likely to have already occurred
(Winiarski, 1991). Many HIV-positive clients, particularly those who
are gay or injecting drug users, belong to communities that have already sustained great illness and death from AIDS. Many clients know
others who have been abandoned by families and friends when their
HIV status was disclosed. Therefore, we should first and foremost
affirm the client's reality—that abandonment could occur. If we notice
that we are trying excessively hard to assure clients that they will not
be abandoned, it may indicate countertransference and the need for
supervision.

When clients raise issues of being abandoned, even at this early
stage, we too are being questioned. Concerns about abandonment
express, albeit subtly, a concern that we might leave. Before assuring
clients that we will not leave them, we need to engage in self-examination: How willing are we to work with clients throughout their
illness? Will we continue to work with them when they become too
weak to come to our office? Will we stay at our clients' deathbed if
requested, even if no one else is there? In asking ourselves these questions we may find that other issues arise. Winiarski (1991) maintained
that to deal effectively with our clients' feelings of abandonment, we
have to deal with our past losses; otherwise, we risk having those
ghosts interfere with the therapeutic relationship. The realities of
abandonment must be addressed with our clients not only in terms of

the possibilities that others may leave them but also in terms of the possibility that we also may not always be there.

Fear of Dying

Once the initial shock of testing HIV positive has worn off, clients may begin to express their fear of dying. For many people living with HIV disease, it is not death per se that frightens them but rather the type of death they anticipate. Winiarski (1991) identified four common concerns: that dying will be painful and labored; that it will entail loss of control of bodily functions; that it will come after a long period of dementia; and that it will occur alone. In addition, fear of physical disfiguration (Kaposi's sarcoma lesions, facial warts) is also prevalent. One counseling strategy is to assist clients in establishing a picture of how they would like to die. Although most such concerns are largely outside our clients' control, many other aspects of the dying process can be planned. For example, clients can decide whether they would like to die at home, in a familiar setting, or in a hospital. Clients can make decisions regarding the degree to which they desire to use life support measures.

Not every client will be emotionally able to make decisions like these soon after testing positive, but for some clients making decisions may be advantageous. Life-support decisions (a living will) in particular are best made in the early stages of HIV infection, when there is little on no HIV-related neural activity. These decisions should be recorded in writing with copies given to prominent people in the clients' life. When clients are estranged from their parents, this becomes particularly important. It may prevent the parents from attempting to legally challenge the clients' wishes based on grounds of mental incompetence.

Although we do not want to force newly diagnosed clients to plan for their death, some will raise the subject on their own. Often making plans helps clients feel more in control and less fearful. In this way, directly addressing the fear of dying may be empowering.

Coping With Uncertainty

After testing positive, one of the difficult adjustments our clients must make involves accepting the unpredictability of life. The course of HIV disease varies greatly from individual to individual, leaving clients little comfort in being able to anticipate how they will be doing in a year,

5 years, or 10 years. Planning for the future becomes a gamble, with potential strength and energy levels drawn into question. This uncertain future causes severe anxiety in many clients. Often this anxiety appears worse in clients who are newly diagnosed and asymptomatic due to the stress associated with first anticipating getting sick (Winiarski, 1991). Our initial step in working with this anxiety is to acknowledge its validity. Only then can we help clients to find ways to make their anxiety more tolerable.

Living Fully

Counseling newly diagnosed clients often includes helping them evaluate and reevaluate their life plans. New, shorter term goals may be developed. Often clients are motivated to attempt activities that they may have been putting off. Thus being HIV positive may force a client to live life more fully. However, we should not assume that all our clients will rush to transform their life for the best. Some clients welcome this transformation, but others are resentful. Take for example, AIDS activist Wayne Karr:

> When people say that AIDS changed their lives, I hate that. Yeah, it changed my life. And yes, it's a learning experience. But it's not a change I wanted, nor is it an experience that I cared to learn firsthand. Is it a change I wanted? Or something that I'm grateful about? Absolutely not. No way. I would have much rather learned about it from reading a book, although I know that the lesson wouldn't have been the same. (Hitchens, 1992, p. 90)

At times it may be extremely challenging to work with clients who resign themselves to a short, unfulfilling life. Clinical experience suggests that a client's adjustment to testing positive strongly reflects deeper characterological traits he or she possessed prior to infection. Thus we need not take our clients' resignation personally; rarely does it reflect our abilities as counselors. Instead we should acknowledge that not all clients want to change after testing positive.

Making Connections

Feeling connected counteracts feelings of abandonment and is important for clients' health and well-being. Support groups for HIV-positive clients are potentially helpful (Grant & Anns, 1988; Macks &

Turner, 1986; Morin, Charles, & Malyon, 1984; Namir, 1986; Tross & Hirsh, 1988). In some parts of the country, primarily in more metropolitan areas, special groups exist for people who recently tested positive. However, although support groups can help clients adjust to being positive, they can also frighten these clients by forcing them to face their illness (Morin et al., 1984). We should exercise some degree of caution in recommending a group to our clients. Before making a referral we should become familiar with the group and its format. Groups that are often most helpful to newly diagnosed clients tend to focus on education, problem solving, and relaxation (Dworkin & Pincu, 1993)

Not all members of groups view their infection in the same way or have the same experience of being HIV positive. Because of their unique issues, women, chemically dependent people, ethnically identified people, adolescents, and teens may benefit from groups created specifically for them.

Women's Issues

Overcoming self-blame and guilt may be a particularly difficult part of the adjustment process for women with HIV disease. Society looks down upon them; conservative members of society label them *promiscuous* and consider their life-style improper (Dworkin & Pincu, 1993). Their role as effective nurturer, caretaker of children, and protector of family values gets called into question (Freiberg, 1991a, 1991b; Nichols, 1989). In addition to overcoming stigma and shame, Chung and Magraw (1992) identified four things that may make the job of adjusting to being HIV positive more difficult for women.

First, HIV-positive women must deal with isolation. In conducting groups for HIV-positive women, Chung and Magraw (1992) found that most women had never met another woman with HIV disease. Women often reported feeling alone due to the frequent portrayal of AIDS as a (gay) male disease. That most existing social and community services for people living with HIV disease are run by or cater primarily to men also contributes to women's isolation (Chung & Magraw, 1992; Gentry, 1993).

Second, women's adjustment may be influenced by their unique relationship to medical issues. The women in Chung and Magraw's groups questioned whether medical caregivers believed their symptoms and illness were real and medically significant. They doubted whether practitioners took their reports of symptoms seriously. The women also experienced their health care providers as lacking knowledge. They felt uncomfortable about having to inform their physicians about gynecological manifestations common to the HIV condition (Chung & Magraw, 1992).

Third, women often hold key roles in households that compromise their ability to adjust to living with HIV disease. The women in Chung and Magraw's groups reported that despite their HIV-positive status, their families continued to view them as caregivers. In addition, group members were troubled by questions regarding the transmission of HIV to other family members even when these fears were not warranted.

Fourth, the dynamics of the mother-child relationship affect some women's ability to adjust to being positive. Chung and Magraw stated that "researchers and caregivers have focused mainly on the transmission of HIV perinatally and often overlook the fact that women who become HIV infected may already have children. In these cases, the issue is not HIV transmission, but how to cope with being both ill and a mother" (p. 893).

In helping clients adjust to testing positive, we should remember that often health is not a priority for women who are caregivers for others. Thus their adjustment process often gets pushed aside for other things that feel more pressing. In an interview with the *Positive Women's Network Quarterly* (1994), Mylo Riley, director of AIDS Vancouver's Women's Programs reiterated that for these women

> *health* isn't on their list of priorities. First of all, women have to make sure their kids have something to eat. After that, they go to work; then they come home and meet the family's needs; and if anyone in the family gets sick, they look after the family before they look after themselves. . . . Their health is low on the list. (Madsen, 1994, p. 28)

In helping HIV-positive women adjust, we need to encourage them to view their own health as more of a priority. At the same time we should acknowledge the primacy of many women's need to give care to others.

Chemical Dependency Issues

Chemically dependent people who test HIV positive face additional challenges to the adjustment process. Recovery programs are often unprepared to provide services to HIV-positive people and may be caught off guard to find that patients in their recovery program have tested positive. Doctors and staff may have strong reactions and objections to treating chemically dependent people with HIV disease. This rejection may exacerbate HIV-positive people's already strong feelings of being out of place. Whenever possible, HIV-positive chemically dependent clients should be placed in a recovery situation with others who are positive. When this is not possible, we may need to weigh the benefits of group treatment in promoting recovery against the potential harm caused by AIDS-related prejudice.

Little has been done to address the unique needs of HIV-positive chemically dependent women. Recovery programs often fail to provide adequate attention to women's special relationship needs, such as responsibilities for the care of children, family, partners, and friends (Wells & Jackson, 1992). When working in a recovery setting, we must remain sensitive to the unique issues women face as they contend both with the struggles of breaking their addiction and the struggles of adjusting to life with HIV disease.

Cultural Issues

People's willingness to accept their HIV-positive status is invariably influenced by their cultural beliefs about AIDS. In a major study of attitudes toward AIDS in the United States, Herek and Glunt (1991) reported that African-American respondents were more likely than white respondents to mistrust what the government, scientists, and physicians said about AIDS. African Americans also believed that the AIDS epidemic was a tool to promote hatred of racial and minority groups. Similarly, Croteau, Nero, and Prosser (1993) found a belief among ethnic people that the HIV and AIDS epidemic is a "genocide attempt by dominant culture" (p. 291). Because of these cultural beliefs, feelings of mistrust and anger that may seem out of proportion to a mainstream counselor may be very appropriate.

The adjustment process must be understood from the clients' perspective. Before attempting to facilitate adjustment, we should first acquire sensitivity to the ways in which our clients' cultural and family milieu influence the adjustment process. We might also ask our clients about referrals to counselors who are of their own culture. Clients may not always want these referrals. Still, it is important for us to have these referrals for the times when they are needed.

Youth Issues

The acceptance process for youth is often made more difficult by their age-appropriate belief in immortality. The thought that one may not have a long life seems incongruous with what it means to be young. After the initial shock of testing positive wears off, teens may have many questions that they may be embarrassed or unable to ask. Often this is exacerbated by a distrust for adults. Building rapport with our younger clients may take extra effort, but it is crucial.

HIV-positive youth often benefit from involvement with other peers living with HIV disease (Shalwitz & Dunnigan, 1989). Because most examples of HIV-positive people with full, rewarding lives are adults, our young clients may think they are the only person their age struggling with HIV disease. Thus we should seriously consider referring adolescent and teenage clients to peer-support groups. These groups take advantage of peer influences in encouraging the development of age-appropriate methods of coping with HIV disease. When no such group exists or transportation becomes prohibitive, we may have to find other ways of linking HIV-positive teens together. One strategy is to take advantage of advances in information technology: if our young clients have access to a computer and modem, the Internet may help link them to other HIV-positive teens across the country.

Conclusion

Although the acceptance process continues throughout the course of HIV-positive people's lives, many tasks arise as soon as the initial shock of receiving positive test results wears off: reducing guilt and shame, containing the fear of abandonment, and coping with an uncertain future. When confronting these issues of adjustment, clients often become emotionally volatile and may attempt to push us away. We, however, must remain present for them.

An important part of adjusting to being positive involves "coming out." The decision to tell others often has great consequences. Our role in helping clients sort through the complex aspects of this self-disclosure is addressed in the next chapter.

CHAPTER 4

Telling Others

*The choice to disclose to others almost always
comes down to perceived cost versus benefit.*

When clients are in the early stages of the HIV continuum, disclosing that they are HIV positive is a choice. They are most likely be asymptomatic; thus they can keep their life with HIV veiled behind their healthy appearance. Still, for these clients a tension prevails: by keeping their positive status to themselves, they are safe but isolated; sharing their status with others may garner support but often feels overwhelmingly risky. As clients examine the wide range of influences that affect their decision to live openly, we must continue to affirm the often contradictory emotions that arise.

Clients who do not tell others that they are HIV positive live with a secret. Often they fear that if one person were to find out, everyone else they know will find out. This is especially the case for clients who have highly visible jobs or live in close-knit communities. The isolation these clients feel can be heartbreaking. It was captured in the experience of Roxy Ventola and her husband Vinnie:

> For a year Vinnie and I were in the closet. When we started telling people, the reaction we got from heterosexuals was horrible. They all dropped us. It was very painful. So we went back into the closet, but that was a different kind of hell. You are living with a wall around you, in isolation. And you're not letting in the people who really could be there to love and help you. (Hitchens, 1992, p. 266)

In considering coming out, clients are forced to reflect on their ability to handle the prejudice and stigma that often accompany being known as someone living with HIV disease. Discrimination against HIV-positive people takes many forms: loss of job, eviction, denial of insurance, denial of public services (including police), denial or delay of health care services, and adverse legislation (Tross & Hirsch, 1988). Wayne Karr recalled the assault he survived after openly disclosing his HIV-positive status:

> I walked into a classroom at LACC [Los Angeles City College] this fall. I had already graduated from there, magna cum laude, number two in a class of 650. I was studying psychology. Anyway, I went back and walked into a classroom this fall. It was a political science class. The first day, the professor made an announcement that if you were late for class, you were out of there, unless you had a doctor's excuse. The second time the class met, I had just come from a pentamidine treatment that had run a little late, so I walked into the class half an hour late. When I did, the professor said in front of the whole room that I was dismissed from the class. I said, "Well, I was at the doctor and I have a doctor's excuse. You said that would be acceptable." And as I went to hand him the excuse he commented that I didn't look sick to him. I said, "Well, I'm a person with AIDS." He said he wished that I hadn't told him that. Then I said, "Why?" He said that he didn't want to handle my papers because they don't know everything there is to know about AIDS.
>
> That was the first time in almost 5 years of living with AIDS that I ever, ever, ever felt dirty, ashamed, defenseless. Most of the other students, quite frankly, were very much on his side. (Hitchens, 1992, p. 88)

Discriminatory and prejudicial attacks have a profound social and psychological effect on clients that cannot be underestimated and should be addressed in counseling.

Clients' ability to come out and to withstand attack is a function of many factors, some current and some historical. Clients who have well-developed support networks may feel more comfortable coming out. Clients who have already disclosed to a trusted person often find disclosing to other new people easier. Some clients' personal histories include sharing personal news and then being abandoned by primary people in their life (i.e., their mother, father, or lover); these clients are often less inclined to disclose. When these clients are placed in a situation where disclosure is unavoidable and imminent, their unresolved feelings often reappear and need to be worked through.

Clients frequently want to spend a number of counseling sessions preparing for major disclosures. During these sessions, we should help our clients develop strength and confidence in themselves. Clients often have difficulty determining the way they want people to react to their disclosure. On one hand, many clients hope that they will be treated with great acceptance as though nothing has changed. On the other hand, when people give little or no acknowledgment of the disclosure's affect on them, clients may feel unimportant, unacknowledged, or ostracized. Our work with clients should help them become clear about the responses from others they most want to receive. It should also help prepare them for the disappointment and anger they may feel in situations where these responses are not given.

Double Disclosure

At times, the disclosure of HIV status involves a second disclosure. For some gay clients, disclosing their HIV status also involves a public acknowledgment of their being gay. When clients who injected drugs tell others they are HIV positive, they too may face a similar situation; frequently the route by which they were infected gets called into question. Working with these clients requires an additional sensitivity to the myriad feelings raised by the disclosure of sexual orientation or drug use (or both).

Disclosing to a Counselor

Disclosure also occurs within the counseling relationship. When clients know they are HIV positive prior to starting counseling, they must decide how and when to tell us—if they choose to do so at all. Before disclosing, clients typically try to determine how comfortable we are working with HIV-positive people. As much as they may want to believe that we are comfortable, they are often hypersensitive for signs to the contrary. One such sign may be our assumption that, unless we are told differently, all our new clients are HIV negative. For clients who are HIV positive, such an assumption could be read as a sign of unwelcomeness. Rather than assuming our clients' HIV status, a better strategy is to ask them directly in a nonjudgmental and nonthreatening way. Doing so conveys our comfort with the topic of HIV. It also extends an invitation to our clients to bring HIV-related issues into counseling.

Clients concerned about disclosing their HIV status to others often turn to us for answers and advice. Winiarski (1991) maintained that before responding we should have our stance on this issue well thought out. He offered us four questions to consider: Do we believe, universally, that no secrets should be kept? Or do we believe there can be exceptions? Why should our clients tell a family member who has always been rejecting? Is there a disparity between our goals for reunion and communication and our clients' goals? Discovering and acknowledging our feelings (i.e., countertransference) around disclosure allows us to respond more readily to our clients' needs and concerns. Understanding and affirming our clients' good reasons for disclosing— or not disclosing—is far more beneficial than offering suggestions or directions based on what we think, read, or heard is best.

Women's Concerns

The still-prevalent misperception that women only become HIV infected if promiscuous (Wiener, 1991) often colors women's decisions to share their HIV-positive status. Thus when our women clients disclose, they must be prepared to have the integrity of their sexual relationships drawn into question. In addition, if they have children, these clients must be prepared for reactions that suggest they are unfit mothers.

The threat of abuse may also temper the decision to disclose. Some women may be vulnerable to violence when HIV-related issues are involved. Research has already established that women's requests for condom use (whether or not they are HIV positive) are often met by verbal and physical abuse (Anastos & Marte, 1991; Gentry, 1993). When they disclose their HIV-positive status to a spouse or partner— a disclosure often more threatening to the partner than a request for safer sex—women may be even more likely to face abuse. Thus we cannot assume automatically that it is better for women to share their HIV status with their partner. Nor can we assume that because HIV-positive clients are lesbians they are at any less risk for abuse (Maroney, 1994). Potential harm to our clients must be seriously considered and assessed. If necessary, we should help clients find protection.

Cultural Considerations

Two factors often intensify the emotional and psychological consequences of disclosure for ethnically identified clients: the family and shame. In many cultures the family (*la familia*) serves as the core unit of emphasis. Often family is broadly defined to include extended relations and kin (Wikinson, 1993). Marin (1991) observed that the Latino community places such a great importance on the family and community that the threat of possible rejection and stigmatization is extremely psychologically burdensome. Chan (1993) observed the same dynamic in Asian-American culture.

In addition to loss of family, another frequently perceived consequence of disclosure is shame. In many cultures guilt, an experience of the individual, is supplanted by shame, a communal experience. Clients may feel that it is their duty to avoid bringing shame upon their family. Because being HIV positive is often viewed negatively, they may assume that it if they came out, their family would be disgraced.

Ethnically identified families and communities are often characterized by a heightened interest in and knowledge of their members. Thus disclosure to anyone even remotely associated with the family or community may be avoided. We should not be surprised to work with clients who are reluctant to talk about being HIV positive even with their closest friends if the friends have ties to the clients' family or community. This factor should be taken into consideration when referring ethnically identified clients to support groups. Although some clients may prefer groups composed of other ethnically identified people like themselves, others may find this type of group too threatening. Similarly, until these clients decide to come out to their families, they may prefer receiving adjunctive services from mainstream AIDS service agencies and providers rather than those which exist within their own community.

Youth Issues

At a time when peer acceptance is crucial, young people living with HIV disease must frequently contend with ostracism. Other adolescents may lack information about HIV and may operate under many false beliefs about its contagion; they may not want to stay in the same room with an HIV-positive person for fear of catching AIDS through casual contact. In choosing to disclose their HIV status, young clients may risk losing the friendships they desperately need at this stage in life. By not disclosing, they may have to suffer in silence as friends make ignorant, destructive, or discriminatory remarks about HIV-positive people in their presence. Young clients who may not be able to garner support from their friends often need additional help. Extra counseling sessions and support groups comprised of others their age may be critical to their emotional and physical health.

Conclusion

Herek (1990) maintained that disclosure makes support and assistance easier to obtain and therefore is associated with higher self-esteem. Similarly, Namir (1986) suggested that avoidance carries with it more distress and depression than does disclosure. However, Dworkin and Pincu (1993) urged caution. They reported that some clients, in an attempt to empower themselves, immediately need to tell everyone about their HIV status, a decision that they may later regret. This holds particularly true for newly diagnosed clients.

Dworkin and Pincu recommended working with clients to make decisions about disclosure carefully, cautiously, and rationally. One strategy is to help clients become clear about the responses they most desire. Another strategy is to work on the skills clients need to cope with responses they do receive—from rejecting to supportive. As long as clients remain healthy, they can selectively share their HIV status with only those who respond supportively. When our clients become sick they are forced to come out to more people. Thus working to help asymptomatic clients develop the ability to depersonalize rejection and internalize love and support serves them well in the long run.

PART TWO

STATUS QUO

CHAPTER 5

Continuing Love Relationships

Relationships that continue do so
in spite of—or because of—testing positive.

The demands of living with HIV disease easily strain even the most committed marriage or relationship. The couple becomes a *ménage à trois*; HIV is the third person at all of their activities—sometimes sitting at the dinner table, sometimes hiding in the corner, but always present. For some couples, knowledge that one or both of them are HIV positive serves to increase an already strong emotional bond. For other couples, this knowledge makes ending a dysfunctional relationship nearly impossible. This chapter explores many of the issues that confront couples living with HIV disease. Because the issues of couples in which both members are infected (sero-concordant) differ from those of couples in which only one member is infected (sero-discordant), they are addressed separately.

Issues for Sero-Concordant Couples

For some HIV-positive clients, knowing that their partner is also HIV positive evokes fantasies of perfect mirroring—of complete attunement and understanding. In reality, this rarely happens. Although sero-concordant relationships can be extremely validating and comforting, it is not always the case that they are easier than sero-discordant relationships. Even in couples in which both partners were infected at about the same time, different individual reactions, approaches, and responses to HIV commonly occur. Although they may prefer to focus solely on their similarities, inevitably sero-concordant couples need to focus on their differences. These differences can be seen in the questions and problems that typically cause concordant partners to argue.

The Question of Who Infected Whom

The question of who infected whom, with its accompanying blame and guilt, cuts to the core of a couple's commitment to each other. When this question arises in the course of counseling, it often provides a vehicle for the couple to address issues as yet unresolved. For example, issues of trust commonly arise: "How can I trust you if you infected me?" If the partners became infected after entering into their relationship together, issues surrounding how they define their relationship arise: "Wasn't this supposed to be a monogamous relationship?" Even if sexual relationships outside of the primary relationship were allowed, becoming infected with HIV may raise new issues: "Wasn't sex outside of this relationship supposed to be safe?" When the question of who infected whom becomes contested, deeper issues of trust, fidelity, and security lie below.

Some sero-concordant couples were not concordant when their relationship began. When HIV-negative partners sero-convert, the question of who infected whom takes on a greater intensity. Partners who were seropositive at the start of the relationship may feel responsible and guilty for infecting the people they love most. This guilt may be extremely overwhelming and may threaten the partners' ability to stay in the relationship.

In these cases, trying to alleviate the clients' guilty feelings is often ineffective. Instead, a better approach is to try to understand how feeling guilty serves our clients. Although our work with these clients should address their feelings of responsibility, it need not necessarily focus on reducing their guilt. Sometimes a simple reframe is helpful. If our clients can come to see their guilt as a reflection of how much they care for their partner as opposed to seeing it as a reflection of their own inherent badness, their guilty feelings often become more acceptable, less threatening, and less disturbing.

Clients in relationships who become infected by their partners may feel extremely angry. A client's anger with his or her partner is often justified and needs to be validated. At the same time, counseling also should consider ways in which this outwardly directed anger compensates for a client's unexpressable inwardly directed anger. If self-directed anger seems present but not voiced, ways must be found to allow for its acknowledgment and expression. Clients who, when infected, were aware of the routes of HIV transmission may not acknowledge but often experience deeply seated self-blame for having failed to use condoms or clean needles. In counseling, these clients can gradually come to see how blaming their partner provides them with a way of avoiding responsibility for their own actions. This awareness cannot be forced. This perspective should be broached with the utmost sensitivity only after the development of a strong, therapeutic relationship. In order for clients to take responsibility for their actions, they must possess ego strength and the ability to admit their fallibility. Therefore, clients must be helped to develop the strength necessary to incorporate their humanness, with all of its shortfalls, into their self-concept.

When clients examine their role in infecting their partner or in allowing themselves to become infected, it frequently produces an exploration of deeper, core issues of self-worth. From the perspective of HIV affirmative counseling, no quick and easy strategy exists to build a sense of self-worth. Offering clients exercises like affirmations often provides an easy fix, providing us relief from the intensity of our clients' feelings. For our clients, however, especially those living with HIV disease, these exercises are often experienced as incongruous with their deeply held feelings of defectiveness. Ironically, if we can provide our clients with room to explore their perceived character flaws, and not attempt to rid our clients of these flaws, the so-called flaws often lose their power. Instead of seeing these clients' character as a problem needing fixing, we can view it as an outgrowth of their life experiences; in doing so we provide clients with the essential affirming environment needed for healing. Of course, resolving characterological issues such as self-worth takes time—if such a resolution is even possible.

When working with couples we should avoid assumptions. We must not presume that because the couple was sero-discordant at the start of their relationship, it was the positive partner who necessarily infected the negative partner. Until ruled out, other routes of transmission (e.g., affairs, undisclosed drug use) are always a possibility.

The Question of Who Is Sicker

Sero-concordant couples sometimes argue about which partner is sicker. In many couples, the person labeled *the sicker* derives huge secondary gains. This may even occur when the only overt symptom of HIV disease is a psychological or physiological fatigue. Being the sicker may allow partners to escape contributing to the day-to-day maintenance of their relationships. When this is the case, resentment may build on the part of well partners who may feel that their health is taken for granted and that their HIV-positive status is ignored. It could also be that adopting a well-sick dynamic provides well partners with a way to escape into a sort of denial whereby their sick partners carry the HIV-related concerns for them both.

In counseling couples where well-sick labeling occurs, a careful and thorough history of the relationship should be taken. Many times current HIV-related patterns merely reflect exacerbations of unac-knowledged prior dynamics. For example, HIV may not have caused the unequal distribution of power and privilege in a relationship; it may merely serve as a catalyst for making a covert issue overt.

In couples in which one partner is truly more severely affected by HIV than the other, we must exercise caution so as not to favor one partner over the other. It is often easy to identify with the burdens of being ill and to overlook the burdens of being the primary caregiver in a relationship. Both partners need validation for their different, yet equally valid, concerns.

Conjoint counseling is helpful, but serious consideration should be given to other adjunctive services. Individual sessions for the partners might provide an additional way for each one to feel understood and validated. Sero-concordant couples support groups can also be helpful. However, sometimes it may be more beneficial to refer partners to different groups for people living with HIV disease so that they may develop their own personal support network.

The Question of How One Copes With Illness

Different ways of dealing with illness become particularly apparent in sero-concordant couples. Variations in coping styles often add strain to the relationship. Most peoples' reactions to illness reflect their early childhood experiences. Clients may think that everyone, including their partner, handles or should handle illness the same way they do. Clients who react to being positive by constantly going to their doctor, or by enrolling in various experimental drug protocols, or by trying various alternative treatments may not understand why their partner refuses to take any action. Clients who always adopt a stoic approach to illness may not understand why their partner worries about getting a cold or the flu. Counseling should encourage clients to see, under-stand, and respect diverse ways of coping with illness. Frequently this entails an exploration of the effects of familial and cultural influences.

The Question of Who Will Take Care of Whom

Sero-concordant relationships are often strained by fears related to providing and receiving care. If clients anticipate that they will fall ill first, they may become anxious over their partner's ability to provide care. The cause of this anxiety lies not in whether the partner is capable of providing care, but rather in whether the partner is capable of providing the kind of care that is desired.

Arguments over anticipated caregiving may become extremely threatening to a couple, especially when partners have different levels of income. It can be quite helpful for clients to recognize that an issue such as "How will you be able to support us on your income?" reflects an issue of deeper concern: "How will you be able to support me?" Arguments about caregiving frequently reflect more complex dependency issues. Couples can be helped to see beyond the immediate issue of care to the deeper issue of dependency. In working with couples, we must be careful to address both sides of the dependency issue: Not only will partners who anticipate becoming dependent experience anxiety, but partners who anticipate being placed in the supportive role may also experience difficult and conflicting feelings.

No Escape: The Problem of Seeing Oneself Reflected in One's Partner

Being mirrored is an inescapable part of being in a relationship. In couples in which both partners are sero-positive, what is often reflected is HIV disease. For many of our clients, having a partner who is HIV positive serves as a painful and constant reminder that they also live with HIV. For example, if their partner gets sick, even with something minor, it can serve to remind them that they, too, will eventually get sick.

HIV-positive couples regularly complain that they lack an escape. As long as their partner is around, they can go no place without being reminded of HIV. One strategy for reducing this constant mental and emotional bombardment is for couples to establish HIV-free zones. Places in the home and times during the day or week can be set aside and maintained for activities having absolutely nothing to do with HIV. Typically, couples have to work hard to make these zones a reality because an enormous number of events and items impinge upon them (e.g., HIV-related literature left scattered, medications set in visible places, calendars marked with doctors' appointments). However, the importance of creating and maintaining a safe refuge cannot be stressed enough.

Issues for Sero-Discordant Couples

In contrast to sero-concordant couples who face issues related to their shared experience, sero-discordant couples often deal with issues of difference. For many couples simply acknowledging differences *in general* causes great tension and conflict. For sero-discordant couples the magnitude of the degree of difference may cause conflict and arguments to occur more frequently. Sometimes this tension becomes too much for couples to endure and their relationships fall apart. Other times sero-discordant couples enter into counseling expressly to deal with their differences. When this occurs we have to make an effort to help couples understand their differences, and also to help them find some common ground. The issues of difference with which sero-discordant couples contend are philosophical and practical; counseling should explore both of these aspects.

Why One Partner Is Positive and Not the Other

Why only one member of a couple is HIV positive epitomizes the issue of difference. For positive partners, the knowledge that their partner escaped infection may compound personal feelings of guilt and shame. It may also give rise to feelings of envy and resentment. For HIV-negative partners, guilt in general, and survivors' guilt specifically, may also be a prime issue. Negative partners' feelings of guilt may be intensified if they engaged in risky activities similar to those of their positive partner.

In counseling sessions, sero-discordant couples should be encouraged to express their feelings—especially feelings of guilt, envy, and resentment. Some couples are frightened to voice what they consider to be negative feelings. They fear that to do so will destroy their relationship. We need to reassure these clients that leaving such painful feelings unexpressed undermines their relationship. When couples do openly discuss their feelings, we need to generously provide validation.

It is not solely the HIV-positive partner in a sero-discordant couple who feels envious. The increasing amount of support programs and assistance available to people living with HIV disease may leave HIV-negative partners feeling excluded and unsupported. In their marriage or relationship, these feelings become intensified when they perceive their partner as receiving more support than they do. Providing these clients with additional support for being HIV negative (e.g., HIV-negative support groups) often proves helpful.

Not Feeling Understood

In sero-discordant couples arguments often arise from feelings of not being understood. HIV-positive clients may find it inconceivable that their partners could understand their experience since they do not harbor the virus in their body. When HIV-positive clients raise this issue in counseling, we may initially react by attempting to prove to them that their partner really does understand; however, this approach is ill advised. A better strategy is to explore and expand upon their feelings: Why do our clients feel misunderstood? What statements or actions give them the impression that they are misunderstood? Although our clients may be understood more than they think, it is important for us to acknowledge that HIV-negative partners do not actually know what it is like to be a person with HIV disease. To work effectively with our clients, we must affirm this reality, not deny it. Ironically, when we validate the actuality that HIV-negative partners cannot understand our clients' experience the same way our clients do, our clients feel understood.

HIV-negative clients who are in a sero-discordant relationship can also feel misunderstood. Compounding this, they often feel unentitled to express their feelings: "How can I complain about feeling misunderstood, when I'm not the one who's HIV positive?" HIV-negative clients must come to recognize that their feelings are valid, and that they also have a right to express their feelings.

When we conduct conjoint sessions, affirmation should be offered to each member of the couple equally. We should validate both the HIV-positive partner's reality and the HIV-negative partner's reality. In doing so, we demonstrate how both truths can co-exist. Our affirmative stance models for couples a way in which the differences in their relationship can be bridged.

The Fear of Infecting the Other Partner or Being Infected

Although the issue of sex and sexuality receives deeper discussion in its own chapter, the subject merits mention here in the context of discussing couples' dynamics. An extremely serious fear for sero-discordant couples is that of transmitting HIV. A twofold strategy to working with this issue is often useful. First, we can acknowledge the unique fears of each member of the couple. Often these fears reflect the anxiety associated with the uncertainty of HIV and AIDS. For example, clients may want assurance that they can practice safer sex and not be infected. However, although practicing safer sex can reduce their risk to negligible levels, it is impossible to say that they will be 100% risk free; even the best condoms fail occasionally (Davidson, 1994). We should validate the frustration our clients feel when they want definite solutions to problems that cannot completely be resolved.

Second, we can help couples explore any concerns they may have about getting close to each other—concerns of which they may not even be aware. Because practicing safer sex and not sharing needles or blood-infected instruments reduce the risk of HIV transmission to near zero levels, the issue of infecting or becoming infected frequently reflects a couple's difficulties with intimacy. An exploration of intimacy issues commonly leads to the discovery of other fears such as the fear of dependency and the fear of loss.

The Fear of Dependency

In sero-discordant couples a heightened fear of dependency often prevails. HIV-positive clients may feel dependent upon their HIV-negative partners. This dependency, whether actual or anticipated, can cause great uneasiness. It is not uncommon for clients to retain unresolved issues of dependency from earlier experiences. These historical issues may cause present feelings to become intolerable. When exploring dependency issues in counseling sessions, we need to focus not only on the presenting situation but also on how the current HIV-related situation taps into feelings from the past.

Dependency is not a one-sided issue. HIV-negative clients may resent being depended on. They may question whether they can actually provide the support required by their partner. They may wonder who will support them. If HIV-negative clients have unresolved dependency issues, the issues are certain to arise just as they do for their HIV-positive partners. Counseling needs to focus on both the current dependency fear and its antecedents.

The Fear of Loss

Closely related to the fear of dependency is the fear of loss. For sero-discordant couples, it may manifest as an intense fear of rejection and abandonment. Jealousy may arise, particularly when one partner seeks assistance and nurturing outside of the relationship from friends or support groups. For HIV-negative clients, the fear of loss also may be translated into anticipatory grief. They may question whether it is worth going through with their relationships, of getting closer to their partner, only to watch the partner die. Counseling should focus on helping clients come to accept that there are no quick antidotes to these fears. Clients must learn to contain the anxiety that these difficult situations engender. To work effectively with clients, we must do the same; we must learn to hold our clients' anxiety while at the same time containing our own anxiety about not being able to solve all of our clients' dilemmas.

An Additional Couples' Issue: The Pressure to Stay Together

Regardless of whether clients are part of a sero-concordant or sero-discordant couple, the issue of feeling forced to stay in the relationship often emerges. HIV-positive clients worry that if they ended their current relationship they might not be able to start another. They may wonder, "Who else would want me?" "Who else would support me?" "Would I even have the strength to build a new relationship?"

When HIV-negative clients consider ending their relationships, they must reconcile their feelings of abandoning someone with a life-threatening illness with their need to go (Forstein, 1994a). HIV-negative clients have their own set of doubts. They may wonder, "Does leaving this relationship when my partner is HIV positive make me a bad person?"

When couples feel forced by HIV to stay together, the resulting tension may be disastrous. In his book, *Constructing the Sexual Crucible*, Schnarch (1991) described a healthy relationship as one in which both members of the couple become differentiated. A highly differentiated couple remains together because each partner makes a conscious choice to commit to the relationship knowing that they could also choose to end the relationship (differentiation); the couple does not stay together because partners feel they could not live without each other (fusion) or because they feel they have no other alternatives. Clients who remain in dysfunctional relationships often do so because they lack the ability to tolerate the anxiety associated with asserting their individual identity.

When counseling clients who are unsatisfied with their relationships yet remain in them because of HIV, it is helpful to assess each member's capacity to tolerate the anxiety associated with differentiation. Caution should be taken so as not to set treatment goals that might, in fact, encourage the couple to become less differentiated and more fused. Even when couples come to counseling to save their relationship, we must not collude with their lack of differentiation. Paradoxically, when we agree to try to keep their relationship together (and not entertain alternative options), we may actually be reinforcing their fusion and making it less likely that the relationship will last. Exploring what might happen if the relationship dissolved provides couples with the opportunity to make choices from a position of differentiation. Our goal with these couples should always be to help them recognize that although it may be difficult, they can always choose whether to stay in or leave their relationship.

To work effectively with couples, we must believe that the decision to maintain the relationship and the decision to end the relationship are equally valid. Most of us are aware that we can only hold this position if we have explored our own biases around this issue. Working with sero-concordant and sero-discordant couples forces us to examine and reexamine many of our established assumptions: Do we feel couples should stay together at all costs? Do we feel couples should dissolve their relationship when differences become too difficult? At what point do we believe that remaining in a conflict-ridden relationship becomes abusive? When do we consider leaving a conflict-ridden relationship avoidance? The clearer we can be about our beliefs, the more proficient we can be in helping couples to define their own beliefs and to act accordingly.

Women's Considerations

HIV-positive women often view their marriage or relationship in ways that differ from men. Some women see their relationship primarily in terms of the risk of abandonment and the impact that being abandoned might have on their lives. Some women focus primarily on their ability to bear children and how it defines their primary relationship.

Sadly, if women develop AIDS-related symptoms before their male partners do, they are likely to be abandoned (Ankrah, 1991). The fear of abandonment may be strongest in women who depend on their partner for material and social resources (Hankins, 1993). When a woman is highly dependent upon her partner, avoiding abandonment may be the only framework from which she is capable of viewing her relationship.

Most women living with HIV disease are of childbearing age. Often their relationship to their partner may be constructed around their reproductive role. HIV-positive women may question their capacity to fulfill this role in light of the risk of maternal transmission of HIV during pregnancy (Shaw, 1989). When married women decide not to have children, they may begin to doubt their value as a spouse or their desirability to their partner (Chung & Magraw, 1992). Partners, too, may harbor such questions.

When counseling HIV-positive women, it is critical to remember that women's experiences of HIV disease are inseparably linked to their experiences as women (Chung & Magraw, 1992). With hetero-sexual clients, this gender effect occurs even when their partners are also HIV positive. Issues of power and socialized concepts of feminin-ity must be taken into consideration as we explore our clients' rela-tionships. We should also remain aware of the many ways in which gender and power issues become part of the counseling relationship.

Cultural Issues

HIV-positive couples who belong to ethnic communities face their own set of issues. First and foremost, HIV-positive ethnic couples often face a lack of recognition and support. Many ethnic communities view AIDS as strictly a problem of the majority culture. Ethnically identified HIV-positive couples may be treated as outcasts. Thus they may have to turn for assistance to organizations that primarily serve the main-stream culture. In many areas they may be the only African-American, Latino, or Asian-American couple in an otherwise all white support group. If the couple is biracial or bicultural, there is less chance that they will find others like themselves in a support group.

Ethnically identified clients may hold culturally influenced ways of dealing with sickness that may not be shared by their partners. Even when both members of the couple share the same ethnic background they may have different levels of acculturation; thus they may not rely upon traditional approaches to healing in the same degree. When couples do not share a common ethnic identity, differences in dealing with sickness often result in conflicts that reflect deeper cross-cultural divergence.

Conclusion

The issues confronting couples living with HIV disease are multidimensional in nature. Some issues take on a personal quality belonging to one partner or the other. Other issues belong to the couple. In working with clients in either individual or conjoint sessions, we should remember that although many issues are HIV related many others are not. Often couples present problems that are long-standing; we should not be misled into believing that historical patterns of miscommunication, discrepant power hierarchies, or codependency resulted only because one or both members of the couple are HIV positive. Helping clients decide when to continue and when to dissolve their relationship becomes far more difficult, yet far more important, when HIV disease is involved. We cannot (and should not) make relationship decisions for our clients, but we can help them develop both the differentiated sense of self and the tools necessary to struggle with their relationships as well as their other issues.

CHAPTER 6

HIV Positive and Dating

Dating epitomizes the classic approach-avoidance conflict.
A date is at once both desired and dreaded.

Most people find dating challenging because it raises all
kinds of powerful emotions. For our HIV-positive clients,
additional HIV-related issues compound dating issues already in existence. Some clients find they must learn how
to date all over again, playing by different rules. Other clients simply
pull away from any social contact that may potentially lead to something more than friendship. This chapter focuses on the clinical issues
of HIV-positive dating. Most of the dating issues cross gender and age
boundaries. Yet others take on unique characteristics when experienced by women and adolescents.

Seeing Oneself as Desirable

Many peoples' experience of dating is inextricably tied to their ability
to feel desirable. Clients living with HIV disease may lose their sense
of desirability—particularly when they unfavorably compare themselves to others. Clients may believe that by virtue of their HIV status,
they lack the qualities necessary to date. As a result of being HIV
positive, they may have lost weight and see themselves as unattractive.
They may feel fatigued and consider themselves unexciting to be
around. They may have little interest in pursuing a high-powered
career and therefore consider themselves a bad catch.

Helping clients find aspects of themselves they can consider desirable becomes a major therapeutic goal of HIV affirmative counseling.
This is best accomplished by trying to avoid refuting clients' critical
self-perceptions. Instead, we should explore the emotions that accom-

pany the perceptions. For example, rather than denying our clients' statements that they are too thin ("You look fine"), it is better to encourage them to talk about their feelings ("How does it feel to be losing weight?"). Focusing on our clients' feelings helps us avoid getting into a power struggle with them. We should also work with clients to help them discover things about themselves that they can continue to hold in high regard. This often involves a painstaking process of self-evaluation—especially when clients' self-esteem was injured prior to their becoming HIV positive.

Deciding Whom to Date

People living with HIV disease frequently question who will find them desirable. In deciding to date, the question of whether to date other HIV-positive people or HIV-negative people usually arises. Neither choice is conflict free.

For some clients dating other HIV-positive people offers a sense of camaraderie. Many things that would ordinarily have to be explained do not have to be. Many fears are elevated. Dianne Rice, a 47-year-old woman with HIV disease described why she prefers dating HIV-positive men:

> . . .Otherwise, in my head, while we're having sex, I'm wondering, is he thinking about *it*? Is he scared? Is he this, is he that? And it ruins the whole thing. He may not be thinking that at all. But I am. So, you know, it doesn't work. (Hitchens, 1992, p. 146)

However, problems arise when clients assume that they will be understood and that things will be easier simply because the person they date is also positive. Clients may need a gentle reminder that everyone's progression and everyone's ways of coping with HIV disease differ.

The decision to date only other HIV-positive people can become extremely taxing. When people live outside of large urban areas where HIV-positive people readily self-identify, finding others to date may take additional effort. Women often find it difficult to meet HIV-positive heterosexual men. Still, the comfort that arises from dating someone in a similar condition often outweighs the obstacles. For many, the alternative of dating someone HIV negative evokes so much anxiety that it does not even seem like an option.

In some social circles dating someone sero-negative has gained acceptance. Various communities (e.g., gay men in large urban centers) may not even question sero-discordant dating. Other communities may view sero-discordant dating as something inconceivable. A 28-year-old hemophiliac described his experiences:

> As much as the hemophilia may make it easier for me to accept having AIDS on a physical level, my heterosexuality has made it much more difficult for me to accept than if I were homosexual. I think that the heterosexual community is very ignorant in a lot of ways about the risk of AIDS and about the people who have it. From what I know from my friends who are homosexual, homosexuals just accept that a person they are interested in dating is either HIV positive or is at least aware that he could be. And if they are or aren't positive, homosexual men are aware and educated enough to practice safe sex. . . . From what I've experienced, straight people will not ask [your HIV status]. You have to tell them, and when you do, it's much harder for them to accept. In the gay community everyone is at least aware of the possibility, and if someone is HIV positive or has AIDS, you can still start a new relationship. In the straight community that's almost impossible. (Hitchens, 1992, p. 190)

HIV-positive clients need to determine their own degree of comfort in dating someone HIV negative. In doing so, issues of rejection often reappear. An aggravation of issues related to feeling misunderstood is also common.

Wanting a Relationship

Faced with a life-threatening illness, many people living with HIV disease reevaluate their priorities and in so doing experience an intensification of their desire for a relationship. Humans strongly need companionship, particularly in times of crisis. Many theorists have written on the profound existential aloneness that arises when facing the inevitability of death. Someone special often acts to counter this loneliness.

Many times clients experience the desire for a relationship at an intensity out of proportion to their pre-HIV dating experiences. Knowledge of our clients' complete relationship history is indispensable. If we are used to practicing slow and intensive long-term counseling, we may find it unrealistic to think that clients with little dating experience can quickly develop healthy intimate relationships. However, our clients' ability to make radical changes in relatively short periods of time should not be discounted. Living with HIV disease can be a powerfully motivating force.

Coping With the Pressures of Time

The intensity with which HIV-positive clients approach dating often stems from the constant pressure of living on borrowed time. Although some clients consider their life to be cut short and may not even consider dating, others strive to maximize every minute and every encounter they have with another person. Understanding our HIV-positive clients' perspective on time proves invaluable. It often provides an explanation for the dynamics driving our clients' dating behavior.

Disclosure

Another dilemma HIV-positive clients must solve is when to let their date know they are positive. Some clients opt for disclosing on the first date. Others postpone telling until they feel that the dating is serious and that a relationship might develop.

The thought that our HIV-positive clients' may be dating and not disclosing may cause some of us considerable concern. The majority of us are painfully aware of the litigious environment in which we practice. We usually feel relieved when we can gain clarity and direction about exactly how we are to approach difficult legal issues like disclosure and the duty to warn. Unfortunately with regards to HIV disease, few ethical and legal guidelines exist; even fewer have been tested in court. Thus, like our clients, we are left to sort through the complex and competing demands and emotions of disclosure.

The Argument for Telling Immediately

Some clients adopt a more proactive stance, letting dates know that they are HIV positive when they are first asked out or when they first get together. These clients feel better knowing their date's reaction before they invest time and emotional energy. Sometimes it is informative to have these clients role-play disclosing in the counseling session. Clients may be surprised to find that despite good intentions the manner in which they present or convey their positive status works to distance them from their date.

The Argument for Delayed Telling

Other clients prefer to save their disclosure for an opening. They may go out a number of times before telling their date that they are positive. Often the subject of being HIV positive gets broached when the date asks about it or alludes to it. One rationale behind waiting lies in our clients' concerns about protecting themselves from stigma and unwanted rumors; this may be particularly important if our clients are only out to a few people. Another rationale is our clients' lack of confidence (often rightly so) that early dating may turn into a more committed relationship. In addition, many people living with HIV disease feel that they do not owe a disclosure to someone on the first date if sexual contact will not occur.

When counseling clients who adopt a wait-to-tell stance, we must exercise caution so as not to convey disapproval. We need not necessarily worry if our clients wait; in general, we are under no legal obligation to force them to disclose. We should, however, address the issue if clients avoid disclosing when asked by their date or when dating involves sex. In raising the issue, we should take care to identify with our clients not with their date. There is no good reason for us to ask our clients how they might feel if they were their date. Instead, we should focus their attention on better understanding the things that make disclosure difficult.

Counselors' Ethical and Legal Responsibilities

The fear of HIV infection has turned many people in the United States to the courts. People—even those who were not infected but were afraid that they might be—have sued everyone from partners to perfect strangers in an attempt to assess blame and receive compensation (Woods et al., 1992a). In these suits, failure to disclose HIV-infection status alone did not appear to be sufficient grounds for a judgment for liability.

> . . . it has become quite clear that HIV-infected people have a legal duty to disclose infection status to those who might be exposed to the virus through some act or behavior by the infected person. This does not mean that they should disclose their status to everyone who comes in contact with them. It does mean that they have a legal obligation to know under what circumstances

they might risk exposing others to the virus, and they have a duty to prevent these circumstances. (Wood et al., 1992a, p. 9)

Even though confidentiality concerns with clients living with HIV disease have generated much scholarly debate, there has been relatively little litigation regarding counselors and their duty to warn (Harding, Gray, & Neal, 1993). The *Tarasoff* (1976) ruling is difficult to apply to HIV cases: establishing that a counselor's failure to warn actually caused a person to contract HIV is very impracticable (Harding et al., 1993; Wood et al., 1992b). In contrast, strong legislation exists which prohibits counselors' breaching the confidentiality of an HIV-positive client (Harding et al., 1993; Wood et al., 1992b). As in any situation where legal standards are not well defined, the ethical codes of our professional organizations must inform our work. Many national and state organizations provide legal guidance to counselors when difficult counseling situations arise.

Rejection

When dating, rejection inevitably occurs. Whether or not HIV status was in reality why they were rejected, clients living with HIV disease often view rejection in those terms. Even a date's subtlest expression of discomfort can get interpreted as a major HIV-related rejection.

When clients do experience HIV-related rejection, it may be far more difficult to cope with than regular rejection. If clients get rejected because they know little about politics, they can always study up on the topic. However, there is nothing HIV-positive clients can do to change being positive. Counseling provides clients with a safe place to vent the frustration they feel when rejected for something that is outside their locus of control.

For many clients the mere anticipation of rejection produces profound fear and prevents them from dating. Sometimes it is useful to conceptualize this fear as a projection of clients' self-disapproval onto others. At the same time we should be careful to not forget that even projections feel real to our clients. Their experiences of dating, both actual and imagined, serve as a window into their feelings about themselves, their illness, and their self-worth. Counseling can focus on helping clients gain insight and self-knowledge through their feelings about dating.

Women's Challenges

Often it is far more difficult for HIV-positive heterosexual women to find a partner to date than for men. The comments of socialite Mary Fisher, an HIV-positive woman best known for her speech at the 1992 Republican National Convention, illustrated this difference:

> I know that relationships are possible after HIV. . . . I have seen women in support groups who have married or formed relationships after finding out that one person's negative and the other's positive. However, the community I come from is not as welcoming for a woman with AIDS as the gay community is to itself. My world in dating and relationships is small to begin with; I'm divorced, widowed, whatever. A mom with two children, fairly independent. You know, you add HIV to it and the pool of potential men goes down to practically nothing. (Dowd, M., 1994, p. 66)

Recognizing the need for social outlets, some metropolitan HIV-service organizations organize monthly parties or gatherings for HIV-positive women (and men) or even dating services. However, although these services are beneficial to some clients, not everyone feels comfortable using them; some clients find the prospect of going to a party where everyone is HIV positive depressing.

Parents' Issues

HIV-positive clients who have the primary responsibility for caring for young children usually find dating extremely difficult. Many times the energy required to care for their children leaves them exhausted and with little strength for social activities. If they do want to date, finding a suitable babysitter or child care person may be impossible if their children are HIV positive. In addition, HIV-positive parents commonly view time with their children as such an incredibly valuable commodity that anything that takes them away from their children, like dating, often gets rejected. Finally, HIV-positive parents—regardless of the children's HIV status—may doubt their ability to find a mate willing to care for their children if they become too sick to do so.

Given this, it is understandable that HIV-positive parents may not date. Still, we should not lose sight of the difference between not dating and having no desire to date. Our single parent clients may not date, but they may still desire the company of another adult. In counseling, we must approach this desire, and the pain deriving from its lack of fulfillment, with great compassion.

Youth Concerns

The greatest factor that distinguishes the dating experience of HIV-positive youth from that of HIV-positive adults is their relative lack of prior experience. Learning how to date constitutes one of the major developmental tasks of adolescence. Thus for adolescent clients, dating becomes an activity filled with questions and uncertainties magnified by the presence of HIV in their life.

Adolescence exacerbates almost all of the issues examined in this chapter. Finding another HIV-positive adolescent to date may be nearly impossible. Rejection has an even more paralyzing and destructive effect on adolescents than on adults as the adolescent's sense of self is still developing. Therefore, when working with HIV-positive adolescents, we must remember to approach their dating problems and concerns from the perspective of a teenager and not from the perspective of an adult.

Conclusion

The desire for contact with others is one of the most human of all desires. Living with HIV disease does not extinguish this desire; instead, for many people, this desire becomes enhanced. In the 1990s HIV-positive dating is more widely accepted. Ted Mischuk, a 49-year-old HIV-positive man, described how dating has changed over the last decade:

> For the last 6, 8, 10 years, the fear has been so prevalent that most HIV-involved people were convinced they could never have another relationship. Now, in the last year or two, with the improvement of the medications and protocols, they're discovering that, Hey, we're liable to end up little old ladies and bag men if we don't do something about it. And now it's not impossible to reach out to somebody and have a relationship without being terrified. It's inevitable. We are all going to die. The only difference is that some of us have a better notion of when. (Hitchens, 1992, pp. 101–102).

Living with HIV disease often provides the catalyst clients may need to revise the way they date. Some clients adopt a new straightforward approach to dating: they refuse to tolerate game-playing, indecisiveness, or the inability to commit to a relationship. Many times, clients' own game-playing is replaced by an increased ability to remain fully present in dating situations. Dating takes on an intimacy previously impossible, thereby opening the door to healthy relationships. However, just as often HIV-positive clients retain their old dating patterns, regardless of how inefficacious they may be.

The majority of the dating issues we see in counseling revolve around our clients' ability to develop and maintain a healthy sense of self. There are many ways in which we can help facilitate this process. For example, if our HIV-positive clients can come to see themselves as desirable and can come to avoid personalizing HIV-related rejection, they stand a better chance of maintaining healthy, life-enhancing social activities like dating. Dating is important in that it provides our single clients with a sense of leading a normal life. In addition, it provides them with the possibility of an active sex life.

CHAPTER 7

Sex and Sexuality

*Living with HIV does not mean
living without sex!*

Sexuality and AIDS are so closely connected that it seems nearly impossible to think of one without the other. This puts many of our clients, and us, in an extremely difficult position: though uncomfortable to discuss, sex and sexuality become topics too salient to ignore. Counseling clients living with HIV disease requires that we not only address issues of sex and sexuality but also that we do so in explicit detail. For example, we cannot simply assume that our clients practice safer sex when they say so; we must ask for a complete description of their sexual encounters (Frost, 1994). Similarly, when assisting clients to alter high-risk behaviors, we cannot back away from graphically exploring alternative sexual fantasies, sexual activities, and even sexual positions.

An exploration of sex and sexuality commonly leads to an investigation of our clients' intimacy issues, desire issues, and performance issues. Living with HIV disease may greatly challenge our clients' prior conceptions of what is intimate. Altering previous sexual behaviors may lead our clients to reject having sex altogether. Modifications in clients' level of sexual desire and performance may leave them feeling nonsexual. Our goal must be to help clients see these changes as opportunities to self-reflect and grow. An HIV-positive diagnosis should not necessitate an end to our clients' sex life. Renowned HIV-positive choreographer Bill T. Jones, in an article profiling him in *Poz* magazine, commented on this point:

> So I say to people if you feel you can't have human contact, pleasure, because of this thing, you're doing that to yourself.

Don't blame it on AIDS. There are areas of subtlety to be explored that are rich. Any barrier you feel, be aware. You are doing it. Nobody else is doing it. Take responsibility for your mental and physical health. Don't blame it on HIV. Don't blame it on the government. I say, Have sex. Sex is a healthy human expression, and if HIV wins over that, that's bad. (Kaplan, 1994, p. 43)

Sex is an integral part of most clients' lives. Our task is to enable them not only to have safer sex but also to have great sex.

Safer Sex Issues

The second decade of the AIDS epidemic brought with it a shift in efforts toward safer sex education. Throughout the 1980s, safer sex education focused on what people could and could not do. Posters, advertisements, and articles included lists of sexual activities assigned to *probably safe, possibly safe,* and *unsafe* categories. These posters, and the approach they represent, are no longer popular. Educating people—whether HIV negative or positive—about using condoms and other restrictive barriers (e.g., dental dams) is still important, though health educators now realize that offering clear concise information about avoiding high-risk activities comprises only a small portion of the intervention needed to modify unsafe sexual behavior. Today, safer sex education and counseling focuses on the decision-making process people undergo when choosing whether or not to engage in sexual activities.

Clients often need our help in establishing which sexual activities they feel comfortable with and which they consider off limits. They need to discover and determine their personal degree of comfort with activities that may or may not transfer HIV. For example, many clients are conflicted over oral sex. Other clients may feel conflicted over the safety of using condoms for intercourse (anal or vaginal) because they know that condoms do, on occasion, break. Clients should be encouraged to speak openly and honestly of their fears and concerns regarding the transmission of HIV. At times we may need to correct our clients' misunderstandings. To do so we need to stay informed and current with research on HIV transmission. Above all, we should assist our clients in developing their own code of conduct. Once this code is established, we need to support our clients in adhering to it, even in the height of passion.

Many of our earlier strategies for encouraging safer sex have failed to consider the reality of sexual interactions: communicating about sex is often painful and difficult. When clients cannot express to their partner what they feel safe doing or are willing and unwilling to do, unsafe sex or no sex is liable to occur. It is crucial that we help clients become more comfortable in expressing their sexual needs, desires, and fantasies. One way to do this is to model a willingness to talk about sex in the counseling session.

If clients do not mention sex, we should bring it up. We need not be polite and avoid asking our clients about their sex life. Attention can be drawn to its absence in session: "I wonder why you never mention feeling sexual." When clients describe their sex life as fine, we should ask, "What do you do, and what makes it fine?" Whenever possible, we should avoid talking in euphemisms. If clients talk about getting intimate or sleeping with a date, we should ask if this means they had sex. We should always try to use the language of our clients; they speak of condoms or rubbers, dental dams and latex, not pro-phylactic barriers. We should take as our goal affirming our HIV-positive clients' need to have sex as well as their ability to talk openly and honestly about this need.

Frequently clients find talking about sex embarrassing. A good strategy is to address the embarrassment as it occurs in the counseling session: "I notice you became embarrassed while describing your fantasy to me. What about telling me that felt embarrassing?" Clients often respond with concerns that we are judging them. We should not be surprised if our clients, even clients more mature in years, have rarely talked about sex to another person in any meaningful way. Many clients were raised in environments where sex simply was not discussed. They often worry that in talking about sex they will reveal their inexperience. If we detect this concern, we should assure our clients that we are not sitting in our chairs evaluating their sexual prowess. Clients often feel comforted in knowing that other people get embarrassed too. By acknowledging their embarrassment, we can help clients discover that the more they talk about sex, the easier talking will be.

When clients give up former sexual activities and adopt new ones, a sense of loss often results. Recalling the good old days is a common experience for clients, especially for clients who were sexually active in the days before AIDS. Because sexual activities express a core aspect of self, losing activities is experienced as a loss of self and can be quite painful. Holding this understanding allows us to validate our clients' sadness at the loss of sexual freedom rather than to label it *immature* or *dysfunctional.*

It is imperative that the continued practice of these risk-avoidant activities be included in our clients' redefinitions of sex. In many metropolitan cities, some people who once practiced safer sex are returning to high risk-activities (Ekstrand, 1992). Clients need to see safer sex as something practiced constantly and consistently. We may want to work with clients to determine, in advance, situations where clients may find practicing safer sex difficult. Many clients find role-playing ways to negotiate safer sex in these situations helpful.

The use of drugs and alcohol poses a great threat to the practice of safer sex. Clients often cite impaired judgment as a reason for engaging in unsafe sex (Marks, 1994a; Springer, 1991). In these cases we want to conduct a complete assessment of our clients' drug-and-alcohol-use patterns. In some cases clients' use patterns may dictate a referral to a recovery program.

It is easy to fall into the trap of focusing solely on helping clients adjust to what they cannot safely do. Clients can be encouraged to explore the range of sexual activities that they can engage in without risking HIV transmission. A session spent on ways to eroticize safer sex is often in order. Many AIDS organizations offer workshops and lectures on hot, erotic safer sex. We may want to recommend these to clients who feel comfortable exploring sexuality in a somewhat public forum.

Safer sex is for everyone. Often our clients believe that because they and their partner are both HIV positive they no longer have to practice safer sex. They are mistaken. Different strains of HIV exist. When two HIV-positive partners engage in unprotected sex, they risk becoming infected with another strain. Viral load theory suggests that the more strains of HIV with which people become infected, the more severely compromised their immune system becomes (Baker, 1994; Siano, 1993). Even though clients are HIV positive, they should take care to practice safer sex so as to not risk further exposure to other strains.

Desire Issues

Desire is a major aspect of sex. In the context of counseling, desire has almost always been used to refer to the request, or hunger, for sex. In sessions clients are often asked, "How often do you want (desire) to have sex?" or "How often do you initiate (desire) sex?" Instead of being construed as a measure of frequency, desire can also be considered as an expression of passion. In this alternative view, the object of desire is not the sexual act but rather those who participate in the act (i.e., clients and their partners). Although it is often easier for clients to focus on wanting sex, Schnarch (1991) suggested that this focus ultimately results in problems of sexual desire. Schnarch maintained that when clients are able to adopt a viewpoint of desire-as-passion and shift their focus to wanting their partner (or wanting to be wanted themselves) the result is fulfilling sex. For many HIV-positive clients, making this shift requires overcoming a major obstacle.

The notion of sexual desire as "ever-increasing passion that people anticipate, hope for, and demand" (Schnarch, 1991, p.18) may be tempered by our clients' pervasive HIV-related feeling of dirtiness. The societal stigma against people living with HIV disease, which runs rampant throughout the United States (Herick & Glunt, 1988; 1991), often comes to be internalized by clients who come to believe that they are bad, wrong, or dirty. These feelings run counter to feelings of passion. At the same time, clients' partners may come to be considered undesirable in that they serve to remind clients of how they became infected. Clients may split off the negative parts of themselves and project them on their partner, identifying them with every negative feeling they have about HIV.

Trying to get our clients to dismiss or reject their feelings of dirtiness is usually ineffective. Instead, a better strategy is to emphasize to our clients the importance of their learning to assuage their feelings. Our task is to help clients develop a capacity to self-soothe, to contain their feelings in a way that reduces fear, anxiety, and feelings of low self-worth. Clients can only learn to self-soothe when we promote the value of attending to feelings of badness, wrongness, and dirtiness instead of superficially rejecting or avoiding them. The degree to which clients can develop the ability to soothe themselves when feeling dirty or wrong ultimately determines the degree to which they are capable of creating and maintaining satisfying sexual relationships in the face of their HIV status.

Helping HIV-positive clients develop the capacity to self-soothe is a formidable task. To work effectively, we must allow our clients to experience and survive their painful feelings. We must avoid rushing in and attempting to reduce our clients' pain no matter how tempting it may be. When clients make room for the pain associated with feeling dirty and undesirable, they often experience other emotions connected to sex. Exploring desire issues may lead to the recollection of early associations to sex that predate becoming infected. Thus, in many ways, examining issues of sexual desire gives us a better understanding of our clients' personality dynamics.

Performance Issues

Issues of performance—a person's ability to function sexually—must be distinguished from issues of desire. Clients may have no desire and yet be physiologically capable of performing. Likewise, clients may desire sex yet be incapable of performing. HIV itself should not impede sexual functioning, but some of the medications prescribed for HIV disease may decrease a person's ability to function or have side effects that do the same. When our clients describe performance issues, we should be certain to inquire about the possible side effects of their medications. We should avoid assuming that all performance issues are psychological in origin. Clients should be encouraged to discuss their inability to perform sexually with their primary physician. Their doctor may need to prescribe additional drugs (e.g., testosterone) to counteract the performance-impeding effects of the other medications.

Intimacy Issues

The relationship between sexuality and intimacy confuses many people; they either divorce intimacy from sexuality or, conversely, see intimacy solely as sexual contact (Schnarch, 1991). If clients can attain intimacy only through sexual contact, they may lose their sole source of closeness when HIV disease leaves them unwilling (or unable) to have sex. Therefore, in examining issues of sex and sexuality it is also necessary to explore intimacy. If our clients' concepts of intimacy are defined narrowly, counseling can focus on helping them become more expansive. Clients can be encouraged to acquire nonsexual means of feeling intimate. For many clients the counseling relationship may be their first intimate relationship from which sex was explicitly excluded. Thus the counseling relationship can be held up as an exemplar, and clients can be supported and encouraged to form other similar relationships.

Women's Issues

When women's sexuality is viewed from the context of their HIV disease, two issues become salient. First, HIV-positive women's physical health often compromises their ability to feel sexual. Second, when HIV is involved, pregnancy becomes an extremely complex proposition.

HIV-positive women regularly suffer from vaginal yeast infections and pelvic inflammatory disease. Unfortunately, these conditions are more severe and less successfully cured than when they occur in HIV-negative women (Hankins, 1993; Vasquez, R., 1994). Therefore, when counseling clients who seem uninterested in sex, the relationship between their physical discomfort and their lack of sexual desire must be taken into consideration.

HIV-positive women make decisions about pregnancy in much the same way that HIV-negative women do. A woman's HIV status does not predict her decision to terminate a pregnancy (Selwyn et al., 1989). Feelings about whether the pregnancy was planned is a far greater predictor. Family pressure, religious beliefs, and the desire to have a child are also important factors.

The decision to become pregnant or to carry a pregnancy to term can only be viewed from within the context of cultural attitudes that often promote childbearing as a means of attaining a sense of identity or status. Data that place the chances of transmitting HIV infection to offspring at 20% to 30% in the industrialized world (Hankins, 1993) help to elucidate the decision to become or remain pregnant. A 20% to 30% chance that the offspring may be infected is also a 70% to 80% chance that they may not. For many women these may be better odds than those they routinely face in other areas of their life (Anastos & Marte, 1991).

When women choose to carry their pregnancy to term, they should be encouraged to visit their obstetrician and physician regularly to discuss ways in which the risk of transmission to the infant can be reduced. Common ways of reducing risk include the use of a Cesarean section as opposed to a vaginal delivery and bottle feeding as opposed to breast feeding.

Women may not always know their HIV status when they become pregnant. Women may learn they are positive from bloodwork accompanying tests used to confirm their pregnancy. In this case, the emotional devastation of testing positive may permeate their feelings about being pregnant.

When HIV-positive clients decide to carry their pregnancy to term, they need substantial support and reassurance. Counseling may be the only place for pregnant women to express fears and doubts about their decision without being subjected to efforts to convince them to terminate the pregnancy. Therefore, if affirming HIV-positive women's right to bear children (or their right to end a pregnancy) presents a conflict for us, immediate clinical consultation is in order. In most cases a referral to another counselor is necessary.

Cultural Considerations

Two factors affect HIV-positive people who are highly identified with mores of African-American and Latino communities: prohibitions against talking about sex and prohibitions against using condoms. These prohibitions also exist for many other people. When adhered to, both of these prohibitions can make practicing safer sex nearly impossible. Cultural prohibitions against talking about sex may also make it difficult for counselors to broach the subject unless they introduce issues gently and build a therapeutic relationship within which feelings of embarrassment and shame can be talked about without fear.

Youth Considerations

Counseling strategies may need to be modified to incorporate the ways in which adolescents view their sexuality. Adolescent clients, some of whom are sexually active, may have received minimal education about human sexuality. What they did learn may have been superficially focused on reproductive aspects of sex. Any formal sex education that adolescents were exposed to may have contained little of substance about safer sex other than to suggest abstinence. Many times counseling needs to supply the missing details about physiological, psychological, and emotional aspects of sex.

Adolescents are often unprepared for sexual encounters that are frequently unplanned (Strunin & Hingston, 1993). Therefore, HIV-positive adolescents' adoption of safer sex involves a cognitive shift. Adolescents need to feel supported in planning ahead for sexual encounters that require condoms. Although condoms are more readily available now than in the past, younger teens may still find obtaining them problematic. When clients do not feel comfortable getting condoms, the importance of avoiding high-risk activities must be stressed.

Adolescents' sexual standards—what behaviors are acceptable or unacceptable—are often determined by their peers. At this developmental stage, peer influences are primary and may take precedence over the opinions, suggestions, and experience of adults. Thus being urged to act in ways that put the approval of their peers in jeopardy often feels problematic for clients. When we make such recommendations, we risk having our clients view us as their parent rather than their advocate. Instead of offering clients directives—suggestions about what HIV-positive clients should not be doing—a better strategy is to focus on developing skills. A respondent in a Philadelphia study of teenage sexual behavior advised, "Don't tell us what to do, tell us how to do it, step by step, without losing the approval of our peers" (McLaurin & Juzang, 1993, p. 3).

HIV-positive adolescents may also experience great anxiety and uncertainty regarding their sexual orientation. Adolescents may have had some sexual experiences with partners of the same sex but may not yet be gay or lesbian identified. Sometimes adolescents who think they are gay or lesbian engage in sexual activities with partners of the opposite sex so as to avoid being labeled *homosexual*. Fear of other peoples' reactions to their sexual orientation may keep adolescents from talking about their sexuality; this reluctance may appear in counseling.

Gay- and lesbian-identified adolescents who struggle with feelings of self-hatred may be unable to distinguish their feelings of being HIV positive from their feelings of internalized homophobia; they may feel being HIV positive is punishment for being gay. Counseling should focus on helping these adolescents overcome these destructive beliefs. They must be reminded that HIV disease is not a gay disease—that anyone can get it. They must also be helped to develop a healthy attitude toward their sexual and affectional orientation. Gay and lesbian adolescents' access to information about homosexuality, in general, and gay and lesbian sex, in specific, may be severely restricted. Thus, although sex education is a vital element of counseling with many adolescent clients, its importance is increased when working with gay and lesbian clients.

Conclusion

Although significant physical and psychological obstacles may need to be overcome, a healthy, erotic, intensely satisfying sex life is a reality for many people living with HIV disease. HIV affirmative counseling cannot avoid exploring issues of sexuality. To serve our clients truly, we frequently need to expand the amount of knowledge they have about sex as well as their degree of comfort around their sexuality. For many of us, this may entail a parallel process.

When clients believe that their HIV status obligates them to be abstinent, they are mistaken. They may have an increased duty to act responsibly, but sex is in no way prohibited. Sex has the potential to provide clients with an opportunity to touch and be touched, to enjoy and be enjoyed, to value another person and be valued in return. One consequence of life with HIV disease is that human contact—both physical and emotional—often is in short supply; therefore it is particularly tragic when clients feel compelled to give up sex for reasons that hold little merit.

CHAPTER 8

Planning for the Future

*Planning depends on whether the future
is seen as long or short.*

Living with HIV disease is characterized by a pervasive uncertainty regarding the future. Existentially, everyone must eventually die; however, on a daily basis most people do a successful job of denying their death. Denial becomes infinitely more difficult for people living with HIV disease who are forced to acknowledge that their death may come sooner rather than later. Though being HIV positive is no longer viewed as an immediate death sentence, it still causes clients to question and requestion their goals, motives, desires, and plans in light of their awareness of mortality.

This chapter examines the psychological repercussions of trying to integrate HIV into future plans. Clients usually feel pulled in two opposing directions. At times, a sense of pseudosecurity that nothing could happen draws clients into planning far into the future. At other times, living only for today exerts a pragmatic pull. Scott Biggam, a 36-year-old nurse's assistant described this tension:

> I tested HIV-positive in August of 1990. Since then I've been fighting a constant battle between wanting to keep a sense of normalcy in my life, in terms of making future plans and having career goals and things like that, versus—how can I say it?—just sort of letting things go and living for the present. I don't mean that in a decadent way. I guess maybe living a little more just for pleasure, just for enjoying the pleasures of the moment, rather than worrying about what's coming down the line in terms of future plans and goals, as most people my age do. (Hitchens, 1992, p. 138)

Neither approach to planning is exclusive, and we can expect that clients will vacillate between them.

Long-Term Planning

In Western culture, it is nearly impossible to live without plans. The HIV is catastrophic not only because of its ability to destroy the body's immune system but also because of its capacity to disrupt clients' long-term plans. Helping HIV-positive clients reengage in the planning process is a major focus of HIV affirmative counseling. We are called upon to assist clients with two major tasks. First, clients need to overcome HIV-related hurdles that prevent them from feeling entitled to set goals. Second, clients need to shift their criterion for decision making from quantity of life to quality of life.

When clients hear their HIV diagnosis, they often react by feeling as though their life is over. Working from this incorrect, but emotionally justified, premise, many clients interrupt all long-term planning. They often ask, "What is the point if I am not going to live to see the plans carried out?" In counseling, our basic strategy should be to avoid contradicting or refuting a clients' feelings of despair. More often than not, any justification we may give clients for planning ahead is experienced by them as false or ingenuous. Our clients' feelings of having their life cut short have validity and require affirmation.

Everyone walks through life guided by their own internal time clock. Though seldom acknowledged to others, people usually predict how long they will live and use that prediction to determine what they want to accomplish and by what age. HIV forces our clients to recalibrate their internal time clock. Recalibration is not easy and may result in internal turmoil. A good starting place for counseling is our clients' pre-HIV assumptions about their life: What were their goals? We need to encourage clients to make their goals explicit—especially those that only existed implicitly as hopes and dreams. After clients are helped to identify their goals, we can assist them in reevaluating them in the light of HIV: do things once considered important still seem so? We can help clients set new goals (or hold on to old goals) that can realistically be accomplished given the clients' current and projected future health status.

Our clients deserve the utmost respect for the their evolving sense of life-span. Often our clients base their decisions upon a good-years-left calendar; goals are set according to the number of healthy years clients anticipate remaining in their life. For example, in a profile on

HIV-positive world-class swimmer Jim Ballard, Forster (1994/1995) described how Ballard developed a 3-year-plan:

> "The fastest I had ever seen anyone go from testing positive with a healthy T-cell count to a point where they were not able to function was in 3 years," explains Ballard. As a result he holds to his rule that, "If it can't happen in 3 years, it doesn't exist." Rather than make any promises or plans to do something 4 or 5 years from now, Ballard prefers, as he says, "to just keep everything in a time frame that's manageable." (p. 69)

To work effectively, we must come to understand the significance of this number to our clients; at the same time we must remember that the number is not static. Many times clients push the number further into the future as each year after testing positive passes without opportunistic infection.

In planning for the future, clients inevitably come to shift how they decide whether something is worth pursuing. Prior to testing positive, clients can devote equal attention and energy to numerous activities because time appeared unlimited. For younger clients time seems to stretch endlessly. For midlife or aged clients, time still offers many opportunities. Whatever their age, after testing positive, clients may no longer view time the same way; their future suddenly seems foreshortened. Quality supersedes quantity, and goals are based upon their ability to contribute to a greater quality of life.

To adopt quality of life as the criterion for decision making and planning, clients must undertake an exhaustive exploration of their values. Clients often have not considered short-term quality of life as a valid way to live, especially given the achievement and future orientation of Western culture. Clients may come to the painful realization that their life has been organized around things that no longer hold lasting value (e.g., wealth, status, fame). This realization often causes clients to feel ungrounded and directionless. When this occurs, clients need to be reassured that their feelings are typical and represent the first step in the formation of new values that better reflect their life with HIV.

Denying the Future

Upon diagnosis, some clients automatically begin to incorporate HIV considerations into their future plans. These clients often feel easier to work with; we may become anxious when confronted with clients who steadfastly refuse to include provisions for HIV in their future plans. Automatically labeling this behavior *dysfunctional* may be inaccurate. Instead we should distinguish between healthy denial and unhealthy denial.

Many times clients make plans as though nothing will happen to them. Clients may begin things or plan things that in our judgment seem unreasonable or unobtainable. We should remain cognizant of the fine line that exists between denial and hope. Often plans for the future, even if outlandish, keep people alive.

Although hopeful denial can be productive, unhealthy denial can prove damaging to our clients' physical and mental health. Clients cross the line between healthy and unhealthy denial when health maintenance is compromised. We must confront denial when it prevents clients from establishing a relationship with a physician, taking prescribed medications, paying bills, or acting responsibly. Confronting unhealthy denial can be especially tricky, particularly when clients have constructed their entire belief system around the denial of HIV. Counseling must maintain a balance between validating our clients' need to believe that nothing will happen to them and addressing the consequences of such beliefs.

Short-Term Planning

Clients' ability to make short-term plans also changes when living with HIV disease. Energy level may become the most overriding concern when making such plans. Because energy level can vary from day to day, short term-plans often change drastically. This can frustrate characteristically rigid clients who are accustomed to adhering to schedules at all costs. Counseling can help clients attain greater flexibility around their short-term plans so as to avoid feeling stressed or even guilty when changes need to occur.

Making a Will

Making a will falls squarely between long-term and short-term planning. For most asymptomatic clients, writing a will requires decisions about events that will occur in the long-term future. However, for various reasons, making the will should not be delayed. Clients should constantly update and revise it as situations change. Because wills are only binding if made under sound mind and body, they have sometimes been contested by families and others who do not like the decisions outlined in the will, and who claim that the will was written under conditions of HIV-related organic brain syndrome. Because HIV does cross the blood-brain barrier, people living with HIV disease find it advantageous to make their will before any manifestations of HIV can be detected. It is important that others know the location of the document and have easy access to it.

Clients must also make decisions regarding a Durable Power of Attorney for Health Care and a Medical Directive, also known as a Living Will. Executing a Durable Power of Attorney for Health Care allows clients to appoint another person to make medical decisions for them should they become unable to do so. This legal directive can eliminate delays in clients' medical treatment and ensure that their wishes are carried out. Counseling can play an important role in assisting clients to identify whom they trust to make personal health care decisions. Moreover, as the AIDS Health Project (Wood et al., 1992b) has maintained "a sensitive mental health practitioner may be the only person with whom an HIV-infected patient feels comfortable discussing such emotional and personal issues as withdrawal of life support, consent to an autopsy, funeral arrangements, and concerns a patient's family and friends might have about these issues" (p. 117).

A Medical Directive sets out the desires of the client to avoid life-sustaining measures and allow for natural death. Counseling should assist clients in exploring their feelings about plans for response to possible future pain and suffering as well as any moral and emotional considerations they may have about the termination of life support (Wood et al., 1992b).

Clients often need assistance in the preparation of legal documents that delineate their health care wishes. Referrals to legal counsel familiar with HIV-related issues is often necessary. In many metropolitan cities, AIDS service agencies have legal departments designed to help clients with these matters. When such assistance is not available, we may need to link clients to lawyers in their community. We need to become acquainted with lawyers who have experience in these matters and who will work with HIV-positive clients at a reduced fee if necessary.

Parents' Issues

An integral part of HIV-positive parents' plans for the future is securing their children's welfare. Insuring that their children are cared for may be their top priority, coming even before their own health concerns. Before clients get too ill (or lose the opportunity due to a court decision), they must arrange for their children's future physical and emotional needs.

For some clients, other family members may be available (or be persuaded) to care for their children during their illness and after their death. Other clients who are estranged from family and friends have no choice but to plan for foster care or adoption. This may be even more complicated if the children are, themselves, HIV positive. Although the American Academy of Pediatrics Task Force on Pediatric AIDS (Centers for Disease Control and Prevention [CDC], 1993) clearly stated that children with HIV infection deserve the same access to foster care and adoption as other children, this does not always occur. Walker (1992) noted that a shortage of foster homes has resulted in hospital wards filled with AIDS babies. Clients need an enormous amount of support as they struggle to arrange for their children's future. We must be attentive to the hurt that arises in making those arrangements.

HIV-positive parents also worry about their children's emotional well-being. In planning for the future, many clients struggle with how to ensure that their children have something inspiring to remember them by. One strategy is to help clients engage in the process of making memories now (Corea, 1992). We can encourage clients to document their present activities through photos, videotapes, or journals. We can also encourage clients to create letters, tapes, and cards that can be given to their children in future years (e.g., a birthday card for a 15-year-old's 21st birthday). In some areas, groups exist that hold onto these future memories and deliver them when appropriate.

Most of the activities involved in our clients' planning for their children's future take time and energy, commodities that become less available as our clients' illness progresses. We should support clients in working on these issues as early as possible. Attending to these issues is likely to raise many deeply emotional issues (e.g., loss); however, knowing that their children are provided for often assuages HIV-positive parents' fears and provides a sense of relief.

Conclusion

Whether acknowledged or not, much work in counseling takes place against a background of conscious and unconscious assumptions about time. Even the counseling process itself is time limited; thus it is affected by the ways our clients' sense of time shifts when confronting the progression of their illness. To work skillfully with clients, we must become familiar with their perspective on time. We must become clear on how our clients' assumptions about their remaining healthy days affect their ability to make both long-term and short-term plans. Our clients' personal sense of time is not static, but changes, sometimes from day to day depending upon their energy level, physical health, and emotional state. Monitoring these modifications is helpful. Drastic changes commonly indicate that further issues need attention and care.

CHAPTER 9

Preventive Treatment

Dealing with the side effects, both psychological and physical,
can be the most difficult part of preventive treatment.

Eventually clients face the troublesome decision of whether to begin preventive treatment. Although prophylactic intervention is often cited as one of the reasons clients should get tested for HIV, deciding to initiate such treatment depends on many factors. Medically, clients' current level of immune suppression, typically measured by CD_4 count (done as part of a blood workup), is the most common deciding factor. Doctors and clients should also, however, consider the psychological repercussions of starting treatment.

Although the extreme importance of staying current with preventive medications and their side effects cannot be overly emphasized, individual treatment regimens are not included in this book. The wide variety of treatments and the ever-changing state of experimental drug protocols makes such inclusion impractical. In addition, when working with HIV-positive clients it is important that we exercise caution so as to remain within the scope of our training and practice, which usually does not include prescribing medication. Instead, this chapter focuses on a more crucial counseling issue: the decision-making process by which HIV-positive clients decide to undertake preventive treatment.

There are two major approaches to current preventive treatment for HIV disease: traditional pharmaceutical treatment and alternative treatment. The decision-making process for each approach has distinctive elements. A more recent hybrid approach combines traditional and alternative therapies and has become more widely accepted.

Deciding to Begin Prophylactic Drugs

Conflicting information beguiles clients trying to decide whether or not to begin prophylactic drugs. Their doctor says one thing. The latest edition of *AIDS Treatment News* reports something else. Friends on the drugs report feeling great. Other friends are so nauseous from the drugs that they can barely eat. How then can we help clients sort out all of the various reports and make an informed decision they can live with? First, we can help clients understand and synthesize the barrage of information and, more importantly, feelings associated with the start of treatment. Four practical aspects of pharmaceutical intervention come under consideration: timing, efficacy, toxicity, and cost. We can help clients in these areas as well as those that arise when experimental drug protocols are considered. Throughout all of this, we must monitor and address one significant psychological effect of considering prophylactic treatment: the breaking down of our clients' denial system.

Timing

Over the last few years, the question of when to begin treatment has become exceedingly complex. When the Food and Drug Administration released ZVD (brand name AZT) for wide distribution in the 1980s, physicians commonly placed patients on some type of prophylactic medication almost immediately upon testing positive. More recently, data presented at the IX International AIDS Conference in Berlin in 1993 drew into question the effectiveness of such early intervention (Follansbee & Dilley, 1993; Van der Horst, 1994). This led some clients to stop taking antiviral drugs and other prophylactic medications. More recent advances in physicians' ability to determine whether clients' viral load (the amount of virus in their system) is increasing, decreasing, or remaining stable over time has renewed the promise of early treatment (Baker, 1994).

Clients frequently vacillate between agreeing to start treatment and postponing it. They need room to express and explore these ambivalent feelings. Counseling must be a neutral place where clients do not feel pushed to act one way or another. Thus even when we have strong biases regarding the importance or worthlessness of prophylactic interventions, we must keep them to ourselves.

Sometimes clients straightfowardly ask for our opinion. Other times they inquire, "What are your other clients doing?"—veiling their desire for direction. In spite of how inviting it may be, we should take care to avoid giving advice. Giving advice changes the dynamics of the counseling relationship. When we encourage clients to begin treatment, they can no longer explore their ambivalence without feeling as if they are disobeying, rejecting, or disappointing us. A better strategy is to work closely with clients and their primary physicians in addressing the rationale and underlying feelings of any decision. Of course, to work collaboratively with any of our clients' other health care providers requires the clients' informed consent.

Clients occasionally interpret a doctor's suggestion that they begin drugs as a omen that they will soon fall ill. Clients may avoid discussions of prophylactic treatment in order to defend against an unconscious fear of becoming sick. This may occur even when clients consciously know they are healthy. Therefore, it is important that counseling explore both spoken and unspoken fears related to starting on drugs.

Efficacy

Questions about prophylactic drugs' ability to fight HIV disease are often problematic for clients. They want assurance that if they begin treatment it will be effective. Of course, this guarantee cannot be given. One helpful counseling strategy is to invite clients to talk about how they might feel if the treatment were ineffective. Clients can then be encouraged to suggest alternative plans. Having other alternatives in mind may lessen clients' emotional attachment to having any single drug be successful.

Toxicity

A number of the currently used drugs produce toxic side effects. For many clients the side effects, which range from nausea to liver damage, may be reason enough to prevent them from choosing treatment. Yet the side effects vary from person to person and cannot always be predicted. It is not uncommon, however, for clients to base their decision to avoid drugs on inaccurate information, or hearsay, or the experience of a single acquaintance. Whenever possible, we should assist clients in obtaining accurate information regarding the toxicity of treatments. We can also help clients conduct a cost-benefit analysis to determine whether the drug's virtues outweigh its side effects.

Clients may also need to be reminded and reassured that treatment regimens can often be changed if undesirable side effects appear.

It is useful to frame the decision to begin taking preventive drugs as a decision on quality versus quantity of life. For some clients, living a long life will be important and side effects will be more easily tolerated. Other clients will prefer living a life free of limiting side effects even if that means dying sooner. Regardless of the decision clients make, there will be people in their lives telling them they made the wrong choice. Counseling must act as an antidote to such judgments. We must help clients see their choice as an expression of their personal values; as such their choice has an integrity that cannot be challenged.

Cost

Much of the previous discussion on whether or not clients feel they should begin drug treatment assumes that they can financially afford such treatment. Prophylactic drug treatment is not cheap. Tragically, many clients cannot absorb the expense.

In an amazing reversal of fortune, insured clients may fare worse in this respect than uninsured clients. Some cities or counties have programs that provide prophylactic drugs for clients without health insurance. Many of the major drug manufacturing companies are privately owned and make huge profits from the sales of HIV-related drugs; historically, they have provided some quantity of subsidized drugs to those unable to afford their normal cost. Some clients, of course, have health insurance with a prescription plan that covers HIV-related drugs; however, some of these clients do not want to use their health plan for drugs, particularly if they are concealing their HIV status from their insurance company or place of employment.

Experimental Protocols

On an experimental basis, new drugs in developmental stages often get offered to people living with HIV disease. People participating in these drug trials typically receive free medical care and lab work, thus making the trials highly attractive. The decision to begin an experimental trial becomes particularly complicated because fewer guarantees are made about the efficacy of the treatment or about side effects that may be experienced. In addition, many times the requirements of an experimental protocol restrict any outside treatments. Despite the

drawbacks of experimental protocols, the undeniable element of helping the fight to find a new cure may be empowering to clients.

There are many intricate details for clients to examine when considering an experimental protocol: Might they receive a placebo? Will
they receive treatment if the drug is determined effective? If the drug
is effective, will they continue to receive it after the study ends? Will
they be pulled off the drug if side effects arise? Who makes this decision? How long will the experimental protocol run? What happens if
the drug proves ineffective? When will they receive notification of the
study's outcomes? Often our clients do not even know what questions
to ask, let alone understand the answers. In that case, we need to
educate clients about drug studies in general, and then assist them in
understanding the specifics of any study they may consider joining.

Deciding to Begin Alternative Treatments

Alternative approaches to the early treatment of HIV disease run the
gamut from nutritional programs to non-Western medicine, from
herbs to the use of healing visualizations. A whole underground network exists to inform HIV-positive people of the latest trends in alternative treatments. Because our clients have more access to this
information than we do, we should not feel embarrassed or hesitant
to ask them about the details of any nontraditional treatment they are
considering. Rumors about alternative treatments spread quickly;
ascertaining the source and reliability of clients' information is important. Knowing experts to consult with when questions arise is beneficial. Many of the issues presented in the previous sections on pharmaceutical prophylaxis also apply to alternative treatment. In
addition, three unique questions arise: Is the treatment reliable? How
qualified is the practitioner? Is a cure promised?

The question of an alternative treatment's reliability parallels the
issue of efficacy for pharmaceutical treatments, albeit with some significant differences. Although proponents of alternative treatments
proclaim their effectiveness, few alternative treatments have been evaluated through the same stringent Western scientific tests as pharmaceutical drugs. Clients who choose to use alternative treatments must
rely on faith (or word of mouth) regarding the efficacy of the treatment. Faith is important and may cause a placebo type effect, but it
can also be harmful. For example, when an alternative treatment appears not to work, faith may prevent clients from changing to another
type of treatment.

The methods of administering alternative treatments often lack reliability. Many clients obtain treatments through informal channels, resulting in a great variation in suggested dosages, treatment schedules, and treatment modes. As various alternative treatment regimes sweep across the nation (e.g., bitter melon enemas or drinking kombucha mushroom tea) the result is a more serious version of the grade-school telephone game in which the end receiver's message sounds quite different from that of the original sender.

Although clients may consider such over-the-counter treatments harmless, many may have side effects as severe or more severe than those of pharmaceutical drugs. Herbs and vitamins can become toxic when taken improperly. This may be information clients are either unfamiliar with or choose to disregard. They may erroneously consider a treatment safe based solely upon its alternative label.

Sometimes clients follow an alternative treatment on their own. When clients adopt their own regime, we might gently inquire as to whether their primary health care provider has been informed. Letting health care providers know about all preventative treatments undertaken may prevent harmful drug interactions from occurring if additional medications are prescribed. Other times clients are under the care of a practitioner. If clients receive care from an alternative practitioner, we should try to form an alliance as we do with the client's physician.

The regulation of alternative practitioners varies depending on type of practice and geographic location. Some states license chiropractic doctors. Some states require a license to practice traditional Chinese medicine and prescribe herbal remedies. However, in some states, the only thing necessary to distribute herbs for medicinal treatment is the herbs. Clients may want to try to determine their practitioners' qualifications. They may want to find out where practitioners studied, or with whom. Knowing what professional organizations, if any, they belong to may help ease a clients' concerns about practitioners' integrity.

Warning signs of potential problems with alternative practitioners may present themselves in counseling sessions. A common one is for practitioners to tell clients that their way is the only way to fight AIDS; clients are required to quit any other treatments they may be undergoing. This may include a prohibition against Western medicine (including visits to physician). Clients are asked to rely only on the alternative practitioner. An even more harmful variation of this occurs when practitioners brings clients' faith into play: They may lead clients to believe that they do not respond to treatment because they do not try enough. Fortunately, not all alternative practitioners work this way. Many highly ethical, highly trained, highly compassionate health providers work in non-Western, nonpharmacological ways. Unfortunately, they may remain less visible than opportunists who recognize the vulnerability of people living with HIV disease. Many of the same warnings may apply to clients dealing with the Western medical system. Therefore, counseling must help clients develop into good consumers of any type of treatment they may consider.

Occasionally a new alternative treatment arrives on the scene touted as the definitive absolute cure for AIDS. The false promise of a cure harms clients in at least two ways. First, if clients are required to undergo the cure exclusively, they may miss a valuable opportunity to begin another treatment that may actually help. Secondly, the promise of a cure raises clients' hopes and expectations. When the cure fails, clients may succumb to feelings of disappointment and hopelessness. Clients may not only be disappointed in the treatment but also in themselves for acting gullibly and believing in the cure. Rather than attempting to deny our clients' credulity, a better strategy is to reframe it as hopefulness and to work with clients to become more selective in where they place their hope.

Pharmaceutical and Alternative Treatment: The Perfect Combination?

Rather than approach preventive treatment from a bifurcated position of either a pharmaceutical or alternative approach, many clients are adopting a combination of methods. This trend is becoming more acceptable to practitioners as well (Botkin, 1984; Simerly & Karakashian, 1989). Clients may forget that many alternative treatments complement pharmaceutical treatments. For example, the use of herbs may strengthen the immune system and may help lessen nauseous side effects of ZVD. Acupuncture can be effectively used to reduce pain, augmenting other analgesics (Shealy & Cady, 1993). Clients can find ways to use both types of treatments to supplement each other. For example, a Western-trained physician can monitor the success of an Eastern treatment and determine the treatment's effectiveness using objective methods, not guesswork or intuition. An increasing number of Western licensed physicians have also received training in alternative methods. If they are not knowledgeable themselves, many physicians refer to alternative practitioners with whom they feel comfortable working. Although combining treatments may alleviate some of the questions raised regarding the safety and effectiveness of preventive treatment, it still will not necessarily relieve the psychological effects of deciding to fight HIV actively and aggressively.

The Psychological Breakdown of Denial

Beginning treatment—even prophylactic treatment—often brings clients a deeper acknowledgment of their HIV-infected status. Taking medication, once, twice, and even more times a day serves as a continual reminder to clients that they are living with HIV disease. Healthy denial mechanisms may weaken, leaving clients vulnerable to bouts of fear and anxiety. When denial breaks down, the therapeutic task becomes helping our clients learn to live with the emotions aroused by taking medication.

Women's Issues

Many of the psychological issues discussed in this chapter also apply to women living with HIV. However, prophylaxis is another area in which women and men have received disparate treatment. Currently, established treatment regimens have been developed and tested primarily on men. Researchers and physicians know very little about how women may respond differently to drugs. Women may also experience different side effects and toxicities from HIV medications (Anastos & Marte, 1991). Therefore, women clients often experience further frustration and anger when considering preventive treatment.

Women seldom have access to experimental preventive drugs through drug trials in the same way men do. Denenberg (1992) maintained that women are typically implicitly and explicitly excluded from drug trials. In many cases women fail to meet gender-biased qualifications. In other cases the burdens of life as a woman and mother may make participation prohibitive.

> [Women] . . . are required to give proof of contraception or sterilization to enroll; they are tested for pregnancy during enrollment. Trial sites do not generally consider women's special needs for child care, for appropriate transportation, and for appointments that match their needs for caring for children and other family members. (Denenberg, 1992, p. 73)

Corea (1992) also elaborated on the obstacles women face in trying to obtain experimental drugs and added two further points. First, the requirement that participants have a private physician excludes the majority of women with HIV/AIDS who, for lack of money, use public health facilities. Second, decisions on where to locate the trials effectively keep women out. Federal trials often ignore cities with the highest caseloads of HIV-positive women.

Much work needs to be done to make preventive treatments meaningfully available to women. As long as many women's lower earning potential prohibits access to treatment, beginning treatment may not even be an option, let alone a choice (Christensen, 1992). As long as women find the financial or practical costs of participating in drug trials prohibitive, beginning treatment may not be an option. Additional work must be undertaken to help women gain access to treatment. Counseling HIV-positive women requires a sensitivity to the ways in which the constraints of their external world affect their internal, emotional world.

Class Issues

The relationship between social class and health care is quite clear in the United States. Lower class clients are often shut out of the health care system. They may find that proactive treatment to boost their immune system and prevent the progression of infection, whether pharmaceutical or herbal, is unobtainable. In working with disenfranchised clients, it may be useful to adopt a case manager role akin to that of social workers and actively help clients search for previously unexplored resources (e.g., experimental treatment programs, drug scholarships, governmental assistance, local AIDS service agencies). Unfortunately, even after searching, many people from oppressed communities may still have no access to preventive treatment. Tragically, we may be left with no other option but to acknowledge the validity of our clients' rage at being left out of the system.

Cultural Considerations

Particularly around issues of the medical treatment for HIV disease, we must cultivate an exceptional sensitivity to our clients' cultural views of healing. Clients' cultural beliefs regarding illness and appropriate medical treatment provide essential information for nonethnic counselors working with clients from outside the mainstream culture (Jackson, 1990). Some clients may prefer their traditional cultural healing arts to white, middle-class, Western-biased treatment (Jue &

Kain, 1989; Tharp, 1991). Clients may also take religious beliefs into consideration when choosing treatment (Durand, 1992; Parés-Avila & Montano-López, 1994). To work effectively, we must stay attuned to the many cultural influences that contribute to clients' decisions.

Youth Issues

In many ways, young people face the most severe difficulties when deciding to begin preventive treatment. The effects of drug treatments on youth have received even less research attention than the effects on women. Dosages and side effects have not been carefully studied, nor have the effects of drugs on young people's normal physiological development.

Youth commonly gain access to medical care through their parents. Who, then, decides what treatment a youth should receive and when the treatment should begin? Counseling can play a crucial role in helping young clients sort through the myriad emotions that may arise as decisions get made for them or as they get asked to make adult decisions for which developmentally they may be unprepared. Family counseling may be in order. These sessions may be a potentially effective way of sharing between the parents and the youth the responsibility for treatment decisions.

Conclusion

Deciding to begin preventive treatment is one of the many milestones that lie along the path of living with HIV disease. Clients must determine whether the benefits (actual or anticipated) of initiating treatment outweigh the costs (side effects, psychological stress, and financial cost). Throughout this complex process, support, validation, and affirmation are crucial.

Weighing the benefits and costs of traditional and alternative treatment need not always be complicated. Sometimes clients make decisions for purely idiosyncratic reasons. Take, for example, Michael Callen who authored the book *Surviving AIDS*:

> I have a lot of friends who are New Age [oriented] and who are holistic. They just don't know what to make of me. I eat like a pig and I eat really well. But sugar is one of my three or four main reasons for living. I'm a classic Coca-Cola addict. Aside from yoga, I have not dabbled much in so-called alternative, homeo-

pathic forms of medicine. Many long-term survivors of AIDS have.
I am simply not among them. (Hitchens, 1992, p. 32)

However, decision making does become more severely complicated
when gender, class, culture, or age get factored into the process.

Regardless of whether clients consider pharmaceutical or alternative treatment, they must become well informed. An important goal
of counseling is to help clients learn how to become good consumers
of treatment. We should encourage clients to assert their right to know
as much as possible about any proposed course of action.

Deciding to begin preventive treatment can empower clients. Instead of feeling helpless and hopeless, clients may feel strengthened by
proactively doing something to help their body fight HIV. We should
support our clients in their treatment choices unless they are unques-
tionably harmful. Our clients' hopeful mental state may contribute to
their sustained health as much as, or more than, the treatment.

CHAPTER 10

Living Healthier

Reduce stress. Live healthy.
Easier said than done!

The relationship between stress and illness (dis-ease) is widely accepted. People living with HIV disease are repeatedly admonished to reduce their level of stress by doctors, lovers, friends, and family. At the same time they are told to find ways to live healthier. We, too, are not immune from offering our clients this advice.

Living a life free of stress is no easy task, especially in face of a life-threatening illness. We may be surprised to find that some clients have no concept of how to reduce stress or live healthier. This chapter examines practical ways people living with HIV disease can modify their life-style. Although the responsibility for living healthier rests ultimately on our clients, we can do many things to assist them in this quest.

Stress Reduction

Counseling can be extremely instrumental in helping HIV-positive clients discover ways to reduce stress. Behavioral and cognitive behavioral techniques are quite useful in this regard. Many traditional stress-reduction techniques can also be employed, often with great success.

To reduce stress, clients must first identify the copious stressors in their life. Though it may be tempting, it is best not to rush clients through this step and on to the next step of implementing stress-reducing exercises. Unless clients are given the opportunity to exhaust the process of identifying the sources of stress in their life, valuable information may be missed. We must not assume to know the things clients perceive as stressful, or to what degree they are experienced as such. We may find that many items on clients' stress lists only tangentially relate to HIV. Everyday events that caused a mild but tolerable level of stress and anxiety for clients when they were HIV negative often produce increases in intensity and discomfort after clients test positive. Many times it is a combination of things—waiting for a doctor, regularly getting blood drawn, always feeling tired, constantly being examined—that causes clients to stress out. In counseling, great care must be taken not to diminish the importance of any sources of stress in clients' lives. Clients' feelings of stress and frustration must be validated. Clients may already feel unentitled to express their feelings, afraid that others think they complain too much.

After identifying stressors, clients can be encouraged to find ways to reduce the stress. In some cases, simple interventions are possible. If shopping for food causes stress, finding someone to assist in that task may reduce stress. Other times reducing stress becomes more difficult because its source cannot be changed or modified (e.g., having blood drawn). In these situations, clients may find relaxation techniques helpful. Clients, especially those unfamiliar with relaxation techniques, may benefit from direct instruction. We may need to shift from a nondirective therapeutic stance to a more educative stance by actually teaching clients how to relax. When appropriate, biofeedback and visualization can also be incorporated into counseling sessions; both methods of stress reduction have been shown to be particularly helpful to people living with HIV disease.

When addressing more global stress, clients can be encouraged to pursue a relaxation program on a regular, perhaps even daily, basis. Meditation, yoga, and exercise exemplify activities that produce a demonstrated reduction in physiological and psychological stress levels. Clients unfamiliar with these activities can learn about them through books and courses.

An HIV-free zone is also an effective stress reducer. Oftentimes we need to give clients permission to forget about HIV and AIDS for a while. HIV-related reminders like medications, pamphlets, and appointment slips can quickly overtake clients' living quarters and create a suffocating stressful environment. Instead, a favorite room or area can be created where nothing about HIV and AIDS is allowed. Once this safe space has been established, clients can go to it as a refuge from the stresses of their life.

It is important not to pathologize stress inadvertently. Stress is a normal part of life, even more so for people living with HIV disease. Above all, clients must feel free to come into counseling and talk about stress. Sometimes our enthusiasm in teaching stress reduction backfires, unintentionally giving clients the impression that they are good clients only if they are calm and relaxed. Sadly, if clients cannot discuss stressful events in their life, then our good intentions have been worthless.

Exercise

Exercise plays an important part in an HIV-positive client's life not only because of its stress-reducing properties but also because of its many beneficial physiological qualities. Without exercise, many clients living with HIV disease may experience losses in strength and muscle mass, part of the problem of wasting (Capaccioli, 1993). Regular physical training facilitates protein retention and strength maintenance and thus should be encouraged (Cappaccioli, 1993; Harris, 1994; Rigsby, Dishman, Jackson, Maclean, & Raven, 1992).

People living with HIV disease may want to consider an approach to exercise that includes both resistance training and endurance training. Resistance training such as weight lifting helps build crucial muscle mass. Endurance training such as brisk walking or aerobics helps increase lung capacity, improve appetite, and improve bowel habits (Cappaccioli, 1993). Regardless of the activity they engage in, HIV-positive clients must remain sensitive to their individual limitations and their current health state. Exercise physiologists or certified trainers who work well with HIV-positive clients are not uncommon in some parts of the country; referring clients to them is often useful.

Nutrition

For people living with HIV disease, proper nutrition constitutes a crucial part of living healthier. Nutrition is particularly important because several HIV-related infections affect the gastrointestinal tract, minimizing optimal nutrient intake, absorption, and metabolism (Physicians Association for AIDS Care, 1993). This suboptimal nutrient availability leads to malnutrition, which in turn impairs the immune system.

Issues related to food and eating frequently get brought into counseling. For example, losing weight often frightens people living with HIV disease. When weight loss affects clients' physical appearance, their self-esteem may be lowered. Lack of appetite or nausea, a common side effect of prophylactic medication, may affect clients' emotional outlook on many issues. Because of the interrelation of clients' nutritional states and their psychological states, we may want to form an alliance with a good nutritionist who specializes in working with HIV-positive people.

Clients' seeming preoccupation with food safety may be highly appropriate and not necessarily obsessive. Clients have good reasons for worrying about eating contaminated foods (e.g., inadequately cooked meats, raw foods like fish or eggs, leftovers). It is extremely important that people with compromised immune systems avoid food-borne diseases because these can be difficult to treat, hasten the progression of HIV disease, and even be fatal (Physicians Association for AIDS Care, 1993).

At times, however, we may be called upon to help keep clients' food safety concerns in balance. Because eating is important, steps should be taken to help clients avoid becoming germ-phobic or coming to food as an enemy. An article on food in *Being Alive: People With HIV/AIDS Action Coalition Newsletter* illustrated this dilemma:

> The prospect of traveling around the world in an "unprotected bubble" is scary. That's what it's like having an impaired immune system in a "dangerous world." On the other hand, living in a protective bubble can create unnecessary stress and unhealthy isolation in the HIV-infected individual. (Jensen, 1993, p. 7)

At times counseling includes helping clients plan a strategy for dealing with difficult (and potentially dangerous) situations like being a dinner guest or traveling outside of the United States. Clients who have high anxiety levels around food contamination can be encouraged to become knowledgeable about food safety and to employ their knowledge in a way that provides them the maximum freedom of movement—not in a way that is overly restrictive.

Moderating Substance Use and Stopping Substance Abuse

Understandably, HIV-positive people embrace a wide range of attitudes and behaviors with regards to the use of mind-altering drugs and alcohol. Often, as part of our work with clients, we are called upon to address their substance use. Counseling strategies differ substantially depending on the degree to which clients use or abuse drugs and alcohol. Therefore, our first task is to distinguish between clients who are seriously chemically dependent and those who are recreational or social users. Because rates of HIV infection among injecting drug users are high (Friedman et al., 1993), severe chemical dependency is not uncommon among people living with HIV disease.

HIV-positive addicts and alcoholics face two challenges. They must stop using their drug of choice. In addition, they must overcome any HIV-related adjustment problems that they may be experiencing. For most clients, the consequences of drug and alcohol abuse may far overshadow those of being HIV positive. The continued abuse of drugs or alcohol can significantly compromise clients' physical health, psychological functioning, and socioeconomic situation (Fischer, Jones, and Stein, 1989). Therefore, in counseling, examining recovery issues must often take precedence over HIV-adjustment issues.

In counseling substance-abusing clients with HIV disease, four major treatment issues deserve special attention. The first issue concerns clients' use of denial. Nonabusing clients often use denial in a healthy way to help them defend against extreme HIV-related anxiety. In contrast, abusing clients' use of denial is unhealthy and forms the psychological defense that allows them to continue using drugs or alcohol. With nonabusing clients we may overlook denial (or at times even encourage it), but with abusing clients denial must be confronted and discouraged. However, these clients do not easily abandon denial as a defense; Fisher, Jones, and Stein (1989) noted that HIV-positive substance abusers may remain in denial throughout the entire course of their HIV illness.

A second treatment issue concerns clients' ability to receive proper care. Becoming HIV positive often forces clients to acknowledge a drug or alcohol problem. If clients admit to a substance abuse problem, they face the double stigma of being both an addict and HIV positive. This stigma may drive clients away from treatment (Fisher et al., 1989). Substance abuse counselors and treatment staff at hospitals and recovery programs are not immune from rejecting HIV-positive clients. Faltz (1988) listed common responses given by recovery program staff when asked to work with HIV-positive clients: "'What's the use, the client will die anyway?' 'My job is to help people get healthy, not to die,' 'I have no experience in this kind of counseling,' 'In addition to all my other work, I'm supposed to counsel dying people too?'" (pp. 217–218). Breaking their addiction will be difficult enough for HIV-positive clients without also having to contend with ignorant and hateful attitudes from people who are supposed to be helpful. When it becomes necessary to refer a client to an alcohol and drug recovery program, we want to make certain that the program's staff are well informed about HIV and are comfortable working with HIV-positive clients.

A third treatment issue concerns clients' ways of handling difficult and painful emotions. Living with HIV disease often engenders strong feelings of anxiety, anger, guilt, and depression. Substance abusers historically find these feelings intolerable (Fisher et al., 1989). As HIV-related feelings become more demanding, clients may try to resort to old patterns of self-medication with drinking and drugging (Fisher et al., 1989). Even with clients who have remained abstinent for long periods of time, we must remain attentive to signs of relapse.

A fourth treatment issue concerns finding appropriate support for HIV-positive clients' continued abstinence from drugs or alcohol. Many people in recovery rely upon group support like 12-step meetings to stay clean and sober. HIV-positive clients commonly need groups that are not only geared to recovery issues but also sensitive to the special issues that arise for them as people living with HIV disease. One good example is the HIV-oriented meetings of Alcoholics Anonymous and Narcotics Anonymous that can be found in urban areas heavily affected by HIV.

Treating substance abusers living with HIV disease often demands specialized knowledge about recovery from drugs and alcohol beyond the scope of this book. When working with this population, we should secure additional information such as that found in Shernoff's (1991) *Counseling Chemically Dependent People With HIV Illness*; Quackenbush, Benson, and Rinaldi's (1992) *Risk and Recovery: AIDS, HIV, and Alcohol*; or Fisher and Needle's (1993) *AIDS and Community-Based Drug Intervention Programs: Evaluation and Outreach*. Continued supervision and consultation may be necessary.

In our work, we also come into contact with clients who drink alcohol or use recreational drugs but whose actions do not meet the clinical definition of chemical dependency. Although some clients (and their doctors) believe there is no harm in sporadic use of alcohol or drugs, other people take a stronger position. In a section of his book, *No Time to Wait: A Complete Guide to Treating, Managing, and Living With HIV Infection*, Siano (1993) addressed recreational drugs and alcohol in relation to HIV:

Whenever I see a patient who has just come back from using drugs for a couple of days, weeks, or months, blood is drawn to measure the immune system's strength and the measurements have usually dropped significantly.

These numbers are very difficult to rebuild—*almost impossible if the person continues to use drugs.* Laboratory tests have shown why. In a test tube, HIV replicates approximately 20 times faster in a solution containing cocaine than it does in a cocaine-free environment. With alcohol, the rate of replication is 5 times the control rate. Replication rates in other drug environments have not been tested, but I am convinced from personal observation that recreational drugs are dangerous for HIV + s. (p. 49)

Another danger of recreational drug and alcohol use often goes unacknowledged. Cabaj (1994) noted that the use of alcohol, drugs, or even abused prescribed medicines alters judgment and allows for disinhibition in sexual behaviors. HIV-positive clients who use alcohol or drugs, even occasionally, run the risk of reinfecting themselves (or infecting others).

For most clients, the decision whether or not to drink or use recreational drugs occasionally epitomizes yet another quality-of-life decision they must make. Many acknowledge the possibility that their choice may compromise their immune system's functioning, but they may feel that the enjoyment that comes from an occasional letting loose with friends is emotionally compensatory. In counseling, we should invite nonabusing clients to make thoughtful choices. We should also remain alert for signs that an occasional drug or drink is becoming habitual.

Contact

One of the most overlooked aspects of living a healthy life is the need for contact with others. This holds particularly true for people living with HIV disease who often feel isolated. At times, clients keep themselves from being with others, even though they may be hungry for contact. With these clients, we should not only examine the immediate circumstances but also explore their historical relationship patterns. In encouraging clients to make and maintain contact with others, we can focus on three major areas.

The Counseling Relationship

For some HIV-positive clients, the counseling relationship may serve as their only source for affirmation, closeness, and support. Regardless of our theoretical orientation, we should acknowledge this directly with clients at an appropriate point in the relationship. Since these clients often feel that they burden us, bringing the topic out in the open and into the session helps prevent a client's premature termination of counseling. Unless they are truly burdensome, clients must be reassured that they are not asking too much of us and that we are willing to provide them with the human contact they need. We can then offer the counseling relationship as a model for the supportive relationships with others clients wish to develop. By learning to ask for and receive affirmation, closeness, and support from us, clients develop the skills needed to obtain affirmation, closeness, and support from others.

Support Groups

In many urban areas and in an increasing number of nonmetropolitan areas, organized support groups exist for people affected by HIV and AIDS. These groups often run the gamut from full-spectrum groups to asymptomatic groups, from sero-discordant couples groups to women's groups. For many HIV-positive people, these groups fill several important roles. They provide a sense of belonging, countering the ostracism many HIV-positive people face. They provide an ongoing support network of people clients can turn to when they feel down, or in need of assistance. They provide a necessary source of mirroring, countering clients' feelings that they are the only person with HIV. They also provide clients with an information network on the latest treatments.

In spite of the many benefits they offer, support groups are not appropriate for all clients. Some clients feel extremely uncomfortable in a support setting. Therefore, it is best to consider the appropriateness of a group setting for a specific client rather than to make a referral to a support group part of our standard treatment protocol. Often we need to work with clients to prepare them for group sessions, especially when clients have never before been in a support group. If we do refer clients to groups, we should look for ways to incorporate the material that arises for the client in the group setting into the work of individual counseling.

Supportive Relationships

Strong, intimate, healthy relationships with a partner or with close friends provide another important source of contact for people living with HIV disease. We can often be helpful in assisting clients to maintain relationships in the face of HIV-related obstacles. We can also encourage clients to create new types of supportive relationships, especially when they have been abandoned by people traditionally thought of as sources of support (e.g., parents, partner, husband, wife).

When clients are not in relationships, we might encourage them to take advantage of buddy programs offered by AIDS service agencies. In many cities these agencies provide buddies or emotional support volunteers who have been expressly trained to provide a nurturing, supportive relationship to HIV-positive people. Many times a buddy can furnish the emotional, physical, and spiritual support clients living with HIV disease vitally need to remain healthy—and the support they need as their health begins to decline.

Conclusion

Unlike the early days of AIDS, when being HIV-positive meant certain death and clients could do little to prevent the disease's progression, HIV-positive people have many opportunities to bolster their health. A well-established relationship between stress and illness exists, particularly with respect to HIV disease. One of the greatest contributions people living with HIV disease may make to their longevity is to reduce stress and live healthier.

There are many ways we can assist clients to create a more healthy life. We can educate clients on ways to reduce stress. We can help remove clients' blocks toward engaging in physical activities. We can assess clients' nutritional knowledge and make appropriate referrals when necessary. We can provide a supportive therapeutic relationship and help clients find ways to create other supportive relationships in their lives.

When working with clients around issues of living healthier and reducing stress, an inherent paradox arises. Stress reduction itself risks becoming stressful if promoted too vigorously. We must make certain that our expectations and the expectations of our clients do not become an unexpected source of stress.

Just like our clients, we must also remember that living with HIV disease is, by its very nature, stressful. Not all sources of stress can be reduced. The next chapter examines a common source of stress: the workplace.

CHAPTER 11

The Workplace

A work-related crisis is a life crisis.

I n the United States, paid work constitutes a central role in many people's lives. When people are healthy, a major portion of the day may be allocated to their job. Many people, particularly those who closely adhere to the Protestant work ethic (e.g., middle class, male), may organize their whole life around work: they prepare for a career, actively pursue that career, and look forward to reaping the rewards of that career. The progression of HIV disease disrupts that cycle. Because for many people, especially men, personal identity develops synchronously with their career development, work-related crises often result in personal crises.

Clients who hold jobs outside of the home often come in contact with people who find it uncomfortable (or unacceptable) to work with someone HIV positive. The emotional reactions of bosses, co-workers, and others in the work environment may greatly affect the emotional state of our clients. Although the Americans With Disabilities Act supposedly protects people with HIV and AIDS from overt acts of discrimination, HIV-positive clients may still encounter less open, but no less painful, expressions of insensitivity or overt and covert discrimination.

In counseling we must validate the immense impact of work-related issues on employed clients' lives. HIV-positive clients' ability or inability to provide for themselves financially has staggering psychological implications. This chapter examines four workplace issues that afflict people living with HIV: discrimination, insurance, disability, and stigma. It also considers the increasingly complex situation that arises when HIV-positive clients work as health care providers.

Discrimination

Federal legislation makes it illegal to discriminate on the basis of HIV status. Title I of the Americans With Disabilities Act (ADA) is designed to protect people living with HIV or AIDS from discrimination in job application procedures, hiring, promotions, discharge, compensation, and job training (Zavos, 1992). In some situations, the implications of the law are quite unequivocal. For example, employers may not legally inquire into an applicant's HIV status when conducting job interviews (Zavos, 1992). However, in other situations the mandates of the ADA are not as clear-cut. By law an HIV test may only be required when the test is job related. Although Zavos (1992), writing for the American Bar Association's AIDS Coordination Project, maintained that "HIV tests are almost never job-related" (p. 2), employers may feel and act differently.

In spite of the protections offered by the ADA, people living with HIV know that covert discrimination still occurs. It is not uncommon for clients to feel that if they were to apply for a new job or a promotion their HIV status might become an issue. Clients may get passed over for promotions, or fail to get jobs, because they are supposedly unqualified. Clients' only recourse is often a costly legal battle that requires the public disclosure of their HIV status. Although under the ADA clients are entitled to legal recourse, they may be hesitant to exercise that right. Clients may decide that the harassment they might be subjected to in the course of a trial overshadows any compensation they stand to gain from winning their case.

Counseling can help clients cope with the traumas of job-related discrimination. We can validate our clients' assessment of the AIDS-friendly climate of their workplace. We can assist clients in distinguishing between realistic paranoia (fact based) and exaggerated paranoia (fear based) with regards to discrimination. We can help clients establish appropriate responses to any HIV-related discrimination that does occur. Clients need to be affirmed regardless of whether they choose to address job-related discrimination actively or simply choose to ignore it. Although it may be difficult for clients to overlook discrimination, they may feel that they need to do so to remain employed.

The Americans With Disabilities Act requires employers to make reasonable accommodations to a work environment or in the way things are customarily done. These accommodations must permit a person with HIV or AIDS to apply for a job, perform essential functions of a job, gain access to a work site, and enjoy equal privileges and benefits of employment (Zavos, 1992). Clients may be unfamiliar with this portion of the law; they may not understand how the concept of reasonable accommodation applies to them. For example, clients may be unaware that they are allowed regular rest periods or time off on a regular basis for HIV-related medical treatments. Although the ADA does not require employers to adjust a job in a way that would impose an undue hardship on them, it does require employers to make changes to allow people living with HIV to perform their functions. Clients need to be informed of their rights, especially when their physical condition begins to interfere with their ability to work. When clients decide to request accommodations from their employers, they often feel anxious and threatened. Our understanding and support is essential.

Stigma and Rumors

In many work environments where explicit discrimination is outlawed, implicit discrimination remains uncontrolled in the form of stigma and rumors. Clients may come to counseling doubting their sanity. They may have been assured by their employer that they are accepted and respected yet sense that they are being ostracized because of being HIV positive. In counseling sessions it is important not to add to our clients' confusion by challenging or doubting their experiences; instead we should help clients become more aware of the many ways discrimination may be present yet hidden.

Work environments give rise to rumors. When a person living with HIV disease enters a workplace, rumors commonly arise because many people remain unknowledgeable about HIV and its transmission. Acting out of ignorance at best, and hatred at worst, workers find ways to stigmatize HIV-positive co-workers. It is not surprising then, that clients come to counseling with examples of offhanded offensive comments made by supervisors and other employees while clients were within earshot. Clients need to develop ways to cope with the feelings of hurt and anger that arise from these comments. Under some circumstances clients may decide that a direct confrontation of the perpetrator of the comments is appropriate; under other circumstances clients may prefer to play dumb. We should affirm our clients' decisions and note the valid reasons that inform our clients' response.

In attending to job-related discrimination, our energies need not be limited to the consulting room. An enormous amount of education needs to be done in work environments themselves. Fear about transmission, and the hatred it spawns, must be combatted with clear, concise information. With proper preparation we can use our ability to work with people to act as consultants to businesses. Teaching workers how not to fear people living with HIV disease may reduce many of the traumas that occur in the workplace.

Insurance

An enormous number of people rely upon employers as their sole source of health insurance. Thus for many clients, work-related issues become intricately intertwined with issues of health care. Clients may shun objecting to an injustice suffered on the job because they feel that to make a conflict public may risk their link to medical treatment.

The Americans With Disabilities Act specifically outlaws denying employment to a person living with HIV disease because insurance costs may increase (Zavos, 1992). However, it is unclear whether employers are required to include individuals with HIV or AIDS in a health-insurance plan. Furthermore, the ADA permits preexisting condition clauses that limit the coverage for HIV and AIDS as long as they are not designed to evade the act's purposes (Zavos, 1992). Court rulings regarding the interpretation and implementation of the ADA are pending. Therefore, we should make every effort to stay current with judicial decisions that may pertain to our clients.

Ironically, even when clients have health insurance they may feel too frightened to use it. Clients may worry that if they decide to use their health insurance for HIV-related expenses, their employer will catch on and either fire them (citing non-HIV reasons) or put a cap on their benefits. Clients often need our help to sort through their feelings about this complex issue. Clients need to determine how long they can wait to use their insurance without jeopardizing their health. Some clients are capable of paying their medical expenses out of pocket. Other clients need to find alternative low-cost sources of health care. Clients may have to ask that the reports their physicians send to insurance companies are written in such a way that the justification for any procedure is general and not HIV specific. Even still, many clients may be distraught and worry that by using their health insurance they are hurting themselves. As with other troubling emotions clients share in counseling, we must avoid discounting these feelings (i.e., consoling clients by telling them they have nothing to worry about). A better strategy is to assure clients that their feelings are justified.

Disability Leave

Leaving work on disability results in multifaceted consequences. When clients go out on disability, they free up time and energy to use for boosting their immune system. They can also engage in other life pursuits. Simultaneously, stopping work is another recognition that HIV has encroached upon their life. When clients are strongly tied to career for their self-identity, taking disability leave may throw them into a profound despair

When clients' health insurance depends upon their active employment, leaving work may mean the loss of continued medical and psychological care. Many clients cannot afford the steep cost of health insurance without an employer's co-payment. Often they are forced to obtain new policies. Some clients find it difficult to find a policy at an affordable price. Others find that new policies only offer reduced services.

Once working ceases, even clients with good disability benefits may worry about how they will manage financially. Clients' fears of exhausting their benefits hang heavy. We want to encourage clients to voice their fears. When counseling these clients, an effective strategy is to help them focus on making concrete plans to prevent the fears from materializing. Clients can be encouraged to keep well informed of the status of their benefits; knowing specific details (e.g., the limits to their benefits) can prevent unconscious fears from running rampant. Clients can also be encouraged to explore any other forms of assistance that they may be eligible for.

Leaving work on disability can exact not only a financial toll but also an emotional one. Many clients have to adapt psychologically to life without work. Often they need to articulate new goals and directions. If clients do not have a strong design for spending the time they once devoted to their job, lethargy and boredom may result. No matter how much clients look forward to stopping work, we should closely monitor them for signs of depression once they are out on disability.

When a Health Care Professional Is Positive

Many of the work-related issues discussed in this chapter are compounded when HIV-positive clients are health care professionals. Clients' choices regarding continuing to work must take into consideration the guidelines set forth by their professional organizations as well as any legal restrictions that apply. If clients are in the position of being forced to leave their current position (or to close down their practice), exploring with them alternative ways of using and channeling their education, training, and energy is often beneficial. This is especially true when clients remain asymptomatic.

If a health care worker does not presently have to stop working (for example, an asymptomatic psychologist), the issue still exists of when in the future to do so. Clients who are nurses or physicians may come to counseling to explore the issues related to closing a practice or ending an association with a medical facility: the appropriate way and time to inform their patients is often a monumental concern. Developing a supportive relationship with these clients cannot be overemphasized. Because of the consequences associated with disclosing to others, we may be the only person the health care workers can turn to, to share their thoughts and concerns.

Parents' Challenges

For many single parents employment depends on child care. Finding child care for an HIV-positive child may prove difficult and may prevent single parents from working. If their child is frequently ill and needs constant attention, clients may find themselves unable to hold down a steady job. Even if their child is not HIV positive, the stigma of having a parent who is may make child care unobtainable. Because these clients often feel oppressed and misunderstood, we should take painstaking measures to insure that we understand their experiences and validate any feelings that arise such as frustration or anger.

Culture and Class Issues

Most of this chapter has been written under the assumption that the worker is a United States citizen and thus eligible for work-related benefits. Some noncitizens, in the United States legally or illegally, do migrant work or day labor and receive no health insurance, no benefits, and no disability even when injured on the job. For these people, not working may not be an option. Many times the survival of their family rests on their bringing home a day's wages. Hiding their HIV status may be crucial, and working paramount, even when it means destroying their health. In counseling, we should endeavor to see things from the viewpoint of these workers. We need to work proactively and may find ourselves taking on a case-worker role.

Youth Concerns

HIV-positive young people face their own version of workplace concerns. Many of the issues adults face at work, for example, discrimination and stigmatization, occur for youth in the schoolyard and in the classroom. Adults may have had previous experience with prejudice, but young people may not. They may be unprepared for the pain inflicted by cruel remarks and actions.

School plays an important role in the development of young people, providing them with opportunities for learning as well as socialization with peers. For HIV-positive youth, these opportunities may be severely restricted; instances where local school districts have barred children with HIV disease from attending school are well known (Walker, 1992). In some cases it is the community, through acts of harassment, that effectively keeps HIV-positive youth out of classrooms.

An article in the October 1993 issue of the *Pediatric Infectious Disease Journal* and reprinted in the *CDC National AIDS Hotline Training Bulletin* (CDC, 1993) emphasizes that restricting HIV-positive youth from schools not only causes great suffering and anguish for the youth and their families but also propagates the unfounded notion that HIV is likely to be transmitted in schools. No cases of HIV transmission in school have been reported, and children with HIV disease should be able to participate in all school activities with the same considerations as other children to the extent that their health permits (CDC, 1993). No reason aside from fear exists to justify excluding HIV-positive youth from school. The prevalence of fear and widespread misinformation regarding the inclusion of HIV-positive youth in school activities often necessitates our taking on an advocacy role, educating school boards as well as parents and the wider community.

Confidentiality of the youth's HIV status in the school is an important and sensitive issue. State and local laws protecting privacy must always be followed. Three recommendations are included in the article reprinted in the *CDC AIDS Hotline Training Bulletin* (CDC, 1993): First, persons aware of the youth's HIV status should be limited to those who need such knowledge to care for the child (e.g., the school medical adviser, school nurse, and teacher). Second, the youth should be encouraged to self-administer medications because their administration by a school nurse or medical adviser may compromise confidentiality. Finally, young people should be allowed to use nearly all services for youth with special needs without revealing their HIV status. Because many parents may be unaware of the full extent of HIV-related confidentiality legislation, it is often appropriate for us to work with young people's parents to ensure that confidentiality is protected at school.

Two other issues often arise with regards to an HIV-positive youth's participation in school. Teachers, administrators, and parents are often concerned about what should happen if young people get cut and bleed. Similarly, they often worry about permitting young people's participation in athletic programs. Two guidelines should be followed (CDC, 1993): First, schools should use principles of universal precautions (gloves and disinfectants) when handling blood exposures; this should be a uniform policy for any blood exposure (e.g., nosebleeds, fights, unintentional injuries) from any young person. Second, HIV-positive youth should be permitted to participate in competitive sports. Although participation in some contact sports may result in laceration or abrasion, the risk of HIV transmission during sports is probably extremely low. However, the American Academy of Pediatrics has recommended that an HIV-positive youth interested in participating in football or wrestling consider another sport (CDC, 1993). Of course, any decision regarding an HIV-positive youth's participation in athletics should include the youth's physician.

HIV-positive clients who attend school need an enormous amount of support from us. For most young people, school is stressful enough without the additional burden of worrying about their HIV status. Counseling can provide youth with a place to give voice to the concerns and hurts they may have experienced at school. For example, young clients may worry that they can pass on the virus to other kids at school. In working with young clients, our job is often to speak openly and frankly about HIV (e.g., how HIV is and is not transmitted). Other people in young clients' lives may be unprepared, unwilling, or unable to speak directly to these concerns. In working with young people we must recall what being in grade school or high school is like and how important issues like peer acceptance and athletic prowess can be.

Conclusion

Many of the larger issues facing HIV-positive people—fear, stigma, loss—crop up in the work arena. Although legislation protects the rights of HIV-positive people to earn a living, ignorance and prejudice still exist in the workplace. At some point in counseling, most employed clients want to discuss HIV-related work issues. Therefore, we should stay informed of the various legislative rulings that affect HIV-positive people in our state and city.

To counsel effectively, we must understand and respect the fact that for some clients, quitting a job is better than enduring a level of hatred or harassment that has become intolerable. We must also be able to empathize with clients who prefer to suffer the indignities of HIV-related discrimination in order to maintain a steady income. We must allow clients to express their pain and anger regardless of whether they leave work or stay.

Because many people's health care is provided through their employment, work-related issues take on even greater weight. The continuance of health care is a primary interest for people living with HIV disease. Thus, anything that could potentially threaten their health care causes alarm. We must also acknowledge that, tragically, some people have neither health insurance nor employment. Whenever job-related issues arise, we should anticipate that they will be accompanied by health care concerns.

Adult clients' job-related issues and young clients' school-related issues often require us to step outside of our traditional role as counselor. At times we may have to help clients establish links to community agencies that can provide them with legal, financial, and medical assistance. We may also need to act as client-advocates in courtrooms or at schoolboard meetings. In addition, we have a duty to use our education, expertise, and status as professionals to educate people in our clients' work and school environments. We must do everything we can to eradicate the stigma and discrimination that burden our clients' lives.

CHAPTER 12

Fortifying the Spirit

*HIV disease is spiritual. It asks people to question
the essence and meaning of their life.*

H IV disease is most frequently described as a disease of the
body, and yet it also affects the soul. HIV-positive clients are
often confronted with the larger questions of human existence: "Why me?" "What is my purpose?" "What happens
after I die?" For many clients the only safe place to grapple with the
answers to these questions is in counseling.

Just as clients need to fortify their bodies to defend against the
physical attack of HIV, so too they need to fortify their spirits to rally
against the disease's emotional and psychological assault. Many times
we are called upon to join clients on their spiritual journey. Those of
us who identify as pastoral counselors may be familiar with incorporating spiritual issues into our counseling sessions; still, we may not
fully understand the unique dimensions of the spiritual issues facing
people living with HIV disease. Others of us may believe spiritual
issues do not belong in the counseling session. Regardless, clients
present AIDS-related spiritual issues. It is as Winiarski (1991) maintained: for people living with HIV "issues of connection to a greater
reality; blame, shame, or guilt, based on religious beliefs; and the role
of God become prominent issues in psychotherapy" (p. 183).

Spirituality and Religion

Religion and spirituality often provide HIV-positive people a framework from which to view their life. Although some clients may see
religion as a source of solace, others may see religion (or at least certain

religious leaders) as a source of pain and condemnation. Sometimes clients' negative experiences with religion color the way they view spirituality; they may reject both. Other times clients may have positive experiences with organized religion that serve as the core for their spiritual pursuits. Some clients have no religious background yet consider themselves to be highly spiritual. Of course, some clients are interested in neither religion nor spirituality.

Drawing a distinction between religiosity and spirituality is crucial when HIV-positive clients have become estranged from organized religion. In his book, *Ministry to Persons With AIDS: A Family Systems Approach*, Perelli (1991) noted that HIV-positive people often erroneously presume that because they are disconnected from organized religion, they can no longer have their own personal spirituality or personal relationship with God. However, once these clients come to understand the difference between spirituality and religiosity, they often feel freer to pursue spiritual interests.

In his book *AIDS-Related Psychotherapy*, Winiarski (1991) defined religiosity as "a stereotypically patterned, unquestioned following of rules or 'walking through the pace' concerned primarily with external practice" (p. 185). Winiarski (1991) noted that there are dangers associated with "acting religious": clients may give little concern to understanding what lies beneath their external practice. He suggested that many of the condemnatory and punitive messages directed at clients mark beliefs and activities based in religiosity rather than spirituality. As such, religiosity may play part in a client's bargaining process (Kubler-Ross, 1969). Clients with strong religious beliefs may see being HIV positive as punishment. They may feel that if they act more religious they will be forgiven and spared the ravages of HIV disease. Winiarski (1991) stated that in some cases "fear of further retribution requires the individual to avoid questioning, exploring, or disagreeing with beliefs of practice" (p. 185).

According to Winiarski (1991), spirituality is an "inner generated, thoughtful, and sometimes skeptical search—a process rather than a product—for universal connections, with no *quid pro quo* from a higher power sought or intended" (p. 186). Perelli (1991) described spirituality as a dimension of the human experience that transcends the immediate awareness of self. He maintained that clients enter the spiritual realm when questioning the meaning of life, when confronting personal limitations, or when experiencing the unconditional love of another person. "Spirituality is concerned with issues of meaning, hope, freedom, love, forgiveness, truth, and the image of God" (p. 22). Given this definition, we may find that spirituality plays a much bigger role in clients' lives than even they recognize.

The Role of Spirituality in Clients' Lives

It is helpful to understand how religious or spiritual beliefs originally manifested in clients' lives. Sometimes clients' dedication to a religious or spiritual path has continually provided them with comfort; other times this dedication is a more recent reaction to their HIV status. Religion and spirituality can be punitive and contribute to self-hate, or they can provide clients with a profound sense of connectedness. Examining spiritual and religious beliefs in the context of clients' personal histories can help us determine whether clients are using these beliefs in the service of growth or in the service of self-retribution. When it is the latter, we need to encourage clients to discover ways in which their religious or spiritual beliefs and practices can be used to promote compassion and healing.

Facing Death and the Acceleration of Growth

At times we may be surprised to witness the dedication and drive that some HIV-positive people bring to counseling sessions. Often a remarkable growth can occur when clients face the limited nature of their lives. Facing death creates a crisis of the spirit; what can result is often, though not always, miraculous. In his personal account of spiritual growth, "Savage Grace: The Spirituality of Illness," Matousek (1994) wrote:

> While it is true that our lives have been shattered by the HIV virus, it is also true that within this destruction, profound insights have led to a deepening of vision, purpose, and faith. Knowing that we may die very soon, we've been forced to look toward eternity; to come to treasure what we have; to realize, as a monk once wrote, that if the cardinal's flight from bank to bank were less brief, it would also be less glorious. (p. 105)

Even though clients' accelerated movements toward happiness and spiritual maturity may seem joyful and promising, we should remember that often they effectively obscure a deeper fear. Unlike the common anxiety of daily living, this fear has a most profound source: "Knowing that my own funeral could be next, I panicked, for fear not only of dying, but of dying completely ignorant of my inner life" (Matousek, 1994, pp. 105–106). Thus in counseling sessions we are amiss to acknowledge our clients' growth and to not also acknowledge their fear.

Many times clients arrange their experiences in ways that highlight how they have benefited from living with HIV disease. Matousek, reflecting upon his state as a person living with HIV disease, wrote:

> For me, this has been the ideal predicament: carrying a potentially fatal bug (with its urgent message not to waste time) while remaining asymptomatic. I've often said that HIV has actually saved my life, propelling me to change, encouraging me to confront what's difficult, urging my fascination with things divine. There is nothing Pollyanna in this; it does not imply that I'd have chosen this virus, or that I would not cure it tomorrow if I could. But there have been undeniable benefits to having the myth of immortality exploded. Like thousands of others living in this limbo, I've found depths and doors and potentials in extremes that I didn't know existed before. Forced to look beyond the body for metaphysical meaning, I've learned that within the horror lies a tremendous mystery. (1994, p. 107)

Although it is easy to join clients in glorifying their spiritual and psychological growth, we should remember that the process by which they obtain this growth is often grueling.

HIV disease propels many people along a spiritual journey, but we should not assume that because clients are HIV positive, they will become spiritual. According to Matousek (1994), the concept of a spiritual element in living with HIV disease is untenable to some in the AIDS community. The continued spread of the epidemic and the increased suffering that results make it difficult for some people to conceive of there being any benefit to AIDS—spiritual or otherwise.

Toxic Beliefs

Sometimes clients come in for counseling with religious beliefs that punish rather than promote spiritual growth. Winiarski (1991) observed that many HIV-positive people internalize proclamations by religious leaders, such as "we love the sinner but hate the sin," and transform these statements into a self-condemnatory and intrapunitive attitude. Before she died in 1992, Sonia Singleton described her experience:

I thought that God had betrayed me. God had abandoned me. I'm not a deeply religious person, but I was brought up to believe in a power greater than myself. And I just didn't consider myself a person worthy of getting something as cruel as this. I felt like a low animal. I took on all the ugly, nasty things that society was saying about people with HIV or AIDS. I took everything they projected and ran with it. That was my fault. I didn't have to accept that. I didn't have to believe that. I needed to have a greater understanding of who I was and what this virus actually was. (Hitchens, 1992, p. 245)

We must remember that not all toxic beliefs stem from clients' pasts. Instances exist where a client's family and friends (and even doctors, nurses, and other health care workers) have used threats of punishment by God to urge conversion to or alignment with religious beliefs.

Fortunato (1993) maintained that a good counseling strategy is to counter toxic beliefs by using antidotes from within the client's own religious tradition. For example, most religious traditions contain portrayals of a compassionate God. When clients see God as damning, they see only an incomplete picture of God. The Christian tradition, and many others, also conceive of God as merciful.

If we are not knowledgeable about a particular religion, or feel uncomfortable sharing the knowledge we may possess, we should consider consulting with a carefully chosen clergy person (Winiarski, 1991). It is often helpful to choose a person who comes from the same religious or spiritual tradition as our clients. At times we may also want to put clients, and their families, in touch with AIDS-affirmative clergy.

New Age Spirituality

Since the beginning of the AIDS crisis, many people living with HIV disease have found solace in what could best be described as New Age spirituality. The scope and range of these various New Age paths vary, but they have in common an effort to "rally people away from victimhood toward the possibilities of self-healing and survival" (Matousek, 1994, p. 107). They often employ numerous techniques like affirmations, visualizations, and mirror work, not at all incompatible with counseling. At their best, they offer people living with HIV disease an uplifting alternative to a despairing and meaningless approach to death.

Concerns must be raised over some possible side effects of New Age spirituality, however. When a New Age spirituality preaches notions of self-created reality and urges people to take responsibility for their illness, it runs the risk of being misinterpreted. Clients with unresolved guilt issues over becoming infected ably transform taking responsibility for their illness into blame and self-punishment. Getting ill is seen as a result of and testament to their negative outlook on life. These clients take what could be a liberating spiritual philosophy and turn it into another source of guilt: "If I had only done more affirmations, my T-cell count would not have dropped." When counseling these clients, an effective strategy is to help them separate their own self-deprecating interpretations of New Age philosophy from the original healing intent of the path. This commonly leads to an examination or reexamination of clients' beliefs about why they became infected.

Another danger of New Age spirituality is that it often enjoins a one-sided optimistic view of life (Winiarski, 1991), leaving no room for negative emotions such as anger. When clients view anger as unspiritual, they may hold inside their outrage at the injustices they face rather than expressing the rage and pain in a psychologically healthier manner. Paul Monette, the author of the renowned AIDS memoir, *Borrowed Time*, is quoted as saying "by taking anger away from people, some forms of spirituality keep people from becoming part of the political battle. Anger against injustice is the most significant emotion an adult can feel" (Matousek, 1994, p. 109).

When working with clients who uphold the belief that negative emotions are bad and should not be expressed, we will do best to try to work from within their framework. Challenging or discounting a client's spiritual beliefs, regardless of how unhealthy they may seem to us, typically engenders resistance; clients justifiably feel that their beliefs are being devalued by us. A more useful strategy is to remind clients that a spiritually perfected state without anger is a goal for which to strive. Even the most enlightened beings experienced and expressed anger on their spiritual pathways. Some clients can come to use New Age spiritual beliefs and practices in a manner more accepting of emotions. For example, clients can construct affirmations in ways that are inclusive of a wide range of human feelings: "All parts of me, including my anger, work for my highest good!"

Sometimes we simply need to remind clients that it is okay to be human. We should not lose sight of how risky this may feel to clients involved in spiritual communities that frown upon the expression of raw emotion. For some clients, counseling sessions provide a solitary place in their lives where crying, yelling, and worrying is not only condoned but also supported and encouraged. We must remain mindful of how important and sacred counseling sessions may become to our clients. In the end, certain clients may feel most comfortable seeking spiritual truth and guidance from New Age teachers and human groundedness from us.

Pastoral Counseling

Many people living with HIV disease make concerted efforts to integrate psychospiritual healing with the realities of living with a compromised immune system (Matousek, 1994). As the number of long-term survivors increases, it becomes more and more imperative that we support people living with HIV disease in their struggle "to cultivate hope during this twilight period of pessimism and uncertainty" (Matousek, 1994, p. 110). Pastoral counselors may find themselves singled out for this task.

Bennett and Henrickson (1993) defined pastoral care as "the care of the soul" (p. 5). They distinguished it from psychotherapy or counseling by virtue of the explicit introduction of God into the client's explorations. Although pastoral counselors are often ordained in a religious tradition, not all pastoral counselors are clergy people. Pastoral counselors differ from other counselors in that they approach counseling in a value-neutral way as opposed to a value-free way (Bennett & Henrickson, 1993, p. 6). Bennett and Henrickson elaborated on this difference between counselors and pastoral counselors when they wrote that pastoral counselors "listen and speak the language of 'God-talk' while always encouraging clients to articulate their own spiritual concerns in their own vernacular" (p. 6).

Bennett and Henrickson (1993) maintained that in pursuing the goal of a value-free approach to clients, traditionally trained mental health providers avoid raising issues of spirituality and thus miss out on what may be a key organizing component of their clients' lives. They suggest that, at a minimum, secular counselors need to ask questions like "Does spirituality play a part in your life?" or "Is your thinking about your disease shaped by your religious tradition?" (p. 6).

Pastoral counselors are not free from blocks to their effectiveness. In order to provide care to all people living with HIV disease, those who are pastoral counselors must find ways to overcome whatever difficulties they may have with controversial issues like homosexuality, premarital sex, or abortion. For example, some pastoral counselors may feel uneasy about dealing with gay or lesbian HIV-positive people because of conflicts between the theology of pastoral care of the sick and the teaching of their church on homosexuality and homosexual behavior (Perelli, 1991). Pastoral counselors with conflicts of this nature need to refer clients to a clergy person who does not feel burdened by these pressures.

Regardless of whether we are recognized as a pastoral counselor or not, we may be called upon to minister to clients struggling with spiritual concerns, such as what happens after they die. To be helpful, it is important that we do not use clients' denominational affiliations to form an opinion about their belief systems about what happens after death (Fortunato, 1993). In discussing eschatological beliefs, Fortunato (1993) wrote, "Many a Catholic has confessed to me his or her belief in reincarnation; many a Jew has affirmed a belief in heaven" (p. 3). It is always best to ask clients for help in defining what a particularly religious or spiritual affiliation means to them.

We need not agree with clients' religious beliefs in what happens after death. Fortunato maintained that we may even hold no notion of continued existence after death (an atheistic belief) and still help our clients with spiritual issues: "perceiving a client's eschatological beliefs as illusory is fine, as long as the caregiver understands that they are useful, functional illusions (and as long as the caregiver can respect the client's perception of atheism as equally illusory)" (1993, p. 3).

Bennett and Henrickson (1993) took a different stand. They maintained that we should not attempt pastoral counseling unless we are specifically trained in pastoral counseling, nor should pastoral counselors engage in psychotherapy. In the end, we may find that for HIV-positive clients the lines between spiritual and psychological issues are not as clearly demarcated as with other clients. This is not to imply however, that we should stop being attentive to the differences between the spiritual needs and therapeutic needs of people living with HIV disease (Perelli, 1991).

Healing Versus Curing

Many times clients turn toward spirituality or religion as part of the bargaining process that many people with life-threatening illnesses go through: "If I pray each day, I will get better." Although this type of bartering may ease clients' immediate fears and discomfort, for people living with HIV disease it is rarely successful for any length of time.

In working with these clients, it is often useful to distinguish between healing and curing.

Because of counseling's early links to the medical model, most of us tend to work out of a cure model whether or not we are aware of it. The medical model maintains that an illness is cured when its symptoms no longer return after a period of time. For example, agoraphobia is cured when the client can leave his or her house.

Healing, however, is different. As Sardello (1982) wrote, "Let us be clear: healing does not necessarily bring the individual release from disease; healing is not to be confused with cure of symptoms." According to Bennett and Henrickson (1993), most spiritual traditions define healing as the restoration to wholeness. "Symptoms are cured or not cured, but it is a person who is healed or not healed" (p. 6). Given this definition, our task should center on helping clients become more whole. The relationship between healing and wholeness can be seen in the statement of a 51-year-old HIV-positive man:

> I think that a lot of people, after they've been diagnosed, give up whatever their life is. They throw away the good parts of their life, and they don't address the bad parts. I've kept all of the good parts, and I realized that I had to address all the bad parts. I had to look at them, I had to own them. I had to forgive myself for them, and then I had to let them the f—k go. And then I could get on with my life and get on with my healing to whatever degree I was able to heal myself. (Hitchens, 1992, pp. 238–239)

We should remember that healing can happen even while HIV-related symptoms worsen. Instead of removing clients from the reality of their illness, healing restores their freedom to make choices even in the presence of continuing disease (Dubos, 1978). Bennett and Henrickson (1993) wrote that "healing occurs when a person discovers that the sacred which transcends this world is also manifest in his or her life, thereby sanctifying life and making it more real" (p. 6).

If we have not already made the shift, we must move to conceptualizing our work with clients as healing rather than curing. Sometimes this shift is quite difficult. It is often hard to let go of the belief that counseling is beneficial and helps our clients live longer. Certainly cases exist where clients start counseling and their immune systems became stronger. Yet, in spite of counseling, clients' immune systems also continue to become more compromised over time. We can promise no cures for HIV disease; we can, however, help with a deep process of emotional and spiritual healing.

A Caveat

In her article, "Sometimes It's OK to Be Sick: The Benefits of Poor Health," Duff (1994) wrote that "our concepts of physical and psychological health have become one-sidedly identified with the heroic qualities most valued in our culture: youth, activity, productivity, independence, strength, confidence, and optimism" (p. 108). It is often easy to encourage clients to become spiritual heroes—to allow them their choice of spiritual or religious path but prescribe an active attack. We may forget the value in passive approaches to spirituality and healing.

We must take care so as to not focus our clients' spiritual and religious lives strictly on outward or public activities. Duff (1994) warned:

> In our infatuation with health and wholeness, illness is one-sidedly identified with the culturally devalued qualities of quiet, introspection, weakness, withdrawal, vulnerability, dependence, self-doubt, and depression. . . . Many sick people are shamed by friends, family, or even their healers into thinking they are sick because they lack these "healthy" attitudes, even though illnesses often accompany critical turning points in our lives—times when it is necessary to withdraw, reflect, sorrow, and surrender in order to make needed changes. (p. 108)

We should be mindful of the ways in which we may attempt to aggrandize spirituality. It is important not to forget that what is most profound about spirituality is often its simplicity. Introspection often occurs in solitude. Spiritual revelations often arise out of stillness. Even when clients do not appear highly engaged in activities commonly deemed spiritual, they may still be leading inwardly spiritual lives.

Cultural Issues

Fortunato (1993) wrote that the distinction between psychological and spiritual growth or healing is Eurocentric. Other cultures, such as Buddhist or Native American cultures, see no such difference. This is only one example of the extent to which our cultural sensitivity and awareness of our own cultural biases are crucial when working with clients from ethnic communities other than our own.

It is important for us to remain conscious of the broad cultural spectrum in many religious and healing traditions. Bennett and Henrickson (1993) pointed out the example of the *botanicas*, the herbal and spiritual healing centers of many Latino cultures. Similarly, Parés-Avila and Montano-López (1994) wrote of the importance of respecting the manner in which Latinas and Latinos with HIV disease meet their spiritual needs, "whether that is through affiliation with the more formal religions or an adherence to some form of folk-healing belief system" (p. 348). In an article in *Seasons*, a publication of the National Native American AIDS Prevention Center, Harris (1991) also addressed the importance of respect for cultural spiritual traditions.

> For . . . Native person[s] to obtain services in New York City, they must go through intake procedures at a number of agencies. They will not be asked if they are Native American; however, chances are the intake worker will ask if they need a Spanish translator. You will never see "traditional medicine" as an option, and your request for a spiritual guide will most likely be answered by a choice of Eurocentric religions. "Burning Sweet Grass or Sage Allowed" is a sign you will not find in any of the medical institutions in New York City. (p. 2)

Familiarity with and respect for ethnically diverse clients' traditions, beliefs, and practices about spirituality and healing are essential to the counseling process (Jue & Kain, 1989).

Conclusion

For many clients, living with HIV disease awakens an interest in things of a spiritual nature. Some clients find comfort in traditional religious beliefs; others turn to alternative paths. In facing their death, many clients come to question the meaning of their life and turn to counselors, secular as well as pastoral, for assistance.

When counseling HIV-positive clients, we should remain open to the wide variety of paths that the quest for healing and wholeness may take. For clients raised in orthodox religious traditions that condemn people with HIV disease, finding meaningful spiritual direction may be difficult. Distinguishing between spirituality and religiosity is often helpful.

Many of us may consider dealing with spiritual issues out of place in the counseling session. We need to remember that many people living with HIV disease may feel alienated from all sources of spiritual guidance; the counseling session may be the only place where they feel comfortable enough to risk elaborating on issues of faith. At times we may be surprised to find that when we provide clients with the room to pursue spiritual matters accelerated psychological growth often occurs. This makes sense, for in many ways and in many cultures, there is no distinction between psychological and spiritual growth.

CHAPTER 13

The HIV Emotional Roller Coaster

The emotional course through HIV disease is not a straight path, but one filled with twists and turns, ups and downs.

Just as our clients' physical states may vary, so too may their emotional states. One week clients may come to our offices optimistic, cheerful, and serene; the next week they may feel hopeless, depressed, and agitated. These fluctuations may even affect clients who have worked hard to adjust to living with HIV disease. Thus we should not be shocked when clients express sentiments like those of Marc Wagenheim, who battled AIDS for almost 6 years before dying: "I have times when I'm very brave and strong and manage to climb out of a seemingly bottomless pit, and I have times when I'm very afraid" (Hitchens, 1992, p. 97).

This chapter examines the emotional roller coaster of life with HIV disease. Three emotions—fear, anger, and hope—are examined in the context of three major environmental influences: CD_4 cell counts, politics, and the promise of a cure. For almost every client a direct relationship exists between these environmental influences and these emotions: any change in the first is likely to result in a major mood swing. We need to be aware of these patterns for two reasons. First, we should avoid pathologizing these mood swings; when viewed in context, they represent natural and appropriate reactions within the ever-changing world of HIV disease. Secondly, by understanding these patterns, we can help our clients better anticipate and prepare for them.

This chapter also examines depression. For clients, emotional responses to many events, people, and changes in the environment often take the form of depression. There is a high incidence of depression in HIV-positive clients. Therefore, understanding the many ways depression manifests in relation to HIV disease is critical.

Monitoring CD$_4$ Cells

For many clients, the consequences of closely monitoring their CD$_4$ count is an endless alternation between fear and relief or fear and despair. Basic knowledge of the mechanics of CD$_4$ cells is essential to understanding this emotional pattern in HIV-positive clients. Knowledge of attribution theory and experience working with irrational thoughts is also helpful. Because the lives of people with HIV disease are filled with uncertainty, everything can be taken for an omen— particularly CD$_4$ cell counts.

CD$_4$ Cell Counts and Their Implications

Although HIV attacks many kinds of cells inside a host's body, doctors and researchers place most attention on the infection of CD$_4$ cells. These cells, alternatively known as T-helper cells or T-4 cells, provide essential support for many of the other cell types in the immune system (Krowka, 1989). CD$_4$ counts represent generally accepted markers of immune functioning because many of the other cell types of the immune system cannot function effectively without their assistance.

CD$_4$ cell counts fall in a range. Non-HIV-infected individuals commonly have approximately 500 to 1,500 CD$_4$ cells per cubic millimeter (Krowka, 1989). HIV-positive people may have counts that continue to fall within that range but often drop below it; greater losses of CD$_4$ cells are incurred with time. CD$_4$ cells dynamically adapt to the various stresses placed on the body; in both HIV-negative and HIV-positive people, CD$_4$ cells fluctuate even on a daily basis. The procedures used to count CD$_4$ cells may vary from laboratory to laboratory. Differences in procedures may cause differences in test results when doctors change labs.

For many people living with HIV disease, the decline of their CD$_4$ cells does not take place in a straight line (Krowka, 1989). No single change is determinative; nonetheless, a CD$_4$ cell count provokes much justifiable anxiety. CD$_4$ cell levels still remain a common criterion for many medical decisions, such as when to begin zidovudine (ZDV) or other prophylactic treatments. In addition, as of January 1994, the Centers for Disease Control and Prevention modified the definition of AIDS to include people whose CD$_4$ count dropped below 200. This may exacerbate the anxiety some HIV-positive clients already associate with their CD_4 cell counts. For some clients and their physicians, the negative emotional impact of CD_4 cell monitoring influences them to choose other measures of immune compromise. If clients exhibit severe anxiety over CD_4 tests, simply changing to another measure may do little to reduce fear. However, one strategy that is often effective is for clients to request that their doctor notify them only when a change in CD_4 cells requires a change in medical treatment; this way clients are spared worrying about insignificant fluctuations.

Attribution Theory and Its Application

Many clients monitor their CD_4 cells in spite of the limitations to this measure. In an excerpt from her journal, Patti Wetsel, M.D., a physician caring for AIDS patients who is herself HIV positive, described her astonishment at realizing the psychological effect of changes in her CD_4 count:

> The HIV roller coaster is climbing uphill for a change! My CD_4 count is now 565! I felt terrific before this but now I feel even better—yeah, yeah, yeah, as I told my patients, it's just a number, but now it's *my* number! (Wetsel, 1994/1995, p. 87)

Whether the results show CD_4 cells increasing or decreasing, clients have an emotional reaction and explain or rationalize the results with characteristic patterns of thinking. It is often very useful to pay close attention to these thought patterns. When counts are lower than before, clients frequently attribute the results to external sources: laboratory techniques, normal fluctuations that everyone has, or environmental stressors. In this way a drop in CD_4 cells can be seen as the result of some random force outside of the clients' body. Many clients may go to great extremes to avoid seeing the drop as a sign of further destruction of their immune system.

When results show an increase in CD_4 cells, clients commonly make an internal attribution. Clients may identify anything they did—from a change in nutritional habits to leaving work on disability to falling in love—as the reason for the increase. Although we may feel frustrated by the lack of consistency in this attributional process, the process is crucial to our clients' ability to maintain hope. By attributing gains in CD_4 cells to things within their sphere of influence, clients increase their sense of control; by attributing drops in CD_4 cells to factors outside of themselves, they retain the hope that things within their power may still restore their immune system. Given the inherent fluctuations of the CD_4 count and the demonstrated relationship between the mind and the body, we serve clients best by respecting their attributional process.

Working With Irrational Thoughts

The high anxiety associated with CD_4 cell counts and the complex medical knowledge needed to understand their functioning fully furnishes clients with many opportunities to engage in irrational thinking. Common irrational beliefs include:

1. "If my CD_4 cell count drops below 200, I am certain to get an opportunistic infection."
2. "My CD_4 cell count was 150 last month and dropped to 100 this month; in 2 more months I'll be dead."
3. "Nobody lives with less than 10 CD_4 cells."

Before challenging a client's irrational belief, we should make certain that we understand in what respect the belief is irrational. We must be able to present clients with information they will respect, and must present it in ways that they can integrate. With regard to the first irrational belief, we might inform our clients that "some people do get opportunistic infections when their CD_4 cell count drops below 200, but no hard and fast rule exists for all people. CD_4 counts are only general indicators and cannot predict infections with the certainty implied by your belief." In response to the second irrational thought, we may remind clients that drops in CD_4 cells are not linear. Whenever possible it is particularly effective to use the progression of clients' own CD_4 counts as an example of how CD_4 cells fluctuate. Finally, we can remind clients espousing the third belief that with less than 10 CD_4 cells they will be dead, that there are people who have very few CD_4 cells and still manage to lead productive lives (Siano, 1993). At the same time we address the irrational nature of our clients' beliefs, we must be certain to affirm the validity of their emotions.

The cycle associated with CD_4 cell counts often produces extreme anxiety for clients. Over time we, too, may come to share in our clients' investment in high or stable counts. We should stay alert for evidence that an interest in our clients' CD_4 cells may compromise our role as counselor. If we become over identified with our clients' good health, it may signal a need for supervision or consultation with a colleague.

Anger and HIV-Related Politics

Clients are influenced in many ways by the political climate in which they live. Clients who were calm one week may come into a counseling session in an uproar the next in response to a news story or other report of an AIDS-related political development. From its very discovery, AIDS has been a political illness. Many clients are as influenced by the politics of AIDS as they are by HIV status.

Rarely is politics conceived of as a bona fide factor in clients' mood states, yet many HIV-positive people become outraged by the politics of the world around them. Often clients present this anger in counseling. Sometimes their anger is linked to specific political events. Other times, or for other clients, anger appears more generalized, and it is left to us to ask clients if recent political events (e.g., the election of a well-known AIDS-phobic official) has anything to do with their current feelings. We are most helpful when we stay current with AIDS-related politics.

For many of us, the connection between clients' anger and AIDS-related politics means expanding the ways we approach anger. Often clients' anger is an appropriate response to a system that has long been neglectful of their needs. We should take care not to view this anger immediately as pathological or overblown. Even when the anger seems inappropriate, upon closer examination we may find that it is not the anger that is inappropriate, but rather the way in which it gets expressed. One strategy for helping clients cope with anger is to assist them in finding healthy modes of expression. Many political action groups exist for the sole purpose of providing people living with HIV disease (and others) a way to vent their anger. Though some people may find the way in which these various groups conduct themselves controversial, some clients may find these groups a useful and effective way of dealing with their anger.

The Hope for a Cure

News about a possible cure for HIV disease exerts a strong influence on HIV-positive people's mood states. Many clients live each day with the hope that it will bring them closer to a cure. Thus news of a breakthrough drug, a breakthrough treatment, or a breakthrough vaccine may increase clients' hopefulness. In the same way, news of a new drug's ineffectiveness or toxic side effects may cause clients to feel despondent and hopeless. We, too, may find ourselves reacting to reports about new treatment discoveries in similar ways.

An example of the effect of medical treatment news on clients is the emotional response to studies presented at the International AIDS Conference. People living with HIV disease and their health providers usually look toward the annual international conference with anticipation of breakthroughs in HIV disease treatment. However, in 1993, researchers at the conference in Berlin presented several studies that "dampened these expectations" (Follansbee & Dilley, 1993, p. 1). In their report from the AIDS Conference, Follansbee and Dilley (1993) wrote

> . . . research has left resignation where only 2 years ago there were high hopes. For mental health and medical practitioners alike, the first task may be dealing with the emotional responses of clients to this information.
>
> People with advanced HIV infection, who have been undergoing antiviral therapy and have developed side effects to these medications, may feel a sense of hopelessness of the failure to see new treatment options emerge. . . . For others, particularly those ambivalent about medications, the data may evoke a renewed sense of hopelessness and loss of control over the course of infection. (pp. 2–3)

The mood of gloom and doom that dominated these proceedings was so pervasively felt that it has been labeled the *post-Berlin syndrome* (Baker, 1994).

In response to the ever-changing treatment news and accompanying mood fluctuations, we can encourage clients to remain focused on the single thing that remains constant and within their power: how they wish to live their life until a cure is discovered. When disappointing research findings are announced, nothing is more needed and less available than hope. Often it is left to us to remain hopeful and work towards a cure.

Depression

People living with HIV disease may be frequently besieged by episodes of depression. In assessing symptoms of depression, we must take care not to dismiss these as simply "understandable psychological responses" (Baker, 1993). We must be alert for signs that the symptoms are indicative of a major mood disorder.

The list of symptoms for a formal diagnosis of major depressive episode includes many common physical complaints mentioned by people living with HIV disease, thereby making it difficult to diagnose depression accurately. Many HIV-positive clients already have three or four of the five symptoms required for diagnosis of major depressive episode, solely by virtue of their physical condition (Winiarski, 1991). People with advanced HIV disease may exhibit decreased interest or pleasure in previously enjoyable activities, sleep disorders, and appetite and weight loss as a result of the physical effects of the virus or antiviral medications. The contributions and interactions of physical illness and social factors also make symptoms difficult to evaluate (Baker, 1993).

Making a differential diagnosis of depression can be difficult. For example, diminished ability to think or concentrate, a common symptom of depression, can also indicate HIV dementia. It is important that we distinguish between depression and signs of early dementia; a referral for formal neuropsychological testing may prove helpful (Dilley & Boccellari, 1989). Winiarski (1991) maintained that the diagnosis of depression in people living with HIV disease should be established less on the basis of physical manifestations, and more on the basis of the client's feelings and thoughts.

Strategies for working with clients who manifest signs of depression center around providing emotional support during times of heightened stress and fear. We should also seriously consider referring clients for medical evaluations for antidepressant medication. People living with HIV disease often find these medications quite beneficial for two reasons. First, they provide clients with "emotional space and strength to gather their resources" (Winiarski, 1991, p. 74). Second, the side effects of antidepressants, generally mild, may be taken advantage of (Baker, 1993). For example, sedation, a common side effect of many antidepressants, may prove helpful to people with insomnia.

A number of different types of antidepressant medications exist, including tricyclics, selective serotonic uptake inhibitors (SSUI), and monoamine oxidase (MAO) inhibitors. Antidepressants differ in their side effects and mechanisms of action. MAO inhibitors and psychostimulants are contraindicated if clients are also taking any of a long list of other medications, many of which are used in the typical course of treating HIV disease (Baker, 1993). Hence these types of antidepressants are prescribed less frequently.

Whether or not we condone the use of psychotropic medication, we must remain open-minded to its use with HIV-positive clients and make appropriate referrals when necessary. Although individual and group therapy have been shown to be effective for depression (Baker, 1993; Levine, Bystitsky, Baron, & Jones, 1991), the use of antidepressant medication has also been shown to be important for many clients. In spite of any personal biases we may hold against the use of antidepressant drugs, we should avoid acting in ways that add to the burden of treatable conditions.

Conclusion

Fluctuations in mood states, sometimes drastic, are not uncommon in people living with HIV disease. Anger, anxiety, and hopelessness may result from factors beyond our clients' control, such as fluctuations in CD_4 cells, AIDS-related politics, or the lack of a cure. Many clients may turn to us to have their feelings validated. They may need our assurance that their mood swings are normal. In addition to individual counseling, some clients benefit from sharing their feelings in support groups or group counseling.

We should take seriously our responsibility to make referrals to psychiatrists when psychotropic drug intervention seems necessary, especially in the case of major depression. We can help our clients overcome any shame they may feel in taking such drugs; clients face a tough enough battle without needing to feel they must do it all on their own. Until researchers discover a cure, clients living with HIV disease continue to travel an emotional path filled with high spots and low spots. Our job is to travel with them.

PART THREE

TRANSITIONS

CHAPTER 14

Receiving an AIDS Diagnosis

If testing positive is getting engaged,
then receiving an AIDS diagnosis is getting married.

L abels have great power, and the AIDS label is no exception. Receiving an AIDS diagnosis makes everything concrete. For many, the AIDS label conjures up images of men and women, aged before their prime, wasting away and dying with a multitude of unpronounceable infections. Some clients, particularly when they are first told they have AIDS, forget that many people continue to live productive lives long after their AIDS diagnosis.

Receiving an AIDS diagnosis marks a transition, and with this transition comes a host of physical and psychological repercussions. To counsel clients effectively we must understand the complex determinants of the AIDS diagnosis. We must also recognize the negative effects of labeling. Finally, contradictory as it may seem, an AIDS diagnosis produces positive benefits; we must understand these, too.

The AIDS Diagnosis

What might seem like a relatively straightforward process—being diagnosed with AIDS—is actually more complex. To receive an AIDS diagnosis clients must meet some part of the definition handed down to physicians by the Centers for Disease Control and Prevention. As of 1995, this definition has three parts: an original, pre-1993 index of disorders, a list of four disorders added in January 1993, and a criterion based upon CD_4 cells. Each part of this definition includes features that generally are life threatening, although some discrepancies exist with regards to urgency (Keeling, 1993).

The Original Centers for Disease Control Definition (Pre-1993)

Up to January 1993, the Centers for Disease Control and Prevention defined AIDS as the manifestation of one of a list of disorders in four major categories of illness (Keeling, 1993). This list was determined by surveillance reports that tracked the most common manifestations of HIV disease, including opportunistic infections, neoplasms, neurologic disease, and wasting.

Opportunistic infections are infections caused by typically innocuous microbes that take advantage of the immune suppression of the HIV-positive person. Many of the agents of opportunistic infections exist normally in the environment, but they rarely affect people to any degree until the usual protective power of immunity is lost (Keeling, 1993). The causative agents for opportunistic infections include a wide range of bacteria, viruses, fungi, and protozoa that produce a variety of clinical patterns. We cannot be expected to have a physician's depth of knowledge regarding these infections, but it is important that we become familiar with the most common infections.

Mycobacterium avium complex (MAC or MAI) is the most common form of bacterial infection in people with HIV disease (Update, 1993). Its symptoms include malaise, fevers, night sweats, weight loss, and diarrhea. The bacteria that cause MAC may disseminate to the lungs, bone marrow, blood, liver, and other organs (Winiarski, 1991). Current treatment includes various drugs taken singularly or in combination (a drug cocktail).

Cytomegalovirus (CMV) is a herpesvirus that can affect many different parts of the body. In the eye, CMV affects vision and can lead to blindness. Doctors treat this condition using such drugs as Ganciclovir and Foscarnet. Various methods of administering these drugs are under investigation (Update, 1993). CMV may also affect the gastrointestinal tract and the central nervous system where it is far more difficult to treat (Winiarski, 1991).

Cryptosporidiosis (crypto) is a protozoan infection causing severe diarrhea and abdominal pains. Extreme weight loss may often occur. The development of safe and effective treatments for this infection continues to be a slow and arduous process (Update, 1993).

Pneumocystis carinii pneumonia (PCP) is a pneumonia most often caused by a protozoan. Bactrim/Septra and pentamidine are drugs proven quite effective in treating and preventing PCP infection. In 1992, the Food and Drug Administration approved a new drug, Atovaquome, for use with people intolerant of the sulfa-based Bactrim/Septra.

Neoplasms or cancers happen far less frequently in AIDS than do opportunistic infections (Keeling, 1993). Even when neoplasms are present, it is still usually an opportunistic infection that causes death. Although neoplasms may not be fatal as often as some of the infections, they frequently produce physical disfigurement and can have a huge psychological impact on clients.

Kaposi's sarcoma (KS) is a tumor typically found on the skin but also affecting the lungs and other parts of the body. People with KS may have purplish, bruise-like lesions, commonly on their face, neck, and lower extremities and in their mouth (Keeling, 1993). Doctors commonly treat KS with chemotherapy. Keeling (1993) reported that although KS was common in the United States at the beginnings of the AIDS epidemic, its incidence has recently decreased significantly due to the more common use of early prophylactic antiviral drug treatments.

Lymphomas, tumors of the lymphoid tissue, have become more frequent in people with AIDS (Keeling, 1993). AIDS-related lymphomas tend to occur in unusual locations and are commonly resistant to usual therapies (Beral, Peterman, Berkelman, & Jaffe, 1991). A trend in the incidence of lymphomas has been observed: as better therapy results in longer survival for people living with HIV disease, the incidence of lymphomas rises (Moore, Kessler, Richman, Flexner, & Chaisson,1991).

Neurologic abnormalities are common to people with AIDS (Snider et al., 1983). Signs of neurologic symptoms should always be attended to as studies have shown that abnormalities occur in HIV-positive people well before the appearance of clinical deficits (Koralnik et al., 1990). Common early symptoms include forgetfulness, difficulty concentrating, confusion, balance problems, leg weakness, dysphoric mood, and behavioral changes (Winiarski, 1991). HIV-associated dementia complex, a common and severely limiting neurologic manifestation of HIV disease (Tross & Hirsch, 1988), is discussed in chapter 17.

Wasting is often the dominant manifestation of AIDS (Keeling, 1993). People in the severe phase of HIV disease often loose large percentages of lean body mass and weight. The use of anabolic steroids may help some people to maintain muscle mass (Smith, 1994).

The Revised 1993 Centers for Disease Control Definition

The pre-1993 definitions of AIDS were developed from frequently observed symptoms of those infected with HIV disease. These definitions neglected women because early in the AIDS epidemic most HIV-positive people in the United States were men. The 1993 revision added cervical cancer to the list of diagnostic criteria, but other women's conditions continue to be neglected (see the Women's Issues section in this chapter). The 1993 revision also added HIV-related pulmonary tuberculosis and HIV-related recurrent bacterial pneumonia, two opportunistic infections not commonly seen at the start of the AIDS epidemic.

The expanded 1993 definition further included a criterion for diagnosis that is irrespective of any particular manifestations of infection: a CD_4 cell count below 200. Because of this added criterion, implementation of the revised definition meant that on January 1, 1993, many people considered to be asymptomatic HIV positive became people with AIDS.

This change in the AIDS definition continues to be confusing and often presents a great psychological challenge for clients (Marks, 1993). Some people with CD_4 counts below 200 have only mild to moderate symptoms not usually associated with an AIDS diagnosis. Thus adjusting to an abrupt change from asymptomatic to an AIDS diagnosis may be quite traumatic. These clients may need more time and more support before they can accept the new label. O'Dowd (1993) reported that many asymptomatic clients who meet the new definition choose to ignore it, minimizing its threatening implications. Asymptomatic clients whose CD_4 counts drop below 200 have widely varying reactions to receiving an AIDS diagnosis. We must remain sensitive to the needs of the individual. It is crucial to set aside any preconceived assumptions in order to explore clients' associations, both conscious and unconscious, to the diagnosis of AIDS.

The Effects of the AIDS Label

In the early days of the AIDS epidemic, any sentence that included the word *AIDS* also included the idea of impending death. This association still lingers, in spite of medical advances prolonging the life-span of those living with AIDS. Even in well-informed clients, an AIDS diagnosis brings with it deeply rooted conscious and unconscious fears of immediate death.

Many clients may hold a huge investment in the identity *person living with HIV* as opposed to the identity *person with AIDS*. They are acutely aware of the power behind the words. Michael Callen spoke to this distinction:

It has been incredibly frustrating for me to see people lose respect for the distinction between being sick and not being sick. When you have HIV, you are not necessarily sick, nor will you necessarily get sick.

I'm not denying that there are similarities between the experience of finding out you're HIV positive and finding out that you have AIDS. I'm merely begging people to honor the distinction between having HIV and feeling well, and having AIDS and not feeling very well. To me, to use the terms interchangeably is deeply offensive. And I also believe that, in a sense, it can become a self-fulfilling prophecy, you know? (Hitchens, 1992, p. 34)

Receiving an AIDS diagnosis may mystify clients who receive the diagnosis simply by virtue of a drop in their CD_4 cells. Physically they feel as healthy as they always did. They may experience no overt internal changes, yet they are considered a person with AIDS. When counseling clients newly diagnosed with AIDS, it is often useful to focus on helping them determine how much and what sort of importance they wish to place on the label and how much emphasis they wish to place on their own experience of their level of health or illness.

At the time of their diagnosis with AIDS, clients may exhibit many reactive psychological symptoms, including depression, anxiety, and preoccupation with illness. Tross and Hirsch (1988) observed that these symptoms often take the form of transient and situational adjustment disorders. The AIDS diagnosis may throw clients back to issues that were examined at the time clients first received their HIV-positive test results. Counseling may need to readdress fears of death and abandonment as well as issues of finding meaning and purpose in life (Tross & Hirsch, 1988). After receiving an AIDS diagnosis, clients may display keener hypervigilance for physical symptoms. Encountering new infections or treatment failure can throw clients into a serious depressive state. In many cases, medical evaluation for antidepressant drugs may be indicated. Passive suicidal ideation is common (Tross & Hirsch, 1988) and should be closely attended to.

Receiving an AIDS diagnosis greatly reduces many clients' ability to deny death. Death becomes increasingly more real with each new symptom, infection, or drop in CD_4 cells. Often a twofold counseling strategy is useful. First, we can acknowledge and validate how traumatic it is for clients to confront that their death may arrive sooner than expected. Second, we can encourage clients to consider how they want to live out their remaining years, months, weeks, or days. When adopting this approach, we should remain sensitive to the ways in which clients may construe us as nonunderstanding, trivializing, or condescending. Unless we are HIV positive, clients are correct when they tell us we do not really know what they are going through. Even if we are HIV positive, we still make empathic failures. Instead of reacting defensively when clients feel we are unempathic, a better response is to acknowledge our empathic failure and to look for ways to better understand not only how this failure is experienced by our clients but also the entire spectrum of issues with which the client is trying to cope.

The Benefits of an AIDS Diagnosis

We should take care not to assume that all clients react to their AIDS diagnosis negatively. Ironically, for some clients a diagnosis of AIDS comes as a relief. This is especially likely for clients who have little to no access to treatment and assistance. Many states and counties restrict various types of medical and financial assistance exclusively to people with an AIDS diagnosis. For clients in these states and counties, receiving an AIDS diagnosis affords them a host of material benefits not previously accessible. Even though the availability of medical and financial benefits may result in an immediate reduction of clients' stress and anxiety, we should watch carefully for signs of depression that may also occur as the reality of living with AIDS sets in.

Women's Issues

Women's bodies differ from men's. If women manifest with the same infections as men (e.g., Pneumocystis carinii pneumonia), doctors may recognize it as AIDS. However, many women living with HIV disease also suffer from symptoms like severe, reoccurring pelvic inflammatory disease and treatment-resistant vaginal yeast infections. Yet, according to the Centers for Disease Control and Prevention, no one of these symptoms alone is enough to secure a woman an AIDS diagnosis. Anastos and Marte (1991) compared vaginal yeast infections to thrush (a yeast infection of the mouth identified as a symptom of AIDS) and asked, "Does it make sense that the same infection in another orifice— an orifice not present in men—is not categorized as an AIDS-related condition?" (p. 191).

The implications of this gender discrepancy are enormous. Women get excluded from many health-related services, including mental health care, at major AIDS agencies across the nation because they cannot demonstrate an AIDS diagnosis. Even if they are physically ill, without a diagnosis women receive few of the resources available to men.

Tragically, until the Centers for Disease Control and Prevention further expands its definition of AIDS to include opportunistic infections common in women, many HIV-positive women will continue to struggle without governmental assistance. When working with women, we should acknowledge the extreme hardships they face even when attempting to get accurately diagnosed with a life-threatening illness. We must validate the hurt and anguish that arises when women must constantly battle for visible recognition, support, and assistance.

Conclusion

Recognizing and understanding the complex issues that arise upon receiving an AIDS diagnosis is an important part of the counseling process. Many clients experience the stigma of the AIDS label as worse than the infections or loss of immune function that resulted in the diagnosis. Often issues of death and dying, hope and hopelessness, meaning and meaninglessness, first discussed when clients originally tested positive, become salient again.

At this juncture in our work with clients, it is common for strong feelings to arise. Especially if we have been counseling clients since they first tested positive, we may feel saddened or angered by the onset of their first opportunistic infection. Even at this stage, we may find our ability to connect with clients threatened by our own need to distance ourselves from their eventual death. We may find ourselves denying that our clients have AIDS—even when they have accepted their diagnosis. As clients move into the next stage of their illness, we are often pushed to the limits of our capacity to be present with our clients. The support of other colleagues is crucial. Frequent consultation and supervision may be invaluable in helping us find ways to reach out to our clients while accompanying them along the next leg of their journey.

CHAPTER 15

Hospitalization

The hospital is not home.

Until doctors and researchers make major advances in the medical treatment of HIV disease, sooner or later most people living with HIV disease require hospitalization. Hospitalization represents yet another transition; it marks a total disruption of clients' normal daily functioning. When hospitalized, clients must also make drastic psychological adjustments. Counseling can play a big part in easing the pain associated with these changes.

Depending on their location, hospitals can be attuned to the needs of people with advanced HIV disease, or they can be indifferent. Money also affects the type of care clients receive, with public health settings typically providing less personalized and comfortable care than private settings. Some hospitals in major metropolitan settings have established specialized immune suppression units with a supportive environment for clients; many of these offer extended visiting hours, allow same-sex partners to stay in the hospital room overnight, and employ nursing and support staff who enjoy working with HIV-positive people. Staff who work on these units tend to be knowledgeable about HIV and its transmission, so unnecessary and excessively protective behaviors and reactions (e.g., leaving a person's food outside the door) rarely occur. In many other hospitals, however, clients with HIV and AIDS may encounter ignorance, homophobia, and harsh or punitive policies and regulations.

Regardless of the setting, once clients are hospitalized their task becomes clear: they must adjust to life inside the hospital. We too must adjust; we must consider our therapeutic stance when clients are hospitalized. Will we visit clients in the hospital? If so, how frequent will our visits be? What type of sessions will we conduct? What will we do if clients do not have a private room? These issues are best thought through and discussed with clients prior to hospitalization. In that way expectations can be articulated and disappointments can hopefully be minimized.

For the client, adjusting to hospitalization has many components. The Center for AIDS Prevention Studies at the University of California San Francisco (McKusick, 1992) identified several tasks of people living with HIV disease who are hospitalized for the first time. They must confront disability and impairment, deal with surrendering control, and counteract depression. They must gather more sophisticated information regarding opportunistic infections, reevaluate their health maintenance routines, and engage in pain management. Hospitalized clients must also reevaluate their support system.

Similarly, when working with hospitalized clients, we have a number of tasks to attend to (McKusick, 1992). We must provide continuity of contact. We must help clients deal with thoughts and fantasies of death. We must assist in reassessing clients' expectations. Finally, we must nurture hope.

Client Tasks

AIDS-related hospitalization immediately forces most people with HIV disease to change their self-perception. Hospitalization confronts clients accustomed to viewing themselves as healthy, strong, and physically capable with a new vision. Confined to a hospital ward at best or a hospital bed at worst, clients must grapple with the disabling and impairing consequences of HIV.

One strategy that is often useful in facilitating clients' adjustment to the changes of hospitalization is to help clients distinguish between permanent and temporary impairments or disabilities. For example, a client who is hospitalized for excessive dehydration, who is too weak to leave his or her bed, needs to adjust temporarily to this impairment. In situations like these we can help clients remain aware of the short-term nature of their restricted status. In contrast, a client who, during his or her hospitalization, has a PICC-line (a direct intravenous tube that allows self-injection of medication) placed must adapt permanently to a level of discomfort and restricted physical movement. In cases like these, we must help clients make a long-term psychological adjustment. Even when an impairment is temporary, clients' emotional and psychological reactions may be long-lasting.

At times we need to offer two seemingly contradictory responses to our clients. We need to acknowledge the loss of mobility, versatility, and freedom they suffer when hospitalized. Simultaneously, we need to urge clients to find new ways of experiencing and asserting the mobility, versatility, and freedom they still possess. We should be certain to balance interventions that affirm hospitalized clients' feelings of loss with interventions that empower them.

Surrendering Control

Upon entering the hospital, clients are confronted with another task. Most hospitals, by their very nature, strip clients of personal control. Clients must eat at certain hours. They must wake up at a certain time. They must go for this test or that treatment. Many clients may find coping with the loss of control painful and difficult.

Clients often need a safe space in which to express the rage, sadness, and frustration that arise from not being allowed to make their own decisions. Many clients may repress these feelings because they feel unsafe voicing their feelings in the hospital. They may worry that getting angry or frustrated with the hospital staff could jeopardize their treatment. We may be the only people with whom clients feel they can share their feelings without fear of reprisal.

Many clients can be encouraged to assert the control they still have even while hospitalized. We can support clients in retaining their self-determination and personal authority. Some clients may need help becoming more assertive with their needs and desires. Other clients may have no problem voicing their needs and desires. These clients may only need our assistance when their needs go unacknowledged.

Countering Depression

When clients are hospitalized they often become depressed. Depression may naturally arise from the physical and emotional losses associated with hospitalization. Depression can also result from conscious and unconscious thoughts and fears that hospitalization may engender.

When depression arises from the realistic constraints of hospitalization, we must take a supportive approach. Often ways can be found to address particular problems so that clients' depression may be alleviated. For instance, if clients become depressed because they are alone, we can work with clients to try to ensure frequent visitors. We can also remind clients that although the feelings they experience in the hospital are valid, they may not feel the same way once they return home. This is not done to discount our clients' feelings but instead to acknowledge again their time-limited nature.

In other instances, depression may arise from irrational thoughts. Clients may believe that no one who enters the hospital ever gets to leave. They may think that the doctors and nurses don't like them. They may assume that they are in the hospital to die. In working with these clients, we must assess the amount of validity there is to each belief. Are clients likely to die during this hospitalization? If this is the case, we can help clients cope with the reality of their approaching death. Are clients doing something that might be off-putting to the medical staff? If so, we can help clients become aware of the impact of their behavior on others. If clients' thoughts have no factual basis, then we can help clients recognize the irrationality of their beliefs. Cognitive-behavioral approaches are often helpful in these situations. However, no matter how unreal clients' beliefs may seem, they still comprise the clients' reality and must be treated as such. We should consider challenging clients' beliefs only after we validate clients' good reasons for possessing them and for experiencing any associated feelings.

Gathering Information About Opportunistic Infections

Prior to hospitalization, clients' levels of knowledge about opportunistic infections vary. Even when extremely knowledgeable before they are hospitalized, most clients psychologically distance themselves from the information. Clients read or hear about infections that affect others, not themselves.

In light of their hospitalization, information about opportunistic infections takes on new meaning. Clients may find their knowledge base insufficient to understand their current situation. Clients who previously showed no interest in learning about opportunistic infections may find they lack the resources needed to become better educated. Sometimes fear prevents clients from thinking clearly; clients may need help formulating questions for their doctors. Sometimes we need to provide educational resources, or to explain information that may be beyond clients' comprehension levels. Although we may be tempted to downplay our educational function in favor of deeper work, gaining information is vitally important for most hospitalized clients. Part of what may disturb clients most about hospitalization is the mystification that arises when information is communicated in unclear ways or in ways insufficient to meet clients' needs. Becoming well informed may greatly reduce clients' levels of anxiety and depression. However, it is worth noting that some clients may have a different cognitive style; they may prefer not knowing about their condition. Unless this style poses harm to the client, it should be respected.

Reevaluating Health Maintenance Routines

Hospitalization itself requires a drastic modification of clients' previous routines to stay healthy. Clients may face many new decisions: What type of new medications should I take? What about their side effects? What about nonmedical treatments? Many times clients may not feel strong enough to make these decisions alone. Many times we may be called upon to lend ego strength, especially when a strong therapeutic relationship has been established.

It is important to look for ways in which clients may blame themselves for being hospitalized. Counseling should focus on what lies beneath this blame. Sometimes the self-blame reflects internalized feelings about being HIV positive. Other times self-blame is related to issues of self-control: for some clients the illusion of having control over their health is hard to relinquish. For these clients, the acknowledgment that they actually have little control over HIV's effect on their body is difficult and painful.

Pain Management

Pain is common in people living with HIV disease. Almost 50% of HIV-positive people experience pain, and it is the second most common reason for hospitalization (Patt, 1993). Pain is not caused by HIV infection itself but by any number of diseases to which clients are susceptible (e.g., esophageal ulcers, herpes zoster, lymphoma). Common treatments like chemotherapy and radiation can also cause pain.

Clients often feel lost when confronted with physical pain. Most clients were raised in a society that adheres to an excessively negative view of the experience of pain (Fertzinger, 1986). Patt (1993) wrote that "traditionally tolerance of pain has been viewed as a demonstration of strong character. In reality, pain is a legitimate component of disease that deserves attention and treatment" (p. 1). When hospitalized, clients have to take inventory of their beliefs and desires related to pain and its management. Clients may operate under the misguided notion that pain is felt in direct proportion to the physical effect of disease, forgetting that pain is also strongly affected by their past experience (Patt, 1993). Some clients may have had experiences that have led them not to trust or believe that appropriate treatment to ease physical pain will be offered or is even possible (Forstein, 1994b).

Clients who abused drugs frequently report low thresholds of pain. Ironically, due to their history of abuse, physicians are often less willing to treat these clients' pain despite the fact that successful pain management for former addicts is especially crucial (Faltz & Madover, 1988; Winiarski, 1991). Gottlieb (1992) maintained that refusing to prescribe pain medications to former addicts in pain often leads them to engage in aberrant drug-seeking behaviors. He suggested that a realistic goal for medically ill patients with past drug use and pain is to restore patients to their baseline state rather than aim for abstinence.

Some clients may need help remembering that the subjective nature of pain does not make it less legitimate. Any persistent pain should be assessed and treated (Patt, 1993). To this end, we should encourage clients to talk to their physicians and nurses about the pain they experience. Some clients frequently try to avoid medication until pain becomes unbearable (Patt, 1993). These clients engage in what Patt (1993) called *clock watching*, anxiously monitoring how long they are able to deny help. Often these clients fail to appreciate the risks associated with ignoring pain; studies have demonstrated that pain can have a very potent negative effect on immune functioning (Gottlieb, 1992; Patt, 1993). Uncontrolled pain has a negative impact on basic functioning and enjoyment of life.

Although various interventions can considerably reduce HIV-related pain, many hospitalized clients still experience some degree of pain. Clients have to face the reality that there are limitations to their physicians' ability to mitigate pain. They have to realize that physical distress is a difficult part of HIV disease (Nuland, 1994). Our work with these clients by necessity focuses on helping them learn to live with persistent or recurrent pain. With these clients validation become extremely important; often they feel that nobody understands or believes their experience of pain. They feel angry, frustrated, and dispirited that nothing can be done to spare them pain.

Reevaluating Support Systems

During their hospitalization, the actual level of strength of clients' support systems becomes apparent. Clients may be surprised to find that their support system is stronger or weaker than anticipated. Either condition may require emotional adjustment.

Just as there are many different types of family dynamics, there are many different ways in which families or other support systems can respond to clients' hospitalization. In some cases friends, partners, and relatives who supported healthy clients disappear when clients are admitted to the hospital. This actual abandonment often comes as a huge blow to clients. It may also compound any unresolved abandonment issues from a client's past. With regard to abandonment, it is important to remember that clients often consider us part of their support system. If we do not visit clients in the hospital, or at least maintain contact via phone, we may be seen as abandoning.

There are numerous means for us to help clients whose support system has left them. We can help clients vent the anger and pain they feel at having been abandoned. We can offer to conduct a conjoint, family, or group session either in the hospital or when the client gets released. This session can focus on the partner's, family's, or friend's reluctance to visit, and we can support clients in expressing how bad it felt to be left alone in the hospital. We can help clients make explicit the ways in which they need their partner, family, or friends to support them.

For some clients, hospitalization encourages those close to them to come closer and act more supportive. Families may visit, sometimes arriving from great geographical as well as emotional distances. Husbands, wives, or partners may reaffirm their vow to provide care in sickness and in health. Friends may cancel other engagements to spend time in the hospital. Although the support may come as a surprise and feel good, some clients may also respond angrily. Clients may want to know where people were when they were feeling good. They may question people's motives: why are they just now showing up? Clients may be unable to understand or unwilling to accept a sudden display of caring, particularly when it comes from people who have previously expressed condemnation of clients' sexual and affectional orientation, drug use, life-style, or HIV status. A family, conjoint, or group session, if possible, may provide clients with an opportunity to express their anger and hurt. At the same time families and friends may be given a chance to make amends and reestablish connections.

Some clients may never have established a support system. They may literally be left alone in the hospital as in the world. Even while they are in the hospital, plans can be made to help these clients find ways to garner support. Many cities have AIDS organizations that offer emotional support services such as "buddies." When clients who have no support system respond with reticence to the suggestion of a buddy, we may need to explore any underlying reasons clients have for wanting or needing to remain isolated. Some clients may feel unlovable or unworthy due to their hospitalization or their HIV status. Alternatively, current feelings may reflect longstanding, core feelings exacerbated by hospitalization. Once the immediate crisis of hospitalization recedes, counseling can focus on repairing a client's devalued self.

Tragically, sometimes people in clients' support systems are prevented from offering them support. This particularly holds true when clients' primary support givers are not conventional family members and may not have their visitation rights assured. Some hospital units, usually those accustomed to working with people living with HIV disease, allow visits from anyone clients choose; others, not so liberal in their policies, restrict visitors to the conventional immediate family only. This becomes problematic for gay, lesbian, or unmarried clients who want their mate to visit. Problems may also arise when nuclear family members unaccepting of a client's mate or friends act to have them prohibited from visiting.

It is prudent to deal with visitation problems prior to hospitalization. We can help clients anticipate any problems and take action so as to prevent them. Clients can be encouraged to make clear statements about whom they want to visit them. If their doctor has admitting privileges at a hospital that does not recognize these wishes, we can advocate that clients bring this to their doctor's attention and work toward some resolution.

A client's hospitalization often changes the nature of the counseling relationship, expanding it to include interactions with partners, family, and friends. We must recognize the difficult issues that arise for those who love and care for people living with HIV disease. Caregivers often have to adjust their picture of their loved ones—from seeing loved ones as strong and healthy to seeing them as hospitalized and ill. This shift may be particularly difficult when caregivers are HIV positive. Hospitalization may cause some caregivers to doubt their ability to provide ongoing care. Other caregivers may question whether or not they want to continue providing care, and if they are bad for deciding to stop. When clients are hospitalized their family, friends, and loved ones may become scared, anticipating the clients' death. They may be embarrassed by this fear and concerned that it represents a lack of hope. Husbands, wives, partners, and children of hospitalized clients may wonder who will care for them. Sometimes it may feel appropriate to invite caregivers into clients' counseling sessions. Other times we may choose to uphold our primary responsibility to our clients; we may feel that to include others may compromise the integrity of the counseling relationship. We may also feel that caregivers are best helped by having time away (i.e., counseling sessions) from those people to whom they provide care. It is crucial that we have resources and referrals available for caregivers and offer them whenever necessary.

Counselor Tasks

When clients are admitted to the hospital, we must strive to provide continuity of contact. For clients, everything has changed: their surroundings, daily schedule, and health status. Contact with us may be the one thing that remains constant. As previously mentioned, we need to decide the amount and type of contact we are willing to provide and capable of providing. The precise form and timing of the contact is often less crucial than providing a feeling of continuity. Clients need to feel they can count on us to be present for them. Some clients may even view hospitalization as a test of our capacity to stand by them till the end. This testing is best addressed directly with clients when we sense it occurring.

Our ability to provide continuity of contact may be threatened if no arrangements have been made with clients before they are hospitalized; we may not even know our clients are in the hospital. Clients in advanced stages of HIV disease may wish to make some type of arrangement so that we receive notification if they are hospitalized. These arrangements should contain contingencies for situations in which the client cannot personally contact us. At the very least, we should know what hospital clients will go to if seriously ill and should obtain clients' permission to call the hospital if clients are suddenly absent from scheduled sessions for a prolonged period of time. Above all, in making these arrangements we must remember our obligation to protect clients' confidentiality. Therefore, it is particularly important that these details be explicated before clients are first hospitalized.

Dealing With Thoughts of Death

Another of our tasks is to help hospitalized clients confront and cope with their thoughts and fantasies of death. To start, clients must recognize that people commonly think about death when hospitalized for an opportunistic infection. Often clients' fears stem not only from their thoughts and feelings but also from the realization that they have those feelings. This meta-level awareness can produce more distress than the original thoughts and fantasies, causing clients to view themselves as mentally ill or deranged. Therefore, we should be certain to address both overt thoughts and feelings and covert meta-level thoughts and feelings.

When clients admit to thoughts of death, we can help them engage in reality testing. Often these thoughts, and the fear that accompanies them, have at the base some element of reality and thus need to be honored, not simply discarded in total. For example, embedded in clients' recurring fantasy of dying in their sleep in the hospital is an element of truth; the possibility exists that this may happen. Nevertheless, we can help clients see that their fear may be disproportional to the probability of the event occurring. We may also be able to assist clients to see that these thoughts and fears could reflect lots of other fears, including, for example, dying per se or loss of control.

Many times clients refrain from asking their doctors for information about their prognosis. By not obtaining cogent information regarding the progression of their illness, clients can leave themselves wide open to morbid rumination. Information often serves as an antidote to fear. Helping clients overcome the obstacles that prevent them from staying informed is often extremely beneficial.

Reassess Expectations

Prior to hospitalization clients may hold many expectations for the progression of their life. Hospitalization will undoubtedly challenge these. Clients often need assistance in reassessing their expectations in light of their revised medical condition. Many of the goals that clients previously established in counseling will change. What was once important to clients may be cast off and new involvements may ensue to take their place.

When clients are hospitalized, we too must reassess our expectations. We may have been operating from the belief that our clients will live infection-free for many more years, or that clients will continue to be strong enough to come to our office weekly. These and many other expectations may become severely challenged by clients' hospitalization. To help our clients establish new expectations, we must first let go of our own.

Nurturing Hope

When counseling hospitalized clients, one of our most critical tasks is to sustain hope. At any given time in the therapeutic relationship, at least one person must hold the hope for the other. When clients become hospitalized, the onus falls on us.

Nurturing hope is a complicated matter. We cannot force clients to be hopeful. We can, however, support and nurture whatever hope exists for clients, even when clients are unaware of this hope. Many times hospitalization obscures any hope clients hold consciously (Carson, Soeken, Shanty, & Jerry, 1990). We must then hold onto and remind clients of their earlier hopes, if they are still appropriate. Sometimes this is unnecessary; it is enough for clients to know that we remain hopeful even when they cannot.

Youth Issues

The issues addressed in this chapter also apply when HIV-positive youth are hospitalized. In addition, four youth-specific issues arise. First, for some young people, their HIV-related hospitalization may be the first time, since birth, that they have been inside a hospital. The entire hospital environment may seem mysterious, confusing, and anxiety provoking. If young people are placed on a standard immune suppression unit, it is likely that they will be the only young person there. They may feel isolated, as though they do not belong. We should consider ways in which young clients' isolation may be eased. Retaining contact with friends, if possible, is often helpful.

For some young clients, hospitalization may also mark their first time away from home for an extended period of time. They may miss their family, pets, or the simple comfort of their own room. It is important to let young clients know that this homesickness is natural. We can encourage parents or caregivers of young clients to bring items from the youth's room to the hospital to serve as transitional objects. Whenever possible, young clients should be supported in dressing in their own clothes or pajamas, as opposed to a hospital gown.

Hospitalization for HIV-positive youth differs from that of HIV-positive adults in one other major way. Unlike adults, children and adolescents cannot legally make binding decisions for themselves. Parents or guardians determine the course of treatment for youth regardless of the youth's wishes; youth need not even be consulted. For older adolescents, this lack of power may serve to exacerbate feelings of losing control. Developmentally, teens are in the process of individuating from their parents; when hospitalized they may be forced back into a dependent relationship that is difficult and painful. Counseling should attend to the emotional impact of this renewed or increased dependency. When appropriate, we should propose to parents a collaborative model of decision making that allows more mature youth to remain informed and have some degree of say in their treatment.

Conclusion

Hospitalization may be devastating to clients because it removes nearly all distractions. While in the hospital, almost nothing prevents clients from evaluating and reevaluating their medical treatment, their support systems, their future. Even when clients return home from the hospital, knowing that they have been hospitalized has a transforming effect. Hospitalization makes living with AIDS a concrete reality. The adjustments people living with AIDS must make in the hospital foreshadow the adjustments they will have to make once released, or in the future.

During hospitalization we need to provide clients with hope, with perspective, and with reassurance. Often we need to extend the same support to caregivers struggling to adjust to their loved one's hospitalization. When clients are hospitalized we, too, must make adjustments, altering expectations for them that we may have held. We may find that intense emotions arise. When working with ill clients, it is easy to concentrate on making sure that they are well cared for and ignore our own need for emotional comfort and support. If we overlook this need, we become susceptible to burnout. It is essential that we take steps to insure that our feelings get attended to. As clients move into more severe stages of HIV disease, we must be certain that our support network is in place.

CHAPTER 16

Loss

*Large losses take their toll, but the
cumulative sum of small losses suffered daily is often greater.*

Loss permeates the late stages of HIV disease. In the early
stages, life flowed with little daily disruption, but in the advanced stages life becomes constricted and increasingly more
complicated. In the early stages counseling focused on the
clients' adjustment to life with HIV, but in the advanced stages counseling often focuses on clients' adjustments to life without many of the
things upon which they have depended. In the early stages, HIV disease
robs clients of their identity as a uninfected person, but that identity
is at least supplanted by an identity as a person living with HIV. In
the late stages clients suffer many more losses, and few of them are
replaced.

As they approach the end stages of their illness, people living with
HIV disease and AIDS face many losses large and small. We should
take care not to underestimate the power of small losses; the adage
that the sum of the parts is greater than the whole certainly holds true.
The pain and terror of losing the things one holds dear is enormous,
and when these losses continue regularly, without stopping, the results
are devastating. Counseling can help clients cope with the many forms
their losses take.

Loss of Physical Attractiveness

People in today's Western society are particularly focused on maintaining their physical appearance. They may spend vast amounts of
time and energy exercising, grooming, and dressing to look their best.

People may go to any lengths possible to keep their physical appearances from deteriorating.

Many HIV-related infections result in painful changes in clients' physical appearance. Lesions may appear. Warts are not uncommon and may appear on the face. Extreme loss of weight may leave once muscular persons so depleted that their bones show through the skin. In other cases, the side effects of medications and treatments for opportunistic infections may cause appearance to be altered. For example, hair loss from chemotherapy can occur. Although these cosmetic losses may seem small compared to larger losses, they feel large when placed in the context of a society that favors those who look good.

Radical and unwanted changes in appearance also affect clients' body image and sense of self, often in very disturbing ways. In grasping the significance of this trauma, it is important to understand the degree of importance clients placed on their looks when they were healthy. Only with this understanding can we comprehend clients' reactions to changes in appearance; otherwise, clients' reluctance to be seen in public places may appear disproportionate. In some cases, action can be taken to compensate for or correct the loss. Some facial warts can be removed. Some lesions can be covered up with makeup. Hair loss can be hidden with hats or wigs. Counseling may provide valuable and much needed support for clients as they seek ways to overcome the challenges to their physical appearance.

Concerns about loss of physical attractiveness sometimes mask the presence of deeper issues. Clients' negative feelings about their appearance may be related to embarrassment or shame for being HIV infected. Lesions, weight loss, or any other conspicuous signs of HIV disease leave clients unable to hide their illness easily. Often it is this "scarlet letter effect" that is most disturbing and painful.

Loss of Job

At some point our clients' illness may force them to cease working. Some clients feel too fatigued to work. Other clients may stop working because of a doctor's order to go on disability. HIV-related treatments may become extremely involved and time-consuming, prohibiting some clients from holding down steady, full-time jobs. Other clients simply make a personal decision to spend their time pursuing activities other than work. Regardless of the rationale for ending employment, doing so often results in great loss.

For clients who have worked a large portion of their lives, the relief that immediately arises from not having to assert the energy to go to work each day may initially overshadow the pain associated with leaving their career or job. At first, clients may consider fighting HIV a better use of their energy. However, as time passes some clients may also manifest signs of loss, depression, and anxiety. Unless clients' finances are extremely well established, leaving work probably elicits fears about their ability to provide for themselves. We may be called upon to help clients find ways to reduce these anxieties or at least cope with them.

For many clients, the place of employment provides a social support network that disappears when they leave. Clients may not even realize the importance of this social aspect of work until they are gone. It is often beneficial to assist clients that are considering not working anticipate this aspect of loss and make contingency plans.

For many clients living with HIV disease, work furnishes them with a time and place focused on matters other than AIDS. When clients stop working, the amount of time that becomes available to think about their illnesses often comes as a shock and surprise. Taking into consideration the constraints of clients' health, we might encourage clients to find other activities that can provide a diversion from dwelling on AIDS as well as prove meaningful. For example, when clients leave their jobs yet are still healthy enough to do some work, we can explore other avenues besides full-time paid employment where clients can use their skills. Many times "retired" HIV-positive clients find it comfortable and rewarding to volunteer at AIDS service agencies where the time and energy demands of staying healthy are expected and understood.

Over time, many clients, particularly middle-class males, become highly associated with their careers; their careers often become their identity. When clients' careers end the result is often a loss of ego strength. Dependency issues may resurface, particularly in clients who have been socialized to find their self-worth in the traditional role of financial provider. Anticipating or actually being dependent may cause painful and difficult feelings to arise. One strategy for helping clients through these complex reactions is to frame feelings in the context of grieving. Clients can be encouraged to grieve for their old job or their old career. Clients frequently need assurance that although many people they know may eagerly anticipate retirement, the sadness they feel about losing their job is normal, appropriate, and understandable considering their circumstances.

Loss of Mobility and Physical Functioning

As HIV disease progresses, many clients' ability to move around is severely hampered by fatigue, muscular pain, or the effects of neuropathy. Other clients may retain the physical ability necessary to move around but prefer remaining at home because of conditions such as persistent diarrhea. Treatments that require clients to remain stationary for hours at a time also render some clients immobile. In the late stages of HIV disease, other clients are able to move, but only with the assistance of a cane, walker, or wheelchair.

Loss of mobility and physical functioning translates to loss of freedom and independence. Clients who are truly homebound must rely on others to help them with their daily life. They must find someone to shop for them, help them with their laundry and other chores, and take care of their day-to-day affairs. Even clients who can move with assistance must now make special arrangements for simple tasks like going to doctor's appointments or coming to counseling. Some clients may become overwhelmed by the sheer amount of energy needed to accomplish even the littlest task and may find themselves frustrated when unable to obtain assistance.

Counseling should offer clients a place to vent their frustration. Often clients feel they have no one to complain to because the very people they want to complain about are the people they depend upon for help. Because our therapeutic stance provides clients with a place to vent, we should take care to maintain clear boundaries and be cautious about providing physical assistance to clients ourselves. For example, we probably do not want to personally drive clients to appointments, even if clients find it difficult to get another ride. Although clients might express their appreciation for the ride, they might not subsequently be as free to express other feelings to which the break in the therapeutic frame gave rise (e.g., anger related to feeling more dependent upon us). A better approach is to link immobile clients to any and all community resources available. Many agencies provide free transportation to important appointments for people living with HIV disease.

Many immobile clients need support to examine their feelings about being dependent. We may find it helpful to work developmentally exploring current feelings in the context of clients' other earlier dependent relationships. The experience of being literally dependent on others for food, safety, and movement often reactivates conscious and unconscious early dependency issues. Many clients can more easily adjust to their current situation when they understand their feelings in relation to earlier events and relationships.

Loss of Others

Because of their associations with others who, like themselves, are HIV positive, clients may face a disproportionate number of deaths, especially when they are long-term survivors. The loss of someone to AIDS-related complications is never easy, and it takes an enormous psychological toll on clients who are themselves HIV positive. They must not only deal with the grief of losing someone, but they must also contend with a reflection of their own anticipated death. This can be especially excruciating when the friend's death involved a great deal of physical or emotional suffering.

For many HIV-positive clients, the grieving process may never end (Remien, Katoff, Rabkin, & Wagner, 1993). Sometimes the people whom clients found most supportive are the people the client most often loses. In their study of long-term survivors, Remien, Katoff, Rabkin, and Wagner (1993) offered a long-term survivor's description, typical of many people living with HIV disease, of the toll of losing others:

> One of the hardest things is watching your friends die. And that is the wearing part, that is the exhausting part, after a while it is grief beyond belief. I mean you're conscious something is very wrong. Or you go to pick up the phone to [call] someone who isn't there anymore. And that's part of being a long-term survivor. That's one of the hardest parts. All of a sudden your support systems aren't there anymore. The people that were your extended family aren't there anymore. And one by one you watch them go. That's the hardest part. You know there are going to be physical limitations when you're diagnosed. You know it's gonna get worse physically. But it's along the way that the people that you love, the people that are friends, the people that you tend to lean on, all of a sudden they aren't there anymore. That's one of the wearing factors that's tremendous. The sense of constant loss. And the longer you live with this thing, the more losses there are. There seems never to be a reward for being a long-term survivor. (pp. 8–9).

Many times clients who have sustained multiple losses appear to lack an emotional reaction to further losses. There is often great survival value in this psychic numbing. Many clients cannot grieve for those they have lost; to do so is too threatening and too overwhelming. When we work with these clients, we should avoid even subtly pressuring them to emote.

Whether clients become highly emotional or anaesthetized over the loss of others, we must provide them with something extremely important: a sense of stability and continuity. When we see signs that clients perceive these qualities to be lacking, we should directly address this issue. When we anticipate being unable to provide clients with stability or continuity (e.g., because of a vacation), we should take care to inform the client well in advance, pay special and explicit attention to clients' feelings about the break, and make appropriate contingency plans as necessary.

For clients in advanced stages of HIV disease, these contingency plans take on even greater importance. We must be certain that anyone who covers for us while we are away is well versed on HIV-related issues. Prior to our absence, some clients may prefer meeting or knowing about whomever will be covering for us. If possible, and when appropriate, we may want to arrange to introduce clients to the counselor who will be covering our practice. The more familiar clients feel with our replacement, the better he or she will fill the role of transitional object.

Loss of Future

Especially in the advanced stages of HIV disease, clients need room to mourn their losses of opportunities, promises, and future plans. Experiencing this loss of the future may throw clients into an existential crisis. According to existential theory, as death moves closer, clients are forced to face the consequences of the choices they made or did not make during their life (Yalom, 1980). Considering these unrealized and unactualized choices, plans, and aspirations may produce overwhelming guilt and profound remorse.

The most effective counseling approach avoids pointing out the things clients did in fact accomplish and thus diminishing the weight of this guilt; to do so will invalidate clients' present reality. Instead, existential guilt and remorse is considered an appropriate reaction to a crisis of meaning. Many clients in the late stages of HIV disease are thrust into the position of questioning the meaning of their life, especially when things remain unfinished or undone. Clients can be supported in their attempts to put their life in perspective and find meaning in the reality of what their life has been. It is not our job to suggest to clients either directly or indirectly what they should find meaningful. Clients must find this meaning for themselves. We should provide not solutions but structure and support for the inquiry.

Loss of Self

The cumulative effect of small losses can best be understood by using the theory of self-psychology. The repeated losses that people living with HIV disease sustain constitute a conscious and unconscious loss of self. Clients may literally no longer know who they are.

A client's job, physical appearance, family relationships, and friends may become internalized as pieces of the self, or self-objects. A client then literally experiences the loss of these self-objects as the loss of self. The psychological structure of the client's personality is deconstructed, often resulting in severe disorientation and intense emotional distress (Abramowitz & Cohen, 1994).

With most clients we should consider the deeper ramifications of the repeated loss of self-objects. We can work with clients to help strengthen what remains of their self-structure. While facilitating this process, we must remain aware of the role we play in fortifying our clients' sense of self. Over the course of counseling, we often become an internalized self-object for our clients.

The stability of the counselor-client relationship becomes of utmost importance as other self-objects are lost. Clients may question our permanence. We should take this concern to heart and address it with great sensitivity and respect. When we become one of the few self-objects remaining in a client's life, empathic failures (e.g., running late, misunderstanding the client's communications, or being unable to reschedule a client's appointment) are likely to be experienced as a shock to the client's sense of self (Abramowitz & Cohen, 1994). Addressing them as such helps clients acknowledge the importance of the counseling relationship and the work they have done in counseling, and also helps clients reconsolidate and stabilize their self-structure.

Conclusion

Working with HIV-positive clients coming to terms with the many losses in their lives brings us face to face with our own limitations. We cannot possibly prevent our clients' losses. At best, we can help clients learn to better cope with the many losses they encounter, and will continue to encounter, as their illness progresses.

As our clients continue to lose the things closest to them, the counseling relationship becomes substantially more important. We should pay special attention to how our clients' emotional reactions to loss play themselves out in the counseling session. We should address these dynamics with clients whenever appropriate.

We are naturally affected by our clients' losses. Witnessing clients lose their physical attractiveness, job, mobility, physical functioning, friends, future, and sense of self is often excruciatingly painful. The demands of serving as clients' primary source of support may emotionally overwhelm us. Therefore, it is especially important that we regularly obtain supervision or consultation whenever we work with clients in advanced stages of HIV disease.

CHAPTER 17

Neurobehavioral Impairment

*Changes in cognition wax and wane throughout
the course of HIV disease. It is during the lucid periods
that clients often feel the most anguish.*

One of the most horrific aspects of living with HIV disease is anticipating or braving neurological impairment. Clients often become terrified awaiting the deterioration of their memory, muscle control, and personality. Family and friends often fear that their loved ones will lose the ability to recognize them. When cognitive or motor impairment does occur, some clients, as well as the people around them, may try to ignore it for as long as possible. Although their need to overlook HIV-related neurobehavioral changes is understandable, it may prevent clients from gaining much needed care.

Researchers, neurologists, physicians, and psychologists presently view the neurobehavioral aspects of HIV disease much differently than they did in the mid-1980s. A new conceptualization of impairment distinguishing among the many gradations of cognitive impairment was created in 1991 by a working group of the American Academy of Neurology AIDS Task Force (Working Group, 1991). For adults, the new term *HIV-associated dementia complex* replaces the previous term *AIDS dementia complex.* HIV-associated dementia complex refers to a brain disorder characterized by intellectual and/or motor deterioration that severely inhibits a person's ability to function at work, at home, or out in the world. An additional term, *HIV-associated minor cognitive/motor disorder,* is now used to describe mild cognitive and/ or motor impairment that may not necessarily develop into severe dementia.

These changes in definition have many implications for people living with HIV disease and their counselors. First, they challenge previous findings that up to 50% of all people with HIV disease are affected by dementia (Keeling, 1993). Second, they demystify what was once known as AIDS dementia, breaking it down into two components that are neither equal in severity nor interchangeable. Third, they increase the importance of differential diagnosis. Finally, the changes in definition have resulted in changes in how treatment is conceptualized across the spectrum of neurobehavioral manifestations of HIV disease.

The technical language used to describe the neurobehavioral aspects of HIV disease often prevents clients from realistically understanding much about cognitive and motor impairment; therefore, many clients rely upon word-of-mouth to ascertain their odds of becoming demented. Because information from misinformed sources is often alarming and damaging to clients, we have a responsibility to provide clients with clear descriptions and definitions of the neurobehavioral aspects of HIV disease, as well as with information about the likelihood of becoming impaired. Although many of the tests used to diagnose these impairments definitively may lie beyond the scope of our customary training and expertise, we should still understand and engage in preliminary assessment. Once either minor or major impairment has been diagnosed, we must provide clients and their caregivers with appropriate care. This frequently involves relying on a more directive counseling approach. We are often in the best position to detect changes in a client's cognitive and/or motor functioning; because neurobehavioral impairment may be the first sign of HIV-related symptomology, it is crucial that we do so.

The Prevalence of Dementia

Accurate information presented to clients paralyzed with fear over becoming demented can effectively reduce their levels of anxiety. Estimates of the prevalence of HIV-related cognitive and motor impairment vary due to the myriad ways impairment has been defined and measured. Early studies estimated the occurrence of cognitive impairment in people diagnosed with AIDS in ranges from 66% to 90% (Macks, 1989) and the rate of incidence of AIDS-related dementia at more than half (Keeling, 1993). Mapou and Law (1994) wrote that these early studies did not differentiate between AIDS dementia complex and less clinically significant cognitive changes, thus "grouping together individuals who were frankly demented with those showing only mild impairment" (p. 135). More recent studies using the new, two-level classification system for cognitive and motor impairment suggest a lower prevalence of AIDS dementia complex than originally reported (Mapou & Law, 1994). In addition, recent studies suggest that the use of the drug zidovudine (ZDV) may also reduce the occurrence of AIDS dementia complex/HIV-associated dementia complex (Mapou & Law, 1994).

Mapou and Law (1994) stated that it is currently unclear whether cognitive impairment occurs when someone is HIV positive and asymptomatic. Studies that do show impairment in asymptomatic people suggest that from 20% to 30% of medically asymptomatic people living with HIV disease may manifest detectable impairment. For people showing symptoms of HIV disease, 50% to 70% of them may show signs of neuropsychological impairment. However, this does not imply that all of these cases meet the definition of HIV-associated dementia complex. According to Mapou and Law (1994), the actual prevalence may range from approximately 5% to 35%, substantially lower than earlier findings. Given this uncertainty regarding the frequency with which HIV-associated dementia complex occurs, we can assure clients that becoming demented is not inevitable.

Demystifying Dementia

A critical part of our work with HIV-positive clients is to demystify dementia. People generally misunderstand the term *dementia*. Boccellari and Dilley (1989) wrote that "for some, the term implies images of insanity and violent, out-of-control behavior; for others, the image is one of the frail and helpless elderly person" (p. 188). The American Psychological Association's HIV Office of Psychology Education (Barret, Pawlowski, & Washington, 1993) also acknowledged that the term *dementia* produces fear, attributing it to the colloquial use of the term to mean "weird," "frightening," or "disgusting." A good counseling strategy is to ask clients and their caregivers to discuss their notion of dementia in order to clear up any misconceptions they may hold.

Now that the term *AIDS dementia complex* is falling out of use, clients may need to be introduced to prevailing terms and instructed in how these terms differentiate severity of impairment. This information needs to be presented in a form easily assimilated by clients;

unless we are clear, concise, and assuaging, talking about dementia raises, not reduces, clients' anxiety levels.

When describing **HIV-associated minor cognitive/motor disorder** to clients, it is extremely important to stress that it may not necessarily develop into severe dementia. People with HIV-associated minor cognitive/motor disorder maintain important functioning abilities. Boccellari (1991) gave a cogent description of this disorder:

> Individuals with this disorder demonstrate only mild difficulty in their ability to pay attention, concentrate, and remember details. Family and friends may describe a sense that individuals have "changed" in ways that are subtle but important. They may feel that patients were less interested in things that were formerly satisfying, or that they are not as talkative or as "sharp" as before. Patients themselves report similar observations, such as "thinking more slowly" and having difficulty performing complex tasks. (p. 13)

Clients may also report motor disturbances such as problems with balance and coordination. They may experience decreased physical activity, apathy, and social withdrawal. However, clients usually remain fully oriented to day, date, and time. They continue to walk and typically retain the ability to speak easily (Boccellari, 1991).

HIV-associated dementia complex includes symptoms in three different areas: cognitive, motor, and behavioral (Dilley & Boccellari, 1989; Winiarski, 1991). Early stage symptoms of cognitive impairment include poor concentration, slowed mental processing, and forgetfulness. Early stage manifestations of motor impairment include slowed movement of eyes and limbs, abnormal reflexes, balance problems, and leg weakness (peripheral neuropathy). Early stage behavioral symptoms include apathy and social withdrawal, dysphoric mood, and personality changes.

Late stage symptoms of cognitive impairment include global cognitive dysfunction (in severe cases), slowed verbal responses or mutism, wide-eyed staring, and what Winiarski (1991, p. 86) referred to as "quiet confusion." Late stage manifestations of motor impairment include generalized muscle weakness, peripheral neuropathies, and incontinence. Late stage behavioral symptoms include agitated psychosis. Despite these symptoms, clients generally retain an awareness of people and activities in their surroundings (Dilley & Boccellari, 1989).

Clients with HIV-associated minor cognitive/motor disorder or the early stages of HIV-associated dementia complex often continue to function reasonably well and live relatively autonomously. However, once clients progress to the late stage of HIV-associated dementia complex, they cannot live independently. "They have lost their ability to adapt creatively to their disability" (Boccellari, 1991, p. 13). When this is the case, the responsibility for caretaking must shift from the client to others in their immediate care network.

It is important to remember that a diagnosis of any type of dementia requires evidence of impairment in everyday social and occupational functioning in addition to neuropsychological impairment (Mapou & Law, 1994). Thus Mapou and Law (1994) recommended caution when communicating neuropsychological findings to clients. They maintained that even when impairment is present, it is not known currently whether it is prognostic for subsequent development of dementia.

It is also important to recognize that various opportunistic infections manifest symptoms similar to those of HIV-associated minor cognitive/motor disorder and HIV-associated dementia complex (Mapou & Law, 1994). Opportunistic infections like toxoplasmosis (*toxo*—a protozoan infection passed by contact with infected cats and ingestion of raw or undercooked meat or unpasteurized dairy products), progressive multifocal leukoencephalopathy (*PML*—a viral infection), or cryptococcal meningitis (*crypto*—caused by the inhalation of a yeast-like fungus found worldwide, often in soil) also result in cognitive and motor impairment, as does central nervous system lymphoma (Siano, 1993; Winiarski, 1989). Some of these conditions, especially those caused by the cryptococcal fungus and the toxoplasmosis protozoa, can be treated with medications. Therefore, it is critical that an accurate diagnosis and assessment of a client's condition be made.

Assessment of Neurobehavioral Aspects of HIV Disease

Given that we may spend more cumulative time with clients than do physicians, we must remain cognizant of signs of cognitive and/or motor impairment. When clients demonstrate mental status or personality changes, we should begin to consider the presence of HIV-associated minor cognitive/motor disorder or dementia complex. Dilley and Boccellari (1989) recommended that clients suspected of hav-

NEUROBEHAVIORAL IMPAIRMENT

ing HIV-related neurological complications receive complete medical and neuropsychiatric evaluation.

Dilley and Boccellari (1989) also suggested that we regularly perform a thorough mental status exam with HIV-positive clients. "Assessing orientation, attention, memory, language ability, and judgment should be a part of any evaluation" (p. 148). Many of these factors can be assessed unobtrusively. However, brief screening exams often fail to detect early and subtle deficits associated with HIV-associated dementia complex.

The diagnosis of HIV-associated dementia complex is always a diagnosis of exclusion (Dilley & Boccellari, 1989). We must rule out all other possible causes of impairment and must work collaboratively with clients' physicians before making a definitive diagnosis. We must take caution when using changes in mood state as part of our diagnosis criteria. Mood disturbance does not always indicate central nervous system involvement. In fact, mood disturbances have been known to confound performance on neuropsychological measures and produce false signs of dementia (Mapou & Law, 1994).

Dilley and Boccellari (1989) wrote that it is extremely difficult, yet extremely necessary, for us to distinguish between early symptoms of HIV-associated dementia complex and functional depression. Mapou and Law (1994) stated that because coping with a life-threatening illness often causes symptoms of depression and anxiety, such symptoms may account for the neuropsychological impairment seen in HIV-positive people. However, they caution that "complaints of cognitive difficulties by an HIV-positive individual should never be attributed benignly to the stress of the illness without first being addressed as possible neurobehavioral symptoms to be investigated" (p. 137).

Treatment

The most effective and appropriate treatment for clients with HIV-associated cognitive and/or motor impairment or HIV-associated dementia complex builds on a stage model, with different strategies utilized with different degrees of impairment. The most common approaches involve a two-part treatment model that includes adaptation and compensation (stage one) and environmental engineering (stage two) (Boccellari & Dilley, 1989; Boccellari, Kain, & Shor, 1989). However, before we can even suggest an intervention, we must generally first deal with denial in clients and their caregivers.

Denial of Impairment

Often clients and their caregivers play down the seriousness of emerging symptoms (Boccellari & Dilley, 1989). For the client, denial may protect against the awareness of what is happening. Alternatively, it may represent what Boccellari and Dilley (1989) referred to as "organic denial," in which clients "lose the ability to appreciate fully the impact of their behavior on themselves or other people because of their brain dysfunction" (p. 191). Partners, families, friends, and other caregivers may also engage in denial if the painful reality of their loved one's illness becomes too overwhelming.

Because of the potentially harmful consequences of leaving symptoms untreated, we must help clients and their caregivers overcome denial. When clients and their caregivers continue to deny the seriousness of cognitive and/or motor impairment, and symptoms such as disorientation or confusion occur, clients are put in potentially dangerous situations. We must remain alert for ways in which we, too, may deny the presence of neurobehavioral impairment. We may find ourselves unconsciously underestimating the severity of a client's impairment or ignoring it altogether. To do so is to collude with the client's denial. Again, this may place the client in danger.

Ironically, the exact opposite reaction may occur, particularly in caregivers. Overvigilance, or overcompensation for a client's cognitive and/or motor difficulties, may be equally as harmful. When caregivers act as though clients can do nothing independently, they promote unnecessary feelings of helplessness in the client (Boccellari, 1991). We, too, must be careful not to do the same to our clients.

Interventions for HIV-Associated Cognitive/Motor Disorder: Adaptation and Compensation

At this early stage of impairment, the fact that clients can actively participate in treatment and management decisions should be taken into consideration (Boccellari, 1991). Keeping clients involved increases their self-worth and decreases their feelings of isolation. Interventions at this stage should focus on encouraging and reinforcing clients' remaining cognitive and emotional strengths (Boccellari & Dilley, 1989).

Emotional support becomes extremely important at this stage because of the high incidence of depression and anxiety. Clients must cope not only with any other challenges caused by HIV but also with the awareness of their inability to perform tasks that once came easily. In addition to individual counseling, medication may help to relieve much of the depression and anxiety. When clients appear anxious or depressed, it is often wise to recommend that clients see a psychiatrist or consult with their primary doctor to be evaluated for psychotropic medication.

Clients also may find group therapy helpful. Sharing their experiences and knowing that they are not alone is important to clients facing increasing psychoneurological impairment (Mapou & Law, 1994). Couples groups for clients and their partners may also be beneficial (Boccellari, 1991). These groups can help to address and support the many role changes that occur within relationships as impairment increases.

When working with clients with HIV-associated cognitive/motor disorder, the scope of our enterprise expands to include educating and informing clients and their caregivers of the many strategies used to help compensate for cognitive problems. Six major strategies are writing down reminders, slowing down, keeping mentally active, avoiding fatigue, monitoring tasks verbally, and anticipating stressful situations.

Clients can be encouraged to keep lists, or memory journals, or notebooks (Boccellari, 1991; Boccellari & Dilley, 1989; Sohlberg & Mateer, 1989). When clients write down appointment times and other important information, the result is often an increased sense of competency. Because clients with cognitive impairment often find multiple tasks difficult, encouraging them to slow down and work on one task at a time decreases the number of mistakes made. In addition, slowing down may reduce clients' feelings of frustration and may enhance their feelings of mastery (Boccellari, 1991).

To stimulate and reinforce concentration, clients can be encouraged to play games such as Scrabble, cards, checkers, or even video games, and to make jigsaw puzzles (Boccellari, 1991; Boccellari & Dilley, 1989). However, care must be taken so as to choose games and activities that are not too difficult or frustrating for clients. Fatigue often exacerbates cognitive and memory problems and causes irritability and emotional outbursts (Boccellari, 1991). We can encourage clients to get plenty of rest. It is also important that clients learn to schedule important appointments for times when they feel less tired (Mapou & Law, 1994).

Clients often find that they are better able to focus their attention when they monitor tasks verbally. We can encourage clients to think aloud when working (Boccellari, 1991; Boccellari & Dilley, 1989).

Clients need to learn to anticipate stressful situations. Avoiding or minimizing exposure to stressful environments is also often helpful (Boccellari, 1991; Boccellari & Dilley, 1989). Clients can be encouraged to go to public places during uncrowded hours when clients are apt to feel less disoriented, frustrated, and scared.

In addition to these six major strategies, we can suggest other methods of combating cognitive decline. For example, exercising may help reduce stress and keep clients involved in the world (Boccellari & Dilley, 1989); clients may retain motor and coordination skills longer when these skills are used (Boccellari, 1991). Permitting clients to manage their own medication for as long as possible allows them to feel actively involved in their own treatment and increases their feelings of competence (Boccellari, 1991; Boccellari & Dilley, 1989). Avoiding tasks that have become impossible to complete helps prevent frustration (Boccellari, 1989; Boccellari & Dilley, 1989). Finally, setting realistic daily and short-term goals increases feelings of competency (Boccellari, 1991).

Interventions for HIV-Associated Dementia: Environmental Engineering

Losing the ability to remain mentally flexible, to adapt and adjust to changes, and to deal with new situations is a painfully difficult challenge for clients with HIV-associated dementia complex (Boccellari & Dilley, 1989). Since clients have less ability to adapt and change, their external environment must be altered to compensate. Environmental engineering, or the process of providing external structure for a client's world, acts to minimize danger, confusion, and other results of a client's failing abilities (Boccellari, 1991; Boccellari & Dilley, 1989). Boccellari (1991) and Boccellari and Dilley (1989) offered many suggestions for environmental changes that can offset a client's increasing confusion and memory problems, speech problems, and movement problems.

Clients and those close to them may become frightened by the heightened disorientation, confusion, and lack of memory that often occur as the severity of dementia increases. Clients may lose track of time and may not even recognize those close to them. To offset these lapses, it is often helpful if clients are provided with frequent reality and orienting cues such as easily viewed calendars and clocks and reminders throughout the day. Installing nightlights may help reduce the nighttime confusion that often occurs. Before beginning any new activity, it may be beneficial to explain to clients what will happen; this often makes changes more predictable and less confusing.

Part of our work is to teach caregivers how to respond when clients become confused or act in a bizarre manner. Partners, family members, and friends often need to be told that challenging people when they are confused merely exacerbates confusion. Caregivers need to learn that the clients do not always know why they act in a particular way. We can recommend that caregivers learn to remain calm and redirect clients from inappropriate behaviors in a firm but nonthreatening manner.

In counseling sessions that include caregivers, we can stress the importance of keeping the client's environment structured and familiar. This is particularly important when clients receive care away from their own home (Boccellari, 1991). Familiar objects, like photographs, may provide clients with a sense of security and may trigger pleasant and comforting memories. To the extent possible, people who care for the client should not change. Keeping furniture and personal objects in the same positions often helps reduce confusion. In addition, keeping the environment uncluttered by objects and reducing the number of visitors may help prevent overstimulation, which can lead to confusion, agitation, and apprehension.

As HIV-associated dementia complex progresses, expressive speech may become more difficult. Clients may begin to speak more slowly or slur their words. In the most severe cases, clients may become mute and unresponsive to questions. When this loss of functioning occurs we need to teach clients, their loved ones, and their caregivers ways of compensating. Boccellari (1991) and Boccellari and Dilley (1989) suggested that when clients attempt to speak, others should not rush or interrupt them. Those needing to communicate with clients should think simply, asking questions that require yes and no answers rather than complex responses. Some clients may find writing down information easier than attempting to respond verbally.

HIV-associated dementia complex also causes balance and coordination problems. These can stem from generalized weakness, memory failure, or damage to parts of the brain that control movement (Boccellari, 1991). Clients may need canes or walkers to help them move around. They may need special assistance when getting out of a seated position. Caregivers must remove any objects that may cause clients to slip or trip. We, too, should not forget to ensure that our offices provide easy accessibility for motor-impaired clients. Clients may need to modify such day-to-day activities as getting dressed so as to require fewer motor skills; Boccellari (1991) gave as examples wearing slip-on shoes or drinking soup from a cup with handles as opposed to using a bowl and spoon. When clients appear to be stuck, caregivers may find it helpful to give a gentle reminder of the appropriate behavior.

The emotional and personality changes that accompany dementia often cause clients and those caring for them immense difficulty. Distractibility, stubbornness, and emotional volatility are among the behavioral changes attributable to HIV-associated dementia complex. Whenever possible we should help those close to the client recognize that these behaviors are often not deliberate and are usually beyond the impaired person's ability to control (Boccellari, 1991). If a client experiences panic-stricken states, we can help caregivers learn to notice what stimuli triggered the reaction. We can encourage the use of time outs and the reduction of overstimulation.

Similarly, limited insight combined with environmental misperceptions and emotional reactions may cause clients to act suspiciously and irrationally, and accuse caregivers of things they did not do (Boccellari, 1991). Those close to the client may need to be reminded that clients are usually unaware of their paranoia. Arguing with a client does no good. Instead, those close to the client should offer simple observations and solutions (Boccellari, 1991). When clients display suspicious or paranoid behaviors that indicate possible psychosis (e.g., delusional thinking, hallucinations, or illusions) they should be thoroughly evaluated by their physician (Boccellari, 1991). Occasionally these symptoms may be the result of side effects of medications. Otherwise, they may indicate acute illness that needs immediate treatment. Regardless of the cause of a client's suspiciousness or paranoia, adopting tactful responses rather than confrontive ones works best.

Caregivers

The burden of adjusting to a client's impairment often falls on the client's partner, family, or friends. If the client is to remain at home, caregivers' participation is essential (Mapou & Law, 1994). Just as clients often find counseling helpful in aiding their adjustment to cognitive and motor impairment or dementia, caregivers, too, may find counseling beneficial.

The needs of caregivers are extensive. Caregivers usually need information about the effects of HIV-associated dementia complex; in many cities organizations exist that offer psychoeducation about dementia. Caregiver support groups may also be helpful. Often caregivers resist obtaining help, feeling that they cannot afford to leave the impaired person. We should stress the importance of respite for care-givers. It is crucial that caregivers have time out from their caregiving role, and a place to express their emotional reactions.

Caregivers may need to learn how to depersonalize the impaired person's behavior. Often caregivers feel that the impaired person's inability to answer questions, ability to remember things from the past but not the present, or paranoid attacks are purposefully intended to annoy the caregiver. Sometimes caregivers feel that they are owed an apology for an attacking or hurtful comment or behavior. However, an apology is most likely to be beyond the cognitive capacity of the client. Although we should be certain to empathize with the caregiver's feelings, we must also remind caregivers that the impaired are often unaware of what they are doing and mean no harm by their actions.

Strong emotions naturally arise in caregivers. They may feel helpless as they watch their loved one's condition decline. They may feel lonely and miss the companionship the loved one provided when he or she was more cognitively, physically, and emotionally available. They may feel fearful, and wonder what HIV-related complication will strike next. They may feel grief in anticipation of the death of their loved one. In addition, it is very common for caregivers to have negative feelings about their loved one. Caregivers may find themselves becoming angry or frustrated with their loved one's impaired behavior. They may feel exhausted by and resentful of the demands of providing care. Caregivers may become conflicted when ambivalent feelings arise; these feelings may not fit their concept of the good caregiver. Caregivers often need our reassurance that their emotional reactions are normal.

HIV-associated minor cognitive/motor disorder and HIV-associated dementia complex can affect anyone with HIV disease. In addition to knowing the generalized information and interventions presented in this chapter, we need to become familiar with complexities faced by culturally identified clients and youth. Assessment and treatment for these clients can vary from that already presented.

Culture, Class, and Language Considerations

In assessing the presence and severity of HIV-associated cognitive/motor disorder and HIV-associated dementia complex, great reliance is placed on standardized test batteries. For certain clients the cultural relevance of the tests in these batteries may come into question. Considerations such as whether English is a client's second language may confound testing (Winiarski, 1991). Social-class factors may also influence test results. Sometimes those who administer test batteries may not be aware of the influence of these variables on the testing process. When this is the case, we must take an advocacy role and help clients receive culturally sensitive and appropriate assessment.

Youth Issues

The developing nervous system of infants and children responds to HIV differently than that of adults. Levenson and Mellins (1992) reported that HIV disease in the pre- and perinatal periods may cause diffuse brain injury that affects verbal processes as well as auditory short-term memory and attention. The experience of both researchers and clinicians suggests that HIV-exposed children are at significantly higher risk for developmental delays and cognitive deficits and disability (Spiegel & Mayers, 1991). Assessment for HIV-associated minor cognitive/motor disorder or HIV-associated dementia complex is usually based on the loss of behavioral milestones progressing over weeks to months. In assessing a child, however, it is important that all other causes of neurological damage, such as infection, be considered and excluded (Dilley & Boccellari, 1989).

The treatment of youth with cognitive and/or motor impairment also differs from that of adults because many young people still need to attend school. Young people may require special classes if impairment becomes too great. Levenson and Mellins (1992) maintained that HIV-positive children who participate in special education may benefit from smaller classes with fewer distractions and more direct instruction and remediation. We may need to act as parent advocates when the special educational needs of a child are not being met.

The needs of cognitively impaired HIV-positive youth may give rise to a modification in our approaches to counseling young people. Levenson and Mellins (1992) noted that cognitive disabilities and receptive and expressive language deficits may preclude the use of traditional verbal and play psychotherapies. Spiegel and Mayers (1991) suggested behavior therapy as an alternative.

Conclusion

Dementia is one of the most difficult HIV-related complications that clients and their caregivers face. Current reconceptualizations of the progression of neurological impairment in people living with HIV disease suggest that a wide range of impairment occurs and that milder forms do not always progress to full-blown dementia. Knowledge about the progression of dementia and the interventions that can be used may help clients and their loved ones cope with anxiety and with other hardships associated with neurologic impairment.

When we work with clients living with HIV-associated minor cognitive/motor disorder or HIV-associated dementia complex, we often shift from a nondirective therapeutic stance to a more directive one. Although the exploration, validation, and affirmation of clients' feelings still remain important, behavioral interventions become predominant. The interventions described in this chapter can help clients and their partners, families, and friends adjust to clients' diminishing abilities. In addition, they help keep clients safe. When clients experience psychoneurological impairment, their safety must be the primary concern.

Often clients do not function in counseling sessions they way they did prior to impairment. Providing an uncluttered, structured, supportive therapeutic environment becomes extremely important. Many of the suggestions made for clients' day-to-day caregivers also apply to us. This includes the recommendation for outside support. The heartache and difficulty of ministering to clients with severe cognitive impairment is yet another compelling reason for us to obtain supervision or consultation with colleagues sensitive to HIV-related issues.

Above all, it is important for everyone associated with clients to remember that although clients may become severely demented and unable to communicate, they still retain awareness of people and activities around them. Clients with dementia benefit greatly from signs of affection and comfort. Partners, families, and friends must bear in mind that touching, holding hands, hugging, or simply sitting together convey love and support to impaired people in a way that they remain capable of comprehending. To the extent that we feel comfortable, we too can engage in many of these activities. Even when we are left with no alternative but simply to sit quietly with them, severely impaired clients often experience our caring presence as deeply meaningful.

CHAPTER 18

Depending on Others for Care

As independent-living skills fade,
dependency issues intensify.

As clients progress along the path of HIV disease, they ultimately reach the point where they can no longer care for themselves. Fatigue, the demands of intensive medical treatments or neuropathy erode independent-living skills and drive clients to become dependent upon others for their daily care. Although briefly addressed in previous chapters, becoming unable to live independently carries such an enormous emotional charge that it merits further examination.

When clients lack the ability to care for themselves, issues arise not only for them but also for those people expected to assume the caregiver role. Clients face dependency issues—both existential (in the here and now) issues and historical (unresolved developmental) issues. Husbands, wives, partners, families, and friends face myriad emotional and practical issues associated with being depended upon to provide care. One such practical issue, legal affairs, frequently becomes increasingly important and demanding as clients become less autonomous.

Receiving Care

Three kinds of issues arise as clients become less able to care for themselves. They may contend with existential or present-day issues of being dependent upon a caregiver. They may also come to terms with childhood dependency issues that remain unresolved. Finally, they may grapple with feeling infantilized, an issue that bridges both the past and the present.

Existential Dependency Issues

Clients often have strong reactions to very real and present aspects of the current situation of being cared for. In the late stages of HIV disease, care is often gained at the expense of clients' independence. Clients' emotional reactions to receiving care are often complex. They may experience intense gratitude for the care; simultaneously, they may deeply resent caregivers for having so much authority.

Although clients may accurately perceive the contradictory nature of their feelings (both angry at and dependent upon their caregivers), they may feel capable of expressing only their appreciation for the care. When this occurs, their resentment and other negative emotional reactions to being dependent become internalized, expressed only in outbursts of anger, if at all. These internalized feelings often become transformed into depression or apathy, and create an endless loop. As clients become increasingly more depressed or apathetic, they need increasingly more help. The more help they receive from their caregivers, the more resentful they feel. Many times clients are unaware of this loop; drawing attention to the pattern and validating associated feelings often help to break the cycle. We can also help clients move away from dichotomous thinking—either they are resentful or they are appreciative—and move toward more holistic, inclusive thinking where they can be both angry and grateful.

Historical Dependency Issues

Early childhood issues that relate to being nurtured and cared for often become reactivated when clients are placed in a dependent position. Adult clients who in infancy or early childhood survived the loss or lack of a primary caregiver often feel that nobody could possibly take care of them. These clients may feel abandoned when their current caregiver seeks respite. They may fear that if they express what they are needing, their caregiver will regard them as excessively demanding and leave. Thus they may give their caregivers little indication of the type of care they truly desire.

Clients whose early infancy or childhood care served to fill a narcissistic need for their primary caregiver often experience their current care as wrong. These clients feel that they are not being cared for in the right way. They may feel that caregivers are more concerned with their role as caregiver than about actually tending to their needs.

Clients often experience these re-injuries on a deep and unconscious level. They may be unaware of why they react so irrationally to being cared for. It is often rewarding for these clients to explore their present feelings in light of their early childhood experiences. By placing feelings in a historical context, clients may become better equipped to respond directly to the current situation, and to do so with less emotional reactivity. They may feel more entitled to ask for the care they need, and to incorporate the care they are offered.

Infantalization

When caregivers overcompensate for clients' deficiencies, clients are being infantalized. It is important that clients hold onto as much control and involvement in their life as possible for as long as possible. To avoid infantalization, clients often need to express assertively their desire to remain involved in decisions about their treatment and their care. Sometimes clients must convince their caregivers that they can still make decisions. If clients have not asserted themselves in the past, avoiding infantalization may be even more difficult. We should look for ways to help clients express how bad it feels to be infantalized. During conjoint, family, or group counseling sessions we can also encourage caregivers to allow clients to participate actively in treatment and management decisions to the extent clients are able.

Providing Care

Caregivers face their own set of issues resulting from the experience of being depended upon. Providing constant and exacting care—cooking meals, giving baths, pushing wheelchairs, administering medications—concretizes the recognition of their loved one's declining health. This recognition is often heartbreaking. Caregivers may also struggle with pain that arises from doubts about their own capacity to continue to provide care.

Caregivers have a specific role to play, a role which in most cases they have narrowly defined as precluding signs of weakness. Caregivers often see themselves as the strong one. To allow themselves to be vulnerable and to express their emotions may be very threatening and extremely difficult. Thus we must give caregivers permission to express themselves in ways that cannot be construed as exhibiting weakness. It is often helpful to describe common reactions of others placed in the position of caregiving. We should assure caregivers that we understand their need to stay strong and that everything they feel is appropriate and valid.

We should be aware that beneath the facade of strength, caregivers often suffer with feelings of loss. At the same time they are working hard to attend to the physical and emotional needs of their loved one, partners, family members, and friends are also trying to adjust to the realization that their loved one can no longer be there for them as in the past. Acknowledging a loved one's unavailability can be a particularly traumatic recognition for caregivers who may be used to thinking of their relationships as equal partnerships.

Caregivers often also struggle with doubts regarding their ability to be a good caregiver. The responsibility of providing care to a person with HIV disease may quickly become overwhelming. Todd Husted, who is HIV-negative, described a portion of what providing care for his partner, Craig, entailed:

> And the medication. There were times when Craig was taking as many as 20 different pills a day. We had to write down each individual pill and when they were taken just to keep track of them all. It became a full-time job monitoring the callous, lackadaisical doctors and getting the insurance company to fulfill its contractual obligations, a never-ending nightmare-blizzard of paperwork. (Hitchens, 1992, p. 40)

Caregivers may also worry that if their loved one's condition should worsen, the amount of care needed will prove to be too demanding. Caregivers often need help in bringing their focus back to the present. Although their fears for the future are valid, caregivers are often calmer when they focus on getting through their responsibilities a day at a time.

Sometimes caregivers feel resentful that they have been pulled into the role of caregiver. Feelings of frustration and resentment naturally occur. We may need to explain to caregivers how expressing these feelings in a support group or during their own counseling session reduces the likelihood of these feelings being expressed or acted out in unconscious or insensitive ways.

Because many caregivers remain so invested in maintaining a strong front, they may be unaware of symptoms of burnout. We should monitor caregivers for warning signs of burnout, which include increased isolation, increased irritability, sleep disturbance, reliance on tranquilizers and alcohol, and devotion to the care of the loved one to the exclusion of all other activities (Dilley & Boccellari, 1989). Burnout may severely compromise a caregiver's ability to provide care; we should do everything we can to ensure that caregivers find the means to obtain time away from their caregiving role.

Many caregivers display vehement resistance when the suggestion of respite is made. These caregivers may use the experience of providing care to contain their own painful feelings. Being in control of their loved one's care may result in a sense, albeit false, that caregivers can control their loved one's destiny. Caregivers may also use the experience of providing care as a way to feel special and important. Caregivers may feel that they are the only ones capable of providing care. Caregivers may also have to deal with their own guilt and abandonment issues before they can find a way to share the caregiving responsibilities with others. Caregivers need support and encouragement to come to terms with their own limitations and their own need for care. Caregivers must hear the message that they are also entitled to help and support, and that they need not be alone (Dilley & Boccellari, 1989).

Legal Issues

Counseling can often help caregivers sort through the complex feelings that arise in the process of putting a loved one's affairs in order. Particularly during the end stages of HIV disease, emotional support may be invaluable because the number of decisions caregivers need to make can feel overwhelming; power of attorney, custody decisions, wishes regarding life support, and funeral arrangements must all be discussed and documented legally (Macks, 1989).

Tragically, many times family disagreements about sexual orientation, drug use, or life-style result in a contesting of legal decisions. Legal challenges are often unpredictable and unexpected. Ida Hoffman, a 45-year-old HIV-positive woman recalled her experience with Arthur:

> We lived together for 15 years. We weren't married, but we were living in common law. We got married just before Arthur's death. The hospital didn't feel that he was competent to make up his mind about the marriage, and I had to go through a legal battle with the hospital and his family. They finally determined that he *was* competent. And he wanted to come home. So he came home and we got married. He died on November 1, 1989. (Hitchens, 1992, p. 108)

As experts in human behavior, we may be asked to support our clients' positions if legal action is brought to discredit the validity of their decisions. We may be called to testify before a judge to our clients' competence to execute legal decisions (Wood et al., 1992a). If we do get called as a witness in court proceedings, we should avail ourselves of the legal counsel provided by various professional organizations like the American Counseling Association, the American Psychological Association, the National Association of Social Workers, or the American Association of Marriage and Family Therapists. We should also refer to publications from the AIDS Health Project of the University of California San Francisco such as *AIDS Law for Mental Health Professionals: A Handbook for Judicious Practice* (Wood et al., 1992a) and the newsletter that updates the handbook, *Judicious Practice: An Update to AIDS Law for Mental Health Professionals* (with Wood, Marks, & Dilley as editors).

Women's Issues

Women are often socialized to view themselves as nurturers, as providers of care. Benson and Maier (1990) reported that for HIV-positive women, the basic needs of their family often take priority over their own treatment. Some women may continue to struggle to care for those dependent upon them well beyond the point where it is healthy for the women to do so.

Changes in status associated with the decline in their ability to care for themselves may have an huge emotional impact on women. Women who, when healthier, maintained a career and were self-sufficient, may experience painful emotional reactions to becoming economically and physically dependent upon their families or social service and public health care systems (Benson & Maier, 1990). Women who primarily identified with the traditional caregiver role may struggle with intense anguish as they move into the role of being cared for. Changing roles from caretaker to being cared for may imply a loss of respect and self-respect for many women (Benson & Maier, 1990).

It is vitally important that HIV-positive women be in contact with other HIV-positive women. Support groups, where available, are often beneficial. Although clients' declining health may make leaving their home more difficult, it should not be allowed to prohibit less intricate forms of connection (e.g., phone calls). Many women need to hear from other women that they are not alone in their struggles with the physical and emotional effects of HIV disease. This is particularly true when these effects are gender influenced.

Parenting Challenges

When they become too impaired to care for themselves, HIV-positive parents must also make alternative arrangements for the care of their children. Even if a partner or other family member cares for the children, parents must still face the loss of their role as maternal or paternal caregiver. We must help these clients reinvent their role; we must help them acknowledge that they will always be their children's parent. Because the identity of mother or father is powerful motivation to stay strong and hopeful, we must also work to find ways for parents to continue to see themselves as mothers and fathers even when they cannot care for their children as in the past.

When no friends or family can be called upon to take custody of the children, the children typically become wards of the state. Rarely is a parent psychologically prepared for this to happen. When it occurs, we must help parents deal with the heartrending loss they experience. This may be a difficult role for us to fill because there is little we can do to rectify the situation or reduce our clients' grief. Still, we must address parents' pain, validate their feelings, and support them in any way possible. For many parents, feeling understood proves invaluable.

Cultural Considerations

For some clients there exists a cultural overlay that shapes their reactions to becoming increasingly dependent upon others. In some cultures children are raised to take care of their elders, and to provide for their parents until their parents' death. If, in the course of their illness, adult clients become dependent upon their parents for care, they may be thrown into a cultural crisis. For other clients, culturally related elements in emotional and family reactions to dependency may be subtle and difficult to identify. This is especially the case when clients or their families are not strongly identified with their culture of origin. Thus we should be careful not to embrace as solely unresolved issues of individuation and dependency what are actually deeper culturally influenced issues. Likewise, we should not discount the consideration of those dependency issues that cross cultural boundaries. At all times, we should try to maximize our sensitivity to the issues of clients from cultures other than our own. When appropriate, we should help clients find access to support groups or networks within their culture that potentially can help them come to terms with issues of receiving or providing care.

Conclusion

When clients are living with advanced HIV disease that impairs cognitive or motor skills, dependency upon others is almost certain. Current feelings about being cared for may mix with past feelings of dependency and may create an unwavering emotional reaction. We can work to ease the situation by helping clients explore both past and current feelings about receiving care.

When our clients can no longer take care of themselves, we must also attend to the emotional and physical needs of their caregivers. Individual sessions with caregivers may become necessary in order to provide a place where they can vent their feelings. Referral to a support group may also be beneficial. We should encourage the expression of all feelings attached to caregiving, even those caregivers deem unbecoming or bad. Often caregivers do not acknowledge the warning signs of burnout, thinking that they must continue to provide care alone. We should stay alert to symptoms of burnout and work with caregivers to find ways to attain respite.

Gender and cultural influences may affect some clients' ability to receive care and not provide care. Women, who are firmly entrenched in a social system that conditions them to be caregivers, may sacrifice their own health to continue to uphold their role as nurturer. Similarly, clients who identify with cultural norms that place great importance on an adult's responsibility to care for aging parents may find it difficult to accept care. In counseling clients with these issues, we should explore their feelings through the lenses of gender and culture.

At the most primitive level, feelings of dependency are often linked to a fear of abandonment. When clients become increasingly dependent upon others, they may fear that the other will leave them. This dynamic occurs in the counseling relationship as well. As clients become increasingly unable to care for themselves, more demands are often placed upon us (e.g., for changes in appointment times, home visits, or hospital sessions). Clients may fear that we will stop seeing them. Therefore, we need to address the issues discussed in this chapter not only in terms of how our clients' inability to care for themselves affects their relationships with others, but also in terms of how it affects their relationship with us.

CHAPTER 19

Rational Suicide

The question is not whether clients should or should not kill themselves; the question is to what extent counselors should assist.

I n her article on compassion in dying, Susan Dunshee (1994) observed that people with late stages of HIV disease come to one of three decisions. Some people, the fighters, try everything they can to beat the illness. Others, the limit setters, fight up to a certain point after which they feel it is better to let the disease take its natural course. A third group of people, focused on the quality of their lives, actively choose to end their lives before wasting away from HIV-related infections. This chapter focuses on the issues raised by this third group of clients who contemplate or carry out rational suicide.

Like many of the topics in this book, rational suicide may raise as many issues for us as for our clients. When clients consider rational suicide, we are forced to balance their right to competent professional mental health care, which traditionally has included preventing clients from harming themselves, against their right to die with dignity (Goldblum & Moulton, 1989). Obviously, in order to work well with clients considering rational suicide, we must become clear about our personal feelings regarding suicide as well as prevailing legal and professional guidelines.

AIDS has seriously challenged the way we view suicide. Although many adhere to the position that suicide can never be rational (see Winiarski, 1991, p. 78), others, including members of the National Association of Social Workers (NASW), are willing to consider the question of an appropriate level of involvement in suicide for counselors whose clients have life-threatening illnesses. Rather than focusing on the philosophical question of whether rational suicide is right or wrong, this chapter focuses on the practical questions we encounter when clients raise this possibility. In working with clients contemplating rational suicide, three major counseling issues arise: determining whether the anticipated suicide is rational; working with a client's ambivalence toward dying; and helping partners, families, and friends. After examining these issues, this chapter considers legal and ethical dimensions of our potential involvement in assisted suicide.

Assessing Whether Suicide Is Rational

Clients with HIV disease have many reasons for considering suicide. The decision to stop living may reflect clients' profound experience that the quality of their life has declined to an intolerable level (Jones & Dilley, 1993) or may be a rash response to their experience of feeling socially isolated (Motto, 1994). Therefore, a major charge of HIV affirmative counseling is examining clients' rationales for wanting to end their life and assessing whether or not the impulses are rational.

Although some people maintain that suicide is never rational, over the last few years, with the rising membership of the Hemlock Society and the amazing success of the suicide how-to book *Final Exit* (Humphry, 1991), definitions of rational suicide have begun to take shape. Motto (1994) in his article on rational suicide defined it as a decision based "on a thorough and realistic assessment of all the available and pertinent facts" (p. 2). He maintained that we, as well as our clients, must carry out such an assessment.

To assess a client's suicidal intention for rationality, Motto (1994) suggested that we first review with the client all aspects of his or her life in order to establish "both a clear perception and a realistic interpretation of the facts" (pp. 2–3). The inquiry should include whether suicide is compatible with the client's personal and spiritual philosophy. It should examine what approaches the client has used in the past to problems that seemed insoluble. We should also explore the possible effects of the suicide on others in the client's life, especially if children are involved. In addition, we should inquire into any unfinished projects or goals or any unfulfilled obligations.

In order to screen out any irrational reasons leading HIV-positive clients toward suicide, we must consider possible psychological origins for the suicidal impulse. Compassion in Dying, a Seattle, Washington, group at the forefront of the movement to validate the concept of rational suicide for the terminally ill, has suggested paying close attention to "red flags" that may indicate irrational motivation (Dunshee, 1994). An obsessive focus on suicide with no willingness to discuss other options, a history of nonmedically related suicide attempts, and a history of clinical depression all suggest that the suicidal ideation may not be rational (Dunshee, 1994).

In his article, "Rational Suicide and AIDS: Considerations for the Psychotherapist," Werth (1992) proposed two defining characteristics for rational suicide. First, clients must possess a realistic appraisal of their situation. To assess this, Werth suggested we determine whether clients understand their prognosis and are aware of potential resources and alternatives (e.g., better pain management, hospice services). Werth maintained that our assessment also requires the passage of a period of time during which clients consider and reconsider suicide. This suggestion is echoed in the protocol used by the group Compassion in Dying, which requires that people considering suicide make requests to Compassion in Dying, in writing or on videotape, on three separate occasions with an interval of at least 48 hours between the second and third request (Dunshee, 1994).

According to Werth (1992), the second defining characteristic for rational suicide is that "mental processes leading to a decision to commit suicide must be unimpaired by psychological illness or severe emotional distress" (p. 7). In light of research findings that suggest some degree of clinically evident cognitive impairment in many people with AIDS, we must take efforts to screen for psychological illness seriously. In their article "AIDS and Rational Suicide: A Counseling Psychology Perspective or a Slide on the Slippery Slope," Rogers and Britton (1994) reported that it is often difficult to identify accurately psychological, emotional, or cognitive impairment in order to rule out irrational motives for suicide. Some mental status examinations may lack the sensitivity to detect early, mild neurocognitive impairment (Rogers & Britton, 1994).

In contrast to Rogers and Britton (1994), Motto (1994) believed that with regards to rational suicide, "a clear state of mind in and of itself is not sufficient, and the presence of a cognitive deficit does not necessarily preclude it" (p. 2). He maintained that after having examined all the facts, our criterion for determining rationality is ultimately our "intuitive judgment, faulty as it may be, as to whether the patient's awareness and interpretation of those facts is realistic" (p. 3). We may not agree with a client's decision to kill him- or herself, but it deserves our respect if it is "the best the patient can make while in control of his or her ability to reason" (Motto, 1994, p. 3).

Working With Clients' Ambivalence About Dying

When clients engage in the process of considering rational suicide, ambivalent feelings often arise. This particularly holds true for clients who do not currently experience acute suffering. Often we can make great use of this ambivalence to ensure that alternatives to suicide get explored; one useful strategy is to advocate temporizing (Motto, 1994, p. 3). While setting a tone of profound respect for the finality of the suicidal act, we can help clients find other alternatives temporarily bearable and consider them first. Temporizing is often most effective when we remind clients that delaying the act of suicide does not require relinquishing it as an option.

It is important to remember that last-minute reversals of suicidal intent often occur. What may be most important to clients is knowing that they could end their life if they so choose. As an HIV-positive man stated,

> One of the only things people with AIDS never lose control of is the choice of how you want to live or die with this disease. It is a very personal choice, but it is your choice, and nobody has the right to take that away from you. (Hitchens, 1992, p. 114)

Motto (1994) maintained that it is often not until the last second that the full implications of the contemplated suicidal act become clear; thus one client stated, "The great thing was, once I knew I could do it, life became valuable again. I was back in charge" (Motto, 1994, p. 4). Although we should always talk about suicide seriously, we can also remember that there is a difference between contemplation and action; encouraging clients to talk through their thoughts and feelings about suicide often deters them from acting. Thus we should take care so as not to discourage clients from discussing suicide in sessions.

Partners, Families, and Friends

Clients need to recognize that the decision to commit rational suicide has a wide-ranging effect on those close to them. Motto (1994) recommended that, with the clients' consent, we should work with their partners, appropriate family members, and close friends. Including others in counseling sessions creates an opportunity for the client to discuss alternatives to suicide. If the decision for rational suicide is firm, it allows all those who are likely to be impacted to discuss the psychological preparation needed, and to create a mutual support system that will be helpful in avoiding feelings of guilt and isolation.

People close to a client may need support in coming to terms with the client's decision to commit suicide. Loved ones may experience ambivalent feelings about the decision: given the client's health and future prognosis, they may understand the rationale for not wanting to live and publicly support the suicide; yet they may have personal reasons for not wanting the client to die and may privately wish the client would continue to fight his or her illness. Alternatively, a client's loved ones may feel bad for wanting the client to die and may wonder if it is unnatural or abnormal not to demand that the client continue living. Counseling may help loved ones reconcile these competing feelings and desires. Loved ones often need to know that the wide range of feelings a client's contemplated suicide engenders is natural. They can be encouraged to explore all of their feelings, not just those they feel may be socially acceptable. When appropriate, they may find it helpful to share their ambivalence with the client.

If clients do take their lives, those who survive them may question to what degree they are responsible for the suicide. Especially when their ambivalent feelings were not addressed, they may feel that they could have done more to convince clients to live. When partners, family members, or friends were adamantly against the suicide, they may feel regret and guilt for having not been more forceful in expressing their views or in taking more direct action. Often this guilt may interfere with survivors' ability to go through the bereavement process. Sometimes focus can be shifted away from the guilt; survivors may come to acknowledge that although they feel conflicted over the means by which it was accomplished, they find comfort in knowing that their loved one's intense suffering has ended.

Counselors' Involvement in Rational Suicide

Openness is the cornerstone of the counseling relationship. What then do we do when clients ask us for information about how to end their life? Unfortunately, there is no standard practice prescribed for such a situation (Motto, 1994). At the core, however, is the understanding that being open with our clients ensures that they will be open with us (Motto, 1994).

Although the legal limits of the counselor's role in rational suicide will eventually be determined in the courts, we can, in the meantime, turn to two contemporary developments for assistance in the decision-

making process. The first development is the pioneering work of Compassion in Dying, the Seattle organization that is, in many respects,
paving the way for the creation of national guidelines for the appropriate behavior of people assisting terminally ill clients who wish to
end their life. The organization has carefully created an approach that
navigates the territory between lawful and unlawful behavior:

> What Compassion members will do is almost limitless: offer
> advice on lethal doses, counsel bereaved family members, con
> vince wary doctors, literally hold a patient's hand at the moment
> of death. What they will not do is simple: they will not provide
> or administer drugs. (Belkin, 1993)

According to the 1993 *Judicious Practice: An Update to AIDS Law
for Mental Health Professionals* (Wood, Marks, & Dilley, 1993), Compassion in Dying basically provides practical, psychological, and spiritual support for clients who are clear in their intentions to commit
suicide. What is revolutionary about Compassion is that in the past,
suicide, even assisted suicide, has usually been a solitary act. Any
involvement in this act has been perceived as morally questionable.
Compassion in Dying has transformed old interpretations of the act
of assisting suicide, releasing participants from the condemnation that,
in the past, generally resulted from involvement.

A second development from which we may also draw guidance is
the action of the National Association of Social Workers. In 1994, the
NASW adopted new guidelines that state a position similar to that of
Compassion in Dying and affirm "the right of the individual to determine the level of his or her care" (NASW, 1994). The guidelines
delineate appropriate ways of being involved with clients who are
contemplating suicide:

> The appropriate role for social workers is to help patients express
> their thoughts and feelings, to facilitate exploration of alterna
> tives, to provide information to make an informed choice, and
> to deal with grief and loss issues. . . . [They] would thoroughly
> review all available options. . . . Social workers should act as
> liaisons with other health care professionals and help the patient
> and family communicate concerns and attitudes to the health care
> team to bring about the most responsible assistance possible.
>
> It is inappropriate for social workers to deliver, supply, or
> personally participate in the commission of an act of assisted
> suicide when acting in their professional role. If legally permis-

sible, it is not inappropriate for a social worker to be present
during an assisted suicide if the client requests the social worker's
presence. (NASW, 1994)

The NASW new guidelines make social work the first of the counseling professions to consider it ethical for practitioners to attend the
assisted suicide of a client (Marks, 1994b). This change may have
significant implications for counselors working with clients ravaged
by the physical complications of HIV disease. The new guidelines
recognize that we often develop long-term professional relationships
with clients and that our support may be particularly important in
easing the transition from life to death (Wood et al., 1993).

In spite of these developments, there have been past court decisions
from around the country that have promoted the position that mental
health professionals have a duty to prevent suicide (Wood et al.,
1992a). If a case were brought to court in which a mental health
professional had been charged with assisting suicide or criminal neg-
ligence, the prosecutor would need to prove "the practitioner's intent
to assist or act negligently; *and* causation—that but for the practitioner's actions, the suicide would not have occurred" (Wood et al., 1992a,
p. 71). Given the nature of suicidal ideation and the unpredictability
of suicidal behavior, it is difficult to prove that our inaction caused a
rational suicide. It is also worth noting that, as counselors, our inaction is judged against the standard of care common among the prudent
counselors in our community dealing with similar situations (Wood
et al., 1992a). Courts typically first consult professional codes of ethics
to determine the standard of care. Guidelines such as those of the
National Association of Social Workers are useful in creating a standard of care that restricts our personal participation in the commission
of an act of rational suicide but makes no requirements with regard
to the prevention of a rational suicide.

Although much has been written about the strong feelings that arise
for partners, family members, and friends when HIV-positive clients
contemplate suicide, little has been written about our reactions. Many
of us have intense emotional responses to clients' determination that
life has ceased to have value. These feelings may arise even when the
we understand and consciously agree with our clients' decision. We
may privately entertain psychological reasons and theoretical justifications for why clients should continue to live. For example,

> we interpret the wish to die as a weakness, a failing, a capitula-
> tion to the narcissistic injury. Even when there is no hope for

recuperation or for a reversal of illness, we search to find meaning in the life that is left to live, no matter how painful it may be. In the absence of any psychological reason for holding on to life at any cost, we look to spiritual reasons to justify the pain of continuing to live. We search aggressively for a way in which to understand that decision to die as an aberration, a momentary loss of reason. (Forstein, 1994b, p. 124)

Unless they are attended to, our feelings may prevent us from being fully engaged with our clients. Coming to terms with our own feelings about suicide is crucial. If it is our belief that, as a rule, suicide can never be rational, we may have an obligation to acknowledge our position to clients candidly; the most appropriate time to do this is early on in the counseling relationship when other legal and ethical topics (e.g., our duty to report child and elder abuse, or our duty to keep clients and others from harm) are discussed.

Because ethical and legal guidelines regarding suicide often fail to address specific HIV-related issues, we should seek the advice and guidance of colleagues and supervisors. Keeping accurate and complete case notes is also important. Finding a forum where we can explore our professional and personal concerns should be a priority. Attending a support group for counselors working with HIV-positive clients may prove helpful.

Conclusion

Rational suicide brings issues of life and death into vivid focus. Late in the stages of their illness, when the quality of their life is diminished to intolerable levels, clients may contemplate suicide. They may call upon us to help them sort out their feelings and their affairs, and to assist in the suicide process.

Legal, ethical, and professional guidelines regulating our involvement in rational suicide remain in flux. Recent developments suggest that we are within the realm of professional practice to explore openly with clients in a nonjudgmental manner their desire to kill themselves. These developments also suggest that failing to prevent clients in advanced stages of HIV disease from rational suicide may no longer be considered negligent action on our part. In fact, the time may quickly come when being present at the time of our clients' rational suicide is included as an accepted part of our professional responsibilities.

People unfamiliar with the issues surrounding rational suicide often worry that policies that allow us to assist clients considering suicide will make suicide too easy. They also worry that people might commit suicide due to manipulation by those who want to assist them. Although there is some reality base for this concern, it seems equally likely that clients may be harmed by our refusal to discuss suicide-related issues. As Robert Marks, editor of *Focus: A Guide to AIDS Research and Counseling*, wrote "In the end, bringing suicide out of the closet and into therapy, even up to the moment of death, enables mental health professionals to protect against poorly considered suicides or shadowy attempts to influence dying clients" (1994b, p. 2).

CHAPTER *20*

Hospice and Home Care

For some clients there is no place like home.
Others may find a hospice setting more desirable.

I n general, most clients come to live out the final stage of their illness in one of six locations. Some clients, particularly those with extremely demanding AIDS-related complications, are confined to an immune suppression unit of a hospital. When no immune suppression unit exists, they may be placed in another ward of the hospital. Those who are financially indigent may land in a state or county hospital or out on the streets. Other clients may choose a residential hospice setting. Still other clients may prefer to die at home—this can be their own home, their family's home, or even a friend's home. The decision of where to die is comprised of many practical, emotional, and sometimes financial factors.

For many reasons, residential hospice and home health care have become widely accepted and often preferred by HIV-positive people and their loved ones. Advances in health care have insured that most, if not all, of the medical needs of clients in the final stage of HIV disease can be treated at home or in a residential hospice. Although hospitalization may mean sparing a client's family from dealing with the unhygienic aspects of death, it may result in increased isolation for the client and a loss of control for both the client and the family of medical decisions and of access to each other. However, although dying in a hospice or at home provides clients and people close to them with substantial emotional and practical benefits, these settings are not without their costs.

Residential Hospice Care

Clients in the end stages of HIV disease are typically eligible for hospice care when their life expectancy is 6 months or less. Ideally, residential hospices offer carefully designed programs of care that recognize and respond to the needs and rights of the terminally ill. Several tenets are followed (Murphy & Donovan, 1989). The patient and family compose the unit of care. An interdisciplinary team of doctors, nurses, social workers, pastoral caregivers, and counselors manage the care. Trained volunteers often supply supplementary support. After the client's death, hospices often make bereavement care available to loved ones.

In many parts of the country, residential hospice facilities exist specifically for people in the final stage of HIV disease. These facilities are responsive to the unique issues produced by HIV disease. Hospices in areas that have not been as greatly affected by HIV disease may accept clients with HIV disease but may not be as sensitive to a client's special situation and needs. In addition, in these facilities hospice staff may not have had the opportunity to become well informed about HIV disease and may still harbor misconceptions. Actions that stem from unaddressed fear and ignorance may adversely affect clients.

Often one of the most painful issues for clients entering a hospice is the unavoidable acknowledgment of their approaching death. At the point they enter a hospice, clients may have yet to fully accept the terminal nature of their condition; knowing that hospice facilities take only clients in the end stages of their illness makes denial almost impossible. In being confronted by their death, clients may experience a great deal of previously unexpressed anger and sadness. Many questions may arise for clients regarding the dying process, especially questions clients were unprepared or embarrassed to ask prior to making the decision to enter the hospice. Questions should be encouraged, and attempts should be made to provide satisfying answers.

Although residential hospices may offer clients many comforts in their last months, weeks, and days, hospices also have drawbacks. To varying degrees, hospices divorce clients from the things with which they may have come to feel most identified and familiar. When placed in a residential hospice, clients no longer have the sense of security afforded by their home, their room, their bed, and their belongings. Receiving visitors may feel strained and awkward; although visitors may be welcome at the hospice, it may be difficult to ensure that visits are private.

Visitation takes on intense implications when the clients have a spouse or partner. The psychological well-being of clients is often affected by whether the hospice facility allows their spouse or partner to stay overnight, to be involved with their care, and, particularly in the case of gay or lesbian clients, to display affection openly. Clients in residential hospices may be unprepared for the strain that is placed on their personal relationships. They may have never anticipated how lost they may feel without the constant presence of their partner, families, or friends.

Some residential hospices may be highly sensitive and responsive to the needs of people in the final stage of HIV disease. Facilities based on a "wellness community" model may offer residents a place to celebrate their last days. In addition to residents' medical needs, these facilities may be may particularly attentive to residents' psychological, emotional, and spiritual needs. Hospice staff and volunteers may take great pride in helping residents make the transition from life to death.

Of course, the level of care and treatment received by residents varies from hospice to hospice. Tragically, in some hospices residents spend more time in front of the television than anywhere else. When residents spend all day watching television or engaged in some vaporous activity, their souls may starve. Residents may encounter psychological, emotional, and spiritual death long before physical death arrives. Although it is true that residents' bodies may be declining rapidly, their minds and emotions may be highly functioning. Even residents with symptoms of HIV-associated dementia complex may retain some level of cognitive functioning that should be respected. Whenever possible, we should be certain a residential hospice is capable of meeting the psychological, emotional, and spiritual needs of residents before recommending the hospice to clients and their families and friends. If hospice choices are limited, we may need to suggest to family and friends ways in which they can enhance the quality of their loved one's care.

One of the purposes of hospice care is to help the terminally ill come to terms with death. Residential hospices have come to adopt a wide range of approaches to this task. Some residential hospices honor death. These facilities take time to prepare residents for both their own death and that of their fellow residents. They may have even created traditional rituals for saying goodbye. However, other facilities play down death, almost to the point of ignoring its existence. When a resident dies, the other residents may not even be told; they may wake up to find the resident missing with no words of explanation or con-

dolence given. Little may be said to console the dead resident's roommate. Instead, a new roommate may be quickly put in place. If hospice
staff are overworked or suffering from burnout or multiple-loss syndrome, they may be too depleted themselves to facilitate residents'
acceptance of death. When death is avoided or ignored, there is a
strong possibility that residents will become inhibited in expressing concerns about their own death. In our work with these clients, we may
need to give even greater attention to death and dying issues, particularly
in relation to any feelings aroused by the hospice experience.

Residents are not the only ones who benefit from quality hospice
care. Residential hospices assume the huge physical burden of caring
for someone with a debilitating illness that often exhausts residents'
families and friends. Some family and friends may find solace in the
knowledge that their loved one receives constant professional medical
care. Not having to attend personally to their loved ones' physical
needs may even allow these caregivers to become more emotionally
available and supportive.

Other family and friends may initially consider placing a loved one
in a residential hospice a failing. They may feel that they should take
care of the client at home by themselves, even when they may be unable
to do so. Often family and friends' guilt feelings obscure core feelings
of helplessness and loss. Counseling may be helpful in addressing these
underlying issues. In addition, counseling may often assist family and
friends in redefining their role as primary caregiver, and in coming to
find new ways to continue to provide care to their loved one.

Home Care

Advances in medical care have made caring for people with late stages
of HIV disease at home a reality. Home infusion has become a regular
procedure in many parts of the country and costs substantially less
than when the treatment is administered in a hospital; thus clients can
receive intravenously everything from total parenteral nutrition (TPN)
to a morphine drip without leaving their bedroom. For clients who
decide to refuse life-sustaining measures, these advances may allow
them to live at home while their illness runs its course. The biggest
advantage of home care is that it allows clients to die in the presence
of the physical embodiment of the life they created. Clients are not
forced to look up from a hospital bed at a sterile environment artifi-
cially brightened by flower arrangements. Clients are not forced in the
last months, weeks, or days of their life to adjust to the new surround-

ings of a residential hospice. Instead they can remain in a comfortable and familiar place. This may be particularly helpful for clients who suffer from HIV-associated dementia complex.

Dying at home often eliminates many of the restrictive policies of some hospitals and residential hospices. Spouses or partners may talk to their loved ones at any time, stay with them for as long as they like, and, when treatment allows, even sleep with them in the same bed. Unlike the semiprivate rooms of hospitals or community rooms of residential hospices, in their own homes clients retain privacy.

Keeping clients at home also allows spouses, partners, families, and friends to retain a significant degree of control over the clients' care. In many cases, loved ones can remain an integral part of a client's health care, administering injections, changing bed sheets, and cooking meals. Because people they know and trust play an extremely intimate role in providing health care, some clients may feel less apprehensive about their imminent death.

Home health care also has its disadvantages. Keeping someone in the end stages of HIV disease at home, away from the hospital, in some ways simply brings the hospital home. Special equipment may clutter living room and bedroom areas. Intravenous lines and racks may be constant intrusions. Special beds may need to be rented. A nurse or attendant is often present around the clock. Although it is still home, paradoxically it is not.

Bringing the trappings of a hospital to the home seriously impinges upon the others who share the home environment. When home is the primary location for clients' care, there is no familiar place for spouses, partners, and often family members to go for respite. In addition, most spouses, partners, and family members are unprepared and often uncomfortable with some tasks of giving care to a homebound person with AIDS, such as administering shots or changing adult diapers. Hiring an attendant, when financially feasible, is often a welcome reprieve from these tasks. Whenever possible, we should inquire into the psychological and emotional state of our clients' spouses, partners, and families. When appropriate, we should remind them of significant other and family support groups.

Caring for someone in the end stages of HIV disease is not merely emotionally exhausting. An enormous amount of physical energy must be expended attending to a homebound loved one. Sometimes spouses, partners, and family members are extremely reluctant to allow others into the home to assist, even when to do so provides them with needed rest. They may feel guilty or ashamed that they need outside help.

They may feel some level of pride and accomplishment in being able to care for their loved one without assistance; this feeling of accomplishment may compensate for feelings of helplessness and powerlessness. When appropriate, we should remind these spouses, partners, and family members that it is natural to need rest from caregiving responsibilities. However, we must also acknowledge, particularly to ourselves, that not everyone is disposed to take a break even when it is sorely needed.

Considerations for Counselors

Once clients enter a residential hospice or are confined to their home, we often have to refine elements in our approach to counseling, particularly the way we handle boundary issues. We may need to consider how and when to visit clients. Will our meetings become more or less frequent? Will they last longer than our normal session? How will we fit into our office schedule seeing clients at a residential hospice or at their home? If necessary, how will changes to existing financial arrangements be made? It is best to gain clarity on these issues before we begin counseling clients living with HIV disease. Discussing these issues with colleagues who work with HIV positive clients may be helpful. Unfortunately, there are no easy solutions to these boundary dilemmas; each of us must, with due consideration given to our professional and ethical responsibilities, determine the answers for ourselves. We may find that our position is not rigid and that it becomes modified when warranted by our relationship with each specific client. Although therapeutic boundaries take on new dimensions when working with clients in a residential hospice or at their home, the more explicit we can be about our limits to ourselves and to our clients, the more prepared we may be for times when these limits are challenged by our clients' declining health.

Parenting Concerns

The presence of children in an HIV-positive client's life may make the decision of where to die more complicated. On one hand, dying at home provides parents with the opportunity for constant contact with their children. On the other hand, it may expose children to aspects of the parent's illness that parents prefer to keep hidden. Hospitalization or residential hospice care may prevent the children from being constantly affronted by some of the harsher elements of the end stage of HIV disease, but these may also separate them from their parent. Hospitalization or residential hospice care may make death something foreign, whereas dying at home may have a demystifying effect.

For parents in the end stages of HIV disease, any decision regarding where to die is likely to have emotional repercussions. We can often help parents engage in a careful consideration of the pros and cons of their options. Although some clients may never feel confident that they made the right choice, they may come to take comfort in knowing their decision was mindful. Clients should be helped to feel that any choice they make is valid; one choice does not necessarily make them better (or worse) parents than any other choice.

Cultural Issues

The importance of cultural traditions about death and dying come to the forefront as clients consider the decision to die at home, in a residential hospice, or in a hospital. How strongly clients identify with and adhere to cultural beliefs may influence their decisions. The culturally determined role family members play in helping a client to die peacefully is often also important.

For ethnically identified clients who choose hospice care, special issues may arise. Ethnically identified minority clients may find they are the only person from their ethnic group at a residential hospice; this may result in painful feelings of difference and isolation. If English is not a client's first language, difficulties in communicating may arise, especially when the effects of HIV disease further restrict language use. This may also be problematic if the client's loved ones have difficulties speaking or understanding English. In addition, clients closely identified with the foods and customs of their culture may find a culturally mainstream residential hospice uncomfortable and foreign.

When working in a residential hospice·setting (or hospital setting), we should remain vigilant to signs of culturally related discomfort clients or their loved ones may be experiencing. We need to remember that some clients may quickly become so immersed in the hospice milieu that they may not be able to process their discomfort as arising from cultural factors, although unconsciously they feel that something is wrong or that they do not belong. We also need to pay close attention to ways that being unaware of our own cultural assumptions may cause us difficulty in perceiving culture-related aspects of clients' hospice or home care decisions.

Youth Considerations

For young people, one of the most distressing aspects of the end stages of their illness is that of being developmentally unprepared for decisions related to their death. Still, it is important that young people with HIV disease be offered the respect that others at older ages receive in the same situation. For many young children, simply being away from home produces extreme anxiety, particularly if there have been painful hospital experiences earlier in the course of the disease. Thus any location that takes young children away from the comfort of their own room, toys, and family may be undesirable. However, because the medical conditions for youth may require specialized care, remaining at home may be prohibited. In this case, we must look for ways to help young people, and their parents, adjust to the hospital environment.

Conclusion

When clients are in the medical, financial, and psychological position of being able to decide where they want to spend their final days, many factors come under consideration. Each choice, whether it be hospitalization, residential hospice, or home care, has advantages and repercussions. Competing interests must be weighed: for example, residential hospice care may relieve spouses, partners, families, and friends of the physical demands of providing home care, but it may restrict their ability to interact naturally with clients; home care may provide a sense of familiarity and security, yet it may also turn the home into a virtual hospital. When clients move into the final stage of HIV disease, irrespective of the location they choose to live out the end of their life, our role is often that of watchdog—remaining attentive both for feelings of exhaustion and burnout on the part of caregivers, and feelings of neglect on the part of clients.

When clients are hospitalized, placed in residential hospice, or kept at home to die, counseling may take on increased meaning. Frequently, our work centers on nonverbal activities. Bleezarde (1995, personal communication) gave an example of her work with a 24-year-old hospice resident named Gerald:

> As the weakness and pain increased, and the loneliness from being set apart in a hospice enveloped Gerald, he looked so forward to my visits. Slowly, all his fears, disappointments, sad-

nesses, and anger came out. But I had to listen carefully, for not all of it was in words spoken—some was in the silences between the words. In Gerald's case, underlying all of his anger was a youthful resentment of his illness, which had found no means of expression prior to our work. Toward the end of our sessions together, we designed what Gerald wanted on his Names Quilt panel.

At this stage in our clients' illness, our presence at their side, our empathic understanding, and our heartfelt desire for their psychological and physical comfort may be a profoundly affirming experience for clients. This sort of affirmative stance may be very helpful in carrying clients through the final episode of their lives: letting go.

CHAPTER 21

Letting Go

Life is not over until it is over.

With time, clients' bodies reach a point when they can no longer sustain the ravages of HIV disease. Clients' desire to live is tempered by their bodies' need to rest. Clients living with HIV disease may anticipate death from the moment they test positive, but they must still face many tasks in their actual dying days and moments.

The concept of living with HIV is a crucial component of HIV affirmative counseling. For example, we often encourage clients to focus on quality of life issues or to make the time they have left meaningful. At the same time, we must take care so as not to address only superficially the important issue of encountering death. To do so would be unfortunate, in that death is a time when the counseling relationship can be most beneficial and most sacred. We have much to offer clients in their final days. At the same time, we can learn many things from our dying clients.

Clients often approach their death in the same manner they approached their lives. Some clients deny death up until their last moment. Other clients take active steps throughout their lives to prepare for death. We should take our cues from our clients and explore death at their pace. When clients seem afraid to address directly issues of dying, it may be helpful to extend to them an invitation: we can convey our willingness to talk about any fears or concerns they may have relative to dying. We should take great care to ensure that both our words and tone of voice convey an attitude of compassionate interest—without any element of demand to discuss issues about which clients may not be ready to talk.

Clients close to death face four challenges. First, clients must work to find self-acceptance (Walker, 1991). Second, clients must make clear their wishes for final medical treatment (McKusick, 1992; Walker, 1991). Third, clients must attempt to deal with and hopefully heal rifts with family and friends (Walker, 1991). Finally, clients must find a way to say goodbye and yield to death (McKusick, 1992; Walker, 1991). Counseling can be instrumental in helping clients with these challenges.

People close to the client also must prepare for the client's death. If spouses or partners, family members, and friends have not already done so, they need to work to accept who the client is as a person (Walker, 1991). Coming to accept the client's wishes for medical care, as well as any wishes related to activities after his or her death, are also important. Reviewing everyone's life together is also helpful in preparing for the loved one's death. Since significant others in the client's life may not possess the emotional or psychological abilities to make these preparations on their own, we may need to assist.

As our clients near death, we must also work through our own set of tasks. Four such counselor tasks can be identified (McKusick, 1992). First, we need to deal with the negative aspects of anticipatory grief—in the client, the client's immediate circle, and in ourselves. Second, we need to provide a safe space for clients to explore the implications of their death. Third, we need to provide clients who wish them with specific techniques to promote comfort and release at the moment of death. Finally, we need to say goodbye to our clients.

Client Challenges

For many clients, the battle to accept themselves as they truly are will be hard fought. Acceptance issues may resurface as death draws near. Clients may come to realize the many ways in which they have split off unacceptable parts of themselves and may try to reintegrate these parts.

A core aspect of self-acceptance is the recognition that failures as well as successes make up the drama of being human. We can help clients take elements of their lives they believe reflect personal failure and reframe them as no more than an expression of their humanness. This is particularly significant for clients who were injecting drug users or clients who still feel guilty for becoming HIV positive. We can encourage clients to reflect back on their life and review difficult lessons they may have learned. Often sharing these lessons of life with others—a spouse or partner, son or daughter, parent or sibling—may help clients reintegrate these experiences in a more positive light.

In their struggle for self-acceptance, some clients have to overcome the notion that death represents failure. This issue may be particularly difficult for clients identified with the Western cultural values of mastery, doing, and overcoming nature. The HIV-positive community often places much emphasis upon living, fighting, and surviving HIV disease. Although this approach may at first instill hope, it often backfires as clients come closer to death. Clients may feel that in dying they disappoint people around them. They may feel guilty for not living longer and may look for ways to blame themselves. This may be particularly true if they have subscribed to the New Age notion that they are responsible for their illness. Clients who skipped taking their medication may feel they are at fault. This may also hold true for clients who pursued traditional medicine as opposed to alternative medicine, or alternative medicine as opposed to traditional medicine. In working with these clients, one useful strategy is to help them find their personal answers to the question of what it means to be a success in life. We may also want to help these clients distinguish between physical well-being and emotional or spiritual well-being as death approaches.

For some clients, fully accepting their sexual and affectional orientation may still be an issue. This may be particularly true for clients who in the face of death rediscover their traditional childhood religious beliefs. Working toward clients' greater self-acceptance may include helping them find a way to affirm their sexual identity. To do this, we may need to enlist the help of sensitive and supportive clergy who are familiar and comfortable with sexual orientation issues as well as HIV-related issues.

Planning for Death

As the reality of death approaches, some clients want to create a plan for their death. Although this may seem morbid to some people, the process of planning their death may provide clients with a sense of participation—and hence life—right up to the end. The sense of participation is extremely significant because it provides clients with respect and dignity even as they die. Some decisions, like who will hold power of attorney, should already be arranged by this point; if not, clients should work out the details immediately. Other decisions only arise as clients near death.

One of the biggest decisions clients must consider is at what point to reject curative treatment and adopt palliative care (Martin, 1991). For many clients, it is important to have an ongoing choice to receive morphine, a drug widely administered to reduce discomfort. Some clients may reject the dulling effect of the drug on awareness. They may prefer to allow their body to give out while retaining consciousness for as long as possible. Others may see a morphine drip as a perfect way to accomplish letting go. We can help clients make choices that offer them the kind of comfort they most desire in their final hours. Often clients feel uncomfortable discussing these decisions with their loved ones. They may ask us to help them find a way to express their decision to their spouse or partner, family, and friends. They may also ask us to help their loved ones adjust to and support their decision.

Some clients want to plan their own funeral or memorial. Working with clients to plan their funeral or memorial may provide an opportunity for us to engage clients in a life-review process. Clients can think of how they want others to remember them. Clients can review what they feel they have been and have accomplished. They can reflect on the things in their life they deem important. Rather than influencing clients to cling to life, this process often facilitates the letting-go process by putting life in perspective. Clients also often find knowing they will be memorialized by others in the manner they have chosen comforting.

Healing Rifts With Significant Others

In their final days, some clients often feel an inner impetus to reconcile past hurts with family, friends, and significant others. Recognizing that little time remains to take care of unfinished business, many clients try to find ways to connect with those from whom they feel estranged. The significant others in the client's life may reciprocate if they too are seeking to reconnect and say goodbye.

Many times clients and significant others will not feel capable of settling past differences by themselves, due to the deep-seated nature of the rift. In this situation, we may be asked to facilitate a family session. Holding this type of session may be a great challenge for us especially when only a single meeting is planned. Walker (1991) maintained "when family members come to visit a dying child, these sessions are overdetermined, the pressure on both the therapist and the family intense" (p. 229).

Clients can easily get caught up in believing that this one-time encounter can or should be able to resolve the rift (Walker, 1991). This rarely occurs because past hurts often have complex beginnings and continued additions over time. This is especially the case when the family finds a client's sexual and affectional orientation or drug-using life-style unacceptable. When the client is gay, lesbian, bisexual, or a drug user, the parents and client may anticipate that the encounter will focus solely on sexual orientation or drug use. The anticipatory dynamic of the session is clear: "The adult child wants his [or her] parent's acceptance; the parent often feels guilt, failure, and distaste for his [or her] child's lifestyle. Both feel that sexual orientation or other behaviors have caused a rift for which they feel guilt" (Walker, 1991, p. 229). Often clients and their parents enter such a session defensively.

In these family sessions, we want to avoid focusing specifically on the issues of sexual orientation or drug use. To do so will draw attention to what White and Epston (1990) referred to as the "problem saturated narrative," which assumes that being gay or using drugs is the totality of the client's identity. Thus other aspects of the client are overshadowed. As an alternative approach we can try to facilitate building relationship bridges in less controversial areas of shared experience (Walker, 1991). This approach deemphasizes problem solving in favor of acknowledging whatever connections do exist. By shifting the focus to areas in which each party may, in some small way, feel connected to the other, a new and different type of exchange may arise.

Saying Goodbye

Some clients may begin the process of saying goodbye many months before they are actually on their death bed. Clients can be encouraged to find the ways they feel best address their need to say goodbye. Sometimes in the process of saying goodbye, clients find that a significant person is not, or cannot be, physically present. We can give clients permission to voice their goodbye anyway, aloud or perhaps in writing. Of course, other clients may have no desire to say goodbye.

For some clients the effects of morphine or the neurologic impairment of the end stages of HIV disease complicate their ability to say goodbye. Clients may be incoherent, unable at times to speak. Spouses or partners, family members, and friends may need to be reminded of the client's ability to understand and appreciate their presence. Clients often float in and out of consciousness. In their moments of lucidity, they may find the strength and words to say goodbye. In his article "On Being a Caregiver," Denny Paterno described how he and his lover Michael said goodbye:

> During his last 4 months, Michael was confined to the house. In addition to CMV, he was diagnosed with mycobacterium avium intracellulare (MAI). This caused intense pain, recurring bouts of spiked fevers, wasting syndrome, and extreme fatigue. . . . When Michael's pain became overwhelming, about 3 weeks before he died, the doctor prescribed liquid morphine. This caused a coma-like state. . . . It became clear that it was important to me to communicate to Michael how much he had given me. I also believed it was important to care for Michael's mind as well as for his body. From that point on, I spend the better part of each day holding his hand and recounting our history. . . . Even though he was not able to respond, I knew that he heard me. The day before he died, the infusion nurse stopped by to check his catheter. I was sitting on the bed, and Priscilla was just buttoning Michael's pajamas. He opened his eyes for a moment, looked at me, and said in a shaky voice, "Thank you for everything, Den, I love you." His final words told me I had done the right things. (1992, p. 6)

Letting Go

Permitting their loved one to let go intentionally is a final way spouses or partners, families, and friends can show their respect. It also provides clients with one last gesture of dignity. We may need to introduce clients and their families to the possibility of intentionally letting go. McKusick (1992) wrote that those who have learned to let go generally die more easily than those who continue to hold on tenaciously. Letting go can be facilitated by having clients select the people they want around them. Clients' favorite music may be playing or favorite flowers may be nearby. It also helps if those present give clients explicit permission to go in peace. Steven Paul described how he helped his lover Will let go:

> Once everybody in his family had time alone with Will, I asked him if he was ready to go, and he shook his head no. I tried to let him know that I would be all right. Will was worried that I

wouldn't be able to take care of myself, and so my last words to him were, "Will, when you're ready to take off, don't worry about me. I'll be OK. When you're ready, just take off." (Hitchens, 1992, p. 198)

Those around the client can often ease the client's transition by reassuring them that they will be capable of taking care of themselves once the client has died. Steven Paul continued, describing how Will's best friend Karen helped provide the assurance needed for Will to let go:

Karen told me that when the spirit leaves the body, it goes through the top of the head and that sometimes it has trouble finding its way. The way to help is to direct it to the scalp. So I got a hairbrush and I started to gently comb Will's hair. He started to take off, and then I heard this person wailing. It was me. It was like an animal coming from the pit of my stomach. Will heard me wailing and came back into his body and opened his eyes. Karen said to him, "No, Will, take off. You are the light, you are the love. Steven will be fine. Now, take off." And he did. (Hitchens, 1992, pp. 198–199)

At times we will be the only ones with clients when they die, and it will be up to us to support them as they let go. Other times clients are surrounded by their loved ones, and it is the loved ones who need our support.

Unlike the ideal staged version, sometimes clients have a hard death. In his book *How We Die: Reflections on Life's Final Chapter*, Nuland (1994) dispelled the classic deathbed image.

In dying, however, there is only affliction. Its brief respites and ebbs are known always to be fleeting and soon succeeded by a recurrence of the travail. The peace, and sometimes joy, that may come occurs with the release. In this sense, there is often a serenity—sometimes even a dignity—in the act of death, but rarely in the process of dying. (p. 268)

At times we need to acknowledge to clients and their loved ones that death can be awful for all parties involved. We may need to help loved ones accept death in whatever form—hard or easy—it comes. This may be particularly difficult for loved ones in situations when they were not present at the time of the client's death.

Significant Others' Tasks

As clients near death, their families and friends often find it necessary to come to terms with the nature and course of the client's life. When family members have been estranged or geographically distant, there may be many things about the client's life of which they are unaware. Whom a client truly is and what elements have truly comprised the client's life may be an abrupt shock to significant others, especially those who arrive in the client's final days or hours. These surprises may compound any difficulty families and friends may already be experiencing in accepting merely that the client is dying. If significant others are unfamiliar or uninformed about HIV disease, the acceptance process may be made even more difficult; when this happens we may need to inform the clients' significant others about the sociopolitical complexities of HIV disease, so that clients are not to be blamed for contracting HIV.

Accepting the totality of a client's life may be too difficult for some significant others to do in such a short period of time, or ever. We can encourage these family members and friends temporarily to set aside elements in the client's life they find objectionable, and to direct their attention to the elements that they can accept; other elements can always be worked on at a later time. We can encourage family members to join support groups, either immediately or after the client's death.

Support groups like those offered by Mothers of AIDS Patients (which also welcomes fathers and siblings) or other AIDS service agencies may be very effective in helping family members feel less isolated with their experience. These groups are often particularly helpful when family members come to attend to their loved one from out of town and must leave their personal support networks behind. Support groups are also often helpful when family members are unable actually to be with the client and must try to accept the client's death from a distance. Being with others who are mothers, fathers, or siblings of someone dying of AIDS complications may greatly assist family members who feel ashamed and reluctant to share the details of the client's HIV infected status, sexual and affectional orientation, or drug-using past with others they know.

Accepting the Client's Wishes for Care

Spouses or partners, family members, and friends may need assistance in coming to terms with a client's decision to avoid intrusive life support measures. Often these significant others may feel that unless they fight to keep the client alive, he or she will not know they care. Along with validating this concern, we should also try to help significant others come to see that accepting the client's wishes is an expression of care.

Clients' loved ones may find it difficult to accept the arrangements clients may make for funerals, memorials, and care of their body after death. This may be especially troublesome for families when clients' desires conflict with previously established family traditions, such as when, for example, clients request cremation as opposed to burial in a family cemetery plot. Often it is beneficial to help the family see this conflict not in terms of who is correct but rather in terms of bestowing dignity and respect upon the client. Spouses or partners, families, and friends may become more willing to accept a client's wishes if they believe they are doing something to ease the client's process of letting go.

Reviewing Shared Times

Just as clients need to say goodbye, so too must those people closest to the client. One way in which this is often accomplished is by reviewing shared times. This may be an exceptionally effective way of finding closure, especially when a client may not be verbally responsive. We can suggest that significant others spend time alone with the client, reviewing their shared history together. Often this life-review process is valuable not only to the significant other but also to the client.

Counselors' Tasks

When clients are in the final stage of HIV disease, one of our tasks is to assuage the anticipatory grief of people around them. Grief is certainly an appropriate reaction to the death of a loved one. However, at times people close to a dying client become swept away by grief before the client dies. This anticipatory grief can keep those in the clients' inner circle as well as the client from attending to their final tasks. Rather than focusing on the presence or absence of anticipatory grief, we want to consider the intensity of the grief and how adaptive a response it provides (Gaies & Knox, 1991).

We must remember that we, too, may experience anticipatory grief for our clients. When we have lost many clients, friends, or loved ones to HIV disease, our feelings of anticipatory grief may be greater. In order to counsel effectively, we must find ways to work through this feeling. Gaies and Knox (1991) maintained that we need to find balance between a true sense of presence with our clients and a sense of separation from our clients' lives. To do so it is necessary to find ways of acknowledging our feelings about the lives and deaths of our clients to ourselves and to others who can assist us. Maintaining outside support for our professional lives and enrichment in our personal lives is crucial.

Exploring Implications of Death

Another of our tasks is to explore with clients the process of death and its implications. This discussion may include focusing on such issues as fear of death and dying, and existential and spiritual aspects of life and death (Gaies & Knox, 1991). In these discussions, we should respond to questions as honestly and openly as possible. More often than not, clients do not expect a definitive answer to what will happen after they die or an account of our beliefs. Instead clients desire reassurance that dying will not be too painful. We can most often pledge to clients that every step possible will be taken to help ease their transition to death.

We often play an extremely important role in relieving a client's death anxiety. Gaies and Knox (1991) maintained that "a person who perceives death as a peaceful escape from mortal existence will respond differently than a patient who sees death as painful, punishing, or empty nonexistence" (p. 1). By virtue of the facilitative nature of the counseling relationship and the shared understanding that has developed, we may be the only person with whom the client feels comfortable enough to discuss death openly. McKusik (1992) warned that we must be certain to be available for clients for such discussions and not to withdraw out of our own fear and grief or because of misconceptions about the boundaries of the therapeutic relationship.

Walker (1991) also acknowledged the important role we play in clients' explorations of death. She maintained that when we work with clients near death, we should help them to make plans both for their dying and for the future of the people they love: "The therapist's challenge is to open a space that allows this crucial dialogue to take place" (p. 222). Walker conceded that often people in a client's life are not in synchrony with the client in terms of accepting his or her death. When this occurs, communication channels close down and responsibility for encouraging and facilitating a client's planning process and explorations of death falls wholly on us.

Promoting Comfort

In their final hours, clients may feel comforted not so much by what we say or do but by our presence and our attitude toward death. Our most important task at this juncture is to encourage clients to relax and release. When working with clients in their final dying moments, Sogyal Rinpoche (1992) suggested encouraging them not to waste their time or energy trying to change things that irritate them or make them feel uncomfortable. Instead we can encourage clients to focus and refocus on things—people, places, times in their life—that bring them comfort or inspiration. It is clear that in order to help clients find comfort in death, we must find in ourselves a place of comfort with dying from which to work. Addressing those who counsel and care for the dying, Sogyal Rinpoche (1992) wrote "through the strength and peace and deep compassionate attention of your presence, you will help them awaken their own strength. The quality of your presence at this most vulnerable and extreme moment is all important" (p. 211).

Saying Goodbye to the Client

Although many of our tasks are likely to continue after the client's death (e.g., counseling to those who survive), our final task with respect to a dying client is to say goodbye. Understandably, the strong feelings our clients' deaths engender may cause us to attempt to distance ourselves from our clients. Winiarski (1991) listed a number of plausible justifications that we may offer when retreating: "the press of schedule, the impossibility of geography, and the need to adhere to therapeutic frames" (p. 132). Often excuses conceal deeper emotional concerns. These may be anxious feelings related to our own unresolved issues of abandonment or death. There may be doubts and accompanying guilt related to whether we have done enough for our clients. Winiarski (1991) maintained that when strong feelings arise we need to explore them in supervision or in our own personal therapy.

There is no set way for us to say goodbye to clients dying from complications of HIV disease. We have to find our own approach for each client. As a rule, a good farewell reflects upon the time spent with the client and offers affirmation and appreciation of the work accomplished.

We should be prepared when in some cases our desire to say goodbye goes unnoticed. Sometimes clients in their encounter with us do not provide us with an opportunity to say goodbye; instead they emotionally move away from us. Winiarski (1991) attributed this either to a general denial of death or to a security in the therapeutic relationship that allows clients to pursue personal agendas. Winiarski cautioned against taking such distancing personally.

> As hard as it is to gauge when death will come, it is equally fruitless to gauge your worth to the client by the client's behavior in the dying moments. You have helped the person to the threshold. The client moves across it as his or her own abilities allow. (p. 131)

Youth Considerations

Young people must be helped to prepare for death in a manner consonant with their psychological developmental capacities (Barlow & Mok, 1993). Elliot (1993) noted that many adolescents have yet to develop the capacity for abstract thought, including a full understanding of the irreversibility of death. We must consider the inflexibility of the adolescent's cognitive style, and the anxiety that may accompany it, when examining issues of letting go and dying.

When counseling young people, discussions of death should start with a thorough exploration of preconceived notions they have about dying (Elliot, 1993). In preparing adolescents for death, Elliot recommended that we avoid euphemistic terms like *passing away*; talking about death directly communicates comfort to the youth. Adolescents can be asked if they have given thought to dying and to what it might feel like (Elliot, 1993). With some young clients it may be useful to ask them to think about what they will be missing and what will remain unfinished in their lives (Elliot, 1993). We can ask mature teens about their preferences in regard to living wills, health care proxies, and burial or cremation, giving them an opportunity to express their wishes.

We should take into consideration and make accommodations for the limited nature of some young people's verbal expression skills (Elliot, 1993). Some youth may find writing easier. Others may prefer drawing. Younger children may feel more comfortable talking through a doll or puppet. We should take advantage of the wide variety of ways in which young people communicate.

Although some people may hold concerns that talking so openly about death may raise a youth's anxiety level, Elliot (1993) maintained that such talk frequently relieves anxiety. Many times the young person is already thinking about death. The youth may feel afraid to verbalize his or her concerns for fear up upsetting family, loved ones, and friends. When young people sense the discomfort of others (including us), roles quickly become reversed; by not talking about their death they take care of the very people who are reputedly taking care of them. When we sense that this is occurring, we should help the youth and family members deal with their feelings in more productive ways.

It is important to assist families in finding age-appropriate ways to ease a young client's death. Young clients also can be introduced, albeit differently than adults, to the possibility of intentionally letting go. Imagery is often a powerful tool for helping young clients die peacefully. This is evident in the poignant work Shevawn Avila did to prepare her 8-year-old son Troy for his death:

> One of the things Troy and his brother Aaron and I used to do was to sit around and go, "We wish we had a house," because we lived in an apartment. It was like, "God, if we had a house it would be so cool," you know? "Everybody can have their own room and we'd have this backyard, and we'd have a pet." There were times when we didn't have any money and I would go, "Boys, we just don't have any money. What can we do?" And so we'd go on walks or pack a lunch and go spend all day at the beach. Or just sit and talk and fantasize about one day getting a house. In the Bible it says, "In my father's house there are many mansions"—and I thought about that. I told Troy that night in the hospital, "Troy, it's going to be so cool. You're gonna have your own house. You can have everything in it that you want, and all the food you want to eat." I just laid it on. When I put him to bed, he said, "Mommy, you made me so happy." "Why?" I said. And he said, "You told me I'm going to have my own house. I'm not afraid to die anymore." (Hitchens, 1992, p. 59)

Conclusion

Clients walk a complex path from first testing positive to dying. Much of the work that allows a client to say goodbye, let go, and pass gently into death takes place prior to the client's final decline in health. Still, numerous challenges arise for clients, their loved ones, and even us in a client's final days, hours, and moments.

We play an enormous role in facilitating a client's death. As with issues presented in previous chapters, our role should expand to contain the needs of the significant others in the client's life. We should also pay close attention to our own feelings, concerns, and needs as our clients die.

Although death closes a chapter in the life of the client, our life goes on, and our work with the client's spouse or partner, family, and friends often continues. For them, as for us, death is not only an end, but it is also the beginning of a new life without the client. As the last part of this book puts forth, we are often instrumental in ensuring that this new life is a positive one, in spite of the emptiness the loss of the client represents.

PART FOUR

RENEWAL

CHAPTER 22

Surviving

Life goes on.

When someone dies from HIV-related complications, those who survive are left with memories—some good, some bad—and pain. People expect many things while preparing for the death of a loved one, yet one thing is rarely foreseen. In discussing the relationship between truly loving someone and death, Schnarch (1991) wrote "the most terrible part of all, that few people anticipate, is that the loved one is not there to comfort you through their own death. This each of us must do alone" (p. 594). Grieving the loss of a loved one is difficult in the most common of circumstances; the unique characteristics of HIV-related death often complicate those difficulties.

The bereavement process can be thought of as the ongoing work of reconciling two opposing forces. One force drives people who are grieving to hold on to the deceased. The other demands that they release the deceased, incorporating the loved one into their thoughts, memories, and actions as life goes on without him or her. Clients often need our assistance as they attempt to find some balance between these forces.

Although a generalized description of bereavement is somewhat helpful, people who grieve the death of someone from HIV-related complications often also face a unique set of issues. First, the mourning process is affected by the fact that most people succumb from HIV-related complications at young ages. Second, the stigma that still surrounds HIV disease and AIDS affects those mourning the death of a loved one. Third, the stress of caregiving takes its toll on survivors' ability to grieve. Fourth, when survivors are themselves HIV positive, worry about their own health status may confound bereavement. Finally, survivor guilt may make grieving nearly impossible.

A Generalized Model of Bereavement

According to Lifton (1983), the task of bereavement is to accomplish both separation from the deceased and also a sense of deep connection. Thus models of bereavement tend to reflect these two somewhat contradictory goals. Rather than approaching bereavement from a more traditional perspective with strict developmental stages, current models of bereavement allow for the flexibility of each individual's experience—which is crucial when working with people who have lost a loved one to HIV-related complications. These newer models are also framed in terms of the task of reconciling the opposing impulses of holding on and releasing.

Holding On to the Deceased

Parkes and Weiss (1983) provided a four-stage theoretical framework for understanding the bereavement process. The first three stages of grief—numbness, pining, and disorganization—reflect a survivor's desire to hold on to the deceased. According to Parkes and Weiss, people may go through one or more of these stages and may oscillate from stage to stage.

The initial shock of death may be accompanied by psychic numbing (Lifton, 1980), a state of partial emotional denial, which enables those who survive to make whatever funeral or memorial arrangements necessary. This numbing may not be entirely encompassing, and periods of intense grief may interrupt denial of the loss of the loved one. Once survivors no longer need the numbing, the process of intense grieving, of pining, and of disorganization may begin; this process is often accompanied by depression. In describing this process, Walker (1991) wrote, "Initially the work must contain a ruminative preoccupation with thoughts of the lost person, a tireless examination of the events preceding illness or of the last weeks or the last day, when the cause was lost. It is as if remembering the bereaved could reverse the flow of time and redo the events" (p. 257). Dreams or fantasies where the dead person is present are not uncommon.

In "The AIDS Bereaved: Counseling Strategies," Weiss (1989) divided the process of grieving into three phases. The first two of these, the shock phase and the working-through phase, encompass the desire to hold on to the loved one. The shock phase usually lasts from the time the survivor learns of the death until the final disposition of the loved one's body. There is often, although not always, support from friends, family, or community during this phase. "The survivor often describes this period as one in which there is little time to appreciate the fact that the loss is real, and the absence of the loved one is often experienced as temporary or unreal" (p. 268).

The working-through phase usually lasts from several weeks to several months after the death. Here somatic symptoms and emotional suffering are common. The bereaved person may withdraw from external events, "feeling inadequate or unable to take care of the details of living or simply 'go on' without the deceased" (Weiss, 1989, p. 269). Since formal rituals around death and dying have been completed, this is often the time when survivors are left alone with their grief.

We can play an important role in helping clients with this second phase of the bereavement process. Because of the youth of many who die from HIV-related complications, some young survivors may have had limited experiences with death and dying and may not understand that their emotional responses are normal, particularly the desire to hold on to the deceased. Thus we should validate their feelings and affirm their experience as common and predictable. Even clients who have experienced many AIDS-related losses may need their feelings validated; often they incorrectly assume that because they have been through the grieving process before they should not want to hold on. When family and community support for those mourning is limited, we can provide ongoing care. AIDS bereavement groups, by themselves or as an adjunct to individual or family counseling, are often helpful in putting survivors in contact with other people who share a similar experience of loss. Survivors who reside out of town may find a referral to a bereavement group in their geographic area useful.

Release and Incorporation of the Deceased

In contrast to the desire to retain the loved one who has died, another force tends toward realization of the loss and internalization of the loved one. This force, encompassed in Parkes and Weiss' (1983) fourth stage of recovery and in Weiss' (1989) third phase of reestablishing balance, can also be facilitated through counseling. In traditional psychodynamic terms this force reflects the process of incorporation. According to Walker (1991), "The resolution of grief requires identification of experiences that allow the relationship to be completed: The living are able to let go of the dead knowing that they both *have* and *have not* lost them" (p. 257). Walker maintained that the notion that mourning should end in connection to the loved one (as opposed to decathection) is a crucial one for therapeutic intervention. If the mourning goes well, remembering the loved one changes over time from a source of sadness and pain to gradually becoming a celebration of cherished aspects of the relationship. A new, postbereavement identity is gradually formed, using internalized aspects of the relationship as a foundation. Survivors take over roles and tasks previously performed by the deceased, using as a model their memories of witnessing the loved one engage in the activities as a model.

Often we must help survivors find ways to celebrate the loved one and incorporate him or her into a newly forming identity. Ritual often plays an important part in this process. An effective strategy is to encourage survivors to find personally appropriate and meaningful ways to honor the deceased. Perhaps one of the greatest examples of AIDS-related ritual is the creation of the Names Project AIDS Quilt. Survivors can decorate panels as a living memorial to their loved one. These panels become part of a larger quilt on display throughout the world. The healing power of the quilting process, which is often done in the company of others, cannot be underestimated. The recognition that the deceased in some way lives on in the shape of the quilt and in the hearts of those surviving is incredibly powerful. However, we must remember that a ritual as public as the AIDS Quilt may not be appropriate for every survivor. Many survivors prefer creating their own private rituals, and these also should be supported.

Most models of bereavement maintain that with enough time, survivors begin to reinvest emotionally in activities and interests. However, these models may be deceptively simplistic, particularly when the loved one has died from HIV-related illnesses. Issues unique to HIV disease often complicate the bereavement process, increasing both the time and support necessary for a person to grieve.

Issues Specific to AIDS-Bereavement

Although a generalized model of bereavement may help identify some of the issues facing those who survive the loss of a loved one to HIV disease, it is incomplete. The unique dynamics surrounding HIV disease significantly impact the grief process. Schwartzberg (1992) maintained that the need to reconceptualize grief in the context of HIV disease is in keeping with a trend of challenging traditional models of grief to allow for greater interpersonal and intergroup variability. He noted that clinicians "need to better understand the patterns, expressions, and sequelae of AIDS-related grief" (p. 428) if we are to meet the needs of clients in the difficult years ahead.

Though not an exhaustive list, five major issues can be identified specific to AIDS-related bereavement. These issues arise from the heart-wrenching combination of factors that comprise deaths caused by complications of HIV disease: age and stage differences, stigma, stress of caregiving, identification with the deceased, and survivor guilt. These issues complicate the bereavement process and make counseling all the more necessary.

Age and Stage Differences

Walker (1991) noted that even though loved ones anticipate HIV-related deaths, "they remain out of synchrony with the patient's expected life cycle" (p. 251). Although people accept on some level the fact that those who have lived a long life will die, it is more difficult to acknowledge the death of someone young. This may be especially the case for parents mourning the death of a child in his or her 20s, 30s, or 40s. Evidence suggests that the intensity of grief of parents is greater when they lose an adult child than when the child lost is an infant (Gorer, 1965).

Outside of the deceased's parents, those who mourn the loss of a loved one from HIV-related complications are also likely to be young. Many will not be prepared psychologically to deal with death. At an age when death is most commonly denied (Becker, 1975), many young men and women must face the death of not one but numerous friends and loved ones. Developmentally, people in their 30s strive to create successful intimate relationships and occupational satisfaction (Erikson, 1963). AIDS forces young people to interrupt these concerns in order to face death, a task that is developmentally untimely.

When counseling survivors, we must keep in mind that the death of a young person may severely challenge survivors' ability to cope and function. We should be alert for signs that they feel guilty or responsible for the premature loss of the loved one. This guilt, if not addressed, can result in physical and psychological illness (Walker, 1991). We should also be sensitive to signs of truncated mourning. We want to explore gently the reasons why those who survive have cut short the mourning process. In both cases we want to acknowledge the hardship of losing someone young and the shock and concomitant wave of feelings this particular type of death causes. Knowing that strong emotional reactions are appropriate can often help a client better navigate through the bereavement process.

Stigma

Another factor that distinguishes HIV-related bereavement from other types of grief is the stigma associated with AIDS. People who lose those they cared for to old age, cancer, or accidents feel free to mourn openly with the support of those around them. AIDS, however, carries with it a stigma that applies not only to the deceased but also to those who survive, often preventing them from freely mourning. Moreover, AIDS draws attention to a number of cultural taboos, including sex and death; and when grief is linked to such taboos, normal bereavement may be disrupted (Weiss, 1989).

Families may contend not only with the feelings of losing a son or daughter, brother or sister, father or mother, but also with the feelings of wanting to keep the cause of death secret. When they live in communities far away from major metropolitan centers, or in conservative and intolerant communities, family members may fear encountering ignorance, hostile reactions, and moral judgments. Families may also decide to keep the loss of a loved one secret or invent another cause of death when they fear rejection and ostracism from their friends or colleagues at work. Many times family members fail to anticipate the emotional toll of keeping the death of a loved one a secret. They fail to recognize how secrecy disrupts the process of grieving. For example, family members may reject attending a support group for fear that their secret will become public. In cases where the cause of a loved one's death is kept secret, we may be the only person who truly knows, recognizes, and understands the full nature of the family's grief. Affirming their internal reality becomes even more critical.

Many gay men and lesbians who survive the loss of their partner to AIDS experience intensely real discrimination. Rarely will a company or workplace acknowledge the impact of the loss of anyone other than a blood relative or legally married spouse. Thus gay men and lesbians must grieve the loss of their partners on their own time, with little support or comfort from those for whom they work. Similarly, their own family may not recognize the legitimacy of their relationships and thus may not support them during their time of mourning. Many gay men and lesbians have no one to turn to for support but others in the gay and lesbian community; unfortunately, these gay men and lesbians are often coping with the effects of their own losses and may not be as available as needed.

Stress of Caregiving

AIDS bereavement also becomes complicated when the person grieving served as primary caregiver to the deceased. Weiss (1989) maintained that "the work required to keep the dying person fed, clean, and medicated appropriately along with the emotional strain and disruption of usual life activities can be overwhelming" and result in "survivors' fatigue" (p. 272). This fatigue may be heightened in caregivers who had a difficult time feeling entitled to take time off from attending to the needs of the dying person to see to their own personal affairs.

In working with these clients, our foremost task is to help them find ways to rest. This may not be easy to do, particularly if the survivor's personal life was put on hold while providing care. These survivors often feel a real urgency to plunge back into their daily activities; they may be unaware of how emotionally and physically depleting caregiving was to them. Survivors' urgent need to become extremely busy extremely soon after a loved one's death may also serve survivors in an additional way; when used as a defense, avoiding rest gives survivors a means to deny emotional reactions to the death. When we become aware of this type of defensive behavior, we should look for feelings of guilt that may lie below the surface of survivors' conscious awareness. We should also look for unacknowledged feelings of anger; it is not uncommon for caregivers to feel angry at the deceased, incensed that their loved one dared to die after they provided enormous amounts of care. Unless survivors can acknowledge and explore such emotions, they will have a difficult time with the grieving process.

Identification With the Deceased

When counseling HIV-positive survivors we should be sensitive to the complex nature of their emotional responses (Shelby, 1994). These survivors often face not only the task of grieving over the loss of a loved one but also the anticipatory grieving of the loss of their own health (Weiss, 1989). This often holds true for survivors who have not been tested but operate under the assumption that they are most likely infected. Therefore, we must read beneath the typical expressions of loss and grief and inquire whether survivors also worry about their own health. We should encourage clients to address this fear directly. Giving voice to these fears dilutes the potency they have when kept secret.

Particularly with this group of survivors, we must remain attentive to signals of suicidal ideation. When someone close to an HIV-positive survivor dies from HIV-related complications, feelings of helplessness and hopelessness may arise, leading the survivor to question the point of continuing to live. In this situation, our best strategy is to handle this issue directly; we should immediately ask about the survivor's plans to take his or her life. Although suicidal thoughts are common in people living with HIV disease, when they occur soon after the HIV-related death of someone close to an HIV-positive survivor, they are of special concern. We must decide if the suicidal ideation is the typical consideration of someone living with HIV disease or if it is a more serious indication of the survivor's full intent to end his or her life. We can only make this assessment after exploring in depth the unique nature of the survivor's grief. Often an HIV-positive survivor's thoughts of suicide become exacerbated by the fear that nobody will be left to care for him or her. When this is the case, we can draw on the strength of the therapeutic relationship as a means of countering the survivor's feeling of isolation.

Survivor Guilt

For many people, survivor guilt compromises the AIDS-bereavement process. Lifton (1980) held that survivor guilt—response of survivors of massive death experiences—is epitomized by the question, "Why did I survive when everyone else died?" Survivors, particularly those who are HIV negative, may be steeped in survivor guilt, which prevents them from fully engaging in the bereavement process. Thus it is important to help survivors identify and acknowledge any guilt feelings they may have related to their survivor status.

One strategy for counseling clients with survivor guilt is to explore their internal explanations for why they were spared. That neither we nor our clients can determine the nature of fate should not deter us from exploring why they believe they are still alive. If HIV-positive clients believe that they survive due to a particular behavior—for example, because they take high doses of antioxidants—we should support them in that behavior. The behavior may or may not have contributed to the client's health, but the belief that it did is most likely beneficial. This holds especially true when HIV-negative clients believe they survived because they avoided certain sexual behaviors. HIV-negative clients, particularly those that feel survivor guilt, need an enormous amount of additional encouragement from us to maintain AIDS risk-reduction behaviors.

Facilitating the Grief Process

Although the bereavement process is distinctive and different for each survivor, some common counseling strategies for facilitating the grief process have been identified. In its manual on the medical, psychological, and social aspects of HIV disease, the American Psychological Association HIV Office for Psychology Education suggested eight ways in which we can help clients grieving an HIV-related loss (Barret et al., 1993). First, we can actualize the loss for the survivor through talking and ritual. Second, we can encourage the survivor's expression of feelings. Third, we can assist survivors in developing skills for living without the deceased. Fourth, we can facilitate overcoming emotional withdrawal. Fifth, we can encourage specific times for grieving. Sixth, we can normalize grieving behavior. Seventh, we can allow for individual and cultural differences in grieving. Finally, we can identify nonproductive coping and pathological grieving. However, in facilitating the bereavement process our overarching task must be to validate the clients' feelings and affirm their experience of having lost someone to HIV-related complications. We must take care to not become so focused on established technique—for example, encouraging specific times for grieving—that we lose sight of the idiosyncratic nature of expressing grief.

Many issues arise for us in the course of counseling clients who have lost someone close to them. Once we have invited clients to share their bereavement process with us, we must sit with them and their pain. Bereavement counseling is bound by the reality that "lost is lost." The American Psychological Association HIV Office for Psychology Education lists three consequences of this reality: we cannot fix our clients' grief; we cannot take away our clients' depression and sadness; and we will often feel helpless, as will our clients. Often our best counseling strategy is to sit with clients, witnessing their tough feelings while continually giving them permission and encouragement to grieve (Barret et al., 1993). As the HIV Office for Psychology Education maintained, "Just listening is often the best intervention—sometimes you don't have to do or say anything" (Barret et al., 1993, p. 89).

In facilitating the bereavement process we must remember that clients feel safest to grieve when they know the grief can be expressed and contained (Barret et al., 1993). Clients need to know experientially that we can contain their grief. Often we tend to make accommodations to the therapeutic frame when clients appear deeply hurt and grief-stricken; for example, we may allow sessions to run overtime. Although this may appear to be beneficial to clients, in most cases it is not. When we maintain the therapeutic frame and contain feelings of grief, we convey to clients that they will be able to contain their grief. If we break the therapeutic frame, we convey implicitly to clients that their grief is so intense it is beyond control. Thus we must pay attention to the subtle elements of our work, the meta-communication of our actions, especially when counseling clients with AIDS-bereavement issues. In order to do this, we must first examine and expand upon their own capacity to contain painful grief-related emotions.

Women's Challenges

Although it is true that others may face the same problem, women who survive the death of a spouse or partner have a higher likelihood of having to adjust to severe socioeconomic changes following the loss. This is particularly the case when women were entirely dependent upon their partners' income. If women have young children, the strain of the partners' death increases; not only will they need to find a way to console their children, but they will also need to find a way to support them emotionally and financially. If the child is HIV-positive and needs extensive care, the spouses' or partners' death often means there is no one to share the burden (Walker, 1992). If the woman is herself HIV positive, a spouse's or partner's death becomes even more difficult; she must also find emotional and financial support in case she becomes ill. For women, survival needs may take precedence over the need to mourn. We must appreciate this and assist clients in finding financial and social support.

Parents' Challenges

We need to understand and be sensitive to the special issues of parents who have lost their mates, and find ways to accommodate their needs. Parents who are left to care for young children by themselves may no longer be able to make regular appointments; we need to adjust our schedules to be more flexible. In some cases parents may need to bring their children with them to sessions; we need to find some way to adapt sessions to the children's presence. Moreover, children need help with the bereavement process as well. For some parents, the needs of their children take precedence over their own need to mourn. We must appreciate this, and consider creating ways in which both parents and their children have opportunities to grieve.

Cultural Considerations

Culture strongly determines how a client approaches bereavement. We must be aware of our own personal culturally based assumptions about what mourning should be like. We need to be aware of and open to the wide variety of culturally appropriate ways in which clients may choose to mourn. Cultures and subcultures that do not accept homosexuality generally also severely stigmatize people infected and affected by HIV disease. Clients who identify with these cultural norms may find it difficult to accept the HIV-related death of a loved one. In addition, even when they are able to acknowledge the HIV-related nature of their loved one's death, finding support from within their own community may prove impossible.

Youth Issues

For many young people, especially those who have had no prior experience with death, the loss of a loved one raises many feelings and much confusion. Young people must be assisted to understand death as a part of the life cycle. Especially with an HIV-related death, where the youth may have witnessed the physical deterioration of the deceased, many aspects of dying may have been frightening or confusing. We can encourage youth to ask questions or voice any concerns about HIV disease or death they may have. Many things about the grieving process (e.g., dreaming of the deceased) may seem strange to a young person. Young people need repeated affirmation that their bereavement experience is typical and as expected.

According to McKelvy (1994), when young children suffer the loss of one or both parents to complications of HIV disease, five specific developmental tasks are critical to their bereavement process. First, the children must evolve a new sense of personal identity that includes some positive identification with the lost parent. We must work with young clients so that their identification with their parent is not entirely negative. Often the children's disturbing memories of their parent's illness obscures any recollection of their parent as healthy. Second, children must reinvest in emotional relationships without fear of loss. Restoring children's ability to form emotional bonds is often a slow and painful process. We may be the sole person in the children's life whom they trust will not leave them; thus some children's capacity to bond may begin with their attempts to form a relationship with us. Whenever possible we should make sure that external threats to the counseling relationship (e.g., missed sessions) are minimized. Third, children must consolidate and maintain an internal relationship with the lost parent that will last over time. Some children have few memories of their lost parent. We can encourage these young clients to create a symbolic representation of their parent that will provide them with an inner sense of connection. Fourth, children must return to age-appropriate tasks. Most children must continue to go to school; they may need our assistance in finding ways to manage painful feelings of loss while in a classroom or on the playground. Finally, children must find ways to contain the resurgence of difficult feelings arising from the loss of their parent. Holidays, birthdays, and family celebrations may be especially difficult for young children. "For children who experience disappointment around these holidays, the therapist should be particularly attentive—even giving gifts, when appropriate" (McKelvy, 1994, p. 153).

If young people are left orphaned by the death of a parent, we have not only to help them mourn the loss of their parent but also to adjust to a new living situation. When this occurs, consistency is of great importance. When a new living situation is established, maintaining regular counseling sessions with us provides the youth with the structure and continuity that are crucial to the youth's healthy development. When necessary, we should take a proactive stance to ensure that to the greatest extent possible counseling sessions continue on a regular basis.

Conclusion

The idea that grief is a time-limited process proceeding in discrete stages has greatly influenced both professional and popular beliefs about what is normal or healthy grief (Schwartzberg, 1992). When working with clients grieving the loss of a loved one due to complications of HIV disease, we must take care so as not to adhere to these models too rigidly. AIDS bereavement is highly individualistic and is a function of many factors, including survivors' ages, survivors' ability to overcome HIV-related stigma, survivors' cultural traditions about mourning, and survivors' HIV status.

In addition, stage models suggest that there is an end or resolution to the grieving process. For many people who survive the loss of a loved one to HIV-related illnesses, there is no complete resolution, and no return to the identity they had before the loss. Instead, the grief work may evolve into different forms and "become integrated into the fabric of a person's life" (Schwartzberg, 1992, p. 427). Knowing someone who has died from HIV-related complications changes one indefinably. We must not forget, nor allow our clients to forget, that this change, though painful, can also be invaluable and life affirming.

CHAPTER 23

Multiple Loss and the Search for Meaning

*Multiple loss challenges people to find meaning
in the face of absurdity.*

Aspecial variation on loss has become so prevalent that it bears additional consideration. As the AIDS crisis continues well into a second decade, more and more people struggle to contend with the cumulative effects of multiple loss. People everywhere are losing friend after friend and loved one after loved one to AIDS-related illnesses.

The phenomenon of multiple loss owes its recognition to psychological studies of war-time survivors (Lifton, 1980). The term *multiple loss* refers to the overwhelming task of living in a situation where continual loss has become commonplace. Often the time necessary to grieve the loss of one person becomes interrupted by the demands of caring for or mourning the loss of another person.

Living in a state of multiple loss challenges people to find meaning in the face of absurdity. Once the fundamental rules by which people have previously guided their lives are shattered, the only thing they can do is to search for meaning (Schwartzberg, 1992). This search often becomes the central focus of counseling people who have sustained multiple losses.

Multiple Loss Syndrome

The compounding psychological and spiritual effects of surviving loss after loss cannot be underestimated or overlooked. Lifton (1980) identified five common psychological responses that make up the experience of multiple loss. First, people suffer from indelible mental images of death and dying, stemming from the enormity of the loss. Neugebauer et al. (1992) in their study of bereavement reactions among gay men experiencing multiple losses from AIDS reported that men with greater numbers of losses described more preoccupation with the deceased than did men with fewer losses. Second, people suffer from survivor guilt rooted in the randomness of the situation. In the context of multiple loss, survivor guilt is rarely the sole property of HIV-negative people; Boykin (1991) reported that though survivor guilt was common in HIV-negative gay men, HIV-positive gay men tended to have even higher degrees of survivor guilt. Third, people with multiple loss syndrome often experience a diminished capacity to feel, known as psychic numbing. Fourth, Lifton (1980) reported they also often experience a suspicion of counterfeit nurturance. People who have survived multiple losses often crave special sustenance; however, the identity of victim is often highly defended against. Therefore, nurturance given in response to a survivor's multiple losses is often not seen as real and is rejected because it unconsciously reinforces a feeling of victimization. Finally, people with multiple loss syndrome actively search for meaning. Schwartzberg (1992) maintained that multiple loss syndrome is extremely relevant to grief in an HIV-immersed subculture. For example, "it can be an overwhelming experience to be simultaneously mourning a recent loss, remembering several past losses, and anticipating still others to come, yet this is the reality of grieving for many gay men" (p. 423).

Although multiple loss syndrome is an inherent part of the AIDS crisis, many clients may be unfamiliar with its manifestations. They may have little conscious awareness of how the frequent and continuous loss of friends and loved ones influences their emotions and behaviors. Depression, uncertainty about and loss of faith in the future, and a worn-out commitment to safer sexual practices may all be the result of multiple loss (Dilley & Moon, 1994). When we notice these, or other issues we believe are related to multiple loss, we should bring them to our clients' attention. We should help clients understand how these issues reflect and express their experience of living in a constant state of bereavement.

Bereavement Overload

Many clients who experience multiple loss also experience bereavement overload (Carmack, 1992; Weiss, 1989). One of the most difficult aspects of bereavement overload is "overlapping grief" (Schwartzberg, 1992, p. 426). Clients rarely have sufficient time to mourn the loss of a friend or loved one before they must mourn, or at least prepare for mourning, the loss of another.

Many clients cope with recurring patterns of anticipated and actual loss by emotionally numbing themselves. It is as if there is literally no internal psychological space for them to grieve—it has all been consumed. For most clients psychic numbing plays an extremely important protective role. Thus we should avoid viewing numbing as a defensive stance or as resistance to grieving that should be broken down. Instead we should respect our clients' psychic numbing: it is often the only way clients living with multiple loss can continue on with their daily life and not be in a paralyzed state of overwhelming pain.

A useful strategy for counseling clients engaged in psychic numbing is to validate their ability to take care of themselves by withdrawing emotionally; simultaneously we should invite them to explore their grief *if and when they so choose.* It may be helpful for clients to consider ways to alternate successfully between disconnecting from their experience of grief and engaging in their experience of grief. Until clients are ready to work on bereavement issues, we need to remain attentive to ways in which psychic numbing may also obscure other important issues. For example, research findings suggest that sustaining multiple losses may increase a client's likelihood of committing suicide (Goldblum & Moulton, 1989). Thus we should maintain a heightened sensitivity to indications of suicidal intention.

The Search for Meaning

Clients suffering from multiple loss and bereavement overload often struggle to find meaning in what appear to be meaningless circumstances. The tragedy of HIV disease dramatically assaults fundamental assumptions that previously guided clients' lives (Schwartzberg, 1992). It challenges clients' beliefs about such core issues as self-esteem, personal safety, and the purpose of life. The world may no longer make sense.

Counseling these clients centers on the difficult task of helping them construe new meaning for their lives. Frankl (1992), drawing on his experiences in the death camps of Nazi Germany, wrote in his book *Man's Search for Meaning* that the ability to find meaning in suffering, to find spiritual purpose, is vital for optimal human functioning. Similarly, Schwartzberg (1992) wrote that "in a community beset by AIDS, the need to find meaning in what could otherwise be perceived as a senseless and meaningless ordeal is a psychological task of great importance" (p. 427).

In studies on successful grief resolution, Schwartzberg and Janoff-Bulman (1991) found that people's need to find meaning in death and minimize the disruption to their basic beliefs is more important than the means by which people accomplished this. Clients need not feel restricted, therefore, in the ways in which meaning is sought. Political activism, community involvement, and spiritual pursuits all provide viable options. Often supporting clients' efforts at restoring meaning to their lives becomes the overriding focus of counseling. "For individuals living in ordinary times and circumstances, a search for meaning may be of personal benefit; for those living amid AIDS' constant onslaught of bereavement, finding a personal framework of meaning may instead become a fundamental necessity. In the face of AIDS, the search for meaning may be inextricable from the process of grief" (Schwartzberg, 1992, pp. 427–428).

Conclusion

Each day the AIDS crisis forces people to struggle with the simultaneous and contradictory emotional demands of mourning the dead, nursing the ill, and maintaining a sense of optimism for themselves and for the healthy. The experience of multiple loss brought about by AIDS is unlike anything experienced outside of war or natural disasters. The emotional and spiritual toll of bereavement overload is high. People, lacking the time and energy needed to process the deaths of those close to them, often cope only by numbing themselves.

We can provide a great service to clients living with multiple loss. Deaths of friends and loved ones pose a major challenge to clients: how to find meaning in the midst of absurdity. Although it is true that clients must come to find their own ways to restore meaning to their lives, we need not leave them to engage in this process alone. We should provide clients with a safe, supportive, and understanding environment in which to conduct their search for meaning.

Accompanying clients on their psychological and often spiritual quests to find meaning amidst their experience of intense grief can be deeply moving. Tragically, for many clients, this search will continue until a cure for HIV disease is discovered. Schwartzberg (1992) stated that "an individual's grief will not end as long as the possibility of ongoing loss continues, i.e., as long as AIDS is present and fatal" (p. 427). Until a cure is found, finding meaning in the face of HIV disease is crucial for clients. It is also crucial for us.

CHAPTER 24

Continuing to Care

Our work is not easy.
It does, however, have its rewards.

C learly we can play a crucial role in the physical, emotional, and even spiritual health of clients living with HIV disease and their loved ones. When we work with HIV-positive clients and other clients also affected by HIV disease, we face challenges that differ from those of typical day-to-day counseling. Just as clients are asked to confront issues of quality of life and meaning in life, so, too, are we. While we nurture, support, and sustain these clients, who sustains us?

We cannot engage in the practice of HIV affirmative counseling without taking time to reflect upon our experiences. Periods of self-examination are critical to our work because they allow us to see what parts of our self have been depleted and need replenishment, and what parts are abundant and may be shared more readily. The process of self-reflection provides the foundation for our ability to continue working with people living with HIV disease.

The range of issues and emotions we need to reflect upon both professionally and personally is wide in scope and highly idiosyncratic. Five issues, however, hold universal import: our own grief, countertransference and other feelings, burnout, the rewards of AIDS-related counseling, and the importance of not giving up hope. Attention to each is crucial to our ability to continue to contribute to clients' well-being.

Our Own Grief

Weisman (1981) wrote that "there is no reaction among patients that cannot also occur in caregivers" (p. 165). Clients often are acutely aware of this; we, however, often are not. When a client we have been working with dies from HIV-related complications, we may acknowledge our feelings of loss and grief only reluctantly, if we acknowledge them at all. We may believe we have no time for grief—that people who continue to live with HIV disease need us. We may feel somehow that grieving signifies lapses in our ability to maintain therapeutic objectivity and distance. We may feel that we no longer have any energy left with which to grieve.

When we counsel people living with HIV disease, we must find ways to process our grief. Unless we do so, we will not be able to provide our clients and others with the quality care and compassion they need. Four tasks are integral to the process of coming to terms with our own HIV-related grief: knowing for whom to grieve, giving ourselves permission to grieve, finding time and space to grieve, and finding a way to grieve.

Knowing for Whom to Grieve

We need to know for whom to grieve. The simplicity of this statement belies the complex task it prescribes. Many times clients living with HIV disease disappear from our practice. Often they terminate treatment because they have made as much progress as they desire at a particular time. At other times, they drop out offering little to no explanation.

It is important that we find ways to follow former clients when they leave treatment. Without knowing that a former (and potentially returning) client is still alive and well, we can easily assume the worst. When we have a large caseload of HIV-positive clients, the burden of assuming that clients who have terminated treatment have also died becomes unbearable. Asking clients when they terminate to keep in touch periodically by mailing a post card or leaving a phone message often helps to alleviate our stress of not knowing how they are doing.

If contact with a client breaks suddenly, we may want to follow-up and find out whether he or she is still alive. Receiving news that a client has died may be difficult, but it provides a concreteness that enables us to place some closure on the work we did with him or her. As long as we remain uninformed about former clients' health status we cannot say goodbye. When we can realize the finality of past counseling relationships, we can then provide psychic and emotional space for new clients.

Giving Ourselves Permission to Grieve

The counseling relationship is a unique type of relationship allowing for an intimacy rarely felt in other realms. If the work we did with our clients was good, we will feel grief when clients die. Having strong feelings about our clients' deaths is to be expected, not avoided. Tragically, many of us assume that strong feelings about a client are a sign of incompetence, or that we have not maintained sufficient distance between ourselves and our client. Although distance may be an appropriate model for some counseling relationships, this model does not hold when working with HIV-positive clients. Given that HIV disease often evokes in clients the most basic human need to be touched physically, emotionally, and spiritually, we must find a way to connect with clients deeply; it is in this connection that the true work of HIV affirmative counseling occurs. The cost of connection is loss. Thus we must come to see our need to grieve as a sign that we did meaningful and good work and give ourselves permission to grieve.

Finding Time and Space to Grieve

Once we can recognize our need to grieve, we must find time and space to allow the bereavement process to unfold. Many times we may feel that this is an impossible task—especially when our caseloads include high numbers of people living with HIV disease. Winiarski (1991) noted, "How little we sit with death. How quickly we adjust to the news, and then go on with our lives" (p. 133). The tendency to over-book ourselves or constantly attend to clients in crisis is common. When a client dies, there is often a long list of others waiting for counseling. The promise of a new client, filled with hope and energy, often entices us to take on clients before we are actually ready—before we have had time to process our losses.

When taking on a new client after a client has just died, we should consider the health status of our current caseload (Barret et al., 1993). Are any of the clients we currently see in the end stages of HIV disease? Is it likely that any of our current clients will die in the near future? How many of our current clients are hospitalized or housebound and, therefore, need special arrangements for sessions? Although it is tempting to think that when a client dies, filling his or her appointment time with a new client is the most helpful thing we can do, often we can be more helpful to ourselves and our clients if we leave the appointment temporarily unfilled and use the time in ways to facilitate our bereavement process. In addition, if we provide training or educational workshops and lectures, we may want to reevaluate our schedule when a client of ours has died. When we fail to make room in our lives for the natural emotional reactions that come from working with people living and dying from HIV disease, we do ourselves and our clients a disservice.

Finding a Way to Grieve

We may find that due to the unique dynamics of the counseling relationship we need special ways of grieving the loss of clients and acknowledging the loss of the counseling relationship with its special roles and special intensity. Sometimes we may find attending the funeral or memorial of a client makes us uncomfortable. At times the confidential nature of the counseling relationship may mean that we are not even invited. If we are invited to the funeral or memorial we may be considered an outsider, even though we may know more than immediate family about the deceased.

Frequently we are left to create our own rituals, our own ways of memorializing our clients (Gaies & Knox, 1991). There are no right or wrong ways for us to honor the clients we have lost to HIV disease. Sometimes this can be done with pictures of clients, candles, or letters. Other times it can be done in a private ceremony or at a public space like the Names Quilt. However we do it, we must find a way to remember our clients and recognize their place in our lives.

Countertransference and Other Feelings

The question of what does and does not constitute countertransference is widely debated within psychodynamic and other therapeutic communities. What cannot be questioned is that in working with clients living with HIV disease we experience strong personal feelings. We must examine these feelings, understand these feelings, and, when possible, use these feelings to improve the quality of our work. Although the range of emotional reactions to working with people living with HIV disease reflects our varied personal experiences, four common types of reactions stand out: countertransferential reactions, "tough-enough" reactions, rescue fantasy reactions, and directiveness reactions.

Countertransferential Reactions

Sometimes we are able to respond appropriately to the situations and issues an HIV-positive client presents; other times unresolved issues from our past color our responses. We need to become aware of our sensitive spots, the life issues that continue to bring us pain. Although we can never resolve completely our personal issues around death and dying, quality of life, and the meaning of suffering, clearly those of us who have done more work around these and other similar issues can more easily separate our personal experience from that of our clients. When we have not explored these issues, we risk attributing the source of a strong emotional reaction to a client's life situation when in fact it resides in our personal history.

We must recognize that although many times the term *countertransference* has negative connotations, working with countertransference is a necessary and important part of HIV affirmative counseling. Winiarski (1991) urged us not to judge our own and our colleagues' predispositions and reactions to clients; instead, he recommended that when we feel angry or hostile towards a client (or experience any other strong feeling), we should ask why. For example, if we feel upset with an HIV-positive client because we feel the client has lost hope, we must determine whether the feeling arises from our own desire to have the client act or be a certain way (happy, hopeful, optimistic) or our emotional reaction to the client's lack of compliance. Consultation may be necessary in order to sort out these feelings and should not be avoided or stigmatized. Understanding our reasons for feeling strongly negative or strongly positive toward a client allows us to gain an important perspective on our motives and behaviors and can help us avoid becoming overidentified with, overinvolved with, or overly responsible for clients living with HIV disease.

Tough-Enough Reactions

It is common for us to question whether we are tough enough to be engaging in HIV-related work. This reaction may occur at any time—when we first consider counseling people living with HIV disease, when a client shows up for an initial session, or when a client's health takes a turn for the worse. The difficulty with this reaction is that it is "built on the belief that one handles difficult issues (living, dying, and death) by building a suit of armor and hiding within" (Winiarski, 1991, p. 115).

The notion that we must be tough for our clients can be one of the most damaging beliefs we hold. The type of strength clients living with HIV need is not that which encourages us to shut down feelings, or to become or remain emotionally detached. All clients—but particularly HIV-positive clients and their loved ones—need us to be empathic and to resonate with them emotionally. We cannot do this if we are being tough. We will find that we are doing our best work when we let down our guard. When we cry, laugh, and feel with our clients, we are modeling the strength to remain responsive in the face of the tough work of living with HIV disease.

Rescue Fantasy Reactions

A common, though subtle, reaction for many of us counseling HIV-positive clients is the fantasy that somehow our work can save these clients. Winiarski (1991) noted that these rescue fantasies take two forms. One is that we often believe that successful counseling may lead to greater longevity, or that the therapeutic relationship will promote a cure. The difficulty with this fantasy is that when a client's health begins to decline, we feel increasingly impotent.

The other form of rescue fantasy is the notion that the counseling relationship will change characterological aspects of our clients' personality and thereby lead them to a better death (Winiarski, 1991). Although this type of change may be our goal, it is rarely the clients' goal. Clients' personalities take many years to form, and it is highly unlikely that core attributes will be changed in a short period of time, despite the motivating factors of HIV disease. In fact, part of the rescue fantasy is the assumption that HIV-positive clients enter into counseling because they want to change their basic personality; this is not typically the case. Many times clients come to counseling with short-term, specific needs such as stress reduction or crisis intervention. More often than not, changing characterological traits is not part of clients' agenda. When it is part of our overt or covert agenda but not part of our clients' agenda, we are likely to be disappointed. Most clients die the way they lived: those who lived angry lives often die angry; those who lived contented lives often die contented. Meeting clients' HIV situation with fantasies of transforming their personalities and rescuing them from a terrible death ensures that we will feel helpless, incompetent, and dispirited.

Directiveness Reactions

Counseling HIV-positive clients can engender in us extreme anxiety. If we have not yet developed a tolerance for this anxiety, we may resort to unduly directive approaches with clients as a way of reducing our own anxious feelings. While giving clients homework assignments and other proposals for action is appropriate at certain times, directive assignments are inappropriate when done to offset our own anxiety or helplessness. If we do assign homework or suggest concrete plans for clients, we must take care to avoid gauging our efficacy by the client's compliance or lack of compliance (Winiarski, 1991). Otherwise, we set ourselves up for feelings of failure. It is much more helpful for us to acknowledge feelings of helplessness and anxiety, and find ways to work with these outside sessions.

In order to avoid acting from countertransferential feelings, from our need to be tough, or from our need to become unduly directive, we must find ways to cope with two major emotional stresses of HIV affirmative counseling: ambiguity and information overload. Inherent in this work is a tremendous amount of ambiguity about both the course of the disease and the course of counseling. Silven and Caldarola (1989) maintained that because we experience a state of ambiguity that often parallels what clients experience, the result can be an increased capacity to empathize with our clients. However, they add that "for the counselor who has particular difficulty accepting ambiguity, the risk of inhibiting the client's freedom to recognize and experience the uncertainty of the situation must be carefully watched" (p. 23). Failing to detect our discomfort with ambiguity may result in our colluding with clients who attempt to find quick-fix solutions where none exist.

Similarly, we must become aware of the phenomenon of information overload. When we cannot tolerate feelings of confusion—either our own or our clients'—we often respond by trying to become better prepared, better equipped, and better informed. According to Silven and Caldarola (1989), this can lead us to invest a considerable amount of time and energy in attempts to stay up-to-date with research and treatment issues. The vast amount of conflicting information about HIV disease released each day ensures that we can never know everything there is to know. The scope of the issues related to living with

HIV disease is so broad that we will inevitably become frustrated by trying to absorb the amount of information that exists. Silven and Caldarola maintained that the overwhelming amount of information available also places us at risk for becoming seriously overextended: "the counselor must be willing to accept his or her own limitations, including the limits of one's expertise" (p. 23). We have a professional responsibility to stay current with advances in the field, but an excessive drive to do so is worth examining to ensure that it does not represent an attempt to avoid feelings of ineffectiveness.

Working with people living with HIV disease inevitably causes strong feelings to arise for most of us, but counselors who themselves are HIV positive may face additional emotional reactions that reflect their sero-status (Shernoff, 1994). These counselors need to be on guard for overidentifying with HIV-positive clients. Although sharing the fight against HIV disease often allows these counselors to empathize more easily and more fully with clients, it also makes them more susceptible to overinvestment in their work.

Counselors who are HIV negative must also remain alert for the rise of specific issues related to their sero-status. These counselors are susceptable to survivor guilt, particularly when clients lash out in sessions at "uninfected people who couldn't understand what it's like to be HIV positive." Ironically, if instead of coming to terms with their feelings about being negative, these counselors become trapped in survivor guilt, they may not genuinely be emotionally available and understanding of their clients. Whether HIV positive or negative, we must devote time and energy to reflecting upon our physical, emotional, and spiritual state. Otherwise, we are likely to burn out and be of no assistance to clients.

Burnout

Counseling HIV-positive clients and their loved ones can be physically, emotionally, and spiritually depleting. The intense nature of HIV-related issues ensures that even when we are doing good work, we eventually can feel drained. In his book *AIDS-Related Psychotherapy*, Winiarski (1991) wrote that "quality practice also guarantees that the clinician will ache for herself or himself" (p. 134). If we ignore the fact that we will ache, burnout results.

Unfortunately, we often do not recognize burnout until it has engulfed us. We may wonder why we seem constantly irritable, short with our loved ones, or tired and ill at ease; we may never think to connect these emotional conditions with burnout. In order to provide continuous quality care over an extended period of time, we must identify and attend to the forces that lead us to burn out.

Although the external forces of HIV disease that lead to burnout are important, internal factors may be even more significant. Many times we are unaware of the beliefs, feelings, and motives that influence our work. We stand a better chance of preventing burnout if we can identify the elements within ourselves that leave us vulnerable to burnout. The following 10 factors are among those most frequently responsible for burnout.

1. **Remaining Unaware of Our Motives.** Until called to examine them, we often remain unaware of our reasons for wanting to counsel people living with HIV disease and their loved ones. Unexamined, our reasons may leave us vulnerable to burnout. When we become aware of the core, underlying forces that motivate us to counsel these clients, we often have to acknowledge that we expect something in return for our efforts.

   Before we begin counseling HIV-positive clients and their loved ones we should understand why we feel drawn to do so. We should look below the surface of simply wanting to help for deeper motivations. Perhaps we have lost a friend or loved one to AIDS complications. Perhaps we have tested negative for HIV. Perhaps we are anticipating that some day we will need other people's help. Inherent in most of our motivations is an element of quid pro quo. For example, we may want and expect our work to enable us to feel less helpless, less guilty, or less out of control. Unfortunately, the harsh realities of HIV disease often creates situations where we do not receive what we expect. Instead, we are likely to feel frustrated and disappointed—emotional states that lead to burnout.

2. **Imposing Our Goals on Clients.** Frequently our therapeutic goals for HIV-positive clients lead to burnout. It is important to examine these goals for ways in which they reflect our personal values. For example, our goal may be to help clients adjust to being HIV positive; often inherent in this goal is our notion of the best way for clients to live with HIV disease. Our goal may be to help clients have an easy death; often inherent in this goal is our idea of how clients should approach dying. Our goal may be to help our clients' families support them; often inherent in

this goal is our notion of how our clients and their family should interact.

Although we may consciously and unconsciously operate from the belief that we know what is best for our clients, our clients will not do things the way we want them to—nor should they feel obliged to. Winiarski (1991) wrote that

> the goal-driven therapist who wants to "make a difference" and who must see manifest proof of change can be continually thwarted by the client's illness, or by the client's inability to respect and gratify the clinician's grandiosity. If in one's grandiosity, the therapist dares to enter into a power struggle, death and its foreshadowing always win. (p. 136)

When we maintain goals that are unrealistic or contradict those of our clients, we leave ourselves vulnerable to burnout. In addition, by imposing our goals and values on clients we rob them of the opportunity to find in counseling a safe place—a place free of demands to be or act a certain way.

3. **Failing to Set Limits.** Sometimes we find ourselves in the position of pushing our personal limits. For example, we may feel obliged to accept every HIV-infected client we are referred, or we may schedule HIV-positive clients during times we have reserved for ourselves. Often these actions reflect our belief that clients need us. Our belief may arise from situations where we are genuinely needed, but we should examine this belief for potentially narcissistic sources. We should be certain that we are not making exceptions to our established limits in an attempt to get certain of our needs met in the counseling session (e.g., increasing our feeling of specialness by accepting another HIV-positive client) that could be better met elsewhere. We should not forget that other counselors and resources are available to people living with HIV disease. To avoid burnout, we must learn to set limits that prevent us becoming overextended.

4. **Failing to Take Care of Our Own Health.** Oftentimes we continue to see clients even when we feel run down, or we may skip a meal to squeeze in another appointment. Acts such as these are often guided by the belief that clients can't live without us. For financial reasons we may be unable to survive without clients, but clients will survive without us! We cannot afford to ignore our health.

In our quest to always be there for our clients, we often ignore the warning signs of burnout and end up sick in bed—totally unavailable. In addition, if we work when we do not feel well, we may expose clients to germs that their compromised immune system may be unable to ward off. Thus for many reasons it is important that we engage in activities like walking, running, swimming, or aerobics that promote health and prevent burnout.

5. **Ignoring Our Soul.** Since HIV disease is as much a disease of the spirit as it is of the body, we must nurture and develop our spiritual side. Frequently we believe that this is unimportant. Nevertheless, in that working with clients around issues of death and dying is spiritually demanding, taking care of our soul is crucial. To prevent burnout, we must devote time and energy to our spiritual side, however we conceive it. Meditation, prayer, quiet time, attending 12-step meetings, spending time in nature, or reading an uplifting book may serve this need for restoration, centering, and deep experiences of life's meaning.

6. **Hiding Our Feelings.** Many times we believe that clients need us to be strong and so avoid sharing our feelings with them. We leave our feelings unexpressed, creating an internal emotional condition that leaves us vulnerable to burnout. Clients living with HIV disease do not need us to be strong so much as human. HIV disease is characterized by a lack of human regard. Therefore, it is important that we respect our clients' humanity. The best way to do this is to be human ourselves. When we are touched by something clients do or say, we can let them know. For example, we can share with clients how much we will miss them after they die. In this way, clients come to know that they still impact others. By sharing with clients some of our feelings, we take steps to prevent burnout. This does not mean we should indiscriminately self-disclose; we must always remain cautious and cognizant of the appropriateness of our disclosure to our clients' needs. When done in the right way at the right time, however, sharing feelings provides a meaningful experience for all parties involved.

7. **Devoting Our Entire Practice to HIV Disease.** When all of our clients are HIV positive (or caregivers and loved ones of people living with HIV disease), we are extremely vulnerable to burnout. Even those of us who consider HIV disease our specialty should

remember that specialty need not imply exclusivity. We should consider scheduling clients without HIV-related problems on days when we see many HIV-positive clients; this is particularly important when clients are in end stages of the HIV disease. In a similar vein, Winiarski (1991) noted that as we get immersed in AIDS work, our involvement begins to spread into other areas besides counseling such as fundraising, advocacy, and political lobbying. He warns about the cost of an "AIDS-related life-style" (p. 140) and maintains that "individuals must also temper their zeal, and allow themselves the energy for the long run" (p. 140).

8. **Failing to Use Resources.** It is easy to get drawn into believing that we should provide our clients with all the support they need. Given the magnitude and complexity of the issues confronting people living with HIV disease, no one person (and perhaps not even one agency) can provide all the necessary care. Many community agencies offer excellent support services for HIV positive people and their loved ones. To prevent burnout we must know places where clients can receive adjunctive care, and we must refer them there when appropriate.

9. **Failing to Seek Consultation.** At times we may seek out the advice of other clinicians only reluctantly. We need to overcome our fears around asking for help if we want to prevent burnout. "To practice generally without supervision is dangerous enough. But to treat HIV-positive persons without assistance is to invite technical problems and countertransferential interference of the sort that leads one into incompetence" (Winiarski, 1991, p. 137). Regular meetings and the establishment of a good working relationship with a colleague can help us overcome our reluctance to share our anxieties, concerns, and failures. However, we should be sure that the people we approach for consultation not only have experience in working with people living with HIV disease but also have learned to take care of themselves and are not burned out.

10. **Avoiding Counselor Support Groups.** Counseling can be a very insulating activity—it is just our clients and us. The intense emotional demands particular to working with HIV-positive clients may cause us to feel extremely lonely and isolated. The support of other counselors doing the same type of work is crucial to

preventing these feelings from turning into burnout. In many communities support groups have formed for counselors working with people with HIV disease. The support of others is so imperative that if no groups exist near our offices or homes, we should consider starting one ourselves.

If we intend to continue for any length of time counseling clients living with HIV disease, we must consider preventing burnout our priority. Burnout is a natural part of being a helper and of doing this type of work. Therefore, we must take care not to add to the injury of burnout by blaming or attacking ourselves for being burned out. Burnout can be viewed as our psyches' way of asking us to be compassionate with ourselves. Once we have shown ourselves compassion, we will undoubtedly be able to show more compassion to others. Burnout is painful, but we must remember that with attention, care, and time it passes.

Rewards of HIV Affirmative Counseling

As the end of this book draws near, it is important to reflect upon the many rewards of providing counseling to those living with and dying of HIV disease, and their families, friends, and loved ones. Although some may consider it self-centered to look at what we can receive from working with people facing a life-threatening disease, none of us can continue to do this work without gaining something in return. Those of us who have devoted our professional lives to working with people living with HIV disease know that the rewards are not what we expected when we first began. We know that the rewards of working with clients living with HIV do not make a us *self*-centered but rather self-*centered*.

When we first begin to work with clients living with HIV disease, we often do so for personal reasons and personal rewards. Many times we feel frustrated by the overwhelming lack of attention given to the AIDS crisis and feel that by working with clients living with HIV disease, we will make a difference. Sometimes we first start the work because we feel that counseling people who are HIV positive and their loved ones provides us with a way to give back to our communities. At other times, we lack the awareness of particular feelings for beginning work: we know only that we feel we have something to share and want to do so.

As we continue to work we often come to find out that our original reasons for wanting to do the work reflect our own ego needs such as the need to feel potent, to feel full and capable of giving, or to feel good. If we continue to practice HIV affirmative counseling long enough, we discover that we rarely receive these rewards. Sadly, the frustrations stemming from the current limitations of medical treatment for HIV disease spill over into the counseling arena. If we are looking to make a difference on the large scale, we find that we can just barely make a difference on a small scale. Although we may feel better about ourselves by giving, we quickly find that we can give only on our own limited terms while the AIDS crisis continues to demand caregiving in big ways. Those of us who feel we have something to offer indeed find that this is true. Rarely, however, are our contributions what we originally envisioned.

What then are the realistic rewards of counseling people with HIV disease? Although many rewards exist, and ultimately each one of us finds our own, three are common: we learn the value of life; we learn to how to become more human; and we learn the true greatness of the human spirit.

Learning the Value of Life

Working with people living with HIV disease puts life into perspective. If we open up to learning from our clients, witnessing our clients' struggles to determine the shape and quality of their lives will transform our values. Although it is easy for us to get caught up in the day-to-day tribulations of life, HIV-positive clients remind us that these little things are not important in the large scope of what it means to really live. They remind us that life must not be wasted. They also remind us that if something needs to be accomplished, it is best done today.

As clients demonstrate, these lessons do not always come easy. If we are truly open to learning the value of life, we will be made constantly aware of the myriad ways we discount life's value, ignore life's opportunities, and take life for granted. Our reluctance to take risks in our life will be challenged by our clients' risk-taking behavior and our clients' resulting growth. As much as we want to believe that we model growth for our clients, working with people living with HIV disease provides us with the opportunity to learn that modeling growth is a mutual process. We have as much to learn about life from our clients as our clients do from us.

Learning How to Become More Human

Over the years, many of us have come to rely on our education and experience to provide us with the tools and techniques needed to counsel those in emotional pain. Working with people living with HIV disease challenges what we know about how to do counseling. Many of us come to find our catalog of rehearsed responses or favorite exercises ineffective when offered to HIV-positive clients and their loved ones.

HIV disease strikes at the core of what it means to be human. Clients have their sense of humanness challenged; many people in their life do not want to look at them, be with them, or touch them. In the face of these challenges, we find that there is only one appropriate response: to be as human as possible. A client does not want or need a technician for a counselor. He or she needs a genuine feeling, caring, compassionate human being.

Even those of us who take what we perceive to be a humanistic approach to counseling find ourselves stretched to be more human when working with clients living with HIV disease. Ironically, our clients may be the best teachers for how to go about becoming more human. When we work with clients who throw themselves into a devoted, loving relationship, overcoming past inhibitions to intimacy in the face of knowing that they have less than a year to live, we witness what it means to be human. When we work with the spouses or partners of clients who, despite their loved ones' physical disfigurement, fevers, and intravenous tubing, lie next to them each night when they go to sleep, we witness what it means to be human. When we work with clients who plan on adopting an infant with HIV disease knowing full well that they may not see the infant grow to be an adult, we witness what it means to be human.

Working with people living with HIV disease, we quickly realize that what we have to offer clients is not a wealth of information or a collection of methods for feeling better. What we have to offer is ourselves. As clients call for counseling sessions that consist of nothing less than an authentic encounter of two human beings, we are given the opportunity to find what it means to be more human.

Learning the True Greatness of the Human Spirit

Working with people living with HIV disease is an incredible and humbling experience. If we are open to the experience, we can come to realize that the human spirit possesses an unlimited capacity to transcend suffering and pain, and to experience hope and joy. We can experience in the struggles of our clients the indomitableness of the human spirit firsthand. If we are open, we can learn how to have a truly compassionate presence, and how to truly love another person.

Working with clients living with HIV disease provides us with the opportunity to cast off our misperceptions of the limited capacity of people to feel, hope, hurt, and care. Clients face the dark night of the soul not once but many times over the course of their illness. They question how they can continue to live, how they can continue to find meaning, and how they can continue to find love. We who are privileged to witness this process may find even answers to our own spiritual questions. We may find that a client's faith inspires our own faith.

If compassion is one of the highest spiritual qualities, as is suggested by many great teachers and spiritual paths, counseling people living with HIV disease will provide us with many opportunities to exercise and expand upon our capacity to be compassionate. Compassion has been described as the "tender opening of our hearts to pain and suffering" (Dass & Bush, 1992, p. 4). Thus, to be compassionate we must give up our false notions of what it means to help another person; instead these must be replaced with the ability to open our hearts and be with a person who suffers or is in pain and who needs our physical, emotional, and spiritual presence. If we have not figured out how to do this before we start working with clients living with HIV disease, the work itself teaches us.

There is much that can be learned from working with people living with HIV disease. HIV affirmative counseling can be growth promoting for us as well as our clients. The rewards of working with HIV-positive clients and their loved ones do present themselves to us. They may not be what we anticipate when we begin this work, but they must not be discounted. When acknowledged, accepted, and incorporated into our lives, these rewards are precious, life altering, and filled with grace.

The Importance of Not Giving Up Hope

A discussion of the ways we can fortify ourselves for the magnitude of the work ahead of us stands incomplete without recognizing the importance of hope. Just as clients waste away without hope, so, too, do we. Many times it is us to whom clients look for hope. How then can we maintain hope?

Hope is fostered in community. The support, nurturance, and hope we may receive from other people working with clients living with HIV disease cannot be underestimated. We cannot do this work alone. When we feel discouraged and despairing we must have people in our lives who can help to replenish hope. Supervision and consultation are not optional when we minister to HIV-positive clients, their spouses and partners, their families, and their friends; it is required.

Hope is found in the realistic balancing of the disappointments of the present state of the AIDS crisis and the potential for new break-throughs. Any time we focus on one at the expense of the other, authentic hope is likely to be lost. Hope can only be found in remembering that while the potential for a cure exists, it must be worked toward through efforts that are never easy or without setbacks.

Hope is found when we take time to nurture ourselves. Often we become so involved in taking care of others that we forget to take care of ourselves. Often we become so competent at taking care of others that we forget how to let others take care of us. Hope, an inherently spiritual quality, gets nurtured by contact with things of the heart. In order to maintain hope, we must not lose our connections with those people, places, and things, that offer us comfort of spirit and heart.

Hope is found when we are strong. HIV affirmative counseling demands a strength that has its source at the core of our being. It is the strength to allow ourselves to be human, the strength to allow ourselves, as counselors, to be vulnerable with clients. It is the strength that knows that no matter how badly it hurts, life is precious.

As HIV disease continues its course through communities previously untouched by its destruction, the need for HIV affirmative counselors can only increase. Those who have not yet counseled people living with HIV disease will be asked to do so. Those who have will be asked to continue. Everyone will be asked to envision a more promising future. Hopefully reading this book will leave us feeling more prepared for the tasks ahead of us.

By the time this book appears in bookstores and on bookshelves, much may already have changed in the field of HIV disease. There is little doubt, however, that the need for hope will still remain. May we find the strength to remain hopeful and the courage to share it with those in need.

RESOURCES FOR HIV AFFIRMATIVE COUNSELORS

A nonexhaustive diverse listing of organizations,
hotlines, publications, and electronic bulletin boards

National Agencies and Organizations

AIDS Action Counsel
1875 Connecticut Avenue, NW,
    Suite 700
Washington, DC 20009
(202) 986-1300

AIDS National Interfaith Network
110 Maryland Avenue, NE, Suite
    504
Washington, DC 20002
(202) 546-0807

AIDS Treatment Data Network
611 Broadway, Suite 613
New York, NY 10012
(212) 260-8868

**American AIDS Political Action
Committee**
1775 T Street, NW
Washington, DC 20009
(202) 462-8061

CDC National AIDS Clearinghouse
1600 Research Boulevard
Rockville, MD 20850
(800) 458-5231

**National Association of People With
AIDS**
1600 Research Boulevard
Rockville, MD 20856
(202) 898-0414

National Hemophilia Foundation
110 Greene Street, Suite 303
New York, NY 10012
(212) 219-8180

**National Leadership Coalition on
AIDS**
1730 M Street, NW, Suite 905
Washington, DC 20036
(202) 429-0930

National Minority AIDS Council
300 I Street, NE, Suite 400
Washington, DC 20002
(202) 544-1076

**National Native American AIDS
Prevention Center**
2100 Lakeshore Avenue, Suite A
Oakland, CA 94606
(510) 444-2051

1433 East Franklin Avenue, Suite 3A
Minneapolis, MN 22404-3046
(612) 872-8860

Pediatric AIDS Foundation
1311 Colorado Avenue
Santa Monica, CA 90404
(310) 395-9051

National Hotlines

AIDS Clinical Trials Information
(800) TRIALS-A
(800) 243-7012 (tty/tdd)

CDC National AIDS Hotline
(800) 342-AIDS
(800) 344-SIDA (Spanish)

National AIDS Hotline for Hearing Impaired
(800) 243-7889

National Hospicelink
(800) 331-1620

National Native American AIDS Hotline
(800) 283-2437

Project Inform National Hotline (AIDS treatment information)
(800) 822-7422

Counselors should be sure to also check local and state hotlines.

Publications

AIDS Treatment News
PO Box 411256
San Francisco, CA 94141
(800) TREAT -1-2

AmFAR Treatment Directory
733 Third Avenue, 12th Floor
New York, NY 10017
(212) 682-7440

AIDS Care: Journal of the Physicians Association for AIDS Care
101 West Grand, Suite 200
Chicago, IL 60610
(312) 527-2025

Being Alive/Los Angeles
3626 Sunset Boulevard
Los Angeles, CA 90026
(213) 667-3262

BETA: Bulletin of Experimental Treatments for AIDS
San Francisco AIDS Foundation
25 Van Ness Avenue, Suite 700
San Francisco, CA 94102
(415) 863-2437

The Body Positive
2095 Broadway, Suite 306
New York, NY 10023
(212) 721-1346

CRIA Update
Community Research Initiative on AIDS
31 West 26th Street
New York, NY 10010
(212) 889-1958

Journal of Acquired Immune
Deficiency Syndrome
Raven Press
1185 Avenue of the Americas
New York, NY 10036
(212) 930-9604

Notes From the Underground
150 26th West Street, Suite 201
New York, NY 10001
(212) 255-0520

Positively Aware
Test Positive Aware Network
1258 West Belmont
Chicago, IL 60654
(312) 472-6397

POZ
349 West 12th Street
New York, NY 10014
(800) 9-READPOZ

Project Inform Perspectives
Project Inform
1965 Market Street, Suite 220
San Francisco, CA 94103
(800) 822-7422 national
(800) 334-7422 California
(415) 558-9051 San Francisco

PWA Coalition Newsline
31 West 26th Street, Fifth Floor
New York, NY 10010
(800) 828-3280

STEP Perspectives
127 Broadway East, Suite 200
Seattle, WA 98102
(800) 869-7837

SIDA Ahora
31 West 26th Street, Fifth Floor
New York, NY 10010
(800) 828-3280

Treatment Issues
Gay Men's Health Crisis (GMHC)
Medical Information
129 West 20th Street
New York, NY 10011
(212) 337-3541

Women Being Alive
Being Alive/Los Angeles
3626 Sunset Boulevard
Los Angeles, CA 90026
(213) 667-3262

WORLD
Women Organized to Respond to
  Life-Threatening Diseases
3948 Webster Street
Oakland, CA 94609
(510) 658-6930

On-Line Electronic Services (Bulletin Boards)

HIV/AIDS Information BBS
(Southern California)
modem: (714) 248-2836

HNS HIV-NET
modem: (800) 788-4118

Fog City BBS (Northern California)
modem: (415) 863-9697

Black Bag Medical BBS (Delaware)
modem: (302) 994-3772

**Midwest AIDS/HIV Information
Exchange** (Illinois)
 modem: (312) 772-5958

Critical Path AIDS Project
(Pennsylvania)
modem: (215) 463-7160

AIDSNet (New York)
modem: (607) 777-2158

REFERENCES

Abramowitz, S., & Cohen, J. (1994). The psychodynamics of AIDS: A view from self-psychology. In S. A. Cadwell, R. A. Burnham, Jr., & M. Forstein (Eds.), *Therapists on the front line: Psychotherapy with gay men in the age of AIDS* (pp. 205–221). Washington, DC: American Psychiatric Press.

Anastos, K., & Marte, C. (1991). Women—the missing persons in the AIDS epidemic. In N. F. McKenzie (Ed.), *The AIDS reader: Social, political, ethical issues* (pp.190–197). New York: Meridian.

Ankrah, M. (1991). AIDS and the social side of health. *Social Science and Medicine, 32,* 967–980.

Baker, J. (1993). Treatment of mood disorders. *Focus: A Guide to AIDS Research and Counseling, 8* (8), 1–4.

Baker, R. (1994). Prospects for a new strategy for HIV treatment. *Focus: A Guide to AIDS Research and Counseling, 9* (11), 1–4.

Barlow, K. M., & Mok, J. Y. (1993). The challenge of AIDS in children. In L. Sherr (Ed.), *AIDS in the heterosexual population* (pp. 113–124). Langhorne, PA: Harwood Academic.

Barret, R., Pawlowski, W., & Washington, R. (1993, September). *Medical, psychological, and social aspects of HIV disease.* Washington, DC: American Psychological Association, Office on AIDS.

Becker, E. (1975). *Denial of death.* New York: Macmillan.

Belkin, L. (1993, November 14). There's no simple suicide. *The New York Times Magazine,* pp. 49–75.

Bennett, T. A., & Henrickson, M. (1993). Pastoral counseling. *Focus: A Guide to AIDS Research and Counseling, 8* (7), 5–6.

Benson, J. D., & Maier, C. (1990). Challenges facing women with HIV. *Focus: A Guide to AIDS Research and Counseling, 6* (1), 1–2.

Beral, V., Peterman, T., Berkelman, R., & Jaffe, H. W. (1991). Kaposi's sarcoma among persons with AIDS: A sexually transmitted infection? *Lancet, 335,* 123–128.

Boccellari, A. (1991, May). Care at home for people with dementing illness. *Bulletin of Experimental Treatments for AIDS,* pp. 13–20.

Boccelari, A. S., & Dilley, J. W. (1989). Caring for patients with AIDS dementia. In J. W. Dilley, C. Pies, & M. Helquist (Eds.), *Face to face: A guide to AIDS counseling* (pp. 186–198). AIDS Health Project, University of California San Francisco.

Boccellari, A., Kain C. D., & Shor, M. D. (1989). Caring for people with AIDS dementia complex. In C. D. Kain (Ed.), *No longer immune: A counselor's guide to AIDS* (pp. 153–167). Alexandria, VA: American Association for Counseling and Development.

Botkin, M. C. (1994). Chinese medicine takes root. *Poz, 1* (4), 52–53, 68.

Boykin, F. F. (1991). The AIDS crisis and gay male survivor guilt. *Smith College Studies in Social Work, 61,* 247–259.

Braine, N. (1994). An activist's perspective on AIDS in the lesbian community. *Focus: A Guide to AIDS Research and Counseling, 8* (9), 5,6.

Cabaj, R. P. (1994). HIV and substance abuse in the gay male community. In S. A. Cadwell, R. A. Burnham, Jr., & M. Forstein (Eds.), *Therapists on the front line: Psychotherapy with gay men in the age of AIDS* (pp. 405–426). Washington, DC: American Psychiatric Press.

Capaccioli, A. (1993). Exercise. *Lifetimes* [Special issue on wasting]. (Available from Stadtlander Drug Company, tel. 1-800-238-7828)

Carmack, B. J. (1992). Balancing engagement/detachment in AIDS-related multiple loss. *IMAGE: Journal of Nursing Scholarship, 24* (1), 9–15.

Carson, V., Soeken, K. L., Shanty, J., & Jerry, L. (1990). Hope and spiritual well-being: Essentials for living with AIDS. *Perspectives in Psychiatric Care, 26* (2), 28–34.

Centers for Disease Control and Prevention (1993, December 6). Caring for HIV-infected children in and out of the home. *HIV/AIDS Prevention: CDC National AIDS Hotline Training Bulletin.* Atlanta, GA: Author. (Reprinted from *Pediatric Infectious Disease Journal,* October 1993)

Chan, C. S. (1993). Issues of identity development among Asian-American lesbians and gay men. In L. D. Garnets & D. C. Kimmel (Eds.), *Psychological perspectives on lesbian and gay male experiences.* New York: Columbia University Press.

Christensen, K. (1992). How do women live? In C. Chris & M. Pearls (Eds.), *Women, AIDS, and activism* (pp. 5–15). Boston, MA: South End Press.

Chung, J. Y., & Magraw, M. M. (1992). A group approach to psychosocial issues faced by HIV-positive women. *Hospital and Community Psychiatry, 43,* 891–894.

Corea, G. (1992). *The invisible epidemic: The story of women and AIDS.* New York: HarperPerennial.

Croteau, J. M., Nero, C. I., & Prosser, D. J. (1993). Social and cultural sensitivity in group-specific HIV and AIDS programming. *Journal of Counseling and Development, 71,* 290–296.

Dalton, H. L. (1991). AIDS in blackface. In N. F. McKenzie (Ed.), *The AIDS reader: Social, political, ethical issues* (pp. 122–143). New York: Meridian.

Dass, R., & Bush, M. (1992). *Compassion in action.* New York: Bell Tower.

Davidson, C. (1994). Does reality bite? *Poz, 1* (4), 54–55.

Denenberg, R. (1992). Treatment and trials. In C. Chris & M. Pearl (Eds.), *Women, AIDS, and activism* (pp. 69–79). Boston, MA: South End Press.

Dilley, J. W., & Boccellari, A. (1989). Neuropsychiatric complications of HIV infection. In J. W. Dilley, C. Pies, & M. Helquist (Eds.), *Face to face: A guide to AIDS counseling* (pp. 138–151). AIDS Health Project, University of California San Francisco.

Dilley, J., & Moon, T. (1994). Supporting uninfected gay and bisexual men. *Focus: A Guide to AIDS Research and Counseling, 8* (6), 1–4.

Dowd, M. (1994). Proud Mary. *Poz, 1* (4), 32–35, 65–67.

Dowd, S. (1994). African-American gay men and HIV and AIDS: Therapeutic challenges. In S. A. Cadwell, R. A. Burnham, Jr., & M. Forstein (Eds.), *Therapists on the front line: Psychotherapy with gay men in the age of AIDS* (pp. 319–338). Washington, DC: American Psychiatric Press.

Dubos, R. (1978). Health and creative adaptation. *Human Nature, 1*(1), 82.

Duff, K. (1994, March/April). Sometimes it's OK to be sick: The benefits of poor health. *Utne Reader,* pp. 108–109.

Dunshee, S. J. (1994). Compassion in dying. *Focus: A Guide to AIDS Research and Counseling, 9* (5), 5–6.

Durand, Y. (1992). Cultural sensitivity in practice. In C. Chris & M. Pearl (Eds.), *Women, AIDS, and activism* (pp. 85–90). Boston, MA: South End Press.

Dworkin, S. H., & Pincu, L. (1993). Counseling in the era of AIDS. *Journal of Counseling and Development, 71,* 275–281.

Ekstrand, M. L. (1992). Safer sex maintenance among gay men: Are we making any progress? *AIDS, 6,* 875–877.

Elliot, A. S. (1993). Counseling for HIV-infected adolescents. *Focus: A Guide to AIDS Research and Counseling, 8* (9), 1–4.

Epstein, R. (Director), & Friedman, J. (Director). (1989). *Common threads: Stories From the Quilt* [video]. Home Box Office Video.

Erikson, E. (1963). *Childhood and society* (2nd ed.). New York: W. W. Norton.

Faltz, B. G. (1988). Counseling substance abuse clients with human immunodeficiency virus. *Journal of Psychoactive Drugs, 20,* 217–221.

Faltz, B. G., & Madover, S. (1988). Treatment of substance abuse in patients with HIV infection. *AIDS and Substance Abuse, 7,* (2), 143–157.

Fertzinger, A. P. (1986). Death and growth: The problem of pain. *Loss: Grief and Care, 1* (1–2), 141–49.

Fisher, D. G., & Needle, R. H. (1993). *AIDS and community-based drug intervention programs: Evaluation and outreach.* New York: Harrington Park.

Fisher, G., Jones, S. J., & Stein, J. B. (1989). Mental health complications of substance abuse. In J. W. Dilley, C. Pies, & M. Helquist (Eds.), *Face to face: A guide to AIDS counseling* (pp. 118–126). AIDS Health Project, University of California San Francisco.

Follansbee, S. E., & Dilley, J. W. (1993). Report from the International AIDS Conference: AIDS treatment after Berlin. *Focus: A Guide to AIDS Research and Counseling, 8* (10), 1– 4.

Forstein, M. (1994a). Psychotherapy with gay male couples: Loving in the time of AIDS. In S. A. Cadwell, R. A. Burnham, Jr., & M. Forstein (Eds.), *Therapists on the front line: Psychotherapy with gay men in the age of AIDS* (pp. 293–315). Washington, DC: American Psychiatric Press.

Forstein, M. (1994b). Suicidality and HIV in gay men. In S. A. Cadwell, R. A. Burnham, Jr., & M. Forstein (Eds.), *Therapists on the front line: Psycho-*

therapy with gay men in the age of AIDS (pp. 111–145). Washington, DC: American Psychiatric Press.

Forster, E. (1994/1995). Liquid lunch: World record holder James Ballard makes a splash. *Poz, 1* (5), 24, 69.

Fortunato, J. E. (1993). A framework for hope. *Focus: A Guide to AIDS Research and Counseling, 8* (7), 1–4.

Frankl, V. (1992). *Man's search for meaning: An introduction to logotherapy* (4th ed.). Boston, MA: Beacon Press.

Friedman, S. R., Des Jarlais, D. C., Ward, T. P., Jose, B., Neaigus, A., & Goldstein, M. (1993). Drug injectors and heterosexual AIDS. In L. Sherr (Ed.), *AIDS and the heterosexual population* (pp. 41-65). Langhorne, PA: Harwood Academic.

Frost, J. C. (1994). Taking a sexual history with gay patients in psychotherapy. In S. A. Cadwell, R. A. Burnham, Jr., & M. Forstein (Eds.), *Therapists on the front line: Psychotherapy with gay men in the age of AIDS* (pp. 163–183). Washington, DC: American Psychiatric Press.

Gaies, J. S., & Knox, M. D. (1991). The therapist and the dying client. *Focus: A Guide to AIDS Research and Counseling, 6* (6), 1–2.

Gentry, J. H. (1993, Winter). Women and AIDS. *Psychology and AIDS Exchange, 1* (11), 6–7.

Goldblum, P. B., & Moulton, J. (1989). HIV disease and suicide. In J. W. Dilley, C. Pies, & M. Helquist (Eds.), *Face to face: A guide to AIDS counseling* (pp. 152–164). AIDS Health Project, University of California San Francisco.

Gorer, G. (1965). *Death, grief, and mourning in contemporary Britain.* New York: Doubleday.

Gottlieb, M. (1992, December). Pain management in PWAs. *Being Alive Newsletter.* (Available from Being Alive/Los Angeles, 3626 Sunset Blvd., Los Angeles, CA 90026)

Grant, D., & Anns, M. (1988). Counseling AIDS antibody positive clients: Reactions and treatment. *American Psychologist, 43,* 72–74.

Gretzel, G. S., & Mahoney, K. F. (1993). Confronting human finitude: Group work with people with AIDS. *Social Work With Groups, 18,* 27–41.

Gutierrez, F. J., & Perlstein, M. (1992). Helping someone to die. In S. H. Dworkin & F. J. Gutierrez (Eds.), *Counseling gay men and lesbians: Journey to the end of the rainbow* (pp. 259–275). Alexandria, VA: American Association for Counseling and Development.

Hankins, C. (1993). Women and HIV-infection. In L. Sherr (Ed.), *AIDS and the heterosexual population* (pp. 21–40). Langhorne, PA: Harwood Academic.

Harding, A. K., Gray, L. A., & Neal, M. (1993). Confidentiality limits with clients who have HIV: A review of ethical and legal guidelines and professional practices. *Journal of Counseling and Development, 71,* 297–305.

Harris, C. (1991, Summer). All night subway ride: One perspective on the health care crisis in the Native community in New York City. *Seasons,* reprint No. 6. (Available from National Native American AIDS Prevention Center, 3515 Grand Ave., No. 100, Oakland, CA 94610)

Harris, R. (1994, June). Sports for all . . . That means you! *Body Positive, 7* (6), 10–13.

Herek, G. M. (1990). Illness, stigma, and AIDS. In P. T. Costa & G. R. Vandon Bos (Eds.), *Psychological aspects of serious illness: Chronic conditions, fatal diseases, and clinical care/Master lectures* (pp. 105–150). Washington, DC: American Psychological Association.

Herek, G. M., & Glunt, E. K. (1988). An epidemic of stigma: Public reactions to AIDS. *American Psychologist, 43,* 886–891.

Herek, G. M., & Glunt, E. K. (1991). AIDS-related attitudes in the United States: A preliminary conceptualization. *The Journal of Sex Research, 28* (1), 99–123.

Hitchens, N. (1992). *Voices that care.* New York: Lowell House.

HIV . . . afraid of knowing? (1993, September 24). *Frontiers,* p. 3.

Humphry, D. (1991). *Final exit: The practicalities of self-deliverance and assisted suicide for the dying.* New York: Carol.

Jackson, A. M. (1990). Evolution of ethnocultural psychotherapy. *Psychotherapy, 27,* 428–435.

Jensen, J. (1993, May). Food is not the enemy. *Being Alive Newsletter.* (Available from Being Alive/Los Angeles, 3626 Sunset Blvd., Los Angeles, CA 90026)

Jones, J. R., & Dilley, J. W. (1993). Rational suicide and HIV disease. *Focus: A Guide to AIDS Research and Counseling, 8* (8), 5–6.

Jue, S., & Kain, C. D. (1989). Culturally sensitive AIDS counseling. In C. D. Kain (Ed.), *No longer immune: A counselor's guide to AIDS* (pp. 131–148). Alexandria, VA: American Association for Counseling and Development.

Kain, C. D. (Ed.). (1989). *No longer immune: A counselor's guide to AIDS.* Alexandria, VA: American Association for Counseling and Development.

Kaplan, L. (1994). Bill T. Jones on top. *Poz, 1* (2), 40–44, 69.

Keeling, R. P. (1993). HIV disease: Current concepts. *Journal of Counseling and Development, 71,* 261–274.

Koralnik, I. J., Beaumanoir, A., Hausler, R., Kohler, A., Safran, A. B., Delacoux, R., Vibert, D., Mayer, E., Burkhard, P., Nahary, A., et al. (1990). A controlled study of early neurologic abnormalities in men with asymptomatic human immunodeficiency virus infection. *New England Journal of Medicine, 323* (13), 864–870.

Krowka, J. F. (1989). T-Cell tests and other laboratory mysteries. In J. W. Dilley, C. Pies, & M. Helquist (Eds.), *Face to face: A guide to AIDS counseling* (pp. 36–47). AIDS Health Project, University of California San Francisco.

Kubler-Ross, E. (1969). *On death and dying.* New York: Macmillian.

Levenson, R. L., & Mellins, C. A. (1992). Pediatric HIV disease: What psychologists need to know. *Professional Psychology: Research and Practice, 23,* 410–415.

Levine, S. H., Bystritsky, A., Baron, D., Jones, L. D. (1991). Group psychotherapy for HIV-seropositive youths with major depression. *American Journal of Psychotherapy, 45,* 413–424.

Lifton, R. (1983). *The broken connection: On death and the continuity of life.* New York: Basic Books.

Lifton, R. J. (1980). The concept of the survivor. In J. E. Dimsdale (Ed.), *Survivors, victims, and perpetrators: Essays on the Nazi holocaust.* Washington, DC: Hemisphere.

Lurie, R. (1992). Teenagers. In C. Chris & M. Pearl (Eds.), *Women, AIDS, and activism* (pp. 135–138). Boston, MA: South End Press.

Lynch, A. A., & Palacio-Jimenez, L. (1993). Progression of an illness: The life course of AIDS. *Clinical Social Work Journal, 21,* 301–317.

Macks, J. (1989). The psychological needs of people with AIDS. In J. W. Dilley, C. Pies, & M. Helquist (Eds.), *Face to face: A guide to AIDS counseling* (pp. 2–14). AIDS Health Project, University of California San Francisco.

Macks, J., & Turner, D. (1986). Mental health issues of persons with AIDS. In L. McKusick (Ed.), *What to do about AIDS: Physicians and mental health professionals discuss the issues* (pp. 111–124). Berkeley: University of California Press.

Madsen, J. (1994). AIDS Vancouver women's programs: Speaking with each other. *Positive Women's Network Quarterly, 1* (1), 26–29.

Mapou, R. L., & Law, W. A. (1994). Neurobehavioral aspects of HIV disease and AIDS: An update. *Professional Psychology: Research and Practice, 25,* 132–140.

Marin, B. V. (1991). Hispanic culture: Effect on prevention and care. *Focus: A Guide to AIDS Research and Counseling, 6* (4), 1–2.

Marks, R. (1994a). The Brighton Conference and HIV prevention. *Focus: A Guide to AIDS Research and Counseling, 9* (12), 5–8.

Marks, R. (1994b). Different ways of dying [Editorial]. *Focus: A Guide to AIDS Research and Counseling, 9* (5), 2.

Marks, R. (1994c). Seronegatives and scarcity [Editorial]. *Focus: A Guide to AIDS Research and Counseling, 8* (6), 2.

Marks, R. (1993). State of the science [Editorial]. *Focus: A Guide to AIDS Research and Counseling, 8* (6), 2.

Marks, R., & Goldblum, P. B. (1989). The decision to test: A personal choice. In J. W. Dilley, C. Pies, & M. Helquist (Eds.), *Face to face: A guide to AIDS counseling* (pp. 49–58). AIDS Health Project, University of California San Francisco.

Martin, J. P. (1991). Making terminal care decisions. *Focus: A Guide to AIDS Research and Counseling, 6* (6), 3–4.

Maroney, T. A. (1994, Spring). Lesbians, HIV, and violence. *Lesbian AIDS Project Notes, 1* (2), 10.

Matousek, M. (1994, March/April). Savage grace: The spirituality of illness. *Utne Reader,* pp. 104–111.

McKelvy, C. L. (1994). Counseling children who have a parent with AIDS or who have lost a parent to AIDS. In W. Odets & M. Shernoff (Eds.), *The second decade of AIDS: A mental health practice handbook.* New York: Hatherleigh.

McKusick, L. (1992, June). Counseling across the HIV spectrum. *HIV Frontline.* (Available from Center for AIDS Prevention Studies, University of California San Francisco)

McLaurin, P., & Juzang, I. (1993). Reaching the hip-hop generation. *Focus: A Guide to AIDS Research and Counseling, 8* (3), 1–4.

Moore, R. D., Kessler, H. Richman, D. R., Flexner, C., & Chaisson, R. E. (1991). Non-Hodgkin's lymphoma in patients with advanced HIV infection treated with zidovudine. *Journal of the American Medical Association*, *265*, 2208–2211.

Morin, S. F., Charles, K. A., & Malyon, A. K. (1984). The psychological impact of AIDS on gay men. *American Psychologist, 39*, 1288–1293.

Motto, J. A. (1994). Rational suicide: Then and now, when and how. *Focus: A Guide to AIDS Research and Counseling, 9* (5), 1–4.

Murphy, P., & Donovan, C. (1989). Modern hospice care. In C. Kain (Ed.), *No longer immune: A counselor's guide to AIDS* (pp. 187–205). Alexandria, VA: American Association for Counseling and Development.

Namir, S. (1989). Treatment issues concerning persons with AIDS. In L. McKusick (Ed.), *What to do about AIDS: Physicians and mental health professionals discuss the issues* (pp. 87–94). Berkeley: University of California Press.

National Association of Social Workers (1994). Client self-determination in end-of-life decisions. *Social work speaks* (3rd ed.). Washington, DC: Author.

Neugebauer, R., Rabkin, J. G., Williams, Remien, R. H., Goetz, R., & Gorman, J. M. (1992). Bereavement reactions among homosexual men experiencing multiple losses in the AIDS epidemic. *American Journal of Psychiatry, 149*, 1374–1379.

Nichols, M. (1989). The forgotten 7%: Women and AIDS. In C. D. Kain (Ed.), *No longer immune: A counselor's guide to AIDS* (pp. 77–92). Alexandria, VA: American Association for Counseling and Development.

Nuland, S. B. (1994). *How we die: Reflections on life's final chapter.* New York: Alfred A. Knopf.

O'Dowd, M. A. (1993). Coping with HIV over the course of disease. *Focus: A Guide to AIDS Research and Counseling, 8* (6), 5–6.

Ofman, W. V. (1976). *Affirmation and reality: Fundamentals of humanistic existential therapy and counseling.* Santa Monica, CA: Western Psychological Services.

Parés-Avila, J. A., & Montano-López, R. M. (1994). Issues in the psychosocial care of Latino gay men with HIV infection. In S. A. Cadwell, R. A. Burnham, Jr., & M. Forstein (Eds.), *Therapists on the front line: Psychotherapy with gay men in the age of AIDS* (pp. 339–362). Washington, DC: American Psychiatric Press.

Parkes, C., & Weiss, R. (1983). *Recovery from bereavement.* New York: Basic Books.

Paterno, D. (1992). On being a caregiver. *Focus: A Guide to AIDS Research and Counseling, 7* (12), 7–8.

Patt, R. B. (1993, June/July). Pain management in HIV persons with HIV/ AIDS. *Medical Alert, 1* (4).

Perelli, R. J. (1991). *Ministry to persons with AIDS: A family systems approach.* Minneapolis, MN: Augsburg Fortress.

Physicians Association for AIDS Care. (1993). *HIV disease nutrition guidelines.* Chicago, IL: Author.

Quackenbush, M., Benson, J. D., & Rinaldi, J. (1992). *Risk and recovery: AIDS, HIV, and alcohol.* AIDS Health Project, University of California San Francisco.

Remien, R. H., Katoff, L., Rabkin, J. G., & Wagner, G. (1993, August 24). *A follow-up study of AIDS long-term survivors: Multiple loss and coping.* A presentation at the 1993 annual meeting of the American Psychological Association, Toronto, Canada.

Rigsby, L. W., Dishman, R. K., Jackson, A. W., Maclean, G. S., & Raven, P. B. (1992). Effects of exercise training on men seropositive for the human immunodeficiency virus-1. *Medicine and Science in Sports and Exercise, 24* (1), 6–12.

Rogers, J. R., & Britton, P. J. (1994). AIDS and rational suicide: A counseling psychology perspective or a slide on the slippery slope. *Counseling Psychologist, 22,* 171–178.

Sardello, R. J. (1982). The suffering body of the city: Cancer, heart attack, and herpes. *Spring: A Journal of Archetype and Culture, 146.*

Schnarch, D. M. (1991). *Constructing the sexual crucible: An integration of sexual and marital therapy.* New York: W. W. Norton.

Schwartzberg, S. S. (1992). AIDS-related bereavement among gay men: The inadequacy of current theories of grief. *Psychotherapy, 29,* 422–429.

Schwartzberg, S., & Janoff-Bulman, R. (1991). Grief and the search for meaning: Exploring the assumptive worlds of bereaved college students. *Journal of Social and Clinical Psychology, 10,* 270–288.

Selwyn, P. A., Schoenbaum, E. E., Davenny, K., Robertson, V. J., Feingold, A. R., Shulman, J. F., Mayers, M. M., Klein, R. S., Friedland, G. H., & Rogers, M. F. (1989). Prospective study of human immunodeficiency virus infection and pregnancy outcomes in intravenous drug users. *Journal of the American Medical Association, 261,* 1289–1294.

Shalwitz, J., & Dunnigan, K. (1989). Youth and HIV: No immunity. In J. W. Dilley, C. Pies, & M. Helquist (Eds.), *Face to face: A guide to AIDS counseling* (pp. 249–259). AIDS Health Project, University of California San Francisco.

Shaw, N. S. (1989). HIV disease: Issues for women. In J. W. Dilley, C. Pies, & M. Helquist (Eds.), *Face to face: A guide to AIDS counseling* (pp. 241–248). AIDS Health Project, University of California San Francisco.

Shealy, C. N., & Cady, R. K. (1993). The history of pain management. In R. S. Weiner (Ed.). *Innovations in pain management* (pp. 3–21). Orlando, FL: Paul M. Deutsch.

Shelby, R. D. (1994). Mourning within a culture of mourning. In S. A. Cadwell, R. A. Burnham, Jr., & M. Forstein (Eds.), *Therapists on the front line: Psychotherapy with gay men in the age of AIDS* (pp. 53–80). Washington, DC: American Psychiatric Press.

Shernoff, M. (1991). *Counseling chemically dependent people with HIV illness.* New York: Harrington Park Press.

Shernoff, M. (1994). Therapists' disclosure of HIV status and the decision to stop practicing: An HIV-positive therapist responds. In S. A. Cadwell, R. A. Burnham, Jr., & M. Forstein (Eds.), *Therapists on the front line: Psychotherapy with gay men in the age of AIDS* (pp. 549–559). Washington, DC: American Psychiatric Press.

Siano, N. (1993). *No time to wait: A complete guide to treating, managing, and living with HIV infection.* New York: Bantam Books.

Silven, D., & Caldarola, T. J. (1989). The HIV-positive client. In J. W. Dilley, C. Pies, & M. Helquist (Eds.), *Face to face: A guide to AIDS counseling* (pp. 15–25). AIDS Health Project, University of California San Francisco.

Simerly, R. T., & Karakashian, S. J. (1989). Psychotherapy with HIV-positive, ARC, and AIDS patients: Clinical issues and practice management. *Transactional Analysis Journal, 19* (4), 176–185.

Slater, B. R. (1989). Special needs of today's adolescents. In C. D. Kain (Ed.), *No longer immune: A counselor's guide to AIDS* (pp. 93–113). Alexandria, VA: American Association for Counseling and Development.

Smith, D. (1994). When did steriods become our friend? *Poz, 1* (3), 42–45.

Snider, W. D., Simpson, D. M., Nielson, S., Gold, J. W., Metroka, C. E., & Posner, J. B. (1983). Neurologic complications of Acquired Immunodeficiency Syndrome: Analysis of 50 patients. *Annals of Neurology, 14*, 403–418.

Sogyal, R. (1992). *The Tibetian book of the living and dying.* New York: Harper Collins.

Sohlberg, M., & Mateer, C. A. (1989). *Introduction to cognitive rehabilitation.* New York: Guilford Press.

Spiegel, D. (1993). *Living beyond limits: New hope and help for facing life-threatening illness.* New York: Random House.

Spiegel, L., & Mayers, A. (1991). Psychosocial aspects of AIDS in children and adolescents. *Pediatric Clinics of America, 38*, 153–167.

Springer, E. (1991). Effective AIDS prevention with active drug users: The harm reduction model. In M. Shernoff (Ed.) *Counseling chemically dependent people with HIV illness* (pp. 141–157). New York: Harrington Park Press.

Strunin, L., & Hingson, R. (1993). Adolescents. In L. Sherr (Ed.) *AIDS in the heterosexual population* (pp. 125–138). Langhorne, PA: Harwood Academic.

Tarasoff v. Regents of the University of California, 131 Col. Rptr (1976).

Tharp, R. G. (1991). Cultural diversity and treatment of children. *Journal of Consulting and Clinical Psychology, 59*, 799–812.

Tross, S., & Hirsch, D. A. (1988). Psychological distress and neuropsychological complication of HIV infection and AIDS. *American Psychologist, 43*, 929–934.

Update on opportunistic infections. (1993, July). *Project Inform Briefing Paper* (No. 3). (Available from San Francisco Project Inform, 1965 Market St., No. 220, San Francisco, CA 94103)

Van der Horst, C. (1994). A personal response to therapeutic nihilism. *Focus: A Guide to AIDS Research and Counseling, 9* (11). 5–6.

Vasquez, C. (1994). The myth of invulnerability: Lesbians and HIV disease. *Focus: A Guide to AIDS Research and Counseling, 8* (9), 1–4.

Vasquez, R. (1994). Don't wait to get sick: Women's OIs. *Positive Women's Network Quarterly, 1* (1), 10–14.

Walker, G. (1991). *In the midst of winter: Systemic therapy with families, couples, and individuals with AIDS infection.* New York: W. W. Norton.

Walker, J. (1992). Mothers and children. In C. Chris & M. Pearl (Eds.), *Women, AIDS, and activism* (pp. 165–171). Boston, MA: South End Press.

Weisman, A. D. (1981). Understanding the cancer patient: The syndrome of caregiver's plight. *Psychiatry, 44,* 161–168.

Weiss, A. (1989). The AIDS bereaved: Counseling strategies. In J. W. Dilley, C. Pies, & M. Helquist (Eds.), *Face to face: A guide to AIDS counseling* (pp. 267–275). AIDS Health Project, University of California San Francisco.

Wells, D, B. V., & Jackson, J. F. (1992). HIV and chemically dependent women: Recommendations for appropriate health care and drug treatment services. *The International Journal of the Addictions, 27,* 571–585.

Werth, J. L. (1992). Rational suicide and AIDS: Considerations for the psychotherapist. *Counseling Psychologist, 20,* 645–659.

Wetzel, P. (1994/1995). Caro diario: How one doctor tackles her own HIV. *Poz, 1* (5), 86–87.

White, M., & Epston, D. (1990). *Narrative means to therapeutic ends.* New York: W. W. Norton.

Wiener, L. S. (1991). Women and human immunodeficiency virus: A historical and personal psychosocial perspective. *Social Work, 36,* 375–378.

Wilkinson, D. (1993). Family ethnicity in America. In H. P. McAdoo (Ed.), *Family ethnicity: Strength in diversity.* Newbury Park, CA: Sage.

Winiarski, M. G. (1991). *AIDS-related psychotherapy.* New York: Pergamon Press.

Wood, G. J., Marks, R., & Dilley, J. W. (1992a). *AIDS Law for mental health professionals: A handbook for judicious practice.* AIDS Health Project, University of California San Francisco.

Wood, G. J., Marks, R., & Dilley, J. W. (Eds.) (1992b, Fall). *Judicious practice: An update to AIDS law for mental health professionals.* AIDS Health Project, University of California San Francisco.

Wood, G. J., Marks, R., & Dilley, J. W. (Eds.) (1993, Fall). *Judicious practice: An update to AIDS law for mental health professionals.* AIDS Health Project, University of California San Francisco.

Working Group of the American Academy of Neurology AIDS Task Force. (1991). Nomenclature and research case definitions for neurologic manifestations of human immunodeficiency virus-type 1 (HIV-1) infection. *Neurology, 41,* 778–785.

Yalom, I. (1980). *Existential psychotherapy.* New York: Basic Books.

Zavos, M. A. (1992). *Americans With Disabilities Act: Business responds to AIDS.* (Available from Centers for Disease Control and Prevention, as part of the Labor Leader's or Manager's Kit, tel. 1-800-458-5231)

INDEX